France

The International Library of Politics and Comparative Government

General Editor: David Arter
Associate Editor: Gordon Smith

Titles in the Series:

France
David S. Bell

Italy
Mark Donovan

Germany
Klaus H. Goetz

Revolution and Political Change
Alexander J. Groth

New Politics
Ferdinand Müller-Rommel
and Thomas Poguntke

Legislatures and Legislators
Philip Norton

European Union
Neill Nugent

Nationalism
Brendan O'Leary

Transitions to Democracy
Geoffrey Pridham

The Media
Margaret Scammell and
Holli Semetko

Parties and Party Systems
Steven B. Wolinetz

France

Edited by

David S. Bell
University of Leeds

Dartmouth
Aldershot • Brookfield USA • Singapore • Sydney

Published by
Dartmouth Publishing Company Limited
Gower House
Croft Road
Aldershot
Hants GU11 3HR
England

Dartmouth Publishing Company
Old Post Road
Brookfield
Vermont 05036
USA

British Library Cataloguing in Publication Data
France. – (International Library of
Politics & Comparative Government)
  I. Bell, David Scott II. Series
  320.944

Library of Congress Cataloging-in-Publication Data
France/edited by David S. Bell.
            p. cm.— (The international library of politics and
      comparative government)
      Includes bibliographical references and index.
      ISBN 1–85521–346–X
      1. France—Politics and government—1958. 2. Political science–
–France. 3. Political leadership—France. 4. Gaulle, Charles de,
1890–1970—Influence. I. Bell, David Scott. II. Series.
JN2594.2.F694 1995
320.944—dc20   94–48072
                                                                      CIP

ISBN 1 85521 346 X

Printed and bound in Great Britain at the University Press, Cambridge

Contents

Acknowledgements

The editor and publishers wish to thank the following for permission to use copyright material.

American Political Science Association for the essays: Joseph A. and Mildred Schlesinger (1990), 'The Reaffirmation of a Multiparty System in France', *American Political Science Review*, **84**, pp. 1077–101; Frank L. Wilson (1983), 'French Interest Group Politics: Pluralist or Neocorporatist?', *American Political Science Review*, **77**, pp. 895–910.

Blackwell Publishers UK for the essay: Martin Harrison (1990), 'The French Constitutional Council: A Study in Institutional Change', *Political Studies*, **38**, pp. 603–19.

Blackwell Publishers USA for the essays: Michael Keating (1988), 'Does Regional Government Work? The Experience of Italy, France and Spain, *Governance: An International Journal of Policy Administration*, **1**, pp. 184–204; Roy Pierce (1991), 'The Executive Divided Against Itself: Cohabitation in France, 1986–1988', *Governance: An International Journal of Policy and Administration*, **4**, pp. 270–94.

Butterworth-Heinemann Limited for the essay: Mattei Dogan and Daniel Derivry (1988), 'France in Ten Slices: An Analysis of Aggregate Data', *Electoral Studies*, **7**, pp. 251–67. Reproduced with the permission of Butterworth-Heinemann, Oxford, UK.

Cambridge University Press for the essays: Sylvia B. Bashevkin (1984), 'Changing Patterns of Politicization and Partisanship Among Women in France', *British Journal of Political Science*, **15**, pp. 75–96; George Tsebelis (1988), 'Nested Games: The Cohesion of French Electoral Coalitions', *British Journal of Political Science*, **18**, pp. 145–70; Ezra N. Suleiman (1987), 'State Structures and Clientelism: The French State Versus the "Notaires"', *British Journal of Political Science*, **17**, pp. 257–79.

Frank Cass Publishers for the essays: Roger Duclaud-Williams (1981), 'Change in French Society: A Critical Analysis of Crozier's Bureaucratic Model', *West European Politics*, **4**, pp. 235–51; Robert Elgie and Howard Machin (1991), 'France: The Limits to Prime-ministerial Government in a Semi-presidential System', *West European Politics*, **14**, pp. 62–78; Yves Mény (1984), 'Decentralisation in Socialist France: The Politics of Pragmatism', *West European Politics*, **7**, pp. 65–79.

Comparative Politics for the essays: Pierre Bréchon and Subrata Kumar Mitra (1992), 'The National Front in France: The Emergence of an Extreme Right Protest Movement', *Comparative Politics*, **25**, pp. 63–82; Kay Lawson (1981), 'The Impact of Party Reform on Party Systems: The Case of the RPR in France', *Comparative Politics*, **13**, pp. 401–19.

Preface

French politics is perhaps an acquired taste, but I, personally, have always found the subject of passionate interest and the issues raised by the intensity of debate fascinating and challenging. This volume is a collection of essays published in English-language journals covering some of the main research topics in the study of French politics. The collection is illustrative of the political science research currently being conducted on the French political system and, as such, is part of a much wider debate in the academic community. No translations have been included; the lack of material from French professional publications means that the French political science community is under-represented. However, I hope that the collection is both rigorous and varied enough to give the reader an idea of the richness of the research currently being undertaken on French politics, and also why French political developments are of concern to scholars in the university world.

As the editor of this volume, I would like to thank the series editors for their help and encouragement and particularly our long-suffering publisher, John Irwin, for his patience and advice.

D.S. Bell

Series Preface

The International Library of Politics and Comparative Government brings together in one series the most significant journal articles to appear in the field of comparative politics in the last twenty-five years or so. The aim is to render readily accessible to teachers, researchers and students an extensive range of essays which, together, provide an indispensable basis for understanding both the established conceptual terrain and the new ground being broken in the fast changing field of comparative political analysis.

The series is divided into three major sections: *Institutional Studies, Thematic Studies* and *Country Studies*. The *Institutional* volumes focus on the comparative investigation of the basic processes and components of the modern pluralist polity, including electoral behaviour, parties and party systems, interest groups, constitutions, legislatures and executives. There are also collections dealing with such major international actors as the European Union and United Nations.

The *Thematic* volumes address those contemporary problems, processes and issues which have assumed a particular salience for politics and policy-making in the late twentieth century. Such themes include: democratization, revolution and political change, 'New Politics', nationalism, terrorism, the military, the media, human rights, consociationalism and the challenges to mainstream party political ideologies.

The *Country* volumes are particularly innovative in applying a comparative perspective to a consideration of the political science tradition in individual states, both large and small. The distinctive features of the national literature are highlighted and the wider significance of developments is evaluated.

A number of acknowledged experts have been invited to act as editors for the series; they preface each volume with an introductory essay in which they review the basis for the selection of articles, and suggest future directions of research and investigation in the subject area.

The series is an invaluable resource for all those working in the field of comparative government and politics.

DAVID ARTER
Professor of European Integration
Leeds Metropolitan University

GORDON SMITH
Emeritus Professor of Government
London School of Economics and Political Science

Introduction: French Politics and Political Science: Out of the Mainstream?

The Fifth Republic, 'de Gaulle's Republic' as it used to be called, was introduced by referendum in September 1958 and the General became its first President on 21 December of the same year. The impact of its founder on subsequent politics can hardly be underestimated, de Gaulle's legacy included the rise of the presidency as the principal political office. French Republicanism was traditionally suspicious of over-powerful presidents and preferred to see the Assembly as the repository of popular sovereignty, reserving for the president the tasks of a 'constitutional monarch'.

However, not the least of the ironies of the Fifth Republic is that it has become the Presidential 'république des partis'. This is ironic because de Gaulle affected to despise political parties, although of course he founded one, the RPF, in April 1947, and owed his power to another (variously named UNR, UNV^c and UDR) which dominated the Assembly in the early years of the new republic. The Fifth Republic has witnessed a progressive bi-polarization of party politics. Starting with the coalition around de Gaulle, which consolidated French conservatism, marked a break with the right's instability in the Fourth Republic and provoked a reaction from the left (around Mitterrand's presidential bids), the Fifth Republic appeared on the road to an 'Anglo-Saxon' style left-versus-right 'alternation'. The creation of the Socialist Party in 1969 and its extraordinary rise under Mitterrand (after his 1971 takeover) seemed to confirm this tendency, though in reality things were not so simple.

First, the 1970s were a peculiar interlude, resulting in large part from the fact that President Pompidou died intestate. Had Pompidou lived to anoint a dauphin, the subsequent story might have been very different. As it happened, the 1974 presidential election was won by the centrist Giscard d'Estaing which both revived the centre parties (which had never been entirely happy with gaullism) and started a rivalry on the right between centrists and gaullists (and presidential hopefuls in each camp) which was not resolved. This rivalry was one reason for Giscard's defeat in 1981. After 1981 the 'orthodox' or conservative right had to contend with the loss of power as well as with its divisions and then, in 1983, with the rise of the extreme right under Le Pen. The National Front divided the orthodox right and prevented it from capitalizing on the Socialist government's mistakes.

On the other side of the divide, on the left, the position was also quickly revealed as one of internal coalition rivalry. The signature of the Communist and Socialist joint manifesto (the 'Common Progamme') in 1972 was followed by the unexpected rise of the French Socialist Party which, following Mitterrand's narrow defeat by Giscard, quickly established itself in 1974 as the dominant force in the coalition. The Communist Party decided that it could not tolerate being the junior partner and ended the coalition in September 1977. The apparent symmetry of the 'bi-polar quadrille' (or 'gang of four') was thus short lived (1974–77), with the politics of the two coalitions becoming even more intricate in the 1980s.

The 1981 election victory by the Socialist candidate Mitterrand together with the Socialist Party victory in the Assembly elections produced an unexpected result – the vertiginous decline of the Communist Party. Long before the fall of the Berlin Wall, the French Communist Party had started to collapse and, by the elections of 1988, it was sidelined. By contrast, the Socialist Party at this time appeared poised to become a 'party of government'. An internal change of political values to embrace social democracy (including the elimination of marxist rhetoric) and an end to its continual factional warring could have consolidated the new Socialist Party and confirmed it as the dominant party around which alliances revolved – in a mirror image of the gaullists of the 1960s. This did not happen. The party was content with its position in power, but could not master its internal squabbles and was plunged into a series of debilitating finance scandals. It became evident by 1991 that the party would be humiliated at the polls in 1993 (which duly happened). The only slight uncertainty was whether the rise of the ecologists who were themselves split (into the 'Greens' and 'Generation Ecology') would be able or willing to support the Socialists. The ecologists were not able to use their ephemeral popularity, while their ability to provide a reliable component for a governing coalition was always in doubt.

In institutional terms, the Fifth Republic has seen the rise of reliable, stable, presidential majorities; if these did look prone to periodic destabilization, the institutional settlement of 1958 has not been reopened. The movement of power from president to prime minister and back in the 1980s was politically, but not institutionally, difficult. The following pages will touch on the nature of the new constellation of forces as well as on institutional and party structures.

French Government

French government is one of the staples of political science; a student taking a 'political science' degree is almost certain at some point to encounter French politics. The reason for this is that France, along with the United States and the United Kingdom, has been a significant site for the development of representative democracy, with many of France's problems and solutions having a direct bearing on the parallel evolution of other western societies. France has therefore faced many of the major questions of government in the same spirit as Britain, America and the smaller western democracies – the extension of the franchise, orderly reform, welfare state construction, and the protection of human rights.

However, France has had a more turbulent political history than either Britain or America, and French politics have always exhibited some curious features (viewed from an 'Anglo-Saxon' perspective) – hence French 'exceptionalism' is a well-established research theme.[1] The massive French Communist Party (PCF), the curious rise of protest movements, quasi-revolutionary upheavals and so on are typical indications of the continuing paradox of French political life: it is clearly in, but not quite of, the western pattern.

It had been thought that the Fifth Republic would perhaps put an end to this 'exceptionalism', The first indications were that de Gaulle had removed one of the main obstacles and had created a modern mass conservative party (the 'gaullist party'), but the development of an adventurous foreign policy, the 'events' of May '68 and the collapse of gaullism created as many problems as they resolved, thus confirming France as the exception to many generalizations about western Europe.[2] The study of French politics raises many substantial methodological conundrums and difficulties of interpretation which bolster its status as a political science test bed. The passion of French politics, along with its personal as well as ideological distinctiveness, mean that it is likely to remain a centre of research attention; moreover, the intellectual rigour of the research work on France means that French political science will remain an essential part of the 'political science community'.

The Challenge of Comparison

There is a broad strand of study in political science labelled 'comparative'. However, as Jean Blondel and others have pointed out, its methodology never became as 'comparative', as sophisticated, as in anthroplogy and sociology.[3] Cross-cultural research does, however, present notorious difficulties, and political science lacks the 'unified field theory' which would enable concepts and events to be related and compared. In particular two rival candidates for theoretical hegemony in political science – marxism and functionalism – both turned out to be seriously misleading dead ends. (About the third aspirant, 'rational choice theory', see below.)

Comparative politics as a practice sought to build up generalizations and paradigms and indulged in model-building on a small scale. However, the study of comparative politics still suffers from the cultural problem: how do we take account of cultural factors? Human beings are not inert objects of study; they have ideas about what they are doing, how they behave and how they should behave. These perceptions, even if objectively mistaken, have to be taken into account otherwise behaviour is inexplicable. As has been posed before: can you understand banking as a whirl of paper, or do you have to know what people's notions of credit, exchange and so on actually are?[4] Similarly, politics is action and actions are taken (so the argument goes) with a mental map which will differ from society to society. How is this mental map to be discovered so that its influence can be gauged – or controlled for – so that an equivalence of actions can be established? If the cultural factor could be understood, then (so it is argued) a properly cumulative series of case studies could be built up – an advance of the first importance in comparative politics. At present its pursuit is bedevilled by the 'non-additivity' of isolated, culture-bound studies which neither relate to a general theory nor allow for larger generalizations. There are various ways of dealing with this problem but one, inspired by a long tradition of research and of concept-building, is the political culture approach. 'Political culture' is therefore the first topic to which attention must be turned.

French political culture presents some distinctive features, of which more later, but the first problem is the general and methodological one: how can 'political culture' be investigated and its influence determined? In Chapter 10, 'The Study of French Political Socialization', F. Greenstein and S. Tarrow analyse empirical research on the 'socialization' of French children into French political culture. The topic, as they point out, is replete with paradox; thus it is necessary to have a clear conceptual understanding and a sound empirical methodology if the influence of political culture is to be accurately gauged. The studies of French political culture, still in an early state, do not entirely avoid these problems, although they can, in principle, be resolved.

In their review of the research on French political socialization, Greenstein and Tarrow identify a number of continuing problems in the study of French politics (substantive as well as methodological). They consider a series of assumptions and hypotheses about French political culture and the values behind political cleavages, as well as the particular methodological problems of research into socialization. The idea of 'paradox' at the heart of the debate on French political culture together with many of the assumptions about political culture generally are analysed, but their main conclusion is that, in dealing with an object as protean as political culture, no one investigative technique will ever be sufficient. Rather, only a large case-study basis will enable theories of change to emerge. This empiricism will be, as they say, one means of ridding the study of French politics of its more 'mystical' tendencies – a task not yet complete.

In 'Change in French Society' (Chapter 6), Roger Duclaud-Williams examines Michel Crozier's powerful and persuasive view of French society. Crozier's model, very much dependent on the cultural variable, is that in France the political culture is pervaded by bureaucratic values (sometimes characterized as the alternation between routine and crisis).[5] The argument Crozier elaborates in *The Bureaucratic Phenomenon* (London: Tavistock, 1964) is that bureaucratic values lead to peculiar modes of change in France – rigidity followed by upheaval. In this view, 'May 1968' was a typical product of this bureaucratic political culture and was in fact caused by it. Duclaud-Williams argues that, examined in detail and stripped of conceptual and methodological ambiguity, the Crozier bureaucratic organizational model is not convincing when applied to politics. The 'fit' between reality and Crozier's general theory of change through routine, interspersed with the periodic crises of the French political system, appears persuasive at first sight (because of the cyclical nature of these crises), but it is not clear that the French Assembly was gripped by a bureaucratic culture, as he states, or that the upheaval of 1958, for example, was a general social crisis. Duclaud-Williams argues the case for a less ambitious approach, one based not on a general theory of change but on 'arenas of power' – identifying the obstacles to change and 'mapping out' where these impediments are serious and where they can be overcome. The key to change, argues Duclaud-Williams, is the extent of state involvement in different sectors of national life. Crozier's model remains persuasive because it is based on a general theory of organizational change, but Duclaud-Williams' analysis represents an important challenge to Crozier.

Also under the heading of 'change' comes the Constitutional Council. The Fifth Republic Constitutional Council is not strictly comparable to the US Supreme Court because it does not interpret the Constitution *post facto*; instead, legislation under consideration can be referred to it. It was not an immediately successful institution (for about a decade, it made absolutely no impact).[6] Whatever the intention of its framers, however, the Constitutional Council has steadily grown in importance and stature; by the 1980s it had come to display a blend of 'audacity and prudence' and had developed human rights legislation in France. This evolution came about partly by intention (President Giscard's reform, giving access on demand to 60 parliamentarians, was crucial) and partly through accidental political developments. Martin Harrison's 'The French Consitutional Council: A Study in Institutional Change' (Chapter 11) analyses the Council's development in a system resistant to 'rule by judges' and the Council's own acute awareness of its delicate position. The Council has few equivalents, but this discussion gives an important insight into a key Fifth Republic innovation, perhaps illustrating Thucidides's 'law' that institutions will expand over time to the utmost limit of their power. More importantly, it demonstrates the important political position of the law and of lawyers. As Martin Harrison shows, this must not be understood in a crude 'we are the masters now' politicization of law, but as a more subtle balance of outlook, persuasion and appreciation of the political role which law can play.

Frank L. Wilson's 'French Interest Group Politics: Pluralist or Neocorporatist?' (Chapter 25) is an exercise in comparative analysis. Wilson's is an important contribution to the lively discussion of interest group representation in France inspired by the 'neocorporatist' model of Lehmbruch and Schmitter. One of the most astute analysts of French political structures, Wilson places France in context. The models of interest group behaviour, usually presented as mutually exclusive representations of reality, are not appropriate to western Europe. The inability of western European systems to measure up to the 'pluralist' model (the United States) is frequently presented as a lapse (either moral or pre-modern, or perhaps both) and has led observers to propose a 'neocorporatist' model of interest representation.[7] However, the 'neocorporatist' model, which does not allow for the neutrality of the state, is also deficient since the interest group and the government both retain their autonomy; the relationship is thus a search for consensus – that is a bargaining, not a command, relation. If both 'pluralism' and 'new-corporatism' are unhelpful models – or actively misleading – then so too are the marxist and 'protest' accounts of interest group activity. The 'protest' relationship and the marxist (dominated/dominator) models have strong supporters amongst academics in France, but there are good grounds, as Wilson says, for proposing that the only appropriate representation of reality would be a judicious mixture of all four models.

Elections and Voting

France is the birthplace of the discipline of electoral geography. The seminal study by André Siegfried's *Tableau politique de la France de l'Ouest*, published in 1913, showed the conservative nature of voting habits and the relation between patterns of voting and social structures. Since that time voting studies have become more sophisticated and more technical, using a range of techniques (opinion polls, for example) which were unavailable to the pioneer Siegfried. French political science has a deserved reputation for extensive polling and statistical analysis.

However, Mattei Dogan and Daniel Derivry challenge one trend in polling studies when they argue, in 'France in Ten Slices', that national averages are insufficiently sensitive to the causes of political change. In Chapter 5 they argue that the social context explains much of the variation and that, in a country as diverse as France – one of the most heterogeneous in the European Union – only an analysis of local society can explain changes in variables.[8] Using the *canton* (the smallest administrative unit) as the basis of analysis, they place France's 2,450 cantons into ten categories or 'deciles' (each of 245 units) and analyse the cultural and social data for each. Slicing France into 'deciles' has the methodological advantage of 'demonstrating the impact of the social context on individual behaviour' showing, for example, the importance of religious practice. It also avoids the 'ecological fallacy' and is a ground-breaking method in electoral research.

Dogan and Derivry conclude that national averages are highly misleading because they hide very wide diversity in causal relations. Surveys based on individuals abstracted from the all-important social context are subject to a misplaced inference – the 'individualistic fallacy' (a mirror image of the 'ecological fallacy' which infers the characteristics of individuals from group data). They argue that it would be impossible to understand the rise of the extreme right National Front without an appreciation of the correlation between the proportion of Muslim immigrants and the vote for the extreme right. They go further to suggest that the territorial diversity of France explains the poor organization of French national political parties, although their study again brings out the importance of religion as an indicator of political outlook. The authors make some large claims for their statistical method, but also suggest some possible lines of future research (combining individual and aggregate data). Overall this is an important paper for both the study of France and elections.

In 'Economics and the French Voter' (Chapter 17), Michael Lewis-Beck engages both with the long-term debate about French voting patterns and with the fashionable 'rational choice' approach to political events. Is the evidence worldwide consistent with rational choice assumptions? In particular, do voters support governments which put money into their wallets (the so-called 'pocketbook vote')? At one level it is clear that voters are influenced by the condition of the economy, but that is not what the argument is about: the question is whether there is a direct link between their personal circumstances and their vote. A deteriorating economy, as Lewis-Beck acknowledges, does push voters into opposition, but selfish calculations – the fat or thin wallet – do not directly enter the considerations of the voter. In sum, people distinguished what was best for society from what was best for themselves; the vote was a social not a selfish one; people voted for the social interest.

Lewis-Beck distinguishes between American and French voting patterns, but the argument has subsequently widened (to take in other societies) and progressed. The methodological problems are considerable, involving a need to differentiate the effect of the economy on voters from the selfish vote. This research is also part of the testing of 'rational choice' assumptions and predictions and for this reason, too, is important. Rational choice theory has proposed a number of precise, falsifiable, postulates which are simple but not easy to test. For what it is worth, and the jury is still out, the most important of these rational choice hypotheses (budget maximizing bureaucracy, vote maximizing politicians and 'pocketbook voting') have not been corroborated by empirical studies.[9] The implications for France were an unusually high number of 'economic malcontents' prior to the 1981 elections which, combined with high unemployment and inflation, produced a low subjective index of well-being. Lewis-Beck's investigation does not cover the Socialist government except to note that, as of 1982, the new Mitterrand presidency was not succeeding on these fronts.

Research on women's political involvement has touched France as it has other political systems. However, as Bashevkin points out in 'Changing Patterns of Politicization and Partisanship Among Women in France' (Chapter 1), shifts in women's opinion have to be related to, and analytically disentangled from, the broader patterns of change. Bashevkin employs a much wider range of survey data than is usual and uses multiple indicators. Her general conclusion is that French women have become increasingly politicized since being enfranchised after the Second World War and that a trend towards increasingly left-wing attitudes occurred over the 1968–78 decade. By 1978 a majority of women in France were expressing a preference for the left, hence the conclusion that the reliance on assumptions about 'private' or domestic isolation is no longer warranted. The comparative implications are clearly important to researchers on other societies.

'Flash', 'surge' or protest parties (of which the 'Poujadist' movement of the mid-1950s is the most famous) were once a feature of French politics, but again it was thought that the French extreme right-wing current had dissipated by the time of the Fifth Republic.[10] However at the European elections of 1984, the National Front made a spectacular breakthrough (polling 11.2 per cent of the votes), with other elections of the 1980s confirming its place as a central actor on the French political stage. If the National Front has been the subject of extensive research, its origins and dynamics are still an object of controversy in the academic world. There are many aspects to this controversy, but Pierre Bréchon and S. K. Mitra deal, in particular, with its emergence and, especially, with its implantation in the town of Dreux (which subsequently became a solid base for the National Front). Chapter 3 distinguishes the National Front's core support from the fluctuating part of its vote (which is sizeable) and looks at how it is able to use specific incidents to play on what the authors call a 'latent deviant xenophobia' in France.

Political Parties

The 'deviant' aspect of French political life that the Fifth Republic was partially able to remedy was the absence of a major mass conservative party. Patriotic, capitalist and parliamentary conservatism in France was traditionally split into warring fragments (the ideal typical threefold division is set out in René Rémond's *The French Right*) and was poorly organized. Gaullism, the foundation of the Fifth Republic and over 12 years its dominant party, emerged as the conservative party, very much on the 'Anglo-Saxon' (or at least the British) model. However, the unexpected death of President Pompidou truncated the evolution of gaullism and plunged the French right into internecine conflict, which, even in 1995, it had still not resolved.

The gaullist party (under different names) provided the motive force for successive governments of the right and was the magnet for right-wing, centrist and conservative politics. This stability was abruptly overturned by the collapse of the gaullist party in 1974, the year after Pompidou's death, and then by its reshaping by Jacques Chirac in 1976 into the *Rassemblement Pour la République* (RPR), 'Chirac's' party (sometimes called 'neo-gaullist') and the direct descendant of the General's gaullist party. The problem tackled by Kay Lawson ('The Impact of Party Reform on Party Systems') is that of setting out parameters for long-term rivalry on the right (Chapter 16).

Although both the Socialist Party (in 1981) and the gaullist party (in 1968) won absolute majorities, the Fifth Republic's politics are still coalition-based, though more stable than in the Fourth Republic. Using a game theoretic framework, George Tsebelis develops the concept of 'nested games' in which parties pursue strategies in two different but connected areas. In Chapter 24, Tsebelis argues that the 'nested game' theory accounts for the cohesion of coalitions, that game theory accords with the empirical research and supports the hypothesis that there is a difference in behaviour according to whether the 'game' is visible to the electorate or not.

As with French conservatism, the French left stands out from the 'normal' western

European pattern in that it does not have a social democratic party. French socialism evolved from a sectarian base and had to contend with a big Communist Party on its left from 1921 onwards. The consequences of this were both the failure of a reformist, consensual social democracy to take root and an extreme factionalism in the French non-Communist left. This factionalism is analysed by A.M. Cole ('Factionalism, the French Socialist Party and the Fifth Republic').[11] The *Parti Socialiste* (PS) prefers, for political presentational reasons, to refer not to its 'factions' but to its 'tendencies' ('tendencies' being more acceptable divisions). All the same, it was an extreme factionalism which eventually caused the party to implode and was a reason for its crushing setback at the polls in 1993. In Chapter 4, Alistair Cole anatomizes the factions of the French Socialist Party into organization factions, parallel factions and external factions, locating the origins of factionalism in the old SFIO (in effect, a rather unstable conglomerate of parties). This essay advances the work on factions undertaken by Sartori and by Beller and Belloni, and embellishes their conceptual categories.

Within the *Parti Socialiste* the factions themselves composed a minor party system, the new factor in the Fifth Republic being the rivalry between personalities in search of presidential nomination. To a large extent this was disguised by the extreme ideological polarization of Socialism in the 1970s; its subsequent de-ideologization (partially as a result of the collapse of Communism) revealed, in 1990, a Namierite paradise with no Burke to interrupt the clash of naked self-interest. This spectacle caused the disenchantment of public opinion with the *Parti Socialiste*.

The Problems of Presidentialism

What kind of Republic is the Fifth Republic? Institutional stability, much touted as a gaullist success story, was dependent in its initial years on the General's political skills and then, from 1962–85, on relatively secure parliamentary majorities. In Chapter 8, Duverger characterized this period as 'semi-presidential government', not because the Presidents (de Gaulle, Pompidou, Giscard and Mitterrand) were in any way half-hearted in their exercise of power, but because the regime had neither the clear division of powers of the US nor the division between power and representative function characteristic of a proper parliamentary system. The fusion of presidency, executive and parliamentary majority produced almost unlimited presidential power, despite a constitution that should be read as Prime Ministerial.

The Prime Minister's power in the Fifth Republic in 'normal times' (outside the so-called '*cohabitation*') depends, not on the parliamentary majority, but on the President. This is a political, not a constitutional, fact whose scope is analysed by Elgie and Machin in their 'The Limits to Prime-ministerial Government in a Semi-presidential System' (Chapter 9).

The National Assembly, so bitterly criticized for its 'irresponsibility' in the Fourth Republic, was downgraded by the Fifth Republic constitution, but then began to work its passage back after de Gaulle's departure. The parliament's supine position towards executive authority could hardly be expected to change completely, given that the executive emanates from the parliamentary majority and that they stand or fall together, but the National Assembly has begun to assume a more central position in public debate. In this it joins the West European mainstream in which the national parliament is a principal forum for political controversy. The French National Assembly of the 1990s did play a more important role as initiator and focus in political life than in the 1960s; this limited power (rather than US-style Congress or Fourth Republic Assembly) is not dramatic, but is crucial in French politics. In an empirical study entitled 'Parliament's Capacity to Expand Political Controversy in France' (Chapter 2), F. Baumgartner draws attention to these changes in the status of the National Assembly in the Fifth Republic. Baumgartner argues that the Assembly can affect the policy process by moving debate from the technical level (where the outcome is decided by experts behind closed doors) to the ideological level (where it becomes public property). In the cases examined (which are from the Socialist era of 1981–86), the government was forced to back down. Grounded on Riker's work in 'rational choice' theory, this essay contrasts 'contractors', who limit debate to small groups, with 'expanders' who move onto (what is for them) the more favourable territory of symbols and ideology.

In 1951 Maurice Duverger made the famous prediction that, under certain circumstances, France could develop a bi-polar party system (this appeared in *Les Partis Politiques* in 1951). In 1995 this prediction still appears wide of the mark. In their study, 'The Reaffirmation of a Multiparty System' (Chapter 20), Joseph and Mildred Schlesinger explore the impact of electoral competition on the various parties, using a 'rational choice' framework. They conclude that Fifth Republic electoral competition forced the restructuring of parties and that the distinctive two-ballot elections in single-member constituencies for the Assembly ensured that 'the legislative group would be the core party unit in a multi-party system'. In a comparative study with the Third Republic, the researchers conclude that similar electoral rules produced similar organizations and, more broadly, that the French electoral system enables voters to express compromise choices – that is, to reject political extremes – a feature that has often been overlooked. The Schlesingers' work points to a slightly different conclusion than continuing bi-polarization, one that fits better with the contemporary reality of French politics.

Chapter 8, 'A New Political System Model' by Maurice Duverger, is a comparative study of presidentialism in western liberal democracies. The emergence of the presidency as the principal focus of political power and competition in the Fifth Republic has led to a series of attempts to characterize the new institution and to place it in context. In 1978 Duverger asked what would happen to the presidency were the left to hold the majority in the Assembly? Both Giscard (in a speech at Verdun-sur-le-Doubs in 1978) and Duverger came up with the same answer: that power would 'cross the river' from the Elysée palace of the President to the Matignon residence of the Prime Minister. Giscard's presidency was never put to the test because his supporters won the 1978 Assembly elections; in consequence, presidential supremacy was not challenged until 1986.

However Duverger's research on 'semi-presidential' regimes continued. These are located somewhere between presidential and parliamentary regimes and occur where a president is elected by universal suffrage and a government is dependent on a parliamentary majority. There is thus potential institutional tension between the president elected by universal suffrage (as developed during the Fifth Republic) and the government supported by a parliament of a different political composition from the presidential majority. Duverger identifies three types of semi-presidential regime: where the president is a figurehead, where the president is all-powerful, and where the president can share power with parliament. Using the comparative method and four explanatory variables (the constitution, tradition, politics and the nature of the parliamentary majority's relation to the president), Duverger's essay tries to explain why similar constitutions lead to radically different outcomes. If Duverger's transformational grid is a convincing explanation of the practical outcome of constitutional mechanisms, Georges Vedel is more persuasive in his view that France represents, not a semi-presidential synthesis', but an alternation between presidentialism and parliamentarism (the '*cohabitations*' of left-wing president and right-wing Assembly of 1986–88 and 1993–95 being parliamentary). Duverger's chapter nonetheless remains essential to the debate concerning the nature of presidentialism and the functioning of the French constitution.

The main constitutional innovation (or experiment) of the Mitterrand Presidency was the period of so-called '*cohabitation*' between a president supported by a majority of one persuasion and a parliamentary majority of a conflicting persuasion. In the period 1986–88 Mitterrand had been elected president by a left-wing (principally Socialist) electorate, where-as the parliament had a neo-gaullist and centrist majority which imposed Jacques Chirac as Prime Minister. President Giscard d'Estaing (who probably coined the term '*cohabitation*') had faced the problem of an incongruous majority during his term 1974–81, but one which was not so divergent: Giscard, a centrist, faced an Assembly which broadly supported him, but which was dominated by neo-gaullists, not his own centrist party.

'*Cohabitation*' was not the *pons asinorum* of the Fifth Republic (the loss of clear Assembly majorities is that) because the constitution was clear. Moreover, it could be said that the period of 1986–88 marked the first time in which the constitution worked as its framers intended. The interest in '*cohabitation*', as Pierce shows in Chapter 19, was therefore not constitutional but political. The battle between a president (whose office and person the right could not afford to humiliate) and a majority of the Assembly impatient to kick out the *ancien régime* was a 'war of movement' – a guerrilla war in which Mitterrand at first appeared to have been trounced (but fought back to win the presidential election of 1988). The victory of the left and Mitterrand's second term as president were built from the unpromising '*cohabitation*' setback at the polls in 1986, and from a vigorous right-wing majority. As Pierce underlines, there were very few constitutional powers open to the president at this time: Mitterrand delayed, but could not prevent, the passing of legislation. The '*cohabitation*' of 1986–88 was nevertheless popular with public opinion (which appreciated what it saw as bi-partisan solidarity) and was relatively productive. If the experience of 1986–88 shows that '*cohabitation*' can work, there were special circumstances then prevailing which do not guarantee that it will succeed in the future. The Socialist Party's defeat in 1993 and the return of another conservative majority forced a second '*cohabitation*' period for President Mitterrand until 1995.

Local and Regional Power

As is often said, France has more units of local government than the rest of the European Union put together. Recently, under the 1981–86 Socialist government, it added elected regional assemblies to the existing municipal and departmental tiers. These regions were widely canvassed in the Fifth Republic, with reform on the cards from the mid-1960s onwards, but it was left to the government of 1981 (in one of its two major reforms – the 'Defferre decentralisations') to give the 22 regions an elected membership and a clear statute.[12] The French regions are not a major political force and are situated within a unitary state; nevertheless, the right's victories in the first regional elections (of 1986) consolidated its position, as Yves Mény points out in Chapter 18 – 'Decentralisation in Socialist France'.

In 'Does Regional Government Work?' a comparative study of regionalism in France, Italy and Spain (Chapter 15), Michael Keating observes that the creation of a unified nation was more effective in France than in Spain or Italy, with the result that supporters of regional devolution were intially relatively weak. However, because of their long period in opposition coupled with their tenure of local office, the French Socialist Party leadership had become convinced regionalists. The net effect of the Socialist 'Defferre reforms' was less to create regional powers than to reinforce politicians against the civil service, especially the big city mayors (the Minister responsible, Gaston Defferre, was mayor of Marseilles). In Italy there are problems of the North/South contrast and the South's underdevelopment. Italian regions work efficiently in the North, where they have acquired startling political support against the central authorities (and against the South), allowing the regions to become one component in the list of possible political changes on the agenda in Italy. In Spain, the post-Franco regime was faced with the need to reconcile regional movements to the new central state. The Spanish regions were less homogeneous and more politically demanding than the French regions ever were (Corsica excepted); Spanish regionalism also had a long political history. The new Spanish central state began a period of negotiation which resulted in different powers for different regions, but also provoked constant argument in the Constitutional Court. In Spain and Italy revenue-raising powers for the regions are a problem, but in France, with weaker regional movements, this issue has not become politically salient.

The research by Keating brings to light the tension between regionalism and centralism. While decentralization has been the trend in the modern nation-state, the central authority has proved remarkably resistant. Regional power could develop, but other political preconditions had to be met first. In 'Decentralisation in Socialist France: The Politics of Pragmatism', Yves Mény analyses the *'grande affaire du septennat'* – the Defferre decentralization measures which created new institutions and which overall represented a wide-ranging and profound change in decision making. The reforms were not, however, as revolutionary as they appeared at first sight; they confirmed many existing practices and certainly did not devolve power directly to citizens. The effect of the reforms was to shift the balance of power to local representatives. The same tension noted by Keating, between regionalism and centralization, was evident in the Defferre reforms which are an attempt to recast the state so that it could manage modern France.

In 'State Structures and Clientelism: The French State Versus the "Notaires"', Ezra N. Suleiman looks at another aspect of the centralized state and asks whether a decentralized state is more accessible than a centralized one. The case study in Chapter 21 is of the reform of the notaries (*'notaires'*) which was resisted by the professional group. In France public notaries have a monopoly over the drawing up of legally binding contracts. In a long history of attempts to change their institution, the government elected in 1981 intended to open up entry into the profession, end the practice of notaries proposing their own successors and increase competition by freeing up the fee structure. However, the profession organized itself sufficiently for the reforms to be abandoned in 1984. The failure of this reform is an object lesson in political and administrative power. The Ministry of Justice became protector of the profession, the reform ceased to be given priority, and the centralized state facilitated a strong clientelism (ostensibly in contradiction with the overseeing and supervising role – the '*tutelle*'). By concentrating his analysis on the state, Suleiman illustrates the limits to state power and how that power can fluctuate; he also shows how the state's policy can be changed, how the state is open to influence and how the policy process is political and not 'managerial'.

The Communist Party

During the Cold War, Communist parties, which polled respectably in many countries in 1945, disappeared or became small minorities in most of western Europe, yet the French political system has exhibited one very distinctive feature: the persistence of a large and strictly orthodox Communist Party. Until the brief Indian summer of the Italian Communist Party in the 1970s, it was the French Communist Party which held the record for the highest Communist vote in free elections (winning 28.6 per cent in 1946). The USSR was, it must be remembered, an ideological superpower during the Cold War and this influenced – or even determined – the analysis and understanding of the Communist phenomenon in France. Where they did not become entangled with party politics, debates were dominated by a wholly inappropriate marxist model.

At the forefront of the reassessment of a Communist movement in a country where 'the industrial proletariat was small and lacking in homogeneity' and where the socialists had only a 'weak purchase upon such industrial workers as there were' is Tony Judt. In Chapter 14, Judt examines the dominant paradigms of the PCF, both his own and that of Professor Kriegel (whose work dominates the study of the PCF), as well as the Party's own curiously rigid dogma. The feature of PCF history which has still to be disentangled, and which may be more fully studied as a result of the opening of the Soviet archives, is the Party's close links with, and subservience to, the Communist Party of the Soviet Union. The major question which Judt raises for marxist historiography, and one more or less evaded until very recently, is the link between marxism and Communism. As Judt remarks, from Marx to Marchais (the PCF's leader after 1971) is a vertiginously descending trajectory, but the tracks are surely there.[13]

Political Protest

The May '68 'events' were, by any reckoning, an extraordinary phenomenon.[14] For about a month, in an advanced industrial society, government simply ceased to function and the streets were filled with demonstrating students. There are a number of unsolved problems about the French May '68 'events', but the topic tends to be dominated by the accounts of those who participated and by the ideologically committed (usually marxists). The objective analysis of May '68 and its problems has, rather surprisingly, been neglected; until recently, the heady rhetoric of the barricades has been prevalent in many accounts.

Sidney Tarrow ('Social Protest and Policy Reform') tackles one of the puzzles concerning the problems of May '68: what impact did the events ultimately have? In Chapter 22, Tarrow follows one specific reform of immediate relevance to the student demonstrators – the *loi d'Orientation* on the reform of higher education in France. Tarrow argues that a protest movement, even one the size of May '68, is not sufficient to initiate change; instead, reform requires an opportunistic elite group ready to take advantage of whatever situation arises.

Even so, the 'window of opportunity' is limited and soon closes. Touching on a number of comparative themes in addition to the policy process, protest and leadership, Tarrow's essay is an important contribution to the study of a society whch has experienced many waves of spontaneous mobilization (1936 or, more recently, 1986). Tarrow concludes with the suggestion that the opportunity provided by May '68 was insufficient to guarantee its success, which in turn could explain the continuing crisis in French higher education.

Leadership

The French political system has been characterized by the appearance of what Stanley Hoffmann calls 'heroic leadership' (ascribed to France's political culture)[15] and is yet another dimension along which France differs from Britain, the 'Old Commonwealth countries', Scandinavia and the US. The study of leadership – its sources, powers, style and impact – has therefore formed a notable part of the investigation of the French political scene.

On the Fifth Republic, the research turns principally on the legacy of its founder, General de Gaulle. What was de Gaulle's real contribution? Can we categorize the General's form of political leadership? What was de Gaulle's 'grand design' and what were his political principles? These are all continuing debates. Although less politically highly charged than in the 1960s, they are germane to understanding the nature of the Fifth Republic.

'Gaullism', thought to be a passing phenomenon, outlasted its founder. In 'Continuity and Change in Gaullism: The General's Legacy,'[16] David R. Cameron and Richard I. Hofferbert analyse the mass support for de Gaulle and the subsequent rejection of the founder of the Fifth Republic. A key concept here is Weber's notion of 'charismatic leadership'. Charismatic leaders are those whose authority emanates from the superhuman gifts 'imputed to them' by their followers and whose authority is thus essentially personal. 'Charisma' is a slippery concept and one which is difficult to operationalize. Charismatic leadership as a phenomenon appears to fit many figures on the French political scene (from Boulanger to de Gaulle) and is a very suggestive hypothesis. One of the key questions about charismatic leadership is how, if at all, it can become stable (because, dependent on miraculous results, the leadership type is seen as essentially unpredictable). Any charismatic leadership will have to be institutionalized, to cease to be purely personal, if it is to survive.

In studying the General's 'legacy', Cameron and Hofferbert attempt to show the transformation of charismatic mobilization into routine and non-personal support, as well as the corresponding convergence of de Gaulle's vote with that of the gaullist party. The reason for this shift was, they contend, located in the partisan realignment of 1962–67, itself a result of presidential politics. This research on the transformation of gaullism was concluded before President Pompidou's untimely death in 1974, but it remains a substantial empirical investigation into charisma and charismatic routinization, as well as into mass gaullism.

In addition to the constitution and the gaullist party, de Gaulle's other enduring legacy was to French foreign policy. This is sometimes summed up as the politics of '*grandeur*' captured by the famous images on the first page of de Gaulle's war memoirs: 'France cannot be France without "*grandeur*"'. However, in addition to the striking rhetoric of the General's foreign policy, there were the separate dimensions of nuclear and European policy. We will concentrate here on the most active part of French policy – the so-called European 'theatre'

– and on the ramifications of de Gaulle's outlook.

First is the famous contrast between 'General de Gaulle's Europe and Jean Monnet's Europe', brought out forcefully by Professor J.B. Duroselle in Chapter 7. Stripped of its imagery (which made it so attractive as a mobilizing political vision), de Gaulle depicted a Europe of nation-states acting in the manner of 18th-century monarchies, performing a stately balance-of-power minuet. As an all-purpose political justification, this vision – which allowed each power its place, its dignity and its respect – was rhetorically effective, being both flexible and capable of giving a sense of creative purpose to foreign policy – something notoriously elusive for middle-ranking powers. However, de Gaulle's image was counterposed with another (as it happens, equally French) concept of Europe – that of Jean Monnet (which of these two was the 'realist' and which the idealist might not be immediately evident). As Olivier Guichard noted with candour, de Gaulle was more than a little influenced by the romantic monarchist ideology of the extreme right and, taken at face value, his vision was completely divorced from the contemporary realities of international power (whereas Jean Monnet's was not). In many ways, Europe is still precariously balanced between these two outlooks.

However, de Gaulle did establish a political consensus around French foreign policy whose powerful *succès d'estime* made it difficult for subsequent presidents to change, whatever their outlook.[17] Consensus might be good in theory, but it was consensus around a grand, not to say grandiose, vision appropriate, perhaps, if France had been a superpower, but which in the circumstances was far too ambitious.

If the Cold War positioned France as the political and diplomatic energizer of Europe, then problems were raised for it by the unexpected elimination of superpower rivalry on the continent. In 'France in the New Europe' (Chapter 23), Ronald Tiersky looks at the problems posed for France by the collapse of the Cold War order which de Gaulle had so ably exploited. De Gaulle worked within a Europe divided between the Cold War antagonists; while he claimed to be pursuing a policy of overcoming these divisions (wrongly imputed to the Yalta conference settlement), he was adroit at exploiting the opportunities they provided.[18] The paradox is that, thanks to Jean Monnet and European institutions, France's position in the new Europe will be more important than it was in the 1930s. The old gaullist ideals, such as an assertive foreign policy, have begun to be challenged. This area is explored by Tiersky who analyses Europe and France's position after the 1991 Maastricht agreement (which envisaged steps to a common defence and foreign policy) on European union. In particular, as Tiersky notes, how has the reunification of Germany affected France and French foreign policy? There is, of course, not a straight answer in what is a rapidly evolving situation. In this Mitterrand, a figure no less sibylline than de Gaulle, may have scored some points, but France is now moving in a very different direction from that dictated by de Gaulle.

In 'The Political Principles of General de Gaulle', Douglas Johnson brings French political traditions and the General's own upbringing to bear on the question of the consistency – or otherwise – of de Gaulle's political action (Chapter 13). The General in this account is seen as a political thinker of some substance, with a distinctive, dynamic and (for 'Anglo-Saxons') unfamiliar political philosophy from which a set of principles was derived. These principles are identified and scrutinized in this attempt to discover the foundations of de Gaulle's politics.

One way of looking at de Gaulle is as a leader of vision and structured theory pursuing a well-defined project. This is the impression which de Gaulle's use of rhetoric sought to convey and which was largely successful in suggesting that the statesman-General, unlike mere 'politicians' of the Fourth Republic, did follow a high-minded and detailed blueprint. Since it is unlikely that any politician can have clairvoyance, another interpretation is suggested by S. and I. Hoffmann in their 'The Will to Grandeur' (Chapter 12). In this de Gaulle is interpreted as a 'political artist' fashioning French foreign policy 'creatively' from the materials to hand. Less important than the political blueprint, say the authors, was his use of opportunities which arose in the international system through which to underline the arrival of the new France of the Fifth Republic – a France of 'grandeur'. Thus, for example, the French veto of the UK's first application to join the European community in January 1963 was an adroit use of a stalemate situation to enhance France's position. The negotiations between Britain and the six had irretrievably stalled, but neither wanted to draw the obvious and invidious conclusion – that here were two incompatible positions which could not be reconciled. De Gaulle, however, was willing to be resolute, thus giving the negotiating gridlock a positive purpose – his own, of course – spiced with anti-Americanism. France did not keep Britain out (Britain's agricultural policy did that), but de Gaulle drew substantial strength from what appeared to be hopeless deadlock. This example shows how political 'artists' can use even the most intractable material for their own ends.

Conclusion: A French Science of Politics?

French political science has a long and distinguished history of major, indeed crucial, contributions to the development of the discipline. If the broadest and longest-term view of the history of political science is taken, then the French contribution has, of course, been in the front rank. The list of pioneers includes philosophers, empiricists and researchers such as Rousseau, Montesquieu, de Tocqueville and so on (the roll-call is virtually endless). Much of the early path breaking was French.

However, if we narrow the time scale and look at the exponential growth of the discipline of 'political science' since the Second War, then the French contribution has been less central (although also distinguished). As it has grown since World War II, political science has been US dominated. The political world may have been bi-polar, but the political science world has been uni-polar with one superpower. This is probably the case for a number of reasons, some of them intellectual (the domination of French academic culture by marxism) and some organizational. The American political science community, which has had as its aim the development of an objective universal science (an aim it shares with the mainstream European discipline), has not been 'ring-fenced' from outside; all the same the size and resources of the profession have given the US the lead and ensured American domination. Yet if political scientists in many small cultures have contributed to the building of the modern discipline, French political scientists have tended not to be so conspicuous in the mainstream.

Hence in political science, as in natural science, there have been European centres of excellence and individualistic contributions, but the two revolutions of behaviouralism and rational choice were American. Where does France stand in this context? French 'political science' as a discipline is as distinguished as its counterparts in the other main European academic centres. But France is not an academic superpower. The one area where French researchers made a highly distinctive contribution and one which, for historical reasons (a few emigrés apart), is not dominated by the US is the marxist tradition. However, marxism is now regarded as a social science backwater, especially by French intellectuals, and its contribution to the mainstream (other than by reaction against its postulates) has been minimal. Spin-offs from French marxism and from the more fanciful of French social philosophers have achieved some success in literary fields, but not in political science.

The areas of political research developed in the mid and late 20th century have included game theory, rational choice, functionalism, behaviourism and voting studies, with a drive to quantification and comparative analysis. Whereas there have been many remarkable studies in all of these areas, the main effort has again been American. The same must be said of the areas of the discipline in which France has a particular interest, including strategic studies. Individual French political scientists have contributed to animating the worldwide debate and have contributed powerfully to the course of its development. An obvious name here is Professor M. Duverger whose book on *Political Parties* set the framework for subsequent researchers, initiating an argument concerning the 'Duverger thesis' (linking proportional representation and multi-party systems) which is still in progress. There have also been contributions on power, elites, electoral analysis, socialization and political ideology which have been profoundly influential within the discipline. In addition to authors in this volume, prestigious names include Professor G. Lavau and Professor Annie Kriegel who have made impressive contributions to the understanding of the phenomenon of Communism. The widespread use of French as a 'second language' in the discipline means that technical studies have made their way relatively easily into the professional political science community.

The pressures facing political science are only partially academic and are not the same in France as in other countries. For example, the drive of UK research councils to promote collaborative research in large-scale projects is not replicated elsewhere in Europe. By the same token, gaps in the professional field are a mirror of its strengths: French political science has a strong juridical tradition and electoral studies are highly developed, but the theoretical debates which have shaken the discipline have had less effect in France (this may be positive, but France does lie outside the mainstream here).[19] French political science studies of local government, of the structure of power and of the sociology of elites are seminal. Yet in both political philosophy and empirical theory, the French contribution has been more limited; pursued within a largely national context, it has had fewer implications for the world community of political science.

A good deal of French intellectual energy of the last 50 years has run into the sands. Political science in France (as with economics, sociology, history and the 'softer' arts and humanities) has been diverted by the marxist agenda. It is tempting to be dismissive about the calibre of this work, turning as it does on abstruse problems of marxist theory (which to 'the non-marxist' are not problems). There are two issues here. The first is that, even within that limited remit and apart from a proliferation of neologisms, French marxism has made few fresh contributions.[20] Such contributions as were forthcoming were borrowings from 'bourgeois theory' to bolster the marxist synthesis. In Althusser, the marxist paradigm found its last fundamentalist, even if one at the service of the Communist Party. Other variations of marxism were based on the opposite mistake to that made by purist fundamentalists: that marxism was compatible with other intellectual trends. These syntheses were imposed on the pre-1848 Marx (which Althusser repudiated) and the spiritual/Hegelian aspects of the 1848 manuscripts. For example, the Christian-marxist dialogue (promoted by the Communist Party for political reasons) was based on this Marx-before-Marx misunderstanding: after 1848, Marx held that religion was an ideology which supported the exploitative relations of production.

The second aspect of this marxist intellectual tradition, and one which, as Judt points out, shows up a weakness in French political philosophy, is its emanation from a culture which looks for total – all-embracing – theory.[21] Despite the discovery of liberalism (and 'totalitarianism') in the 1980s, French intellectuals incline to system building on a grand scale. These post-war systems mainly derive from marxism, if at some distance. French political science, although not rich in 'master thinkers' like Malraux, Sartre, Camus, Mounier, Lyotard, Darrida and Foucault, has been subject to the same system-building pressures.

There is, of course, the towering figure of Raymond Aron. Aron must rank as the principal conservative philosopher of post-war Europe, but he was a teacher, a master of exposition and synthesis, and not an empiricist. Aron's astonishing clarity and refinement of conceptual categories are not to be underestimated. It was said of F.D. Roosevelt that he could take a subject like banking and explain it so that even bankers understood it. Aron, in turn, could take the baffling 'theological' nuclear strategy debates conducted across the US and explain them so that even strategists understood. This is a talent for analysis and commentary or exposition, but does not advance the discipline in a creative way. The importance of Aron internationally is his elegant elaboration and systematic ordering of material; in the French context, it was the contrast with Sartre (who 'left the darkness of the subject unobscured') which really mattered. If we focus on the political science mainstream and leave aside Cold War battles between intellectuals (important though they were), Aron is an isolated figure. In sum, French political science is active and thriving and continues to make a distinguished contribution to the discipline. All the same, whilst there is political science in France, there is no French political science.

So why study French politics? Leaving aside the obvious and urgent need for an extended comparative field, there are still reasons why France should continue to be one of the 'big four' analysed by political science students everywhere. One is the drama of French politics, along with its intense and endlessly self-reflective capacity. French politics is distinctive in nature, in content and in style, a distinctiveness which has not lessened with the decline of the French Communist Party or the departure of de Gaulle. The rise of the National Front and the ecologists is one aspect of this 'exceptionalism'; the nature of leadership is another.[22] France has retained its capacity for political surprises as well as for highly-charged issue politics which remains fascinating to the student of politics.

The impermanence of the French institutional settlement – France's inability to find a constitutional and political point of equilibrium – is another reason for the interest in French politics as a research area. The bitter but unsettled nature of French political action has also meant the politicization of much wider areas of French civil society than has traditionally been the case in Britain (and also, possibly, America). Institutions which in Britain have been outside political pressures, like the civil service and the electronic media, have not escaped them in France. (This is perhaps an oversimplification, but remains broadly accurate.) Thus the extent of politicization and the rapid escalation of problems into political issues must be of interest to 'political science'.

Then there is the position of the state in France. The state – the central study of the discipline – has developed very differently in France. The active developmental state will continue to concern political science, and France is the classic example of the 'interventionist' state (and not just in economics). Whereas in Britain and America the Industrial Revolution was achieved by the apparent retreat of the state from economics and society, this was not the case in France which lagged behind the major 19th-century powers. France had to use the state to impel and promote industrialization, and this remained a role of the state even under the right. By the same token, the creation of France itself was the work of the state in a way which it was not in England (where a sense of English identity and stable boundaries were established at a very early date). Thus French conservatism was as mindful of the centrality of the state as was the left, which puts the French state in a very different political position to Britain or America. The bureaucracy in France, much studied, and French local government will remain topics of continuing interest; indeed, France must be the testing ground for comparative studies in these areas.

However, the attractiveness of France as a country of study must lie, partially at least, in its accessibility and in the openness of its institutions to research. The French political science discipline is not as suffocating as it is in the US; institutions are not as closed as they are in the UK, and the subject is one which can be tackled by an ambitious researcher.

France is both too big and too small. Its very recent past as an intellectual superpower gives its intellectuals a self-confidence they would not otherwise have, but the nation has also retained a certain self-sufficiency into the *fin-de-siècle*.[23] In other words, much of French political science engages a Franco-French debate. Techniques, concepts and methods are imported and applied with perception and skill (one thinks here of the magisterial electoral studies), but they look inward and not outward. Had France been smaller like, say, the low countries or Scandinavia, the intellectual community would not have been able to isolate itself and would have had to engage more closely with the wider political science community. (The interventions of Rokkan, Lijphart, Daalder and others are testimony to this effect.) Where the UK has been unable to avoid the impact of the American science of politics because of the ease of elite interaction, the French have an – unintentional – linguistic protectionist barrier.

It must again be underlined that none of this is a denial of the quality of French political research, of its relevance to national concerns or of its contribution to wider French culture. The point is somewhat different: French political science has stood outside the mainstream, but it has had an impact and has an elite of distinguished practitioners.

Notes

1. See J. Lovecy (1992), 'Comparative Politics and the Fifth French Republic', *European Journal of Political Research*, **21**(4), June, pp. 385–408 and Anne Stevens (1992), *The Government and Politics of France*, London: Macmillan.
2. See, for example, S. Bartolini (1984), 'Institutional Constraints and Party Competition in the French Party System', *West European Politics*, **7**(4), October, pp. 103–27.
3. Jean Blondel (1981), *The Discipline of Politics*, London: Butterworth. On the methodology of comparative analysis, see Arend Lijphart (1971), 'Comparative Politics and the Comparative Method', *American Political Science Review*, **65**, September, pp. 682–93 and R.K. Yin (1981), 'The Case Study Crisis: Some Answers' *Administrative Science Quarterly*, **26**, March.
4. W.G. Runciman (1963), *Social Science and Political Theory*, Cambridge: Cambridge University

Press.
5. The French civil service has long been an object of study by foreign (in particular British and American) political scientists who have undertaken a number of comparative studies as well as others inspired by the neo-corporatist paradigm. There are many aspects to such investigation, including the administrative courts, the private offices of politicians and the 'impulsive' role of the state. Amongst the most important in English are two works by Ezra N. Suleiman (*Elites in French Society*, Princeton University Press, 1978 and *Politics, Power and Bureaucracy in France*, Princeton University Press, 1974); L.N. Brown and J.S. Bell (1992), *French Administrative Law*, Oxford University Press; D.A. Clark (1984), 'The Ombudsman in Britain and France: A Comparative Evaluation', *West European Politics*, 7(3), October; J. Hayward (1986), *The State and the Market Economy*, Brighton: Harvester; Yves Mény (1989), 'The National and International Context of French Policy Communities', *Political Studies*, 37(3), September; H. Machin in J. Richardson (ed.) (1982), *Policy Styles in Western Europe*, Unwin. E.J. Feldman's (1985) comparative study of British and French decision-making, *Concorde and Dissent*, Cambridge University Press, is exemplary. In addition, the French Plan is the subject of a substantial literature, amongst which may be signalled S. Estrin and P. Holmes (1983), *French Planning in Theory and Practice*, London: Unwin, which has a technical economic aspect; D. Green (1978), 'The Seventh Plan – The Demise of French Planning?' *West European Politics*, 1, pp. 66–76; P. Cerny and M. Schain (eds) (1980), *French Politics and Public Policy*, London: Methuen.
6. A. Stone (1989), 'In the Shadow of the Constitutional Council', *West European Politics*, 12(2), April, pp. 12–34.
7. In both abundance and complexity, the academic literature on the problematic concept of neo-corporatism is set to rival the community power debate of the 1960s. For an overview, see A.G. Jordan (1983), 'Corporatism: The Unity and Utility of the Concept?', Strathclyde Papers on Government and Politics No. 13, University of Strathclyde (Glasgow); the *locus classicus* is G. Lehmbruch and P. Schmitter (eds) (1982), *Patterns of Corporatist Policy-Making*, London: Sage.
8. Mattei Dogan's electoral and statistical work is renowned. However, the comparative dimension to Dogan's work is unusual within the French discipline. France is an obsessively opinion-polled society and its analysis of polls, elections and public opinion movements is correspondingly sophisticated. In the area of mathematical techniques and polling research, the French political science community is second to none. However, the intensity of focus on French politics and the importance of the Franco-French debate mean that very little of this work travels beyond the 'event horizon' of the 'Hexagon' which is metropolitan France. The European testing of American postulates (on 'partisan dealignment', for example) has been largely accomplished elsewhere. It remains the case that the Armand Colin/FNSP series of election analysis is amongst the best European work in this area, and that French electoral research centres (CEVIPOF, for example) are very highly regarded.
9. The testing of rational choice assumptions, to which Lewis-Beck contributes powerfully in his studies of 'pocketbook voting', lies outside the domain of this survey. However, rational choice has been tested in various studies, for example whether politicians' behaviour is 'vote-maximizing' and whether bureaucracies are 'budget maximizers', See, for example, P. Whitley (1986), *Political Control of the Macroeconomy*, London: Sage; G.A. Boyne (1987), 'Bureaucratic Power and Public Policies', *Political Studies*, 35, pp. 79–104; J. Bendor (1988), 'Review Article: Formal Models of Bureaucracy', *British Journal of Political Science*, 18(3), pp. 553–95; and, in particular Leif Lewin (1991), *Self-Interest and Public Interest in Western Politics*, Oxford: Oxford University Press.
10. The literature on the National Front is already substantial. In English see M.A. Schain (1987), 'The National Front in France and the Construction of Political Legitimacy', *West European Politics*, 10(2), April, pp. 229–52; J.G. Shields (1987), 'Politics and Populism', *Contemporary French Civilisation*, XI(1), Fall/Winter, pp. 39–52; K von Beyme (1984), *Right Wing Extremism in Western Europe*, London: F. Cass; S. Mitra (1988), 'The National Front in France – A Single Issue Movement?', *West European Politics*, 11(2), April, pp. 7–64; and J. Marcus (1994), *The National Front and French Politics*, London: Macmillan.
11. See also B.D. Graham's comparative study of factionalism and D. Hine (1982), 'Factionalism in West European Parties', *West European Politics*, 5, pp. 36–52.

12. S. Biarez (1982), '"Aménagement du Territoire" in France: State Intervention or Regulation?', *West European Politics*, **5**(3), July, pp. 270–86; D.E. Ashford (1990), 'Decentralising France: How the Socialists Discovered Pluralism', *West European Politics*, **13**(4), pp. 46–55.

13. Amongst the abundant literature on the French Communist Party, see in particular A. Kriegel (1966), *The French Communists*, Chicago: Chicago University Press; also the detailed and radical comparative work of the University of Nanterre group and its journal, *Communisme*.

14. Most of the material was written in the immediate aftermath of the May '68 'events' themselves and subsequent analysis – in English-language journals as well as French – is thin. C.E. Zirakzadeh (1989), 'Traditions of Protest and High-School Student Movements in Spain and France in 1986–87' (*West European Politics*, **12**(3), pp. 220–37) looks at the student movement of the mid-1980s from a comparative angle.

15. See L.J. Edinger (1967), *Political Leadership in Industrialized Societies*, London: Wiley.

16. In *American Journal of Political Science*, **XVII**(1), February 1973, pp. 77–98.

17. See S. Hoffmann (1984–85), 'Gaullism by any other Name', *Foreign Policy*, No. 57, Winter, pp. 38–57 for one approach, and M. Harrison (1984), 'Mitterrand's France in the Atlantic System', *Political Science Quarterly*, **99**(2), Summer, pp. 219–46 for a more balanced view.

18. D. Thomson (1965), 'General de Gaulle and the Anglo-Saxons', *International Affairs*, **41**(1), January, pp. 11–21.

19. The Old Adam, the legal training of many French 'political scientists', is very evident in the high quality of juridical analysis of the Fifth Republic Constitution. In English see J.S. Bell (1992), *French Constitutional Law*, Oxford: Oxford University Press.

20. On French marxism in general, see L. Kolakowski (1978), *Main Currents of Marxism, Vol. 3: The Breakdown*, Oxford: Oxford University Press; on post-war French marxism, see George Lichtheim (1966), *Marxism in Modern France*, London: Methuen. There is also E.P. Thompson's (1978) polemic against Althusser *The Poverty of Theory*, London: Pluto, which is from a putative marxist standpoint. The literature on the variants of French marxism is voluminous, impenetrable and mostly literary rather than 'political science'.

21. Again possibly as a result of its marxist/theoretical bias, French political science has made little impact on empirical theory (even though one of the leading comparative researchers is Professor Jean Blondel). Tony Judt's charge, made in *Past Imperfect* (Oxford: University of California Press, 1992, pp. 75 ff.), is that French politics lacks a political philosophy yardstick or a tradition of enquiry into such a measure, by which to judge political action. For Judt, the denial of universal criteria of truth and justice is a catastrophic failure in French political thought.

22. There is a substantial imbalance in the study of French political parties: the literature on the Communists is voluminous (understandable in the light of the Cold War, perhaps), but then so is research on the National Front. Articles on the Socialists are adequate, but there is virtually nothing in English on the modern neo-Gaullist Party (the principal party of the Fifth Republic) and only a few articles on the centre party (the UDF) which has played a key role in the years since its creation by President Giscard. French research reflects the same imbalance, if to a lesser degree. But see A. Knapp and P. Le Galès (1993), 'Top Down to Bottom-up?', *West European Politics*, **16**(3), July, pp. 271–94 and A. Cole (1993), 'The Presidential Party and the Fifth Republic' *West European Politics*, **16**(2), April, pp. 49–68; A. Knapp (1994), *Gaullism Since de Gaulle*, Aldershot: Dartmouth.

23. As might be expected given the cultural emphasis on the importance of the French language, French political science is innovative in textual and content analysis. Many studies could be mentioned but see, for example, the work by Monica Charlot and the book by J. Mer (1977), *Le parti de Maurice Thorez*, Paris: Payot. In English, see J. Gaffney (1989), *The French Left and the Fifth Republic*, Basingstoke: Macmillan.

[1]

B.J.Pol.S. **15**, no. 1 (1984), 75–96
Printed in Great Britain

Changing Patterns of Politicization and Partisanship Among Women in France

SYLVIA B. BASHEVKIN*

During the past decade, political researchers have devoted growing attention to women's political involvement and, to a somewhat lesser extent, their political attitudes in Western cultures. This interest has been a response in part to contemporary feminist movements and, more specifically, to the increasingly visible role of women as social activists, partisan elites and governmental decision makers in Western European and North American society.[1]

In the French electoral literature, recent analyses of women's political attitudes have addressed two major empirical phenomena, namely the extent of female politicization during the 1970s compared with the immediate post-war years, and patterns of partisan preference in this same chronological period.[2] Such studies generally conclude that French women are increasingly politicized and, at the same time, increasingly leftist in their partisan beliefs.[3]

Despite the consensus which has emerged around both of these trends, the development of women's attitudes in France remains in need of systematic attention. On a conceptual level, many existing studies have failed to relate shifts in female public opinion with broader patterns of political and social change in modern France. Such factors as the decline of traditional religiosity,

* Department of Political Science, University of Toronto. Research for this study was supported by doctoral and post-doctoral fellowships from the Social Sciences and Humanities Research Council of Canada. Earlier drafts of the article were presented at the Second Annual Conference of Europeanists (Washington, D.C., 1980) and the Sixth Annual Southwestern Ontario Comparative Politics Conference (McMaster University, 1982). I am grateful to Naomi Black, Alan D. Levy, and an anonymous reviewer for their helpful comments, and to Brenda Samuels for her expert typing of the manuscript.

[1] Major studies in this area include Jeane J. Kirkpatrick, *Political Woman* (New York: Basic Books, 1974); Melville E. Currell, *Political Woman* (London: Croom Helm, 1974); Jane S. Jaquette, ed., *Women in Politics* (New York: Wiley, 1974); and Margaret Stacey and Marion Price, *Women, Power, and Politics* (London: Tavistock, 1981).

[2] See, for example, Janine Mossuz-Lavau and Mariette Sineau, *Les Femmes françaises en 1978* (Paris: CORDES, 1980); Gisèle Charzat, *Les Françaises, sont-elles des citoyennes?* (Paris: Denoël/Gonthier, 1972); Albert Brimo, *Les Femmes françaises face au pouvoir politique* (Paris: Editions Montchrestien, 1975); Monica Charlot, 'Women in Politics in France', in Howard R. Penniman, ed., *The French National Assembly Elections of 1978* (Washington: American Enterprise Institute, 1980), pp. 171–91; and David R. Cameron, 'Stability and Change in Patterns of French Partisanship', *Public Opinion Quarterly*, XXXVI (1972), 19–30.

[3] Longitudinal comparisons in this area are based upon older survey data reported in Mattei Dogan and Jacques Narbonne, *Les Françaises face à la politique* (Paris: A. Colin, 1955); and Mattei Dogan. 'Le comportement électoral des femmes dans les pays de l'Europe occidentale', in *La Condition sociale de la femme* (Brussels: Editions de l'Institute de sociologie Solvay, 1956).

the emergence of a 'new left', and the development of contemporary feminism have generally been overlooked in the literature, even though a number of analyses suggest that older explanations of female attitudes – related to theories of clerical and spousal (i.e. husbands') influence – are no longer relevant to female public opinion.[4]

This conceptual issue is linked with important methodological problems in the existing literature. Established studies have frequently employed only two data points in comparing early post-war with contemporary findings; for example, many present data from one year in the early 1950s and one in the late 1970s.[5] This telescoping of female attitudes does not facilitate systematic longitudinal study of either politicization or partisanship, which is essential in order to relate the evolution of women's views to major social and political changes which have occurred during recent decades. Moreover, in examining patterns of politicization, a number of studies rely upon single, as opposed to multiple, indicators of this phenomenon.[6]

The present article employs existing survey data from the period 1951–78 in a detailed examination of changing patterns of politicization, measured in terms of political interest, voter turnout, and survey response, and party identification among women in France.[7] Our discussion considers both attitudinal phenomena in relation to ongoing changes in French society and politics, a difficult and complex project which is only begun in this study, but which remains promising as a source of new insights and hypotheses for future research.

[4] For a consideration of clerical and spousal influences, see Mossuz-Lavau and Sineau, *Les Femmes françaises en 1978*, Chaps 3 and 4; Brimo, *Les Femmes françaises*, pp. 75–9; Charlot, 'Women in Politics in France', pp. 174–80; and Charzat, *Les Françaises*, pp. 42–9, 53–5.

[5] Examples include Charlot, 'Women in Politics in France', Tables 6.1 and 6.3; and Margaret R. Inglehart, 'Political Interest in West European Women', *Comparative Political Studies*, XIV (1981), Table 5.

[6] The most common indicators employed in this literature are political interest (including frequency of political discussion) and voter turnout. See Inglehart, 'Political Interest in West European Women'; Mossuz-Lavau and Sineau, *Les Femmes françaises en 1978*, Chap. 1; Charlot, 'Women in Politics in France', pp. 172–4; and Charzat, *Les Françaises*, Chaps 1 and 2.

[7] The major data sources employed in this study are firstly, the 1958 French Election Study, directed by Georges Dupeux, François Goguel, Jean Stoetzel and Jean Touchard, which was gathered from a cross-sectional sample ($N = 1,650$, weighted to 1,870 cases) during three survey waves: pre-referendum, post-referendum and post-election. Approximately two-thirds of the sample was interviewed at each point in time. Secondly, data from the 1970 European Communities Study, directed by Ronald Inglehart and Jacques-René Rabier, are introduced. This survey included 2,046 French cases gathered from a national cross-section of respondents age 16 and over. Thirdly, Euro-barometres #6 (October/November, 1976) and #10 (October/November 1978), conducted by Jacques-René Rabier and Ronald Inglehart, are used. The former sampled 1,355 French respondents drawn from a stratified national quota sample. Since the rural population was under-represented in this sample, rural cases were duplicated in the ICPSR dataset (used in this analysis). The French sample in Euro-barometre #10 included 1,038 French respondents weighted to a total of 1,194 cases. These datasets were made available by the York University Institute for Behavioural Research, in co-operation with the Inter-University Consortium for Political and Social Research. Neither the original investigators nor the IBR not the ICPSR bears responsibility for the analyses or interpretations presented here.

The article is organized as follows. Firstly, we review briefly the background to female enfranchisement in 1944 as well as subsequent social and political changes affecting women's attitudes, in order to develop a series of hypotheses regarding politicization and partisanship from the immediate post-war years through the late 1970s. Secondly, we introduce data on political interest, electoral abstentions, and survey non-response in order to examine patterns of politicization in the early 1950s and following. This section relates an overall decline in gender differences and growth in female politicization between 1951 and 1978 to broader developments in religion, family life, the labour force and party politics, arguing that these wider social and political processes contributed to the emergence of an increasingly active and independent female electorate.

Thirdly, the article introduces a similar contextual argument in considering longitudinal trends in French partisanship. Using empirical data from 1958 and 1968 electoral studies, and from 1970, 1976 and 1978 Euro-barometre studies, we explore patterns of female party identification since the early post-war period. This part of the discussion suggests that longitudinal change in women's political attitudes – and most notably the recent growth in moderate leftism – is a generational process which merits careful attention by students of French public opinion.

THE BACKGROUND TO FEMALE ENFRANCHISEMENT

In a comparative study of women's political history in Western democracies, Richard Evans maintains that traditional values regarding the role of women were more deeply entrenched in Catholic than in Protestant cultures, and that efforts by late-nineteenth and early-twentieth century feminists to alter conventional gender norms were therefore more effective, and at an earlier date, in the latter than in the former.[8] Evans demonstrates as well, that the political as well as clerical opposition to legal reform – including the granting of the vote to women – was stronger in Catholic than in Protestant systems.

The lengthy struggle for enfranchisment in France offers useful support for this argument. In the late nineteenth and early twentieth century, French feminist and especially suffragist initiatives were strongly opposed by Church authorities, who supported hierarchical family organization under the direction of a male *chef de famille*.[9] The role assigned to women by this tradition was primarily maternal, centred around responsibility to the family and loyalty to Roman Catholicism. Historically, this set of duties was enforced by the Church, its schools, and affiliated organizations, and by restrictive laws

[8] Richard J. Evans, *The Feminists* (London: Croom Helm, 1977).

[9] On French family organization and the role of women within it, see Theodore Zeldin, *France, 1848–1945* (London: Oxford University Press, 1973), Vol. I; and Catherine Bodard Silver, 'France: Contrasts in Familial and Societal Roles', in Janet Zollinger Giele and Audrey Chapman Smock, eds, *Women: Roles and Status in Eight Countries* (New York: Wiley, 1977).

such as the Napoleonic Code of 1804, which limited women's rights in marriage, education, property ownership and political life.[10]

Clerical and legal traditions thus exerted a profound effect upon French women through the modern period, even though revolutionary action in the eighteenth century had enfranchised men and began a process of secularization and radicalization among them. The important role played by religious tradition within the lives of women is emphasized by Langlois, who argues that the influence of a revolutionary tradition upon males, combined with that of clericalism upon females, contributed to 'the progressive feminisation of the permanent cadres of Catholicism'.[11] This pattern is reflected in the growth of Women's Catholic Action (ACGF), which aimed to renew family life, to promote increased social welfare provisions, and to foster the mission of the Church in French society. Notably, ACGF attained a membership of some two and a half million during the early 1900s.[12]

Challenging established views regarding the role of women was therefore extremely difficult, including within the French left. During the late nineteenth century, activist Hubertine Auclert attempted to build a coalition between feminism and the socialist movement; her efforts established the Socialists as the first party to include social and political equality for women in their programme. However, Auclert's work was complicated by two factors which continued to affect the treatment of women by leftist organizations through the post-war decades: first, a widespread perception among Socialists that feminism was a bourgeois phenomenon which avoided the central issue of economic, and specifically class exploitation; and second, a generalized belief in French society that the majority of women were clericalist and therefore not promising material for left-wing mobilization.[13]

Efforts to enact female suffrage during the early decades of the twentieth century thus confronted many older, and fairly negative perceptions. In particular, parties of the left tended to favour suffrage in an ideological sense but feared its electoral consequences, while the Church and its allies generally opposed changes in the status of women, at the same time as they believed that female enfranchisement might aid Christian Democratic and other moderate political elements. The latter group therefore argued that women voters would neglect their children, oppose their husbands, and become ugly and unfeminine, while the former (and especially members of the Radical party) maintained that enfranchisement would 'strengthen clericalism and endanger the Republic'.[14] After rejection by the Senate in 1919, 1929, 1932 and 1935, female suffrage was finally decreed by General de Gaulle in 1944.

[10] For a discussion of the Napoleonic Code, see Maïté Albistur and Daniel Armogathe, *Histoire du féminisme français* (Paris: Editions des femmes, 1977), Chap. 2.

[11] Claude Langlois, 'Les effectifs des congrégations féminines au XIXe siècle', as quoted in Evans, *The Feminists*, p. 126.

[12] Michael P. Fogarty, *Christian Democracy in Western Europe, 1820–1953* (Notre Dame, Indiana: University of Notre Dame Press, 1957), p. 281.

[13] See Charles Sowerwine, *Les Femmes et le socialisme* (Paris: Presses de la FNSP, 1978).

[14] Evans, *The Feminists*, p. 134.

His decision is widely viewed as an acknowledgement of the important role played by women in the Resistance, and as part of an effort to establish a revitalized French Republic after the Second World War.[15]

The implications of these developments for women's attitudes in the immediate post-war period are complex but can be broken down into two main hypotheses. Firstly, it is notable that early feminist arguments for legal emancipation, including the vote, were opposed by clerical and political authorities for reasons which generally had to do with the perceived fate of particular French institutions – were women to gain increased rights. Feminist claims therefore became wedged within wider systemic disputes involving right and left, clericalism and anti-clericalism, such that French women themselves were hardly an independent political force either during these debates or following the formal granting of political rights in 1944.[16] This problem, combined with the fact that legislation to enfranchise females was introduced more as a clearing of the national agenda after the Second World War then as a reflection of either mass-level or elite-level consensus regarding their political rights, probably contributed to a profound hesitancy or ambiguity *vis-à-vis* politics among French women. This background to suffrage informs our discussion of female politicization in the years after the Second World War, in which we employ existing survey data on political interest, electoral abstentions and survey non-response.

Secondly, because debates about women's rights in France tended to be wedged in broader systemic cleavages, it is unlikely that the actual granting of the vote in 1944 altered established relations between females, on the one hand, and politically influential institutions, on the other. The relatively close attention paid to women by the Church and its affiliates, combined with a more masculine, class-orientated focus within trade unions and parties of the left, could therefore help to explain greater female support for such confessional groupings as the Mouvement Républicain Populaire (MRP), as well as lower female identification with leftist parties. Our re-analysis of 1958 French survey data, reported below, evaluates this proposition in relation to early post-war influences upon French voters.

THE CHANGING CONTEXT OF FEMALE POLITICIZATION AND PARTISANSHIP

An important question which follows from these two hypotheses concerns the impact of subsequent changes in French society and politics upon women's attitudes. For example, if such traditional institutions as the Catholic Church

---

[15] See Dogan and Narbonne, *Les Françaises face à la politique*, pp. 13–14. It should be noted that the 1944 Assembly vote on female enfranchisement was overwhelmingly in favour of suffrage.

[16] For a more detailed treatment of this period, see Jane Jenson, 'Women on the Agenda: Mobilization for Change in France', paper presented at Conference of Europeanists (Washington, D.C., 1982), pp. 7–21.

began to weaken by the early 1960s, then what implications did this process hold for female politicization and partisanship? In this section, we examine briefly the broader context of French public opinion, focusing in particular upon the period 1958 through 1978.

A useful starting point for this discussion is the 1958 establishment of the Fifth Republic which, according to Bourricard, corresponded with a series of governmental measures designed to achieve 'conservative modernization'.[17] In general social terms, France following 1958 became an increasingly urban, industrial and national society, as access to the mass media, consumer goods and a modern transportation system widened. Levels of formal educational attainment and non-agricultural employment grew rapidly, at the same time as migration to the cities reduced population in many heavily 'christianized' rural areas.

Since the consequences of social modernization in France were numerous and varied, we shall focus here upon the specific implications of change for the female electorate. First, in reference to confessional political organizations, modernization was associated with rural depopulation and the rise of television, both of which worked to diminish the circulation of clerical publications.[18] Industrialization and urbanization also drew such established groups as Catholic Action 'closer to the positions of the radical left', a process that was reflected in the declining electoral fortunes of confessional political parties.[19] The MRP received approximately 4,600,000 votes in 1945, but was reduced to less than 2,500,000 as the Centre Démocrate in 1968.[20]

At least part of this decline in confessional politics may be related to concurrent changes in the social and economic status of French women. In demographic terms, many older women who had been traditional practising Catholics, and who may therefore have supported such parties as the MRP, passed from the electorate. They were replaced by new cohorts whose political perceptions were likely to be shaped by exposure to more secular, and potentially radical influences, including higher education, paid employment and left-wing political organizations.[21] The impact of education and

[17] François Bourricurd, 'The Right in France since 1945', *Comparative Politics*, x (1977), p. 13. For a more general treatment of social change in France, see John Ardagh, *The New French Revolution* (New York: Harper and Row, 1968).

[18] See Vincent McHale, 'Religion and Electoral Politics in France', *Canadian Journal of Political Science*, II (1969), 292–311.

[19] Bourricurd, 'The Right in France', p. 23.

[20] Eric Cahm, *Politics and Society in Contemporary France* (London: George G. Harrap, 1972). On the radicalization of Catholic Action groups, see Renaud Dulong, 'Christian Militants on the French Left', *West European Politics*, v (1982), 55–72.

[21] According to Juillard, 'between 1962 and 1968, the number of working women increased by 6·89 percent; the number of employed males by 5·58 percent ... more women in France work than in any other Western European country.' See Joelle Rutherford Juillard, 'Women in France', in Lynne B. Iglitzin and Ruth Ross, eds, *Women in the World* (Santa Barbara: Clio Press, 1976), p. 118. On the important linkage between female employment and education, on the one hand, and exposure to leftist influences, on the other, see Cameron, 'Stability and Change', p. 29.

employment was especially significant among married women, who gradually gained increased financial and social independence, as reflected during the 1960s in legal changes which enabled them to open bank accounts without their husband's authorization, and to obtain equal rights and responsibilities in marriage.[22]

This apparent shift in the conditions which had earlier produced a less politicized, relatively confessional female electorate was accompanied by a second set of changes emanating from the French left. That is, the initial decades of the Fifth Republic were marked by considerable ferment in radical circles, notably among intellectuals who opposed the rigid, undemocratic theory and practice of conventional leftism. The growth of a 'new Left' in France, culminating in the events of 1968, thus provided a critical milieu within which student, anti-war, environmental and women's movements could develop – sharing as they did a common opposition to the class reductionism of the old Left. In the words of Jenson,

the status of women could not be derived *only* from the desire of capital to have a pool of cheaper, less organized, and more exploitable labour. The experience of women in the modern capitalist system ... raised questions of domination and subordination between men and women in work, in the family, in the couple, and in sexuality – issues which the traditional Marxist analysis ... could not answer.[23]

The women's movement of the 1960s and following thus posed a major challenge to conventional French political thought and practice, especially on the left, since its mobilizational focus was a group of citizens who had long been considered confessional and depoliticized in orientation.

In partisan terms, the response to this feminist challenge was mixed. PCF strategists, who recognized the value of a united (left) front approach in the mid-1960s, ultimately agreed to support reformed contraception and abortion legislation; their revised positions on social policy suggested that the shift toward Eurocommunism within the party as a whole might be accompanied by a more feminist, and less class reductionist commitment to women *qua* women.[24] Indeed, the PCF paid growing organizational attention to women through the mid-1970s, since party membership was 32 per cent female in 1976, compared with 25·5 per cent ten years earlier.[25]

[22] Legislative reforms are discussed in Juillard, 'Women in France', pp. 116 ff.

[23] Jane Jenson, 'The French Communist Party and Feminism', in Ralph Miliband and John Saville, eds, *The Socialist Register 1980* (London: Merlin Press, 1980), p. 125 Emphasis in original.

[24] For a thorough review of these processes, see Jenson, 'The French Communist Party and Feminism' as well as Jane Jenson 'The New Politics: Women and the Parties of the Left', paper presented at Conference of Europeanists (Washington, D.C., 1980), pp. 32–44.

[25] By way of contrast, female membership in the PS and PSU reached approximately 25 per cent in the early 1970s. See Roy Pierce, *French Politics and Political Institutions* (New York: Harper and Row, 1973), p. 155; Charzat, *Les Françaises*, pp. 58–9; R. W. Johnson, *The Long March of the French Left* (London: Macmillan, 1981); Yann Viens, 'Femmes, politique, Parti Communiste Français', in *La Condition féminine* (Paris: Editions Sociales, 1978), pp. 347–82; and Charles Hauss, *The New Left in France* (Westport, Conn.: Greenwood Press, 1978).

This seeming receptivity to feminist principles within the PCF, however, began to falter with the decline of Eurocommunism generally. As Jenson demonstrates in her case study of a women's commission in Paris South, 'the retreat to *ouvrierisme* after 1977' meant in part that the PCF rejected its new strategy *vis-à-vis* feminism, and adopted 'the old responses of dismissal, fear, and challenge'.[26]

By way of contrast, the governing alliance of Giscard d'Estaing consistently sought support from a liberal stream within French feminism. In 1974, Giscard appointed Françoise Giroud as Secretary of State for the Condition of Women, Simone Veil as Minister of Health, and two other females as members of the Government. These appointments, combined with divorce, abortion and anti-discrimination legislation passed during the Giscard presidency, helped to strengthen the image of the centre–right among reform-orientated feminists. More sweeping demands for publicly-funded abortions, however, and for an end to 'tokenism' in the fields of employment and party politics were frustrated by the essentially cautious, incremental approach of the Giscard government – a frustration reflected most clearly in the 1978 formation of Choisir, a separate feminist political party.[27]

These dual problems of retrenchment inside the PCF, and growing discontent among feminists with the Giscard Government provided valuable political opportunities for a third player, namely the Parti Socialiste (PS). Under the leadership of François Mitterrand, the Socialists initiated in 1971 an aggressive recruitment drive among younger, urban, white-collar voters, including women.[28] Unencumbered by the rigid doctrines and organizational strategy which characterized the PCF, the PS developed a party platform (including internal party affirmative action) which could be expected to attract feminist voters during the 1970s. Notably, through its critique of the policies of the Giscard government, which alleged that *la condition féminine* was widely studied but only marginally improved, the PS won support among feminist groups which had previously remained aloof from what they viewed as 'the patriarchal state'.[29]

This growing attention paid to feminist concerns by parties of the left, including during the Eurocommunist period in the PCF and more generally in the PS, suggests one basis for a major attitudinal shift among women voters.

---

[26] Jenson, 'The French Communist Party', p. 144.

[27] Wayne Northcutt and Jeffra Flaitz. 'Women and Politics in Contemporary France', *Contemporary French Civilization*, VII (1983), p. 187. The major policy positions of Choisir were presented in Gisèle Halimi, *Le Programme Commun des Femmes* (Paris: Bernard Grasset, 1978).

[28] On the rejuvenation of the Socialist left following 1971. see William Safran, *The French Polity* (New York: David McKay, 1977), pp. 86–91; and Howard Machin and Vincent Wright, 'The French Left Under the Fifth Republic', *Comparative Politics*, X (1977), 35–67.

[29] Margaret Collins Weitz, 'The Status of Women in France Today: A Reassessment', *Contemporary French Civilization*, VI (1981–82), p. 213. For the PS critique of Giscard's policies, see Northcutt and Flaitz, 'Women and Politics'. One prominent feminist group which endorsed the Socialists in 1981 was Psychanalyse et Politique. founded in 1968.

More specifically, we would expect the attempts of leftist parties to mobilize among an increasingly independent, politicized and secular female electorate to be reflected in longitudinal change in party identification through the 1970s. New cohorts of women, who were exposed to different politicization influences than those which had operated during the enfranchisement period, are especially salient to this hypothesis, since these younger females tended to be less religious, less socialized to traditional social (including gender role) norms, and more receptive to the increasingly leftist tenor of French electoral politics. We would therefore predict that the partisan attitudes of French females as a group, and of younger women in particular, became increasingly leftist through the late 1970s.

We shall now turn our attention to patterns of female politicization in the post-war years and following.

PATTERNS OF FEMALE POLITICIZATION

Existing studies of women's attitudes in France have frequently relied upon single indicators of politicization (generally political interest) drawn from a limited number of time points (usually two) during the past three decades. In the present section, we shall introduce quasi-longitudinal data from the period 1951–78 in order to examine in detail changes in political interest, electoral abstentions and survey non-response. The main purpose of this discussion is to establish major trends in women's politicization during the decades following enfranchisement, and to relate these trends to important social and political developments in France in this same period.

As reported in Table 1, gender differences in political interest in post-war France were generally large, reflecting considerably higher levels of interest

TABLE I   *Political Interest Among French Women and Men, 1953–78**

	1953	1958	1965	1969	1970	1976	1978
Women	40	47	53	53	31	60	59
Men	72	69	64	66	47	78	72
Difference (Women – Men)	−32	−22	−11	−13	−16	−18	−13

* All data are derived from nationwide samples with the exception of the 1965 figures, which are drawn from a study of Boulogne-Billancourt, a working-class area of Paris. Each entry represents the percentage of respondents professing any level of interest in politics, except for the 1976 and 1978 results which combine the percentage of cases reporting frequent or occasional political discussion.

Sources: 1958 French Election Study; Euro-barometres #6 (1976) and #10 (1978); Dogan and Narbonne, *Les Françaises face à la politique*; Guy Michelat, 'Attitudes et comportements politiques dans une agglomération de la région parisienne', in Gérard Adam et al., eds, *L'Élection présidentielle des 5 et 19 décembre 1965* (Paris: A. Colin, 1965); Charzat, *Les Françaises, sont-elles des citoyennes?* Philippe Braud, *Le Comportement électoral en France* (Paris: Presses Universitaires de France, 1973); and Mossuz-Lavau and Sineau, *Les Femmes françaises en 1978*.

among males than females. As might have been expected given the background to women's suffrage, the largest gender difference in political interest
in Table 1 (32 per cent) appears in 1953, the first year for which data are
available, while the highest absolute level of female political interest (60 and
59 per cent) is obtained in 1976 and 1978, the most recent years for which
figures are reported. While gender differences in interest tend to fluctuate in
the 11 to 32 per cent range during the years between 1953 and 1978, it is
notable that women's interest increased nearly twenty percentage points
through this period, at the same time as relatively little change occurred
among men. Females therefore became increasingly interested in politics
between 1953 and 1978, even though their absolute level of interest in 1978
remained substantially less than that of men.

In light of figures in Table 1, it would seem that the growth in female
political interest between 1953 and 1978 was fairly systematic. That is, except
for the 1970 data which show major declines for both men and women, female
interest tended to increase by approximately 7 per cent during three periods,
namely 1953–58, 1958–65 and 1969–76. By way of comparison, male political
interest generally declined over the period 1953–70, and peaked in 1976 (78
per cent), at the same time as female interest rose quite steadily to a 1976–78
plateau of approximately 59 per cent.

The relatively consistent growth in women's political interest, particularly
during specific chronological periods following the end of the Second World
War, was probably related to broader historical changes of direct relevance to
French females. The years 1953–65, for example, are widely identified by
political scientists with recurring constitutional crises of both the Fourth and
Fifth Republics.[30] In social terms, however, this same period was characterized by twin processes of modernization and especially female secularization,
and the passing of pre-enfranchisement cohorts, which probably contributed
to a 13 per cent increase in female political interest between 1953 and 1965
(see Table 1).

Similarly, in 1968 and following, France experienced social and political
conflict on a scale which Ehrmann and other analysts have termed
'traumatic'.[31] In specific reference to women, however, these same events and
processes seem to have had a reverse, distinctively liberating effect, since new

[30] On political instability during the Fourth Republic, see Philip M. Williams, *Crisis and
Compromise: Politics in the Fourth Republic* (London: Longmans, 1964); Philip M. Williams,
Politics in Post-War France (London: Longmans, 1958); and Duncan MacRae, Jr., *Parliament,
Parties, and Society in France, 1946–1958* (New York: St Martin's, 1967). For an overview of
French constitutional crises, see Pierce, *French Politics and Political Institutions*, Chaps 1–3, 5;
and John S. Ambler, *The Government and Politics of France* (Boston, Mass.: Houghton Mifflin,
1971), Chaps 1, 10.

[31] Henry W. Ehrmann, *Politics in France* (Boston, Mass.: Little, Brown, 1976), p. 211. On the
traumatic implications of 1968, see also Pierce, *French Politics and Political Institutions*,
pp. 129–40; and Lowell G. Noonan, *France: The Politics of Continuity in Change* (New York:
Holt, Rinehart, 1970).

left movements of the 1960s provided a major organizational and ideological base from which contemporary French feminism has developed.[32]

From an attitudinal perspective, the events of 1968 and the subsequent growth of feminism and a revitalized French left exposed younger female cohorts to an increasingly aggressive, radical political milieu. The growth of women's political interest to a level of nearly 60 per cent in 1976, representing an increase of twenty percentage points over the base figure of 40 per cent reported in 1953, suggests that these broader social processes influenced, and indeed enhanced the level of female politicization in France through the late 1970s.

Data on electoral abstentions during the period 1951–78, reported in Table 2, offer somewhat less direct evidence of growing female politicization over time. Comparing figures on non-voting in 1951 and 1973 legislative elections, for example, we find little change in the turnout levels of either men or women, such that the gender differential in both years remained at a level of 7 per cent.

One possible explanation for the relatively consistent pattern of French electoral abstentions since 1951, as compared with changes in political interest during this same period, is that parallel short-term influences affected non-voting among both men and women.[33] That is, although females had lower levels of political interest than males, they were probably encouraged to vote in the 1950s through the 1970s by clerical and rightist political organizations, at the same time as men received similar cues from left-wing parties and trade unions. This explanation is supported by the 1969 entries in Table 2, which show that in one presidential election where both the Communists (PCF) and Unified Socialists (PSU) recommended that their supporters abstain from voting, male abstentions slightly exceeded female (by 2 per cent). In 1969, therefore, the specific electoral cue given to men apparently differed from that offered to women, such that the regular pattern of male–female abstentions shifted somewhat. Over the longer term, differences were generally in the opposite direction, with female non-voting slightly higher than that of males.

Available data on 1977 and 1978 abstentions, however, indicate that these older gender differences may be disappearing. Since limited figures in Table 2 from Paris municipal and Vienne legislative elections show non-voting differed by only 1 to 2 per cent, it would seem that the exit of older female cohorts and the entrance of younger women who came of age politically after

[32] On the development of contemporary French feminism, see Elaine Marks and Isabelle de Courtivron, 'Introductions' to *New French Feminisms: An Anthology* (Amherst, Mass.: University of Massachuesetts Press, 1980), pp. 28–38; Albistur and Armogathe, *Histoire du féminisme français*, pp. 477–73; Jean Rabaut, *Historie des féminismes français* (Paris: Editions Stock, 1978), 333–80; Annie de Pisan and Anne Tristan, *Histoires du MLF* (Paris: Calmann-Lévy, 1977); and Naty Garcia Guadilla, *Libération des femmes: le MLF* (Paris: Presses Universitaires de France, 1981).

[33] This hypothesis is drawn from Alain Lancelot, *L'Abstentionnisme électoral en France* (Paris: A. Colin, 1968), p. 179.

TABLE 2 Electoral Abstention Among French Women and Men, 1951–78*

Year	1951	1953	1958	1962	1962	1965	1965	1967	1968	1969	1969	1973	1977	1978
Type of election†	L	M	R	R	L	PM	P	L	L	R	P	L	PM	VL
Female abstention	24	25	53	27	30	32	18	24	27	23	32	25	31	19
Male abstention	17	13	47	17	18	24	11	17	14	16	34	18	30	17
Difference (Women – Men)	7	12	6	10	12	8	7	7	13	7	-2	7	1	2

* Cell entries represent the percentage of electoral abstentions, with figures on presidential elections derived from the second round of voting.

† L = legislative; M = municipal; R = referendum; PM = Paris municipal; P = presidential; VL = Vienne legislative.

Sources: Georges Dupeux, Alain Girard, and Jean Stoetzel, 'Une enquête par sondage auprès des électeurs', in Mattei Dogan et al., eds, Le Référendum de septembre et les élections de novembre 1958 (Paris: A. Colin, 1960); Guy Michelat, 'Attitudes et comportements politiques à l'automne 1962', in François Gougel, ed, Le Référendum d'octobre et les élections de novembre 1962 (Paris: A. Colin, 1965); Alain Lancelot, L'Abstentionnisme Électoral en France (Paris: A. Colin, 1968); Charzat, Les Françaises: sont-elles des citoyennes? Brimo, Les Femmes françaises face au pouvoir politique; Mossuz-Lavau and Sineau, Les Femmes françaises en 1978; and Monica Charlot, 'Women in Politics in France', in Howard R. Penniman, ed., The French National Assembly Elections of 1978, (Washington, D.C.: American Enterprise Institute, 1980).

1968 has reduced remaining disparities. This generational view is confirmed by results reported in Mossuz-Lavau and Sineau, which indicate that the gender difference in municipal non-voting among Parisian respondents born before 1900 was considerably higher than in the overall sample (14 vs. 1 per cent).[34]

A third measure of female politicization in France is provided by data on survey response or, more accurately, non-response. The extent of non-responses among women in post-war surveys was widely noted, including in one study which claimed that females constituted 63·5 per cent of those who held no opinion about the 1958 Constitution.[35] In fact, the problem of ascertaining women's electoral preferences provided a major impetus for experimentation with separate ballot urns for men and women in France.[36]

TABLE 3   *Non-response to Party Identification and Party Preference Items, 1958–78*

Year	% Women (n)	% Men (n)
1958	54·5 (606)	40·5 (521)
1968	21·7 (871)	17·7 (837)
1978	21·2 (621)	17·6 (574)

* Cell entries represent the percentage of cases reporting no response to party identification (1958, 1968) and party preference (1978) items.

Sources: 1958 French Election Study; July 1968 IFOP survey reported in David R. Cameron, 'Stability and Change in Patterns of French Partisanship', *Public Opinion Quarterly*, xxxvi (1972), Table 3; and 1978 (#10) Euro-barometre study.

Non-response data from the first wave of the 1958 French Election Study, reported in Table 3, offer a useful baseline from which to analyse this phenomenon.[37] They show that the proportion of women professing no party identification or stating that they did not know their identification was 54·5 per cent, compared with 40·5 per cent among men. Notably, levels of non-response in 1958 exceeded 64 per cent among rural, university-educated, and younger women (under 29).

[34] Janine Mossuz-Lavau and Mariette Sineau, 'Sociologie de l'abstention dans huit bureaux de vote parisiens', *Revue française de science politique*, xviii (1978), 73–101. The levels of non-voting among women and men born before 1900 were 32 and 18 per cent, respectively.

[35] Georges Dupeux, Alain Girard and Jean Stoetzel, 'Une enquête par sondage auprès des électeurs', in Mattei Dogan *et al.*, eds, *Le référendum de septembre et les élections de novembre 1958* (Paris: A. Colin, 1960), pp. 119–93.

[36] A report on one such experiment is presented in Madelaine Grawitz, 'Le comportement féminin à Lyon, d'après une expérience d'urnes separées', in François Goguel *et al.*, eds, *Le référendum du 8 janvier 1961* (Paris: A. Colin, 1962), pp. 205–9.

[37] The first wave of the 1958 survey is employed because it included the largest number of female respondents (n = 606), compared with 395 in the second and 522 in the third waves.

Comparing these 1958 figures with patterns of non-response in 1968 and 1978, we find that significant changes occurred during the two decades following the establishment of the Fifth Republic. In both the 1968 IFOP and 1978 Euro-barometre (#10) surveys, approximately 21 per cent of women reported no party identification, which represented less than half the level obtained in 1958 (see Table 3). Moreover, gender differences in non-response for both 1968 and 1978 were in the 3 to 4 per cent range, as compared with 14 per cent in 1958. These major reductions in both the level of female non-response, as well as gender differences in non-response, indicate that a considerable politicization of French women occurred between 1958 and 1978 and, more specifically, during the years 1958 through 1968.

Additional 1968 data reported by Cameron indicate that non-responses among younger respondents in that year were relatively low, and did not differ at all by gender.[38] Moreover, comparing women age 21–9 in 1958 and 1968 samples, Cameron shows a very considerable drop-off in non-response from 69·0 to only 17·4 per cent, which suggests once again that younger female cohorts in 1968 and following were relatively interested, aware and as politicized as younger males.

To summarize this discussion of changing patterns of female political interest, abstentions and non-response in France, we would conclude that substantial shifts have occurred in all three indicators of politicization. Firstly, in reference to political interest, we have shown that the absolute level of female interest increased considerably during three periods between 1953 and 1978, while the relatively extreme gender differences in interest which existed during the 1950s decreased in these same years. Secondly, in terms of non-voting, the data indicated that although levels of male and female abstention were relatively similar from 1951 through the 1970s, both 1977 and 1978 figures suggested that even these residual differences were disappearing, probably as a result of the entrance of new cohorts to the female electorate. Thirdly, in analysing patterns of non-response, we demonstrated the magnitude of this phenomenon among women in 1958, and showed that the extent of female non-response as well as gender differences in non-response had both diminished considerably during the decade 1958–68.

Now let us turn to the background to female partisanship in post-war France.

CLERICALISM, LEFTISM, AND PARTY IDENTIFICATION

The historically close relationship between women and clericalism, and men and leftism held major implications for political attitudes in post-war France. The present section reviews these contextual influences briefly, arguing that institutional factors related to the Catholic Church and parties of the left played a significant role in shaping partisanship after the Second World War.

[38] Cameron, 'Stability and Change', Table 3. In 1968, non-response among men and women aged 21–9 was 17·4 per cent.

We then introduce 1958 public opinion data in order to examine empirically the impact of these factors.

Theodore Zeldin's study, *France, 1848–1945*, provides an excellent review of the treatment of women by major social institutions.[39] Zeldin maintains that female political behaviour during the first half of this century is best understood in terms of an important coincidence between the concerns of the Catholic Church, on the one hand, and the traditional responsibilities of French women, on the other. In Zeldin's view, because women were encouraged to love God, the Church, and their families at the same time as the Church was attempting to establish a social foundation for its religious mission, a strong alliance developed between institutional Catholicism and large numbers of French females. This alliance was reflected in the growth of Church schools and in such organizations as Women's Catholic Action (ACGF), which encouraged French women following the Second World War 'to collaborate in the Church's apostolic mission . . . in its present efforts to bring the weight of [ACGF's] 2,300,000 members to bear on public opinion and institutions'.[40] According to subsequent studies, Catholic Action had fairly specific objectives which included providing civic education to French women, ensuring state aid to Church schools (the *écoles libres*), increasing social welfare provisions, and publishing materials 'of Catholic inspiration'.[41]

The extent to which this alliance between women and the Church had identifiable political effects, however, is complicated by the shifting electoral strategy of French Catholicism in the post-war years. In a 1955 report for UNESCO, Dogan and Narbonne contended that clerical leaders were explicit in their condemnation of all left-wing candidates, including those of the Radical, Socialist, and Communist parties.[42] By way of contrast, a later study of the 1958 elections by Rémond argues that while the Church and its affiliated organizations formally condemned non-voting as well as the PCF, they did not explicitly endorse either the confessional MRP or other parties of the centre-right and right.[43]

In spite of this variation in electoral cues, there existed a systematic overlap between the policy positions of organized French Catholicism and those of the post-war Mouvement Républicain Populaire. Established as a centrist, Christian Democratic party after the Second World War, the MRP promoted

[39] Zeldin, *France, 1848–1945*, pp. 292–3, 343–62.

[40] *Annuaire* of Catholic Action in France, 1950, as quoted in Fogarty, *Christian Democracy in Western Europe*, pp. 281–2.

[41] William Bosworth, *Catholicism and Crisis in Modern France* (Princeton, N.J.: Princeton University Press, 1962), p. 142.

[42] Dogan and Narbonne, *Les Françaises face à la politique*. The French study was part of a larger four-nation project commissioned in 1953 by UNESCO, at the request of the United Nations Commission on the Status of Women. See Dorothy Pickles, 'The Political Role of Women', *International Social Science Bulletin*, v (1953), pp. 75–104; and Maurice Duverger, *The Political Role of Women* (Paris: UNESCO, 1955).

[43] René Rémond, 'Les catholiques et les élections', in Dogan *et al.*, eds, *Le Référendum de septembre et les élections de novembre 1958*, pp. 99–116.

90   BASHEVKIN

a series of moderate social reforms in such areas as family allowances and social security.[44] These measures would, in the view of party leaders, eliminate fundamental injustices in French society and thus the need for socialist and Marxist parties. In the words of Fogarty, the MRP thereby sought 'to become the king pin of a "third force"' between right and left.[45]

By way of contrast, leftist institutions in post-war France gave less consistent organizational attention to women voters. As described above in our discussion of the nineteenth-century suffragist Hubertine Auclert, parties of the left were historically distrustful of both women voters generally, who were presumed to be incurable clericalists, and feminist activists more specifically, whose arguments did not fit neatly within the male-dominated organizations or class-orientated ideologies of the left. This uneasy relationship between women and the left was reflected quite clearly during lengthy legislative debates over enfranchisement, when the relatively small Radical party (RGR) opposed female suffrage on the grounds that women voters would 'punish' parties of the left and reward those of the centre and right. Notably, the RGR sponsored very few female candidates in legislative elections following enfranchisement. In 1946, for example, 12·1 per cent of the RGR slate was female, followed by 7 per cent in 1951. These figures compare unfavourably with the percentage of women candidates advanced by the MRP (13·3 and 11 per cent, respectively) – a result which is especially notable in light of the traditional social ideology of the Popular Republicans.[46]

The two major parties of the French left after the Second World War, the Socialists (SFIO) and Communists (PCF), were considerably more sympathetic toward women than the Radicals. As outlined by Dogan and Narbonne, both expressed ideological support for the rights of women and also maintained women's affiliates in the Union des Femmes Françaises (UFF), allied with the PCF, and the Action Démocratique et Laïque des Femmes, sympathetic to the SFIO. As well, both major parties of the left actively promoted women candidates, particularly the widows of Resistance fighters, in post-war elections.[47]

This formal record in support of women, however, was accompanied by less favourable treatment inside the institutions of the Socialist and Communist left. Although much of this treatment is only beginning to receive scholarly attention, research by Bacot and Jenson suggests that women's groups on the

[44] See François Goguel, 'Christian Democracy in France', in Mario Einaudi and François Goguel, eds, *Christian Democracy in Italy and France* (Notre Dame, Indiana: University of Notre Dame Press, 1952), pp. 109–224; and R. E. M. Irving, *Christian Democracy in France* (London: Allen and Unwin, 1973).

[45] Fogarty, *Christian Democracy in Western Europe*, p. 336.

[46] Data on female candidacies are drawn from Dogan and Narbonne, *Les Françaises face à la politique*, Chap. 9.

[47] According to Dogan and Narbonne, the proportion of female candidates in 1946 and 1951 was highest in the PCF (19·7 and 25 per cent, respectively), followed by the SFIO (12·7 and 15 per cent, respectively). Approximately two-thirds of female legislators who were elected during the Fourth Republic were Communists.

left were generally auxiliaries of the main party organizations; as auxiliaries, they were neither intended nor expected to challenge men's prevailing organizational and ideological dominance of the left.[48] Moreover, given their long-standing distrust of both women voters and feminist 'agitators', the post-war PCF and SFIO did not vigorously pursue the mobilization of women on mass or elite levels, even though each party sponsored female candidates and separate party affiliates during this period.

TABLE 4   *Distinct Party Identifications (%) Among Women and Men in September, November and December 1958**

	Wave I		Wave II		Wave III	
Party	Women	Men	Women	Men	Women	Men
Communist	8·6	9·7	11·2	8·1	8·0	7·1
Socialist	25·3	39·4	20·6	32·1	12·9	28·1
Radical	12·7	13·1	6·5	12·5	3·8	5·6
Popular Republican	20·8	11·6	14·1	9·8	11·1	4·5
UNR/Gaullist	13·6	10·0	22·9	20·7	52·4	43·5
Indep. Farmers	19·0	16·2	24·7	16·8	11·8	11·2
(*n*)	(221)	(259)	(170)	(184)	(288)	(267)

* The *n*s reported in this table reflect only those respondents offering a distinct party identification. All missing data, including political tendencies, have been excluded.
   Source: 1958 French Election Study.

In the light of this contextual background, it is not suprising to find that in 1958, the partisan attitudes of women in France were substantially less leftist, and more favourable toward the MRP and other centre and right parties than those of men. As reported in Table 4, the overall level of leftist partisanship among females was, across the three waves of the study, considerably less than among males. Comparing PCF, SFIO, and RGR support in the final phase of the survey, for example, we find a gender difference of 16·1 per cent, with 40·8 per cent of men and only 24·7 per cent of women expressing identification with any of the three parties. The vast majority of this difference is attributable to large disparities between male and female support for the Socialists, which reached 15·2 per cent in the third wave of sampling. In comparison, levels of PCF and RGR partisanship were fairly similar among both sexes, although the general pattern was for men to be more communist as well as more radical than women.

Data in Table 4 also show that women were somewhat more supportive of the MRP than men in all three waves of the 1958 study, with gender differences ranging from 4·3 to 9·2 per cent over the three waves. As well, these figures show that while the absolute level of both female and male MRP

[48] Paul Bacot, *Les Dirigeants du Parti Socialiste* (Lyon: Presses Universitaires de Lyon, 1979), Chap. 4; and Jenson, 'The French Communist Party'.

92   BASHEVKIN

TABLE 5   *Mean Levels of Agreement with State Aid to Church Schools,*
               *1958**

Group	Mean	Standard error	Standard deviation	(*n*)	Prob.
Men	2·53	0·06	1·20	(481)	≤0·001
Women	2·83	0·05	1·16	(493)	≤0·10
MRP women	3·32	0·20	0·89	(19)	

  * Respondents were asked whether they agreed or disagreed with the following statement:
'The state ought to subsidize *les écoles libres.*' The difference of means test was employed to
determine significance of differences between women and men in aggregate, and between women
in aggregate and MRP identifiers.
  Source: 1958 French Election Study, Second Wave.

identification declined between September and December of 1958, with the
very pronounced growth in Gaullist strength, the lowest point of MRP
support among women (11·1 per cent in the third wave) was only slightly less
than the initial level of male support (11·6 per cent). Moreover, Table 4
indicates that the proportional decline in MRP partisanship over the three
waves was less among women than men, such that the party's support base
grew from 60·5 per cent female in September of 1958 to 72·7 per cent female
in December of that year. These figures compare with earlier results
indicating that the MRP electorate was between 53 and 61 per cent female in
the late 1940s and early 1950s.[49] The gender imbalance in MRP support which
was present immediately after the Second World War thus increased following the exit of voters, particularly men, from the party's electorate during the
fall of 1958.

TABLE 6   *Party Identification (%) of French Women by IFOP Regions*
               Code, 1958

Party	Paris	West	Northeast	Southeast	Southwest
Communist	8·7	4·7	11·4	8·1	8·3
Socialist	26·1	20·8	27·1	13·5	35·4
Radical	8·7	7·0	14·3	13·5	16·7
Popular Republican	8·7	39·5	21·4	10·8	16·7
UNR/Gaullist	13·0	11·7	11·5	24·3	10·4
Indep. Farmers	34·8	16·3	14·3	29·8	12·5
(*n*)	(23)	(43)	(70)	(37)	(48)

  Source: 1958 French Election Study, First Wave.

  [49] These 1958 percentages were calculated by summing the total number of respondents who
identified with the MRP in each survey wave, and then determining the proportion of each total
which was composed of women. Older survey data are drawn from Dogan and Narbonne, *Les
Françaises face à la politique*, as well as *Sondages*, XIV (1952).

In addition to these specific findings concerning gender and MRP support, our data also point toward a number of related conclusions regarding confessional influences upon partisanship. As reported in Table 5, women were significantly more supportive of state aid to Church schools (the *écoles libres*) than men and, quite interestingly, female MRP identifiers were significantly more inclined toward the pro-Church view than women in aggregate. Combined with data which show a strong relationship between pro-Church attitudes toward education and residence in confessional regions of France (see Table 6), on the one hand, and centre/right partisanship, on the other, these results suggest an important clerical dimension in women's attitudes.[50] That is, the congruence between women's perceived interests and those of the French Catholic Church in the post-war period contributed in part to particular patterns of female public opinion, including lower levels of leftist partisanship, greater female support for Church views regarding education, and higher rates of MRP identification, as well as a strong positive correlation between centre/right partisanship and clericalist influences.

Clearly, factors other than a confessional interest in women voters also contributed to these trends. The relatively limited education and paid employment of French women in the post-war years, for example, as well as the generally masculine, class-based orientation of leftist political organizations, helped to shape female public opinion in a manner distinctive from that of men.[51] As reflected in Table 6, however, the interest in women shown by parties of the left and corresponding levels of female party identification varied by region, such that PCF support was highest in two regions where its women's affiliate, the UFF, was most active, namely Northeastern France (11·4 per cent) and Paris (8·7 per cent). While these figures are only heuristic, they do suggest that the inattention of the French left to women generally had negative attitudinal consequences, but that where some form of organized mobilization occurred (and here the case of the UFF may be instructive), female public opinion reflected its impact.

The last group of hypotheses outlined above concern longitudinal change in female partisanship in France. We shall now turn our attention to this subject.

CHANGING PATTERNS OF FEMALE PARTISANSHIP

The 'conservative modernization' of France following 1958, which involved important changes in both social structure and political life, held major

---

[50] Among females residing in the highly confessional West of France, 39·5 per cent identified with the MRP, while among those living in the Northeast region – which included the heavily christianized area of Alsace-Lorraine – 21·4 per cent identified with the party. These figures coincide with older regional data reported in Bosworth, *Catholicism and Crisis in Modern France*. Data on the relationship between attitudes toward the *écoles libres* and female partisanship, not presented in tabular form, show that 61·5 per cent of women who were in complete agreement with state funding were centre or right partisans, compared with only 22·2 per cent of those who were not at all in agreement. The level of leftist partisanship increased systematically, from 8·2 to 44·4 per cent, with opposition to state aid.

[51] See Cameron, 'Stability and Change'.

94   BASHEVKIN

TABLE 7   *Party Identification and Party Preference Among French
Women, 1958–78**

	1958	1968	1970	1976	1978
Left	24·7	33·3	42·8	51·6	56·0
Centre/Right	75·3	66·7	57·2	48·4	44·0
(*n*)	(288)	(682)	(739)	(501)	(479)

* Each cell entry represents the percentage of female respondents professing left or
centre/right party identification (in 1958 and 1968) and party preference (in 1970, 1976, and
1978).
Sources: 1958 French Election Study, Third Wave; 1968 IFOP survey reported in Cameron,
'Stability and Change in Patterns of French Partisanship'; 1970 European Communities Study;
and Euro-barometres #6 (1976) and #10 (1978).

consequences for women's partisan attitudes.[52] As we have argued, these
changes probably affected female perceptions of both the confessional right
and parties of the left, such that by 1968 women could be expected to
evidence lower centre and right identification, and correspondingly greater
leftist support. Indeed, as reported in Table 7, 33·3 per cent of French women
in 1968 identified with a leftist party, compared with less than 25 per cent in
1958. This growth was particularly apparent among younger women (age
21–9), where 46·3 per cent expressed leftist identification in 1968. By way of
contrast, the extent of centre and rightist identification among women
between 1958 and 1968 declined from 75·3 to 66·7 per cent and, among
younger respondents in 1968, this figure dropped to 53·7 per cent.[53]

This same general process of partisan change continued through the 1970s.
As reported in Table 7, French women became increasingly leftist in their
political preferences through 1978, at the same time as the female pillar of
support for centre and rightist parties continued to erode. Roughly speaking,
the ideological division of female preferences in 1978 represented the reverse
of the 1970 pattern, since a majority of women favoured centre and rightist
parties in 1970, an approximate 50–50 split existed in 1976, and a majority
endorsed leftist parties in 1978.

Over the longer term, we find that the two-thirds to three-quarters support
of women for centre and rightist parties which existed prior to 1970 had
dissipated to a level of less than 45 per cent by 1978. More importantly,
among the youngest female cohort (under age 30) in the 1978 survey, only
36·8 per cent expressed preference for a party of the centre or right,
compared with 53·7 per cent among a comparable group in 1968. This decline
in centre and rightist support among young women, accompanied by an
increase from 46·3 to 63·2 per cent in leftist support during the same ten-year
period, suggests that generational change helped to produce a major partisan

[52] Bourricard, 'The Right in France Since 1954', p. 13.
[53] These figures were adapted from Cameron, 'Stability and Change', Table 3.

realignment among French women in the Fifth Republic and, more specifically, in the decade following 1968.

Data from the Euro-barometre surveys also indicate that the French Socialist party gained disproportionately from women's shift toward the left. Between 1970 and 1978, the PS increased its share of the female vote by approximately fourteen points, from 23·8 to 37·7 per cent, at the same time as the PCF gained slightly, the PSU remained more or less at the same level, and the MRG lost substantially relative to its small base. Comparing levels of Socialist strength over the longer term, we find that female support for the party nearly tripled during the twenty years following the establishment of the Fifth Republic, since it grew from 12·9 per cent of total female preferences in the fall of 1958 (as the SFIO) to 37·7 per cent in the fall of 1978 (as the PS). During this same period, PCF support among women increased far less significantly, from 8·0 to 12·5 per cent.

This last finding sheds important light on the relationship between attitudinal change among French women, on the one hand, and broader transformations of the party system, on the other. On the basis of this discussion, we would propose that the overall decline of traditional Catholicism and its confessional affiliates, combined with a generalized shift away from Gaullist and neo-Gaullist conservatism in the direction of moderate leftism (i.e. the PS) have been mirrored quite clearly in women's attitudes. This point permits us to speculate that the future of female partisanship – and especially of moderate leftism – rests partly in the ability of the present Socialist regime to accomplish meaningful reforms and, in particular, in its ability to grant feminists and other newly mobilized groups effective political influence within that process. As the apparent benefactor of increased female politicization and leftist partisanship during recent decades, the PS seems compelled to respond to these changes by widening the numerical and substantive representation of women within French government.[54]

CONCLUSIONS

This discussion has examined changing patterns of female politicization and partisanship in France, in the context of broader social and political developments during the post-war years and following. On an empirical level, the study indicates that French women have become increasingly politicized in the period since the end of the Second World War and, in particular, that levels of political interest and survey response rose especially in the decade 1958–68. Moreover, our analysis of political partisanship has shown a trend toward increasingly leftist attitudes – primarily in the decade 1968–78.

These findings suggest that growing female politicization in the years immediately after the establishment of the Fifth Republic was followed by a

[54] See Hannah Fenichel Pitkin, *The Concept of Representation* (Berkeley: University of California Press, 1967).

pattern of rising leftism, such that changes in politicization may have laid the groundwork for major alterations in party identification and preference. More specifically, the entrance of new female cohorts in the years 1968 and following, combined with the exit of older and more politically conservative groups, would seem to have transformed the attitudinal contours of the female electorate, to the point that a majority of women respondents in 1978 expressed preference for a party of the left.

On a conceptual level, the relationship between these shifts in female public opinion and broader changes in French politics and society provides a significant challenge for future research. Firstly, this linkage suggests that established approaches to women's attitudes, which frequently rely upon assumptions regarding a changeless, ahistorical condition of 'private' womanhood, are no longer relevant to attitudinal research.[55] Claims to the effect that domestic isolation produced a situation wherein women were exposed only to the political cues of their spouses and religious leaders, need to be supplanted by a more rigorous evaluation of family roles, clerical and leftist influences, and the complex changes which have affected these factors across time. The growing literature on women's political and social history in France and elsewhere provides a useful starting point for re-considering the contextual background to female attitude formation.

Secondly, the comparative implications of a revised approach to women's views are varied and important. A recent effort to relate patterns of female partisanship to broader social changes in Quebec has produced remarkably similar results; that is, the treatment of women by politically influential institutions (especially the Church and major party organizations) appears to be linked closely with Francophone attitudes over time and, once again, the entrance of younger cohorts has tended to alter major features of female political partisanship.[56]

If employed in other traditionally Catholic cultures, such as Italy, or in such Protestant cases as the Anglo-American democracies, this contextual approach could help to clarify the significance of women's political experiences to their political perceptions and, in more general terms, could address the relevance of changing structures and norms to the development of modern public opinion.

[55] For a critique of this older literature, see Sylvia B. Bashevkin, 'Women and Change: A Comparative Study of Political Attitudes in France, Canada, and the United States' (doctoral dissertation, York University, 1981).

[56] See Sylvia B. Bashevkin, 'Social Change and Political Partisanship: The Development of Women's Attitudes in Quebec, 1965–1979', *Comparative Political Studies*, XVI (1983), 147–72. Similar approaches to American and English Canadian public opinion are developed in my 'Social Feminism and the Study of American Public Opinion', *International Journal of Women's Studies*, VII (1984), and *The Last Frontier: Women and Party Politics in English Canada* (forthcoming), respectively.

[2]

FRANK R. BAUMGARTNER

Texas A & M University

Parliament's Capacity
To Expand Political Controversy
In France

The French parliament generally plays a limited policy-making role in the Fifth Republic. However, on occasion it can play a greater role by generating controversies about governmental actions and by stimulating debates on issues which would otherwise be considered only by specialists. Policy makers know that the outcome of a policy debate is decided in large part by the arena in which it is considered. They use sophisticated rhetorical strategies to force consideration of an issue into the arena of policy making which is most favorable to them. The national legislature plays a central role in these strategies even in France, where its impact on the policy process is otherwise limited.

Generally speaking, politicians become involved in political questions, and civil servants and other experts decide technical ones. The definition of what is "political" and what is "technical" is anything but straightforward, however. In fact, the definition of the issue is the battlefield on which strategic policy makers maneuver. Those on the losing side of a conflict within a specialized community of experts attempt to demonstrate that the issue has broad political implications so that political generalists will become involved, thus changing the balance of power in the policy community (Schattschneider, 1960). These policy makers are called "expanders." "Contractors," on the other hand, dominate the specialized policy arenas and attempt to portray issues as narrow technical measures appropriately left to the "experts" to decide. Expanders focus on easily understood symbols, of which some examples are "liberty," "equality," and "anticommunism." Contractors use the most arcane and incomprehensible vocabulary possible so that nonspecialists cannot even understand the questions being discussed. Almost all issues involve some political and some technical aspects, and strategic policy makers portray issues in contrasting ways, depending on whether they want to expand or to contract participation. The result of the rhetorical battle between expanders and contractors determines where the issue will be considered and therefore what the outcome will be.

Politicians and other policy makers are adept at manipulating arguments to suit their needs (Kingdon, 1984). One of the first major controversies of the Chirac government in 1986 involved the proposed sale of a state television channel. Socialist opponents of the measure transformed it into a broad question indeed: "The proposal . . . has already generated the widest public protest of any Government measure so far, with many groups here contending that the state-owned stations are an inalienable part of the national cultural heritage" (Bernstein, June 12, 1986). Selling off the national cultural heritage is not a popular position in France, and opponents of the sale will have killed it if they succeed in portraying it that way, whether or not they believe that it actually is related to France's cultural traditions. U.S. politicians are just as adept as their French counterparts at manipulating arguments to their advantage. In order to stop the Defense Department from transporting potentially hazardous nerve gas through his state, one senator was able to persuade his colleagues that the plan actually represented "an unconstitutional usurpation of the Senate's power to ratify treaties." Since his fellow senators were not willing to vote against their own power to ratify treaties, this strategic politician transformed his minority position into the majority one (Riker, 1986, p. 110). Policy makers seeking funding for education in the United States showed their strategic skills when they established a link between the Soviet space program and the U.S. education system.

The fact that Sputnik spurred our primary space effort is from the standpoint of the student of policy initiation an expected outcome, since anybody can see the connection between the Soviet space effort and the United States space effort. The task of leading official thinking to make a connection between the perceived "threat" of imminent Soviet space exploration and inadequate funding of schools and colleges is of a different order of complexity, and suggests that entrepreneurial talent of a very high order was at work (Polsby, 1984, p. 170).

The parliament plays an especially important role in the expansion of national debates in France, since it represents one of the best opportunities for expanders to generate large amounts of news coverage and to force an item onto the general political agenda. In concert with expanders outside of parliament, allies within parliament can use the legislative debate to create a massive public controversy where none existed before. It is no coincidence that street demonstrations and other publicity-generating techniques are timed to coincide with parliamentary consideration of a bill. The deputies and the senators of the opposition are natural allies of expanders within the specialized policy communities. Parliamentary expanders are often less interested in the substantive content of the bill than in the opportunity to embarass the government. The interests of these "procedural" expanders in parliament and the "substantive" expanders from within the specialized policy communities coincide in important ways, though they do not overlap completely, as this article will illustrate.

All efforts at the expansion of an issue are not successful, and many bills are passed through parliament with little or no public controversy. On occasion, however, the combination of parliamentary and nonparliamentary tactics can lead to complete policy reversals—quite some power for a supposedly powerless legislature. This article shows how the French parliament can play an important, though a sporadic, policy role even under the tight constitutional strictures of the Fifth Republic.

Description of the Study

This article compares three pieces of legislation considered by the French parliament between December 1982 and July 1984. It is drawn from a larger study which compared 30 cases of policy making in the field of education. Over 100 interviews were conducted with upper civil servants, members of parliament, and interest group representatives as part of the larger study. This article compares only the three cases where extensive debates occurred in parliament. The fact that the national legislature held extensive debates in only 3 of the 30 cases in this larger study says much about the limited policy role of that body. Though the deputies and the senators are often completely absent from the policy process, this article seeks to demonstrate the sporadic, but essential, role which they sometimes play.

Leaders from each of the four parliamentary groups identified members from their party who were especially active in the three bills studied here. This produced a list of 18 Socialists (PS), 2 Communist (PC), 1 Conservative (UDF), and 6 Gaullist (RPR) members. Published reports and transcripts of committee sessions and of floor debates corroborated this selection of specialists. Interviews were conducted with 12 PS, 2 PC, 1 UDF, and 3 RPR members; 17 were deputies and 1 was a senator. Five staff members (two PS, one PC, and two RPR) were also interviewed. While the over-all response rate among members of parlia-

ment was 67% successful interviews were conducted with each of those
most centrally involved; for example, respondents included each of the
committee *rapporteurs*. In addition to the 23 parliamentary respondents,
civil servants and interest group representatives involved in each of the
three cases were also interviewed. The civil servant with the most direct
responsibility for the bill was interviewed first, then others mentioned as
playing an important role in the policy. In all, interviews were conducted
with 50 policy makers involved in the three cases studied here (16 for the
medical schools reform, 15 for the higher education reform, and 19 for
the private school bill). Documentary sources such as the legislative
debates, and administrative and interest group reports were also consulted.

The Limited Policy Role of Parliament

The framers of the 1958 constitution deliberately reduced the
policy role of the national legislature because they perceived the powerful
parliament of the Fourth Republic to be the source of instability. The
constitution of the Fifth Republic restricts the areas of policy where the
parliament may legislate, which were unlimited in the Fourth Republic,
to an enumerated set. The government has control over the parliamentary agenda, the power to accept or to reject amendments, the power to
make any vote a motion of confidence, and the power to force a
"package vote" on government bills with no amendments accepted. In
the budgetary process, parliament has strict time limits on debate, and
the government's proposed budget enters automatically into effect if the
parliament is unable to reach agreement within the specified time.
Deputies are forbidden from offering bills or amendments which would
decrease revenues for the state or increase expenses. "Under the Fifth
Republic, the French parliament, 'once among the most powerful in the
world, became one of the weakest'" (Williams, 1968; see also Wahl,
1959; Andrews, 1962; Chandernagor, 1967; Suleiman, 1973; Masclet,
1982; Safran, 1985; Bréhier, June 13, 1986; Converse and Pierce,
1986).
     The degree of control which the government enjoys over the
National Assembly can be illustrated by a few simple statistics. Between
1968 and 1983, 80% of the bills which the parliament passed into law
were of governmental origin, with the figure reaching 95% in 1981, the
year the Socialist party arrived in power (calculated from France,
Assemblée Nationale, 1984). There are more member bills (*propositions
de loi*) introduced in the typical session than government bills (*projets de
loi*), but the government bills are almost assured passage while the
member bills have less than a 1% chance of success. In 1983, for exam-

ple, there were 650 member bills and 159 government bills, but 115 of the government bills were approved while only 5 member bills made it to the end of the legislative road. Also, since members may not introduce bills or amendments which would increase government expenditures or decrease revenues, their bills tend to be limited in policy importance.

Since the government can accept or reject member amendments, it can insure that its bills are not altered significantly during consideration by the Assembly. Sixty-six of the 115 government bills passed into law in 1983 were subject to no amendments whatsoever. Even when amendments are accepted, they generally come from the government itself or from its allies in the majority. Of the government amendments, 89% were passed, as were 92% of the amendments offered by the committees. Within the committees, the *rapporteur* (and therefore the majority party) dominates. Of 2,600 amendments accepted in committee in 1983, almost 2,300 were from the *rapporteur*. Of the amendments offered by Socialists, 64% passed, but only 14% of Communist-supported amendments. Less than 5% of the amendments offered by the opposition parties were successful (cf. Andrews, 1978, pp. 484, 489).

Another aspect of the dominance of the executive branch over the legislative lies in its control of information. Except for the committee *rapporteur,* few individual legislators in France have the personal expertise or the staff resources to conduct an investigation independent of the party. By U.S. standards, the staff resources of French deputies are minuscule (Campbell and Laporte, 1981; Ranney, 1981). Most deputies interviewed for this study indicated they relied on a single staff aid for their legislative work and on another for their district case work. The minimal staffing levels of the parliament as a whole and of the individual legislators in particular make it easier for the government and the parliamentary majority to control debates, thereby adding to an already impressive set of constitutional advantages of the executive over the legislative branch.

The constitutional reforms of the Fifth Republic and the limited staff resources of the parliament make its policy role smaller than that of the U.S. Congress or the parliament of the Fourth Republic. The reforms have no effect on the parliament's role as a focal point for national debates, however. Indeed, the reduced role of parliament in substantive and detailed policy decisions creates incentives for the deputies and the senators to contribute to the policy process in other ways. Members of parliament are natural expanders of policy debates, and the parliament as a whole plays its greatest role when it generates or amplifies controversy. The members of the governmental majority only rarely play this role. Opposition members seize almost any opportunity to criticize governmental policy, so they are the natural allies of policy

38   Frank R. Baumgartner

expanders hoping to shift an issue from the specialized to the general
political arena.

Parliament and the Expansion of Conflict

Media coverage of an issue increases dramatically whenever
parliamentary debate focuses on it. Especially when combined with
public demonstrations and other activities outside of parliament, the
parliamentary debate can explode an issue onto the front pages of the
newspapers and onto the national political agenda. The parliament is one
of the few places where credible and respected spokesmen regularly
criticize governmental policy and is therefore routinely canvassed by
reporters (Sigal, 1973). Because of the privileged access to the media
which the parliament enjoys, those on the losing side of a debate within
the specialized policy communities can expand the issue and force it onto
the national political agenda. This section discusses three bills which illustrate the special role parliament plays in the expansion of debates
within the French policy system.

The Medical School Law

In response to rules adopted by the European Community in 1975
(European Community, 1975a, b), the government of Prime Minister
Raymond Barre passed a law which would increase the level of training
of general practitioners and specialists (law no. 79-565 of July 6, 1979
relative aux études médicales et pharmaceutiques). Before this law was
applied, however, the Socialist electoral victories of 1981 occurred, and
the new government decided to pass a different law. A small group of
Socialist legislators interested in health questions established an informal
working group shortly after the 1981 elections, and this group worked
closely with the government in preparing the new law. Each member of
this group was a doctor, a pharmacist, or another type of health professional by training. They met with ministerial officials before the submission of the bill and steered the legislation through parliament with only
minimal debate. The leader of this informal group, Louis Lareng, a
Socialist deputy and a medical doctor himself, became the *rapporteur* of
the bill on medical studies. Law no. 82-1098 *relative aux études médicales
et pharmaceutiques* was passed on December 23, 1982. Up through the
passage of the bill, participation was entirely restricted to specialists. Officials from the Ministries of Health and National Education, the deans
of the medical schools, and the small group of Socialist deputies with expertise in the health area completely dominated the process. The bill was
a model of policy making by specialists.

On deputy closely associated with the passage of the law described in an interview how the bill sailed through parliament. "Frankly, it was not a law which led to a great debate at the National Assembly. It encited no passions. The law was very technical and could only interest a few specialists." Another Socialist deputy gave his own explanation for the limited participation which surrounded the bill.

There were about ten deputies who followed this bill. As long as there is no conflict among the Socialist deputies following the bill in the committee, or between the [Socialist] Group and the Government, then there is no problem. The larger group will ratify the decisions of the smaller. When there is conflict, then the question must be brought up at the weekly party caucus [and the party leaders and other nonspecialists will become involved].

Consensus within the community of experts led to the automatic ratification of each decision by the next higher group. This system is similar to that described by Fenno (1973, p. 96) in the U.S. House Appropriations Committee: in the absence of conflict, specialists dominate; where conflict is greater, those on the losing side appeal to outside allies and participation increases. In the case of the medical studies, no single actor had an incentive to expand the debate because of the consensus among those involved in the specialized negotiations. The issue was portrayed as a complex technical question rightly of interest only to medical professionals. Other deputies eschewed participation in the debate, considered themselves unqualified, and saw no reason to question a policy proposal which was the subject of consensus among the specialists.

Shortly after the medical school law was passed, the issue of medical studies reform suddenly appeared on the nation's political agenda. Medical students went on strike and took to the streets in protest against the new law. The issue was transformed from a technical to a highly political question, as the nightly newscasts showed students from the most prestigious Parisian medical schools in their lab coats protesting the law in the streets of the capital (see "De nombreux étudiants. . . ," February 17, 1983; "Le mouvement de grève. . . ," February 18, 1983; Nau, April 9 and May 23, 1983).

A member of parliament remarked in an interview, "The question was being treated within the community of those interested in medical and health questions, but when the people saw all the *blouses blanches* (lab coats) in the streets, things changed." Parliamentary leaders of the opposition were quick to support the striking medical students and used the forum of parliamentary debate to generate publicity for their cause. The medical students' strike marked one of the first opportunities for the opposition to criticize the government in defense of an identifiable, mobilized, vocal, and highly visible constituency. The fact that they had not made a major issue of the bill when it was passed in December 1982 and that many considered the Socialist bill to be very similar to their own 1979 law did not stop the opposition from assailing the government in the spring of 1983. Their interests meshed perfectly with those of the medical students. The students saw the generation of controversy as the only way to alter the legislation, and the opposition hoped to capitalize politically on the show of public displeasure with the government. When the medical students took to the streets, therefore, opposition figures in parliament helped them gain publicity by participating in the demonstrations, by making speeches in parliament, and by generating articles in the press.

Medical students had been excluded from the negotiations leading up to the 1982 law because they lacked a representative organization. The government consulted those groups which did exist, "but these groups are very unrepresentative of the medical students," according to the Education Ministry official most closely involved in the negotiations. "One of our big problems was to find a reliable and a representative partner" among the students, a governmental negotiator explained in an interview (see also Lorenzi, March 16, 1983). Without organized representatives, the medical students could not participate in the specialized negotiations leading up to the 1982 law. When the students found out about the law, therefore, they had to shift the debate out of the specialized community of health experts and onto the national political agenda.

The combination of noisy demonstrations in the streets and daily speeches by the national leaders of the opposition created a major national issue on a topic which months before had been voted through parliament with the sustained interest of only a handful of legislators. The students' strategy was successful.

Many will only remember the image of the students in lab coats taking to the streets, neutralizing the toll booths on the freeways, occupying the Ministry of Health, and disturbing everything they could possibly disturb . . . . In this sense, the action committees will have fully reached their goal: to focus the attention of the media and to popularize . . . a conflict which is difficult for the larger public to understand (Nau, May 23, 1983).

Even though the government had already passed its law with very little controversy, it now named a special body of mediators which gave in to the students on several key demands. Later, amendments attached to an unrelated bill rescinded provisions of the 1982 law. Specialized actors in parliament and in the civil service complained bitterly in interviews about the intrusion of nonspecialists into the process, but the government had to do something to defuse the political controversy. They preferred to give in to some of the students' demands rather than to allow a national controversy to continue to rage. Despite the constitutional arsenal which the government enjoys over the parliament in France and despite the fact that this bill had already been voted into law, opponents forced the government to back down on aspects of a reform by altering the public perception of the issue.

The Higher Education Law

The Savary higher education law (law no. 84-52 of January 26, 1984 *sur l'enseignement supérieur*) dealt with a broad range of issues, including the relations between junior and senior faculty, the development of ties between the universities, the *grandes écoles,* and industry, the question of competition between universities, and the distribution of authority within departments and colleges. Just as each of the deputies and senators involved in the medical school reform during its first consideration had been a health professional, most members taking an active role in the Savary higher education law indicated that their involvement stemmed from professional experience. Socialist and Communist participants were almost all university teaching personnel. Opposition involvement was not limited to specialists at all, however. From the beginning of the debate on higher education, party leaders of the opposition became involved.

The government and the majority tried to keep discussion limited to specific points of the law, but the opposition continually raised more general objections with constant references to such broad symbols as "academic freedom" and "national independence." The debate became a rhetorical battle between opponents of the law, who attempted to demonstrate that the issue was broadly political, and proponents, who wanted to show that it was a technical measure of interest only to specialists. A Socialist deputy closely associated with the bill said in an interview after the debate in parliament,

The specific points of the law were not of very much interest to the opposition. What they were interested in was the conflict with the government. The relative power of the full professors vis-à-vis the junior faculty, the idea of competition between universities, and selection of students were important points of conflict. But for the opposition, they were especially interested in making the debate last as long as possible in order to prolong the discontent with the government after the law on medical studies. So while the debate took place formally on the merits of this one text, in fact, or for the opposition at least, it was a continuation of the other debates, on the nationalizations, medical studies, and more. The debate took place on the level of symbols, and was often very far removed from the text which deals with precise questions.

A member of the cabinet of Education Minister Savary with personal responsibility for much of the bill demonstrated the strategy of the

42   Frank R. Baumgartner

FIGURE 1
Newspaper Coverage of University Reform
In *Le Monde,* 1983-84

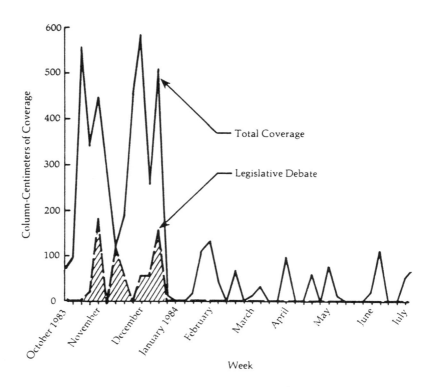

minister when he said in an interview, "What really surprised me in the
parliamentary debate was the violence of the political attack by the opposition to what was a very technical bill, or at least one which was
presented as such by the minister."

Expanders within the parliament followed two tactics. First, they
spoke at a higher level of generality, avoiding questions of precise levels
of enrollment and focusing on "national independence," "freedom of
choice," and the "quality of French science." No one but a specialist
could become excited about a debate focusing on precise enrollment
levels in different areas of study or on the specific composition of university committees, but many nonspecialists could become interested in a
debate which focuses on questions of academic freedom, equality, and
national independence. Second, they generated publicity through

parliamentary maneuvers and obstruction. They shunned specialized negotiations in committee or with ministerial officials but sought the broadest forums to mount their generalized attack on the government and its bill.

The opposition succeeded almost completely in expanding the debate from the specialized to the general political arena. The National Assembly considered nothing else for over three weeks, as the opposition proposed over 2,000 amendments on substantive and grammatical points during 133 hours of floor debate and used the bill as the focus of a general political attack on the government (see Chabord, 1983). The parliamentary debate provided the forum for a much larger discussion of the issue.

Figure 1 shows weekly coverage levels of the university reform in France's leading newspaper, *Le Monde*, for the period from October 1983 to July 1984. The upper line indicates total levels of coverage, the lower line coverage specifically on the parliamentary debates. Newspaper coverage of the debates in the Assembly accounted for only 638 column-centimeters of coverage (the equivalent of just over two full pages); total coverage of the issue during this period was over 3,900 column-centimeters (over 14 full pages). There was five times as much coverage of the issue during the three months of parliamentary consideration of the bill as there was during the seven following months. While coverage in *Le Monde* is not by itself sufficient to indicate increased public awareness or interest in the topic, differences of this magnitude which coincide with coverage in other printed and electronic media clearly indicate a shift. The parliamentary debate had moved the issue from the specialized to the general political arena.

Key to the success of the parliamentary opposition in generating such a debate were the coordinated activities of other opponents to the bill outside parliament. Students and others showed their objections by protesting, sometimes violently, in the streets of Paris. The Fields Prize-winning mathematician, Laurent Schwartz, published a book entitled *To Save the Universities* in which he said that "the degradation of the universities is leading us towards under-development" (see Bolloch, October 7, 1983). Schwartz became the leader of a group of noted scientists and professors, who came to be known as the 55 *sages* (wise men). They went public with their objections to the bill by purchasing full page ads in *Le Monde* ("*Appel au Président. . .*" of November 23, 1983 and "*Les 55 sont déjà mille*" of December 16, 1983). One member of this group, a leading political scientist, used his position as columnist at *Le Monde* to publish his views on page one of that paper (Duverger, November 25, 1983).

The combination of parliamentary and nonparliamentary tactics caused an explosion of the issue onto the front pages of the newspapers and elevated it directly to the highest levels of the state. The adverse publicity generated around the issue made it politically impossible for the government to ignore the appeals of the professors. Presidential advisors, many of whom had been students of the professors at the most prestigious *grandes écoles* now heard their appeals. Naturally, they were more sympathetic than the education specialists within the Socialist party or in the Ministry of Education who had proposed the reform in the first place. Despite the assured passage of the bill through parliament, and indeed over the objections of the Socialist deputies in parliament, the government made several concessions to the disgruntled professors. For the president, the minister, and the government, the prospect of Nobel and Fields Prize-winning intellectuals making public statements and taking out full page ads in *Le Monde* in opposition to their higher education policies was distasteful in the extreme.

Education ministry officials responsible for the bill were instructed to include representatives of the 55 *sages* in their working groups and to make sure that they were aware of planned reforms well before they were made public. Socialist deputies and other supporters of the government's bill were openly resentful of the *Elysée*'s more conciliatory attitude (Bréhier, November 24, 1983). After going through the long process of preparing a bill which they expected to see enacted into law with little or no change, they saw the highest leaders of the government give in to the demands of those whom they had just defeated in the specialized negotiations. The Socialist *rapporteur* of the bill complained about the tactics used by the opposition.

Usually, work is done in committee, and when the text gets to the floor, it is all set [*bouclé*]. In this case, however, the opposition was mute during the committee work, and then suddenly became very talkative when the bill got to the floor. They presented over 2,000 amendments, and dragged the debate on for weeks . They are making fools of everybody, making a sham of the parliamentary process.

An Education Ministry official involved in the negotiations before the parliamentary debate said, "The opposition showed a much more conciliatory attitude in private. When the [ministerial] committee received these people in private, many of them had much experience in the area, and were very constructive. When the issue became a public debate, however, they changed to systematic opposition to the reform." Union officials who supported the reform complained in interviews and in public of the enlargement of the policy community to include these newcomers and questioned their claims to represent the views of a majority of professors.

The resentment of union officials, of Education Ministry officials, and of Socialist deputies who had been responsible for the reform is easy to understand. While they had dominated the policy process when it was limited to the specialized community of experts, they no longer enjoyed the same power after the issue had moved onto the general political agenda. The opponents of the bill had shifted the balance of power by forcing the issue from the specialized policy community to the general political arena.

Government negotiators prefer to encounter criticism in private rather than in public. In both the medical studies and the higher education reforms, government negotiators indicated in interviews that they would have been happy to include more people in the specialized negotiations within the ministries and to give in to some of their demands rather than to see their policies ridiculed and attacked on the front pages of the nation's newspapers. In both cases, however, the lack of organized representatives for these groups precluded their systematic participation in the specialized negotiations. When disgruntled policy makers attempted to expand the debates, they found a natural ally in the parliamentary opposition. The parliament functioned as a court of last appeal for expanders in their efforts to generate publicity and to shift the debate from the specialized to the general political arena. Attempting to determine the relative importance of the many tactics used by those opposed to the bill is less important than realizing that the debate in parliament provides a prime opportunity for opponents both inside and outside of the legislative to expand the debate.

The Private School Bill

The private school bill *(Projet de loi no. 574 relatif aux rapports entre l'Etat, les communes, les départements, les régions et les établissements d'enseignement privés* of May 24, 1984) was a major national controversy even before it reached the National Assembly. Nonetheless, parliamentary consideration of the issue provided the opportunity for expanders to generate more and more adverse publicity. In fact, the parliamentary debate became the subject of so much controversy that President Mitterrand withdrew the proposal and soon received the resignations of both the Education minister and the premier.

The private school bill was the opposite of policy making by specialists. Only 2 of 17 deputies interviewed with respect to this issue indicated that their involvement was related to their personal or professional background. One deputy explained his participation this way:

I am not even a member of the commission which would have had jurisdiction . . . I became

46   Frank R. Baumgartner

interested in this debate from the moment when it became a major political problem. I intervened not as a specialist in the matter, but rather as a person with national political responsibilities.

Reform of the relations between the state and the private school system was a long-standing plank in the Socialist party platform. Private schools enroll about 17% of all school children in France, and 95% of all private schools are associated with the Catholic church. Since 1959, private schools have benefitted from considerable subsidies from the state, including the payment of all teachers' salaries. This and other grants allow the private schools to keep their tuition levels extremely low by U.S. standards, thereby appealing to a broader clientele than would otherwise be possible. In one highly selective private school, for example, tuition ranges from $18 to $125 per trimester, depending on parents' ability to pay (Bernard, March 4-5, 1984). These large state subsidies have long been opposed by the parties of the left, and by the Socialist party in particular.

The slogan of the Socialist Party in the 1960s had been *fonds publics à l'école publique* (public monies for public schools), and private school supporters were worried about what might happen to their subsidies when the Socialists took power in 1981. The party had considerably amended its policies since the 1960s, however. In fact, state subsidies to the private schools rose from 10 billion francs ($1.4 billion) in 1980 to 18.5 billion francs ($2.3 billion) in 1984, 68% increase during a time of Socialist rule (Rollat, July 1-2, 1984; see also France, Ministry of the Civil Service and of Administrative Reforms, 1983, p. 39; Arditti, June 8, 1984). The 1983 Socialist proposal did not call for a reduction in subsidies to church schools, but rather for stricter controls over how the money would be spent. Municipalities which had refused to contribute to the private schools under the previous law would even be forced under the new law to do so. Cardinal Lustigier of Paris referred to the proposal as a historic occasion, since it was the first time that a government of the left recognized the legitimacy of state support for the private schools ("Une 'chance historique'. . ." March 3, 1984; Lhomeau, March 16, 1984).

On the other hand, the bill would increase state control over the private schools in a number of ways. In particular, the management of personnel would be affected with the creation of a new corps of civil service position for the private school teachers. Paradoxically, the private school teachers were in favor of this provision, since it would guarantee them the greater job security enjoyed by French civil servants. Private school leaders, however, feared that over the years they would lose control over hiring, firing, and transferring their teachers. In addition, the bill would limit the use of public money for the creation of new private schools in areas where a public school did not already exist. Under the previous law, any private school that opened and stayed in operation for a specified period would automatically receive state funds, even if enrollment levels were low. Public schools, on the other hand, had to meet many requirements before they could receive money for additional classes. The bill would have forced the private schools to meet the same requirements for opening new classes as the public schools did.

Governmental negotiations on the private school issue were conducted in the utmost secrecy during the two years following the 1981 elections. At the end of 1983, the government finally was prepared to go ahead with its bill, and it used all its constitutional powers to force the bill through parliament in the shortest time possible. First, it insisted on the creation of a special committee in order to avoid possible delays in the 120-member Cultural Affairs Committee and possible jurisdictional claims by other committees. Second, it cut short the work even of this committee and forced the bill to the floor before one quarter of the articles had been discussed. Finally, after forcing the bill to the floor, it used article 49-3 of the constitution to call for a package vote with no amendments accepted (Lhomeau, March 16, 1984; Bréhier, May 19, 1984).

Even the extraordinary parliamentary tactics used by the government failed to defuse the debate over this bill. During the two years of negotiations with the Catholic and lay forces, Education Minister Savary had drafted a proposal which may or may not have been the basis for an acceptable compromise. Just before it was introduced in parliament, however, a group of Socialist deputies closely associated with the lay forces obtained the addition of several symbolically important amendments. These made the bill unacceptable to the clericals, prompting them to organize massive public demonstrations, to which the *laïques* responded in kind. The debate, which had been highly-charged all along, was elevated to an even higher level during the debate in parliament. Anticlerical activists who were unhappy with the governmental proposals appealed first to allies in the Socialist party who had not been involved in the ministerial negotiations and were able to obtain some satisfaction. This shift created a reaction by the Catholics, however, as they appealed to their own parliamentary allies.

Opposition leaders in parliament were quick to join the private school forces in attacking the government and were relentless in their attacks on the government's bill. Just as with the two other bills, the coordination of parliamentary and nonparliamentary opposition was important in causing the government to withdraw or alter its proposal. Opponents of the bill expanded the issue by focusing on broadly political aspects and by portraying the issue in the most symbolic terms possible. They focused especially on the theme of liberty. A leader of one of the largest *laïque* organizations complained, "From the moment when one begins to use the term 'liberty', it becomes a huge trap. . . . One of the greatest successes of the opposition has been to pose the debate in these terms."

The opposition also attached great symbolic importance to aspects of the bill which would have very little concrete impact. For example, the provision that public monies would not be used to create private nursery schools in areas which did not already have either a public or a private nursery school would have affected only a few areas of the country and only a small number of children, but opposition leaders seized on it for its symbolic potential. A Socialist deputy complained, "Everything in this law has taken on such a symbolic quality that nothing can be done. Take the nursery schools for example. This represents almost nothing in concrete terms, . . . and yet it has become a major issue. . . . It is completely irrational." Another Socialist referred to the same symbolic aspects, noting how the issue had been elevated to such a level that the whole nation appeared to be in trauma.

The question has become purely symbolic. Take for instance the question of the nursery schools. . . . When there gets to be such a huge debate about the possibility of opening up new nursery schools, you know it has very little to do with the actual number of children and families who might be affected, but rather it has a great symbolic importance, since people believe that the other side is "indoctrinating" the children from an early age . . . . In this area, no matter what the facts, or no matter how little practical effect some of these measures may have, there has been an enormous psychological shock. We are now engaged in a collective national psychodrama.

Political leaders found it more difficult to generate mass mobilization around the substantively important aspects of the bill. The creation of a new corps of civil service positions for the private school teachers already on the state payroll and the composition of the local boards which would control the state funds for the private schools were by far the most important practical aspects of the proposal, and they generated great debate within the specialized community of those closely involved in the question. These issues were too complex to explain to the general public, however. "Freedom of choice for parents" is a more effective rallying cry than "No integration of private school teachers into the civil service." Mass mobilization and national controversy require easily understood symbols. Members of the parliamentary opposition understood this and spoke always in the most general terms.

The efforts of the opposition to create a massive public debate on the private school issue were not always appreciated even by the supporters of the private schools. The alliance between the procedural expanders in the parties of the opposition and the substantive expanders in the private school organizations and in the church was strained from the beginning. While the opposition wanted to raise the level of the debate and to keep it in the headlines, private school leaders preferred some resolution to the conflict, and they realized that no agreements could be reached when the issue was treated in such an ideologically-charged atmosphere. A leader of the main private school parents' federation who was closely involved in negotiations complained that

the opposition is mistaken in wanting to transform this debate by always crying, *"liberté!"* By making caricatures, they only cause the *laïques* to make caricatures in return. The problem will not be resolved with this kind of debate. In order to resolve it, we will have to come down to a level below that of ideological debate.

While the issue might not be resolved by ideological debate, no resolution of a conflict is preferable to a resolution against one's interests, reasoned the expanders of the private school debate. According to this respondent, parliamentary leaders were more interested in provoking public opposition to the government in order to help them at the next elections than in finding a solution to the problem. Procedural and substantive expanders share some interests, but this alliance can be strained by the different foci of the two groups.

Expanders of the private school issue were extremely successful. No other issue dominated the news in France as the private school issue did. *Le Monde* coverage of the issue totalled almost 26,000 column-centimeters (the equivalent of 106 full pages) from October 1983 to July 1984. These figures can be put into perspective by comparing them with those for the higher education reform described in Figure 1. Coverage of the higher education reform reached a peak of about 600 column-centimeters per week just before the passage of the law in January 1984; the private school issue regularly generated over twice this amount each week during spring of 1984 and reached peaks of over 2,000 column-centimeters per week, or more than one full page of coverage per day. The combination of parliamentary debate, massive demonstrations by both the lay and Catholic forces in the spring of 1984, and the European Elections of June 1984 led to the explosion of the issue and to a political catastrophe of the highest order for the government. President Mitterrand withdrew the bill from parliament despite its assured passage and called for the resignations of both Education Minister Alain Savary and Prime Minister Pierre Mauroy.

Frank R. Baumgartner

Conclusion

The debate in parliament presents the best opportunity for the expansion of an issue in France, and skillful policy makers outside of parliament take advantage of this whenever they believe they will lose a battle if it remains confined to the specialized arena. They cultivate relations with party leaders in parliament so that they can appeal to them when they need to expand a debate. For those who wish to keep an issue restricted to the specialized arenas, the results of a lively parliamentary debate can be disastrous, as they were for the Socialists in each of the three cases described in this article. In each case, a combination of parliamentary and nonparliamentary maneuvers led to the explosion of the issue into a major political controversy. Parliamentary debate may not be enough in itself to push an issue onto the national political agenda but, when combined with public demonstrations and other activities outside of parliament, it can be very effective. Parliamentary debate served as a focal point for wider discussion of the topics considered here, and strategic politicians focused on easily-understood symbols in order to create these national controversies. Despite the constitutional regime of the Fifth Republic, which gives great power to the government over the opposition in parliament, the parliament can nonetheless play an important role in the policy process by lifting issues from the specialized to the general political arena.

In explaining the dominance of the government over the parliament in the French Fifth Republic, Andrews (1978) wrote that the "political situation" was more important than the constitutional advantages enjoyed by the executive. This article also emphasizes the importance of "politics" in determining policy. Controversies widely reported in the press and in the electronic media can force a government to alter its plans, even if the government has the legal and the constitutional powers to go ahead with its proposals. Since the parliament is in a privileged position to generate such publicity, it plays an important role in the policy process in France, despite the constitutional limits on its activities.

One of the biggest points of contention between Socialist President François Mitterrand and Conservative Prime Minister Jacques Chirac during the first weeks of shared rule in 1986 was whether Chirac would be allowed to rule by decree or be forced to pass laws through parliament (Bréhier, March 22, 1986; Duverger, March 22, 1986). The argument sounds pointless, since the prime minister has a majority in parliament and is therefore assured of the passage of the laws which he demands. This article shows why the debate is important, however. The political debates which can surround the parliamentary consideration of a bill can have a catastrophic effect on the political standing of the government. Mitterrand found this out himself with the three bills considered here, and he hoped to force Chirac to share this unpleasant experience.

The tactics of expansion of a parliamentary debate often consist of obstructing the debate by procedural maneuvers and grammatical amendments. Three weeks of parliamentary debate dominated by arguments over the relative merits of semicolons and commas is not a pretty sight and appears to play no policy role (see Bréhier, June 13, 1986). These tactics are far from devoid of policy importance, however. They are the means by which the parliamentary strategists drag on the debate and keep the issue in the headlines. Putting issues in the headlines not only has important political implications, but also great policy implications, as this article has shown. Given the limited role of the French parliament in the policy process in general, this is the means by which it can play its greatest role. Even the constitutional restrictions placed on the parliament of the Fifth Republic cannot take this function away from it.

The relations between civil servants in France and their political counterparts (both political executives and elected officials) have been the subject of sustained interest among students of French politics. In particular, researchers have noted the disdain with which high civil servants in France view the roles of the elected members of the legislature. Suleiman (1973, p. 731) has written that "there are probably few democratic societies where the deputies are held in such derision by the civil servants as in France." Noting the different roles which each group plays in the policy process explains much of this dislike. The upper civil service tends to dominate the specialized policy communities in France. Its members have their greatest power when the public is unaware of the decisions they are making. In concert with the largest interest groups and other organizations in their sectors, they make most decisions with only minimal input from their political superiors. Members of parliament, on the other hand, play their greatest role when they use the legislative debate to generate and amplify the controversy surrounding governmental plans. They attempt to shift debates out of the specialized communities, where the civil servants and certain outside groups dominate, onto the national political agenda, where the civil servants lose their control. There should be no mystery surrounding the dislike of civil servants for the "intrusion" of politicians in the policy process in France. Each time the parliament succeeds in its efforts to create controversy, the civil servants and other specialized actors lose influence.

It is important not to overstate the policy role of the legislature in the Fifth Republic. In the larger study from which this article is drawn, the vast majority of policy cases were decided with no parliamentary in-

52   Frank R. Baumgartner

volvement whatsoever. In addition, many bills are discussed in each legislature, but only a few become the subject of great debate in parliament or elsewhere. The question of why certain issues become expanded while others do not is beyond the scope of the present article. It has to do with the intensity of conflict surrounding the issue, with the organization of interests both within and outside of the government, with the rhetorical skills of the expanders and the contractors, and with the political context of the time. This article has pointed out that the parliament plays an essential role in this process by helping to push some issues onto the national political agenda. This is a sporadic influence, however, and is not always successful. The French parliament is not the center of policy making by any stretch of the imagination. It is the center of politics, however, and politics can have a great impact on policy.

Frank R. Baumgartner is Visiting Assistant Professor of Political Science, The University of Iowa, Iowa City, Iowa 52242.

NOTE

Research was supported by the French government, by the Horace H. Rackham School of Graduate Studies at The University of Michigan, and by the *Institut de Management Public* in Paris. The author thanks Professors Roy Pierce, Jack Walker, Joel Aberbach, and Jean Carduner of The University of Michigan, Jerry Loewenberg of The University of Iowa, and two anonymous referees for their comments and help. Finally, thanks to the dozens of members of parliament, staffers, civil servants, and organizational representatives who gave their time to be interviewed for this study.

REFERENCES

Andrews, William G. 1962. *French Politics and Algeria: The Process of Policy Formation, 1954-1962*. New York: Appleton-Century-Crofts.
_____ . 1978. The Constitutional Prescription of Parliamentary Procedures in Gaullist France. *Legislative Studies Quarterly*, 3:465-506.
Appel au Président de la République. November 23, 1983. *Le Monde*.
Arditti, Catherine. June 8, 1984. M. Savary tente d'apaiser les défenseurs de l'école privée. *Le Monde*.
Bernard, Philippe. March 4-5, 1984. La mobilisation pacifique. *Le Monde*.
Bernstein, Richard. June 12, 1986. Bills Introduced in France on Immigrants and TV. *New York Times*.
Bolloch, Serge. October 7, 1983. La dégradation de notre Université nous conduit au sous-développement affirme M. Laurent Schwartz. *Le Monde*.

Bréhier, Thierry. November 24, 1983. Une partie des députés socialistes s'inquiètent des positions de l'Elysée sur la réforme de l'enseignement supérieur. *Le Monde.*

———. May 19, 1984. Une opposition frustrée. *Le Monde.*

———. March 22, 1986. Le Parlement dessasi, le Conseil constitutionnel écarté. *Le Monde.*

———. June 13, 1986. L'Assemblée nationale malade de l'obstruction: Le droit d'amendement est menacé. *Le Monde.*

Campbell, Stanley, and Jean Laporte. 1981. The Staff of Parliamentary Assemblies in France. *Legislative Studies Quarterly,* 6:521-531.

Chabord, Olivier. 1983. Le débat parlementaire sur l'enseignement supérieur. *Regards sur l'actualité,* 94:34-42.

Une "chance historique" existe pour régler cette question, affirme le Cardinal Lustigier. March 3, 1984. *Le Monde.*

Chandernagor, André. 1967. *Un parlement pour quoi faire?* Paris: Presses Universitaires de France.

Les 55 sont déjà mille. December 16, 1983. *Le Monde.*

Converse, Philip E., and Roy Pierce. 1986. *Political Representation in France.* Cambridge: Harvard University Press.

Duverger, Maurice. November 25, 1983. La fronde des professeurs. *Le Monde.*

———. March 22, 1986. Le président de la République n'est pas obligé de signer les ordonnances. *Le Monde.*

European Community. 1975a. *Directive du Conseil des Communautés Européennes du 16 Juin, 1975 visant à la coordination des dispositions legislatives, réglementaires et administratives concernant les activités du medecin.* Brussels: European Community. June 16, 1975.

———. 1975b. *Déclaration et recommandation de ce Conseil relatives à la formation du medecin.* Brussels: European Community. June 16, 1975.

Fenno, Richard F., Jr. 1973. *Congressmen in Committees.* Boston: Little, Brown.

France, Assemblée Nationale. 1984. *Bulletin de l'Assemblée Nationale, Numéro Spéciale, Statistiques 1983.* Paris: Secrétariat général de l'Assemblée nationale.

France, Ministry of the Civil Service and of Administrative Reform. 1983. *La Fonction Publique en 1982.* Paris: La Documentation Française.

Kingdon, John W. 1984. *Agendas, Alternatives, and Public Policies.* Boston: Little, Brown.

Lhomeau, Jean-Yves. March 16, 1984. Un compromis historique? *Le Monde.*

Lorenzi, Antoinette. March 16, 1983. Le Professeur Seligmann: "L'examen n'est pas un barrage." *Le Matin.*

Masclet, Jean-Claude. 1982. *Un député pour quoi faire?* Paris: Presses Universitaires de France.

Le mouvement de grève des étudiants en médecine continue à s'étendre. February 18, 1983. *Le Monde.*

Nau, Jean-Yves. April 9, 1983. Nouvelles actions spectaculaires des étudiants en grève. *Le Monde.*

———. May 23, 1983. Les étudiants en médecine reprendront les cours mardi 24 mai. *Le Monde.*

De nombreux étudiants en médecine sont en grève dans plusieurs hôpitaux parisiens. February 17, 1983. *Le Monde.*

Polsby, Nelson W. 1984. *Political Innovation in America: The Politics of Policy Initiation.* New Haven: Yale University Press.

Ranney, Austin. 1981. The Working Conditions of Members of Parliament and Congress: Changing the Tools Changes the Job. In Norman J. Ornstein, ed., *The Role of*

54   Frank R. Baumgartner

the *Legislature in Western Democracies.* Washington, DC: American Enterprise
        Institute.
Riker, William H. 1986. *The Art of Political Manipulation.* New Haven: Yale University
        Press.
Rollat, Alain. July 1-2, 1984. Le Premier Ministre au Vatican. *Le Monde.*
Safran, William. 1985. *The French Polity,* 2nd ed. New York: Longman.
Schattschneider, E. E. 1960. *The Semi-Sovereign People.* New York: Holt, Rinehart &
        Winston.
Sigal, Leon V. 1973. *Reporters and Officials.* Lexington, MA: Heath.
Suleiman, Ezra N. 1973. L'Administrateur et le député en France. *Revue Française de
        Science Politique,* 23:729-757.
Wahl, Nicholas. 1959. *The Fifth Republic: France's New Political System.* New York:
        Random House.
Williams, Philip. 1968. *The French Parliament: Politics in the Fifth Republic.* New York:
        Praeger.

[3]

The National Front in France

The Emergence of an Extreme Right Protest Movement

Pierre Bréchon and Subrata Kumar Mitra

The rise of extremist movements with a cultural or religious edge to them poses a basic challenge to liberal democratic societies because of their intransigent opposition to tolerant pluralism. The political agenda of these movements often harkens back to the preindustrial past, from which, taking advantage no doubt of the very openness of political democracy, they cull out and use unresolved issues of identity, ethnicity, and religion in their pursuit of power. By successfully presenting themselves as the exponents of popular action and advocates of issues not articulated by major parties, they undermine the authority of established intermediate structures such as political parties, interest groups, and the media. Even more serious, their very presence in the midst of functioning democracies raises a cruel dilemma of how far to tolerate the intolerant without seriously compromising the institutions of free speech and full freedom of political action and association and of where to draw the line between the values of ethnic identity and exclusiveness, on the one hand, and liberty and human rights, which are the essence of liberalism, on the other.

Though postwar Europe has experienced political movements at both extremes of the ideological spectrum, the activities of the extreme right have caused greater concern because of their temporal proximity and ideological affinity to a past with which Europe has not yet fully come to terms. While the presence of an extreme right movement is by no means unique to France, the French case is of particular interest because of the remarkable electoral achievements of the National Front and its links with the bitter legacies of Vichy.[1] The objective of this article is to bring together the evidence associated with the rise of the National Front in France, drawing on public opinion on significant political issues, aggregate data, and information on its territorial implantation. This is supplemented with a detailed study of the issue of the Islamic headscarf in French state schools and the electoral constituency of Dreux, which many consider to be the key to the fortunes of the National Front. An attempt is made to assess the implications of the rise of the National Front and the factors leading to it for the overall context of French politics.

The Electoral Context

It is important at the outset to clarify the concept of the extreme right because of the lack of scholarly agreement on its political connotations.[2] Nineteenth-century usage distinguished between "conservatives," who wished to retain the status quo, and "reactionaries," who intended to restore the status quo ante, if necessary by force. The latter are sometimes broadly classified as extreme right. The definition followed in this article differs partly from

Comparative Politics   October 1992

the earlier usage in the sense that the extreme right is characterized here as a movement which seeks a comprehensive ideological change without, however, questioning the legitimacy of the constitution and established institutions of the state. The *raison d'être* of the French National Front, according to Jean-Marie Le Pen, rests on its total identification with French culture and identity, which he claims are inadequately or incorrectly represented by all political parties and the media. Once we accept this definition, in which the extreme right distinguishes itself from other political forces in terms of the values it considers essential for political community and its position on the nature and structure of political representation but not on the legitimacy of the state (where it is in agreement with others), the issue of historic continuity between the contemporary extreme right and the extreme right of the 1920s and 1930s becomes rather unclear.[3]

The French case is of particular interest because of the complex legacy of the French Revolution and the declaration of universal human rights, on the one hand, and the equally potent if less well known authoritarian tradition of the right, on the other.[4] This dual legacy continues to affect the political system and political parties, both of which are placed within the respectable bounds of legitimacy. The National Front, however, is uneasily suspended at the margin of the political system, drawing its support in the name of traditions much older than the constitution of the Fifth Republic, as well as in its capacity as a political party competing within the political arena with others like itself and seeking to maximize support by promoting specific interests.[5] The complex profile of the National Front is reflected in the scholarly literature, which attributes its rapid rise to a diversity of factors: "the resurgence of an old national-populist tradition at an opportune moment;"[6] the personality, character, and mobilizing and oratorical skills of its leader, Jean-Marie Le Pen;[7] political and contingent factors like the electorate's exasperation with the Socialist government, the system of proportional representation, and the fragmentation of the moderate right;[8] and finally, the political consequences of the economic crisis of the 1970s.[9]

The spectacular success of the National Front in the European elections of 1984 is explained in a variety of ways. First of all, it is argued that this election, not being of much political importance to domestic politics, made it possible for more people to vote free from the customary constraints of party affiliation, political partisanship, and social class. Second, proportional representation made it possible for parties without large followings nevertheless to campaign nationwide rather than concentrate only on areas of strength. This, compared to the two ballot system prevailing in domestic elections in France, gave an advantage to small parties and to electoral novices like the National Front. Thanks to the oratorical skills of Le Pen and the attention lavished on him by the media, the National Front could present itself as a national alternative with remarkable success (see Table 1). Its enduring presence within the political arena is now generally if somewhat grudgingly accepted. Few, indeed, would claim today that the National Front is merely a transitional "epiphenomenon."[10]

Compared to the past success of the extreme right, which appeared tentative and contingent,[11] its political achievements during the 1980s appear more durable. This is confirmed by its omnipresent leader and cadres in the national, regional, and local political arenas, not to mention the international theatre that stretches from Brussels to Baghdad. Its past performance had seen periods of rapid rise followed by sharp decline. Thus, in the referendum of 1962 the position advocated by the extreme right, which was opposed to

Pierre Bréchon and Subrata Kumar Mitra

Table 1 Electoral Performance of the National Front (percentages)

First ballot or single ballot	National results	Town of Dreux
European elections, 1984	11.2	19.1
Cantonal elections, 1985	8.8	----
Legislative elections, 1986	9.9	16.4
Regional elections, 1986	9.6	16.0
Presidential elections, 1988	14.4	21.8
Legislative elections, 1988	9.8	17.9
Cantonal elections, 1988	5.2	----
Municipal elections, 1989	2.5/10.1 (*)	22.2
European elections, 1989	11.7	21.6
By-election of Dreux, 1989		49.0

Key:

(*)   The National Front was not able to contest the election in all of France's 36000 communes which is why, nationally, its vote share was only 2.5%. However, if we calculate the vote share only on the basis of its performance in cities of 30000 inhabitants or more (there are 219 in France, of which, the Front contested the election in 143), the proportion goes up to 10.1%

granting independence to Algeria, received 9.2 percent of the valid votes. Even three and a half years later, Jean-Louis Tixier-Vignancourt, defending the concept of French Algeria, received 5.2 percent of the vote in the first round of the presidential election. However, following this, the extreme right fell into a precipitous decline that some thought terminal when it won only 0.52 percent of the vote in the legislative elections of 1973. Le Pen received only 0.8 percent of the vote in the presidential elections of 1974. He could not succeed in getting the signatures of 500 elected politicians essential for the nomination of an official candidate in the presidential election of 1981. However, the National Front, created in 1972, managed to receive an "honorable" 10 percent in a handful of communes in the cantonal elections of 1982 and in the municipal elections of March 1983, a trend confirmed once again in the by-elections held towards the end of 1983. In retrospect, its real take-off seems to have come in the elections to the European parliament in 1984, when it registered its first spectacular success in attracting 11.2 percent of the vote.

The National Front repeated its performance of 1984 in the European election of 1989. The result shows that its electoral performance had more or less stabilized. However, two key by-elections in November 1989 in Dreux and Marseille suggested the beginning of a new electoral trend in favor of the extreme right. Though both constituencies are traditional strongholds of the extreme right, the shares of votes received by the National Front (42.5 percent in Dreux and 33 percent in Marseille) were unprecedented. Marie-France Stirbois, the candidate of the National Front in Dreux, received the largest share of the vote, while Madame Roussel, the party candidate in Marseille, placed just after Mr. Mattei, the candidate of the *Union pour la Démocratie Française* (Union for French Democracy, UDF,

65

Comparative Politics   October 1992

a federation of parties led by Valéry Giscard d'Estaing), which, often in alliance with the *Rassemblement pour la République* (RPR, the Gaullist party led by Jacques Chirac), competes in French elections as the moderate right. In the second ballot, all the political parties mobilized their forces against the National Front in both constituencies but failed to stop Marie-France Stirbois from winning with 61.3 percent of the vote.

The Issue of the Islamic Headscarf

Further evidence of the new trend of support for the National Front is seen in a series of opinion polls reflecting popular reaction to key political issues of considerable significance to the National Front (see Table 2). Voting intentions (measured every month by the polling agency BVA), which used to stagnate around 8 to 9 percent, jumped to 11 percent in November 1989 and to 12.5 percent the following month. This sudden increase, both national and local, can be explained on the basis of the convergence of a number of social and political factors. In fact, in October 1989 the incident of the "Islamic headscarf" created a national stir and helped mobilize opinion in favor of the National Front. Three girls of North African origin, all of whom were pupils at a secondary school in Creil in the suburbs of Paris, claimed their right to keep their heads covered in the classroom in conformity with the requirement of Islam. Since French law prohibits all forms of religious propaganda in

Table 2 Voting Intentions in Legislative Elections (percentages)

Period of Survey	Intention of vote for National Front	Possible source of influence
December 1988	8	
August 1989	9	
October 1989	8.5	
November 1989	11	Islamic headscarf
December 1989	12.5	
January 1990	11	
February 1990	10	
March 1990	12.5	Round table on racism
April 1990	15.5	
2 to 5 May, 1990	18	
15 to 19 May, 1990	13	Desecration of Carpentras
June 1990	11	
July 1990	14.5	
31 August to 4 September, 1990	14	
15 to 20 September, 1990	9.5	Stance of Le Pen in favour of Iraq
October 1990	12	
November 1990	14	

Source: Polls of BVA, undertaken every month on a sample of about 4000 people in two waves, first at the beginning of the month and the second a fortnight later. The results are published every month in the newsmagazine Paris-Match.

66

Pierre Bréchon and Subrata Kumar Mitra

state schools, the headmaster, who considered the action of the Muslim girls to be "provocative," asked the girls to cease wearing the headscarfs in the classroom, failing which they would be forbidden to attend school altogether. The three girls insisted on wearing the scarf, were debarred from school for a few days, and were allowed to come back subsequently without the headscarf.

Soon after, however, the girls resumed wearing the headscarf. For a few weeks they were asked to stay in the school library during class hours. When the media made it an issue, the minister of education of the Socialist government, the prime minister, and the leadership of the Socialist Party took an ambiguous position. They suggested a dialogue with the parents of the girls, asking them not to require the girls to wear the headscarf to school. Subsequently, all political parties and several associations for the defense of immigrants and human rights took up positions on this issue. The French Left itself was divided. In the Socialist Party, those who considered themselves to be the defenders of nonreligious education and feminists were generally in favor of a total ban on the headscarf, whereas others, including the wife of President Mitterrand, were for tolerance in the name of the liberty of expression and respect for different value systems. The Right was generally favorable towards the ban on the scarf in the classroom. Valéry Giscard d'Estaing, former president and leader of the center-right, favored respect for prevailing legislation about nonreligious state education. Mr. Millon, president of the UDF parliamentary party, demanded a debate on immigration, expressing the apprehension that the headscarf might spark off a conflict with other forms of religious fundamentalism, leading to a "balkanization" of the national community. The Center of Social Democrats (CDS), the political successors of the Christian Democrats, adopted a more moderate position and asked for tolerance all around, seeking to avoid the emergence of a national polemic on the issue.

The National Front, in marked contrast to other parties, used the incident for political propaganda, arguing that the incident demonstrated a form of religious and cultural colonization of France that threatened her very identity with extinction. Since immigration was the root cause of these problems, the National Front argued, most immigrants should be sent back to where they came from. The issue was then referred to the *Conseil d'Etat*, the supreme interpreter of administrative law in France. The *Conseil* took a compromise position. While the wearing of religious insignia itself did not necessarily contravene the nonreligious tradition of state schools, the *Conseil* suggested that the practice could be forbidden if it formed part of religious propaganda, affected the dignity of the pupil, or disrupted teaching.

That this rather minor incident could attain such great significance in the media and the political system shows that it was only the visible tip of a much larger and more sensitive conflict of basic values, deeply embedded in French society. By affecting the school-going population and the teaching profession, the issue of the headscarf involved the parents because of the key role of schooling in social and economic mobility in France. At the heart of the issue was the position that French society was prepared to accord to immigrants, particularly to those of North African origin. Were they to be accepted on the condition that they assimilated French norms and culture? Or was France ready to recognize the specific religious and cultural identity of the immigrants? The incident also brought to the forefront the problem of the role of religion in French society. Should the state allow religion to incorporate itself into the state school system, or, instead, was religion to be treated entirely

67

as a private affair and therefore excluded from state schools? Lastly, the incident underlined the conflict between deference to cultural diversity and the movement for the equality of status of women in French society. Should the state impose equality of the sexes regardless of race or ethnicity, or should it exempt from the application of the law communities whose norms and practices were different from the mainstream of French society?

The incident of the Islamic headscarf served to catalyze French opinion on the vital issue of the position of immigrants in France, particularly those from North Africa. French opinion was already quite hostile to the immigrants. A poll taken by the polling agency SOFRES for *Le Nouvel Observateur* in November 1984 found that 68 percent of French people favored the prohibition of the entry of new immigrants into France and 25 percent said they would like most immigrants to go back to where they came from; 74 percent were opposed to granting the right to vote in local elections to immigrants who have been living in France, and 64 percent thought that the children of immigrants should adopt, as far as possible, the customs and the values of French society. Another poll taken at the same time by SOFRES for LICRA (the International League against Racism and Anti-semitism) found that 66 percent of the French population thought that there were "far too many North Africans in France." And many polls since then have found that 25 to 30 percent of French people agreed with the ideas of Le Pen on immigration. On the theme of immigration, the leader of the National Front drew the support of a larger group than those who voted for his party.

Incidents like the one over the Islamic scarf symbolize the difficulties regarding the proper recognition of the position and role of the Islamic community in France and the fear of the foreigner, deeply embedded in French society, which become explicit at a time of economic crisis and high unemployment. A section of the public thus viewed its protest against the headscarf as an act of resistance to the march of Islamic fundamentalism. This incident thus helped to activate the latent xenophobia in those sections of French society which extend their support to the National Front and see it as the defender of French identity against the onslaught of Islam.

Territorial Support for the National Front

The territorial composition of the vote for the National Front over the past elections can be used as a benchmark to study its evolution and identify some of the factors underlying these trends. One would expect the support in its areas of strength to go up significantly in reaction to catalytic events like the headscarf and to fall at a lower rate than the average when the National Front experiences a downswing nationally. Thus, when the national level of support for the National Front went up by 4 percent in voting intentions (see Table 2), the corresponding increase from the legislative elections of 1988 to the by-election of November 1989 in the constituency of Dreux was 26.7 percent and in Marseille 12.7 percent. The geographic composition of support for the National Front (particularly the detailed study of Dreux) is helpful in understanding the context in which the vote for the National Front has found potential for rapid growth.

The distribution of support for the National Front by groups of *départements* (see Figure 1) shows a certain amount of stability in the basic trends across regions. The core areas of

Pierre Bréchon and Subrata Kumar Mitra

Figure 1 Percentage Vote for the National Front

Map 1   European Elections - 1984

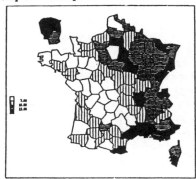

Map 2   Legislative Elections - 1986

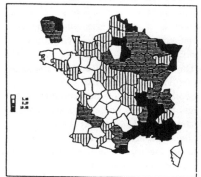

Map 3
Presidential Elections - 1st ballot - 1988

Map 4
Legislative Elections - 1st ballot - 1988

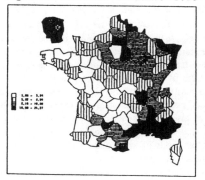

Source : The maps have been generated by the Socio-Political
Data Bank of the CNRS (Centre for the Informatisation of the
Socio-Political Data), Grenoble, unit N° 9919

Key : The maps divide France into four sections, with each
section having the same number of departments according to the
strength of the National Front in a given election. The shades
represent the increasing strength of the Front.

support are to be found on the Mediterranean coast, the Rhône region, a sizable part of the
region around Paris, Alsace, and Moselle. These *départements* partly correspond to the
older industrial and urbanized areas of France, which also contain the largest number of

69

Comparative Politics   October 1992

immigrants from North Africa, attracted during the years of expansion 1950–60.[12] However, they have been most severely affected by the economic crisis that has taken place since then, rendering the immigrant work force surplus manpower, now seen by some as cheap competitors for French workers. These are also the areas of France where the feeling of fear and levels of general insecurity are at their highest, as can be seen from the distribution of violations of the law on carrying firearms.[13] These also are the areas of high incidence of armed robberies, violent crime, and resistance to arrest.

The relationship between fear, a state of general insecurity, violent crime, and the rise of the extreme right is further confirmed by the findings from opinion polls. Questions about the considerations that influenced the decision to vote for the National Front systematically reveal the problem of immigration and the feeling of insecurity as the major factors. The electors of the National Front appear to be much more xenophobic than the average voter. While 55 percent of the sample in a poll conducted in Grenoble in 1985 thought that "there were far too many North Africans in France," 90 percent of the electors of the National Front were of that opinion.[14] Among the electors of the National Front, 63 percent thought immigration to be the cause of unemployment, compared to 26 percent for the sample as a whole. Whereas all National Front electors thought immigrants to be the cause of delinquency, only 51 percent of the population as a whole thought that to be the case. The electors of the National Front are largely favorable toward the idea of sending the vast majority of immigrants back to "where they came from" (53 percent as against 14 percent of the sample as a whole). Above all, the electors of the National Front are quite anxious about the state of general insecurity resulting from the breakdown of law and order: 90 percent of them feel "insecure" as against 75 percent of RPR voters, 64 percent of UDF voters, 24 percent of Socialist voters, and 8 percent of Communist voters.

Thus, the rise of the National Front since the early 1980s has both economic as well as social causes.[15] The cities and regions which have experienced rapid economic development have also witnessed a series of social problems, including the arrival of an inadequately integrated immigrant population, unemployment, the general decay of public facilities, roving bands of idle youth, delinquency, and the clash of cultures in everyday life. In this context, the immigrant becomes the prime target of hostility.

One has to be careful in drawing this broad generalization from aggregate data because, though the correlation between the percentage of immigrants and the vote for the extreme right is statistically supported at the level of the *département,* at levels below the *département* it seems to disappear.[16] It is, therefore, not the mere presence of immigrants as such which is the cause of support for the extreme right but rather fear of the immigrant population. This is more likely to be the case in districts with a heavy concentration of immigrants, as seen from studies of Marseille and Toulouse in the legislative elections of 1986.[17] The neighborhoods which are inhabited largely by the middle and lower middle classes and are close to areas with heavy concentrations of immigrants are areas where the National Front vote is at its maximum. The typical National Front voters are poor whites (*petits blancs*) of lower middle class origin (corresponding in their behavior if not origin to the ethnic whites of American inner cities) who have ambitions for upward mobility but feel threatened by the presence of immigrants, whom they hold responsible for everything that is not right. These people, who live in daily fear of the "devilish" immigrants just beyond the

70

Pierre Bréchon and Subrata Kumar Mitra

periphery of their neighborhood, express their anger and resentment by voting for the National Front.

The Implantation of the National Front in the Dreux Constituency

Some of the conjectures based on statistical evidence and opinion polls can be further reinforced through a detailed study of Dreux, where the National Front has become the dominant electoral force in the span of the past twelve years. Two specific questions to be addressed in this case study are the social base of the support for the National Front and the stability of its electorate.

Dreux is a small town in the *département* of Eure et Loire, administratively a part of the region of the Center but in fact a part of the Paris region.[18] In the early twentieth century Dreux was a large rural trading center with a small ancient industrial sector that employed a skilled work force. It had a stable political and social life of its own, with Maurice Viollette, an independent socialist, occupying the position of mayor for fifty-one years, from 1908 to 1959. Before the second world war, the municipality followed a policy of constructing subsidized "social" housing. After the war, during the period of reconstruction and rapid economic development, Dreux benefited greatly from its proximity to Paris and from the change in the location of production units. The city center expanded alongside the river Blaise. The commercial and industrial units that moved to the area after the war located themselves there. The inhabitants of the area were mostly European shopkeepers (that is, native French, as opposed to immigrants), members of the middle class and politically conservative. Eventually, however, because of the pressure of increasing population, the areas to the north and south of the valley of the Blaise became generally urbanized as well, with large social housing projects for working people, an increasing proportion of whom were colored immigrants. Currently, 47 percent of the population of Dreux live in HLMs (social housing with subsidized rent), which were constructed rather quickly and are generally in a state of disrepair.

Industrialization took place most rapidly in the 1960s, largely in the electronics, engineering, and automobile sectors. Between 1954 and 1975, employment in the industrial sector doubled in size, keeping pace with the doubling of the population from 16,800 to 33,100. With the development of modern industry, the demand for unskilled labor went up as well, from 42 percent of total employment in 1954 to 65 percent twenty years later. The demand for unskilled labor brought in many colored immigrant workers. During the period from 1962 to 1965 large numbers of harkis (Muslims who had fought for France during the Algerian war) immigrated. This tightly knit community found it difficult to mix with other immigrant workers, composed mostly of single men who had come alone to France to work, leaving their families at home. Many other immigrants came between 1968 and 1975, increasing the proportion of immigrants to 15 percent of the total population. They were mostly concentrated in the southern part of the city (where 55 percent of them lived in 1968, increasing to 70 percent in 1975), while the city center lost some immigrants who moved out. The proportion of immigrants in Chamards, one of the neighborhoods of Dreux, went up to 42 percent in 1975. Since then, the proportion of immigrants has gone up again, to about 30 percent of the total population of Dreux (and 60 percent in Chamards). This high

71

Comparative Politics October 1992

concentration of immigrants is resented by the native born French who live there, many of whom feel insecure about their safety.

Dreux has also become a dormitory town, with about 2,000 people commuting to work daily in several large enterprises in the Paris region.[19] The municipality was governed between 1959 to 1965 by Viollette's successor, who conducted affairs very much in the spirit of the past, with little attention paid to social and economic development. In 1965 a list of the Right won the municipal elections with a program of rapid economic development for the town, which the new mayor believed would have 80,000 inhabitants by the end of the century. That was before the economic crisis of 1973, which affected Dreux like many other parts of France. In 1977 the municipality was won on the first ballot with 55 percent of the vote by a list of the United Front of the Left, led by Françoise Gaspard of the Socialist Party.[20] The election showed a clear pattern, with the working and lower middle class neighborhoods voting for the Union of the Left (the Socialist Party and the Communist Party) and the city center and the valley of the Blaise casting its support in favor of the Right. The National Front did not contest the election, nor did it make its presence felt in any other way. The Union of the Left also benefited from a favorable national trend. The 1970s were marked by a general increase in support for the Left, particularly in mid-term elections such as the cantonal elections in 1976 and the municipal elections in 1977, which strongly mobilized the left-wing electorate. The supporters of the moderate Right could use this as an opportunity to warn the Right in office, either through their abstention or even by voting for the Left, without necessarily putting the incumbency of the Right in jeopardy. But the electoral success of Françoise Gaspard had strong local factors behind it as well. The policy of economic expansion advocated by the Right had ceased to be credible during the period of economic crisis and rising unemployment and the social problems to which it gave rise. The Left seemed to further reinforce its control of the local political arena with the election of Françoise Gaspard as a deputy (member) of the National Assembly in 1981, when the Left swept into power, followed by a wave of "pink" legislation.

However, just as the Left was riding the crest of electoral success, the National Front started gradually to establish itself in Dreux. Jean-Pierre Stirbois, the future leader of the National Front in Dreux and Le Pen's subsequent right-hand man, and his wife arrived in Dreux in 1978.[21] They had met as *militants*—active members—of a group supporting the presidential candidate of the extreme right, Tixier-Vignancourt, in 1964–65. Subsequently, they switched over to a splinter group of the extreme right called the *Union Solidariste*, which joined the National Front in December 1977. Extremely militant, anti-American, antiliberal, and anti-Arab, the former members of the *Union Solidariste* found a new focus in the problem of immigration. They were responsible for the creation of the political slogan "A million people out of work are a million immigrants too many" in the legislative elections of 1978. They had correctly diagnosed that the slogan would be effective. It had a sympathetic resonance in middle sized cities caught in the economic recession. Actively propagated, and in conjunction with other factors, it could make it possible for the National Front to establish itself on new political territory.

Jean-Pierre Stirbois and his wife Marie-France set themselves this task. Their first success came in the cantonal elections of 1982, when the National Front won 12.6 percent of the vote in Dreux West and 9.6 percent in Dreux East, levels rarely achieved elsewhere by the party, which could field only sixty-five candidates in the 1,945 cantons in which elections

72

Pierre Bréchon and Subrata Kumar Mitra

took place, receiving 0.2 percent of the total votes cast.[22] In the municipal elections of 1983, the National Front formed part of a joint list with the RPR, a list which joined the UDF in the second ballot.[23] The combined list of the Left led by Françoise Gaspard in Dreux won the election by a slim majority of eight votes.

In a significant development after the 1983 election, the results were disputed, an administrative tribunal set them aside, and a new election was held in September 1983. Because of factional conflict within the Union of the Left, Françoise Gaspard, who had been closely identified with the interests of immigrants,[24] resigned and was replaced by a little known industrialist who belonged to the Socialist Party. In the first ballot, the National Front chose to run alone in order to be able to present its program in an effective and distinctive way.[25] It greatly emphasized the presence of far too many immigrants in Dreux as the cause of high unemployment, delinquency, and the breakdown of public order, problems which could be eliminated only through the reversal of the high level of immigration. The Left won 40.5 percent, the moderate Right 42.8 percent, and the National Front 16.7 percent. The National Front achieved several of its best results in the working class neighborhoods where some traditional supporters of the Left either abstained or switched over to it. In the second ballot, the combined list of the moderate Right and the National Front won an outright victory by a wide margin. The National Front could thus place seven of its members in the municipal council, including three as *adjoints* under the mayor.

Starting with the European elections of 1984, when the national list of the National Front won 19.1 percent of the vote in Dreux, the town became a solid base of the National Front (see Table 1). In the legislative elections of 1986, when Marie-France Stirbois was the candidate from the area,[26] the vote share of the National Front went down somewhat to 16.4 percent.[27] A similar pattern was observed in 1988 when Le Pen as the presidential candidate received 21.8 percent of the vote in the area, whereas the candidate of the National Front won only 17.9 percent in the legislative elections that followed. This phenomenon, which has been observed elsewhere, appears to suggest that the ability of Le Pen to draw in electoral support is superior to other members of the party, even when they happen to be well-established local leaders. However, Dreux contradicted this broad generalization in 1989, when Marie-France Stirbois received 22.2 percent of the vote in the municipal elections, exceeding the 21.6 percent for the Le Pen list in the European election and indicating further reinforcement of the National Front's position in the area. There was an element of sympathy in the share of the vote received by Marie-France Stirbois in this election because her husband had been killed in a car accident shortly before, in autumn 1988. The results led to the inclusion of four National Front members in the RPR-UDF municipal council.

Following the election of the RPR deputy for Dreux to the Senate, a by-election to the National Assembly took place in November 1989. Partly because of a multicornered contest between the candidate of the National Front, an official candidate of the RPR-UDF as well as an RPR rebel, a Socialist candidate, a Communist, a representative of the Left Radicals, and an ecologist, which fragmented the traditional groupings on the Left and the Right, the campaign leading up to the first ballot was rather dull. The participation rate of 55.9 percent was low even by the usual standards in by-elections. The candidate of the National Front, Marie-France Stirbois, came in first with 42.5 percent of the vote (securing 49 percent in the town of Dreux). She had largely outstripped the candidate of the RPR-UDF, whose vote at

73

24.5 percent was 16.4 percentage points less than the alliance had received in June 1988, and the Socialist candidate, whose vote share of 18.1 percent was 15.5 percentage points less than the share of the Socialist Party in June 1988.

This surge in support for the National Front can be explained by the combination of good constituency work by the party in the area, the growing reputation of its candidate, and a national political climate favorable to the National Front. The debate on the Islamic headscarf had presented all the established political parties with a dilemma. Marie-France Stirbois gave prominence to that controversy in her campaign, and Le Pen repeated the theme in his political meetings in the constituency. Faced with this steep increase in the support for the extreme right, all parties except the ecologists called for a concerted effort to stop the rise of the National Front. The parties of the Left even called upon all democrats to vote for the candidate of the moderate right in an effort to stop the election of a member of the National Front.[28] However, this combined effort was not successful in defeating Marie-France Stirbois, who won the election with a majority of 61.3 percent. Abstention went down by about 10 percent. However, the fact that 45.6 percent of people eligible to vote failed to turn out indicates that, despite the claims by the established political parties, the general mobilization against the extreme right fell short of its mark.

Dreux has thus become a veritable political laboratory for the extreme right. The National Front in Dreux has been able to develop a winning formula that combines good constituency work with its anti-immigration theme. This formula has proved effective in small towns of the French "heartland," many of which are caught in the problem of economic crisis and rapid social change. The results of two exit polls by the French Institute for Public Opinion (IFOP) for *Le Figaro* based on a sample of 952 voters and by BVA for *Libération* on a sample of 1,157 electors help us understand the motivations of the electorate. On the basis of these polls, one can see the similarity between the sociological profile of the electorate of Marie-France Stirbois and that of the National Front in general.[29] There are, however, some features specific to her support base.

From the exit polls of 1988, the electorate of the National Front is more likely to be male rather than female and draws support from all age groups, but disproportionately from young people in both the presidential and the legislative elections. Both of these characteristics are quite similar to the electorate of Marie-France Stirbois as well. Like the National Front as a whole, she won some support from all social classes but drew a large percentage of the working class vote in Dreux in her favor. In addition, the BVA poll shows similar tendencies on the part of artisans and tradesmen to support her in large numbers. In contrast, the professionals and higher civil servants of the area have less of a tendency to support the National Front candidate. Thus, the National Front vote in Dreux, compared to its performance at the national level, appears to be drawn from the lower social strata. Many of these supporters from the working classes were probably born and brought up in the countryside and migrated to the town to look for work. They are not properly integrated into urban life and feel that economic modernization leads to the loss of their identity and of the values basic to them. Nostalgia for the past and for the values and sense of identity going back to their childhood attracts them to the National Front, which presents itself as the defender of French identity and stands for the speedy departure of immigrants, seen as the cause of all that is not well. Their removal from French soil would restore the good, stable social order of the past.

74

Pierre Bréchon and Subrata Kumar Mitra

Some of these conjectures are borne out by the political origins of the voters in the second ballot for Marie-France Stirbois and their voting behavior in the legislative elections of 1988 (see Table 3). Compared to 1988, she appears to have retained the full support of her electorate; 98 percent of those who had voted for her in 1988 did so again in 1989, and the same was true of her first ballot voters as well.[30] But she was able to entice voters from both the moderate Right and the Left: four out of ten who voted for the moderate Right in 1988 voted for the National Front in 1989; two out of ten who voted for the Socialists in 1988 voted for the National Front in 1989. The transfer of votes between the first and the second ballots showed that the candidate of the RPR lost 14 percent of his vote to Madame Stirbois. From among Socialist voters of the first ballot, 56 percent admitted having voted for the RPR in the second ballot. Finally, those who abstained in the first ballot appear to have split evenly between the candidate of the moderate Right and its adversary, the National Front.

When asked about which two considerations weighed most in their decision to vote, one factor distinguishes the electors of the National Front sharply from others. Of Stirbois voters, 76 percent suggest immigrants and 36 percent insecurity as the main factors behind their vote, whereas 40 percent of RPR voters indicate the fight against racism as the main factor behind their vote with no clear front runner for the second factor. The vote for the National Front, in Dreux as well as elsewhere in the country, polarized along the lines of the major social issues of the day. Another issue that weighs with National Front electors (see Table 4) is the Islamic headscarf. Whereas almost 60 percent of the Stirbois electorate point to this factor, only 22 percent of the RPR voters mention it among their main considerations. Even more significant is the opinion of the electorate as a whole in Dreux on the issue, for

Table 3 Partisan Voting in the Second Ballot of the Legislative By-election at Dreux, Cross-tabulated by Partisan Voting in the First Ballot in Legislative Election of 1988 and First Ballot of Legislative Elections of 1989 (row percentage)

	Vote in the second ballot, legislative, 1989		
	National Front Mme Stirbois	RPR M. Lethuillier	Wasted ballot or N.A.
Vote in first ballot legislative, June 1988			
- Socialist Party (F. Gaspard)	20	46	34
- RPR/UDF (M Tangourdeau)	41	56	3
- National Front (M F Stirbois)	98	2	-
First ballot, November 1989			
- Socialist Party (C Nespoulous)	5	56	39
- RPR (M Lethuillier)	14	85	1
- National Front (M F Stirbois)	97	3	-
- Abstention/NA	39	42	19

Source: Exit Poll, IFOP (Paris)

Table 4 Issue Positions of the Electorate of the Dreux Constituency, Exit Poll, Second Ballot, Legislative Election, 1989 (percentages)

(The respondent agrees very strongly or somewhat strongly)

Issue items	Total	National Front	RPR	New voters of National Front (*)	RPR voters formerly of the Left (**)
- The debate on the Islamic headscarf has affected your vote	41	59	22	27	18
- Support government policy on immigration	17	4	30	2	49
- Support the RPR/UDF on immigration	26	19	45	32	26
- Support the social policy of the govt.	27	11	42	14	57
- Dissatisfied with the political system	43	59	22	72	13
- Intend to send a warning to the govt. or to express opposition to the govt. through vote	54	76	29	87	11
- Wish that the ideas of the National Front should be taken into consideration by the government	54	79	28	87	14
- Wish that there would be, one day, National Front ministers in the government	27	49	5	41	2
- Wish that there would be a National Front majority in the next legislative election	24	44	4	24	2

Source: Exit poll, IFOP-Figaro

(*)   Those electors of Madame Stirbois who had voted for the RPR or the UDF in the fist ballot of the legislative elections of June 1988, or the first ballot of the legislative elections of 1989

(**)   Those electors of M. Lethuillier who had voted for the Socialist Party or the Communist Party in the first ballot of legislative 1988 or 1989

76

Pierre Bréchon and Subrata Kumar Mitra

73 percent of them would stop the girls wearing the Islamic headscarf from attending state schools altogether. The figure goes up to 86 percent among the voters of the National Front and 80 percent among the electors of the RPR, coming down to 51 percent among the voters of the Socialist Party, according to a poll taken by BVA for *Libération*. The issue of the headscarf, which was seen as a symbol of "conquering Islam" that should not be tolerated, has thus acted as a catalyst that polarized opinion in Dreux. Many saw the position of the education ministry as far too soft, amounting almost to the abandonment of its duty to protect secular French culture and identity.

The electorate of Dreux as a whole is critical of the policy of the government on the issue of immigration, which is approved by only 17 percent of those interviewed, in marked contrast to the French population as a whole where the rate of approval at 40 percent (from a poll taken by BVA for *Paris Match* in April 1990) is significantly higher. Dreux and the area surrounding it thus appear as particularly negative in this regard. Even among the people who voted for the RPR in the second ballot but had voted for the Socialist or the Communist party in 1988 or 1989, only one out of two approve of the immigration policy of the government. The policy of the moderate Right on this issue and on the social policy of the government as a whole does not get any more support from the people of Dreux either, who thus appear to be critical of all established parties. In any case, 43 percent of the electorate of Dreux say that they are dissatisfied with the political system, a figure which goes up to 72 percent among those supporters of the National Front who have abandoned the moderate Right in order to join it. In the BVA-*Libération* poll, 75 percent of the people believe that "politicians strike deals behind the backs of the people" (83 percent among supporters of the National Front, 71 percent among those voting for the RPR, and 51 percent for Socialists). The vote thus appears as a whole to be the manifestation of protest against the policies of the government. More particularly, 31 percent admit that the vote was specifically meant to be a warning to the government, and 23 percent suggest it was meant to show opposition to the government. This attitude is strongest among the voters of Marie-France Stirbois (an approval rate of 87 percent), particularly those who used to vote for the moderate Right in the past.

However, this is not merely a negative vote, as might be construed from the tone of some of the opinions expressed. In expressing their discontentment, 54 percent of all voters and 87 percent of the neophytes of the National Front who have defected from the moderate Right wish that the ideas of the National Front should be taken into consideration by the government in making policy. That, however, is the upper limit on the extent to which the French electorate is willing to accord legitimacy to the National Front as a political force, intent on a radical change of the system. Whenever they are faced with the choice, people are unwilling to see the National Front itself get into power. It is, indeed, strange to find that, even among the Stirbois electors, only 49 percent wish that there would one day be members of the National Front in the government, and only 44 percent hope that the National Front will one day win a majority in the National Assembly.

Since a sizable proportion of the National Front vote consists of protest votes intended to act as a message to the government and thus the result of general discontentment, overall support for it is unstable, particularly when it reaches such high levels in specific elections. When asked about their voting intentions in the next legislative election, it would appear

Comparative Politics   October 1992

from Table 5 that only 27 percent of the people would vote for it in a general election. Even among Stirbois voters, only 50 percent would vote for the National Front in a general election. Fifty-eight percent of the people who have come over from the moderate Right would go back to it in the event of a general election, and only 30 percent of them would vote for the National Front. Fourteen percent of the Stirbois electorate would even go over to the Left, which is where they probably come from. Significantly, 20 percent of the Stirbois electorate place themselves on the four points to the left on a left-right scale with eight points.

Thus, as confirmed by other studies, the electorate of the National Front is composite in character.[31] It contains a hard core characterized by a structured ideology, xenophobia, and the rejection of a political system based on democracy. Forty-nine percent of the supporters of the National Front in the poll taken by BVA for *Libération* agree with the proposition that "democracy is nothing but disorder."[32] But it contains another section which has joined the National Front specifically because of immigration. Every time this issue gains salience in public consciousness and it appears that neither the government nor the established political parties are able to stop the arrival of new immigrants and to assimilate the existing ones into

Table 5 Voting Intentions of the Electorate of Dreux in the Next Legislative Election (column percentages)

"If there is an election of the
National Assembly shortly, Respondent
will vote for ...."

	Total	Electors of			
		National Front	RPR	New voters of Front (RPR/UDF)(*)	RPR voters formerly of the Left (**)
- Communist party or extreme left	4	3	4	-	7
- Socialist Party	25	11	34	3	67
Ecologists	8	3	13	2	17
- RPR/UDF	23	18	38	58	5
National Front	27	52	1	30	-
- N.A.	13	13	10	7	4

Source: exit poll, IFOP-Figaro

(*)   Electors of Madame Stirbois who had voted for the RPR or the UDF in the first ballot of legislative 1988 or first ballot of legislative 1989

(**)   Electors of RPR who had voted the Socialist Party or the Communist Party in the first ballot of legislative 1988 or first ballot, legislative 1989

Pierre Bréchon and Subrata Kumar Mitra

French society, the National Front finds in it a potent political weapon to mobilize voters and increase its political support.

Conclusion

During the early part of 1990, the government of the Left in France made a concerted effort to put into effect a new policy of social integration. A secretary-general for integration was appointed. The government decided to provide additional resources to schools in working and lower middle class neighborhoods to promote social integration through common schooling. New resources were to be made available to generally run down neighborhoods in large cities with a reputation for ethnic conflict. At the same time, the moderate Right was also busy developing an alternative policy initiative. Without directly opposing the integration of immigrants who have already been in France for some time, it wanted to stop all new immigration, make it much more difficult for foreigners to acquire French nationality, and limit the enjoyment of social benefits by foreigners in an effort to make sure that these benefits themselves do not become a cause of the influx of foreigners. Socialist Prime Minister Rocard attempted to develop a consensus on immigration policy among all parties (except the National Front), and a debate was organized in the National Assembly to find ways of fighting racism.[33]

All these measures, however, do not appear very effective to the general public. The intention to vote for the National Front has continued to go up slowly, hovering around eighteen percent in May 1990 (see Table 2). Reflecting the tension that arises out of the conflict between opposing principles of fear of racism, which pushes down the approval rating of the National Front, and fear of immigration, which pulls it up, public opinion seems to fluctuate from event to event. Thus, following the high scores achieved by the National Front in early May 1990, the intention to vote for it tumbled to 13 percent towards the end of May and 11 percent in June 1990 (see Table 2). The cause was linked to the desecration of the Jewish cemetery of Carpentras, a manifestly antisemitic attack which shocked many French people who remember the Holocaust. In response, there were several antiracist demonstrations. Though those responsible for the desecration of the cemetery were not found, the event brought to public attention the danger of the kind of racism propagated by the National Front. In a poll taken by BVA for the French television (TF1 7 sur 7), 47 percent thought that the authorities were partly responsible for the event. Though Jean-Marie Le Pen was prominently mentioned in this context, the "whole political class" was not considered to be above reproach. But the implications for the National Front were quite damning: 52 percent thought that the National Front constituted a danger to democracy.

Democracy is safe in France despite the rise of the National Front, but from the point of view of immigrants France has certainly become less liberal, compared to the high point reached after the victory of the United Front of the Left in the presidential elections of 1981. In their attempts to fend off the challenge of the National Front, politicians of all parties have started using some of its language. This is seen both in the volatility of public opinion and in the politicians' preference for hedging their bets on the issue of rights of immigrant workers. The consequence is a general hardening of attitudes on the issue of immigration.

Since the departure of Michel Rocard, Chirac has made a determined attempt to exploit the issues of immigration and insecurity against the Cresson government on the grounds that it is "soft." She has responded with tough talk. In a television broadcast, "she ferociously attacked illegal immigration, expressed outrage that only a third of captured illegals were actually deported, and proposed that planes be chartered to send them back home."[34] The position taken by the Socialist prime minister has caused a certain amount of consternation within her party. But the general public approves of this shift in policy. Two-thirds of French viewers appear to agree with the policies advocated by Edith Cresson.[35]

The National Front has risen to national prominence because it has succeeded in giving concrete political expression to a latent xenophobia, reinforced by the problem of immigration. It has succeeded in placing this latent xenophobic fear in the context of a general ideology of the extreme right, based on a rejection of established political parties and distrust of democracy. Essentially an able populist politician, Le Pen mobilizes opinion against the political elite, whom he presents as far too soft to provide effective solutions for contemporary problems. By expressing it politically, the National Front has given both reinforcement and legitimacy to xenophobia. Following her success at Dreux, Marie-France Stirbois claimed that her election was a victory against the "foreign invader."

In spite of the latent xenophobia and its expression and reinforcement by the National Front, there is no firm evidence of an inevitable rise of racism and the National Front in France to a position where it can exercise state power directly. In electoral terms, it is possible to envisage a threshold of around a vote share of 15 percent which the National Front is unlikely to exceed in the near future. Paradoxically, the availability of the National Front and the cooptation of parts of its language by its adversaries help create a "normal" issue out of racism, which has to compete with the more established issues of class, material welfare, and partisanship on terms that give a relative advantage to the moderate Left and Right. Some of this can be inferred from the findings reported in Table 2. Voting intentions, highly sensitive to the temporal context, are rarely of an enduring character. Voting intentions for the National Front went up in July 1990 as the effect of the desecration of Carpentras came to an end. The proportions went down in the second fortnight of September 1990 after the stance taken by Le Pen in favor of Iraq but started going up again to 14 percent in October 1990 once the event lingered on.

Public opinion is a battle ground for opposing ideologies in everyday life. Included among the actors present in the arena who are engaged in mobilizing opinion against racism is a range of political groups, associations, trade unions, and church organizations which see themselves as the bearers of the French tradition of human rights and as the representatives of a country which from the beginning of this century has known how to welcome and integrate waves of European immigrants, including Poles, Italians, Spaniards, and Portuguese. However, the fact that the new immigrants are mostly colored and non-Christian puts further obstacles in the way of their eventual integration into French society and adds to the seriousness of the situation. The situation calls for the mobilization of all social forces that could provide an antidote to racism and reinforce the latent traditions of universal human rights and tolerance. As part of the legacy of the Revolution of 1789, they are also present in French society though they have been somewhat stifled during the past years of economic crisis, rapid urbanization, and social dislocation.

80

Pierre Bréchon and Subrata Kumar Mitra

NOTES

We are grateful to Françoise Vibert of the French Institute of Public Opinion (IFOP) and Michel Brulé of the Brulé Ville Associés (BVA) for making available the data on which this article is based. The helpful comments of Jack Hayward, Edward Page, Mike Smith, and three anonymous referees of *Comparative Politics* are gratefully acknowledged.

1. For data on the rise of the extreme right in five postwar European democracies, see Claus von Beyme, "Right-wing Extremism in Post-war Europe," in Claus von Beyme, ed., *Right-wing Extremism in Western Europe* (London: Frank Cass, 1988), p. 7, and Juliet Lodge, *The 1989 Election of the European Parliament* (New York: MacMillan, 1990).

2. For conflicting contemporary definitions of the extreme right, see von Beyme, ed., p. 1.

3. The issue of historic continuity reflects a deeper ambivalence towards the historic legacy in postwar continental Europe. The ambiguity of Le Pen's position arises from his attempts to identify with both the principles of the Vichy regime and the patriotic resistance to the German occupation of France. For the complex ideological origins of the National Front, see Paul Buzzi, "Le Front national entre national-populisme et extremisme de droite," in *Regards sur l'actualité* (La Documentation Française, March 1991), pp. 31–43. The self-perception of the extreme right is not free from this ambiguity. Thus, while claiming continuity with Poujadism, the OAS, and Vichy, Le Pen nevertheless prefers to give his movement the appearance of something new by calling it *"droite populaire, sociale et nationale."* See von Beyme, ed., note 1, p. 4.

4. See R. Eatwell, "Poujadism and Neopoujadism: From Revolt to Reconciliation," in Philip Cerny, ed., *Social Movements and Protest in France* (London: Frances Pinter, 1982), for an analysis of the authoritarian right in France.

5. The complexity of the profile of the National Front is reflected in the composite character of its clientele, which includes unreconstructed apologists of Vichy as well as people who consider themselves to be members of the French Left. For statistical evidence on the various groups present within the National Front, see Martin Schain, "Party Politics, the National Front and the Construction of Political Legitimacy," *West European Politics,* 10 (April 1987), and Subrata Kumar Mitra, "The National Front in France: A Single Issue Movement?," in von Beyme, ed.

6. See M. Winock, "La vieille histoire du national-populisme," *Le Monde,* June 12, 1987. The author traces the origin of the National Front back to the *boulangiste* crisis in an attempt to explain the causes of Le Pen's present prominence.

7. J. Lorien, K. Citron, and S. Dumont, *Le système Le Pen* (Antwerp: EPO, 1986); and Allain Rollat, *Les hommes de l'extrême droite* (Paris: Calmann Lévy, 1985).

8. E. Roussel, *Le cas Le Pen* (Paris: Lattes, 1985).

9. E. Plenel and A. Rollat, *L'effet Le Pen* (Paris: La Découverte-Le Monde, 1984).

10. This is in contrast to the dismissive tone in which the National Front was discussed in 1983: "Emiettée en une myriade d'ilots minuscules, de cenacles impuissants, de cercles fantomatiques, elle [l'extrême droite] ne subsiste qu'à l'état de vestige historique." J. C. Petitfils, *L'extrême droite en France* (Paris: PUF, 1983), p. 123.

11. See Pascal Perrineau, "Les étapes d'une implantation électorale, 1972–1988," in Pascal Perrineau and Nonna Mayer, eds., *Le Front National à découvert* (Paris: Presses de la FNSP, 1989), pp. 37–62.

12. See Frédéric Bon and Jean-Paul Cheylan, eds., *La France qui vote* (Paris: Collection Pluriel, 1988), pp. 249–271.

13. Ibid.

14. From a poll conducted by Pierre Bréchon and Jean-Paul Bozonnet in Grenoble on the basis of a representative sample of 548 electors in 1985. (Grenoble: IEP, 1985).

15. One can even detect a certain element of urban anomie in the rise of the National Front. The breakdown of traditional social structure and networks could give rise to free-floating political behavior which may swell the ranks of urban protest and protest votes in general. See Pascal Perrineau, "Front National: L'écho politique de l'anomie urbaine," *La France en Politique* (Paris: Esprit-Fayard-Le Seuil, 1988), pp. 22–38.

16. On the basis of an analysis of 532 communes in the department of Isère, Gilles Ivaldi shows that the correlation between the two variables is nonexistent and it is weak if the analysis is limited to communes with more than 2,000 inhabitants. See Gilles Ivaldi, *Le Front National dans le Département de l'Isère* (Master's thesis, IEP, Grenoble, 1988).

17. Bon and Cheylan, *La France qui vote.*

18. See the following studies of Dreux: P. A. Hamelin, "Dreux, croissance urbaine et évolution politique," *Les Cahiers de la Loire Moyenne,* 16 (1987), 47–78, and J. Ph. Roy, *L'implantation électorale du Front National en région Centre* (Master's thesis in public law, University of Tours, 1989).

81

19. Ibid.

20. See Françoise Gaspard, *Madame le maire*(Paris: Grasset, 1979), and *Une petite ville en France* (Paris: Gallimard, 1990).

21. For details, see J. Y. Camus, "Origine et formation du Front National, 1972–1981," in Perrineau and Mayer, eds., pp. 17–36.

22. Cantonal elections are held every three years, with only half of the cantons participating in each election.

23. This common list of the extreme and moderate Right was a significant development. It helped bring the National Front a degree of legitimacy. Subsequently, the parties of the Right refused alliances with the extreme right, even local ones. However, tactical alliances between the two continued to exist in those regional councils where the moderate Right needed the support of the extreme right to gain a majority. During the second ballot of the legislative elections of 1988, an accord was made between the National Front and the RPR-UDF in the Bouche du Rhône to avoid splitting votes by avoiding contests through reciprocal withdrawal. However, that accord, which conferred some legitimacy on the National Front, was not electorally beneficial for it because a section of the moderate Right refused to abide by it. The strategy of entering into an alliance with the National Front has been consistently criticized by several leading personalities of the moderate Right, including Simone Veil, Olivier Stirn, and Bernard Stasi, who from the municipal elections of 1983 onwards have recommended abstention in the second ballot instead of voting for the National Front.

24. See Françoise Gaspard and C. Servan-Schreiber, *La fin des immigrés* (Paris: Seuil, 1984).

25. See J. P. Stirbois, *Le tonnerre de Dreux* (Paris: n.d.).

26. Her husband had become the secretary general of the National Front in the meantime.

27. At the same time, Marie-France Stirbois was at the head of the list of the National Front in the regional elections and was elected in the proportional voting, securing 10 percent of the vote in the department (and 16 percent in Dreux).

28. This position did not get full support of all sections within the Left, and the prospect of fighting an election with the help of votes of the Left embarrassed some members of the Right.

29. See, for example, Nonna Mayer, "Why Do They Vote for the National Front?," (Bochum: European Consortium for Political Research, April 2–7, 1990).

30. This, of course, is not true of the electors of Marie-France Stirbois from 1988 who abstained in 1989 because, by the very nature of the exit poll, these persons are not interviewed, the survey being based on those who actually turned out to vote.

31. See Mayer, "Why Do They Vote for the National Front? "

32. Lagrange and Perrineau show that, on scales of attitudes, those who are sympathetic towards the National Front are also characterized by the values of authority, the importance of small groups, strong attachment to self-identity, a rejection of everything that is foreign or different, a rejection of introspection, and a voluntarist attitude. See Hughes Lagrange and Pascal Perrineau, "Le syndrome lepéniste," in Perrineau and Mayer, eds., pp. 228–241.

33. As a part of this consensus, Rocard and Mitterrand agreed to exclude from the agenda the issue of giving the right to vote in local elections to the foreigners settled in France.

34. Mark Lilla, "Mitterrand and Madame Gaffe," *The Guardian,* Aug. 15, 1991.

35. Ibid.

[4]

European Journal of Political Research 17: 77–94 (1989)
© Kluwer Academic Publishers, Dordrecht – Printed in the Netherlands

Factionalism, the French socialist party and the fifth Republic: An explanation of intra-party divisions

ALISTAIR M. COLE
Aston University, U.K.

The modern study of factions in political parties is a relatively novel phenomenon. Academic interest has traditionally centred around the relationship between the 'parts' and the 'whole' of a political system, between political parties and the wider polity. That concentration has tended until recently to take preference over analysis of sub-party units. However, recent research has emphasised the importance of studying a party's internal dynamics as one essential element influencing its overall position within a given political system. The present study continues in that tradition, while attempting to assess the impact of a political system – the French Fifth Republic – upon the internal cohesion of one of its most important parties, the Socialists.

Despite the current interest displayed by political scientists in intra-party conflict, there is no commonly agreed definition of faction. Rose (1964) draws a distinction between factions and tendencies in his analysis of the British party system. Factions are portrayed by Rose as organised, self-aware and disciplined groups; tendencies, by contrast, consist of 'stable sets of attitudes', not corresponding to any organised group of politicians. The distinction between conscious, rival groups completing for power, and general attitudes is a

78

valid one. Our concern in this article is with the former. However the difficulties involved in Rose's distinction underline the essential ambiguities of the concept of faction. Rose implies that only those intra-party groups with a visible degree of organisation should be called factions. How then do we classify those groups which, although clearly recognisable as a stable, cohesive group, are bereft of forms of factional organisation distinct from the party apparatus itself? To label certain groups as factions (or fractions), but to spare others that title would be in itself to impose a negative value-judgement on 'factional' activity.

Certain authors reject the phrase 'faction' altogether. Sartori (1976) or Hanley (1986) reject 'faction' outright for its pejorative overtones and for its specific historical connotations: faction refers to the 'gentlemen's cliques that preceded modern parties' (Hanley 1986: 4), to small power-seeking groups, determined only to serve their members' interests, that became superceded with the development of modern parties. Hanley follows Sartori's lead and proposes the term 'fraction', which he considers 'a purely descriptive term'. In the French context, however, 'fraction' cannot be considered as 'purely descriptive': it is possible the most pejorative manner of labelling intra-party group conflict. While accepting that the term 'faction' has often been used as a insult, and that certain authors have designated as factions only those 'power-seeking groups' that precede party, it is proposed to retain the term faction to label sub-party units. Faction need not necessarily invoke 'overtones of conspiracy and illegitimacy' (Hanley 1986); it is probably the most neutral term available, given its general usage within the language of politics. Moreover, it is questionable whether a generally recognised term can be abandoned without causing overwhelming confusion, especially in relation to the existing body of literature. As for the historical objection, a distinction must be drawn between pre-party and modern party factions.

The Socialist party's official factions (courants) are those groups with which this article is primarily concerned. Nonetheless, the term faction will refer to any group whose existence is widely recognised within the party, even if this group is temporarily allied with others in a leadership coalition. We shall not deal with Rose's 'stable sets of attitudes', which frequently cut across formal divisions between factions (e.g. on nuclear power). Nor or we concerned with Hine's (1982) 'single-issue' groups (e.g. feminist lobby) which have often had the same effect. Because there are clearly different types of faction operating within the PS, conceptual classifications will be made within this category. In terms of the party, all factions thus form a 'part of the whole' and even a majority constitutes only a faction.

The causes of factionalism

From its origins, French Socialism has been marked by its factional nature. The 1905 SFIO, the first unified Socialist party, was formed after a process of fusion between six distinct political groups. Ideology and institutional factors both caused divisions within the unified party. Ideology was of crucial importance in the young SFIO's life. The 1905 party was created, on the orders of the Second International, as a revolutionary party, in total opposition to bourgeois society: the party's role was to prepare itself for the historically inevitable revolution rather than to participate in 'bourgeois' governments, even of republican defence. But in fact 'maximalist' (Guesde) and 'reformist' (Jaurès) wings coexisted within the party, divided by ideology and political strategy (the centre-right sought alliances with advanced elements of the Republican bloc; the 'left' refused). Though the doctrine of non-participation in government remained intact until 1914, the party's political practice (contesting elections, voting for 'progressive' legislation, running local government) already bore little relationship to its revolutionary ideology.

The Tours split of 1920 and the creation of the PCF, reinforced the SFIO's ideological straightjacket: in order to portray its fidelity to the veille maison, the SFIO continued to proclaim itself a revolutionary Marxist party commited to non-participation in 'bourgeois' governments. During the interwar period institutional questions of party strategy (whether or not to enter government) and alliances (with the PCF or Radicals), as well as ideological differences, seriously divided the party between left and right and harmed its cohesion. The 'non-participation' stance encountered increasing opposition from among SFIO deputies. In 1933, a large body of 'neo-socialist' deputies split from the party, in protest against its refusal to join the Radical-led government after the 1932 general election. The interwar period also witnessed the development of opposition left-wing factions: Zyromski's Bataille Socialiste (1926) and Pivert's Gauche Révolutionnaire (1935). The Popular Front government of 1936 finally breached the SFIO's 'non-participation' doctrine, but did not preclude an outbreak of serious factional activity. This was mainly due to left-wing opposition to Blum's government over economic policy, the pace of reforms and whether or not to intervene in the Spanish civil war. Government participation thus provoked factional division, because the party was caught between irreconcilable policy options.

After Guy Mollet's capture of the SFIO from Blum and Mayer in 1946, intra-party dissent was limited during most of the Fourth Republic. That could be largely explained in terms of the constraints imposed by the wider political system: from 1947 to 1951, the SFIO joined with centre and conservative parties in a series of 'third force' governments formed to safeguard the Republic from the anti-regime parties, the PCF and de Gaulle's RPF. The in-

80

stitutional pressures placed on the SFIO were so great that potential opponents preferred not to endanger the leadership in an extremely delicate period. There was felt to be no alternative to the leadership's strategy: other alliances (e.g. with the 'cold war' PCF) were difficult to envisage. Such enforced consensus began to break down from the mid-1950's, with the emergence of a powerful anti-colonialist faction, which strengthened its identity in opposition to Mollet government's Algerian policies in 1956–1957. It finally split to form the PSA in September 1958 (forerunner of the 1960 PSU).

The advent and consolidation of the Fifth Republic and Gaullism, from 1958 to 1962, saw the non-communist left demoralised and disunited. From 1958 until 1971, the old SFIO was largely dragged along by events, outdated as it was by the presidential system, although it remained the best organised force on the non-communist left, with solid roots in parliament and local government. The initiative passed to groups outside of the SFIO: to the burgeoning political club movement (and especially to François Mitterrand, head of the CIR group of clubs after 1964), or to the PSU. Both major forces of the 'new left' were determined to rejuvenate the left from outside its existing 'archaic' structures. In 1962 de Gaulle's referendum introduced the direct election of the presidency which was widely condemned on the left. After the failure of Defferre's bid to stand as a presidential candidate backed by a Socialist-Centrist-Christian Democratic federation, the left-wing parties (PCF, SFIO, PSU) agreed to support Mitterrand as the united left candidate in the 1965 presidential election. That contest revealed the left-right bipolarising pressures of the presidential election when Mitterrand achieved 45.5% on the second ballot run-off against de Gaulle. Mitterrand's performance created a new dual image: that of presidential leader of the left and of proponent of alliance between the non-Communist left and the PCF. His 'presidential' stature gave Mitterrand immense authority, which enabled him to impose his leadership on the non-Communist left, at the expense of Mollet and the SFIO. Mitterrand led the FGDS (SFIO, CIR, Radicals, clubs) at the 1967 and 1968 general elections, on both occasions in electoral alliance with the PCF. Despite the poor FGDS showing in the 1968 election (after the events of May), Mitterrand regained the initiative in 1969, after Defferre's disastrous performance (5.1%) in the 1969 presidential election, on a strongly anti-Communist ticket. That left Mitterrand as the only plausible 'presidential' leader and alliance with the PCF as the only realistic strategy.

In July 1969, Mollet's SFIO allied with Alain Savary's small UCRG group of clubs and transformed itself into a new Parti Socialiste (PS) of which Savary became leader. Most commentators, however, date the rejuvenation of the PS from the June 1971 Epinay congress, at which Mitterrand finally joined and captured control of the new party. Mitterrand's CIR allied in a apparently contradictory manner with the right and left-wings of the old SFIO, represented respectively by Mauroy/Defferre and CERES, against the outgoing Savary/Mollet leadership and the orthodox socialist faction led by Poperen, whose UGCS also joined the PS at Epinay. What united the disparate factions of Mitterrand's future majority was the belief that a genuine party renovation could only occur once Mollet (and his protégé Savary) had been overthrown. For Mollet had come to personify the SFIO's steady decline from 1946 to 1969.

Within the new PS from 1971 to 1981, factionalism was constituted by the competition of rival politicians and intra-party groups, whose main divisions were over personalities (including presidential rivalries), policy/ideology, party strategy, and differing organisational interests. These divisions could not be separated into watertight compartments: all major 'factions' combined elements of interest and principle. Nonetheless, these groups could be distinguished according to their proximity to party power, their strategic relationship vis-à-vis the wider political system, their ideological consistency, and their degree of extra-party organisation. Table 1 outlines the results of party congresses during the party's first decade.

The modern PS was formed after a process of fusion of diverse forces on the Socialist left: the old SFIO, Mitterrand's CIR, Savary's UCRG, Poperen's UGCS and Rocard's PSU (after 1974). Until 1973, Mitterrand's leadership depended on the continuing support of the left-wing CERES faction, whose leader, J.P. Chevènement, largely inspired the 1972 party programme, Changer la vie. However, within the new leadership, the Mitterrand and Mauroy/Defferre factions soon constituted a dominant force, whereas CERES became increasingly isolated, especially after the signing of the common programme with the PCF in June 1972. Mitterrand's leadership was considerably strengthened by the 1972 common programme, which transformed the left into a credible alternative governing coalition. It was consolidated further in the 1973

Table 1. Factions and party congresses, 1971–1979. (percentages rounded up or down to nearest half percent).

Congress	1971	1973	1975	1977	1979
Mitterrand	15	65.5[1]	68[2]	76[3]	47
Mauroy	30[4]	Mitt	Mitt	Mitt	17
CERES	8.5	21	25.5	24	15
Rocard	–	–	Mitt	Mitt	21
Mollet	34[5]	8	3	–	–
Poperen	12	5	Mitt	Mitt	Mitt

Source: Bulletin Socialiste 15 June 1971, L'Unité 22–28 June 1973, L'Unité 7–13 February 1975, Le Poing et la Rose, 63, June 1977, Le Poing et la Rose, 81, May 1979.
[1] Mitterrand, Mauroy, Defferre and Savary; [2] Mitterrand, Mauroy, Defferre, Savary, Rocard and Poperen; [3] Mitterrand, Mauroy, Defferre, Savary, Rocard, Poperen, Mollet's remaining supporters; [4] Mauroy and Defferre; [5] Mollet and Savary.

82

general election, at which the PS obtained 20.8% in alliance with the left Radicals and came close to the PCF's score (21.7%). By the Grenoble congress in June 1973, Mitterrand had emerged as undisputed party leader. The final motion adopted in 1973 was supported (quasi-unanimously) by 92% of party mandates (Mitterrand, Mauroy/Defferre/Savary, CERES, Poperen) with Mollet (8%) left alone to fight a rearguard action against Mitterrand. In his Parties and Party Systems, Sartori (1976: 98) argues that:

'while the electoral system is not a sufficient cause for the multiplication of parties, the electoral system does become a sufficient cause for the multiplication of fractions . . . Simply and practically put, the laws of Duverger may well be wrong for parties and correct for fractions'

While Sartori does not argue that the electoral system is the only cause explaining internal party factionalism, it is nonetheless regarded as perhaps the most important causal factor. More specifically, he stipulates that 'a highly proportional type of electoral system will allow a high degree of fractionism, that is, will encourage and produce fission'. Thus, PR used in internal party elections will lead to a proliferation of 'medium-sized and mini fractions', whereas 'maxi-fractions are unlikely'. In 1971, the PS adopted by a highly proportional system of intra-party election: factions were to be represented on the party's executive organs according to the percentages their motions had obtained at party congress (after all, party members had voted at grass roots level). There was a low (5%) threshold to representation. But there is little evidence to point to PR producing a fissiparous intra-party representation.

That a party's electoral system might help or hinder potential factions is a plausible hypothesis, but extreme caution must be adopted before accepting any causal relationship between PR and the number of factions. By the 1973 congress, a pattern of rallying (rassemblement) to Mitterrand had been established, which endured until 1979 (see Table 2): those factions seeking to join the PS leadership agreed to sign a common motion before congress. In 1973 only CERES refused this procedure yet retained its position in the majority; in

Table 2. Number and nature of official PS factions.

Congress	Number	Maxi (25%+)	Medium (10–25%)	Mini (−10%)
1971	6	2	2	2
1973	4	1	1	2
1975	3	2	0	1
1977	2	1	1	0
1979	6	1	3	2

Source: as for Table 1.

1975 it refused again, and Mitterrand expelled it from his leadership. Mitterrand's success in relation to the wider political system ('his' restoration of Socialist fortunes) had a far greater explanatory value on the number and nature of factions than did the 'rules of the game' of the party's PR electoral system. Such rallying to Mitterrand endured until the 1978 general election defeat, and undoubtedly strengthened his position. The resurgence of open and extensive factional rivalries between 1978 and 1981 owed more to the PS' (and therefore Mitterrand's) generally weaker position in the wider political system, than it did to the PR method of intra-party election.

Mitterrand's domination of the PS leadership became virtually complete after the 1974 presidential election at which he narrowly failed to defeat Giscard d'Estaing for the presidency. Thereafter, the party's main objective became to prepare for the 1978 general election and the probable exercise of power. This objective helped explain the pattern of intra-party relations established at the 1975 and 1977 congresses that of a somewhat artificial division between a politically heterogeneous majority, and a left-wing opposition, CERES. In 1975 Mitterrand finally excluded CERES from his leadership: he now regarded the CERES alliance as incompatible with his 'presidential' interpretation of left unity, which involved the PS marking its distance from the PCF and the radical commitments of the common programme. CERES was replaced in Mitterrand's leadership by Rocard, the former PSU leader who had rallied to the PS (at Mauroy's behest) in October 1974 at the Assises of Socialism. Rocard's promotion infuriated PCF leaders, since the ex-PSU chief had consistently criticised the common programme. Along with Rocard, Poperen was also finally allowed into the leadership in 1975.

Except for CERES, the most important factions again rallied to Mitterrand at the party's Nantes Congress of June 1977, the last one before the 1978 general election. Mitterrand's apparently unshakeable position as leader at the 1977 Congress stemmed from the party's continuing electoral successes, in particular that of the 1977 municipal election, and from his dual status as both probable prime minister after the 1978 general election and PS presidential candidate in any precipitate presidential election. As in previous congresses since 1973, external political circumstances (the PS triumph in the 1977 municipal election; Mitterrand's determination to avoid a renegotiation of the common programme, as demaded by the PCF in April 1977) could account for the internal constellation of alliances, and for Mitterrand's refusal to restore the maximalist (and, he suspected, pro-Communist) CERES to the leadership.

The transformation of Mitterrand's status from 'leader above faction' at Nantes, to leader of the dominant faction at the 1979 Metz Congress, was a gradual process which resulted from two main events: the breakdown of the united left alliance with the PCF in September 1977, and the left's subsequent defeat in the 1978 general election. The left's defeat in 1978 appeared finally to

84

discredit the strategy usually associated with Mitterrand of a PS-PCF alliance based on a detailed programme of government. Mitterrand's position in relation to the wider political system was weakened by this major setback, which in turn had a negative impact on his standing within the party.

The 1978 electoral setback unleashed a series of centrifugal rivalries which had previously been held in check. Before 1978, Mitterrand's 'presidential' authority had provided an essential source of internal party cohesion, however artificial that might have been. This was now openly challenged. The 1981 presidential election and the issue of who would be the party's candidate, now became the PS's predominant concern. That could explain why the rivalry between the party's only two plausible presidential candidates, Mitterrand and Rocard, was so central, and overcame all others in importance.

Nonetheless, a number of other divisions did exist; the most important were over strategy, ideology/policy, and organisational rivalries. In terms of strategy, the PS was divided between those who argued that the party should proclaim its commitment to a Union of the Left alliance in all circumstances, whatever the PCF's attitude (Mitterrand, CERES), and those who believed that the PS must refuse to commit itself too firmly in advance of victory at the 1981 presidential election (Rocard). Divisions over ideology were the hardest to assess, given the shifting ideological positions occupied by the different factions. Broadly speaking, Rocard and CERES offered competing 'moderate' and 'left-wing' poles of ideological attraction, while Mitterrand oscillated between the two. Although he sided with CERES for tactical reasons in 1979, Mitterrand marked his distance as the 1981 presidential election approached. In terms of party policy the winning coalition at the 1979 Congress (Mitterrand, CERES) proclaimed its continuing faith in the most important measures which had been foreseen in the common programme, such as in the nationalisation of the leading industrial groups and the entire banking sector, redistributive fiscal policies, and economic reflation through an increase in popular consumption and public spending. These policies were eventually written into the party's Projet Socialiste of 1980, and (in a watered down form) into Mitterrand's 110 Propositions for the 1981 campaign. Against the 1979 victors, Rocard (and to some extent Mauroy) argued that the left had to temper its reforming zeal by a recognition that domestic and international economic constraints would limit its freedom of action in government: a left-wing government would be doomed to failure if it did not respect the major economic equilibriums (balance of trade, inflation, sound budgetary policy). Mitterrand considered political imperatives (the need to attract PCF voters to the PS) as overriding economic ones.

At the party's 1979 Metz congress – for the first time since 1971 – the leaders of all the major factions presented their own motions. PR certainly enabled this situation of maximal factional competition to materialise, but a comparison with earlier congresses indicated that PR was not a sufficient condition of factionalism. Instead, the central impetus came from the weakening of Mitterrand's hold over the party after the 1978 election defeat, and his determination to defeat Rocard at the 1979 Congress, as a preliminary to neutralising the latters bid for the party's presidential nomination. The 1979 Congress virtually ensured that Mitterrand would secure the PS nomination in 1981. The final stages of the struggle between Mitterrand and Rocard for the PS nomination dominated the party throughout 1980. It was finally decided in Mitterrand's favour in November, when Rocard withdrew his candidacy, rather than go down to certain defeat in internal primary elections. Mitterrand's election as President of the Republic in May 1981 ended the left's relentless crossing of the desert in the Fifth Republic, and suddenly transformed the PS into a party of government.

The structure and location of PS factions
Within the PS, factions are composed of groups of individuals with varying degrees of factional consciousness, organisational cohesion, visibility or durability. Factions have varied in size and in motivation, as in their organisation, their success and their degree of 'coverage' of the party. There have been four major factions within the PS since 1971: Mitterrand, Mauroy, CERES and (after October 1974) Rocard. None of these factions fitted a uniform model or description, but they could each be located in relation to a series of ideal-types. These are the organisation faction, the parallel faction and the external faction.

The term organisation faction is used to describe an intra-party group whose main strengths lay within some aspect of the party's organisation (including support from elected representatives), rather than in organisational structures outside the party. Mitterrand and Mauroy best fitted this description. By contrast, the parallel faction refers to those groups (CERES and Rocard) which maintained a high level of independent factional organisation, parallel to the party's official structures. The term external faction refers to a group or leader (Rocard) who relied primarily on its external popularity to compensate for its relatively weak internal party standing- and to attempt thereby to alter the party balance in its favour.

By 1981 it had become clear that the party's four major factions were of an unequal significance. The contours of that inequality remained broadly stable throughout the Mitterrand presidency. The relative performance of the party's factions could be explained by their location in relation to the wider political and institutional system, by the political space they were able to occupy within the party, and to a lesser degree by the strategies they adopted. These variables gave certain factions long-term strategic advantages over their rivals. Mitterrand was the most favourably positioned both in relation to the wider

86

political system and the space he could occupy within the PS. The strengths of Mitterrand's position lay in his role as First Secretary, in his presidential stature, and in his central party location.

Mitterrand's vital position as First Secretary gave him a considerable influence over the party organisation and leadership. His control of the PS leadership after 1971, combined with his growing political stature, was a superb disguise for promoting his own factional interests. The strategic advantages of this position were obvious: Mitterrand promoted his supporters at all levels of the party, but claimed merely to be developing the party as a whole. His power thus stemmed in part from his position as head of the most powerful organisation faction. Moreover, most new party members tended to align themselves with Mitterrand as party leader, and not as head of a mere faction (such as Chevènement, Rocard or even Mauroy). In these circumstances there was little need to resort to forms of organisation outside of the party. Indeed, they might have proved counter-productive, by reducing Mitterrand's status to that of any 'faction' leader. In January 1981, Mitterrand handed over control of the PS leadership to Lionel Jospin, one of his most fervent protegés. Mitterrandist control of the party's Secrétariat National has remained intact at each subsequent party congress (1981, 1983, 1985 and 1987).

The strength of Mitterrand's position also related to his presidential stature. As presidential candidate in 1965, 1974 and 1981, Mitterrand – first in the FGDS, then in the PS – defined the necessary conditions for the unification of the non-communist left in the Fifth Republic: the collaboration of diverse groups in a common political structure, under a 'presidential' leader, that would be bordered by communism on its left and 'centrism' on its right. At the 1971 Epinay congress, Mitterrand took control of the PS partly because he was its only plausible presidential candidate. His presidential status was further enhanced in 1974, when he narrowly failed to defeat Giscard and illustrated that a PS-dominated left had a real chance of winning power. His 'triumphant defeat' in 1974 restored Mitterrand's position as presidential leader of the entire left and consolidated his control over the PS. After the 1978 general election defeat, the 1979 Metz congress reaffirmed that Mitterrand remained the party's natural leader and best presidential candidate in the eyes of most activists. Mitterrand's election as president in the 1981 presidential election justified their confidence.

Mitterrand's authority stemmed also from his position at the centre of party gravity from 1971 onwards, flanked by factions to his left and right. Mitterrand's central internal party position meant that he could ally with the 'left' against the 'right', or vice versa – a degree of leverage open to no other leader. Moreover, his central location enabled him to pose as guardian of the juste milieu, the party's ideological orthodoxy, threatened alternatively by left and right. Thus in 1975, Mitterrand expelled CERES from the leadership, accusing it of leftist irresponsibility and of siding with the PCF against its own party. At the 1979 Metz congress, by contrast, Mitterrand allied with the 'left' (CERES) to expel the 'right' (Mauroy/Rocard) – accused of revisionism – from the leadership. This completed the triangular mechanism analysed by Bon and Burnier (1974) in relation to the pre-1914 German SPD. Finally, as long as the party remained the fundamentally important factor in the selection of the presidential candidate, as it did in 1980, then this central location was an additional advantage, for it allowed a greater articulation of the various interests and beliefs represented in the PS than would have been possible under Rocard (an ideological anathema to the party's left-wing).

Leadership of Mitterrand's faction was assured by different generations of loyal supporters. These ranged from his Fourth Republic UDSR subordinates (Dayan, Dumas, Beauchamps or Mermaz), and his 1960's CIR Barons (Hernu, Joxe, Estier, Fillioud), to those post-1971 sabras, who had made their careers within the new party (such as Jospin, Fabius, Attali or Quilès). Rivalries between these politicians was frequently intense, as each competed for the leader's favour. Nonetheless, reciprocal loyalties between Mitterrand and his closest political aides overrode divergences over ideology and even strategy. From 1974 onwards, the leader/follower ties developed between Mitterrand and his lieutenants had the aura of a patron-client relationship; politicians who depended on Mitterrand for their political careers generally rewarded their sponsor with absolute loyalty. That strengthened Mitterrand's hold over the PS leadership. At an intermediary and grass roots level, Mitterrand gradually rallied support from his old Molletist SFIO opponents and attracted loyal services from a new generation of party members. Hence, Mitterrand's faction was the most heterogeneous in composition at both leadership and grass roots level. It was also the most ecumenical in terms of ideology, spanning Mitterrand's Radicalism, Poperen's or Joxe's crude Marxism, and Fabius's or Attali's faith in technocratic solutions. Mitterrand's faction was the closest to the 'faction of interest' defined by Sartori (1976: 77): its conscious members were primarily interested in exercising influence, whether within the party, or in government after 1981.

Mitterrand's most dangerous rival after 1971 for the incarnation of a party legitimacy was also his closest ally, Pierre Mauroy. His past within the SFIO, his role in securing the victory of Mitterrand at the 1971 Congress, and his initiative in calling the October 1974 Assises at which Rocard joined the party, all enabled Mauroy to claim to be a unifying force, with deeper roots in the socialist movement than Mitterrand. For Mauroy also headed an organisation faction. He could count on powerful sources of support from within the party organisation and amongst elected PS officials, as the most prominent representative of the old SFIO within the new party. Mauroy's backing came primarily from those areas where the influence of the old party remained

88

strong. Socialist local authorities, traditonally powerful ex-SFI0 federations (especially his own Nord and neighbouring Pas-de-Calais) and amongst mayors and councillors, deputies and senators. His position as National Secretary for Coordination from 1971 to 1979 gave him considerable influence over the central party organisation and relations with the federations. These solid roots meant that Mauroy was able to forgo any forms of parallel factional organisation until 1979, relying instead on a powerful network within the party. Only after 1979 did Mauroy's supporters begin to organise themselves more formally as a 'parallel faction'.

Nonetheless, when the confrontation with Mitterrand finally occurred at the 1979 Metz Congress, Mitterrand was able to claim a party legitimacy far more convincingly than Mauroy, a sign of the renovation of the PS under Mitterrand's leadership during the 1971 to 1981 period. Indeed, outside the few remaining ex-SFI0 strongholds, Mauroy's support was virtually non-existent. Furthermore, he was not a credible presidential candidate- and that was a crucial disadvantage in the Fifth Republic.

Finally, Mauroy was widely perceived to represent the party's traditional, municipal right-wing, on account of the support he achieved from the remnants of the SFI0. This perception was important: it limited the space he could then probably occupy within the PS, and thus his range of possible alliance partners, especially by comparison to Mitterrand. Thus, for example, while CERES would refuse any alliance which included Mauroy but excluded Mitterrand, Mitterrand could if necessary ally with CERES against Mauroy/ Rocard (as in 1979), or with Mauroy and Rocard against CERES (as in 1975 and 1977). More than any other PS faction, Mauroy's supporters were primarily a regional force, concentrated in the few remaining areas of SFI0 strength.

The left-wing CERES faction could rely on no such powerful network within the party organisation. Its number of deputies was consistently weak until the 1981 general election, although it achieved a firm base in local government in 1977. In response, CERES developed its own factional structures, parallel to the official party organisation. The essential facets of CERES' organisation came into existance while it was still a think-tank in Mollet's SFI0, and thus predated the 1971 Epinay Congress. According to its critics, CERES disposed of a national chain of command, in which decisions filtered down from the Secretariat (dominated by Chevenement) in a 'democratic centralist' manner to regional and local groups. The impression of a tightly-organised, disciplined faction was increased by the existence of the CERES's General Assembly, with ultimate decision-making authority, to which delegates were sent from the federations. In addition, CERES had its own national headquarters, held frequent mini-congresses – colloques – and disposed of permanent commissions (staffed by Parisian experts), factional publications, independant finances and outside links with organised labour or with fraternal

parties. In reality, however, the disciplined nature of the CERES' organisation can be exaggerated, and local groups often displayed a large measure
of independence from the national leadership (Wolf interview, 1983). Nonetheless, CERES most nearly approximated the model of parallel faction, as
described by other authors in the Italian Christian Democrat or Socialist
parties (Beller and Belloni, 1978).

If the success of a left-wing faction can be gauged by the influence of its
leaders, by the extent of its audience or by how many of it ideas penetrate the
party, then CERES achieved more than most of its counterparts in other
European Social Democrat parties. It benefited from its status as the dynamic
left-wing of an expanding party to increase its audience from 8.5% of party
mandates in 1971 to 25.4% in 1975. Moreover, its ideas strongly influenced the
1972 party programme, Changer la vie, and the Projet Socialiste of 1980; and
its leader, Chevenèment, occupied important party functions before becoming
a Minister in 1981. Nonetheless, CERES unquestionably failed in relation to
its own ambitious objectives, to construct socialism from within social democracy and to achieve a durable break with capitalism. These objectives implied
either that CERES's political ideas triumphed within the PS leadership, or else
that it could take control of the party itself. Despite its early influence from
June 1971 until June 1972, the first alternative became increasingly remote, as
Mitterrand progressively lessened CERES's influence over party policy. At
the 1975 PS congress, CERES moved into opposition partly in an attempt to
recover its identity as the party's left-wing. The second-maximal- objective
was even more unattainable: it was highly improbable that CERES could ever
by itself conquer an electoral majority and take control of the party 'from the
left'.

The reality of CERES's internal party location was as a self-identified
'left-wing' and as a consciously ideological faction. On both counts, it suffered
strategic disadvantages. As a self-identified left-wing, it limited its range of
possible allies and made its reentry into the leadership after 1975 dependent on
Mitterrand's goodwill. That was forthcoming only in 1979, when CERES had
been reduced to under 15%. More generally, CERES's limited success echoed
a general failure of self-identified left factions in European Social Democratic
and Labour parties to achieve their overambitious objctives (Hanley 1986).

Its highly ideological nature was essential for understanding CERES's
leadership structures (centralised), organisational ambitions (conquest of the
party for socialism) and the motivations of its activists. But both factors meant
that CERES was situated unfavourably for the exercise of significant political
power in a party dominated by the presidentialism of the wider system (which
demanded compromise and a watering down of commitments). Although
Chevenèment relied on CERES as a vehicle for his own presidential ambitions
in 1980, it was highly unlikely that a representative of the party's left would

90

ever capture the PS nomination: no such candidate could aggregate a sufficient range of interests within the PS to be acceptable to the other factions, let alone the electorate. In fact, CERES was condemned either to change (as it would in the 1980s), or to a subordinate or an oppositional role.

At the opposite end of the party's ideological spectrum was Michel Rocard. From the date of his arrival in the PS in 1974, Rocard had scarcely concealed his presidential ambition. To that end, he maintained an elite cabinet of policy advisers, divided into economic, political, social policy and marketing sections that rivalled Mitterrand's (Evin 1979). Moreover, from 1974 onwards, a skeletal parallel national factional organisation existed, through which directives were regularly sent to contacts in the federations, using a network partly established in the PSU.

Rocard's major internal handicap was that he lacked the 'legitimacy' of Epinay, due to his late arrival in the PS at the 1974 Assises of Socialism. That earned him the lasting distrust not only of CERES (Rocard had previously condemned the PS-PCF common programme), but also of Mitterrand's lieutenants, who saw him as a threat to their authority. Until 1978, Rocard indisputedly lacked the political weight to challenge Mitterrand for the status of the party's best presidential candidate, but after the 1978 general election defeat, his star rose rapidly in public opinion: from 1978 until 1980, Rocard could boast a substantial lead over Mitterrand in the opinion polls. Rocard's 'external' strategy represented an attempt to transform his public popularity into internal party support, as a preliminary to making a bid against Mitterrand for the party's 1981 presidential nomination. The showdown between Mitterrand and Rocard occurred at the 1979 Metz Congress, at which the challenger underlined his status as the only plausible PS candidate for 1981 apart from Mitterrand. That was a long-term strategic advantage in the Fifth Republic. But Rocard still trailed Mitterrand badly, and the Metz congress determined the fate of the 1981 PS presidential nomination. His 'external' strategy, the direct appeal to public opinion with scant regard for party orthodoxy, paid insufficient attention to the party patriotism of PS activists. In a presidential political system such as the Fifth Republic, Rocard's popularity might have been expected to compensate for his relative initial weakness within the party. Not so. His failure to win the 1981 PS presidential nomination illustrated that Mitterrand's control over a pivotal PS remained, in 1980, a more important qualification for the selection of the party's presidential candidate than Rocard's public popularity.

Notwithstanding Rocard's 'leftist' past as PSU leader from 1967 to 1973, Mitterrand succeeded in 1979 in portraying Rocard's faction as the party's modernist right-wing, a term of some considerable abuse in the pre-1981 PS. For confirmation of this, Mitterrand pointed to Rocard's past criticisms of the common programme, to his present doubts as to whether any future alliance with the PCF would be possible, and to his pleas for economic 'realism'. Apart from the general unpopularity with PS activists that it caused, the perception that Rocard represented the party's modernist rightwing limited his range of possible allies. Any alliance with CERES, an ideological anathema, was inconceivable and his only chance of overturning Mitterrand's leadership was through a direct challenge in alliance with Mauroy, an alliance Mauroy consistently refused.

Thus in terms of factional structures, the manner in which the party's various factions organised themselves was heavily influenced by their position within the party (degree of proximity to party power); by their own self-conception (e.g. CERES' identity as the party's left-wing encouraged it to 'organise for socialism'); and by their position in relation to the wider political system (hence the elitist, 'presidential' character of Rocard's policy advisers). Those groups able to avoid open factional structures distinct from the party (Mitterrand, Mauroy until 1979) tended to occupy powerful positions within the party organisation. In contrast, those factions with highly visible parallel forms of organisation (CERES), or appealing primarily outside of the party (Rocard) occupied a relatively weak position within the party. To that extent, parallel forms of factional organisation usually testified either to an oppositional or to a minority vocation.

Conclusion

By the late 1970s, rivalries between potential PS presidential candidates had emerged as the most powerful source of intra-party conflict within the PS. That process culminated in the struggle for the party's 1981 nomination fought out between Mitterrand and Rocard from 1978 to 1980. The factions that enjoyed the most success were those headed by présidentiables (Mitterrand and Rocard), whereas those which refused to define themselves primarily in terms of the presidential election (Mauroy, CERES) were gradually weakened. Notwithstanding this, other factors continued to act as important sources of intra-party conflict and gave substance to presidential rivalries: ideology (especially for CERES and Rocard), divisions over strategy, organisational competition, and different historical origins. By contrast, party rules – PR in internal party elections – were perhaps necessary for the free expression of factions, but were in no sense a sufficient condition for promoting factionalism.

No mechanism comparable to the presidential election existed to suggest why factions existed within the SFIO before 1958. During the Third Republic, factional divisions stemmed above all from ideology, from institutional pressures (alliance strategy, competition between the party organisation and the

92

SFI0 deputies) and from the first Socialist experience of government (the SFI0 being caught between irreconcilable policy options[1]). There was no credible challenge to Blum's political leadership throughout the 1920 to 1940 period. That changed during the Fourth Republic. Once Mollet had captured control from Blum in 1946 (by championing ideological 'orthodoxy' rather than by challenging Blum's personal qualities) he faced no substantial threat to his position as party leader. The SFI0's narrow margins of manoeuvre meant that institutional pressures were primarily a source of intra-party cohesion rather than conflict, due to the lack of an alternative strategy and to the SFI0's regular responsibilities in government. Moreover, traditional ideological divisions were no longer as potent a source of conflict, although decolonisation began to perform their role from the mid-1950s onwards. Neither in the Third nor the Fourth Republic did personal rivalries assume the importance they would do in the presidentialised Fifth.

Within the post-1971 PS, despite often powerful sources of cleavage, each faction was probably condemned to cohabit the political space offered by the PS as a reformist Socialist party, bordered by the PCF on its left and centrist conservatism on its right. For as long as presidential and electoral bipolar-isation continued to characterise the Fifth Republic, the PS was the only realistic vehicle through which the non-Communist left could achieve power. No faction either on the party's left (CERES) or right (Rocard) would lightly consider leaving the party: it would probably be condemned to political marginalisation if it did. The institutional system thus acted as a powerful source of enforced intra-party cohesion, despite the counterveiling pressures of the presidential election.

The French PS (somewhat like the Japanese parties described by Sartori, 1976: 91–93) thus belongs to that family of parties created by the fusion of previously existing organisations, whose old rivalries carry over into new factional conflicts. However, fusion is only one explanation for the existence of factions within the PS; others (personality, ideology, strategy, power rival-ries) are of greater significance, especially given the subsequent divisions within the founding organisations, in particular the old SFI0. Moreover, the history and organisation of the PS makes any comparison with other main-stream European Socialist and Social-Democrat parties difficult, in particular because of the absence of 'organic' links with the trade unions, because of the peculiar ideological legacy bequathed to the PS by its SFI0 predecessor, and by having to compete with a powerful Communist party on its left. Indeed, the PS was virtually unique (along with the less important Italian Socialists) in the sense that it was bordered by a powerful Communist party on its left: through-out the first twenty-five years of the Fifth Republic, alliance strategy (attitude towards the PCF) was a powerful divisive force within the non-Communist left. Nonetheless, the PS shared many similarities with other Socialist and

93

Social-Democrat parties. The degree of political space occupied by these parties has usually spanned from extreme democratic left to centre-left of the political spectrum: they have been the centre of attraction for the various reformist forces within society (Hanley 1986). That might explain why Socialist parties appear particularly prone to internal party diversity, or else to the dangers of electoral and ideological stagnation if that diversity is artifically suppressed (the fate which befell the SFIO under Mollet). Notwithstanding this, the PS can be distinguished from its fraternal parties by the conditions within it operates in the French context. Direct election of the presidency has propelled personal rivalries into the forefront of factional divisions, – a development not limited to the left. The presidentialism of the French political system thus creates an additional personal stimulus for intra-party (or intra-coalition) rivalry, which while falling short of the extreme personalisation inherent in USA presidential elections, nonetheless sets the French apart from other Western European party systems

Note

1. The impact of government experience upon conditions for intra-party factionalism appears somewhat contradictory according to whether the Third, Fourth or Fifth Republic is being considered. This question lies outside of the boundaries of the present study.

References

Allouche, G. First Secretary of PS *Nord* federation, Mauroy faction (interview, 1983).

Ayache, G. et al. (1987). *L'identité Socialiste des utopistes à nos jours*, Paris, Syros.

Bell David, S. and Criddle, B. (1984). *The French Socialist Party: Resurgence and Victory*, Oxford, Clarendon.

Belloni Frank, D. and Beller David, C. (1978). *Faction Politics: Political Parties and Factionalism in Comparative Perspective*, Santa Barbara, Clio.

Bizot Jean, F. (1976). *Au Parti des Socialistes*, Paris, Grasset.

Bon, F. and Burnier Michel, A. (1974). 'Qu'elle ose paraitre ce qu'elle est', in Bernstein, E. *Les présupposés du socialisme*, Paris Seuil , pp 255–300.

Bulletin Socialiste (quotidien) (1970–1971).

Bulletin Socialiste (mensuel) (1971–72).

Carraboeuf, J. First Secretary of PS *Calvados* federation, ex-CIR (interview, 1987).

Cayrol, R. (1978). 'La direction du Parti Socialiste: organisation et fonctionnement', *Revue Française de Science Politique* 28: 201–219.

Chapuis, R. et al. (1980). 'L'effet Rocard', *Politique Aujourd'hui* 3–4: 91–104.

Charzat, M. and Toutain, G. (1975). *Le CERES: un combat pour le socialisme*, Paris, Calmann-Lévy.

Cole Alistair, M. (1985) "Factionalism in the French Parti Socialiste, 1971–1981", Oxford, Unpublished D Phil thesis.

Evin, K. (1979). *Michel Rocard ou l'art du possible*, Paris, Simeon.

94

Faire (1975–1981).

Frontière (1974).

Giesbert Franz O. (1977). *François Mitterrand ou la tentation de l'histoire.*

Graham, B. (1982). 'The play of tendencies: internal politics in the SFIO before and after Second WorldWar', in Bell, David S. (ed.) *Contemporary French Political Parties*, London, Croom Helm.

Hamon, H. and Rotman, P. (1980) *L'effet Rocard*, Paris, Stock.

Hanley, D. (1986). *Keeping Left? CERES and the French Socialist Party. A Contribution to the Study of Fractionalism in Political Parties*, Manchester, Manchester University Press.

Hine, D. (1982). 'Factionalism in West European Parties: a framework for analysis', *West European Politics* 5: 36–52.

Hurtig, C. (1970). *De la SFIO au nouveau Parti Socialiste*, Paris, Armand Colin.

Johnson Robert, W. (1981). *The Long March of the French Left*, London, Macmillan.

Juillard, J. (1979). 'La logique partisan: l'example du PS', *Esprit* 9–10: 85–97.

Kergoat, J. (1983). *Le PS de la commune à nos jours*, Paris, Syros.

Lazitch, B. (1978). 'Le CERES ou les singes de Lénine', *Commentaire* 1: 39–51.

Loschak, D. (1971). *La Convention des Institutions Républicaines: François Mitterrand et le socialisme*, Paris, PUF.

Machin, H. and Lagroye, J. (1980). 'Le factionalisme dans le Parti Socialiste Français', unpublished paper presented at the ECPR Workshop on Factionalism in Political Parties, Florence.

Mexandeau, L. Ex-CIR, close to Mitterrand, Minister 1981–1986 (interview, 1987).

Le Monde (1973, 1974, 1975, 1977, 1978, 1979).

Mossuz, J. (1970). *Les clubs et la politique en France*, Paris, Armand Colin.

Nord-Demain (1971–1981).

Le Nouvel Observateur (1975–1980).

La Nouvelle Revue Socialiste (1977).

Parodi, J-L and Perrineau, P. (1980). 'François Mitterrand et Michel Rocard: deux ans de concurrence devant l'opinion', *Pouvoirs* 13: 189–197.

Parti Socialiste (1972). *Changer la Vie: Programme de Gouvernement du Parti Socialiste*, Paris, Flammarion.

Parti Socialiste, Parti Communiste, Mouvement des Radicaux de Gauche (1973). *Le Programme Commun de Gouvernement*, Paris, Flammarion.

Parti Socialiste (1980). *Projet Socialiste pour les années 80*, Paris, Club socialiste du livre.

Parti Socialiste (1982). *Guide de l'adhérent*, Paris, Club socialiste du livre.

Le Poing et la Rose (1972–1981).

Le Poing et la Rose – Spécial Responsables (1975–1981).

Politique Hebdo (1971–1978).

Portelli, H. (1980). 'La guerre idéologique', *Projet* 147: 874–879.

Portelli, H. (1980). *Le socialisme français tel qui'il est*, Paris, PUF.

Repères (1975–1979).

Rose, R. (1964). 'Parties, Factions and Tendencies in Britain', *Political Studies* 12: 33–46.

Sartori, G. (1976). *Parties and Party Systems: A Framework for Analysis*, Cambridge, Cambridge University Press.

Sevin, H. (1983). "La coalition majoritaire du Parti Socialiste de 1971 à 1975", Paris, Unpublished doctorat d'état.

Simmons, H. (1970). *French Socialists in Search of a Role, 1956–1967*, Ithaca, Cornell University Press.

L'Unité (1972–1980).

Viveret, P. Rocard faction, editor of *Faire* (interview, 1984).

Wolf, M. Leader of CERES – *Nord*, 1971–79 (interview, 1983).

[5]

Electoral Studies (1988), 7:3, 251–267

France in Ten Slices: An Analysis of Aggregate Data

MATTEI DOGAN AND DANIEL DERIVRY

National Centre of Scientific Research

The idea that man is a social being is a fundamental principle in all social sciences. The behaviour of an individual cannot be fully understood if he is 'extracted' from his social environment, because it is precisely this social context which gives meaning to his attitudes and opinions. Such an excision is nevertheless performed in survey research, where each person becomes a unit in a sample—except for those rare cases when information is deliberately collected about the social context.

It is therefore not surprising to find, in a bibliography of about fifty survey-based electoral studies published in Europe and the United States during the last twenty years, that relatively few have explained more than one-third of the variance. These studies have failed to explain a greater share of the variance because they focused exclusively on the personal characteristics of the individuals, without reference to the social context. This has been denounced as the 'individualistic fallacy' (Scheuch 1966 and 1969).

Regression analyses based on aggregate data have not arrived at better results. These aggregate studies have been done at the national level, so the differences among regional contexts have cancelled each other out. Neglecting local context is particularly damaging for countries characterized by great territorial diversity: France, Italy, Spain, Portugal, Canada, India, Nigeria, etc. Here we face the 'ecological fallacy'.

For instance, in a previous multiple regression analysis of France we found, as a first cut, a very weak correlation (0.13) between the proportion of industrial workers and the proportion of leftist vote for 2,450 *cantons*, and a strong relationship between religious practice and the leftist vote (− 0.63). In a second research design, the national regression analysis was replaced by 87 regressions in the framework of the 87 *départements*. The new analysis showed the fallacious character of the multiple regression at the national level: the correlation between workers and leftist vote is raised from 0.13 to 0.43 (Derivry and Dogan, p. 547). A similar ecological fallacy has been tested for central Italy (unpublished results).

Some aspects of political behaviour can better be analysed by survey research than by aggregate data. For instance, it is not possible to observe 'class consciousness' in aggregate data. The reverse is obviously equally true: social context, for instance, is better seen in aggregate data than in surveys.

It would not be appropriate to discuss here the advantages and disadvantages of aggregate data analysis *vis-à-vis* survey data analysis. Rather than reviewing the vast literature in detail, and entering into an extended theoretical and methodological debate, we simply wish to propose another methodological approach which overcomes some of the problems of the other two, and to present new data collected by this method in order to demonstrate its explanatory value.

This paper has two aims. The first is methodological, to show that it is possible to demonstrate the impact of the social context on individual behaviour and at the same time to avoid the risk of ecological fallacy by analysing aggregate data in statistically constructed social contexts. The method involved is well known by statisticians, but has almost never been applied in electoral research. This method is based on the distribution of the population in deciles. This is a reaction against the electoral geography traditionally cultivated by many French political scientists.

The second aim is substantive, to show the relation between class, religion, and politics in a France deprived of its physical geography, but nevertheless spatially organized in statistically-created universes. In these universes, the individual finds his social milieu: in a religious environment, even the atheist is affected. The social milieu of this atheist does not appear in survey research.

Analysis by Deciles as Simulated Experimentation

In the natural sciences, the researcher can experiment with the phenomenon under observation and change the parameters according to the hypothesis. In the social sciences, however, the scholar is in a much less favourable situation. Direct experimentation, still conceivable for small groups (as is done in social psychology), becomes impossible at the level of larger groups. But there is a substitute for direct experimentation: the simulated experiment, by creating statistical categories. A better understanding of the logic of simulated experiments can be gained through an illustration. The chemist can analyse a substance by varying its temperature. The social scientist who wants to investigate the relationship between religious and political behaviour cannot change the aggregate data: neither the level of partisanship nor the frequency of church attendance can be modified. He cannot stimulate a dynamic process; he can only simulate one, by taking into consideration various levels of differentiation and by observing the characteristics of each of the artificially created subgroups of a population.

The social scientist, unable to engage in direct experimentation, may instead use experimental classifications. The division of a population into deciles is one such classification. The categories created in this way could be unidimensional, that is to say, built on a single variable. They could also be constructed by including several variables, with the consequent risk of complicating the explanatory process.

How does one divide a population? This depends upon the number of individuals to be included within each subcategory. For instance, it would be possible to divide the population in equidistant levels (for example, every 5 per cent increase in religious practice). The

MATTEI DOGAN AND DANIEL DERIVRY 253

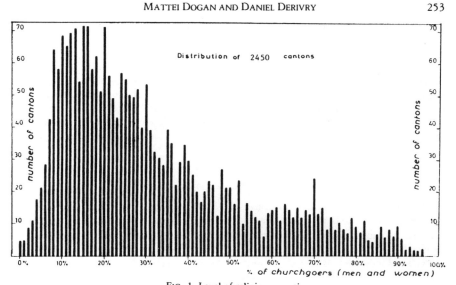

FIG. 1. Level of religious practice.

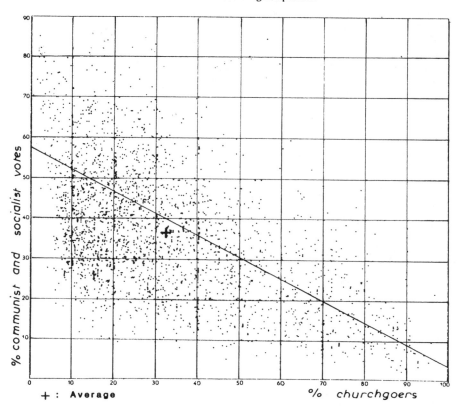

+ : **Average**

FIG. 2. France's diversity: 2,450 reference points.

unequal distribution of individuals among equidistant subcategories presents certain disadvantages.

Another method is to divide the population into numerically equal categories. The
number of categories depends on the absolute size of the population: each category must
contain a meaningful number of cases. In addition, the heterogeneity of each subcategory
should be minimized. These two imperatives are in a sense contradictory: the variations will
be better controlled by dividing the population into 10 or 20 categories rather than into
quartiles. This is the approach taken here. However, we did not divide the population, but
the 2,450 cantons, into deciles, using the aggregate data for each canton. Consequently,
each decile has 245 cantons in it.[1]

Say it with Figures, not in Words

We have compiled an ecological data base for 2,450 cantons, the smallest administrative
units in France. The large cities have been excluded because one of the most important
variables, religious practice, was not available for these cities. We have also assembled, for
each of these 2,450 cantons, quantified data on social structure and on a series of other social
and cultural indicators, as well as electoral results. The data on religious practice have been
collected by Canon Boulard and his associates, with the collaboration of hundreds of parish
priests, over ten years in the 1960s. These statistics on religious practice have not been
updated, so it is not possible to consider here the most recent elections. Instead, the analysis
which follows refers to the 1968 legislative elections.

We have transformed many statistical tables into ten figures, which present in a concise
way our detailed results, and which overcome the need for long descriptions in either words
or in mathematical formulas. This essay is divided into two parts. We will first discuss three
series of deciles: by religious practice, by social structure, and by left-right vote.[2] After this,

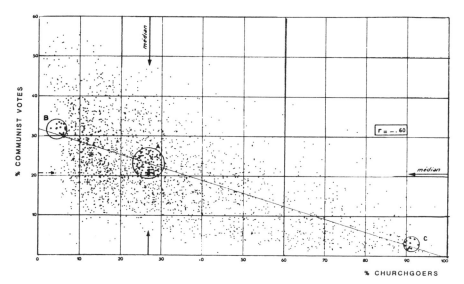

FIG. 3. The Catholic barrier against Communism. A: average normal cantons, B, C: normal cantons in
the extreme contexts.

MATTEI DOGAN AND DANIEL DERIVRY 255

we will look to six extreme deciles: the most rightist decile, the most leftist, the most agricultural, the most industrialized, the most devout, and the most irreligious.

The first three figures illustrate the great diversity of France. Religious practice varies
from 1 per cent to 97 per cent; the leftist vote from 3 per cent to 86 per cent; the communist
vote from 1 per cent to 60 per cent.

Deciles by Religious Practice

As can be seen in Figure 4, the curve of leftist vote declines from decile to decile of religious
practice. From the least religious to the most religious decile, the leftist parties lose two-
thirds of their support (and the Communist Party alone, three-quarters). The left vote
declines by 30 points from the first to the last decile.

We observe a rapid change between the eighth and tenth deciles, whereas from the second
to the eighth deciles, the trend is gradual (with an increase of about four points from one

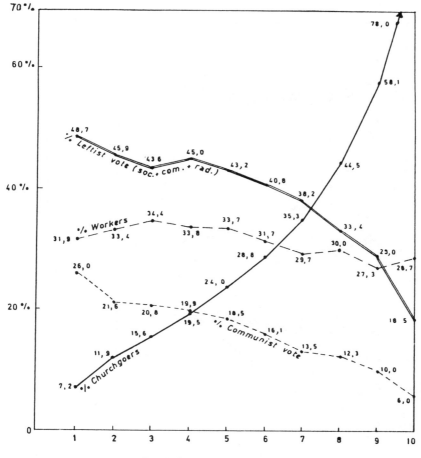

FIG. 4. Churchgoers by deciles.

decile to the next). This exponential tendency at the extreme deciles indicates the impact of
the social context on individual behaviour; beyond a certain level, the difference is not only
quantitative but also qualitative. We will return to this aspect below.

Deciles by Social Class

The proportion of industrial workers indicates the social structure of the ecological units.
This indicator is tied to other variables, such as industrialization or urbanization. The
proportion of salaried workers in agriculture is also a significant indicator, but only for a few
regions of France.

At the national level, social class and voting are weakly correlated, but after a certain
threshold of industrial workers, the relation between class and vote increases (Figure 5).
This can easily be explained. The effect of the working class context is felt after reaching a
certain critical level of worker density. It is mainly in the last two deciles that the impact of
increasing urbanization and working class density reach such a level. In each decile,

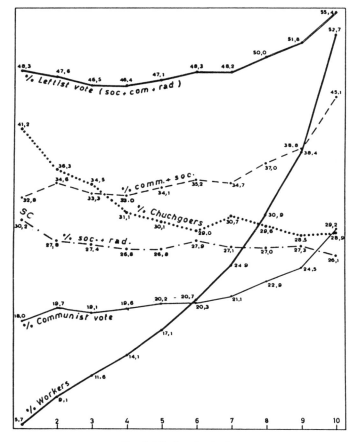

FIG. 5. Workers by deciles.

irrespective of the proportion of industrial workers, the leftist vote is always higher than the proportion of working class voters. As the left vote varies little from one decile to another, the social composition of the leftist electorate varies considerably from the least to the most working class decile.

As Figure 6 shows, the level of communist vote and of total leftist vote change very little from one decile to the next, despite the fact that the composition of the deciles exhibits an increase from 7 per cent farmers to 68 per cent, and a decline from 50 to 13 per cent for the industrial workers. Considering that even religious practice does not vary much according to the social composition, it is clear in Figure 6 that in the first decile the left is composed almost entirely of workers and the lower middle classes and that the tenth decile is predominantly composed of farmers and agricultural workers.

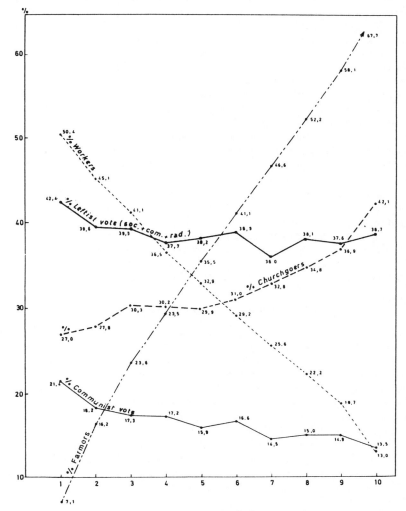

FIG. 6. Farmers by deciles.

Figures 5 and 6 reveal two characteristics of voting in France: the great territorial diversity of the social composition of the leftist electorate, and the importance of the non-working class leftist electorate.

Deciles by Left-right Vote

These deciles (Figure 7) largely confirm what has been observed with regard to deciles by religious practice and industrial workers. Until the fourth decile of leftist vote, the decline of religious practice is correlated with the progression of the left parties. With the fourth decile, when the left obtains over one-third of the suffrage, the level of religious practice declines significantly. Where religious practice is high, the leftist vote is low, and vice versa. However, even though a high level of religious practice is a barrier to the leftist vote, a low one is not necessarily a conduit to it. From the first to the fourth decile, the left passes from 10.7 to 32.3 per cent, and religious practice falls from 64.7 to 28.8 per cent. From the fourth to the last decile, the leftist vote doubles, moving from 32.3 to 65.7 per cent, but religious practice drops only 10 percentage points.

The contrast between the two extremes is striking. In the first decile, where the left is weakest, at least two-thirds of the workers vote conservative; in the last decile, where the left is strongest, at least half of the non-workers vote for the left and thus more of the leftist vote comes from other social strata. In this most leftist part of France, the working class is obviously a minority within the leftist electorate.

Figure 8, concerning the deciles of the communist vote, shows also the distance which separates the communist from the working class. The communist vote exceeds the proportion of industrial workers only in the tenth decile. In the other nine deciles the proportion of communist votes in relation to the number of industrial workers varies from 13 per cent to 80 per cent. In the first five deciles, the communist vote does not reach one-half of the working class vote, even if we admit, for a moment, the absurd hypothesis that the communist electorate is composed exclusively of industrial workers and their wives. This graph refutes a mountain of rhetoric and polemics about the 'communist party as the party of the working class', since in most French cantons the absolute majority of industrial workers did not vote for this party. Although survey research does not reveal this territorial distribution, this graph, based on aggregate data, illustrates a fact as solid as a rock.

Effects of Interaction Between Variables

When a correlation between two variables is calculated, the direct effect of the independent variables upon the dependent variable is measured. Multi-variate analysis requires, however, that the results not be modified by the intervention of other variables. The interference of a third variable could change the initial causal link. Such interference may undermine an otherwise well-established relation.

The relation between class and vote is very sensitive to the level of religious practice. The correlation coefficient between the proportion of workers and the proportion of the communist vote and of the total leftist vote varies from one decile of churchgoers to another. The range of the coefficient is from 0.0 to 0.31 for the communist vote, and from -0.26 to 0.15 for the combined left vote. There is obviously a phenomenon of interaction. In less technical terms, the possibility for predicting the left vote in a series of cantons, knowing the proportion of workers, is not the same in the cantons with high religiosity and in the cantons with low religiosity. This interaction can easily be clarified.

In dividing the population according to religious practice, we are in fact neutralizing the

MATTEI DOGAN AND DANIEL DERIVRY 259

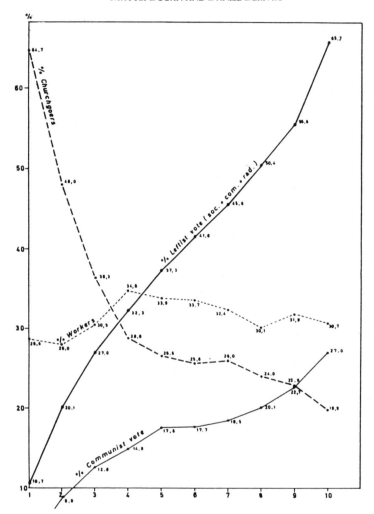

FIG. 7. Leftist vote by deciles.

effect of this variable: the correlations between workers and votes in each of these deciles could present three different configurations.

a. The coefficients may not vary at all, or may vary only a little in relation to the national coefficient—in such a case there is no interaction effect.

b. The coefficients may be higher or lower than the average national correlation. If it is higher, the religious factor disturbs the effect of class on the vote. Liberated of this interference, the relation between social class and voting behaviour finds its true value. If it is lower, the variance which was attributed to the class variable was in reality at least partly imputable to religion. This situation implies an initial relation between the two independent variables. This means that the distorting effect is not the same for the de-christianized cantons as it is for the devout ones.

260 *France in Ten Slices*

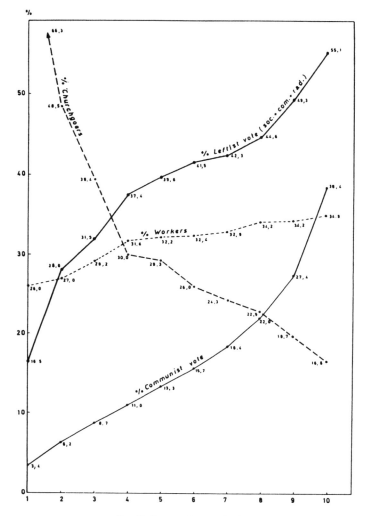

FIG. 8. Communist vote by deciles.

  c. There is also the more complex case where an interaction can be observed between the two independent variables according to the value of the dependent variable. This confirms the difficulty—or even the impossibility—of explaining the partial correlations and confirms the saliency of the analysis by deciles.

The Extreme Slices: Methodological Remarks

For each of the three variables there is a striking contrast between the first and the last decile. The six extreme deciles—the most leftist, the most rightist, the most agricultural, the most industrial, the most devout, and the most de-christianized—each represents an homogeneous universe for its respective variable. This is not to say that these six extreme universes are homogeneous in terms of each of the other variables. The rationale for analysing these unidimensional types is not simply based upon their contrasting characters.

The difference between the first and the second deciles and the difference between the ninth and the tenth are not merely quantitative. The extreme deciles appear as different universes by nature, qualitatively specific, and distinctive. The fluctuations in religious practice from one decile to the next are discriminant for the areas with 'normal' proportions of churchgoers. Above a certain threshold, we are in an ultra-Catholic environment, where even those who never go to church are influenced by the religious culture. Above a certain degree of de-christianization, it is the opposite. In these extreme cases, a variation from 80 to 90 per cent, or a variation from 5 to 10 per cent of religious practice does not make a significant difference. We are then either in a religious environment, or in areas of generalized inter-class anti-clericalism. What is true for the religious variable is equally true for the others. It is for this reason that these extreme deciles could be considered ideal types, quasi-experimental cases.

These six extreme universes represent a relatively important segment of the French nation. As Figure 9 indicates, the two extreme deciles of voting and the two extreme deciles of religious behaviour represent by themselves one-third of all cantons. If we add the extreme deciles of industrial workers and the extreme deciles of the agricultural population—taking into consideration that some cantons belong to more than one of these extreme deciles—all six extreme deciles cover 45 per cent of the total population considered in this ecological analysis.

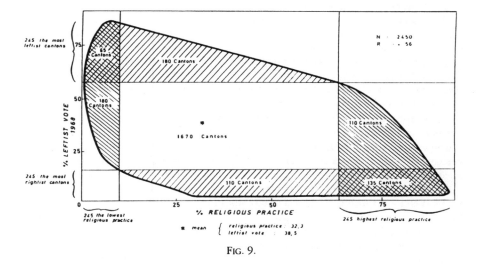

FIG. 9.

The Most Rightist Part of France

This decile includes cantons dispersed among 29 *départements*, but ten populous *départements* group 190 cantons of the 245 belonging to this decile. Many of the cantons in this most rightist slice belong also to the most devout slice; this is to be expected because of the strong relation between religious practice and rightist orientations. It is nevertheless interesting to note that certain cantons deviate from this pattern. There are cantons more rightist than anticipated by the religious variable alone. Some cantons are more conservative than traditionalist, in the sense that the former focuses on economic issues, while the latter refers to religious values.

The leftist vote in this rightist slice varies only from 2.8 to 16.3 per cent, enabling us to say that this is a relatively homogeneous political environment. Nevertheless, in this most rightist part of France, religious practice varies enormously, from 11.8 to 96.1 per cent. Again, we must emphasize the fact that while a high level of religious practice is a barrier to the left, a low level of religious practice is not an unsurmountable handicap for the right.

The Most Leftist Part of France

In this decile, the distribution of leftist votes varies from 59 per cent to 88 per cent, a spread of thirty points. Its homogeneity is lower than the homogeneity of other extreme deciles. The cantons are dispersed among half of the French *départements*; twenty-one of them bring together 189 of the 245 cantons of the decile.

Logically, we would expect a very low level of religious practice in this most leftist part of France and, in fact, only thirteen cantons exhibit the relatively high level of more than 50 per cent churchgoers. Nevertheless, this most leftist decile does not coincide with the most irreligious: the proportion of churchgoers varies from 1.6 per cent to 90 per cent. As one would expect, in only twenty cantons is the proportion of churchgoers higher than 40 per cent, but for the other 225 cantons, the level of religious practice none the less varies from 1 to 40 per cent.

The Communist party, for its part, varies from 3.5 per cent to 57.3 per cent of the vote. In the cantons where it is weakest it represents less than 6 per cent of the total leftist vote; where it is the strongest, it represents 87 per cent. Between these extremes lies a continuum of communist shades.

This part of France characterized by high leftist votes is very heterogeneous. The proportion of industrial workers varies from 7 per cent to 64.4 per cent, but this range does not reveal the real dispersion. A closer observation shows two sub-categories of cantons, one with more than 40 per cent of industrial workers, the other with less than 20 per cent.

By isolating this most leftist tenth of France we can see, in this statistically-created universe, totally liberated from geographic constraints, how the other variables interplay. We observe strong variations along all other dimensions, allowing us to say that the leftist vote and each of its components, Communist, Socialist or Radical, are polymorphic, in the sense that the sociological determinants of this voting behaviour vary from place to place.

Most of the cantons of the first and last deciles are distributed among different *départements*. Yet it is surprising to find that some of the most leftist cantons co-exist with some of the most rightist in the same *départements*. This is the case, for instance, in the *départements* of Finistere, Aveyron and Lozere. French electoral geographers have shaded these *départements* with the same tint in their maps. Considering this internal diversity of some of these *départements* we have to admit that this cartographic technique hides essential information, and is therefore only a rudimentary representation.

The Most Agricultural Part of France

In this decile we are in a truly agricultural universe. Despite a high degree of social homogeneity, the proportion of leftist votes varies from 2.8 per cent to 82.8 per cent, and the Communist vote varies from 0.5 per cent to 49.5 per cent. This enormous political diversity cannot be related to variation by the proportion of industrial workers: 202 of the 245 are comprised of only 10 to 15 per cent industrial workers. This variable is therefore frozen. The size of the presence of middle classes in these cantons varies in a similarly insignificant fashion. We are here in a world of peasants, but they are heterogeneous: small or big farmers, vintners, cattle-raisers, small- or large-scale proprietors, those with rich or poor soil, and so on. Such a diversity of the agricultural population itself could not help but have an effect on political behaviour. It is best not to get involved here in an analysis of the political tendencies of the various strata of the agricultural population. We would risk getting lost among the paths. In any case, the relation between the crops and the vote is certainly overshadowed by the preponderant influence of religious practice, which spans from 2 per cent to 91 per cent. Of all the experimental slices discussed here, this is the most spectacular. The proportion of leftist vote and the proportion of churchgoers in this decile are correlated by a coefficient of -0.70.

For this experimentally homogenized universe we could, without fear of the ecological fallacy, make inferences from the aggregate data to individual behaviour. However, doing this would commit the sin of individualistic fallacy, because these peasants are not like most of the other French peasants: they are peasants surrounded by peasants, people living in a unidimensional world. In such a closed world, religious attitude is the decisive factor for everything in life—particularly on election day.

The 245 cantons composing this most agricultural decile are distributed among 51 *départements*. For some of the latter, regression analysis has shown a high correlation between religious attitude and leftist vote, such as -0.76 for Aveyron. But for other *départements*, de-christianized, the religious factor has little discriminating power: -0.10 for Creuse. So, in this most agricultural statistical slice of France there are areas where the anti-clerical context leaves little room for fluctuations in the relationship between religious practice and vote.

The Most Industrialized Part of France

In this decile the average proportion of industrial workers is 54.4 per cent. The average proportion of leftist votes is 43.8 per cent, that is to say about the same as for the most agricultural decile of France. But this average hides important fluctuations, from 5 per cent to 75 per cent, and the Communist vote varies, for its part, from 1.7 per cent to 51 per cent. This variation could be explained in part by the fluctuating proportion of people belonging to the lower middle classes. It could also be explained by the internal diversity of the working class and particularly by the relative importance of various branches of industry. Yet the essential explanation of the variations of the leftist vote in this most heavily working class decile is, once again, religious practice, which varies, incredibly, from 4.5 per cent to 90 per cent. This is fact. Religious practice and leftist vote are correlated by a coefficient of -0.65, nearly as high as the one we found for the most agricultural slice of France.

Here are the two most contrasting 'worlds' in France, the most agricultural and the most industrialized, and where, nevertheless, the importance of religious behaviour in the explanation of political behaviour is equally decisive.

The Most Devout Part of France

In this most devout decile, the religious dimension is well under our control since the proportion of churchgoers oscillates only from 67 per cent to 97 per cent, with an average of 78 per cent. The average proportion of industrial workers for this decile is 28.7 per cent, varying from 1.3 per cent to 66.7 per cent. Here we have much greater social diversity than in the opposite decile, the most irreligious.

This decile so near to heaven is allergic to the influence of the leftists: more than 200 among the 245 cantons offer less than one-quarter of their vote to the anti-clerical parties. We are not surprised to find that the correlation coefficient between industrial workers and leftist votes is virtually null (-0.06). Social class does not influence voting behaviour where the religious context is so powerful.

The Most Irreligious Part of France

The cantons in this decile, which, as all others, is not a geographical area but a statistical construction, are probably among the most de-christianized pockets in the Western world. Only in Tuscany, Emilia, or some areas of Spain could we find a lower proportion of church-goers. The average is 7.2 per cent and varies from 1 per cent to 10 per cent. We can consequently consider the religious behaviour of these cantons constant, but the other two dimensions have important fluctuations: the proportion of industrial workers varies from 9.4 per cent to 64.3 per cent and the leftist vote varies from 18.8 per cent to 88.4 per cent. The religious factor having been neutralized, we would expect to find the ideal circumstances in which to observe whether the relationships between class and vote are important. In this decile there cannot be cross-pressure between social status and belief. Religious practice being everywhere low, the social foundation of voting should be free to appear . . . It does not. In addition, the correlation coefficient between industrial workers and leftist vote is curiously negative: -0.26. This negative correlation suggests that the most leftist cantons are those which are predominantly agricultural rather than industrial. It seems that the probability of voting for the left is higher for a farmer who does not attend religious services than for an industrial worker who similarly does not. The implication is that abstention from religious practice is ideologically more significant for a farmer than for an industrial worker. In a village, abstention from religious practice can be noticed by everyone. In the anonymity of the city, however, it does not necessarily imply a refusal. Voting, after all, is related as much to the real conditions of daily life as to socio-professional categories.

Usually a decile corresponds very marginally to specific geographical areas; the cantons of a decile are not contiguous, they are located in the north and the south, the east and the west. But, for this particular decile, we find that many cantons are concentrated in a few poor agricultural *départements*. Twenty-one of the twenty-five cantons of Haute-Vienne, and twenty of the twenty-five cantons of Creuse, belong to this decile. In the first *département*, the vote is 72 per cent leftist while the social composition of these cantons is only 29 per cent industrial workers; in the second, the vote is 55 per cent leftist while industrial workers comprise only 18 per cent of the population. Here the 'proletarian' is the peasant, not the industrial worker.

Comparing the most devout and the most irreligious deciles, it appears that when the level of religious practice is very low, all social classes have more or less a preference for the left; when the level of religious observance is very high, religion plays the role of a barrier against the left more or less for all classes.

Last Attempt to Resuscitate the Working Class

According to the basic rules of statistical analysis, the units of a population are presumed to be equivalent in size. It is this principle of equivalence which allows us to compare the position of the units on various variables. But such a situation is rarely found in social sciences. There are very few socio-ecological studies in the international literature that take into consideration the demographic size of the units. The French cantons, as the American counties or the German Bezirke, are of unequal demographic size. The issue of the unit's demographic size arises in the regression analyses. Let us formulate this in very simple socio-logical terms: does the proportion of industrial workers, for instance, have the same contextual significance when they amount to 1,000 or to 10,000 workers? If the signifi-cance is not the same, is there a threshold? Are we not neglecting an essential dimension? The question is whether demographic size is not by itself an important variable.

A few hypothetical examples, illustrated in Figure 10, will help us understand the methodological issue. In the first chart, the correlation coefficient for size is 0.73; in the second, where the largest units, counted twice, are at the periphery of the cloud, the correlation coefficient falls to 0.54; in the third chart, the largest demographic units are situated on the regression line (again, they are counted twice), and the correlation coefficient rises to 0.85. If the crosses representing the largest units were randomly distributed in the cloud we would again find the correlation coefficient of the first example. It is clear that demographic size becomes important only if it intervenes in a given direction. In fact, we found three-quarters of the cantons ranked between 1,000 and 5,000 economically active persons. More than nine out of ten fell within a range of between 500 and 7,500 persons. Consequently, the question of demographic size is really important only for a minority of the cantons, the most populous deciles, where one-quarter of the economically active population is concentrated.

Having ordered the cantons from the least to most populous, we divided them by deciles. Analysis shows there is no correlation between size and the dependent variables. For instance, the leftist vote reached an average of 41 per cent in the least populous decile and 40 per cent in the most populous. Neither is there a correlation between size and church attendance. Religious practice approaches, in the most populous decile, the national average. Only the proportion of industrial workers increases regularly with the size of the canton, passing from 22 per cent to 45 per cent.

Briefly stated, size, which does not exercise any direct influence on the relations between variables for the first nine deciles (except for the trivial relation with the proportion of workers), does intervene for the most populous cantons, the most urbanized ones. We have also conducted an analysis of the largest cities, showing the importance of the lower-middle class vote in the socialist electorate. This is a different tale, for another time. It is sufficient to say that this does not contradict the findings we present here. The regression analysis which takes into consideration size does not modify the relations that we identified without including size. If we weigh the correlation coefficients according to size we obtain for the

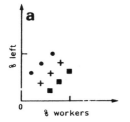
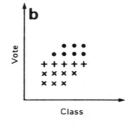
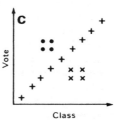

FIG. 10.

entire country a multiple correlation coefficient of 0.69 for religion–class–vote, while a national regression, ignoring size, produces a not very different one: 0.64.

Conclusion: The National Average Fallacy

France is one of the oldest nations to have achieved its national unification and identity (only Spain accomplished it earlier). But its territory has remained one of the most diversified in Western Europe (except maybe Spain, Italy and Portugal). Has this strong territorial diversity been a historical given, or is it still a source of current electoral cleavages? Under the impact of urbanization, the decline of agricultural population and the rise of middle classes, the increasing geographical mobility, the influence of national radio and television networks, and above all the decline of religious practice, the diversity of the French mosaic is slowly paling. The lessening of religious practice everywhere has reduced the influence of this statistical indicator, but the ordering of the 2,450 cantons on this dimension and their distribution by deciles remain more or less the same in 1978 as in 1968. A similar analysis dealing with the legislative elections of 1978 and socio-economic indicators updated in 1975, but using the same census on religious practice (which has not been updated and probably will never be repeated), shows that on the whole the picture here presented—even if in less vivid colours—persisted, with a clear decline of correlation coefficients between religious practice and vote, and a strengthening of the relationship between middle classes and socialist vote.

Nevertheless, today France is still a country of electoral polymorphism, where political behaviour is meaningless if it is not observed in regional contexts. The territorial diversity of causal relations helps explain why political parties in France are not well organized at the national level. They are polymorphic in the sense that the same party has here a mostly agricultural environment and there a mostly industrial one, being here predominantly religious and there, anti-clerical. The electoral system—single member constituency with two rounds—responds to the local symbiosis. This polymorphism has in most areas deep historical roots. New local factors intervene, like the density of foreign immigrants (of non-European background). For instance, it is difficult to explain the flash in the pan of the National Front at the municipal elections of 1983 and at the legislative elections of 1986 without considering the local context: there are for these elections very significant correlations—by cantons and districts in cities—between the proportion of Muslim immigrants and the electoral performance of this xenophobic extreme-rightist movement.

For a country like France, as this analysis based on aggregate data demonstrates, the national averages—particularly those concerning the causal relationships between religion, class and vote—are largely fallacious. The national correlational coefficients are only average relations, and they hide causal relations of various intensities. They are abstractions which cannot reflect the original diversity. However, this spatial diversity is more important than the difference between social classes at the national level.

The same is true for national averages based on surveys. A representative sample collects isolated individuals, defines only individual characteristics, and consequently is unable to detect the social environmental factors in individual behaviour. It would be theoretically possible to replicate the same surveys in different social contexts, but these multiple surveys, whose results would be combined with aggregate data indicating the social context, would be extremely time-consuming and costly. This is none the less a way to avoid simultaneously the individualistic fallacy and the ecological fallacy.

The analysis by deciles proposed here sheds more light on the social context than on individual characteristics. These individual characteristics could be supplemented by

MATTEI DOGAN AND DANIEL DERIVRY 267

double-pronged survey research. The first could consist of six or eight surveys done in specific social contexts, resulting from an analysis by deciles, as the one presented in this article. The results of such contextual surveys would remain to be weighted according to the results of a classical survey of a national sample. Thus, combining ecological aggregate data and results from these two sets of surveys, one should be able to explain a large portion of the variance in voting behaviour, and in other fields as well.

Notes

1. The French cantons are not be confused in any way with the similarly-named Swiss cantons. The French cantons are the smallest administrative units. They have remained unchanged since Napoleon. It is not possible to do ecological research at a lower level, such as that of the commune, because there are 36,600 communes in France. No one has ever attempted such a daunting task.
2. The Leftist vote includes the Communist party, the Socialist party, and a large part of the Radical party. We take the word Rightist in its geometrical sense, as opposed to Leftist parties.

References

Daniel Derivry and Mattei Dogan, 'Unité d'analyse et espace de référence en écologie politique. Le canton et le departement francais', *Revue francaise de science politique*, 21, 1971, pp. 517–70.
Erwin K. Scheuch, 'Cross-National Comparisons Using Aggregate Data', in: Richard Merritt and Stein Rokkan (editors), *Comparing Nations*, (New Haven: Yale University Press, 1966), pp. 131–67.
Erwin K. Scheuch, 'Social Context and Individual Behavior', in: Mattei Dogan and Stein Rokkan (editors), *Social Ecology*, (Cambridge: M.I.T. Press, 1969), pp. 133–55.

[6]

Change in French Society: A Critical Analysis of Crozier's Bureaucratic Model

Roger Duclaud-Williams

Few students of French society in recent years, have attracted as much attention as Crozier and most assessments have been favourable.[1] Nor is there any denying that all that he writes is compelling, persuasive, and extremely closely argued. Nordlinger describes Crozier's first major work, *The Bureaucratic Phenomenon* (Tavistock Publications, 1964), as 'an exceptional study' and goes on to refer to it as 'powerful, elegant and valid'.[2] Stanley Hoffmann has referred to Crozier's work as 'rich and provocative' and goes on to say: 'Thanks to Crozier, we have a convincing model of routine authority as well as change.'[3] The importance of what he has written is greatly increased by the generality of his conclusions. Crozier and his numerous collaborators have assembled a formidable body of research and reflection on the political and social problems of contemporary France. For these reasons it seems difficult to deny the importance of a critical examination of his thought, and in order to give some unity to this discussion, the following argument will concentrate on Crozier's view of the obstacles to change in France and the manner in which they are habitually overcome. The attempt to understand change and the obstacles to it has been at the core of all that Crozier has written and therefore our discussion will lead us to examine both his early writings of the late 1950s and more recent refinements and elaborations of his earlier views which have appeared more recently.[4] Once this has been said, it is nevertheless true that the core of his argument and the seeds of much later discussion are contained in *The Bureaucratic Phenomenon* and it will therefore be necessary to make this study our central concern, remembering always to pursue points elsewhere in his writing whenever necessary.

The argument of *The Bureaucratic Phenomenon* develops in three stages. The first two parts of the book are concerned with an examination of the Post Office Savings Bank and the State monopoly in the production of cigarettes and tobacco.[5] On the basis of these examples Crozier examines the ways in which groups and individuals may relate to one another within organisations. At this stage in the argument there is no suggestion that Crozier is pointing to phenomena that are in any sense peculiarly French.

The second step in his argument is to suggest that there are certain widely espoused values in France which correspond rather exactly to traits in the bureaucratic model which he has just elaborated.[6] This correspondence between the bureaucratic model and the values held more widely in France enables him to suggest that the patterns of behaviour which he has observed within organisations can also be discovered in quite different settings, and it is this move back from culture to behaviour which constitutes the third step in his argument.[7] In other words it is French political culture which makes the link between the case studies and the broader historical examination of certain sectors of French society. The argument of *The Stalled Society,* first published in the late 1960s, proceeds in the same fashion—from a general discussion of the problem of change towards more particular reference to France and to specific sectors of French life.[8] But, since the model and the concepts employed are the same, whether Crozier is discussing organisations, sectors of activity, or society as a whole, it is not possible to treat these separately in our discussion. It will be convenient to begin with the key concept of crisis.

THE CONCEPT OF CRISIS

It may be helpful at the outset to summarise Crozier's view of the way in which French organisations typically adapt to changes in their environment. He suggests that this adaptation is difficult in France but finally can be achieved with reasonable success. It is important to underline this point because a superficial reading of *The Bureaucratic Phenomenon* suggests that it gives support to the notion that France is somehow a country in which it is more difficult to achieve change than in other major western democracies. Crozier has quite specifically rejected any such view. What he does believe, however, is that the mode of adaptation which is typical of French organisations and French society is peculiar to that nation.

The process through which change within the organisation occurs is one in which long periods of routine during which nothing alters are interspersed with crises, and it is these crises which have to bear the entire burden of adaptation. Incremental adaptation of the organisation to its environment cannot occur. There are many reasons for this. The isolation of strata from one another within the organisation means that information which is relevant for reform does not reach the leadership. Those in positions of responsibility exacerbate this difficulty by preparing their reforms in secret. They do so because they fear the conservative consequences of any negotiation or premature disclosure of their intentions. These information problems are rendered more acute by a concentration of formal authority at the peak of the organisation. This excessive concentration increases the distance between those who have the necessary knowledge of current operating difficulties and those who have the power to deal with them. Nevertheless the organisation must survive and when dysfunction reaches an intolerable level the impersonal rules which protect the liberties of members of the organisation must be briefly suspended whilst strongly authoritarian methods are used to put matters right.

It is the contention in the present analysis that Crozier's use of the terms 'crisis' and 'periods of routine' are often ambiguous and their use during the case studies does not correspond with the usage adopted later in *The Bureaucratic Phenomenon*. This is an important criticism if it can be sustained because the case studies constitute the essential supporting evidence.

Crises occur within the Post Office Savings Bank in the following way.[9] The task which occupies most of the staff is the constant updating of subscribers' accounts. The cheques arrive in the morning's post and before the day's work is finished all of them must be checked against the credit in the customers' accounts, the appropriate deduction made, and postal notification of this despatched to the customer. It is a basic rule of the organisation that all post which arrives in the morning must be dealt with during that day's work. Problems arise because at certain times in the year there is a much greater volume of business than at others and this imposes considerable strain on the girls who are doing the routine clerical and tabulating work on machines. In difficult periods they must work faster and probably also stay on for compulsory overtime. These crises when the volume of work builds up are particularly acute because there is no arrangement whereby extra staff employed elsewhere in the branch can be drafted in to help out.

It may be that this description of operations in this Paris branch has already revealed the ambiguity of Crozier's notion of 'crisis'. It would appear that the successive crises which he describes in the Post Office Savings Bank have nothing to do with changes in the character of this organisation. This is so because after an increase in volume of work and the accompanying crisis there is a return to the *status quo ante*. Nothing is changed by these crises. They are in fact part of the *routine* of branch operation.

To sum up on this point, much of the force of Crozier's argument derives from the close correspondence which exists between the difficulties encountered in organisations and those which exist in much broader, less organised sectors of French life such as industrial relations or colonial administration. It is the contention here that the parallelism which Crozier seeks to establish is unreal because it depends upon an ambiguity in the concept of crisis. Crisis in the Post Office Savings Bank is a symptom of malfunctioning and makes no contribution to the better adaptation of the organisation to its environment. Crisis, then, is at one moment a notion used to describe the results of a failure to adapt and at other moments becomes the occasion on which these difficulties can be surmounted.

One of the features of the model is that in periods of routine, relations between strata are largely governed by impersonal rules which effectively guarantee a large measure of independence and security for the individual members of the strata. The rules serve effectively to limit the discretion exercised by supervisory grades. In contrast to this situation, when a crisis occurs and change must be organised from the centre, the inter-strata relations are suddenly modified and a much more authoritarian and discretionary style of management is adopted in order to bring about these necessary changes. Thus Crozier reports in the case of the Post Office Savings Bank that, when the burden of mail increases, the supervisors, who normally have very little to do, become much more strict and authoritarian in their relations with the girls who are actually doing the tabulating work.[10] But the evidence presented by Crozier which concerns the contrast in leadership styles between the routine and crisis periods is rather unconvincing. One is left with the impression that, contrary to the requirements of the general model, relations between the workers and the lowest level of supervisors are routinely rather strict and that there is correspondingly little scope for them to become more authoritarian at times of crisis. He tells us, for example, that it is regular practice for all detected mistakes to be traced to their perpetrators and the division head then has the responsibility of deciding whether or not to demand a written apology from the girl in question. The head may also, if he thinks it necessary, issue an official reprimand, which will then be entered on her official civil service record. Given the atmosphere within the branch, the written apology and the official reprimand both involve considerable humiliation.

The fact that supervisors do have discretionary powers does not conflict essentially with Crozier's insistence that relations between strata are governed by impersonal rules. This is because the powers in question relate only to exceptional incidents and not to the regular performance of the clerical work. The difficulty arises when we come to the examination of what Crozier means by the adoption of a more authoritarian style of supervision at times of crisis. He says that the first-level supervisors put considerable pressure on the girls but he gives us no indication of what this pressure consists. We know that the distribution of tasks within the four-man team is something informally controlled by the team itself and that supervisors do not attempt to intervene in this arrangement. We also know that the rule that all the work which arrives in the morning should be dealt with during that day is generally accepted. We know too that procedures already described in relation to mistakes are regularly employed. It is, therefore, difficult to see exactly what pressure the first level of supervision can bring to bear on the workers, given that Crozier insists that for most of the time when work is at a normal level, they have no need to intervene in performance and have no powers which they normally use to control workers' activities. One is, therefore, left with the distinct impression that Crozier is insisting that the style of management becomes more authoritarian at times of crisis because this is required by the model which he is in the process of constructing.

It might be argued in Crozier's defence that the inconsistency of usage which has been shown is not important because the context in which the term crisis is used makes it quite clear whether reference is made to an unproductive crisis or a productive crisis. If this line of defence is adopted, it would be incumbent on Crozier to show a parallelism between productive crises in organisations and those broader crises in French society in which authoritarian methods are used to accomplish rapid social change. But this defence cannot be sustained. Its major flaw is that there are no productive crises in the operation of the Post Office Savings Bank or any of the other case studies in *The Bureaucratic Phenomenon* or Crozier's later writings.[11] This omission is all the more significant since Crozier constantly stresses the empirical rather than the *a priori* nature of his methodology and all his works, including the most recent *L'Acteur et le Système*, contain a large number of case studies. These cases are invariably informative and full of insights relating to blockages and obstacles to change. But there appears to be none where the ways in which these obstacles can be surmounted through the productive crisis are described.

A second reason for rejecting the defence explained above, one perhaps more telling, is that it seems clear that Crozier does not intend to draw a distinction between the 'unproductive crises' which he described in the working of the Post Office Savings Bank and the 'productive crises' of political life. This is clear because he stresses the increased interventionism and much more authoritarian style which supervisors adopt at times of crisis in the Post Office Savings Bank. There would be no need to emphasise this aspect if he intended us to treat such crises as merely part of the routine operation of the organisation.

Although it has been necessary to concentrate on some rather fine detail of the case studies in order to make certain points about the concept of crisis, it should not be thought that the objections raised relate only to the problem of organisational change. In *The Stalled Society* Crozier makes it quite clear that he regards the student and worker uprising of May and June 1968 as a typical bureaucratic crisis of the French variety.[12] He argues that the concentration during the crisis on free expression and open communication and also the fact that certain very clear, implicit limits to the degree of violence to be used were widely respected are both features of the events of those months which point to the relevance of his own analysis. It will be remembered that he stressed the isolation of strata one from the other and the difficulty of communication between them, and the fact that the bureaucratic structure of many French organisations provides those who work in them with a degree of security which facilitates critical and even rebellious behaviour towards those in positions of authority. Despite these apparent links between the analysis of *The Bureaucratic Phenomenon* and certain features of the events of May 1968 it does not seem that the notion that the May crisis was a bureaucratic crisis on the global societal level can be sustained. Once again the crisis seems to have been singularly unproductive. Crozier himself seems too much of a realist to take his own analysis too seriously because he hesitates between the optimism of supposing that new forms of behaviour really have been learned as a consequence of the experiences of 1968, and the pessimism of supposing that once law and order was restored old habits and attitudes rapidly reasserted themselves. To conclude: organisational and social crises there are, but they are not the answer to the problems created by conservative routine, and the proposition that it is preponderantly through a series of productive crises of adaptation that French society and French organisations adapt to their environment remains to be demonstrated.

EQUALITY

Another difficulty to which it is necessary to refer at this point is created by Crozier's insistence on a strict equality between different members of the same stratum. He insists on this notion at all three stages of the argument, the organisational, the cultural, and at the level of global social change. But his own description of behaviour within the organisations he studied does not bear out his assertion of strict equality. He tells us that, in the Post Office

Savings Bank, the girls work in a team of four and are required by the official regulations to rotate the four posts amongst themselves so that each spends the same length of time on each of the four tasks which make up the team's work. If behaviour conformed to these regulations there would be no difficulty for Crozier but, in fact, he tells us that one of the four girls is tacitly recognised by the team as leader because the pace of work of the whole team depends on her. The full rotation of posts amongst the team is in fact informally limited so that only two of the four girls ever do the most important work.[13] There is also a tendency for girls with greater seniority to occupy the leading post more often than their colleagues. Since the Post Office Savings Bank does not distinguish in its level of payment between girls carrying out different tasks, paying instead according to the exams which individual workers have passed, it would seem that the girls, rather than insisting on an exact equality flout the official regulations in order to establish an informal if rather mild hierarchy among themselves with respect to the performance of the work task.

A similar sort of difficulty arises with respect to the notion of equality when we move from the Post Office Savings Bank to the industrial monopoly. In fact, at no point in his study does Crozier tackle the question of what kind of equality he regards as salient. But perhaps it is not too difficult to reconstruct his view of the kind of equality which is so important to the French worker. At many places in his work, Crozier links the insistence upon equality with the French resentment of dependence and the inability of groups to develop their own leadership structure. This would seem to suggest that what he believes workers are concerned about is equal subjection to the same rules so that all are protected against the exercise of arbitrary authority, and dependence on the goodwill of others is reduced to a minimum. We may ask whether the requirements of equality defined in this way are met within the tobacco and cigarette factories study. The difficulty which arises in this case concerns the relation of the production workers to the maintenance workers. Yet it appears that the factual situation which Crozier describes contradicts the essence of his model. He makes it quite clear that production workers resent the maintenance workers and harbour considerable grievances against them. This arises because, when a machine breaks down, they are unable to repair it themselves and instead must wait and depend upon maintenance workers. This dependence is all the more galling because the behaviour of the maintenance workers is unpredictable and time lost through the machine being repaired must be made up by the worker if he wishes to fulfil his production quota and receive the standard wage. In the eyes of an observer and in the view of the production workers, there is therefore both a differentiation of task and a degree of dependence of production workers on maintenance workers.[14] On the other hand Crozier is quite clear that the production and maintenance workers must be treated as members of the same stratum. This being so, the existence of the dependence of some on others within the stratum seems to contradict Crozier's model.

At this stage in the argument one is tempted to ask how Crozier supposes that strict equality does reign amongst the workers within the factory. The answer to this question is quite simple. He stresses, at a number of points, that the equality to which he refers in this case is exhibited by the fact that the production and maintenance workers both belong to the same trade union.[15] Both harbour certain hostilities towards higher management and the ideology of this trade union is one of an absolute opposition of interest between members of the working class and management. The union's view is that both production and maintenance workers are members of the working class. Equality in this case seems to mean an identity of interest.

Now it might seem possible to save Crozier's argument by accepting the facts as they exist in the tobacco factory and adopting a definition of equality which corresponded with those facts, viz. a perceived identity of interest. Unhappily for Crozier's argument this procedure is not possible. Time and again he stresses that the insistence upon equality within the strata grows out of a fear of dependence upon others and a wish at all costs to reduce this dependence by limiting discretionary authority through the use of rigidly enforced rules.[16] But, as we have seen, the production workers do not seem to have been able, perhaps had not even tried, to develop rules which might protect them against dependence on the maintenance workers. It is quite clear throughout that the equality upon which Crozier is insisting is not to be regarded as a synonym for working-class consciousness because it is said to exist not just in strata near the base but at all levels in organisations and in society at large. Other strata in which this emphasis on equality is said to exist include parliamentary deputies.[17]

Let us then sum up this part of the argument concerning Crozier's notion of equality. We noted first that Crozier does not provide us with an explicit definition of the sort of equality with which he is concerned but that the logic of his model suggests quite clearly what he means by the term. He is referring to an equality which is infringed in two ways, by the development of leaders within a particular stratum which gives rise to a distinction between leaders and non-leaders, and by the subjection of anyone in the stratum to the discretionary and arbitrary authority of someone higher up. We found that, with respect to both of the full-length case studies contained in *The Bureaucratic Phenomenon*, the posited notion of equality was contradicted by the facts described.

CHANGE WITHIN ORGANISATIONS

In this part of the argument reference will be made to some of the difficulties which seem to be involved in Crozier's view of the way in which change can occur within organisations or bureaucracies. This is a necessary preliminary to the discussion of global societal change, and it should also be remembered that Crozier applies essentially the same reasoning to the understanding of change within society as he does to change within the organisation. If that is borne in mind, we are made more aware of the importance of this part of his argument. Let us begin by summarising his argument.

Crozier believes that there is a tendency in all large organisations for the members of each stratum to attempt to reduce their dependence on the discretion of their immediate superiors by the elaboration of a set of rules which limit the exercise of that discretion. In France, and in public administration particularly, this tendency is more marked than in large organisations elsewhere. Crozier holds that, as a result, those who are in the best position to understand the inadequacies in the functioning of an organisation, that is, those at the base and their immediate superiors, will not be able to rectify the faults in the working of the organisation. These immediate superiors will have been deprived of the power to react because of the elaboration of rules which limit their discretion. This restriction means that, if decisions are to be taken to put right problems in the working of the organisation, they must come from much higher levels in the organisation and probably from the very top. This analysis points to two particular difficulties. Because of the isolation of one stratum from another, those at the peak of the organisation who attempt to organise reform will be less well informed than is necessary for the task, and they may have considerable difficulty in imposing solutions on the organisation because of the extent to which it is rule-bound.

The first problem with Crozier's analysis is that it assumes that change must take a particular form. Change, in Crozier's view, seems to involve a process of adjustment whereby organisations can perform more adequately the purposes which they have always sought to perform. This is a rather restricted notion of what change may involve, for it completely overlooks the possibility that an organisation may be called upon to change in order to perform a new task. Even if we narrow our definition of change and concentrate for the moment only on the sort of change to which Crozier is referring, he still seems open to criticism for assuming that inadequacies of performance are most obvious to those working at or near to the base of an organisation.[18] There are clearly certain cases when this will be true, but it does not require much imagination to envisage others when inadequacy of performance is much more easily perceived by those working at higher levels. For example, inadequacy in the performance of an organisation may often be visible because it is possible to compare performance with other organisations performing similar tasks elsewhere, and it is much more difficult for those working at or near the base to make such comparisons.

Another set of circumstances may be cited to contradict Crozier's supposition. Often a particular organisation is only one of a number involved in providing a service for or supporting a particular section of the community. Assessment of adequate performance and the necessary steps to be taken in order to improve it in such cases can never be perceived by any one of the organisations involved, let alone by those at the base of such an organisation. In this situation it is members of the client group who are in the best position to assess performance because they can most easily detect overlapping in the activities of the organisations upon which they depend as well as gaps in the services provided.

One can suggest why Crozier, in *The Bureaucratic Phenomenon*, took this particular and rather partial view of change. In the first case, at least with reference to the Post Office Savings Bank, it would appear that the problems of the organisation corresponded quite closely to his analysis. The main unresolved problem was the irregularity in the load which imposed enormous strain on the clerical staff at moments of peak demand. This was clearly the kind of problem most visible to the workers themselves. It also appeared to be the case that management did not understand how serious the problem was and wrongly believed that the difficulties of the organisation arose from the monotonous character of the work.

In the case of the tobacco and cigarette factories, it is also possible to fit some of the problems of the organisation into Crozier's framework. In this case the difficulty was one of continual breakdowns of the machines and time lost in their repair, which was a problem most obvious to those directly involved. But other problems in the tobacco and cigarette factories, to which Crozier refers, point up the unduly narrow conception of change with which he is working. He mentions that one of the aims of headquarters management was to close down a number of factories and concentrate production.[19] The need to do so arose from changes in transport and marketing which rendered the manufacture of the product, region by region, uneconomic. This is a good example of the sort of change the need for which is not likely to be most easily perceived by those working at the base of an organisation.

But there are other reasons which seem to have led Crozier to take a narrow view of change and they relate to his methodology. He emphasises that earlier students of bureaucracy have not been much concerned with change within organisations but have instead concentrated on their rigidities and their conservative character.[20] He claims that he has advanced the study of organisational and social change by ceasing to concentrate so exclusively on the problems of routine. But despite the priority which Crozier gives to the explanation of change, in *The Bureaucratic Phenomenon* and his more recent writings, it seems that his mode of investigation is ill-adapted to throwing light on this particular problem. The simplest way of supporting this argument will be through an examination of the case studies which he presents in *The Bureaucratic Phenomenon*—case studies to which he returns again and again in his later writings.[21]

The information which he presents derives from questionnaires distributed to the workers and their immediate supervisors, and from extensive interviews with workers and members of the management team in a number of plants. On this basis he constructs his picture of an organisation in which it is extremely difficult to organise change. And then he introduces the notion of the authoritarian reform figure whose presence is necessary in order to break out of the vicious circles which he has just described. In other words, the information which he collects relates entirely to the routine side of the reform cycle and he totally fails to observe directly the process of change which occurs from time to time at moments of crisis. One must ask how observations concentrated at one point in time are capable of illuminating the process of change. It is true that occasionally he refers to important incidents in the history of the two organisations studied but these references are always incidental, are never given any extensive discussion, and do not seem to have played any part in the development of his theory.[22]

The methods of enquiry used by Crozier limit in a number of important respects the character of the evidence produced and these limitations affect his conclusions directly. His concentration on what he sees as the routine phase in the cycle by which an organisation adapts to its environment permits him to elaborate convincingly the nature of the obstacles to change, but it gives him no direct guidance as to how these problems are actually surmounted. It is therefore necessary, in order to complete the picture, for Crozier to introduce the authoritarian reform figure, but the reader has to take this part of Crozier's argument on trust.

Up to this point in the analysis, the work of Crozier and those associated with him has been treated as a whole, consistent in its different parts. But a close reading of his most recent full-length work, jointly authored with Friedberg, seems to indicate, although not stated explicitly, that he feels some of the assertions made in *The Bureaucratic Phenomenon* were over ambitious.[23] The emphasis on the crisis as being the only way in which change can be produced in organisations and in the wider society is dropped. Much more caution is expressed about the possibility of framing a general theory of change. In *L'Acteur et le Système* he makes it clear that he envisages a possibility of crises which do not produce any real change and he relies instead on the notion of *apprentissage collectif* as being the process through which real change can occur.[24] The term *apprentissage collectif* is used to refer to the possibility that the players of a particular game can learn new rules within which they can interact. Emphasis is laid on the fact that the conduct of players is never entirely determined by the rules of the game which they are playing. They can use their freedom to experiment and to make discoveries. The learning to which Crozier refers in his notion of *apprentissage collectif* is not the learning of a traditional sort in which information is passed from teacher to pupil, but a learning of a much more modern character. Players, through their interaction, help one another to discover new forms of behaviour, of which none of them was previously aware. Crozier and Friedberg are here inclined to talk not so much in terms of the specific mechanisms by which change is produced but more in terms of factors which are conducive to change or constitute obstacles to it. For example, they stress that change will be facilitated where a notion of authority is accepted which is not too absolutist; for reform to occur and to be effective it is necessary to bring together the broader view of the planner on high and the particular knowledge of those on the ground.[25] It will be seen from these brief illustrations that in *L'Acteur et le Système* we are far removed from the explicit and detailed model of change which was earlier enunciated and have entered a realm of cautious generalities, not to say platitudes. The whole tenor of the present discussion is not to deplore this vagueness but rather to suggest that it is an inevitable consequence of attempting the impossible—a general theory of change.

In another respect, however, *L'Acteur et le Système* is not a retreat from *The Bureaucratic Phenomenon*, but, on the contrary, continues and elaborates on the approach adopted in the earlier work. The approach referred to here is that which tries to understand broader social change by applying to it the methods and concepts of organisational theory. It is to the difficulties involved in this extension from the organisational to the social that we should now turn.

BEYOND THE ORGANISATION

Crozier is perfectly well aware of the problems that may be involved in extending an organisational mode of understanding to society at large. In his defence he writes: *'Les différences sont beaucoup moins grandes que nous ne pouvions le supposer; entre ce qui se passe à l'intérieur d'une organisation et ce qui se passe en dehors de toute organisation.'*[26] This contention is supported by the argument that organisations are becoming increasingly open to external influences and that global society is necessarily becoming more organised and planned. Hence, he contends, the wide gap which perhaps once existed between the forms of social life in the organisation and the more atomised unstructured society beyond the organisation has reduced to the point where his method of understanding society by applying to it a bureaucratic model becomes entirely appropriate. More specifically, he has two quite different strategies which are designed to cope with the difficulties involved in translating a bureaucratic model from the organisation to the society as a whole. The first of these methods is stated and employed in *The Bureaucratic Phenomenon* and the second, which can be regarded as complementary to the first, is explained at some length in *L'Acteur et le Système* and makes use of the notion of *'système d'action concret'*, which is intermediate between organisation and the global society.[27] We shall examine these two approaches in turn. Jumping ahead somewhat, we may say that the first of these two methods consists in admitting the difference between life within organisations and life outside them, but also suggesting that, because individuals outside the organisation are still committed to the same cultural values which their behaviour within the organisation exhibits, those same behaviour patterns will repeat elsewhere. The first approach is used in *The Bureaucratic Phenomenon.*[28] The second approach exhibited in *L'Acteur et le Système* consists of minimising the difference between inter-organisational and intra-organisational problems.

The first of these two approaches to the problem posed by translation does not seem to be convincing. One of the points that Crozier makes in discussing the Post Office Savings Bank and the cigarette factories is that, in the short and medium term at least, the environment in which they exist is extremely stable. The importance of this fact is that, freed from external constraint, the cultural values to which individuals are committed can find full expression. This line of reasoning suggests that, once individuals are operating in an environment which is not closely controlled by an organisation, the fit between cultural values and individual behaviour will become much less exact. If this is so, it surely suggests that the observation of behaviour within organisations operating in a stable and undemanding environment is a poor guide to the understanding of change in the wider society.

The second approach to the problem of translation from the organisational to the social deserves closer examination. The problem which Crozier sets himself in *L'Acteur et le Système* is to understand the nature of the constraints which arise when men attempt to collaborate to achieve common purposes. This formulation in itself underlines his view that the problems are the same whether one sets up an organisation to solve the problem or whether it seems more sensible to bring about a degree of collaboration between a number of different organisations and groups. Crozier sees the essential problem as one of necessary coordination, and power as the means by which this coordination is achieved. He stresses that power cannot be regarded as an attribute of any individual or group but rather as a relation between two individuals or groups, and who says relation also says structure. These structures may not be as formalised or as explicit as single organisations and that is why Crozier describes this kind as *'système d'action concret'*. Examples of *systèmes d'action concret* which Crozier and his collaborators studied in the 1960s and 1970s include the system of relations which links the French Ministry of Industry to its client companies and industries, the system of relations between prefects, mayors and other administrative officials at the departmental level, and the system of relations which links the Ministry of Public Works to those firms and organisations with which it has dealings on a regular basis. He insists that in the study of these *systèmes d'action concret*, as in the study of organisations proper, the crucial task is to locate and describe power relations and this can best be done by first examining the tacit rules which are accepted by those operating in a particular field. When the rules by which the players abide have been established it will be possible to delimit the areas of predictable behaviour from those areas in which a degree of uncertainty about individual behaviour remains. Crozier and Friedberg contend that power is located around these areas of uncertainty.[28]

Once again, this line of argument seems to be open to the objection that it misapplies organisational methods to non-organisational problems. Within an organisation it is a relatively simple matter to establish the forms of behaviour which are rule-governed and thereby to locate areas of uncertainty. In such a context the notion of freedom of manoeuvre or discretion is a real enough notion, but surely outside the organisation the rules themselves are much less explicit and the notion of uncertainty or discretion a much less sure guide to where power is located. It seems that freedom of manoeuvre is an essential condition for the exercise of power but not a very useful guide to its location since most people, in the world outside the organisation, will have retained a considerable degree of discretion in many matters.

POLITICS

Let us now examine some of the problems posed by the application of a bureaucratic or organisational model to the behaviour of deputies and to relations between government and Parliament.[30] Here we shall have to limit ourselves to the discussion contained in *The Bureaucratic Phenomenon*, because Crozier's later work has not touched directly on the political world.

The facts of the situation as described by Crozier and other observers of French politics are not in dispute. The parliamentary groups of the Fourth Republic and the early years of the Fifth Republic were poorly organised and, with the exception of the Communists, ill-disciplined. For this and other reasons coalitions which commanded a majority in the Chamber in principle were, in fact, often in difficulty in attempting to get their legislation through, and every six or nine months these difficulties were sufficient to upset the coalition and oblige the Premier to resign. How then does Crozier fit this picture into his model of *The Bureaucratic Phenomenon*?

The answer to this question seems to be that the feat is accomplished at the cost of considerable ambiguity. At one moment all deputies are considered members of the same stratum and as such as holding strongly egalitarian sentiments towards one another, sentiments that make it difficult for them to associate in groups and develop effective leadership.[31] So far, this picture is at least consistent with the accepted view of French parliamentary behaviour during the period of interest to Crozier, but a difficulty arises when we refer to another section of his discussion where he stresses the hierarchical division among deputies into three strata, between each of which there is considerable conflict. These are, starting from the base, ordinary deputies, cabinet ministers and ex-cabinet ministers, and Premiers and ex-Premiers.[32] It hardly needs to be pointed out that this part of the discussion is in total contradicition to what has gone before.

How can we explain this apparently rather obvious lack of consistency in Crozier's argument? The answer to this puzzle seems to come in two parts. In the first place, his insistence on equality among deputies was bound to run into difficulties when he came to consider the relationship between the assembly and the government, since the latter was composed entirely of deputies and yet exercised some degree of authority both within the country and within Parliament. He was therefore caught between two possible courses of action in seeking to fit parliamentary behaviour into his model of bureaucratic behaviour. Either he could consider all deputies as belonging to a single stratum in which case he seemed to have an explanation for indiscipline, or he would have to take account of the authority wielded by the government, in which case he would have to regard Parliament as an organisation within which there were a number of distinct strata. Neither of these alternatives is entirely satisfactory for his purposes and he seems to have fallen somewhere between the two, using whichever seemed appropriate at particular points in the argument.

The second reason for the introduction of the notion of distinct strata within Parliament seems to arise out of Crozier's acknowledged indebtedness to Leites.[33] Leites' view of parliamentary behaviour is a personal and rather controversial one. Whereas most commentators insist that the instability of French political life in these years arose in part because of the all too accurate reflection of social conflicts with the Chamber, Leites insists that the conflict between the groups of deputies is artificial and unrelated to real social conflict. The conflict which Leites saw as important was that between governments who wished to remain in power and excluded deputies who wished to become cabinet ministers. The importance for Leites and Crozier of these artificial conflicts between different categories of deputy is that it helps to explain why Parliament was unable to deal with pressing social problems. The argument is that, preoccupied by conflicts that were purely internal to Parliament, deputies were unable or unwilling to give attention to wider social problems. Most observers of this period would prefer to stress the vertical divisions of opinion among deputies and the close, if not perfect, link between the attitudes adopted by these deputies and the attitudes of the social groups which they sought to represent.[34] Crozier cannot adopt such a view of the working of Parliament because it would correspond in no way to his bureaucratic model.

So far we have concentrated our attention on two levels, that of the individual organisation, and that of the sector of national life which is more or less organised. We are now in a position to turn to a third level, that is the level of France treated as a single social and political entity. In moving to this higher level, both in *The Bureaucratic Phenomenon* and in *The Stalled Society*, no concessions are made. Crozier holds that at this level, as at the other two, change occurs by means of the alternation of periods of routine with crises which themselves produce necessary reform. The crucial difficulty at this third level is that, even if we accept his arguments about the way in which change is achieved at the two lower levels, there is no reason to suppose that the crises in each of the organised sectors of national life will occur at the same time. It is clear that, for students of French politics, much of the plausibility of Crozier's account arises out of the way in which it seems to correspond at least in outline, with the events leading up to the establishment of the Fifth Republic. But the events of 1958 can only be seen as fitting in with Crozier's analysis if one supposes that there is some reason for the individual crises in each sector to come to a head at the same moment. It is difficult to see any reason for accepting such a supposition. On the contrary it would appear that the logic of Crozier's analysis would suggest that change would be incremental as seen from the national level.

Strain created by failure to adapt will slowly increase throughout the routine phase of the cycle. At some point it will be necessary for the authoritarian reform figure to impose new rules and in this way secure adaptation. But since the purposes of organisations vary infinitely and the environments in which they exist differ strikingly, some demanding rapid innovation and others much slower change, the frequency of crises will vary greatly from one sector or organisation to another.

It may be useful to illustrate this point by reference to the political crisis of 1958 and the establishment of the Fifth Republic. It is not possible to explain the difficulties of the years immediately before 1958 by aggregating a series of organisational or sectoral crises. There were many areas of French life in which there was no particular crisis prior to 1958 and in which no far reaching reforms were imposed as a consequence of this political crisis. In fact, it is easier to designate those areas of French life which were affected by the political crisis than to list all those that were not. 1958 was certainly a turning point in the relationship between France and her colonies, and the new regime certainly brought important constitutional changes which affected the relationship between government and Parliament in important ways. But it would not be easy to explain changes taking place in other areas of French life before and after 1958 by reference to this political crisis. 1958 is not an important date, for example, in the development of the French educational system or the national system of industrial relations, to cite only two of the examples which Crozier himself uses in *The Bureaucratic Phenomenon*.[35] Nor, to mention two further examples more or less at random, did 1958 bring important reforms in the French Civil Service[36] or significant changes in the character of government intervention in the housing market.[37]

AN ALTERNATIVE APPROACH

It will be clear by now that the present analysis shows little sympathy with any attempt to formulate a general theory of change or even, for that matter, with any attempt to describe nationally-typical modes of adaptation. The question which *The Bureaucratic Phenomenon* seeks to answer (how does change occur in France?) and the question posed in *L'Acteur et le Système* (what is the nature of the constraints on collective human action?) are too general to be capable of attracting a useful answer. An alternative approach is proposed here, but not an alternative theory. The first task ought to be to locate, as accurately as possible, the exact extent of obstacles to change. Once this has been done, it is likely that these obstacles will prove much more serious in some sectors of national life than in others. This approach has the advantage that a map of the sort described might in itself suggest certain explanations. The most obviously dynamic sector of French life since the war has been the economy. At the opposite end of this particular spectrum we might place the educational system and the system of local government. In these last two areas, the changes which have occurred in many other European countries have either not yet occurred in France at all or are occurring with considerable delay. Does this not suggest that one of the keys to the understanding of the varied dynamics of different sectors of French national life lies in the extent and nature of State involvement? In the case of housing, crucial factors promoting or retarding adaptation, are the nature of the relationship between central government and local housing authorities, and between government and the major financial institutions involved in the housing market.[38] There is obviously insufficient space to explore this problem fully here, but it is necessary to emphasise that in attempting to understand change and obstacles to it, one must first take into account the extent and nature of state involvement in the sector under study. This approach is akin to that involved in Lowi's notion of arenas of power.[39] All this is not to say that it is impossible to point to certain general features of the French or any other political system which may form part of an explanation of particular reform successes and failures. But there is a world of difference between doing this and presenting a model which purports to explain phenomena which vary from revolutions and coups at one extreme to congested Post Office Savings Banks at the other.

NOTES

1. See for example, Henry W. Ehrmann, *Politics in France*. N.Y.; Little, Brown & Co., 1968, who refers to Crozier as a 'latter-day de Tocqueville' (p. 131). He specifically adopts Crozier's view of the role of the 'grands corps' (p. 137). He also uses Crozier's model when discussing the labour movement (p. 190) and in analysing obstacles to change (p. 137).
2. E. A. Nordlinger, 'Democratic Stability and Instability: The French Case', in A. Lijphart (ed.), *Politics in Europe*. Prentice-Hall, 1969, p. 166.
3. S. Hoffmann, *Decline or Renewal? France Since the 1930s*. New York: The Viking Press, 1974, p. 71.
4. M. Crozier and E. Friedberg, *L'Acteur et le Système*. Paris: Editions du Seuil, 1977.
5. M. Crozier, *The Bureaucratic Phenomenon*. London: Tavistock Publications, 1964, pp. 13-144.
6. Ibid., pp. 213-36.
7. Ibid., pp. 237-69. This line of argument is clearly adopted in *The Bureaucratic Phenomenon* but in *L'Acteur et le Système*, in this as in many other matters, a more cautious line is taken. Culture is now seen as a less reliable guide to behaviour and regarded instead as a tool which can be used by individuals and groups in many different ways. See M. Crozier and E. Friedberg, *L'Acteur et le Système*. Editions du Seuil, 1977, pp. 167-94.

8. M. Crozier, *The Stalled Society*. New York: The Viking Press, 1973.
9. M. Crozier, *The Bureaucratic Phenomenon*, p. 20. Here Crozier identifies these workload peaks as crises.
10. Ibid., p. 20.
11. This is true of the following cases: The Ministry of Industry (Crozier and Friedberg, *L'Acteur et le Système*, pp. 155-66) and the 'département' ((ibid., pp. 218-33). This is also true of the four examples cited in M. Crozier, *The Stalled Society*, chapter 5.
12. M. Crozier, *The Stalled Society*, pp. 124-36, especially p. 129 and p. 133.
13. M. Crozier, *The Bureaucratic Phenomenon*, p. 18.
14. Ibid., pp. 93-9 and pp. 108-10. In speaking of the production workers feelings towards maintenance workers, Crozier talks of their 'jealousy and resentment', p. 95.
15. Ibid., p. 110 and following.
16. Ibid., p. 53 and p. 222.
17. Ibid., p. 257
18. '*Ceux qui décident ne connaissent pas directement les problèmes qu'ils ont à trancher. Ceux qui sont sur le terrain et connaissent ces problèmes n'ont pas les pouvoirs nécessaires pour effectuer les adaptations ou pour expérimenter les innovations indispensables.*' M. Crozier, 'De la bureaucratie comme système d'organisation', *Archives Européennes de Sociologie*, II, 1, p. 37.
19. M. Crozier, *The Bureaucratic Phenomenon*, p. 62.
20. Ibid., pp. 195-8.
21. See for example the case of the industrial monopoly summarised and re-analysed in M. Crozier and E. Friedberg, *L'Acteur et le Système*, pp. 49-54.
22. For example, on pp. 39-40 he discusses the involvement of Post Office workers in the Civil Service strike of 1953. But the strike changed nothing and therefore we learn nothing about how change can occur within such an agency.
23. M. Crozier and E. Friedberg, *L'Acteur et le Système*, particularly pp. 239-64.
24. Ibid., pp. 338-47. In *Où va l'Administration Française?* he has already introduced the notion of '*apprentissage*' as a necessary condition of change but crises are still seen as unavoidable and as the only escape from a variety of vicious circles. (M. Crozier et al, *Où va l'Administration Française?* Paris: Les Editions d' Organisation, 1974, pp. 26 and 27.
25. Ibid., p. 346.
26. Ibid., p. 205
27. Ibid., p. 207, for a definition and defence of this concept.
28. M. Crozier, *The Bureaucratic Phenomenon*, p. 252. On this point see also M. Crozier, 'The Relationships between Micro and Macro Sociology', *Human Relations*, Vol. 25, No. 3.
29. M. Crozier and E. Friedberg, *L'Acteur et le Système*, pp. 207-16, for a statement of this argument. On these points see also M. Crozier, 'Sentiments, Organisations et Systèmes', *Revue Française de Sociologie*, Vol. 12, (1971), No. Spécial, 2e partie, pp. 141-154. See also M. Crozier et J.-C. Thoenig, 'The Regulation of Complex Organised Systems', *The Administrative Science Quarterly*, XXI, 4.
30. M. Crozier, *The Bureaucratic Phenomenon*, pp. 251-63.
31. Ibid., p. 257.
32. Crozier's inability to decide whether to treat deputies and Ministers as equals and members of a single stratum or members of different strata in conflict with one another is best brought out by contrasting the following two quotations:

   The 'political class', just like the bureaucratic strata, has become an isolated group, extremely equalitarian, rebellious against any kind of authority, unable to build stable leadership and to engage in constructive collective action. *The Bureaucratic Phenomenon*, pp. 256-7.

   Finally the great difference of status between Presidents and ex-Presidents, Ministers and ex-Ministers and, at the bottom, simple deputies, has had a much deeper influence on the strategy of mass participants than their role as members of the majority or of the Opposition. *The Bureaucratic Phenomenon*, p. 256.

33. N. Leites, *On the Game of Politics in France*. Stanford University Press, 1962.
34. Philip Williams, *Crisis and Compromise: Politics in the Fourth Republic*. London: Longman, 3rd edition, 1967, throughout.

35. J. Fournier, *Politique de L'Education*. Paris: Editions du Seuil, 1971, p. 257 and following.

36. Crozier himself would, I think agree with this view of the impact of the 1958 crisis on the Civil Service in France. See for example M. Crozier, 'Pour une analyse sociologique de la planification française', *Revue Française de Sociologie*, Vol. 6, No. 2.

37. R. H. Duclaud-Williams, *The Politics of Housing in Britain and France*. London: Heinemann Educational Books, 1978.

38. My own comparative examination of post-war British and French housing politics exemplifies the sort of approach I am advocating here.

39. T. Lowi, 'American business, public policy, case studies and political theory', *World Politics*, Vol. 16, No. 4. T. Lowi, 'The development of arenas of power' in O. Walter (ed.), *Political Scientists at Work*. Duxbury Press, 1971.

[7]

General de Gaulle's Europe and
Jean Monnet's Europe

J. B. DUROSELLE

I HOPE I shall be excused for having chosen a topic which is related to the names of two Frenchmen; my justification is that both these men, General de Gaulle and Jean Monnet, have played, and are playing, an important part in European international relations. They are as different as two men can be; what they have in common is the influence which they exert. Perhaps behind their differences, in spite of the fact that each of them considers the other's concepts and actions as dangerous, there remains a secret mutual esteem and admiration. But the ways in which they conceive of the future of Europe are contradictory, and it is that contradiction which I would like to analyse.

Concept of Europe

First of all, however, it would seem necessary to stress the ambiguity of any concept of Europe—an ambiguity which derives from geography, history, and political philosophy. Europe is geographically ill-defined in two respects. The northern and southern limits are clear, but there is some doubt about its eastern and western boundaries. Where is the eastern boundary? Europe is a peninsula, and therefore any definition of its borders with Asia is artificial. Herodotus put them at the Tanaïs river (the Don); now it is admitted that Europe reaches to the Ural mountains, as witness General de Gaulle's expression: 'Europe from the Atlantic to the Urals'. But the population of Siberia, if not of Central Asia, is now mostly Russian, and the geographical structure of western Siberia is the same as that of eastern Russia. On the western side of Europe, there is the famous problem of the islands—Iceland, Ireland, and Great Britain. It seems that, on 14 January 1963, General de Gaulle was in unconscious agreement with the Venerable Bede of the eighth century, when he decided that the United Kingdom was not European —at least for the moment. All this shows how artificial and arbitrary is the geographical definition of Europe.

Professor Duroselle is Director of the Centre d'études des relations inter-nationales at Paris and Professor of International Relations in the Faculté des Lettres in the University of Paris; author of *L'idée d'Europe dans l'histoire* (Paris, Denoël, 1965) and other works. This article is the text of the fifteenth Sir Daniel Stevenson Memorial Lecture delivered at the London School of Economics on 22 November 1965, with a postscript added.

Historically, it is obvious that the eastern limits of Europe have changed. In Charlemagne's era, Europe did not extend further than the eastern borders of his ephemeral Empire. In the seventeenth century, Poland was European, but not Russia; in the eighteenth century, however, with Peter the Great, Russia entered Europe. Did the Bolshevik Revolution of 1917 exclude her again? Is the present border of Europe the Iron Curtain, or the Polish-Soviet boundary? Once again, we are confronted with the artificial character of Europe.

In terms of political philosophy, the situation is even more obscure. When the word 'Europe' appeared in the seventh century B.C., there was no sense of a Europe considered as a 'superior community', above cities, tribes, kingdoms, and empires. The Greeks were opposed to the barbarians; and there were barbarians in Europe and Greeks in Asia. The Roman Empire was located around the Mediterranean and did not extend to Northern Europe. With Charlemagne, Europe first appears as a political concept; he is called by poets, 'King, father of Europe . . . Venerable chief of Europe'. From now on, Europe exists, but which Europe? It could be said that there has been an intellectual oscillation between two concepts. One is the concept of a group of independent States which have certain principles in common—a common idea of international law and a common acceptance of the formula of the balance of power.[1] But there is another concept, namely that Europe should be more than an organization of independent States, that it should be united. Plans for the unification of Europe have appeared in every century since Charlemagne. In the Middle Ages, they were the dreams of intellectuals who wanted to re-establish Charlemagne's Empire under the authority either of the Pope or of the Emperor. The lawyers of the first modern States in European history—England and then France—fought consistently against these tendencies, and the principle that 'the king is emperor in his kingdom' prevailed. In modern times, plans for unification, such as those of St Thomas More's *Utopia*, or of William Penn, or of the Abbé de Saint-Pierre, were essays written by pacifists and cosmopolitans. In the nineteenth century, romantic writers tried to merge the rising nationalist tendencies with the idea of a United States of Europe; Mazzini and Victor Hugo are good representatives of these noble but at the same time unrealistic views.

The two men

It is not surprising therefore that people like General de Gaulle and Jean Monnet have taken from this historical complexity what best fitted their personalities and temperaments. For General de Gaulle, the im-

---

[1] Some eighteenth-century writers have elaborated this concept, notably Vattel in his book *The Law of Nations*, Edmund Burke, and, for the definition of the balance of power, William Robertson in his *History of the Reign of Charles V*.

portant factor in Europe's evolution is the State and the Nation, and their traditional organization, which he thinks could be improved. For Jean Monnet, Europe conceived as a potential united Power is much more attractive, and he does not see this as possible without a decline in the power of the individual State and Nation.

Before going more deeply into their opposing points of view, it may be interesting to compare the two men. They are roughly of the same age: Jean Monnet was born in 1888 and de Gaulle in 1890 (Adolf Hitler in 1889). The fact that one was born in Lille and the other at Cognac in southern France is immaterial; the General is not a typical northerner, nor Monnet a typical southerner. What is more interesting is the part they played in 1914. De Gaulle, a tall, strong professional army lieutenant, who had just graduated from Saint-Cyr, fought with enthusiasm and was wounded on 15 August not far from Dinant. Monnet, who suffered from poor health and was not fit for military service, was selling his father's cognac in Canada and England when the war broke out. He immediately thought of the way in which he could be most useful to the Allied cause. As the French Government had moved to Bordeaux at the beginning of September, he paid a visit to Viviani, the Prime Minister, and convinced him that close economic co-operation had to be established with the British. He worked very hard in London during the war, in close co-operation with Sir Arthur Salter, and as the result of an agreement concluded in November 1917 they finally achieved their aim: the creation of the Allied Maritime Transport Executive in which they played a decisive role. For de Gaulle, the war was connected with the 'grandeur' of France; for Monnet, with the idea of close co-operation between allies.

Second World War

In June 1940, it is well known that General de Gaulle's historical role was to keep not only *French soldiers* but, as he clearly understood from the beginning, *France herself* in the war against Hitler. Monnet had been appointed as early as September 1939—once again with Lord Salter—as chief of the Franco-British purchasing committee. He did not join the Free French Movement and preferred to work for the British Government in the United States, where he established intimate relations with Harry Hopkins and President Roosevelt, and was the author of the Victory Programme of November 1941. He went to Algiers at the beginning of 1943 as Roosevelt's envoy and succeeded in persuading General Giraud to merge his movement with the Gaullists and to unify French resistance.

Here again, we see the difference between the two men. De Gaulle was interested in re-creating the French State, Monnet in co-operation and in merging and uniting forces everywhere. They did not agree in

3

July 1940 and de Gaulle has published Monnet's letter in his memoirs.
They disagreed also in their appreciation of the role of the United
States. Monnet won the confidence of Roosevelt and ever since, at least
until President Kennedy's death, he has continued to exert a significant
influence in Washington. De Gaulle, in trying to re-create France, was
an awkward customer. Churchill recognized his greatness and overcame
the irritation which de Gaulle frequently caused him. Roosevelt did not
understand him at all, made jokes about him as a prima donna, and,
blinded by prejudice, paid no regard to his immense popularity in
France. De Gaulle did not understand Roosevelt either; the roots of his
notorious anti-Americanism may well be found in this period.

To complete the picture, it is necessary to add that General de Gaulle
attaches great value to the importance of prestige, that he is a great historian, a great writer, with a splendid style 'à la Bossuet', that he has an
exceptional gift of oratory. Monnet, on the contrary, dislikes prestige, is
constantly looking to the future and not to the historical past, does not
like to write and prefers to telephone, prefers conversations to speeches.
To illustrate these attitudes, a mischievous analogy might be Kaiser
William II and Baron Holstein; I prefer to evoke Louis XIV and Father
Joseph, the 'éminence grise'.

General de Gaulle's Europe

Now, to turn first to General de Gaulle's Europe. He has disclosed his
ideas gradually and, as is well known, he is advisedly ambiguous. He
never says one thing without leaving the door open for some other meaning. For instance, when he said that he was opposed to Britain's entry
into the Common Market, he added: 'It is possible that one day England
may transform herself enough to become a member of the European
Community, without restriction or reservation.' The door is open for an
eventual change not only in Britain's attitude but also in General de
Gaulle's opinion.

In attempting to define General de Gaulle's Europe, I would stress
four points. It is a Europe of independent States, with no supranational
authority; a Europe independent of the United States; a Europe in which
the dominant Power in foreign policy would be France; and a Europe
open to the East.

(i) A Europe of independent States with no supranational authority

This idea is well known; but where does it come from? Probably
from a highly original concept of the State. In General de Gaulle's view
it is very difficult to become a real State. If I may be permitted to exaggerate a little, I would say that there are, in his opinion, only two States in
the full sense of the term, Britain and France: first Britain and second
France. Historically, Britain became a modern State before France did;

this is a rather disturbing fact, but nothing can be done about it. But France must be ranked as high as Britain. One of the most stimulating hypotheses in the interpretation of General de Gaulle's policy is precisely his admiration for Britain, and his deep conviction that the old Franco-British rivalry for precedence continues. After all, the list of similarities between British and Gaullist French policies is astonishing: the small striking force, the objections to the MLF, the recognition of Communist China, the vote in favour of Communist China at the United Nations, etc. I cannot help thinking that General de Gaulle secretly tries to copy Britain in many ways. The enormous difference, however, is in the style of negotiations. *Vis-à-vis* America, General de Gaulle is decidedly in favour of saying 'No', whereas I believe that the British often prefer to say 'Yes, but. . .' The Americans seem less irritated by the latter method, but they sometimes are: see for instance General Wedemeyer's memoirs on the relations between American and British generals in 1942. (Let us note in passing that Jean Monnet also makes this parallel between Britain and France when he says that, in the failure of European unification, the two guilty Powers are France and Britain.)

Other States are, in General de Gaulle's view, far behind these two historical leaders. The United States has a Constitution which goes, as he says, 'cahin-caha'. Russia (the General hardly ever uses the expression 'the Soviet Union') is poisoned by Communism; but he is convinced that Communism will disappear one day, and is only an episode in her history. Italy and Germany are far from being really united. General de Gaulle never speaks of East Germany; he always says 'Prussia and Saxony'.

The results of this idea of the supreme value of individual States are twofold. First, the States—the real ones—are bound to survive ideologies; secondly, they cannot be absorbed or merged into something bigger and supranational. It is well known that, as regards purely economic matters, General de Gaulle is in favour of the Common Market; it is also well known that the strong alliance, whether right or wrong, between de Gaulle and Adenauer in 1958 saved the Common Market from being absorbed into the free trade area proposed by Britain. But now that economic matters, because of the progress of the Common Market, are tending more and more to have political connotations, de Gaulle is increasingly cautious. The breakdown of negotiations on agricultural problems on 30 June last year is probably due to this fact. The powers of the European Commission, 'a technocracy composed of a majority of foreigners', must not be allowed to destroy the individual State's right of self-determination. Majority voting, due to come into effect on 1 January 1966, has to be got rid of by some kind of gentleman's agreement. Whereas Jean Monnet's postulate is that economic integration is good *because it will* necessarily, some day, produce political integration, for de Gaulle, it is good only so long as *it does not* produce political integration.

5

THE WORLD TODAY   January 1966

(ii) A Europe independent of the United States

This is also a well-known aspect of de Gaulle's Europe. He has gradually come to the view that the Brussels Commission is the instrument of a U.S.-dominated Europe. One of the many reasons why he rejected Britain's application to enter the Common Market was because after he had met Mr Macmillan at Rambouillet there occurred the Kennedy–Macmillan meeting at Nassau in which he felt Britain knuckled under to the United States in terms of atomic armaments. Certainly he believes that the Americans, whether consciously or unconsciously, are trying to maintain their 'hegemony' over Europe. He sees signs of this attitude in the theory of nuclear non-dissemination, in the influx of American investment into key industries all over Western Europe, in the so-called Kennedy Round, in the Geneva nuclear test ban, etc.

He has been suspicious of the United States ever since he met Roosevelt at Casablanca in January 1943. He believed then that the United States in her turn had 'yielded to the spirit of intervention', that Roosevelt wanted an 'American peace' dictated on his (Roosevelt's) terms. Though de Gaulle is in favour of the Western Alliance, he never hesitates to denounce these tendencies; and this irritates the Americans because they are not conscious of exercising any hegemony or of wanting to do so. On 23 July 1964 de Gaulle said: 'Many people . . . have suggested for Europe not an independent policy, which indeed they do not conceive, but an organization unable to have such a policy, connected . . . to an Atlantic, that is to say an American, system, and consequently subordinated to what the U.S. call their leadership.' On the contrary, what de Gaulle wants is an independent Europe—a Europe which will be a 'third force'. On 31 December 1964 he rejected 'all the systems which, under cover of "Supranationality", or "Integration", or "Atlanticism", would in fact keep us under a well-known hegemony'.

(iii) A Europe in which the dominant Power in foreign policy would be France

General de Gaulle has never spoken openly of such French leadership. The word 'supremacy' which appears in the English translation of his memoirs is simply a bad translation of 'coopération'. But it is clear that what he calls a politically united Europe is a Europe in which the other partners are willing to accept what he thinks is good sense and historical necessity, that is to say, the policy which he proposes of Europe 'as a third force'. Among the Six, France is the only Power with 'world responsibilities'. French ideas have to be taken into account, therefore, and he seems to reckon on a Europe in which—as Germany did in Adenauer's latter years—the other partners would follow the general line of French foreign policy. The fact that they do the opposite, that, if they feel the necessity of leadership, they prefer the powerful leader—namely, the United States—to France, does not seem to discourage him. In the end he is sure that good sense will prevail, and the European countries will understand that they should cherish a 'European Europe' in which France will definitely be the big brother. (This is one more reason for dismissing the candidacy of Britain, another Power with world responsibilities; it would not be pleasant for France if a second big brother joined the first.)

(iv) A Europe open to the East

General de Gaulle has so often said that France will be faithful to the Western Alliance and he has so violently condemned the Communist system that the idea of a shift of alliances is quite absurd. Such an idea has been conceived only in the minds of American newspaper columnists.

But at the same time, he speaks of a 'Europe from the Atlantic to the Urals'. What does that mean? Very probably, one can assume that he is looking to the long-range future. One day, Europe will be 'united'—an association of States in which France will play her appropriate role. Such a Europe is the only Power which will be able to convince the Russians that the reunification of Germany is unavoidable. One day also, Communism will disappear in the U.S.S.R. Meanwhile, it is possible that China, 'innumerable and miserable', and the 'yellow people' will one day fight against the Soviets, the Europeans, and the Americans. Ultimately they may perhaps conquer Siberia and Soviet Asia. Why should we not imagine that the 'Russia' of that time, freed from Bolshevism, would be delighted to join her old partners, as in the times of the European concert following Peter the Great?

This whole theory has a curious 'yellow-peril' flavour. After all, Charles de Gaulle was fourteen years old when the Russian-Japanese war broke out. I suspect that he must have read an atrocious novel: *L'invasion jaune* by Paul d'Ivoy, in which the yellow armies, commanded by the Japanese, successively defeated Nicholas II, William II, invaded France, where Jean Jaurès had weakened the army, and murdered the population—and I must add this detail, all because of the egoism of Britain and the United States, who refused to join the anti-yellow alliance.

Jean Monnet's Europe

Jean Monnet's Europe has practically nothing in common with that of de Gaulle. It must first be pointed out that Monnet is less interested in a geographical area than in a set of political institutions. For de Gaulle, there is first of all France and her neighbours; Europe is the grouping of those neighbours, and this grouping has to be 'united', with national sovereignties maintained and under the inspiration of France. Monnet, on the other hand, pursues a philosophy bent on changing the nature of human relationships. As men are not good (he is not optimistic in this sense) their minds will not change if they are not induced to do so by new political institutions. Now, why is it that those institutions have to be created in Europe? Because Monnet is French and therefore European? I do not think so. After all, he could just as well have continued his career in the United States in 1943; his influence there was immense. Very probably, his idea of new institutions, created to change the human mind progressively, originated with his European experiences—those with Britain and Italy during the first World War—but it also came from the conviction that Europe needs such institutions more than any other area of the world.

When he wrote the foreword to my book, *The Idea of Europe in History*, Jean Monnet insisted much less on the common culture of Europe than on the European 'spirit of domination'. The Europeans are the only peoples in history who have conquered the world. In Monnet's opinion, this is not an achievement of which to be proud. The spirit of domination is a bad thing in itself, and it has proved itself so by ultimately causing the fratricidal destruction of Europeans by Europeans, and the suicide of Europe. Therefore Europe has a greater need to be cured because Europe is sicker than the other continents.

I would like to summarize my picture of Jean Monnet's Europe, as I did for that of de Gaulle, by stressing four points. Monnet's Europe is: an anti-nationalist Europe; a Europe based upon concrete institutions; a European Community linked to the United States in a strong partnership; an 'open' Europe.

(i) An anti-nationalist Europe

Jean Monnet is a 'good citizen of his own country', but he hates nationalism, because nationalism is equated in his view with the 'spirit of domination'. Nationalism is based on inequality, and what needs to be created is the spirit of equality. As he has said: 'National sovereignties can oppose one another; nationalism in one country fatally provokes nationalism in the others.'[2] While General de Gaulle exalts French nationalism, Monnet deplores it, not so much because French nationalism could be dangerous in itself, but because it encourages German nationalism, which is still potentially dangerous.

The consequence is that Monnet's Europe is not founded upon a new European nationalism which would eliminate local nationalisms, but is based on something quite new. Many pro-Europeans believe that a kind of European nationalism has to be developed in public opinion before Europe can be united. Monnet, who is no sentimentalist but a man of action, does not believe that Europe has a prior need of this new kind of nationalism. After all, Britain, France, and Spain were united before the 'nationalist movement' appeared. And a European nationalism would

[2] Foreword to J. B. Duroselle, *op. cit.*, p. 11.

eventually bring a united Europe into opposition against the other big Powers.

(ii) A Europe based upon concrete institutions

Here I think is Jean Monnet's most original idea, and his greatest contribution to human history. As he said on 3 October 1965 at a ceremony at Scy-Chazelles in honour of Robert Schuman: 'For a long time, people spoke of European unity. But words, general ideas, good intentions were not enough. Concrete action was necessary to bring that idea to reality. That action was started by the Schuman Plan.' It is a well-known fact that the Schuman Plan originated from the ideas of Jean Monnet and was then strongly backed by Robert Schuman, who took the decision and 'made the political choice'.

To create an institution is in itself an action; it is also a source of future creativity. The institution, once it exists, produces concrete effects; those effects produce something new in the minds of men, and this is the important point. An institution is immensely more influential than any amount of propaganda in changing the minds of men. But what sort of institution? Is there any guiding-line to determine what has to be done? Yes, indeed. Jean Monnet discovered this from his experience when he worked in London between 1914 and 1918. He had to convince the Allied Governments that it was better to purchase in common rather than to purchase separately, to set up a pool of tonnage as a remedy for the shortages created by the ceaseless German submarine warfare. The normal reaction of each Government was to act individually. Years of attempts and series of failures were necessary to persuade them to create such pools, the dominant and very simple idea of which was 'common interest'.

Now, in the case of the countries of Europe destroyed and weakened by two wars, the common interest is obvious. National solutions have failed; a common order has to be created. 'Only very recently we have started to accept in the relations between our nations what we accept in the relations between men in one country: that force does not prevail, that differences be resolved by common rules, by common institutions.'[3] When the Coal and Steel Community was created, the means were established for resolving differences by a common set of rules. Jean Monnet was the first chairman of the High Authority, and he contributed immensely to organizing a common line of action and to developing a common spirit. Here we are far from General de Gaulle's concept of cold-blooded individual States, of international relations from which sentiment has to be eliminated; not of course that Monnet is a sentimental man, but he works to create a 'community spirit'.

Monnet likes to demonstrate the consistency of his thinking. He cer-

[3] *ibid.*, p. 12.

tainly had not worked out the concept of 'integration' before 1950. But
always, from the beginning of his striking career, he has believed in
'common interest' fostered by new creative institutions. He played a
great part, as we all know, in conceiving the famous project of 16 June
1940 of Franco-British union. I am convinced that, in the eyes of Churchill and de Gaulle, such a project was unrealistic as such, but they saw that
it could be used to inject some energy into the French Premier, Paul
Reynaud. Jean Monnet went further, however. His idea was: let us try it
and see if it works.

Are institutions conceived out of the blue by intelligent and imaginative men? Certainly this does not seem to be the case. An institution has to
stem from historical necessity. Monnet is convinced that the regrouping
of nations is a historical necessity; that this regrouping is inevitable
sooner or later; that there is at each moment in history an optimum size
for States; and that France, which now is too small, is faced with the
choice between merging into a bigger union or becoming a 'superior
Spain'. He sees another historical necessity in the fact that economic
integration will inevitably produce political integration; hence his
hostility to de Gaulle when the General tries to break this evolution.
Monnet believes that this development will survive de Gaulle's attempts,
or alternatively that France will be excluded from this evolution and that
another 'constellation' of States will be established. He believes that the
movement of history will condemn those who work for isolation.

*(iii) A European Community linked in strong partnership with the United
States*

Precisely because he is against isolation, Jean Monnet does not con-
ceive of Europe as a 'third force' between the United States and the
Soviet Union. He believes strongly in Atlantic solidarity, and denies
de Gaulle's charges that the Americans have secret aims of hegemony.
He is, however, well aware that independence cannot be maintained by
European States at the national level.

At the same time, he is not in favour of the expression 'Atlantic Community', as long as the United States refuses to surrender to a supranational authority a part of her national sovereignty as the Europeans
have to do in the 'European Community'. Jean Monnet prefers the expression 'partnership'. It is interesting that President Kennedy, who
often used the expression 'Atlantic Community'—for instance, in his
message on the State of the Union of January 1962—suddenly abandoned
this expression and from July 1962 used the other, 'Atlantic partnership'.
This change coincided with one of the many visits Monnet paid to the
United States; and this may well be more than a coincidence.

Atlantic partnership means good relations, both politically and economically. But it also has a more concrete aspect. Jean Monnet—and with

him his most distinguished disciples, such as Pierre Uri and Etienne Hirsh—are not only against national striking forces, whether French or British, but are also against the creation of a European nuclear force. They consider that it is sufficient to rely on American protection. For this reason Jean Monnet's 'Committee for the United States of Europe' has taken a firm stand in favour of a 'multilateral nuclear force'—not exactly what the Americans had proposed, but with an increase in the multilateral power of decision.

(iv) An 'open Europe'

As we have seen, institutions are more important than geography. Therefore, in 1950, Monnet and Schuman preferred a small community consisting of six countries *with* supranational powers rather than a community including Britain but without supranationality; hence the very imperfect Europe of the Six. But this Europe must be open. Monnet welcomed the British application to join and condemned General de Gaulle's decision to reject it. Monnet has never seen in Britain's entry into the Common Market an American 'Trojan horse'; on the contrary, he saw it as a way of escape for the British from the embarrassing position of playing a brilliant 'second fiddle'. In his view, however, any application for membership must imply the acceptance of the principle of supranationality.

But the European Community is even more open than this. As Monnet says: 'Now, the European Community is able to become an equal partner of the United States and so to contribute to the consolidation of the Western world, which is indispensable for the progressive establishment of peaceful coexistence between the West and the Soviet Union.'[4] An important difference between de Gaulle and Monnet lies in the fact that de Gaulle believes that Europe *alone*—without the United States—can one day resolve the problem of German reunification, while Monnet thinks that it can be resolved only by a united Europe backed by the United States of America.

Necessity of choice

The two concepts of Europe which I have outlined above are so contradictory that one cannot think of resolving the dilemma by a compromise. It is essential to choose between them. Each of us doubtless has his own personal predilections for one or the other. I myself am much more drawn to the Europe of Jean Monnet, which stems from a creative initiative, rather than to a Europe consisting of a 'Concert of Powers', even if this is improved by close co-operation.

But the choice which history will make does not depend on personal preferences or whims. If there were an overwhelming trend of public

[4] Speech of 3 October 1965.

II

opinion in favour of an integrated Europe, national Governments would
be obliged to take notice of it. But there is nothing of the kind. The
majority of Europeans are probably sympathetic to the idea of a United
States of Europe, but this sympathy is fragile as soon as it comes up
against vested interests; and these tend to become more and more ob-
structive in proportion as integration develops. Just as the Rumanians
objected to the 'socialist division of labour' among the member States of
Comecon, so a French or an Italian industrialist will tend to refuse to
allow his firm to be scrapped on the ground that his Belgian competitors
are showing a higher level of productivity.

In other words, progress towards integration does not depend exclusively on the disappearance of General de Gaulle from the political
scene. The General has applied the brakes by suspending France's participation in the ruling organs of the Common Market on 30 June 1965.
But by his ultimatum tactics, he accelerated the creation and development
of an agricultural common market. The experts will discuss for a long
time to come the question of whether the refusal to admit the United
Kingdom on 14 January 1963, whatever may have been its psychological
aspects, has injured the integration principle, as Jean Monnet maintains,
or has helped it, as André Philip says. Let us imagine that General de
Gaulle suddenly disappeared. Must we deduce from this that everything
would from then on proceed for the best? That the agricultural problems
would be resolved as if by magic? That, with economic integration speed-
ed up in this way, we would arrive painlessly at political integration? I
doubt it very much.

One can accept, and I do accept, that what would appear to be Jean
Monnet's postulate—namely, that political integration follows necessarily from economic integration—is most likely true. But this certainly
does not mean that historical necessity as defined above implies a rapid
and easy passage from one to the other. My guess is that if de Gaulle did
suddenly disappear we should immediately have other trouble-makers
turning up, happy indeed to bring the whole weight of responsibility at
the present time down upon the General. Thus, de Gaulle's Europe of a
'Concert of Powers', matched by growing economic integration, might
simply act as a staging-post, a pause in the building of Europe, a pause
which many businessmen, breathless from competition, would accept
with relief. After which, if historical necessity does in fact exist, the
movement towards integration would be resumed.

In this whole matter, U.S. policy plays a major role. Followed sub-
missively by Germany and to a large extent by France's four other partners, the United States could decide on positive action, on a 'coup d'éclat'.
She could try to set France aside and to bring about another constellation
of Powers. On psychological grounds, one might understand her taking
such a line, since the General appears to do his utmost to irritate her. But

KUWAIT

politically, this would be a disastrous decision for it would stir up doubts all over the world about the Americans' willingness to recognize their allies' independence. One must hope that the French elections, which have finally resulted in the General's re-election, will lead him to reflect and to adjust his policy. The gradual integration of Europe does not depend, in the long run, on the decisions of a few men. But within the time-scale of a decade, Johnson, de Gaulle, and certain others are at liberty to accelerate or slow down its progress.

[8]

European Journal of Political Research 8 (1980) 165–187   165
© Elsevier Scientific Publishing Company, Amsterdam – Printed in The Netherlands

A NEW POLITICAL SYSTEM MODEL: SEMI-PRESIDENTIAL
GOVERNMENT

MAURICE DUVERGER

University of Paris I, France

ABSTRACT

This article aims at defining the concept of "semi-presidential government" and detailing the diversity of its practices. There are in fact three types of semi-presidential regimes: the president can be a mere figurehead, or he may be all-powerful or again he can share his power with parliament. Using four parameters – the content of the constitution, tradition and circumstances, the composition of the parliamentary majority and the position of the president in relation to the majority – the author seeks to explain why similar constitutions are applied in a radically different manner.

In 1970, the idea was conceived of comparing the French political system established between 1958–62 with that of the other countries in Europe where a president of the republic, elected by universal suffrage and given personal powers, co-exists with a government resting on the confidence placed in it by parliament. At the same time it was suggested that these forms of government intermediary between presidential and parliamentary systems should be called "semi-presidential". In addition to that of Paris, there were then five: four operating in Finland, Austria, Ireland and Iceland, with the last having operated in Germany from 1919 to 1933 under the Weimar Republic. Since then, another has been set up in Portugal by the constitution of 1975. The same form of government failed to establish itself in Greece. The constitution of 1975 gave the Head of State considerable personal powers without requiring him to be elected by universal suffrage. It seems that Mr. Karamanlis would have put forward such a reform had he won the subsequent election. Unfortunately, the defeat of the prime minister in 1978 put a check on this de Gaullian process.

Eight years later, the first results of this comparative study were published under the title of *Echec au Roi* (Check to the King), a work

166

of 250 pages, the first part of which traces a general picture of the
countries concerned, and the second part of which is devoted to a more
detailed discussion of the French political system by comparing it with
its counterparts. A seminar of the department of political science at
the Sorbonne is now continuing this comparative analysis of the seven
semi-presidential forms of government, with the help of "assistants" or
students belonging to each of the countries involved. The study is being
conducted in the light of the model described in the work mentioned
above.

This model is based on four essential variables: the constitutional
rules, the make-up of the parliamentary majority, the position of the
president in relation to this majority, and national and contingent
factors. The last three will be examined in more detail later. The first
merits some preliminary explanation. The concept of a semi-presidential form of government, as used here, is defined only by the content of
the constitution. A political regime is considered as semi-presidential if
the constitution which established it, combines three elements: (1) the
president of the republic is elected by universal suffrage, (2) he
possesses quite considerable powers; (3) he has opposite him, however,
a prime minister and ministers who possess executive and governmental
power and can stay in office only if the parliament does not show its
opposition to them.

This definition comes up against several difficulties. In Finland, the
president is not elected by direct universal suffrage. The citizens elect
the "grand electors" by proportional representation and the latter then
elect the Head of State by a three-tiered vote. The system is similar to
that of the United States, in so far as the Finnish "grand electors" are
not elected by majority vote and in so far as they are free in their
choice. In Ireland, the president has very little personal power, in other
words, powers allowing him to make decisions on his own, or to
prevent the prime minister and the government making decisions
without him. His powers are limited to refusing a dissolution proposed
by the prime minister, or referring a law to the Supreme Court so that it
might possibly be pronounced unconstitutional. There was some hesi-
tation at first as to whether this country should be classed among semi-
presidential forms of government. However, when he appealed to the
Supreme Court in 1976, President O'Dalaigh provoked a crisis which
showed that the above-mentioned powers are not inconsiderable.

It is not usual for political scientists to construct analytical models
defined initially by constitutions. However, no-one would dream of
watching a game of football or of bridge without taking into account
the rules of the game. They constitute a fundamental aspect of the

players' strategy and tactics, the framework of which they define. Jurists have obscured this deep nature of constitutions by considering them as sacred texts, capable of only one interpretation, which would be "true", while the others were "false". What I mean of course is that each commentator believes his interpretation — which differs from that of his colleagues — to be the only true one. In actual fact, the interpretation of a constitution cannot be separated from the interrelationship of political forces to which it is applied. If the interrelationship varies, the structure and functioning of the form of government established by the constitution vary at the same time.

The Diversity of Semi-Presidential Practices

Constitutions which lay down semi-presidential governments are relatively homogeneous. It will be seen that they show considerable differences with regard to the powers of the Head of State. These differences, however, remain secondary in relation to the general physiognomy of the system. They are far less important than the variety of political practices, which is the essential feature revealed by comparative analysis of the seven countries concerned. Similarity of rules, diversity of games: such is the two-fold aspect of the pleiad formed by the seven countries to which the model applies. In three of them, the president is in practice a figurehead; in one, he is all-powerful; in the other three, he shares authority with the prime minister.

1. THREE COUNTRIES WITH A FIGUREHEAD PRESIDENCY: AUSTRIA, IRELAND AND ICELAND

The constitutions of Austria, Ireland and Iceland are semi-presidential. Political practice is parliamentary. Although elected by universal suffrage and endowed with personal powers by right of law, the Head of State normally behaves in each of these countries like the modern Italian and German presidents or like the queen of England: that is to say, he ratifies all the decisions which the government puts forward to him, his only real prerogative being in his choice of the prime minister, in so far as his choice is not dictated by the result of the elections. However, several differences between the three countries can be observed. In practice, the president uses his personal powers more in Ireland than in Iceland, and more in Austria than in Ireland.

In Iceland, no deviation can be observed in relation to the normal practice of parliamentarianism. As the parties there are more numerous than in Ireland and Austria, and none ever obtains an absolute majority

168

by itself alone, the Head of State possesses at Reykjavik a greater freedom of action to form a government than in Dublin or Vienna. It rests, however, neither on the prestige of his being elected by universal suffrage, nor on the personal powers which the constitution confers on him, although these latter are very wide. The Icelandic president plays a strictly parliamentary game. He is, moreover, considered not as a committed politician, but as a relatively neutral arbiter, speaking on behalf of the country.

Is this the reason why a curious practice has established itself: that of automatically renewing the term of office of each president when he comes up for re-election if no candidate opposes him? Because of this, only two real elections have taken place since independence, in 1952 and in 1968. The second prevented the transition from a life-president to a semi-hereditary president when the electors rejected the son-in-law of his deceased predecessor, who hoped to succeed his father-in-law. No-one can say if the renewal of tenure for life is the cause or effect of the neutral role of the Icelandic Head of State. One thing alone is certain: the citizens wish to see him play the figurehead role of parliamentary Head of State. However, it is sometimes stressed that he could intervene more actively in the event of acute crisis, for example, what Björnsson (then regent for the king of Denmark) did in 1942: he governed for two years with a cabinet made up of notabilities in the absence of a parliamentary majority.

In Ireland, a single candidate is sometimes put up by agreement between the two major parties which dominate political life ("Fianna Fail" and "Fine Gaël"). This shows clearly the figurehead character of the president, to whom the constitution gives, moreover, very few powers. The candidates are chosen accordingly. The only exception concerns the "father" of the country, Eamon de Valera, architect of independence and national hero, who put forward his candidature in 1959 at the age of seventy-seven. He wanted a kind of gilt-edged retirement, facilitating the accession of a new leader as head of the Fianna Fail. However, his successor at the head of the party and of the government seemed relatively unimportant in relation to himself. In 1966, the reelection of Mr de Valera was not easy. The Irish seem to prefer the president of the Republic to be a figurehead.

In 1976, when President O'Dalaigh wanted to use his constitutional powers by referring a law to the Supreme Court, the move provoked a conflict with the government which culminated in the resignation of the Head of State. This shows that the powers of the Irish president have not fallen into disuse, although they are rarely exercised. No-one then disputed his right to use the prerogatives conferred on him by right of law. The crisis arose from the fact that the president — like all his predecessors and successors — belonged to the Fianna Fail, whose rival (The Fine Gaël) was then in power, which is very rarely the case. The conflict between president and government arose because they were opposed to each other politically. The fact that Mr O'Dalaigh had been accepted by the two parties and invested without competition made the situation more complicated: by exercising his powers, he appeared as a party man again, when he ought not to have done so if he were to remain faithful to his investiture. The situation was diametrically opposed to that in which the first president of Ireland, Douglas Hyde, placed himself. Put forward by the Fianna Fail and elected without competition, he twice used his power to refer a law to the Supreme Court, against the party which had put him forward. He was not put forward again in 1945, and Sean Thomas O'Kelly was elected.

In Austria, the president of the Republic makes some use of his powers. He did so at least up to 1966, when neither of the two major parties (Social-Democrat and Populist) obtained a majority on its own and they governed together within the framework of the "great coalition". This was imposed by the presidents of the Republic, against the will of the Populist Party, which wanted an alliance of the right with the small Liberal Party, then close to the pan-Germanists and the neo-Nazis. In 1953, President Körner pushed strongly in this direction of "great coalition". In 1959, President Schärf followed this example by stating that he would not accept the presence of the Liberals in the government. Several parliamentary Heads of State thus exert pressure to move towards a majority that they prefer; the pressure is less strong, however, because they have less authority.

During this period, certain Austrian presidents played a second role quite outside the conventional parliamentary system. Although they were Socialists, it had been assumed that the chancellor (prime minister) would be Populist, assisted by a Socialist vice-chancellor. In principle, it was the duty of the latter to control the balance of the coalition, particularly in the appointment of high officials, in order to ensure a just division of posts between the two allied parties. In actual fact, President Körner and even more President Schärf tended to ensure personally this Socialist control of the Populist chancellor, instead of leaving it to the vice-chancellor, the official leader of the Social-Democrat Party. As a former leader of the latter party and a former vice-chancellor, President Schärf appeared as the natural rival of the Populist Chancellor Raab, with whom he had negotiated in 1953 the pact of the great coalition. He made full use of his prerogatives with regard to appointments to ensure representation of the Socialist party in the

170

coalition, thus replacing his successor in the duties of the vice-chancellor. As from 1966, when a single party held an absolute majority (exept in 1970–71, when a minority Socialist government was formed), Austrian presidents no longer exercise their real functions, and behave as parliamentary Heads of State.

2. A COUNTRY WITH AN ALL-POWERFUL PRESIDENCY: FRANCE

Amended in 1962 by the introduction of universal suffrage for the presidential election, the French constitution of 1958 does not give great personal powers to the president of the Republic, except in its article 16 which allows him to be a veritable temporary dictator in exceptional circumstances: if "the institutions of the Republic, the independence of the nation, the integrity of its territory or the fulfilment of its international commitments are seriously and directly threatened and if the normal operation of the constitutional Public Powers is interrupted." These conditions are not easily found together, particularly the second, which presupposes an insurrection, an invasion or an atomic attack. Article 16 has been invoked only once, in 1961, after the Algerian military coup of General Challe. It can be disregarded, although much ink has been spilt over its symbolic value.

Apart from article 16, the president of the French Republic can make decisions on his own, without the counter-signature of the prime minister, and without the agreement of the government or of the parliamentary majority, in four cases only: (1) to dissolve the national Assembly, with no further dissolution possible within the same year; (2) to refer to the constitutional Council laws or international commitments which he judges to be opposed to the constitution; (3) to appoint three members and the president of the constitutional Council, on the expiry of the term of office of their predecessors; (4) to address messages to parliament.

Furthermore, the president can refuse his signature to the ordinances and decrees discussed in the Council of Ministers. The ordinances are texts having the force of law, adopted by the government, which is authorised to do so by a plenipotentiary law. The decrees concern the appointment of senior officials: Counsellors of State and Counsel-Masters at the Audit Office, prefects, ambassadors, generals, rectors and directors of central administrations. All the other decrees can be made by the prime minister on his own, for he has executive and statutory power. As for the enactments made by parliament, the president is forced to promulgate them after a fixed period, during which he can refer them should he so wish to the constitutional Council. He can also send them back to the House for a second reading; this decision is subject, however, to a counter-signature, that is to say it cannot be taken without the agreement of the prime minister. The president can also refuse to resort to a referendum even though he is asked to do so by the government or parliament. He cannot have recourse to the referendum, however, without the initiative of one or the other.

It will be noted that the principal powers of the president of the French Republic have a spasmodic character. Apart from participation in the appointment of senior officials, they are not, like legislative and governmental powers, normal prerogatives in general use, but exceptional powers which can be used only infrequently. Furthermore, the majority are not powers of decision. They tend either to prevent a decision in order to submit it to a fresh examination and have its legitimacy checked, or to submit the decision to the French people (dissolution, referendum). They correspond to the concept of arbitration, as referred to in article 5 of the constitution.

In practice, the French president exerts much greater powers. On 31 January 1964, General de Gaulle interpreted the constitution in a highly debatable manner, by proclaiming "that the indivisible authority of the State is entrusted completely to the president by the people who elected him, that there existed no other authority, either ministerial, civil, military or judiciary which has not been conferred and was not being maintained by him, and finally that it was his duty to adapt the supreme domain, which is his alone, to fit in with those, the control of which he delegates to others." These fine phrases fail to take into account that the national Assembly is elected by the people, like the president and that like him it is a repositary of national sovereignty. They ignore the fact that no organ of the State, even though it holds supreme power, has the right to define its own competence and that of the others in relation to itself, since both are laid down by the constitution, which must be observed by all. They also ignore the fact that the government and its head must keep the confidence of the parliamentary deputies in order to remain in office and to exercise their powers, which limits the choice of the president, and the fact that the latter cannot dismiss the prime minister, as the General himself had stated to Paul Reynaud.

However, General de Gaulle's successors have exercised almost the same powers as he did. They have exercised directly the prerogatives conferred on them by the constitution. They have exercised indirectly the prerogatives of their prime ministers and governments, by reducing the latter to obedience. They have thus become supreme heads of the executive and real heads of the government. Professor René Capitant

172

styled the prime minister as "chief of staff of the president of the Republic." The differences of style between the three successive presidents can be noted. The substance of their powers, however, is the same. The authority of Georges Pompidou and of Valéry Giscard d'Estaing over governments has not been less than that of General de Gaulle.

The forms of this authority have varied according to the types of prime minister. Several varieties can be distinguished in this respect. With Michel Debré, Jacques Chaban-Delmas and Raymond Barre, the practice of the French monarchy under Louis XIII or Louis XIV is found: that of a prime minister whom the king allows to govern, while remaining free to dismiss him at any moment. The system has the advantage of removing responsibility from the Head of State. Georges Pompidou, Maurice Couve de Murville and Pierre Messmer were more direct executants of the presidential will. When the strong personality of Georges Pompidou and his actions in May 1968 gave him a personal authority, the president put him "in reserve for the Republic." Jacques Chirac is a special case. Since the dynamism of the man prevented both his being a mere executant and the president having total confidence in him, he was subjected to permanent and niggling control by the "Elysée," which has been described as "super-presidentialism".

It will be seen that the extension of the powers of the Head of State has not involved violation of the constitution. French presidents have only on four occasions disregarded its provisions, and always with the agreement of the prime ministers, the government and the majority in the National Assembly: by refusing to convene parliament in an extraordinary session in 1960, by reducing its prerogatives during the application of article 16 in 1961, by using the referendum under article 11 for a constitutional amendment in 1962 and 1969, and by not putting forward to the referendum or to the Congress the constitutional amendment voted for in 1973. Apart from these cases, the extension of presidential powers has been accomplished within the framework of the constitution by a very simple mechanism: that of the prime ministers and the governments agreeing to comply with the injunctions of the Head of State. If they had refused to do so, and if the president had tried to ignore their refusal, then the constitution would have been disregarded. That has not occurred uptil now, because the interrelationship of political forces did not allow it.

3. THREE COUNTRIES WITH A BALANCED PRESIDENCY AND GOVERN-
MENT: THE WEIMAR REPUBLIC, FINLAND AND PORTUGAL

Semi-presidential constitutions lay down a governmental dyarchy. By
establishing a president put into office by universal suffrage and
endowed with personal powers alongside a prime minister and a government resting on parliament and charged with executive power, such
constitutions introduce dualism into the heart of the State. This
dualism, however, remains purely apparent in four cases out of seven,
as the president is confined to symbolic functions in Iceland, Ireland
and Austria, while the prime minister in France is reduced to the role of
chief of staff. In contrast, dualism operates or has operated in a real
sense in Finland, Portugal and the Weimar Republic.

The latter is normally not highly thought of, because it was unable to
prevent Hitler from rising to power. This is not the fault, however, of
either the election of the president by universal suffrage, or the wide
powers which the constitution gave him. With a conventional parliamentary government, the Weimar Republic would probably have
collapsed sooner than it did. It does not in reality correspond to the
picture usually presented of it. Its first president, Friedrich Ebert, was
not confined to the role of parliamentary Head of State. He made wide
use of his semi-presidential prerogatives. He enacted many ordinances
based on article 48: five in 1919, twenty-two in 1920, twelve in 1921,
six in 1922 and thirty-eight in 1923, year of the collapse of the mark.
He appointed non-parliamentary chancellors, not of any party: Cuno in
1922, Luther in 1925. Cuno — appointed without previous discussions
with the parties and chosen from outside their number — by forming
government where engineers were mixed with politicians, prefigured the
presidential cabinets of 1930—1932. This allowed the Reichstag to
obtain the support of the Social-Democrats on the left and of the
German National party on the right.

Ebert's successor, Marshal Hindenburg, confined himself to more of
a figurehead role during the first years of his presidency. Circumstances
at that time made his intervention less necessary. From 1925 to 1930,
Germany was going through a period of prosperity which lessened
political tensions. Sailing on calmer waters, ministers were more stable
and more effective. Everything changed with the great crisis of western
capitalism, which struck the most industrialised country in Europe
very hard. It required the taking of strong decisions, which were
impossible to make in the absence of a majority. Hindenburg then intervened, as had Friedrich Ebert in the time of the *putschs* and the great
inflation. The Brüning cabinet was from the outset less presidential

174

than the Cuno cabinet, as its head was a politician, the leader of the Centre. It became much more so after the dissolution of July 1930, which opened the Reichstag to 107 Nazi deputies instead of 12. Henceforth, the chancellor could act only through the Head of State, who applied article 48 very widely: forty-three ordinances were enacted in 1931. At the same time, parliament agreed to take a back seat. The Reichstag elected in September 1930 sat twelve days that year, fifty-six in 1931 and ten in 1932. The deputies were not forced into this cold storage. They could meet normally if they wanted to do so. They restricted voluntarily their control over the government and over their legislative activity, to let Brüning act by ordinances. They could do so thanks to the abstention of the Socialists, who disapproved of the chancellor's policy, but tolerated it "in order to prevent the German Republic from sinking into fascist dictatorship."

This strategy was not as absurd as has been said. From 30 March 1930 to 31 May 1932, a single government ruled Germany for two years and two months with the means to make decisions and to legislate to meet the world crisis. Within the same period, five succeeded each other in France, or one every five months. The institutions of Weimar showed themselves to be more effective than those of the Third Republic. In April 1932, the presidential election made it possible for all the opponents of Nazism to be regrouped, except the Communists, who played its game by keeping their candidate in the second round. The halo of the Marshal prevented the old right wing from rallying around Hitler, who was defeated.

The powers of the Weimar president were used at a somewhat irregular rhythm. They were used in the difficult moments when they were necessary. They stayed in the ice-box for the rest of the time. Finland provides the example of another rhythm. Two periods can be clearly seen in the history of the oldest of the semi-presidential regimes, which has been operating for exactly sixty years. From 1919 to 1939, its practice depended above all on the personality of the Heads of State, a weak president regularly following a strong president: Stohlberg (strong) being followed by Relander (weak), who was followed by Svinhufud (strong), succeeded by Kallio (weak). This is to some extent the result of manoeuvring of the political parties during the meetings of the grand electors. After a strong-fisted president, a softer hand was wanted. His incapacity to govern the country then led to an active man, who redressed the balance on the other side. It is probable that things would have followed a different course with a presidential election by direct universal suffrage.

Since 1945, there have been no weak presidents. On the contrary, a constant strengthening of the power of the Head of State can be seen. President Paasikivi played an essential role in foreign policy, which he conducted energetically. In domestic policy, he imposed his will on the government on a very important question: that of the appointment of high officials. All his predecessors had decided some appointments against the advice of the cabinet. Paasikivi did so in a systematic manner. Often it was less a question of promoting his friends, than of restoring the system of promotion by seniority. This also tended to avoid too extensive a weeding out of staff and to maintain the stability of the administration. The ministers finally resigned themselves to this, by proposing candidates likely to please the Head of State in order to avoid differences of opinion appearing within the official proceedings of the Council. The custom did not disappear, however, with the person who had developed it. The appointment of senior officials is now one of the foundations of presidential authority.

Mr Paasikivi stayed in power for ten years, which no president had done previously, his predecessors having carried out only one mandate (six years). His successor, Mr Kekkonen, has been in power since 1956. Only just elected (by a majority of a single vote, with three hundred grand electors) and reelected with difficulty in 1962, he was reelected triumphantly in 1968. In 1974, the Chamber almost unanimously voted for the extension of his powers for four years, in order to save him the fatigue of an election campaign. In 1978, he was triumphantly reelected with the support of nearly all the parties. He has acquired a considerable authority in parliament and in the country. The constitution allows him to participate constantly in the government and in the administration.

Mr Kekkonen uses his presidential prerogatives to urge the parties to build up as large as possible a majority, so that the prime minister and his team have the means to govern. He has a predilection for coalitions of the "green and red" type, which the weakening of the Social-Democrats and of the Agrarian Party forces him to extend to other groups, notably to the Communists. The president wanted to incorporate the latter into normal parliamentary life. This sometimes leads him to break up majorities which he considers insufficient. In May 1975 for example, he cast blame on the Agrarian-Socialist government and forced it to resign by deciding at the same time to dissolve the Chamber. However, the cabinet, disavowed by the Head of State, had escaped *eleven* motions of censure until then. Nonetheless, Mr Kekkonen thought that its majority was too narrow for it to come to grips with the economic crisis.

The elections which followed did not change much in the composi-

176

tion of the Assembly, apart from a slight shift to the right. As the formation of a larger majority was dragging on, the president met the leaders of all the parties together and instructed them to form a "national emergency" government within three days, and gave great publicity to this ultimatum. The time-limit was observed, and a large ministry formed comprising the Agrarian Party, the Social-Democrats, the Communists, the Liberals and the Swedes. It lasted only 293 days, however. For more than seven months it was then necessary to govern with a minority cabinet, resting on a very narrow basis. Eventually, the great coalition desired by the president was set up on 15 May 1977.

The Finnish president is often led to set up minority cabinets, some benefiting from alternating majorities. This is also found in other Scandinavian countries which are parliamentarian. If the situation becomes more difficult, the Head of State forms a government of civil servants and engineers, or a "mixed" cabinet, in which they are combined with politicians, or even trade unionists. These governments enable current business to be dispatched, pending the settling of the situation. They stay in office only as long as the parliament accepts them. They fall when there is a lack of confidence. They undertake transitional duties, until the next elections or the coming of a new majority. The formula is traditional in Finland since Stohlberg used it in 1922 and 1924.

As it has been in operation for less than three years, the semi-presidential form of government in Portugal still enables only a superficial analysis. It shows that the Head of State is neither a figurehead nor all-powerful, but is in the same category as his counterparts in Finland and Weimar. In an early period, president Eanes scarcely exercised the very wide powers conferred on him by the constitution. However, he exercises a discreet, but continuous influence on the conduct of affairs. Portugal first had a minority cabinet set up by Mario Soares, leader of the Socialist party, which represented 35% of the electorate and 40% of the parliamentary seats. To have a wider foundation, Mario Soares and his party then obtained the alliance of the Democratic and Social Centre, a party of the liberal right.

After the defection of the Social and Democratic Centre in July 1978, Mario Soares wanted to stay in power by returning to a minority Socialist government. The president of the Republic refused, dismissed the prime minister and set up a presidential cabinet, not based on any party, which was promptly overthrown by the parliamentary deputies. A second presidential cabinet replaced it, which the parliament agreed not to overturn, in order to avoid dissolution. The Head of State resolved to take such energetic action, because he considered that the

177

previous governments had not taken decisions capable of righting the country's economic situation, which is catastrophic. He wishes to form a majority of the centre, which is difficult to establish.

The Analytical Model of Semi-Presidential Forms of Government

As an analytical model, the purpose of the concept of semi-presidential government is to explain why relatively homogeneous constitutions are applied in radically different ways. It has only four parameters: the actual content of the constitution, the combination of tradition and circumstances, the composition of the parliamentary majority, and the position of the president in relation to this majority. The action of the latter two can be shown in a transformational grid, which suggests the functioning of the regime in all possible situations. In relation to this central mechanism, the first two are somewhat exogenous in character. To some extent they define the environment in which the transformational grid is applicable.

EXOGENOUS PARAMETERS: CONTENT OF THE CONSTITUTION AND TRA-DITION/CIRCUMSTANCES

As constitutions lay down the rules of the game to which the players must adhere, it is clear that their content influences the practical application of the form of government they establish. All the constitutions of the countries concerned outline more or less the same plan for a president elected by universal suffrage, endowed with personal prerogatives, together with a prime minister and ministers, entrusted with the governmental power they can exercise only if parliament leaves them in office. These constitutions are not absolutely identical, however, particularly in the definition of the powers of the president. There are great differences between the Irish constitution, which confers on the Head of State very few personal powers, and the Finnish constitution, which gives him numerous and important prerogatives.

Semi-presidential constitutions fall into three categories. Some give controlling powers only to the Head of State, notably by referring laws to a constitutional Court, use of dissolution and of the referendum, and recourse to Orders in Council in exceptional circumstances; such is the case in Ireland, where some of these prerogatives are found, and in France, where they are all found, exercised sometimes in collaboration with the government. Other constitutions add to the aforementioned powers the right to dismiss the prime minister at the discretion of the president alone. The government can therefore remain in power only if

178

it has the benefit of a two-fold confidence: that of the parliament and that of the Head of State, both being placed on an equal footing. The constitutions of Austria, Weimar Germany and Portugal fall into this category, Austria allowing this supplementary prerogative alone, while the last two provide for others as well.

Finally, the Icelandic and Finnish constitutions make the president a governing, more than a controlling force. He shares in the running of the country, in collaboration with the prime minister and the cabinet. In Iceland, all government decisions must be signed by him, while his own decisions must themselves carry the counter-signature of a minister. In law, both signature and counter-signature can be refused. The president can thus block the government, who can also block him. In Finland, the association of the president and the government is less pronounced, each having his own sphere of responsibility. The Head of State can control the administration, initiate inspections and ask for explanations from departmental heads, without bringing in the ministers. For their part, the latter deal with a large part of government business in Councils held without the presence of the Head of State.

Nevertheless, essential questions are discussed in meetings conducted in the presence of the president of the Republic. He himself takes the majority of his decisions in the Council of Ministers: for example, the initiative in making laws, their implementation by decree, statutory power and the appointment of senior officials. He is not bound by the opinion of the government. He makes decisions on his own. However, his wishes can be carried out only with a ministerial counter-signature, which is also necessary for the conduct of international affairs. The counter-signature, however, can be refused only on grounds of illegality; this limits its scope a good deal and gives great autonomy to the president. Furthermore, he can impose his own point of view, for example by substituting his own draft law for one put forward by the government. The ministers then take responsibility for the presidential decision unless they resign or express a contrary opinion, which is recorded in the official proceedings.

A scale of semi-presidential regimes can be drawn up according to the powers which the constitution confers on the president. The preroga-tives of the Head of State are depicted in the first column of Fig. 1, in descending order from Finland to Ireland; the irregular spaces give a (very approximate) idea of the magnitude of the differences. Juxta-posed (in the second column of Fig. 1) is a scale of the powers in fact exercised in the countries concerned. Comparison of the two is reveal-ing.

It shows two aberrant cases, those of France and Iceland. The French

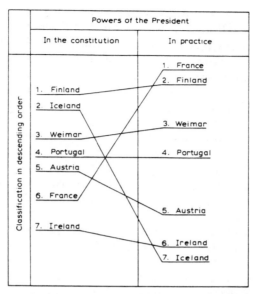

Fig. 1. The powers of the president in semi-presidential regimes.

president exercises in practice much stronger powers than his counterparts, although very few are granted him by the constitution, since he appears sixth in order, or the penultimate, in this respect. In contrast, the Icelandic president appears second with regard to legal powers, just behind his Finnish colleague, but comes last with regard to prerogatives actually exercised, just after, or on the same level as his Irish colleague [1]. Apart from these aberrant cases, the other countries are classified in the same order on the two scales, but not on the same level, except for Portugal since the initiatives undertaken by President Eanes in 1978. In Finland and in the Weimar Republic, practice goes a little beyond the constitutional rules. In Austria and in Ireland, it falls behind.

Although the constitution plays a certain part in the application of presidential powers, this role remains secondary compared to that of the other parameters; the cases of France and Iceland show this in an undeniable way. In both cases, the constitutions are not violated, despite the fairly great differences which separate what is written in the constitutions and actual practices. When practice does not go as far as what is written, this means the president is not exercising the powers which the constitution confers on him. As he has the right to make use

180

of his prerogatives or not, he remains within the framework of the law if he lets them fall into abeyance. When practice goes beyond what is written, this means that the government agrees in fact to submit to the presidential injunctions which it could legally disregard, being able to make free use or otherwise of its own powers, just like the president. Of course, if the Head of State or the prime minister do not exercise all their prerogatives, it is because they find it to their advantage not to do so, in view of the political situation and power relationships.

This leads to discussion of the second parameter, formed by the combination of tradition and circumstances, which are indissolubly linked to each other. In law, the practices of a regime do not really create statute law, unless a general consensus is established in this respect through the course of history. In *Coup d'Etat at Westminster,* two British authors have imagined that a modern English sovereign decided one day to use the immense power granted the crown by the old texts, which have never been repealed, and the antiquated formulae still in use. Thus there would be a restoration of absolute monarchy, which has not been specifically abolished. This fine story of political science-fiction is similar to those which describe the return of the dinosaurs. The rules of the British crown have become fossilised. Their flesh is dead with the world which surrounded them. No-one can bring them to life again. Legal rules which are unapplied, are not dead. They hibernate, and the person who has the necessary skill, can always bring them to life again.

The practices of a regime, however, create a factual tradition, which makes it increasingly difficult to restore dormant legal rules as the years pass by. In 1976, President O'Dalaigh could be forced to resign, because the Irish people had become accustomed to a figurehead, to a Head of State, who did not make use of his constitutional powers. However, he would probably have been able to use his prerogatives with less ill-effect, if he had been more skillful. In Austria, an opinion poll organised by the Populist Party in 1971 showed that the majority of citizens thought that the president had only symbolic representative powers, and that this position was analogous to the German rather than to the French president. When informed of the provisions of the constitution, the majority of those who had been asked replied that the Head of State should act in a discreet and reserved manner, rather than exercise his prerogatives. They declared their satisfaction at his not involving himself in day-to-day politics. Nevertheless, the president is a kind of "reserve controller". The situation is approximately the same in Iceland.

In France, the tradition established by General de Gaulle and his successors has given a contrary picture of the president. The citizens have become more or less accustomed to the idea that he is the real head of the government, who controls policy and reduces the prime minister and his team to a subordinate position. This conception has however always been rejected by the opposition, who have kept the idea that the Head of State must be confined to the (rather strict) framework of his constitutional powers. As this opposition represents about half of the French people, one cannot talk of a "consensus" on presidential powers. Various opinion polls thus show that the presidential image of the Fifth Republic is superimposed on another, formed over thee-quarters of a century during the Third and Fourth Republics. The active head of the new regime, the supreme head of the government and of the majority, who embodies their aims and controls their policies, has not disposed of the easy-going president of the old regime, freed of the contingencies of power, an impotent but impartial arbiter, a decoration at official ceremonies and the symbol of the whole nation. This superimposition could help the regime adapt itself were there to be a realignment of political forces.

Circumstances interfere with tradition. After twenty years of an all-powerful presidency, the majority of French politicians agreed at the beginning of 1978 that the Head of State should resign himself to using only his constitutional powers, if the elections should give victory to the left. By declaring both that he would remain in office and that he could not hinder the implementation of the Common Programme, Mr Giscard d'Estaing confirmed the analyses of the opposition. In October 1978, Mr Michel Debré, the father of the constitution, and Mr François Mitterrand also agreed on this. Legal experts had more difficulty in accepting that a regime could change as radically within the same legal framework.

In the Weimar Republic, the use of the powers of the Head of State in 1919–1926 and 1930–1932, and their dormant status in the interim, correspond to the difference in circumstances: the crises at the beginning and the end encompass a calm and prosperous period, when the parliamentary game did not need presidential correctives. The concept of a "reserve controller" gives a good illustration of the significance of the form of government, devised to counter the difficulties of parliamentarianism, by establishing a point of fixed reference, formed by the Head of State, who is elected by universal suffrage. That he makes use of his prerogatives only on exceptional occasions is in conformity with their actual nature. It is impossible to speak of an unambiguous tradition in an essentially ambiguous form of government, which circumstances can always drive in a different direction from that

182

followed hitherto. Is the parliamentary form of government which operates in radically opposed ways when there is a clear and disciplined majority and when there is none so very different?

ENDOGENOUS PARAMETERS AND THE TRANSFORMATIONAL GRID

Reference will now be made to the tables showing the diversity of presidential practices, compared with the provisions of the constitution. They can be brought together in a comparative analysis of the situation of the parliamentary majorities in the seven countries under consideration. Some quite clear cross-checks then appear, which can be summarised in a few simple formulae. In the countries without a parliamentary majority, there is the greatest coincidence between the constitution and practice, the latter putting the president in an intermediary position, neither figurehead, nor all-powerful. In the countries where coherent and stable majorities are normally found, there is a disparity between the constitution and practice, the latter placing the president either in a dominant position, or in the situation of a parliamentary Head of State, reduced to symbolic status.

Weimar Germany, Finland and Portugal correspond to the first hypothesis. Between 1919 and 1933 in Berlin, and since 1919 in Helsinki, a coherent and stable majority has never been formed. As a result, the governments are normally ephemeral and divided, in other words, weak. The parliament has a formidable blocking power. It cannot make decisions, in the absence of a majority, but it can prevent the executive from making decisions. It cannot promote and uphold strong governments, but it can make them fall. The president does not have the means to act all the time in place of the government. He can give impetus, exercise controls, remedy deficiencies, but not govern himself, except in quite exceptional circumstances. In law, this dyarchy is somewhat similar to that of the blind man and the lame.

Nevertheless, the Head of State possesses a considerable superiority over governments which stem from parliament. He is on his own, and he has durable power. If essential and urgent decisions must be taken and the cabinet, paralysed by the division of the parties which support it, cannot take them, the citizens naturally turn to the president. In Finland, the system clung onto this fixed point after 1944, when the country had to give pledges of hard work, efficiency and of continuing fidelity to its powerful neighbour, of which it formed the natural protective front. Two skilful and strong personalities gradually developed the authority of the Head of State, without rescinding the prerogatives of the government. The Weimar Republic did not have time to reach this equilibrium, while Finland reached it only after twenty-five years, after having first known the alternation of strong and weak presidents. However, if the development of presidential power strengthened the Finnish executive, it could not give stable governments to the country. In sixty years, sixty cabinets have succeeded each other.

Portugal represents a transitional situation. There are fewer parties than in Weimar Germany and Finland, and one of them is in a quasi-dominant position: the Socialist Party, which won 35% of the votes and 40% of the seats in 1976. Three other groups are represented: the Popular Democrat Party (then called "Social Democrat"), which won 24% of the votes and 27.7% of the seats; the Democratic and Social Centre, with 16% of the votes and seats; the Communist Party, with 14.4% of the the votes and 15% of the seats. As the Socialists were divided, they have not been able so far to ally themselves either with the Communists, who are rather Stalinist, or with one of the parties more to the right (as shown by the unfortunate attempt at a Socialist–Democratic and Social Centre majority). A Centrist alliance (which the President of the Republic is endeavouring to promote) seems likely in the long run. In the meantime, circumstances are forcing the President to make use of his powers.

In France, Austria, Ireland and Iceland, there are stable majorities. In Paris, the alliance of the Gaullists, the traditional right and the centrists has regularly won more than half of the seats in the National Assembly since 1962. This majority has adopted voting discipline in votes of confidence, and has gradually given rise to two major parties: the U.D.F. and the R.P.R. In Austria, the majority has belonged to one party since 1966, apart from the brief session of 1970–1971, which separated the Populist majority of 1966–1970 and the Socialist majority, in power since 1971 and recently renewed in May 1979. Previously, neither of the two major parties could govern on its own, the small Liberal group holding the balance. The two major parties governed jointly, however, which gave remarkable stability.

In Ireland, the Fianna Fail have won an absolute majority in five legislatures out of ten, since independence. The alliance of the Fine Gaël and of the Labour Party obtained it once. In the four others, the parliament did not have a majority, although one of the contesting parties or both of them, had come near to doing so; but apart from them there were sufficient independent members or small groups to provide support in such circumstances. The average duration of Irish governments is three and a half years, which shows a quite remarkable stability.

184

Iceland is in a rather different situation, which comes nearer to an absence of majority. No party has ever won more than half of the seats, although one party generally obtains nearly 40% of them. Under the name of the Independence Party, it combines conservatives and moderate liberals who do not feel reluctant to ally themselves with each of the three other major parties, including the Communists. This "quasi-majority" situation guarantees a cohesion and stability of the government equivalent to that of a true majority. Twelve ministers have succeeded each other in Reykjavik in the thirty-three years which followed the advent of the republic (1944–1977), or an average duration of two years and nine months, close to that of the ten legislatures, which lasted three years and four months. During this time, the Independence Party shared power for twenty-six years, thanks to its preponderant position.

In the four countries with a majority or a quasi-majority already described, the presidents have in common a practice far removed from constitutional rules. This distancing, however, is done in opposing directions. In France, a very powerful president plays a much more important role than that provided for by the written constitution. In Austria, Ireland and Iceland, figurehead presidents play a far smaller role than that allowed by their constitutional prerogatives. The difference depends on the position of the Head of State in relation to the parliamentary majority. If he is at the head of it, he becomes all-powerful, like the French presidents. If he is a member of it, without being its head, he becomes a figurehead like the present Austrian president or the majority of the Irish presidents. If he is outside the majority, whether as an opponent or as a neutral figure, he is in a regulatory position, and his actual powers then correspond to the outline of the constitution.

The explanation of these phenomena seems relatively simple. In a parliament with a clear and disciplined majority, the head of the latter governs at the same time the Executive and the Legislature. If the president is in this position, he can thus reduce the prime minister to the position of a chief of staff. This is the case in France, where the majority is originally formed around the Head of State, and where the presidential candidates have been the party leaders. If the president is not the head of the majority party, while belonging to it or coming under it, this means that the party has decided to give its leader the office of prime minister, to whom the real power then belongs. Together with the government, he controls parliament, as leader of the majority party. He thus reduces the Head of State to a subordinate position. This has been the case in Austria since 1971 and in Ireland for most of the time, the parties taking care, in these two countries, to nominate as candidates for the presidency only those holding a subsidiary position, and not their leader.

The third situation would have been represented in France if the left had won the elections of March 1978. Then, a president opposed to the majority would have been reduced to his constitutional powers, which would give him a regulatory role. This was the case in Austria in 1966–1970, when President Jonas was very discreet, in conformity with the national tradition, but nevertheless imposed the appointment of a president of the Supreme Court against the initial will of the government. With this can be compared the constitutional crisis of 1976 in Ireland, when an analogous tradition impeded presidential control. In Iceland, the presidents have also been neutralised by the cultural context, aggravated in the circumstances by renewal of tenure without competition, which reduces them to a symbolic role. They do not therefore exercise their regulating function. However, it could perhaps be exercised in very exceptional circumstances.

All the assumptions about the effect of the make-up of the majorities and the position of the presidents in relation to them can be summarised in a relatively precise "transformational grid", reproduced in Fig. 2. It is not possible to develop here the precise explanation given in connection to it in *Echec au Roi* (Check to the King), pages 120–136. It may simply be noted that box 17 corresponds to the situation in the Weimar Republic, Finland and present-day Portugal (although the latter is almost in box 16, because it is close to a "quasi-majority" of the Icelandic type). Box 9 corresponds to the situation of the Austrian president since 1970 and of the majority of the Irish presidents. Box 5 corresponds to the position of President Jonas in 1966–1970 and box 6 to that of President O'Dalaigh in 1976 (although the latter is also pushed towards box 14, since he has been chosen by agreement of all the parties).

Boxes 6 or 7 would have corresponded to the position of president Giscard d'Estaing had there been a victory of the left in the 1978 legislative elections. Boxes 1, 2 and 3 correspond to the actual situation of French presidents. A more detailed analysis would be necessary in this respect to define the three boxes with greater accuracy; this is now in progress. In particular, relations between Mr Giscard d'Estaing and the R.P.R. since 1978 will have to be studied very closely. Numerically, one is faced with a "balanced coalition". In practice, a lot of Chiracians lean towards the President of the Republic, on whom their re-election or their future depends.

186

Relations Between the President and the Majority		President			
		Leader of the majority	In opposition	Member of the majority	Neutral
True majority	Monolithic	Absolute monarch (1)	Controller (5)	Symbol (9)	Controller (13)
	Coalition with a dominant party	Limited monarch (2)	Controller (6)	Symbol (10)	Controller (14)
	Balanced coalition	Dyarch (3)	Controller (7)	Symbol (11)	Controller (15)
Quasi-majority		Limited monarch (4)	Controller (8)	Symbol (12)	Controller (16)
Absence of majority		⊠	⊠	⊠	Dyarch (17)
⊠ Situation logically impossible					

Fig. 2. The transformational grid.

Conclusion

In a brilliant article, titled "Synthesis or paralysis," our distinguished colleague Georges Vedel wrote that "semi-presidential government, if it could exist in France, would in fact be not a *synthesis* of the parliamentary and presidential systems, but an *alternation* between presidential and parliamentary phases, which is quite another thing" [2]. Who talks of a synthesis between concepts which are only analytical models, arbitrarily constructed by observers? Those who drew up the constitution at Philadelphia did not think of creating a presidential government, nor did all the Englishmen who, brick by brick, built up parliamentary government in London over the centuries know they were creating it — no more than General de Gaulle thought of setting up a semi-presidential regime in France.

The problem is to know whether the concept of semi-presidential government, as it is described, allows us to understand the different ways similar constitutions are applied across the seven countries in which they obtain, and the possible "alternations" in any given country of which Georges Vedel speaks — to understand and predict them. The

187

rest does not matter, even though the research methods used may not be in fashion. In the early sixties, by improving the models put forward in 1951 in *Les Partis Politiques* (Political Parties), it was predicted that France would evolve towards bipolarisation. This intellectual talk was greeted with irony, until the facts confirmed the prediction. In political science, this is rare enough for one not to refrain from emphasising it.

It is not claimed that the model of semi-presidential government operates in just the same way. The evolution of the whole of a political system is much more difficult to comprehend than that of coalitions of parties under the influence of electoral machinery. French citizens have not provided the means of verifying the predictions formulated in *Echec au Roi* (Check to the King) about the evolution of national institutions in the event of a victory of the left in March 1978. The reading of this book was certainly not the sole factor which drove the president of the Portuguese republic to apply the 1975 constitution in the way indicated by the transformational grid already described. For the moment, the proposed model has the merit of explaining fairly well the differences in practical application of an identical constitutional mechanism; neither more, nor less.

Notes

1 In *Echec au Roi* (Check to the King), Ireland appears seventh with regard to powers actually exercised and Iceland sixth. Research done since then results in their order being reversed, or in the two countries being considered as on an equal par.
2 *Le Monde*, 19–20 February 1978.

References

Duverger, M. (1951). *Les Partis Politiques*. Paris: Armand Colin.
Duverger, M. (1978). *Echec au Roi*. Paris: Albin Michel.

[9]

France: The Limits to Prime-ministerial Government in a Semi-presidential System

Robert Elgie and Howard Machin

> I am not the government. Sometimes people confuse me with it, I
> don't know why, but I am not the government. I have it in my power
> to bring certain matters to the attention of the government and if need
> be to give it advice. (François Mitterrand, President of the Republic)[1]

Analysis of the role and influence of the French prime minister since
1958 must start from a paradox: the text of the Constitution indicates
that the prime minister should play the key leadership role as head of
the government, but in practice, for all but the period of 'cohabitation'
between 1986 and 1988, effective direction of the government has been
assumed by the head of state, the President of the Republic. The extent of
presidential leadership may have varied over time as presidents and prime
ministers changed. It may have been exaggerated both by the media and by
the parties in opposition. None the less, it was only during 'cohabitation'
when Chirac, at the head of a Gaullist–Liberal coalition majority in the
Assembly, became prime minister under the incumbent Socialist president,
Mitterrand, that top office-holders in French politics appeared to respect
the Constitution. Our first task is to examine the constitutional position of
the prime minister and the media images of presidents and prime ministers
since 1958.

Our second task is to assess the resources at the disposal of the prime
minister, the president and ministers. This analysis reveals the contrast
between the considerable administrative and institutional resources of
the prime minister (and the relative weakness of the president), and the
enormous political resources of the president as a party and majority
coalition leader. It shows how prime-ministerial resources may be 'borrowed' by the Elysée (the president's residence and office) and how
ministers may wield considerable autonomy either by the institutional
weight of their ministries, their status as leaders of party factions or
coalition parties, or their close personal links with the president.

The third and fourth sections consider two explanations of the variations
in prime-ministerial power, namely personality and differences between
distinct policy areas. Both offer partial explanations and useful insights.
Both lead to the final section which places the trends of the last decade
into the context of longer-term developments in French politics.

CONSTITUTION THEORY AND PRESIDENTIAL PRACTICE

Many of the key clauses of the 1958 Constitution seem unambiguously to
provide for a system of prime-ministerial government. According to Article

20, the government decides and directs the policies of the nation and has at its disposal the administration and the armed forces, while Article 21 stipulates that the prime minister is in charge of the government's actions and is responsible for national defence. The prime minister, therefore, is placed at the head of a government charged with policy-making in the country. Nowhere in the Constitution is there to be found any mention of presidential responsibility for government policy in normal times. The sole exception may be in times of national crisis when, according to Article 16, the president may assume emergency powers for himself and take over the running of the country for a limited period and subject to strict limits.

The prime minister, however, has a range of other prerogatives which serve to back up his basic powers as defined in Articles 20 and 21. Under Article 8, he proposes to the president the names of those he wishes to become government ministers, and the president then officially appoints them. He issues decrees in those areas in which Parliament is not competent to legislate (under Article 21) – a not insignificant power given the restrictions on Parliament. He may call upon the Constitutional Council to determine the constitutionality of a law or treaty (under Article 61). At the same time his counter-signature is necessary for the promulgation of certain presidential acts, such as the nomination of ambassadors. The prime minister must be consulted by the president before a dissolution of the National Assembly (under Article 12) and before the president invokes emergency powers (under Article 16), although he has no power of veto. Finally, the prime minister may propose a constitutional reform (under Article 89), but his proposals would be accepted only if voted by Parliament or approved by a referendum.

Furthermore, the position of the prime minister is strengthened because of the powers of the government in relation to Parliament. In contrast to the parliamentary regime of the Fourth Republic, the prime minister in the Fifth Republic faces a weakened Parliament over which he has almost complete control, as long as he has an effective majority. For example, the areas in which Parliament may legislate are limited by Article 34, while in all other areas the prime minister issues decrees. Moreover, even in the areas in which Parliament is competent to legislate, the government has an impressive range of powers. It sets the legislative agenda (under Article 48); amendments from deputies are declared *ultra vires* if they would result in a reduction of government revenue or an increase in spending (under Article 40); it may ask Parliament to let it issue decrees by ordinance, thus avoiding parliamentary procedure altogether (under Article 38); it can declare a bill is urgent and speed up its passage (under Article 45); and if he deems it to be necessary the prime minister may demand the calling of an extraordinary session of Parliament (under Article 29).

In addition Article 49, clause 3, is used by governments to pass legislation when there is any risk of a defeat in Parliament. Here, the prime minister 'engages the responsibility of the government' on a particular text, and the bill is considered to be passed unless a censure motion is submitted and passed by an absolute majority of the National Assembly. Finally, Fifth Republic governments are much less likely to be brought down than their Fourth Republic counterparts. In part, this stability is because of Article 49, clause 2, whereby once a tenth of National Assembly deputies sign a censure motion (something they can do only once a session), such a motion is only voted upon 48 hours after its presentation, so as to allow tempers to cool. Furthermore, for the motion to be successful it has to gain an absolute majority of the full membership of the Assembly, which means that abstentions are counted as votes for the government.

By virtue of his own powers and of the powers of the government over Parliament, therefore, the prime minister's constitutional position is clear in the Fifth Republic: France should be an example of prime-ministerial government. The 1958 Constitution did, however, include certain provisions which, in favourable conditions, could allow an imaginative and ambitious incumbent of the presidency to usurp prime-ministerial leadership of the government without abuse of the letter of the law. As in the Third Republic (1870 to 1940) the president is empowered both to appoint the prime minister (by Article 8) and to dissolve the Assembly (by Article 12) before the end of its official five-year term (but not twice in any twelve-month period), and no ministerial countersignature is needed for the exercise of these powers. Furthermore, the Constitution provides some legitimation, albeit vague, for presidential leadership of governments; he is commander-in-chief of the armed forces; he is authorised to negotiate and ratify foreign treaties (under Article 52); and, under Article 5, must ensure respect for the Constitution by his 'arbitration' to provide for the regular functioning of public authorities. Article 5 has been the subject of much imaginative interpretation by lawyers of Gaullist sympathies who saw it as their brightest hope of a constitutional justification for presidential government. Moreover, since the constitutional amendment of 1962, the president has been elected by direct universal suffrage, which means that he can claim a mandate from the people – a legitimacy equal to that of the majority in the Assembly.

In practice, while the letter of the Constitution has usually (but not always) been respected, the spirit has not. When General de Gaulle decided to stand for the presidency in 1958 (rather than remain as prime minister) the die was cast: the Constitution was to be interpreted in a generously presidential way. Once easily elected, de Gaulle chose Debré as his first prime minister, which left few in France with any illusions that the prime minister was to be the effective leader of the government. It was instantly clear that, as president, de Gaulle would continue to make policy decisions in those areas he had chosen when agreeing to become the last prime minister of the Fourth Republic: Algeria, foreign policy, defence and institutional reform. Although Debré was a clever and dynamic leader, he was above all de Gaulle's man and a loyal Gaullist. As prime minister he was placed at the head of a government and a majority coalition which had come into existence at the behest of de Gaulle. As a loyal Gaullist he never attempted to usurp de Gaulle's leadership or to refuse to defer to the General's judgements.

FRANCE: A SEMI-PRESIDENTIAL SYSTEM   65

TABLE 1

PRESIDENTS, PRIME MINISTERS AND PARTIES SINCE 1958

President	Prime minister	PM's Party	Lead coalition party
1959 de Gaulle	Debré	Gaullist	Gaullist
1962 de Gaulle	Pompidou	Gaullist	Gaullist
1968 de Gaulle	Couve de Murville	Gaullist	Gaullist
1969 Pompidou	Chaban-Delmas	Gaullist	Gaullist
1972 Pompidou	Messmer	Gaullist	Gaullist
1974 Giscard d'Estaing	Chirac	Gaullist	Gaullist
1976 Giscard d'Estaing	Barre	Giscardian	Gaullist
1981 Mitterrand	Mauroy	Socialist	Socialist
1984 Mitterrand	Fabius	Socialist	Socialist
1986 Mitterrand	Chirac	Gaullist	Gaullist
1988 Mitterrand	Rocard	Socialist	Socialist

When Pompidou replaced Debré in April 1962 the media image of the prime minister was at a low point and subsequently the prestige of the office grew as its incumbent proved a talented debater, an effective party and coalition builder, an election winner and a policy-maker. De Gaulle remained in command but in domestic politics France had some appearance of prime-ministerial government. Pompidou's departure in July 1968 and replacement by the worthy but colourless Couve de Murville led to a sharp decline of prime-ministerial prestige. His brief period of office was marked by the referendum defeat of April 1969 and de Gaulle's immediate resignation.[2]

Pompidou was elected to the presidency and chose Chaban-Delmas as prime minister. Well-liked and dynamic, Chaban-Delmas at first appeared to have assumed Pompidou's erstwhile role as domestic policy leader, while in his new office Pompidou devoted himself to foreign affairs. Within two years, however, the president was assuming effective policy leadership in any area he wished. The prime minister's influence seemed increasingly limited even before he was ousted in July 1973 on the initiative of the president's advisers, Juillet and Garaud. As prime minister for a year Messmer made as much public impact as Couve de Murville in 1968.[3]

Pompidou's death, however, led to Giscard d'Estaing's election to the Elysée and he chose Chirac, then a rising and ambitious star from the Gaullist Party. Two years later, however, Chirac resigned in disgust at being treated as a presidential acolyte. By his own admission he had been unable to play an effective leadership role.[4] His replacement, Barre, fared rather better and established himself as an economic authority at a time when the president was becoming increasingly involved in international statesmanship and monarchical trappings. Mitterrand's three Socialist prime ministers – Mauroy, Fabius and Rocard – have all been seen as presidential choices rather than party or coalition leaders, although Mauroy got on well with both the Socialist Party and its Communist allies and Rocard is well respected by the centrist allies.[5] Only Chirac, however, between 1986 and 1988 clearly established a reputation as the effective leader of the government.

In some ways these images of weak prime ministers and strong presidents are exaggerated. The media and the public know more of the presidents simply because they survive longer in office and in the public eye. The president is in office normally for at least the full seven-year term, although de Gaulle stayed for ten and Mitterrand looks set for a full second term. The prime minister's expectancy of tenure is shorter: Pompidou lasted seven years and Barre achieved only five. Couve de Murville, however, lasted less than a year, Messmer and Fabius remained in office less than two years and Debré and Mauroy, only three years.

The president gains great public prestige by his activities as head of state. De Gaulle established the tradition of visiting every part of France at least once during each term of office, and subsequent presidents have respected the precedent. Such occasions are inevitably covered by the media. So too are the great national occasions – the 14 July Parade, the official opening of new national monuments (frequent under Mitterrand), or new technological triumphs (the nuclear bomb or the high-speed train).

The foreign policy role of the president facilitates the build-up of his image as the key policy-maker. His foreign visits, his major speeches and press conferences on foreign policy inevitably gain wide media coverage. When he speaks on foreign policy he is the 'voice of France', which makes criticism of his positions (by opposition leaders or coalition rivals) difficult for those who do not wish to appear disloyal, if not treasonable.

In contrast, while the prime minister may get wide media coverage for his domestic activities, he may also face much tougher questioning and criticism. Unlike the president, he has to defend his government's policies in parliamentary debates and must reply to parliamentary questions. If the prime minister speaks on television opposition leaders may demand (and sometimes obtain) a right of reply. In contrast, the presidency is often presented, especially by its incumbent, as being over and above politics. The attempt by one prime minister to adopt a similar posture (Fabius, in a televised debate with Chirac in 1985) seemed ridiculous. The prime minister is the leader of a partisan coalition; he is expected to act as such and to take partisan attacks from his opponents. Furthermore, the issues of domestic politics (economic and social policies, law and order, taxes) on which the prime minister makes policy pronouncements are often more divisive – and hence vulnerable – than the foreign-policy issues dealt with by the president.

The foreign-language press and television have a strong tendency to focus on the president rather than the prime minister. They are generally much more interested in French foreign policy than in domestic matters. Foreign journalists and their readers become familiar only with political leaders who occupy high office for long periods. Inevitably the image created and conveyed by the media outside France is that the presidency dominates the entire French political scene.

Neither the constitutional position of the prime minister nor the media image of the president provides an accurate guide to the effective role and influence of the prime minister. They vary with the personalities of the incumbents and the policy sectors involved but always depend on the power resources available to the prime minister and his rivals.

INSTITUTIONAL AND POLITICAL RESOURCES OF THE PRIME MINISTER AND HIS RIVALS

From a cursory examination of administrative law text-books it would appear that the resources at the disposal of the prime minister in official administrative institutions provide him with significant sources of power. In contrast, his rivals for governmental influence, the president and ministers, seem institutionally weak. Appearances, however, may be deceptive: prime-ministerial resources may be effectively commandeered by others while remaining officially under his authority; and in practice political resources are often far more powerful than administrative ones.

In law the prime minister seems to command vast resources whilst the presidency appears relatively under-resourced. One major prime-ministerial resource is organisational: the power to shape the government he leads by fixing the limits of ministerial competences. Statistics indicate that this power has been used generously as the number of ministers and the structures of ministries have varied considerably since 1958. Normally there have been about 50 ministers and 15–20 ministries, but only the ministries of Foreign Affairs, Interior, Justice, Defence, Agriculture, Posts and War Veterans have remained more or less constant in titles and responsibilities since 1958. In 1990 the government included the prime minister, four *ministres d'Etat* (the most senior ministerial rank), 16 ministers, ten *ministres délégués* (assistant ministers but with designated areas of competence) and 17 *secrétaires d'Etat* (the lowest form of ministerial life).

Two major purposes for changing the division of functions between ministries have been to prioritise policy areas (hence there was a ministry for Algerian Affairs until 1962 and a ministry for National Solidarity in 1981) and to adopt the current 'best practice' for efficient organisation (hence the creation of 'superministries' such as Infrastructure in the late 1960s, the splitting up of such ministries in the late 1970s and the sub-division into semi-autonomous agencies in the 1980s). A third objective, however, has been to enhance prime-ministerial influence, and the various re-organisations of responsibilities for financial and economic policy-making appear to illustrate the importance of that goal. The most drastic solution was that of Barre in 1976; he kept for himself the entire Finance ministry, but with a senior Gaullist politician as his *ministre délégué*. After the 1978 elections Barre opted for an alternative strategy, that of 'divide and rule': he split the Finance ministry in two, creating a ministry of the Economy and a Budget ministry. Mauroy in 1981 had a similar but more complex division; he reunited the Finance ministry (under Delors) but appointed a *ministre délégué* (Fabius) with specific responsibility for the budget, and he also set up a Planning ministry (under Rocard) and increased the economic responsibilities of the Foreign Trade and Industry ministries. With policy conflicts thereby institutionalised, prime-ministerial co-ordination and arbitration became essential.

A second major institutional resource is operational: that of direct control of a collection of governmental services. Although there is no 'prime minister's department', the prime minister, from his official residence at the Hotel Matignon, heads a vast array of administrative structures which provide both central and common services to the whole of the government. The key administrative service under his authority is the General Secretariat of the Government, the body responsible for organising, administering, co-ordinating and recording the decision-making work of the government. Its tasks include preparing the agenda for the weekly meetings of the Council of Ministers each Wednesday morning, taking the minutes of those meetings and 'servicing' the main committees of the government.[6] Two other 'core' General Secretariats are also under the responsibility of the prime minister, those of National Defence (the SGDN) and of the Interministerial Committee on European Economic Cooperation (the SGCI). As their titles suggest, both these bodies have important tasks of co-ordination and supervision in crucial policy areas. Other core services include all the official information services; hence both official publications and internal administrative documents are supplied and supervised by the prime minister's agents.

Other core services under the direct responsibility of the prime minister have varied according to the tastes and interests of the different incumbents. In 1988, Rocard, like some but not all his predecessors, included economic planning among his own prime-ministerial responsibilities. Hence, at least in theory, the premier has direct authority over the Planning Commissariat and its consultative committees and can thereby influence the future agenda-setting for governmental action by including items in the medium-term 'Plans'. For similar reasons some of Rocard's predecessors kept direct control over the personnel and training administrations of the civil service, including the prestigious National Administration School (ENA).

The prime minister may appoint several junior ministers to his office to assist running the various different services (Rocard had four junior ministers in 1990). He has the right to establish as large a personal staff (or *cabinet*) as he wishes. The political and policy advisers who form this staff are chosen for their competence and personal loyalty, and their work involves following the work of all ministers and interministerial committees, to facilitate the prime minister's work of co-ordination and arbitration as well as providing political and policy advice. Through the work of his staff as well as through his position in the chair of many interministerial committees (notably those which arbitrate on budget disputes), the prime minister has the means to know and influence most areas of governmental policy-making.

In contrast, the administrative resources of the presidency are relatively weak. The president has no executive office at his disposal at the Elysée Palace and in theory he has no direct dealings with ministries and state agencies, since they are constitutionally responsible to the prime minister and ministers. He has only a relatively small personal staff

FRANCE: A SEMI-PRESIDENTIAL SYSTEM   69

TABLE 2
PRIME-MINISTERIAL SERVICES IN JANUARY 1990

Cabinet (personal staff)

Core central services:

1. General Secretariat of the Government
   - Administrative and Financial Services Division
   - *La Documentation Française* Division
   - *Le Journal Officiel* Division
   - Information Services
   - National Centre for the Computerisation of Legal Texts
2. General Secretariat of National Defence (SGDN)
   - 4 Divisions + 1 Task Force
   - Interministerial Delegation for the Security of Information Systems
   - Institute for Higher Defence Studies
   - Interministerial Committee for Nuclear Security
3. Secretariat General of the Interministerial Committee on European Economic Cooperation (SGCI)
4. Legal and Technical Service on Information (press, radio and television)

Common services:

1. 'The Social Economy' (Co-operatives and mutuals): *Secrétaire d'Etat*:
2. Humanitarian Actions: *Secrétaire d'Etat*:
3. The Environment: *Secrétaire d'Etat*:
   - 4 Divisions + 1 Delegation
4. Economic Planning: *Secrétaire d'Etat*:
   - General Planning Commissariat + 4 research centres
5. Various: a. Atomic Energy Commissariat
   - b. Delegation for towns and urban development
   - c. Delegation for the 1992 Winter Olympic Games
   - d. Delegation on Air Space
   - e. Delegation on the French Language
   - f. Financial Controller

(normally 30–45 in number) most of whom are formally employed in the General Secretariat of the Presidency. Under the supervision of the secretary general, presidential advisers are given specific fields and ministries to cover. Their daunting task is to provide the president with ideas, information and evaluations about all aspects of governmental action and to that end they must keep in close but discreet contact with senior civil servants and even attend interministerial committees if the president is absent. The limited resources of the presidency are also stretched by the president's many duties as head of state: public ceremonies in France and state visits abroad occupy a considerable proportion of presidential time and energies.

The prime minister's resources are relatively great compared with those of his ministers. Each minister's sphere of influence is determined by prime-ministerial dictat. Obviously each minister has a huge bureaucracy at his disposal as well as a small group of personal advisers, but the ministries and ministerial *cabinets* are primarily concerned with policy implementation and management of the field services. Most ministerial perspectives are inevitably highly focused and sectoral. Only the Finance minister shares with the prime minister an overview of all public spending, and thereby of all governmental activity, but several prime ministers have dealt with this possible challenge by a variety of institutional devices.

Furthermore, the prime minister alone is the constitutional representative of the government in dealings with Parliament. He is the only member of the government to share with deputies and senators the right to initiate laws (under Article 39) and only he can declare any bill as a test of confidence (under Article 49 clause 3). In theory, therefore, the prime minister should have the institutional resources by which to dominate governmental decision-making.

The prime minister, however, faces a problem that is not rare in politics: ownership of resources does not always coincide with control. Whether or not he effectively controls these administrative and institutional resources depends on whether or not he owns and controls the key *political* resource – a majority in the Assembly. Only one prime minister since 1958, Chirac between 1986 and 1988, has had his own non-presidential Assembly majority and he alone fully disposed of all his administrative and institutional resources. One of Chirac's first acts was to replace the incumbent general secretary of the government with his own man, thereby announcing to the world that, if hitherto the administration of the government had been answerable to the president, henceforth it was to be accountable only to the prime minister. The president might continue to chair the weekly meetings of the government, as the Constitution stipulated, but those meetings became formal ratifying sessions as decisions were made at Matignon with the prime minister in the chair.

Why was Chirac the exception rather than the rule in leading his own majority against the president, and why did not even Chirac attempt to take full control in those areas where the president could make some vague constitutional claim to influence policy (notably in foreign policy and defence matters)? The answer is largely to be found in the institutional dynamics of the system created in 1958 and 1962.[7]

In 1958 de Gaulle had chosen to resolve the Algerian crisis from the presidency, and until that war was over a majority of those in the Assembly was willing both to allow him to choose whomever he liked as prime minister and to refrain from voting censure motions on the prime minister and government of the president's choice. The members of that first 'presidential majority' may not have accepted its discipline except under the constraint of a threat of military coup or civil war, but the discipline was effective as long as the Algerian crisis lasted.

In 1962, when the war ended, de Gaulle was determined to maintain stable, effective, presidentialised government rather than return to the ever-recurring ministerial and coalition crises of the Third and Fourth Republics. He deliberately chose a new prime minister, Pompidou, from outside Parliament and then precipitated a crisis by proposing to reform the Constitution by referendum so that henceforth the president would be elected by universal suffrage. The referendum was a challenge to parliamentary authority and it forced the deputies to react, to identify themselves as either for or against the president. A majority was against him and voted a motion of censure on Pompidou's government. De Gaulle then used his constitutional power to dissolve the Assembly and offered the electorate a double opportunity to keep him as president and to perpetuate stable government by a '*oui*' vote in the referendum and a vote for a candidate who would be part of a 'presidential' majority in Parliament. He won both his referendum and his majority. By thus making presidential elections the crucial definers of political coalitions he transformed party competition in France.

The president had been given the constitutional initiative to choose the prime minister and to dissolve the Assembly in 1958, but these provisions became crucial to presidential government after 1962 when the *raison d'être* of the majority coalition was that of voting for the government and policies chosen by the president. Thereafter, if a newly elected president faced a hostile incumbent majority in the Assembly he could decree a dissolution and invite the electors to act consistently by giving him a parliamentary majority, as Mitterrand did so successfully in 1981. If an incumbent and popular president were to see his government defeated in the Assembly by a mutiny of his troops he could dissolve Parliament. With the essential political resource of control of a disciplined parliamentary majority in presidential hands the ownership of administrative or institutional resources became immaterial. The president could choose his prime minister on his own terms and know that in the unlikely event of a disagreement the prime minister could not survive without the support of the president's majority in the Assembly. The president gained the powers both to set whatever conditions he chose on the appointments of ministers and the patterns of governmental decision-making, and to dismiss the prime minister whenever convenient. With coalition boundaries set by the president during his election campaign, the prime minister's role in government formation was at worst that of a broker organising the pay-offs for pre-election deals.

De Gaulle, Pompidou and Mitterrand were not only coalition leaders but also the undisputed heads of their own political parties which dominated their coalitions. When in power they used the distribution of ministries to reward the faithful and to soothe their critics. Thus prime ministers often had to face ministers who were party faction leaders (the 'elephants' of the Socialist Party under Mitterrand or the Gaullist 'barons' under Pompidou). Other ministers were sometimes the leaders of coalition partner-parties, imposed by presidential gratitude almost irrespective of the prime minister's preferences. Yet others were close personal friends of the president. Clearly the extent to which a prime minister could effectively control the work of an important faction leader or presidential friend who also held a large and important ministry (the case of Bérégovoy at the Finance ministry under Rocard) was likely to be limited.

Similarly, as each president decided his policy platform as a candidate fighting a presidential election campaign, he determined the programme for his subsequent government, and thus reduced the agenda-setting role of his prime minister. It became unnecessary to modify the institutions of government; the president could commandeer existing institutions at his own convenience. Hence, for example, as long as the secretary general took his instructions from the Elysée, the general secretariat of the government could remain part of the prime minister's services. The European and Defence General Secretariats (SGCI and SGDN) have generally been treated in the same way: officially under prime-ministerial control but actually run by the president dealing directly with their respective general secretaries. In a similar way real policy decisions might well be taken at committees or informal meetings chaired by the president – even in the absence of the prime minister[8] – as long as they were subsequently legitimated by the formal approval of a meeting of the council of ministers. Another convenient side-stepping of the official channels of government was the 'special relationship' which the president might have with particular ministers, and especially with their Foreign Affairs ministers.

The problems of placing such a powerful political resource in presidential hands were two-fold. First, a creditable prime minister was essential to relieve the president of a great deal of inter-ministerial arbitration and co-ordination, to deal with Parliament, to lead parliamentary election campaigns and to act as a screen between the public and the president – a scapegoat for unpopular policies. A prime minister who lacks respect and authority serves no useful function, but the president must often make concessions to keep a talented political leader as prime minister, as Giscard d'Estaing discovered in 1976 when Chirac resigned.

The second problem was revealed in 1986: if the president lost his majority in a mid-term election of the Assembly, he could face a disciplined anti-presidential majority. Such a majority would effectively impose its leader as prime minister and immediately curtail the normal presidential usurpation of institutional and administrative resources. Between 1986 and 1988 France had prime-ministerial government and, if the president did not appear to be completely impotent, it was the consequence of the prime minister's wish not to destroy the prestige of the post he hoped to occupy after 1988, the basic policy agreement between the prime minister and president in some important areas, the shortness of the period of time before the 1988 presidential election and the premier's wish not to precipitate conflicts with the president, as the opinion polls showed that such crises damaged his public image.

None the less, the time-sequence of presidential and parliamentary elections means that cohabitation and prime-ministerial government should, in theory, remain the exception rather than the rule. As soon as he is elected, any president can dissolve the Assembly and expect his coalition supporters to win an absolute majority in Parliament, or at least a 'dominant minority' as Mitterrand's friends did in 1988.[9] He may then choose his own prime minister and govern presidentially. Even if his government and its policies become highly unpopular, he may change his prime minister without a dissolution (as Mitterrand did in 1984 when Fabius replaced Mauroy). It would require highly unusual circumstances to provoke such hostility to the president that a parliamentary majority would censure every prime minister he chose from among his own friends. Recourse to a second dissolution of Parliament should be highly improbable. In normal circumstances the president should lead his own governments, assisted by prime ministers of his own choice for the five years of a normal term of the National

FRANCE: A SEMI-PRESIDENTIAL SYSTEM   73

Assembly. Hence, cohabitation should only occur in those circumstances in which it did in 1986: after an 'ordinary' parliamentary election, at the end of the five-year term of the Assembly and two years before the next presidential election. The Chirac government of 1986 behaved in constant anticipation of the 1988 presidential elections, and in similar circumstances other governments might be expected to do the same.

This 'time-sequence' logic does not, however, provide for all eventualities. In the brief life of the Fifth Republic normal election dates have rarely been respected and there is no reason to presume that the pattern has changed. The first president, having twice dissolved Parliament (the second time was in 1968 after the 'events of May' although his government had not been censured and still held a bare majority), resigned in 1969, less than four years into his second term as president. He bequeathed to his successor, Pompidou, such a huge parliamentary majority that no dissolution was even contemplated. Similarly, when Pompidou died in office in 1974 he passed on a comfortable majority to Giscard d'Estaing, so once again no presidential dissolution took place. Mitterrand has respected the normal election dates, but has spoken positively, if vaguely, of a constitutional reform to reduce the length of the presidential mandate to five years. The time-sequence view may be logical but may not apply most of the time.

PERSONALITY AND PRIME MINISTERIAL INFLUENCE

One approach used to explain the changing influence of prime ministers over time is to account for it through the personalities of the president and the prime minister. According to this approach the relationship between the two changes according to the differing foibles, personal ambitions and perceptions of their roles that the protagonists possess.

Of the different personality-based accounts, the least intellectually seductive and most lacking in scientific rigour bases its conclusions on the psychologies and work habits of the president and prime ministers. Here, the continuing presidentialisation of the regime under Giscard d'Estaing is attributed to the domineering personality of the president whose cold, haughty and overbearing style directed him towards a solitary exercise of power. In contrast, Debré's premiership, marked by an impressive involvement in domestic matters, was said to reflect his wide-ranging interest in administrative reform, his indefatigable workrate and his desire to leave a mark upon domestic policy. Pompidou, however, in 1962 saw himself, it is reported, as an 'outsider' who had to prove himself; hence he deployed his formidable intelligence to become skilled at parliamentary debating but also to impose himself as a government, party and coalition leader. Such factors hardly serve as a basis for a convincing explanatory model.

Slightly more plausible, however, is the notion that the influence of the prime minister and president differs according to the personal perceptions that they have of their roles. It has been argued, for example, that Debré and Pompidou had similar conceptions of their role as prime minister, and the over-riding desire of both was to avoid conflict with the president. They felt that any challenge to the president's authority would serve only to threaten the institutions of the infant Republic.[10] Such an account goes some way towards explaining their deferential attitude towards de Gaulle and at the same time does not discount their desire to control government policy when they knew they had the backing of the General. Chaban-Delmas, on the other hand, did not share the view of his predecessors and approached the premiership with gusto, in some cases determining policy against the wishes of the president, only to be dismissed when Pompidou felt that policy divergences had become too great.

Such an approach is not confined to Gaullist presidents and prime ministers. With the appointment of Fabius in 1984, Mitterrand took the deliberate decision to intervene less in the policy process and devolved more power to the prime minister than previously.[11] Similarly, Mauroy, Fabius and Rocard all publicly declared their double responsibility: in the first place to Parliament and in conformity with the Constitution, and, in the second, to the president, something which has no constitutional basis, but which has become a convention accepted by all prime ministers.[12]

A further personality-based approach focuses on the personal ambitions of presidents and prime ministers. For example, Giscard's desire to stand for a second term in office meant that he could not afford to allow Chirac to assert himself too much as prime minister for fear that he would become too potent a rival and threaten his chances at the next election. Chirac's own presidential ambitions meant that he had to carve a reputation for himself during his time as prime minister and could not simply allow himself to be Giscard's loyal servant. The consequent tensions between the two led to their brutal rupture in 1976. In contrast, the self-effacement of both Couve de Murville and Messmer can be attributed to the absence of any personal presidential ambitions on their part; hence, they contented themselves with simply carrying out presidential commands during their time at Matignon.[13]

None of these personality approaches, however, is ultimately convincing as an attempt to provide a reliable theory of the influence of prime minister and president in the political system, providing instead a largely anecdotal account of their roles. However, in that all three of them highlight the notion that the will of the president is central to the system and show that common to the role of the prime minister is the careful balancing act that has to be undertaken between not destabilising the president and yet not disappearing into obscurity, this approach puts into relief some of the essential qualities of the regime.

PRESIDENTIAL AND PRIME-MINISTERIAL SEGMENTED DECISION-MAKING

In contrast to the previous explanatory proposals, another, a segmented decision-making approach, provides a useful way forward. The argument here is that it is important to disaggregate decision-making sector by sector, so as to identify areas of prime-ministerial and presidential influence constant throughout the Fifth Republic.

First, it is possible to identify a segment of decision-making which is almost always under the control of the president. That there was a reserved domain of policies for which the president alone was responsible was identified as long ago as 1959.[14] At that time the reserved domain was considered to include defence policy, foreign affairs, Algerian and French Community matters. During the Fifth Republic, with the resolution of the Algerian crisis and the abandonment of the French Community, the reserved domain was modified and is now considered to include the EC and currency stability as well as foreign and defence policy. For example, although the General Secretariat of the Interministerial Committee on European Community Affairs (SGCI) is technically one of the services under the prime minister's responsibility, it has regularly been chaired by someone close to the president. Since 1985 this post has been held by Elisabeth Guigou who is Mitterrand's official adviser on European affairs at the Elysée.[15] Indeed, such is the strength of the tradition that these sectors come under the president's control that during the two years of cohabitation Chirac found that he was able to influence policy only marginally in these areas. Indeed, despite the fact that he created a seven-person strong diplomatic unit at Matignon, including experienced advisers such as Jacques Foccart, previously de Gaulle and Pompidou's expert on African affairs, none of the major lines of French foreign policy was changed and the prime minister's influence was limited.[16]

A second presidential segment is comprised of the areas in which individual presidents show a personal interest and in which they take it upon themselves to intervene. For example, Pompidou consistently showed an interest in regional decentralisation reforms, responsibility for which he took out of the hands of Chaban-Delmas and assumed himself. Mitterrand, on the other hand, has intervened on a much more aesthetic level, becoming closely involved with architectural issues and cultural matters. His was the decision to build the cube-like arch at La Défense, while he personally chose the design of the new library, just one of the projects due for completion at the end of his second *septennat*.

In a third segment falls crisis management. Where crises threaten the stability of the regime, or where they touch upon the president's reserved domain, then the president takes control. Thus, de Gaulle invoked Article 16 and assumed emergency powers for himself at the time of the insurrection of the Algerian generals in 1961. During the monetary crisis of March 1983 the prime minister was a mere adviser as the president decided whether or not the franc should be devalued.[17] In times of domestic troubles, however, the prime minister will take charge of matters. Thus, during the wave of public sector strikes in the winter of 1988 Rocard was responsible for bringing the disputes to an end. Even during the protests of May 1968 the decisions about how to react to the growing student and worker discontent were taken each morning at Matignon by the prime minister and a small group of advisers, rather than at the Elysée, until it looked as if the regime itself was in danger. At that point de Gaulle took over in a dramatic way, but once the crisis was passed Pompidou's political solution was adopted (a dissolution and parliamentary elections) rather than the president's referendum (which was postponed until the following year, when it was still a failure).

Finally, there is a segment of decision-making where the prime minister has the responsibility to decide policy relatively free of any presidential interference. In this category it is possible to include the government's relations with Parliament and the annual budgetary process. In the latter, the role of the prime minister is to arbitrate between ministers who demand public money to finance their spending needs and the Finance minister whose desire is to keep spending as low as possible. The result is that the prime minister occupies the position from where he may fashion the main lines of the budget according to his own priorities. Only for a short period at the beginning of the Giscard d'Estaing presidency did the president himself fulfil this function, only to abandon it in 1976 with the arrival of Barre who reinforced his power over the budgetary process by doubling the posts of Finance minister and prime minister.

Outside these presidential and prime-ministerial segments, much policy-making is essentially ministerial, or at least quasi-ministerial. Ministerial autonomy from the prime minister is strongest for those ministers who enjoy privileged relations with the president. Such ministers pursue their own policy initiatives, relatively safe in the knowledge that should they come into conflict with the prime minister the president is likely to arbitrate in their favour. Malraux was said to have the ear of de Gaulle, for example, while Lang is considered to be particularly close to Mitterrand, something reflected in the constant progression of the Culture ministry's budget since 1981. The same was also said to be true of Mitterrand's relations with Defferre at the ministry of the Interior, with Fabius during his time as Budget and then Industry minister from 1981 to 1984 and with Hernu at the Defence ministry.[18] The latter's independence was one of the reasons why neither Fabius nor Mitterrand was more personally implicated in the Greenpeace crisis in 1985.

While this segmented decision-making approach serves to account more fully for the delicate practices of policy-making than most other approaches it is still only a limited analysis. For example, in his budgetary arbitrations from 1988 to 1990 Rocard consistently followed the spending priorities laid down by Mitterrand in his 'Letter to the French' during the 1988 presidential campaign. Indeed, the limits to this analysis are suggested by the positive aspects of the other approaches which were not rejected in their entirety. However, the usefulness of the segmentation approach is that in disaggregating the policy process it successfully identifies several features constant to the practices of the Fifth Republic.

CONCLUSIONS

Many French political scientists have long insisted that France is a special case, a European exception in comparative politics. The shortage elsewhere in Western Europe of similar semi-presidential, or presidentialised, political systems, with prime ministers leading governments responsible to Parliament, has meant that the debates about prime-ministerial government and its limits have had a distinctive flavour in France. Elswhere the discussion has focused on the relations between prime ministers and their ministerial colleagues, their parties and their coalitions. In France, at least until 1986, the debates entirely centred on the president–prime minister relationship and the relative weakness of the prime minister. In this study, however, we have focused on the potential extent of prime-ministerial power. It is clear that during cohabitation the prime minister exercised very considerable power and led in most policy-making processes. It emerges that at most other times a French prime minister, who has the firm support of a president with a disciplined majority in the Assembly, has few reasons to envy many of his foreign counterparts. Certainly most prime ministers of the Fourth Republic, who spent most of their time and talents on surviving in office by holding together their governments and coalitions, had nothing like the policy impact of a Pompidou, a Barre, a Mauroy or a Rocard.

In the institutional logic of the Fifth Republic, the president has a strong vested interest in choosing as prime minister someone of sufficient stature to act as *primus inter pares* in the government, to command and reinforce party and coalition loyalties and to win respect in the electorate as a political leader and policy-maker second only to the president himself. The advantages are great: the president is freed from involvement in the policy-areas which he does not consider interesting or important, in the detailed and time-consuming work of implementing policies (especially in the inevitable annual budget disputes), in parliamentary tactical calculations and in party and coalition conflicts and rivalries (except as an ultimate appeal court). Furthermore, if the prime minister is perceived by the public as having a very major influence on domestic and economic policy-making, and if those policies become unpopular, then presidential popularity, and re-election prospects, may be preserved by replacing the prime minister. But only a visible and respected prime minister can play this invaluable role as a safety valve and scapegoat. The disadvantage is that by choosing and supporting such an effective prime minister, the president may help to create his own heir-apparent and even thereby allow his supporters to envisage his own eventual replacement.

NOTES

The authors wish to thank George Jones, Gordon Smith, Alain Guyomarch, Jacques Lagroye and Brendan O'Leary for their valuable comments and advice.

1. Francois Mitterrand, speech at Brest, 8 October 1985; quoted in English by Olivier Duhamel, 'The Fifth Republic under François Mitterrand', G. Ross, S. Hoffmann and S. Malzacher (eds.), *The Mitterrand Experiment* (Cambridge: Polity Press, 1987), p.160.
2. For a thorough account of the 1958–69 period see Institut Charles de Gaulle, *De Gaulle et ses Premiers Ministres* (Paris: Plon, 1990).
3. Perhaps the best analysis of leadership under the Pompidou presidency is that of F. Decaumont, *La Présidence de Georges Pompidou; Essai sur un régime présidentialiste français* (Paris: Economica, 1979).
4. An interesting account of the 1974–76 period is given in Françoise Giroud, *La Comédie du Pouvoir* (Paris: Fayard, 1977).
5. For a full and enthusiastic description of Mauroy's premiership see T. Pfister, *La Vie quotidienne à Matignon au temps de l'union de la gauche* (Paris: Hachette, 1985).

6. Detailed accounts of prime-ministerial services are provided by M. Long, *Les Services du premier ministre* (Aix-Marseille: Presse universitaire d'Aix-Marseille, 1981), and *Le secrétaire général du gouvernement* (Paris: IFSA-Economics, 1986).
7. See O. Duhamel, op. cit.; H. Machin, 'Political Leadership', in P.A. Hall, J. Hayward and H. Machin (eds.), *Developments in French Politics* (London: Macmillan, 1990), pp.95–113.
8. Chirac asserted that Giscard d'Estaing's decision to agree to the election of the European Parliament by universal suffrage was taken in his absence.
9. A. Guyomarch and H. Machin, 'François Mitterrand and the French Presidential and Parliamentary Elections of 1988', *West European Politics*, Vol.12, No.1 (January 1989), pp.196–210.
10. A first-hand account of Pompidou's view of the prime minister's role may be found in P. Rouanet, *Le Cas Chaban* (Paris: Robert Laffont, 1974), p.347.
12. See Rocard's interview in *Le Point*, No.885 (1989).
13. This approach can be seen most clearly in Pierre Servent's recent book, *Oedipe à Matignon* (Paris: Balland, 1989).
14. The term 'reserved domaine' comes from Chaban-Delmas' speech at the Gaullist Party conference in November 1959.
15. The most complete account of how this committee operates is by C. Luquesne in *Projet*, No.206 (July/August 1987), pp.41–54.
16. For a detailed account of the relations between the president and prime minister during cohabitation see Samy Cohen's article in *Politique Etrangère*, No.3/89 (Autumn 1989), pp.487–503.
17. See Pfister, op. cit., pp.241–73.
18. In an interview to the *Nouvel Observateur*, 30 November 1984 Fabius talked of how he used to 'short-circuit' the prime minister during his time as a minister and how he came to regret this practice because it undermined the authority of the prime minister.

[10]

Review Articles

THE STUDY OF FRENCH
POLITICAL SOCIALIZATION
Toward the Revocation of Paradox

By FRED I. GREENSTEIN AND SIDNEY G. TARROW

(A review article of
Charles Roig and Françoise Billon-Grand, *La Socialisation Politique des Enfants: Contribution à l'Etude de la Formation des Attitudes Politiques en France*, Paris, Cahiers de la Fondation Nationale des Sciences Politiques 163, Librairie Armand Colin, 1968, 186 pp., NF 28.80.)

"WHEREAS in post-war Britain youth has often channelled its energies into violent self-expression, destructive or creative, in France the dominant impression left by all the varying tendencies is of a kind of docile listlessness." A competent British commentator on French politics and society had the misfortune of appearing in print with this assertion about French youth in June of 1968—that is, at precisely the time when many members of France's younger generation were participating in that violent form of self-expression that has come to be called "the Events."[1]

That *les événements* were so unexpected serves as a reminder of a profound void in our knowledge of France: there is virtually no systematic evidence on the political socialization of children and young people in that puzzling system. Such information would of course be relevant to explaining outbreaks like the student rebellion of May 1968. But there are two more basic reasons—both of which apply with special force to France—why under certain circumstances studies of political socialization ought to have especially high priority. Such research is likely to be particularly profitable (1) if the aspects of the system that interest the analyst need to be dealt with by psychological (as distinguished from "structural" or "situational") variables and (2) if these analytically interesting psychological variables are ones that seem to persist from generation to generation.[2]

[1] John Ardagh, *The New French Revolution* (London 1968), 347. Nevertheless, Ardagh provides an excellent introduction to French life in 1968.

[2] This is not to say that political socialization research is relevant *only* to studying intergenerational consistencies. An obvious further point for inquiry is those circumstances under which different generations have undergone significantly different life experiences. A further cautionary note: although political socialization data, and psychological data in general, are often necessary in order to explain individual or group

All behavior is of course dependent upon both structural and psycho-logical determinants, but sometimes it is mainly the "outer" factors, and sometimes the "inner," that are of analytic interest. Thus, psycho-logical variables are not central in explaining why the voting turnout in the United States is lower than it is in Western Europe, a difference that appears to be explicable in terms of variations in voter registra-tion and residency requirements. On the other hand, it has often been argued that the French bring distinctive configurations of political psy-chology (individualism, unwillingness to compromise, hostility to au-thority, etc.) into play in responding to their political world. And it is often held as well that the psychological style of French politics has been strikingly consistent through the years—and through the regimes.[8]

Hence there is great intrinsic interest in the volume under review, a report by Charles Roig and Françoise Billon-Grand of the University of Grenoble on the first major inquiry into the political socialization of French children. Although, as the authors point out, their investigation was exploratory rather than conclusive, it is important both as a con-tribution to the literature on political socialization in different systems and as a source for reflection on the psychological style of French poli-tics. Before we discuss the Grenoble findings and their implications, it will be instructive to note a number of continuing problems in—and with—the study of French politics.

I. France as Paradox: Methodological and Substantive Problems in the Literature

No one denies that France is puzzling. Here is a nation second to none in extravagant expressions of patriotism, but one that appears per-sistently over the years to have harbored substantial numbers of citizens who viewed favorably the prospect that whatever constitution happened to be in force at the moment might be overthrown; a nation with achievements that might seem to be a source of pride and satisfaction,

---

behavior, they rarely are sufficient. Consider, for example, the French national survey finding that President de Gaulle's popularity was *rising* during the months leading up to *les événements.* "La Crise de Mai 1968," *Sondages: Revue Française de l'Opinion Publique,* II (1968) 9. But clearly De Gaulle's aggregate national popularity was less im-portant than his popularity in specific, politically relevant population groups. And even more important, psychological data should not be considered alone—in the absence of data on situational stimuli—in explanations of behavior. On the latter point, see the elegant formulation of M. Brewster Smith: "A Map for the Analysis of Personality and Politics," *Journal of Social Issues,* xxiv (July 1968), 15-28.

[8] This has been argued most forcefully by Stanley Hoffmann. See, in particular, his "Paradoxes of the French Political Community" in Stanley Hoffmann and others, eds., *In Search of France* (Cambridge, Mass. 1963) and "Heroic Leadership: The Case of Modern France" in Lewis J. Edinger, ed., *Political Leadership in Industrialized Societies: Studies in Comparative Analysis* (New York 1967), 108-54.

FRENCH POLITICAL SOCIALIZATION 97

but one that has had five republics, two monarchies, two empires, and a collaborationist government in its unoccupied area, since the demise of the old regime. Yet what is striking about analyses of these and other seeming inconsistencies of French politics is the failure often even to attempt to *explain*. The tendency is to describe, sometimes to exaggerate, and even to *celebrate* the mysteriousness of French politics.

The notion of "paradox"—a term from the lexicon of rhetoric rather than logic—is inordinately common in writings about France:

> There is a paradox in a tradition derived from a revolution which itself was a revolution against traditionalism.[4] [One suspects that revolutionary traditions are no more nor less "paradoxical" in, say, the United States or Mexico. But somehow the task of analyzing *French* politics seems especially likely to evoke references to "paradox."]
>
> The paradox of authority [in France] is that what France needs most is what she has always been least able to breed, and what she must discard is what has been most resilient.[5] [Is this a statement that is in any sense falsifiable?]
>
> In France there are a great many radical electors, a certain number of radical deputies, and a very small number of radical ministers; as for the heads of the bureaucracy, they are all reactionaries. He who properly understands this has the key to our politics.[6] [To what other political system—excepting perhaps the Soviet—is an enigmatic apothegm thought to provide a "key"?]

In part this emphasis on paradox is purely stylistic, but it also seems to result from three related intellectual practices that are common in writings on French politics:

First, much of the writing on France begins with the premise that because France is somehow different from other political systems, the analytic modes used to describe it—the concepts and the ways they are used—need also to be distinctive. This makes evaluation of findings and conclusions difficult, for, as Stanley Hoffmann writes, "the problem of comparison becomes hopeless when the scholar is faced with empirical studies that celebrate the uniqueness of each experience."[7]

An example is "the System," an indispensable concept to analysts of the Fourth Republic. This term appears in the Index of Williams' classic *Crisis and Compromise* forty-eight times, but it is only on page

[4] David Thomson, *Democracy in France since 1870* (New York and London 1964), 11. Our choice of texts is not intended to be representative but merely illustrative of some of the best writing in France.
[5] Hoffmann, "Paradoxes," 108.
[6] Alain (Emile Chartier) *Eléments d'une Doctrine Radicale* (Paris 1933), 25.
[7] Hoffmann, "Heroic Leadership," 113.

201 that we discover that it is being used in neither its scientific nor its commonsense usage, but rather in the very special French sense of "... the System by which a Parliament of multiple parties and shifting coalitions excluded strong personalities from power, and deprived the ordinary citizen of any sense of participation in the government of his country."[8] And concepts are frequently wielded with a curious dialectic of mixed incompatibilities, a sort of Cartesian neither-nor. This mode of argument begins with two polar types like "liberalism" and "authoritarianism," and then affirms that the French style uniquely combines features of both. The difficulty with such assertions is that they cannot be disproved. If a given "style" is seen as a synthesis of two others, then empirical findings may be assigned to either half of the amalgam without invalidating the other.[9]

Second, there is a tendency to use "History" as a sufficient explanation for contemporary political patterns. Thus, one of France's most gifted political scientists writes of the period after World War I: "The weight of the pre-1914 tradition prevented the French political system from reforming itself so as to be able to handle the wholly new problems France had to face after 1914."[10] But why should the "weight of the past" inhibit change after 1914 and not in 1789? Clearly, the political scientist ignores history at his peril, but explanations of the *genesis* of a phenomenon are never sufficient to account for its *maintenance*.

Finally, and subsuming the two previous points, we may note the fundamentally unempirical nature of much writing about France. By this we refer neither to the scarcity of work reporting empirical findings, nor to the tendency of some students of French politics to employ largely deductive reasoning. Rather the difficulty appears to be the absence in much work on France of the appropriate combination of inductive inference from data and deductive predictions about data. When applied by a Tocqueville, or, more recently, a Luethy or a Wylie, unsystematic procedures for considering evidence can lead to brilliant speculations. But the speculations of such writers are too often treated as final verities, rather than being subjected to rigorous assessment.[11] In short, there is insufficient awareness that theorizing and data-

---

[8] Philip Williams, *Crisis and Compromise: Politics in the Fourth Republic* (Garden City, N.Y. 1966), 201.

[9] "Neither-nor" is Hoffmann's phrase; he uses it in a classic instance of polar type analysis: "Paradoxes," 8.

[10] François Goguel, "Six Authors in Search of a National Character," in *In Search of France*, 393.

[11] There seems to us to be too much of this tendency in Michel Crozier's enormously imaginative *The Bureaucratic Phenomenon* (Chicago 1964).

FRENCH POLITICAL SOCIALIZATION 99

gathering need to be employed in a continuing, self-correcting sequence of operations designed to *revoke* rather than evoke paradox.[12]

Three continuing concerns of students of French politics—concerns that have not received sufficiently systematic empirical scrutiny—bear on French patterns of partisanship, conflict, and authority. Each of these matters, as we shall show, raises interesting questions about French political socialization—questions we can now begin to answer as a consequence of the Grenoble study.

(1) PARTISAN IDENTIFICATION

Some writers on France have interpreted partisanship as being so strong that parties or tendencies form "subcultures."[13] Early writers, perhaps because they found that certain geographic regions were electorally stable over long periods, concluded there was an inbuilt *tendance* in the French voter, or even, over the generations, in the French family."[14] Apart from the fact that identification with *tendances* has a different meaning for the political system than would identification with party, and that geographical voting stability can disguise great fluidity in the voting of individuals within an area, the actual importance and meaning to individual voters of *tendance* and party was not empirically established.[15] The result was to build an implicit assumption of high politicization into many of the accepted explanations of French politics.

(2) THE CONFLICT SOCIETY

In part as a result of assuming high frequencies of partisan identification, many writers have drawn an insufficiently clarified or documented picture of the depth of ideological conflict in the French electorate. As one writer puts it, "throughout French political history . . .

[12] See, for example, Herbert Luethy, *France Against Herself* (Cleveland and New York 1968), 3. Luethy writes: "Abstractions can be exhaustively defined, but a personality never. . . . In this respect, France evades all definitions. However sharply and clearly defined her outlines may seem from a distance, she evades the hands that seek to grasp her." Needless to say, works conceived in this spirit are not likely to yield testable—much less tested—hypotheses.

[13] Gabriel A. Almond, "Comparative Political Systems," *Journal of Politics,* xviii (August 1956), 391-409, and Almond and Powell, *Comparative Politics: A Developmental Approach* (Boston 1966), 263-265.

[14] For example, the earliest and perhaps the greatest of these writers, André Siegfried, wrote; "I have observed that the voter knows very well what he wants and even better what he doesn't want . . . he almost always has a *tendance* that marks his behavior." *Tableau Politique de la France de l'Ouest* (Paris 1964 ed.), ix.

[15] A recent study based upon survey data builds its analysis entirely upon a fixed-choice item on *tendance*, without ever ascertaining whether "Extreme Left," "Left," etc., were salient and meaningful to the respondents. Emeric Deutsch and others, *Les Familles Politiques Aujourd'hui en France* (Paris 1966), 11-15.

there have been two 'tempers' which may be called Jacobin or Girondin; each can be found at the same time or in rapid succession *in every sector of French opinion.*"[16] There are several numerical variations on the notion of *les deux Frances,* but common to all of them is an implicit assumption about political socialization and its consequences: that France's internal divisions are profound because individuals are socialized into "ideological families" through family, church, and party, and that these socializing agencies "reinforce one another in their effects on opinion."[17]

(3) THE FRENCH STYLE OF AUTHORITY

Writing mainly in the "national character" tradition, various observers have described a uniquely French set of attitudes toward authority, including political authority.[18] Although such assertions are not of a piece, they typically stress the tightly knit, hierarchical structure of the family *foyer,* its reinforcement in the discipline of the schoolroom, its counterfoil in the peer group's reaction by forming "negative communities," and its culmination in a style of political authority that combines "limited authoritarianism" with "potential insurrection."[19] In short, these writers suggest rather direct links between socialization processes and regularities in French politics. To date, however, their assertions do not appear to have been satisfactorily transformed into falsifiable propositions and appropriately tested.

After an overview of the Grenoble study, we shall return to these three themes, indicating how political socialization research can contribute to their clarification. Certain of the Grenoble findings are relevant to establishing—if not conclusively—the empirical standing of the first two themes. The issues connected with the French style of authority would call for a quite different research design than that used in Grenoble, although a few of the Grenoble findings are germane. It must be emphasized that Professors Roig and Billon-Grand are not to be held responsible for our interpretations of their findings. By and large they present their data without very extensive analytic embellishment,

[16] Hoffmann, "Paradoxes," 18. Italics added.

[17] Gabriel Almond and Sidney Verba, *The Civic Culture: Political Attitudes and Democracy in Five Nations* (Princeton 1963) 133-34.

[18] The basic work here is, of course Crozier, *The Bureaucratic Phenomenon.* Also see Hoffmann "Paradoxes"; Jesse R. Pitts, "Continuity and Change in Bourgeois France," in *In Search of France;* Laurence Wylie, *Village in the Vaucluse* (Cambridge, Mass. 1967, rev. ed. New York 1964); and Rhoda Metraux and Margaret Mead, *Themes in French Culture: A Preface to a Study of French Community* (Palo Alto 1954).

[19] Hoffmann, "Paradoxes," 8.

and those interpretative observations they do make frequently take for granted explanations of French politics we are about to question.

II. THE GRENOBLE STUDY: AN OVERVIEW

(1) THE STUDY AND THE SAMPLE

Two influences led to the appearance of *La Socialisation Politique des Enfants*. One, as Charles Roig points out in his introduction, was a puzzling observation made in the course of his research on French local politics, and the other was the stimulus of a new body of empirical work. The puzzling observation was of the contrast, on the one hand, "between the profound socioeconomic changes affecting" these local communities and, on the other, the "stability . . . of the cleavages and political attitudes of their residents" (p. 13). The body of literature was the halting, exploratory, and sometimes fumbling efforts of American scholars to uncover the nature of children's political learning.[20]

Roig, who was joined by Billon-Grand at the data-analysis stage, was stimulated to carry out a paper-and-pencil questionnaire survey of the political orientations of French schoolchildren. In all, he was able to collect 413 usable questionnaires, administered in the classroom to children in Grenoble and its outlying areas. The children range in age from ten to fourteen, but most are between eleven and thirteen, the equivalents of sixth-, seventh-, and eighth-grade students in the United States. They tend to be from middle-class, nonfarm occupational backgrounds: about two-thirds reported nonmanual paternal occupations, less than a tenth reported farming, and only about a quarter reported manual occupations. The questionnaires were administered early in 1964—that is, in the aftermath of France's disengagement from the Algerian war.

The questionnaire, which was administered by the schoolteachers rather than the investigators themselves, was about evenly divided between fixed-choice and open-ended questions dealing with various aspects of political information and attitudes. Using this instrument and

[20] Roig was first impressed by a paper presented to the Fifth World Congress of the International Association of Political Science by David Easton and Robert D. Hess, "The Child's Political World" (Paris 1961). Easton and Hess were reporting on a national survey of American children that has since been more fully reported in Robert Hess and Judith Torney, *The Development of Political Attitudes in Children* (Chicago 1967) and David Easton and Jack Dennis in *Children and the Political System: The Origins of Political Legitimacy* (New York 1969). Roig and Billon-Grand draw periodically for comparisons on various reports by these investigators and on the study of New Haven, Connecticut children reported in Fred I. Greenstein, *Children and Politics* (New Haven 1965).

procedure it was possible to establish a great deal about the political orientations of French children, although, as we shall see, there are a number of points at which much less structured procedures, probably involving direct interviewing, now appear to be desirable in order to get more precisely at the subjective aspects of political socialization in France.

The authors' findings and presentation also were affected by a pair of obstacles they encountered, which tell us something about both political psychology and the acceptance of social research in France. First, they were forced to content themselves with a smaller and far less representative sample than they had hoped to draw, because of objections that were raised to inquiries into children's partisan orientations.[21] Secondly, they were under considerable financial constraint, and this appears responsible for their failure to introduce certain standard statistical controls in reporting their data, and possibly also for their failure to test for statistical significance. (Significance tests can be useful, even in nonrandom samples, as a rule of thumb for deciding which variations are worth discussing.) Nevertheless, the reader may compute his own significance tests, and the authors do provide information on their sample which helps compensate for the lack of controls.

The information on sample-composition needs especially to be used for estimating the degree to which subgroup differences are real or spurious. The authors' typical table takes the form of a presentation of the responses of their entire sample to some item or series of items, with a further set of comparisons of boys and girls, parochial- and public-schoolchildren, and children at different school-year levels. Since the subgroups differ from each other on more than one characteristic, and since the combined effect of more than one independent variable is rarely analyzed,[22] the reader has to interpret comparisons in the light of possible artifactual biases.

The possible source of bias in the authors' sex comparisons is socio-economic status: the girls are higher than the boys in parental occupational status. The effect of the sampling deficiency would be to enhance the level of political information and involvement found in the female subsample. But in fact the French girls were *less* politicized than the boys, a convincing corroboration of the finding in the United States that adult political sex differences begin to take shape during

[21] As Professor Roig laconically puts it, there were "des pétitions émanant d'associations et de syndicats, des prises de positions diverses, etc." (p. 14).
[22] Chap. IX is an exception, but there the attempt is to discover whether patterns exist among different attitude-questions, and the independent variables of sex, age, or type of school are excluded.

the preadolescent years.[23] Absence of a control for socioeconomic status also must be taken account of in interpreting the parochial-school–public-school comparisons: the parochial-school children were about 10 percent more likely than those in public school to come from non-manual parental occupational backgrounds. Here again, fortunately, the bias does not preclude making use of the findings. If the standard theories about French cleavage are correct, one would expect especially sharp attitudinal differences between the *école publique* and *école privée* children, with the Republican socialization of the former reinforced by their lower socioeconomic origins, and the anti-Republicanism of the latter reinforced by higher status. But as we shall see, it is the mildness rather than the acuteness of the parochial-school–public-school differences that is theoretically interesting.

The Grenoble data on "school year" are multiply confounded by uncontrolled differences in socioeconomic status, school type, and to a lesser extent age. The French school system is partly "streamed" and, as in other such systems, the selection of "high-ability" children for university-preparatory streams at the same time involves an uneven selection of upper socioeconomic-status children into the higher streams. But in the earlier school-year levels the system is unstreamed and socially heterogeneous; furthermore, different regions are at different stages of transition from a traditional streamed to a modern semi-comprehensive system.[24] The Grenoble data are reported in the following school-year categories: (1) socially heterogeneous primary-school students of ages ten and eleven (*cours moyen*), (2) largely middle-class children of eleven and twelve in the secondary schools designed for able children—the *lycées* and *collèges*—and, (3) lower-status children in a school-terminating program (*classe de fin d'étude*). The authors occasionally use the third of these groups as an indicator of lower socioeconomic status, but we have generally avoided this temptation because this group differs from the others in age and school type as well. But we *do* occasionally refer to the older children in the *lycée-collège* category (the *cinquième*, which in the United States would be eighth grade) as a way of estimating the upper limits of preadolescent political learning in France.

[23] Another corroboration: the French girls, like adult females in several countries, are more likely to be "pacifistic" on questions about war, harsh punishment for crimes, and revolution (pp. 69-70, 115). For some American findings on sex differences and a summary of the relevant literature, see Greenstein, chap. 6, and Hess and Torney, chap. 8.

[24] For an introduction to the complexities of French school organization see W. D. Halls, *Society, Schools and Progress in France* (Oxford 1965), chap. 6.

104 WORLD POLITICS

One striking substantive impression emerges from the various sub-group comparisons: *the within-sample variations among the Grenoble children are remarkably slight,* even though many of them are in expected directions. It is a reasonable presumption that sharp, stable, and historically continuous cleavages in adult attitudes would be at least presaged in the preadult years; conversely, it is reasonable to suspect that adult psychological differences, which do not begin to take shape during later childhood, may be of rather low intensity.[25] On the assumption that the limited internal variation in the Grenoble sample reflects a childhood political culture that for some purposes can be treated as homogeneous, we may tentatively compare the overall distribution of responses in Grenoble to overall findings in the United States.

(2) SOURCES OF POLITICAL LEARNING

As in the United States, it seems that most political learning takes place in the child's face-to-face environment and through the somewhat under-appreciated vehicle of the mass media. At the face-to-face level, four-fifths of the Grenoble respondents report having heard conversations about politics among adults. We would expect less exposure to adult political conversation in the United States.[26] There are, as we shall see, important reasons for wanting to know about the level of political communication in French families, and therefore it is unfortunate that this is one of the points at which the methodology of the Grenoble study does not permit a conclusive finding: the political-conversation item was fixed-choice, placing no inhibition on exaggeration, and the principle term—"politics"—was undefined and seems on the basis of other of the findings to be unclear to children.[27]

Television-viewing evidently is as widespread among French as among American children, with virtually every respondent reporting at least some attention to the medium, and, it would seem, to television newscasts.[28] Indeed, the infrequent nonviewing is confined to middle-

[25] For the rationale behind this assertion, see Greenstein, 78-84.

[26] Unfortunately strictly comparable American data are hard to come by, but the American surveys consistently find fewer adults who claim political interest than could possibly generate an 80 percent incidence of overheard political conversations by children. The proportion of American adults who reported that they "talked with someone and tried to persuade him how to vote" was about one-third in the Survey Research Center's 1952, 1956, 1960, and 1964 national surveys. For these and similar SRC findings see John Robinson and others, *Measures of Political Attitudes* (Ann Arbor, Michigan 1968).

[27] The item was "Avez-vous entendu des grandes personnes parler de politique? Souvent-Quelquefois-Jamais" (p. 169).

[28] For a comprehensive study of American children's exposure to television and its consequences, see W. Schramm, J. Lyle, and E. B. Parker, *Television in the Lives of Our Children* (Stanford 1961).

class secondary-schoolchildren, while the highest proportion of viewers was in the lower-class terminal program. Since the diffusion of home television receivers is still far from complete in France, these findings suggest that a good many of the respondents may go to considerable lengths to expose themselves to the medium, a finding of political significance in a system that is ruthless about bending television to government purposes.[29]

The design of the Grenoble study, like that of all other political socialization research until the recent work of Langton and Jennings in the United States,[30] permits no assessment of the effect of formal instruction in civics. The provision for *instruction civique* in French schools appears, as Roig and Billon-Grand note (pp. 180-84), to be met only in a perfunctory way.[31] And the French child gets none of the training in free debate and self-government that is stressed in American schools. But he does receive a catechism of *civisme*—or, more properly, *gallicisme*—in the teaching of history and geography.[32] The emphasis in French schools on nationalism, combined with the lack of emphasis on the actual functioning of the political system, is interesting in that it may lead French children to identify with an abstract entity called "the State," but to have very little sense of obligation to actual governments.[33]

(3) POLITICAL INFORMATION AND PERCEPTIONS

In the United States, the one aspect of the political system that children—even very young children—are certain to be aware of is the Presidency. From this and other evidence, it has been argued that the American Presidency, because it is perceived so early and monopolizes so much of the child's initial learning, provides a basis for organizing further political perception and learning, and contributes to the adult's president-centered vision of the political system.[34] In Fifth-Republic

[29] See Henry Ehrmann's chapter on "Political Socialization through the Mass Media," in his *Politics in France* (Boston 1968), 152-68.

[30] Kenneth P. Langton and M. Kent Jennings, "Political Socialization and the High School Curriculum in the United States," *American Political Science Review*, LXII (September 1968), 852-67.

[31] Also see Jean-William LaPierre and Georges Noizet, *Une Recherche sur le Civisme des Jeunes à la Fin de la Quatrième République* (Aix-en-Provence 1961), 11-12.

[32] Both the francophilia and the lack of training in self-government are unforgettably described in Jean Boorsch's "Primary Education," in the number of *Yale French Studies* entitled "Why Jeannot *Can* Read," xx (Winter-Spring 1958-59), 28, 31-35.

[33] LaPierre and Noizet (pp. 86-89) present the results of interviews with older secondary-school students who exhibit idealized attitudes toward "the State" but rather tolerant views toward "gypping the government, 68-89.

[34] Greenstein, chaps. 3 and 4.

France, it seems likely that, at least during the long tenure in office of its first incumbent, the Presidency had some of the same political socialization function. Only ten of the 413 Grenoble sample children failed correctly to name De Gaulle as the President of the Republic (p. 75);[35] no other piece of political information was so widely shared. Thus the French child of the period of the Grenoble research, like the American child, absorbed information about further aspects of the political system—for example, the legislature—into a mental set in which the Presidency already occupied a central position.

Information about other aspects of the political system was, in fact, *much* less widely distributed than was information about the President of the Republic, at the ages covered in the Grenoble study. Eighty-seven percent of the Grenoble children recognized De Gaulle as a political figure ("*homme politique*") and 82 percent were able to label Pompidou as political in response to a fixed-choice item. But, even though there was nothing in the item to restrain guessing, only 61 percent perceived Guy Mollet, 22 percent Pierre Mendès-France and a mere 9 percent Maurice Thorez as political figures.[36] Fifty-five percent applied "*homme politique*" to General Raoul Salan, who, although influential in the military politics of the late stages of the Algerian conflict, was scarcely a politician. And 11 percent named the television journalist Léon Zitrone. While it is almost axiomatic that children's political information is likely to be low, the poor recognition-rate of such partisan figures as Mendès-France and Thorez, and the identification of Salan and Zitrone as "political," raises the question of what the Grenoble children were thinking of when they reported overhearing adult political conversation. These low levels of political information, which would be no surprise in the United States, are part of a pattern of Grenoble findings that appears inconsistent with the thesis that France is a highly politicized nation.

Our skepticism about this thesis is further increased by findings on the phenomenon commonly referred to by that ubiquitous term in French political studies—"*tendance.*" Apart from their inability to rec-

---

[35] Compare the American findings in *ibid.*, pp. 58-59.

[36] However, the largely working-class children in the terminal program have a slightly higher recognition-rate of the late Communist leader (by 6 percent) and of Socialist leader Mollet (by 7 percent) than the older secondary-school students. Partisan information tends to be lower than other types of political information in French secondary-school children. J.-W. LaPierre and G. Noizet report that, of a battery of twenty political-information questions on international affairs, institutions, current events, and parties, the three items with the highest nonresponse rate are partisan items. See their "L'information Politique du Jeunes Français en 1962," *Revue Française de Science Politique*, xiv (June 1964), 492.

ognize Communist leader Thorez, the Grenoble children were almost totally unable to name any "*homme politique de gauche*," although they had just—in the item described immediately above—been presented with the names of Thorez, Mollet, and Mendès-France. Only 34 percent responded at all; of those who responded, De Gaulle (14 percent), Pompidou (5 percent) and Salan (5 percent) were most commonly said to be of the Left! (Thorez was mentioned by only 1 percent of the children.) If *tendance* were a stable (and highly charged) aspect of French political attitudes, would it not be reflected in greater partisan information?

(4) POLITICAL AFFECT: PREFERENCES AND IDENTIFICATIONS

The Grenoble findings on the affective content of French children's political learning point to the same conclusions as do the findings on sources of learning and levels of political information. The data convey a recognizably French portrait of the political socialization process. But by and large the findings do not appear to be what we would expect from children socialized in a society whose adults are polarized along cumulative lines of cleavage—and the data frequently are somewhat elusive on the specifics of the subjective meaning of politics to French children.

In contrast with American children, for whom the President is not only a well-known, but also a *benign*, symbol,[87] the mere 53 percent of the Grenoble children who responded to a question about the qualities of the President of the Republic were somewhat more likely to mention bad (29 percent) than good (24 percent) qualities (p. 77).[88] The readiness of French children to judge the President unfavorably is consistent with many of the standard expectations about French political culture, but the low level of response is not, unless the view is adopted that failure to respond is a sign of covert hostility. Roig and Billon-Grand advance the rather unparsimonious hypothesis that though the younger children fail to respond out of lack of political interest, the older children are unresponsive out of a desire to conceal

[87] Greenstein, chap. 3, and the citations there of the literature through 1965; Dean Jaros, Herbert Hirsch, Frederick J. Fleron, Jr., "The Malevolent Leader: Political Socialization in an American Sub-Culture," *American Political Science Review*, LXII (June 1968), 564-75; Roberta Sigel, "Image of a President: Some Insights into the Political Views of School Children," *ibid.* (March 1968), 216-26.

[88] Also, when asked whom they would like to resemble when they grow up, only 1 percent of the Grenoble children named De Gaulle; when asked whom they would *not* like to resemble, 10 percent named him (40-42), although as with American children the choice of a political figure as a negative exemplar often indicates reluctance to share the vicissitudes of his office rather than animosity. Greenstein, 142.

their true views. In general, the authors tend to be somewhat *a priori* and *ad hoc* in attributing motives to response patterns. They do not *demonstrate* that covert hostility is behind the failure to respond of any of the children in their sample. Whether covert hostility is concealed by nonresponse needs to be resolved by appropriately open-ended future research.

Unlike the absence of agreement in evaluation of the President of the Republic, consensus was the dominant theme in responses to an item asking for the name of the individual who had done the most for France (p. 64). Out of the eight possible choices, a near majority (48 percent) chose Pasteur, on the face of it the most unpolitical figure on the list, and, we gather, an endlessly praised figure in the elementary-school history curriculum. Another 20 percent chose St. Louis and 12 percent chose Napoleon. There were very few references to past politicians of diverse *tendances* such as Colbert and Gambetta, who were on the list. To what extent does the failure to cite these men, whose names appear on streets everywhere in France, signify an apolitical or anti-political attitude? To what extent does it reflect emphasis in the teaching of history? We do not know yet, and here, again, the Grenoble research now needs to be followed up by work with more probing investigative techniques.

Consensus was also the dominant motif in responses to questions on patriotism (pp. 59-73). The results, similar to those in a number of nations,[39] show that 74 percent would like to live outside of France "only briefly" or "never"; that two-thirds think it is proper for Frenchmen to be prepared to die for their country; that only 22 percent think that traitors to "*la patrie*" should be pardoned, while 38 percent think they should be shot.[40] On the other hand, the divisions on the question "Was the Revolution of 1789 a good or an evil?" were rather striking. Although substantially more children chose good (55 percent) than evil (30 percent), the negative evaluations are impressively large on so fundamental an aspect of a nation's past. We assume that in the United States negative assessments of 1776 would be virtually nonexistent.

---

[39] See the exceedingly valuable review by A. F. Davies, "The Child's Discovery of Nationality," *Australian and New Zealand Journal of Sociology,* IV (October 1968), 107-25.

[40] But the "il faut les fusiller" option should not be interpreted as superpatriotism; small children very commonly use hyperbole. Among the older children interviewed by LaPierre and Noizet, 56 percent thought that conscientious objection was excusable or justifiable; "Les Jeunes Français devant L'objection de Conscience," *Revue Française de Sociologie,* IV, No. 3 (July-September 1963), 259-74.

Again, however, the subjective meaning of the responses is difficult to interpret. The authors, following tradition, tend toward an ideological interpretation, but here they do report open-ended responses, and our impression is that distaste for violence is more common, at least in the children's own explanation of their negative judgments, than are various forms of juvenile anti-republicanism. Statements like "La révolution a fait trop de morts" or "On a coupé la tête à des gens" seem more typical than statements like "Les rois n'étaient pas si mauvais."

Finally, in order to assess the extent to which Left and Right are presaged in children's "latent ideology," the authors—in one of their few cross-tabulations—use the response categories to the French Revolution item as a control for analyzing responses to a large number of other items (pp. 119-22). The findings are mixed: there are only a few items for which "opponents" of the revolution are also "conservative," and these are undramatic. For example, the supporters are eight per cent more likely to consider *laïque* a basic attribute of France, and "opponents" are 10 percent more likely to prefer one-man rule to government by an assembly and 12 percent more likely to choose St. Louis as their national hero. These findings are balanced by a rather larger number of questions on which supporters and opponents of the Revolution either do not differ ("Are there good political parties?" "Should foreigners be made to return to their countries?"), or in which pro-Revolutionary children score higher on "authoritarian" attitudes. ("Must the government always be right against its opponents?" "What should be done with traitors?") Moreover, the absence of controls to partial out third factors further makes the results difficult to interpret as ideological.

Because of these reservations, we cannot share the authors' confidence that "certain political *tendances* appear among individuals with a particular clarity from the age of eleven or twelve" (p. 124). Rather, the findings on political affect lead us to share Henry Ehrmann's general characterization of the findings in *La Socialisation Politique des Enfants*: "Although they came from widely varying family backgrounds, the children's outlook on important historical events and personalities was fairly uniform, a finding one would expect from a society high in consensus. It hardly reflected the divisiveness which historical memories and issues are known to provoke in the adult world."[41]

[41] Ehrmann, 60.

III. French Partisanship, Social Conflict, and Authority
Relations in the Light of Political Socialization Research

(1) orientations to the party system

Major social regularities are sometimes maintained in important ways
by seemingly frail psychological threads. An impressive instance of this
is the effect on the American political system of citizens' "party identifications." The index of this orientation used in America is deceptively
simple: "Generally speaking, do you consider yourself a Republican,
a Democrat, an Independent, or what?"[42] Party identifications in America are potent, even if passionless. The University of Michigan Survey
Research Center has consistently found over the past two decades that
three out of every four adult Americans profess a party identification.
Further, the distribution of preferences for the two major parties has
proved remarkably stable over this period, with the Democrats receiving
roughly a three-to-two advantage. And, finally, a matter of great importance: party identification is closely associated with electoral choice—
it is the best single attitudinal variable for predicting how an individual will vote.

Party voting contributes to so much of the variation in American
electoral behavior that the SRC analysts have come to conceive of a
"normal vote," which is the election outcome that could be expected
if the existing groups of party identifiers were to go to the polls with
the frequencies predicted by their different mean social statuses. By this
way of thinking, election outcomes in the United States can be analyzed
in terms of the degree to which the party identifiers who make up the
bulk of electorate have been led to defect from their parties by issues
that are specific to the campaign, and by candidate appeal, plus the
division among the small group of independent voters, many of whom
are covert identifiers with one or the other of the major parties. In
short, the election is a variant on the normal party vote—and ordinarily
not much of a variant.

The institutional significance of such widespread party identification
is considerable: the predictability of voting behavior makes for fairly
stable connections between politicians and various groups in their

---

[42] The phrase "party identification" was introduced by the University of Michigan
Survey Research Center to describe psychological membership in political parties—that
is, the citizen's feeling that he *is* a Democrat or a Republican (or a Tory or a Radical
Socialist). See the sources cited in Fred I. Greenstein, *The American Party System
and the American People* (Englewood Cliffs, N.J. 1963), chap. 3, and Angus Campbell,
Philip E. Converse, Warren E. Miller, Donald E. Stokes, *Elections and the Political
Order* (New York 1966).

constituencies; the existence of large stable clienteles for the major parties is a major brake on new "third" parties; and the distribution of support between the parties "anchors" election outcomes—from election to election there is less variability than there would be with fewer party identifiers. The variability is especially low in elections that are not dominated by widely publicized national figures—for instance, Congressional elections.

The processes just described, or rather their absence, appear to be of the greatest importance in accounting for certain regularities of French politics—or so it was argued for American readers a number of years ago in a brilliant paper by Philip Converse and Georges Dupeux entitled "Politicization of the Electorate in France and the United States."[43] In particular, Converse and Dupeux pointed to the great volatility of French patterns of party support, including the "rise and fall of 'flash' parties like the R.P.F. in 1951, the Poujadists in 1956, and the U.N.R. in 1958." Although such political patterns have often been considered as evidence of a burning intensity of involvement (if a negative one) in the French electorate,[44] Converse and Dupeux point to evidence suggesting that such parties arise in France and not in the United States because the French are *less* politically involved and not *more* politically involved than Americans.[45]

The major difference between the two electorates is that the frequency of party identification is dramatically lower in France than in the United States. In contrast to the 75 percent of Americans who consider themselves party supporters, less than 45 percent of Converse and

[43] Philip E. Converse and Georges Dupeux, "Politicization of the Electorate in France and the United States," *Public Opinion Quarterly*, xxvi (Spring 1962), 1-23; reprinted as chap. 14 of Campbell and others. Our citations are to the original article. For an earlier treatment see R. D. Masters, "Une Méthode pour Mesurer la Mobilité des Attitudes Politiques," *Revue Française de Science Politique*, x (September 1960), 658-72. For an original application of the Converse and Dupeux analysis to comparative political analysis see James L. Payne, *Patterns of Conflict in Colombia* (New Haven 1968). In France, the fluidity of the party vote and the weakness of party identification was analyzed in several of the "Cahiers" of the Fondation Nationale des Sciences Politiques. See, in particular, Georges Dupeux, "Le Comportement des Electeurs Français de 1958 à 1962," and Guy Michelat, "Attitudes et Comportements Politiques à L'automne 1962," in *Le Référendum d'Octobre et les Elections de Novembre 1962*, (Paris 1965), 173-287.

[44] This seems to be the interpretation given by Wylie to the large Poujadist vote in 1956. "Their vote for Poujade was a vote against taxation; it was an extremist vote against government; it was also a means of differentiating themselves still more radically from their neighbors." Wylie, 1964 edn., p. 329.

[45] On an index of involvement, such as following political news and attending campaign meetings, the French tend in the aggregate to be less politically involved, or no more politically involved, than Americans. Some of the lesser involvement seems to be explained by the lower mean educational level in France.

Dupeux's French respondents identified with parties, while another 10 to 15 percent associated themselves with *tendances*. The responses could not be explained by diffidence or dissimulation; they reveal a fundamental difference "in the flavor of partisan processes in the two electorates."[46] Converse and Dupeux comment that "with a very large proportion of the electorate feeling no anchoring loyalty, it is not surprising that a new party can attract a large vote 'overnight,' or that this base can be so rapidly dissolved."[47]

But what accounts for this aspect of French political psychology? The phenomenon of very low frequency of party identification, as Converse and Dupeux point out, "cannot simply be seen as a necessary consequence of a multi-party system *per se*. Fairly comparable data from Norway, where six parties are prominent, show party attachments as widespread as those in the two-party United States."[48] Converse and Dupeux found themselves turning for an answer to the French political socialization process. They analyzed the recollections by French and Americans adults of the prevailing partisan colorations of their families during their childhood, and especially of their fathers' party preferences. Of the Frenchmen and Americans who reported knowledge of their fathers' party preferences, there was an equal likelihood of holding a party identification. But there were extraordinary differences—much larger than most differences found in surveys—between the two

[46] The authors are especially careful about describing their findings in detail. As they put it, "less than 45 percent of those who did not refuse to answer the question were able to classify themselves in one of the parties or splinter groups, while another 10 to 15 percent associated themselves with a more or less recognizable broad *tendance* ('left,' 'right,' a labor union, etc.). The cross-national differences of 20 to 30 percent are sufficiently large here to contribute to fundamental differences in the flavor of partisan processes in the two electorates. For a long time, we wrote off these differences as products of the incomparable circumstances or of reticence on the part of the French concerning partisanship . . . [but] the hypothesis of concealed partisanship was very largely dispelled by a close reading of the actual interviews. It is undeniable that nearly 10 percent of the French sample explicitly refused to answer the question, as compared with a tiny fraction in the United States. However, we have already subtracted this group from the accounting. Beyond the explicit refusals, the remarks and explanations which often accompanied statements classified as 'no party,' or as 'don't know which party,' had a very genuine air about them which made them hard to read as hasty evasions. No few of these respondents were obviously embarrassed at their lack of a party; some of them confessed that they just hadn't been able to keep track of which party was which. The phrase 'je n'y ai jamais pensé' was extremely common. Others indicated that they found it too hard to choose between so many parties; some indicated preferences for a specific political leader but admitted that they did not know which party he belonged to or, more often, had no interest in the identity of his party, whatever it might be. Others, forming a tiny minority of the non-party people, rejected the notion of parties with some hostility." Converse and Dupeux, 9-10.

[47] *Ibid.*, 1.

[48] *Ibid.*, 11.

national populations in the ability to report a paternal party preference: 86 percent of the Americans, and only 26 percent of the French, were able to do this. Again, as in the respondents' reports of their own nonpartisanship, a close reading of the responses convinced the investigators that they were not merely the victims of some artifact of cross-cultural polling (the French respondents said: "Je n'ai jamais su"; "Je ne lui ai jamais demandé"; "Il ne disait rien à ses enfants"; etc.). And since younger respondents were no better able to report parental party preference than were older respondents, more than inability to remember the names of the mutable French parties must be involved in the lack of information about intra-family political attitudes. There seem, as Converse and Dupeux put it, to be "basic discontinuities of political socialization in the French family."[49]

Convincing as findings based on adult retrospections may be, confirmation based on direct observations of childhood political socialization is necessary. The American side of the confirmation has been available for some time, and now the Grenoble study fills in further details. The American studies all show party identification arising rather early in childhood, taking at least its general shape, although not its full intensity, for most children before adolescence. The specific findings vary somewhat with item-wordings. In New Haven, with an item that probably forces a fairly high level of response ("If you were 21 now, whom would you vote for most of the time? Mostly Democrats. Mostly Republicans. Don't Know."), roughly 60 percent of the children exhibit a party preference from age nine (fourth grade) on through thirteen (eighth grade). This is approximately the incidence of party identifiers found by the Survey Research Center among young adult voters in the United States.[50] In the national survey of American children conducted by Dennis, Easton, Hess, and Torney at the University of Chicago, an item was used that probably reduces identification with party, since the wording permits an "independent" option and also the response "I don't know what Democrat and Republican mean." The Chicago investigators find a 55 percent incidence of party identification during preadolescence, reached by about age ten (fifth grade).[51]

The Grenoble children were never explicitly asked to state a party preference, but Roig and Billon-Grand report responses to four items that together provide convincing circumstantial evidence:

[49] *Ibid.*, 14.
[50] Greenstein, *Children and Politics*, chap. 4.
[51] Hess and Torney, 90.

1. Shortly beyond the middle of the instrument the question "Have you heard of the following groups?" is asked, and the checklist "Communistes, U.N.R., Socialistes, M.R.P." is provided (p. 94). There is no inhibition on uninformed assertions. One bit of partisan information was widely distributed: 85 percent of the sample said that they had heard of the Communists, a figure that rises to 98 percent among the middle-class thirteen-year-olds who make up the oldest *lycée* groups (the *cinquième*). This is consistent with the generally known finding that the Communist–non-Communist cleavage is widely perceived by members of the French adult population.[52] But there was a steep fall-off in awareness of the other three parties: 72 percent said that they had heard of the U.N.R. (80 percent in the *cinquième*); 65 percent said that they had heard of the Socialists (76 percent in the *cinquième*); and a mere 43 percent (57 percent in the *cinquième*) said that they had heard of the M.R.P. (The M.R.P., now defunct, had not run candidates in the Grenoble region in 1962, two years before the survey.)

2. The item immediately following sought to ascertain the child's assumptions about the nature of political parties ("A quoi servent ces groupements?"). Seventy-three percent of the sample (p. 92) was unable to respond, or produced *"divers"* responses, a category the authors use to code answers that miss the point of the question. This inability to respond appropriately is nearly universal (86 percent) among the eleven-year-olds who, along with a scattering of ten-year-olds, constitute the youngest age-group in which the Grenoble findings are reported. Even in the *cinquième*, nonresponse is high, though it goes down to 62 percent. The comparability of American data is imperfect, but the differences are so gross as to be quite convincing: by age ten the proportion of children in the American national sample who say they "don't know what Democrats and Republicans are" shrinks to below 5 percent. By age thirteen the figure is below 2 percent. Many more than 2 percent of these American thirteen-year-olds would no doubt be hard pressed to provide an open-ended description of what "these groups" do, but we assume that the great bulk would at least advance the vague statements made by the few older French children who did answer. (Parties exist "to do political things," "to take power," "they aspire to govern France.")[53]

---

[52] See, for example, the survey evidence presented in Monique Fichelet and others, "Les Français, la Politique et le Parti Communiste," in *Cahiers du Communisme*, No. 12 (December 1967) and No. 1 (January 1968).

[53] Actually, only 33 percent of the *cinquième* children defined "party." The residual 5 percent (and 4 percent of the total sample) made anti-party statements—for example, "ils existent à embêter la France," or "à ennuyer la France."

3. Close to the end of the questionnaire, the question "Are there good political parties?" was asked (p. 98). Again, the incidence of non-response—43 percent—is striking and well over the level we would expect in a population in which party identification is common. Explicit animosity to parties, on the other hand, is relatively rare (9 percent).

4. The previous item was followed by the question, "Name one or several good political parties" (p. 99). We assume that by the age of ten or eleven half or more of a typical American sample would name the Democrats or Republicans—many of them naming both parties. Again, the French "no response" rate is massive—79 *percent*. A further 10 percent mentioned the U.N.R. and 3 percent named various other parties (with responses divided among the parties listed earlier in the questionnaire, the Socialists, Communists, and M.R.P.). Eight percent referred to rough *tendances* of one kind or another.

The Grenoble study, then, appears to corroborate the Converse and Dupeux finding that the great bulk of French children fail to acquire party identifications. It remains for further investigations to corroborate and explain their findings on family political communication.

(2) FRANCE AS A CONFLICT SOCIETY: PAROCHIAL-SCHOOL–PUBLIC-SCHOOL DIFFERENCES

We cannot deal here in detail with the "conflict society" approach to explaining French politics. What seems to be implied in the familiar argument that the ideological cleavages in the French political stratum are deeply rooted in public attitudes is, among other things, that:

1. attitudes are widely held, sharply crystallized, and intensely felt in the French mass public;

2. individuals hold internally consistent attitudes (i.e., revolutionary or reactionary attitudes on issue "a" will be matched by parallel attitudes on issue "b");

3. attitudinal disagreement is high and cumulative (i.e., disagreement on one issue is bolstered by disagreement on the next); and

4. agencies of socialization and membership inculcate and reinforce these attitudinal patterns.

It is not hard to see how propositions of this sort might be tested. To date, while there have been interesting attempts to see if France in fact is divided into homogeneous and opposed "political families,"[54]

[54] Deutsch and others conclude: "The traditional predictors of the Left and the Right have almost all disappeared." 26-29. Also see Pierre Fougeyrollas, *La Conscience Politique dans la France Contemporaine* (Paris 1963).

FRENCH POLITICAL SOCIALIZATION   117

with the exception of scattered findings on "Red" or "White" patches
of voters,[55] the evidence that the French general public displays such a
pattern of attributes has not been found.[56]

One of the principal axes along which French political cleavage is
traditionally assumed to occur is that between a reactionary Catholic
France and a progressive Republican France. Ehrmann, who comments
that "until well into the present century, the opposition between be-
lievers and non-believers has been one of the main determinants of the
political culture," points to the familiar assumption that separate
Catholic education and related institutions significantly contributed to
this aspect of division in France: "The Catholic subsystem existing
within the republic drew its strength from a well-developed network
of private education and associations."[57]

It is still true that, as Siegfried first showed, the geographical areas
where *école privée* attendance is high also tend to vote for the Catholic
Right, and there is survey evidence that the correlation between high
levels of religious practice and right-wing voting is not just an ecological
artifact.[58] But several surveys have turned up little difference in the values
of religious and nonreligious youth, and Catholic organizations—formerly almost uniformly conservative—are now more ideologically heterogeneous.[59] Moreover, even when parochial- and public-school children
are found to differ in political attitude—with the more obvious demographic third factors controlled—this is no sure demonstration of the

[55] On Catholic France, see the classical work of Siegfried, *Tableau*; Laurence Wylie
and others, *Chanzeaux: A Village in Anjou* (Cambridge 1966); Charles Tilly, *The
Vendée* (Cambridge 1964). On "Red" France, see the case studies in Gordon Wright,
Rural Revolution in France (Stanford 1964); Edgar Morin, *Commune en France* (Paris
1967); and J.H.G. Lord, A. J. Petrie, and L. A. Whitehead, "Political Change in Rural
France: The 1967 Election in a Communist Stronghold," *Political Studies*, xvi (June
1968), 153-76. Very little has been written on urban Communist strongholds like those
in the *banlieue* of Paris.
[56] Occasional dissenters, like Nathan Leites, have argued that ideological cleavages
are not the major source of cleavage in the political elite either. See Leites' *On the
Game of Politics in France* (Stanford 1959); also see the evidence presented in
Duncan McRae, Jr., *Parliaments, Parties, and Society in France 1946-1958* (New York
1967), chap. 7.
[57] Ehrmann, 47-49. In his study of western France, Siegfried commented that he
knew of "an imposing number of French towns where the Republican state does not
feel itself fundamentally in charge" because of the dominance of Catholic schools.
Siegfried, 399. The various assertions in the literature on this basis of cleavage seem
to us in general not to distinguish sufficiently between (1) past *versus* present levels
of cleavage and (2) hypothesis *versus* empirical documentation.
[58] The correlation between religiosity and voting for the two parties of the Left during the Fourth Republic was never less than —.45, McRae, 247; for survey data, see,
for example, Michelat and others, 13.
[59] For a summary of the youth survey findings, see Ehrmann, 53. On Catholic organizations see William Bosworth, *Catholicism and Crisis in France* (Princeton 1962)
and Wright, chap. 8.

FRENCH POLITICAL SOCIALIZATION 119

independent effect of parochial-school education, as distinguished from the effects of other factors that preselect parochial-school children (e.g., coming from a religious family, or growing up in a Catholic subculture). A recent study of parochial education in the United States suggests that the Catholic education affects *religious* attitudes, but that it does not affect political attitudes.[60]

While the Grenoble data do not permit an estimate of the independent effect of Catholic education, they do permit comparison by type of school. Using the 5 percent significance level as a convenient way of identifying differences that warrant discussion, we have summarized in Table One a good number of the differences between the two subsamples, emphasizing those that are not likely to be a result of the slightly higher educational level of the *école privée* children.

There are three groups of comparisons in Table One. The first two items are examples of comparisons that seem to generate "real," but for the present purposes uninteresting, differences. These items show that public-school children were more likely than private-school children to list political figures of the past or present as exemplars—the famous people they hope some day to resemble. This imbalance seems to be a consequence of the more frequent references by Catholic-school children to the saints of their church. While we are aware that hagiolatry might under some circumstances become politically significant, we are not inclined to make much of this apparent consequence of different curricular emphases in the two kinds of schools.

The second kind of comparison is made in items three through nine of Table One, which report the main instances of differences that do seem at least partially consistent with the notion that a right-wing Catholic subculture exists and is perpetuated through the school system. The direction of the variance in these items illustrates that some of the kinds of political learning implied in the notion of "two Frances" appears to take place, but its lack of magnitude suggests that the French political socialization process probably does *not* generate and reinforce cumulative ideological conflict. Thus: the public-school children are 12 percent more likely than the Catholic-school children to emphasize *égalité* in defining the term "democracy"; the few children to use the term *laïque*, with its anticlerical implications, to designate France are

[60] Andrew Greeley and Peter Rossi, *The Education of Catholic Americans* (Chicago 1966), chap. 5. Approximately 20 percent of French children attend parochial schools, but such schools are still in the majority in such traditionally Catholic departments as the Vendée, the Haute-Loire and the Maine-et-Loire. Curricular differences have mainly disappeared, as Catholic schools accept government subsidies that require them to tailor their courses to the public school curriculum. See Halls, pp. 80-81.

TABLE ONE

REPRESENTATIVE STATISTICALLY SIGNIFICANT DIFFERENCES $(P<.05)$*
BETWEEN CATHOLIC- AND STATE-SCHOOL GRENOBLE STUDY RESPONDENTS

	Catholic School	State School	Difference
	%	%	%
1. The famous person (living or dead) he would like to resemble is political	13	26	13
2. Person he would *not* like to resemble is political.	34	48	14
3. Chooses "all men are equal" as the best defining characteristic of "democracy" (rather than definitions in terms government of the people, full employment, or the absence of "bosses who direct the workers").	29	41	12
4. Considers *laïque* as the quality that best describes France (rather than *puissante, démocratique,* or *républicaine*).	1	16	15
5. A country should be directed by one man (rather than an assembly).	28	12	—16
6. Disagrees with the statement that the strong will always dominate the weak.	76	84	8
7. Disagrees with statement that the government is always right *vis-à-vis* malcontents.	47	65	18
8. The Revolution of 1789 was good.	41	66	25
9. Wouldn't want to live in the USSR.	26	14	—12
10. Traitors to *la patrie* should be shot.	30	45	15
11. There are (some) good political parties.	55	43	—12
N =	(186)	(227)	

* Chi-square test.

in public school; the Catholic-school children are about 16 percent more likely than the public-school children to assert that a country should be ruled by a single man rather than an assembly; they are less likely (though by only 8 percent) to disagree with the statement that the strong will always dominate the weak (but they also overwhelmingly disagree with this statement); and they are more likely to choose the Soviet Union as a country they would not like to live in.

Finally, children from the two kinds of schools differ the most of all (by 25 percent) on an item we have already discussed: whether the Revolution of 1789 was good. It certainly is of compelling interest (although scarcely a matter for surprise) that France has been unable to develop a neutral, positively valued myth of its own revolution. And it is impressive that this century-and-a-half-old event should be a matter of disagreement among elementary-school children in the 1960's. Nevertheless, the 41 percent of the *privée* children who thought the Revolution an evil were matched by another 41 percent who described it positively, and a fifth of the public-school children were also negative toward the Revolution. And we have further seen that condemnation of the Revolution did not seem to have a strongly ideological quality.

That the divided schools (and whatever else is measured by "school-type") do not socialize consistent or cumulative ideological cleavage at the mass level is further suggested by the third class of finding in Table One. The tenth and eleventh rows of the table are instances of statistically significant differences that can readily be interpreted as showing parochial-school children to have more "liberal" attitudes. These rows show that the public-school children were *more* likely to voice the view that traitors to *la patrie* ought to be shot,[61] and were less likely to approve of at least some political parties. Finally, the two groups did not differ significantly on a variety of items which "could" have generated ideological differences: questions about whether it is normal for Frenchmen to die for their country, about the functions of deputies, about whether foreigners and Arabs should leave France, and about whether the USSR is an enemy nation, among others.

Again the findings, which should be interpreted cautiously because of unmeasured "third-factor" influences, are not what we would expect in a society with deeply etched clerical versus anticlerical conflicts. It is possible that the results would have been very different in the past or in another region—for example, in parts of Western France where the influence of family, class, school, and subculture are cumulative. But those regions of France which are "neatly" Red or White are the exception rather than the rule today. Whether the situation was ever very different is a question for historical research.

(3) AUTHORITY AND SOCIALIZATION IN FRANCE: FROM PARADOX TO PARADIGM

The failure of parochial–state-school differences to produce a consistent pattern of political attitudes in French schoolchildren suggests that we should be skeptical of explanations that attempt to make in-

[61] We may be taxed with having failed to see that the apparently more "liberal" responses of the parochial-school children to this question really disguises a "conservative" response: "Why should we Catholics be willing to die for *their* (the Republicans') country?" We have considered this interpretation but think it too sophisticated to account for children's responses.

ferences from a single agency of socialization to the whole of a nation's value system. This seems to us the major difficulty with the
third theme mentioned at the outset—the amorphous, fascinating, and
often maligned account of national authority style contained in the
literature on "French national character."

The principal accounts in this literature appear to posit that:

1. the French family combines harmony with inequality of status
in a way that leaves the child with a combination of respect for and
distrust of authority;

2. this duality is reinforced in the school by the passivity expected
of the child and the type of discipline—shame before the group—used
as a sanction;

3. the peer group—never legitimized by either family or school—
gains the child's loyalty but not his participation;

4. the child emerges as adult with the patrimony of these dovetailed
experiences—he conforms on the surface, but strikes out against authority when he can; he protects his area of privacy but rejects chances
to change it; he is loyal to his group but will not strive to work within
it; and finally, he projects these attitudes towards life and authority
onto political authority and government, a transfer that allows us to
understand his political behavior in terms of the model, or template,
of his childhood.[62]

The assertions that French childhood—and especially the family—is
an appropriate model for understanding various aspects of political behavior are legion. For example:

On local government:

> The consensus that prevails in most French communes is reminis-
> cent of the harmony characteristic of most French families. The
> resemblance is heightened by the similar authority patterns in
> the two units.[63]

On ideology:

> Growing up, a child learns with what symbols his family identifies
> itself. Beyond the limits of the family he becomes conscious of

---

[62] Some typical citations: Pitts, 249-61; Hoffmann "Heroic Leadership," 114-17;
McRae, 17-19; Wylie, *Village*, 330-37; Metraux and Mead, 1-68; Crozier, Part III. Also
see Mark Kesselman, *The Ambiguous Consensus* (New York 1967); pp. 9-12; Martha
Wolfenstein, "French Parents take their Children to the Park," in Mead and Wolfenstein (eds.), *Childhood in Contemporary Culture* (Chicago 1955); and Wylie, "Social
Change at the Grass Roots," in *In Search of France*, 139-234. A well-balanced blend
of traditional interpretations and recent data will be found in Ehrmann, chap. 3.

[63] Kesselman, 9.

groups of people, of *cercles*, with which he and his family are either associated or not. . . . Within the totality of French culture, these circles are fused into still larger groups, *familles d'esprit* (ideological families).[64]

On group memberships:

The school peer group is the prototype of the solidary groups which exist in France beyond the nuclear and extended family. They are characterized by jealous equalitarianism among the members, difficulty of admitting newcomers, and conspiracy of silence against superior authority.[65]

Finally, Crozier tries to show that in the bureaucracy the protection of personal space and dislike of face-to-face relationships lead individuals to appeal to a higher authority, thereby increasing centralization. And all of this is said to have its source in attitudes toward authority learned in childhood.[66]

Students of political psychology have tended in recent years to be suspicious on formal grounds of theories that hypothesize a chain of causality running from nonpolitical socialization of personality in the primary circles of childhood, through informal associations and memberships, to politics. We need only visualize the number of links in such a causal chain to suspect that the connections among its more remote elements would be weak, or at any rate, complex:

socialization$\longrightarrow$ personality$\longrightarrow$ attitudes$\longrightarrow$ individual
behavior$\longrightarrow$ aggregate patterns of behavior.[67]

Nevertheless, such connections are more likely to be present under some circumstances than others, and whether they obtain is an empirical question.[68] The unanimity of so many talented observers of French society in drawing political conclusions from childhood experiences in France, as well as the prominence of the family in the intriguing empirical findings of Converse and Dupeux, leads us to believe that these relationships are worth exploring.

Thus our disappointment that Roig and Billon-Grand, in their study of Grenoble schoolchildren, were unable to learn a great deal about

[64] Wylie, "Social Change," 231.
[65] Pitts, 259.
[66] The argument is judiciously summarized in Hoffmann, "Heroic Leadership," 114-16.
[67] For a fuller discussion, see Fred I. Greenstein, *Personality and Politics: Problems of Evidence, Interference, and Conceptualization* (Chicago 1969), especially the discussion of "linkage" in chapter 5.
[68] *Ibid.*, chap. 2.

children's attitudes to authority, or even to cross-tabulate children's political attitudes with aspects of family structure.[69] Although the series
of questions on the President of the Republic *might* be interpreted as
evidence on general attitudes toward authority, the authors do not
choose to do so, possibly because their questionnaire seems to have produced rather shallow responses. Answers to the question "What does the
President of the Republic do?" cannot satisfactorily be compared with
American responses to similar items, because of discrepancies in the age-
categories for which data are reported and because of lack of clarity
about the coding criteria used in the Grenoble study. The quotations
presented by the authors suggest rather colorless, if childlike, responses:
"Il organise le pays avec des aides"; "Il administre la patrie" (pp. 52-53).
The children who responded unfavorably to the item asking for evaluation of the President do not seem, in the image conveyed by the literature on national character, to be sniping at authority from the safety
of their *"situations acquises"*—they say, for example, "Il est orgueilleux,
il a un nez trop grand"; "Il a abandonné les pieds-noirs"; "Il n'aide pas
les mineurs" (p. 79).

If the Grenoble data do not permit us to advance generalizations
about French children's attitudes toward authority, they do serve as a
reminder of the special difficulties that may be involved in developing
the operational indicators appropriate for translating the various national-character hypotheses into testable hypotheses. Since it seems to us
that the presently available fixed-choice, paper-and-pencil procedures for
questioning children are not promising instruments for dealing with
the subtle relationships hypothesized in the national-character literature,[70] we conclude with methodological observations about alternative
means of eliciting children's orientations.

IV. CONCLUDING METHODOLOGICAL OBSERVATIONS

Students of comparative political behavior must be grateful to Roig
and Billon-Grand for departing from the literary mode of commentary
on France's paradoxical nature, and conducting an exploratory empirical study of French political socialization. Their achievement is the
more admirable for having been made in the face of obstacles. Not the

[69] The effect of family structure upon children's attitudes is discussed in Hess and
Torney, chap. 3, and in Robert E. Lane, "La Maturation Politique de L'adolescent aux
Etats-Unis et en Allemagne," in the *Revue Française de Sociologie* VII (1956), 598-618.

[70] This seems to us to be a principal shortcoming of what evidently is the only effort
to employ notions from the French national-character literature in political socialization research: Frank A. Pinner, "Parental Overprotection and Political Distrust,"
American Academy of Political and Social Science, Annals CCCLXI (September 1965)
58-70.

least part of that achievement is their demonstration that the obstacles are not insuperable—that research on French political socialization is both feasible and capable of contributing to the study of French politics.

The three kinds of reservations about the book and study that we have remarked on are: the design of the questionnaire, the statistical treatment of the data, and interpretations of the findings. The emphasis on a paper-and-pencil instrument, with fixed-choice items used to ascertain a number of rather elusive orientations, leaves us uncertain at various points about the precise meaning of the children's responses. The absence of controls and partial correlations makes it difficult to ascribe findings to specific causes. And finally, without making their assumptions very explicit, the authors sometimes interpret their findings in terms of inherited expectations about French politics that their data do not clearly support.

An advantage of any kind of empirical research is that it is progressive. The shortcomings of inquiries become part of their contributions, by leading to further research. From our indications of the aspects of the Grenoble study we found problematic, there follow a number of suggestions about the desiderata for further study of French political socialization. One need, of course, is for conducting such work with appropriate attention to controls, and for multivariate analysis in general. Another is for fuller sampling of the diverse groups in the French population: the Grenoble investigators were unable to study many children from the population groups that support the Communist Party or from the still vast small-town segment of the population. And by working in a single region they were unable to examine the question of whether variables such as school sponsorship have a greater or lesser effect in other parts of France. A further need is for measuring instruments that get at some of the more elusive aspects of children's orientations. In conclusion, we develop this last theme further, because of its general implications for comparative political socialization research.

Fixed-choice and other relatively structured and unprobing ways of eliciting response are more problematic in crosscultural research than in research within a single culture. The wider the cultural range of the populations being studied, the more difficult it is to know whether respondents who check the "same" questionnaire alternative in fact mean the same thing. The confusion is compounded when one studies children; because of their disposition to please adult interviewers and get the "right" answer, the investigator is in constant peril of reporting

FRENCH POLITICAL SOCIALIZATION   133

findings that are more a function of his instrument than of any formed aspect of the child's political thinking. Even in crosscultural political socialization research, fixed choice items have their place.[71] But, as David O. Sears points out, they are more appropriate for some purposes (such as "determining the child's affects toward political stimuli") than for others (such as "obtaining the content of his thoughts").[72]

For certain interesting analytic purposes, even the open-ended survey item as it is typically constructed ("What do political parties do?" "What are the good or bad qualities of the President of the Republic?") may be insufficiently sensitive. Thus, for example, on the question of party identification, the Converse and Dupeux data, now supplemented by the Grenoble findings, begin to give us clear evidence on French electoral psychology, but much of what is shown is negative: French voters tend *not* to have party identifications; they seem *not* to have intense, crystallized political ideologies. But we lack a sufficiently subtle and rounded *positive* account of the psychology of French voters. And there is reason to believe that at least at the exploratory stage we may need rather sensitive, quasi-clinical means of obtaining this account.

A reference to "clinical" data-gathering techniques conjures up the psychoanalytic couch, or at least such deep personality measures as the Rorschach ink blot or the Thematic Apperception picture card. But there is a great deal of only partly explored "space" between the standard survey questions and the Rorschach. This space is in part occupied by what are sometimes called the *semi*-projective techniques. Such techniques are closer to the "texture" of day-to-day life and political reality than is the full-blown projective test, but they are, as it were, more unhinged—more suitable for eliciting fantasies, images, and anticipations of behavior—than the usual survey item. The typical semi-projective item consists of a description of an episode of the sort that the individual might encounter in his day-to-day existence: for example, a description of a potentially tense encounter between friends, work associates, family members—or actors in the political arena. The respondent is asked to imagine the outcome of the episode, and, depending upon research interests, it is possible to ask further probing questions about how *he* would respond under such circumstances, about his feelings, about his perceptions of norms, and so forth.

Such techniques, by focusing on archetypical situations, can be pecu-

[71] See, for example, Jack Dennis, Leon Lindberg, Donald McCrone, and Rodney Stiefbold, "Political Socialization into Democratic Orientations in Four Western Systems," *Comparative Political Studies* I (April 1968), 71-101.
[72] David O. Sears, review of Hess and Torney, "The Development of Political Attitudes in Children," *Harvard Educational Review* xxxviii (Summer 1968), 571-78.

liarly useful for getting comparable responses to common stimuli by adults and by children, and crossculturally. The fullness of response, and the possibility through skillful interviewing of drawing out the respondent's full meaning, increases one's confidence that the findings are not merely a function of the instrument. These techniques, which are seldom utilized in political science, have been used by a variety of investigators in other disciplines. Two especially fertile applications, which deserve notice by the student of political socialization, are by Hanfmann and Getzels[73] and by Joseph Adelson[74] and of his associates. Hanfmann and Getzels used a series of episodes about work situations in highly successful comparative analysis of a matched sample of Americans and former Soviet citizens. To a remarkable degree they were able to get both at orientations that were specific to the institutional circumstances each group had encountered and at more general psychological dispositions toward interpersonal relations. Adelson and his co-workers, proceeding in the tradition of Piaget, have interviewed adolescents in a number of countries, using a schedule in which the respondents are asked to imagine the rules of an ideal political system that a group of visionaries are about to set up on a desert island. Adelson's interview schedule covers a remarkable number of the standard issues in political philosophy, in the course of asking how such a political system ought to be organized.

The present reviewers have, in a very preliminary way, used similar techniques for interviewing preadolescent children in France, as well as in the United States and Britain, with a concern for a number of the issues that have led to perennial efforts to compare these three systems. We have asked children to imagine the upshot of a variety of stories, ranging from incomplete episodes about parent-child relations to episodes about aspects of the wider political environment about which we know the children were rather uninformed, but that we wanted to treat as stimuli for imaginative speculations that might reveal implicit cultural assumptions. We have proceeded far enough to be clear that the semi-projective episode-completion stimulus is one that children respond to with interest and enthusiasm, and one that leads them to produce intriguing interview protocols. Consider, for example, the fol-

[73] Eugenia Hanfmann and Jacob W. Getzels, "Interpersonal Attitudes of Former Soviet Citizens, as Studied by a Semi-Projective Method," *Psychological Monographs*, No. 389 (1955).
[74] Joseph Adelson and Robert P. O'Neil, "Growth of Political Ideas in Adolescence: The Sense of Community," *Journal of Personality and Social Psychology*, IV No. 3 (1966), 295-306. Lynette Beall, "Political Thinking in Adolescence," (University of Michigan 1967). Unpublished dissertation.

lowing question about legislative-executive relations, asked of twelve-year-olds in the three nations:

Interviewer: Now I am going to ask you to complete a story about the President and a member of Congress of the President's party. Suppose the member of Congress from your part of the country were asked by the President to vote for a law the member didn't approve of. What would happen? Finish the story. (Roles are varied appropriately for Britain and France).

Boy, Middletown, Conn.: "Well he wouldn't vote for it."

Int.: "Why not?"

Boy: "Because he didn't think it was right."

Girl, Colchester, England: "They have a long talk and an argument and if the MP didn't approve of the new law, he might get chucked out or something like that ... for being against the Prime Minister. Sometimes MP's usually get talked into it."

Girl, Les Baux, France: "The President would ask other people's opinions. They would try to come to an agreement."

Clearly, no one investigative technique, and no one investigation, will be sufficient. We hope that it will be possible a decade from now, out of the pluralism of inquiry, to look back at a long series of political socialization studies, conducted in a variety of systems by a variety of techniques. Once the findings of such studies are synthesized with what is known about the psychology of adult political behavior and about how political systems actually function, we will begin to have documented theories of political stability and change—theories that are *sans* paradox.

[11]

Political Studies (1990), XXXVIII, 603–619

The French Constitutional Council: A Study in Institutional Change

MARTIN HARRISON

University of Keele

Constitutions have a way of confounding both their authors and their critics. Nowhere is this better illustrated than in the evolution of the French Constitutional Council. Little regarded during the constitutional debates of 1958, it now ranks among the most important institutional innovations of the Fifth Republic. Yet although its evolution has received due attention from legal scholars, political science has been slow to recognize its emergence as an actor of some consequence for both the policy process and the institutional balance of the Fifth Republic.[1] The means by which this transformation has been effected and the place the Council now occupies are the principal concerns of this paper.

'Invented' by Michel Debré's task force in the summer of 1958, the Council was one of many devices introduced to keep Parliament in its newly reduced place. It was to review for conformity to the constitution all organic laws and parliamentary standing orders and, on request from the President of the Republic, the Prime Minister or the President of the Assembly or the Senate, any international agreement before ratification or any Act before promulgation. It would also decide, at the request of the government or the president of the appropriate chamber, whether a Bill or amendment under debate lay within the

---

[1] See J. T. S. Keeler and A. Stone, 'Judicial-political confrontation in Mitterrand's France', in G. Ross, S. Hoffmann and S. Malzacher, *The Mitterrand Experiment: Continuity and Change in Modern France* (Cambridge, Polity Press, 1987), pp. 161–81. Also Henry Ehrmann's characteristically perceptive discussion in *Politics in France* (Boston, Little, Brown, 4th edn, 1983), pp. 328–34. Alec Stone's 'In the shadow of the Constitutional Council: The "Juridicisation" of the Legislative Process in France', *West European Politics*, 12:3 (July 1989), 12–34 appeared just as this paper was completed.

0032-3217/90/04/0603–17/$03.00 © 1990 *Political Studies*

'domain of statute', to which Parliament was now confined, or conflicted with a delegation of legislative authority to the government. Finally, the government could ask it to rule that legislation had 'intruded' into the executive's rule-making domain', so enabling it to be modified by simple decree. (Responsibilities relating to elections, referendums and emergency powers fall outside the scope of this paper.)

Although Debré hailed the Council as a 'great and necessary innovation', his intention was no more than that this 'weapon against deviation from parliamentary government' should 'ensure that the rules determining jurisdiction in constitutional matters are respected'. Most early commentators were unimpressed. Avril described it as 'an auxiliary of the executive, making sure its prerogatives are respected'; for Duverger it existed 'not to protect citizens against violations of the Constitution but to prevent one power encroaching on another'. 'The Constitutional Council', lamented Eisenmann, 'amounts to very little'.[2]

Yet the Council embodied a revolution in French public law. Since 1789 the republican tradition had been one of unrestrained parliamentary sovereignty. The Declaration of the Rights of Man proclaimed statute law 'the expression of the general will'. Democratic absolutism combined with suspicion of jurists born of experience of the *parlements* of the Old Regime militated against any external constraints being applied to Parliament. An 'Act' of 16 and 24 August 1790 laid down that 'the courts shall neither prevent nor suspend execution of the decrees of the legislative body on pain of committing criminal abuse of office [*forfaiture*]'. Sieyès was almost alone in asking how respect for the Constitution was to be ensured. His proposal for a 'constitutional jury' was unanimously rejected, stigmatized by Thibaudeau as 'this monstrous power' which would put public institutions in chains.[3]

Sieyès's question never entirely disappeared from view. It was revived periodically by constitutional theorists and (mainly) right-of-centre politicians from Tocqueville to Tardieu – to little avail. Hostility to constitutional review was strengthened by the publication in 1921 of Edouard Lambert's influential *Le gouvernement des juges et la lutte contre la législation sociale aux Etats-Unis*, a critique of the Supreme Court's handling of social legislation. Since then no discussion has been complete without the spectre of a *gouvernement des juges*. In 1946 the MRP briefly advocated a constitutional court, only to be brushed aside by the socialists and communists. The Constitutional Committee which emerged was essentially a device to prevent the Assembly surreptitiously revising the constitution. It made only one ruling in its 12-year existence. To all practical intents and purposes parliamentary sovereignty reigned undiminished.

The creation of the Constitutional Council spelled the demise of that tradition, slow though the consequences were to become apparent. Formerly, the only

---

[2] M. Debré, 'La nouvelle constitution', *Revue française de science politique*, IX:1 (March 1959), 11; P. Avril, *Politics in France* (Harmondsworth, Penguin, 1969), p. 67; M. Duverger, 'Les institutions de la cinquième République', *Revue française de science politique*, IX:1 (March 1959), 120; C. Eisenmann, cited by M. Kajman, *Le Monde* (6 Sept. 1986). But see P. Williams and M. Harrison, *De Gaulle's Republic* (London, Longman, 1960), pp. 131–5.

[3] For historical background see F. Luchaire, *Le Conseil constitutionnel* (Paris, Economica, 1980), pp. 1–11; D. Turpin, *Contentieux constitutionnel* (Paris, PUF, 1986), pp. 9–23; M. H. Davis, 'The law/ politics distinction, the French Conseil Constitutionnel, and the US Supreme Court', *American Journal of Comparative Law*, 34:1 (1986), 46–8; J. Rivero, 'Fin d'un absolutisme', *Pouvoirs*, 13 (1986), 5–16.

restraints on the legislature were those it imposed on itself; now, although it remained sovereign within its domain, it had lost the power to determine the extent of that sovereignty. Once statute reigned supreme; now it 'expresses the general will *only in so far as it respects the constitution*'.[4]

Initially the Council did little to require assessments of its role and potential to be revised. Its vetting of parliamentary standing orders in 1959, apparently based on the principle that anything not specifically authorized in the constitution was prohibited, removed any lingering illusion among members that they were still masters in their own Houses. However, once the first flurry of organic laws had been cleared, the Council's impact on the legislative process was minimal; it was called on to assess the constitutionality of new statutes on average less than once per year. Narrowly drawn, laconic and technical, few of these decisions seemed of much consequence; fewer still made a significant public impact.

In later years a more activist Council would have cause to be thankful that an elliptical style and the caution proper to a fledgling institution had not closed off some of the jurisprudential avenues it was then exploring. For the moment, though, the Council was little known and little esteemed. Governments with loyal majorities rarely felt need of it, while to the opposition it was a partisan body dominated by Gaullist placemen – five of its nine initial members had close links with the General or the Gaullist party – lacking both the will and the capacity to inflict serious embarrassment on the government. Even in its most Gaullist phase the Council's decisions were never a mere resultant of its political complexion and it interpreted the domain of statute more liberally than many had feared. Nevertheless, as Duverger remarked in 1967, it was loved by neither the lawyers nor the public. It was conspicuously lacking in moral authority.[5] The left's suspicions were deepened by the fact that it held none of the posts carrying nominating rights to the Council (Presidency of the Republic or of either chamber). Nor had it access to constitutional review except by the grace and favour of the President of the Senate. At the end of its first decade the Council's future seemed uncertain; even if it survived an opposition victory, its brief and caseload were hardly such as to attract members of a calibre that would ensure that its judgements would command respect.

The first real sign that it might be a force to be reckoned with came in 1971.[6] In 1970 the government had dissolved Gauche prolétarienne, a small revolutionary party. A group of left-wing personalities announced the creation of an Association des Amis de La Cause du Peuple, incorporating the title of the proscribed movement's newspaper. The Minister of the Interior ordered the Paris prefect of police to refuse to issue a receipt confirming that the Association had

[4] 58–197 DC (Decision on conformity to The Constitution under Art. 54 or 61) of 23 Aug. 1986.
[5] *Le Monde* (18 Nov. 1967). The opposition's fiercest criticisms were directed at the composition and system of appointment to the Council; its refusal to invalidate the 1962 referendum (which it had opposed in its advisory role) on the grounds that it lacked jurisdiction and that the sovereign people had spoken, and its handling of election disputes, notably its rejection of complaints based on a broadcast made by President de Gaulle in the 1967 parliamentary elections on the grounds that the President was accountable only before the High Court of Justice.
[6] 71–44 DC of 16 July 1971. See L. Favoreu and L. Philip, *Les grandes décisions du Conseil constitutionnel* (Paris, Sirey, 1986), 4th edn, pp. 239–254; J. Rivero, *Le Conseil constitutionnel et les libertés* (Paris, Economica, 1987, 2nd edn), pp. 9–26; L. Hamon, *Recueil Dalloz-Sirey, Chronique* (1974), 83–90; F. Luchaire, *La Protection constitutionnelle des droits et des libertés* (Paris, Economica, 1987).

supplied the information needed for full legal recognition under the Associations Act of 1901. After an administrative tribunal quashed this decision, the government introduced a Bill empowering prefects to withhold a receipt from any new association deemed to have illegal or immoral aims until the matter could be decided by a court. Once this Bill had been adopted, the President of the Senate, Alain Poher, referred it to the Council. The Council ruled that it violated one of 'the fundamental principles recognized by the laws of the Republic and solemnly reaffirmed by the Preamble of the Constitution' – freedom of association.

In many respects the decision grew naturally out of earlier judgements. From the beginning the Council had adopted an extensive definition of 'the Constitution' by including organic laws and 'organic ordinances' in the *bloc de constitutionnalité* to which legislation must conform. It had taken the significant and adventurous step of adding the Preamble to this in 1970, a concern for civil liberties having been apparent in several early rulings.[7] Nevertheless, the decision was a landmark. While not exactly the Council's *Marbury* v. *Madison*, like *Marbury* it signalled an institution's coming of age. Nicholas remarks that it established beyond question that there were fundamentals that Parliament could neither alter nor contravene.[8] It in fact did far more. This was unmistakably a 'political' ruling, in the sense that its form and style were manifestly tailored to seize a golden opportunity to make a liberal mark and write large a number of points which had previously been written small or remained implicit. By ruling against the government so comprehensively, on so contentious an issue, the Council asserted an independence of spirit that had hitherto been in doubt. It also demonstrated an intention not to remain a mere regulator of the legislative-executive boundary but to be arbiter of a much wider range of norms. Moreover, the message was directed not only at Parliament but even more at the executive, now the *de facto* initiator of the great bulk of legislation.

The terms of the decision are striking. Compared with the terse, narrowly drawn *arguments* of earlier judgements, this was declaratory in tone and couched in the widest possible terms. It invoked both the Preamble, which cross-refers to the rights set out in the Declaration of 1789 and to the Preamble to the 1946 Constitution, and 'to the fundamental principles recognized by the laws of the Republic'. This expression was not in common use. It had been inserted in the 1946 Preamble at the behest of the MRP but even its authors would have been hard pressed to say what exactly it encompassed.[9] Which principles? Which laws? Which Republic? None of the answers was clear. What was clear was that, by evoking so vast and imprecise a range of norms, the Council had transformed both the notion of conformity to the Constitution and its own role and potential.

---

[7] 70–39 DC of 19 June 1970. The opening line of the *visa* cut through debates about whether it could interpret the Preamble with sovereign economy: '*Vu, la Constitution, et notamment son préambule'.* Also Turpin, *Contentieux constitutionnel,* p. 67; J. E. Beardsley, 'The Conseil Constitutionnel and constitutional liberties in France', *American Journal of Comparative Law,* 20:3 (1972); B. Neuborne, 'Judicial review and separation of powers in France and the United States', *New York University Law Review,* 57:3 (June 1982); F. L. Morton, 'Judicial review in France: a comparative analysis', *American Journal of Comparative Law,* 36:1 (Winter 1988).

[8] B. Nicholas, 'Fundamental rights and judicial review in France', *Public Law* (Spring 1978), 89.

[9] It had also been cited in a leading Fourth Republic decision by the Conseil d'Etat, *Amicale des Annamites de Paris,* CE 11 Sept. 1956, Rec. 317. And see Société Eky, CE 12, Feb. 1960, Rec. 101.

Martin Harrison 607

Small wonder that the ruling was apparently reached only after sharp disagreement and by the narrowest of margins.[10]

Whatever the Council's ambitions, its role was bound to remain modest as long as access was limited to only four office-holders. However, in 1974 Giscard d'Estaing assumed the presidency with hopes of securing official recognition for the parliamentary opposition. Almost the only lasting fruit was a constitutional revision extending the right to refer newly adopted Acts to 60 deputies or senators. This generated little enthusiasm. Government supporters feared that the Council would become more politicized, while the left (which now favoured a 'supreme court') dismissed the change as mere tinkering. Few expected it to be of more than minor consequence.[11]

They were soon confounded. Parliamentarians seized on their new power with alacrity. Having dealt with only nine references of ordinary legislation in 15 years the Council had 67 between June 1974 and May 1981, giving rise to 47 decisions (some Bills attracting more than one challenge), 101 under the Socialist governments of 1981–86 (66 decisions) and 34 (26 decisions) under 'cohabitation', between April 1986 and May 1988. Although government backbenchers opposed to liberalizing abortion made the first parliamentary reference, resort to the Council became virtually an opposition monopoly. Of the 236 references under Article 61.2 between June 1974 and December 1989, none was initiated by presidents of the Republic; prime ministers made four and presidents of the Assembly and Senate two each. The remaining 228 were all parliamentary – all but three from the opposition of the day. The Socialists' zeal between 1974 and 1981 was repaid by the right in 1981–86. After March 1986, the Socialists were reluctant to persist with systematic references but the strike rate remained high. The proportion of Bills referred rose from about 1 per cent to around 15 per cent, at which point almost all contentious legislation was being sent for review. Nor was the endeavour futile. Between 1974 and 1981, 29 per cent of decisions under Article 61.2 were total or partial annulments. In 1981–86 and 1986–88 this rose to 51.5 and 58.0 per cent respectively.[12] Reference, or even the threat of it, has become the opposition's most powerful weapon – indeed virtually its only effective weapon during periods of disciplined parliamentary majorities. (Sometimes the outcome is a Pyrrhic victory; a Socialist challenge to a new system of contracts for church schools produced a decision according constitutional status to freedom of education, manifestly not what they were hoping for, while the right's challenge to the Socialists' constituency map for New Caledonia resulted in a ruling that subsequently constrained their own electoral reform. Parliamentarians have been slow to grasp how victories over the government of the day may subsequently thwart them in turn.)

Statistics such as those just cited can be no more than a point of departure for assessing the substantive and institutional importance of the Council's decisions.

---

[10] *Le Monde* (18–19 and 28 July 1971 and 6 Sept. 1986). Favoreu and Philip, *Les grandes décisions*, p. 247, suggest the Council's decision rested on an essentially political judgement that the underlying intention of the Bill was to 'delay, discourage or annihilate attempts to establish or re-establish an association'.

[11] *Journal Officiel, Débats Parlementaires* (S.) 16 Oct. 1974; (A.N.) 17 Oct. 1974 and (Cong.) 21 Oct. 1974. A proposal by Roger Frey, the Council's President, that it have a power of self-reference where public liberties were thought to be threatened was rejected.

[12] For 1977–86, L. Favoreu, 'Les cent premières annulations prononcées par le Conseil constitutionnel', *Revue de Droit Publique*, 1987(2); for 1986–89 my own figures.

It has been prudently sparing with outright annulments – there were 12 between 1974 and December 1989, compared with 66 partial annulments. Although many partial invalidations affect a single, minor clause containing an illicit 'budget rider' or extending legislation to an overseas territory without having consulted the local assembly, some, such as the 1971 freedom of association decision and the ruling on New Caledonia's electoral boundaries, are tantamount to complete rejection. The disallowing of sex quotas for local election lists, which eliminated a central feature of the Socialists' women's rights programme, and of the clauses in their Press Bill aimed at the Hersant newspaper empire, which frustrated its central political objective, are further instances of how the invalidation of a few clauses may have substantial policy consequences.[13]

While most annulments rest on procedural or separation-of-powers grounds, appearing aridly technical at first glance, both process-based techniques of review and those based on *vires* may have important substantive implications. Thus the ruling that proposals for the overseas departments infringed constitutional provisions governing subnational governments seriously impeded Socialist plans for reform.[14] However, many of the Council's most influential decisions take the subtler form of qualified rulings (*conforme sous réserve*), a technique borrowed from the German and Italian constitutional courts. Although appearing in the Council's second decision (on the Assembly's Standing Orders) in 1959, this was not employed in full legislative review until 1976. It reached full flowering during the 1986–88 cohabitation, when it proved especially valuable because, although the practical consequences can be as great as with outright invalidation, the element of confrontation between government and constitutional judge can be perceptibly softened.

Sometimes the Council makes a qualified ruling because it judges that a measure, while not inherently unconstitutional, might be put to unconstitutional ends. A 'neutralizing' reservation can prevent the undesired outcome while leaving the measure itself unscathed. Thus its decision on new contracts for church schools prescribed that the requirement that teachers respect their 'specific character' 'must not be interpreted as permitting any infringement of their freedom of conscience'.[15] 'Constructive' reservations add a positive gloss to the measure or the manner in which it is to be interpreted. For example, the possibility for someone taken to a police station over an identity check to *ask* that the Procureur be informed emerged, through the Council's ruling, as a *right*.

By such means the Council has developed approval 'with reservations' into a method for delivering injunctions to other political actors, whether legislative, administrative or judicial. Favoreu and Philip remark of one particularly detailed ruling on the Security and Liberty Act that it would be difficult for any judge to operate other than along the lines the Council had laid down.[16] The most politically significant instance of the technique to date affected the Chirac government's request for powers to legislate by ordinance in 1986. Possibly suspecting that resort to ordinances was partly motivated by hopes of evading constitutional review, the Council delivered a 40-page ruling that the request was

[13] 82–146 DC of 18 Nov. 1982; 82–181 DC of 10 and 11 Oct. 1984; 81–132 DC of 16 Jan. 1982.
[14] 82–147 DC of 2 Dec. 1982; Favoreu and Philip, *Les grandes décisions*, pp. 576–581.
[15] 77–87 DC of 23 Nov. 1977. The Council doubtless had in mind recent controversies about the lifestyle that might appropriately be required of teachers in such schools.
[16] Favoreu and Philip, *Les grandes décisions*, pp. 507 and 536.

not contrary to the constitution, subject to 'the strict reservation that' the ordinances 'must not have the aim or consequence of dispensing the government ... from respect for rules and principles of constitutional status', and setting out an imposing list of purposes to which they must not be put, including privatization of any 'constitutional public service' – effectively barring privatization of prisons, which was then being mooted. Validation of new constitutency boundaries was 'subject to the strict reservations on interpretation which it [the Council] sets out, and which the rules governing the drawing of constitutional boundaries must respect'. The manner in which the Council set out what was required to meet the constitutional principle of an equal franchise was not unlike the quasi-legislative approach of the US Supreme Court to reapportionment cases. 'Any other interpretation', the Council emphasized, 'would be contrary to the Constitution'.[17]

Another highly influential qualified ruling was on direct elections to the European Parliament. While dismissing Gaullist contentions that these would launch a dynamic process leading irresistibly to an unconstitutional loss of sovereignty, the Council's decision that the agreement was constitutional was subject to 'considerations' going well beyond what was strictly necessary to settle the issue in hand. It spelled out for future governments (and Councils) the limits beyond which moves towards European unification could not go without constitutional revision. One commentator described it as 'a charter of national sovereignty for the future'.[18] As with the freedom-of-association decision, the ruling – reportedly on a 5–4 vote – conveyed a message which was as much 'political' as 'judicial'.

While the Council regularly disclaims any third-chamber role, peppering its judgements with reminders that it was not intended to 'substitute its own assessment for that of the legislator', at times it does precisely that. Striking down the revised constituency map for New Caledonia, it drew on the notion of 'manifest error of appreciation'. Acknowledging that there could be good reasons for variations in electorates, it held that these could 'only operate to a limited extent which, in this instance, has been exceeded'.[19] Decisions on nationalization and privatization invoked the principles of 'just compensation' and 'just price'. In considering the 1984 Press Act the Council held that, where fundamental freedoms were involved, the legislator could only restrict 'existing situations' where this was 'really *necessary* to ensure the realization of the constitutional objective being pursued'.[20] Notions like 'manifest error', 'just compensation' and 'necessity' are well established in French law, reaching back in some instances to the Declaration of 1789. Now, for the first time, they were being applied to Parliament. The ultimate arbiter of the considerable margin for appreciation they allow is the Council.

The final strand in the self-generated expansion of the Council's importance is that where, initially, it examined only such sections of an Act as were specifically challenged, it soon began scrutinizing the entire text, taking up points that referants have passed over, whether from inadvertence or complicity. Thus the

[17] *Le Monde* (28 June, 1 and 4 July 1986).
[18] 76–71 DC of 29–30 Dec. 1976.
[19] 85–196 DC of 8 Aug. 1985.
[20] Favoreu and Philip, *Les grandes décisions*, pp. 516–58, on the nationalization decisions and pp. 644–66 on press enterprises. Also Turpin, *Contentieux constitutionnel*, pp. 324–7.

right-wing challenge to the 1982 revision of the local election code did not question the new sex quota for party lists; the Council picked this up for invalidation on its own initiative. Many 'budget riders' that have been slipped into Finance Acts have suffered the same fate.

So if the Council's emergence to prominence was crucially dependent on the 1974 revision, it also reflects the expansionist spirit it has brought to its task. It has combined an extensive definition of the norms by which constitutionality is assessed with a considerably extended range of jurisprudential techniques, several of them characterized by an imprecision leaving considerable scope for future development. It has, however, closed off one potentially active area by declining to consider the compatibility of legislation with external norms such as the European Convention on Human Rights, the Universal Convention on Human Rights and ILO conventions.[21] Despite this self-denying ordinance, the field of 'rights' is the most striking illustration of the range of issues where the Council's influence is felt. This includes, to list only a selection, decisions on freedom of expression, education, conscience, movement, association and enterprise; the right of asylum, to belong to a union, to strike, to vote and to work; property rights, the presumption of innocence, the protection of privacy and pluralism in the media.[22]

The extent to which the Council has developed its jurisprudence in these matters varies considerably. While equality before the law has featured in over 50 decisions, some areas are as yet represented by only a single case. The boundaries of what the Council considers within its brief are still neither clear nor definitively set. The 1971 freedom-of-association decision asserted its right to interpret the 'fundamental principles recognized by the laws of the Republic'. By the mid-1970s it was referring to 'principles of constitutional status', a phrase embracing not only norms explicitly mentioned in the constitution, the Declaration of 1789 and the 1946 Preamble, but also the 'fundamental principles' and a number of other general principles of French law which have been developed by the criminal and administrative courts. In effect the Council has become the sovereign authority on which norms have constitutional status and the manner in which norms emanating from a disparate range of sources are to be ordered, reconciled, synthesized and 'actualized'. It takes little imagination to glimpse the potential for growth.

Intriguing though such developments may be to specialists in French public law, they would be of only marginal interest to political scientists had they not also laid their mark on every stage of the policy process. The greatest change has been the atrophying of the Council's original central purpose of policing the

[21] 75–54 DC of 15 Jan. 1975; Favoreu and Philip, *Les grandes décisions*, pp. 291–333. Also L. Favoreu, 'Le Conseil constitutionnel et le droit international', *Annuaire français de droit international 1977* (Paris, CNRS, 1978) and Luchaire, *Le Conseil constitutionnel*, pp. 235–65. In 1989, taking a cue from a 1988 Council decision and reversing a long-standing jurisprudence, the Conseil d'Etat indicated it was prepared to judge the conformity of Acts to treaties. This not only removed an obstacle to the operation of international law, particularly Community Law, in France, it also gave the Conseil a role in assessing the validity of statutes. The decision represented a further limitation of national and parliamentary sovereignty as well as tilting the institutional balance in favour of the Conseil d'Etat. See *Le Monde* (21 Oct., 3 Nov. 1989).

[22] Cases discussed in Favoreu and Philip, *Les grandes décisions*, pp. 378–81; Luchaire, *La Protection constitutionnelle*, pp. 173–224; Turpin, *Contentieux constitutionnel*, pp. 299–328; D. Loschak, 'Le Conseil constitutionnel protecteur des libertés?', *Pouvoirs*, 13 (1986).

executive–legislative boundary. Although the 'statutory domain' and the 'regulatory domain' were set out in general terms in Article 34 of the Constitution, it was obvious from the beginning that much would depend on the Council's view of what constituted a 'fundamental principle', to which in many matters Parliament was now restricted, and what was to be the exclusive province of the executive. Some 200 decisions and three decades later, it is clear that Parliament's scope has been limited much less than many initially feared. Indeed, although Article 34 was once bitterly resented by parliamentarians, it has long ceased to be contentious. Once an initial phase of purist enforcement was exhausted, governments have taken a relaxed view. Their domination of the legislative timetable means that since Bills and decrees tend to originate in the same office, what goes into a Bill is often a matter of convenience rather than of any considered assessment of what properly belongs to the domain of statute. Consequently it is not uncommon for Bills to contain clauses which do not belong to the domain of statute and for governments to keep their supporters happy by allowing amendments outside Parliament's competence. Article 41, by which the Council may be called on to resolve disagreements between the government and one or other chamber over whether material contravenes Article 34, has fallen into disuse. It has been used on only 11 occasions, the last being in 1979. The last time a government invoked it successfully was 1966, while a 1982 decision rendered parliamentary challenge to encroachments on the regulatory domain virtually inoperative. Treating such incursions as permissive delegations from the executive – counterparts to delegations to the executive by the legislature – rather than as inherently improper, the Council held that it was not the intention of the Constitution to disallow provisions which intruded into the executive's domain but simply to permit the government to defend its domain when it wished to do so.[23]

The Council has not only been prepared to accept more 'executive' detail in legislation than was initially contemplated; it has frequently adopted a broad definition of Parliament's competence. Although by no means all its rulings have favoured the legislature, it has identified 'fundamental principles' requiring legislative action in fields as varied as taxation, nationalization, labour law, conditions of employment of public servants, creation of new types of public establishments, the administration of the overseas departments, even whether or not VE Day should be a paid public holiday. Indeed its decision on the rules of criminal procedure emphasized that Article 34 *forbade* Parliament to assign to any other body the exercise of powers affecting 'the fundamental guarantees extended to citizens for the exercise of public liberties'.[24]

Further, the Council has treated the statutory domain as being defined not only by Article 34 but also by Article 7 of the Declaration of 1789 ('no one may be arrested except by virtue of a statute'), Article 4 of the 1958 Constitution (citizens are 'voters under conditions laid down by statute'), Articles 35 and 36 (state of emergency), Articles 72–76 (organization of local government), Article 47 (Finance Bills) and Article 53 (ratification of treaties).[25] In one remarkable

[23] 82–143 DC of 30 July 1982; Favoreu and Philip, *Les grandes décisions*, pp. 591–604.
[24] 75–76 DC of 23 July 1975. Also 85–129 DC of 30–31 Oct. 1985 and Turpin, *Contentieux constitutionnel*, pp. 245–59.
[25] Article 7: 73–80 L of 28 Nov. 1973; Article 4: 62–20 L of 4 Dec. 1962 and 82–146 DC of 18 Nov. 1982; Articles 35–6: 85–187 DC of 25 Jan. 1985; Articles 72–6: 75–34 L of 2 July 1975.

decision it even made the spirit of the Constitution prevail over its letter. Rejecting a challenge to an Act dealing with the Plan it remarked: 'While the terms "plan" or "planning" do not figure in Article 34, nevertheless, by its very object the content of a national plan covering several years touches on matters reserved to statute'.[26] The frontier between 'statute' and 'regulations' has become increasingly blurred but has unmistakably shifted in the legislator's favour. Indeed, Eisenmann concludes that 'the limitation of the domain of statutory intervention is practically non-existent'.[27]

Some of the Council's 'separation of powers' rulings – like the decision on criminal procedure cited earlier – have also favoured Parliament. So has its treatment of legislation by ordinance. Early decisions showed a light touch but subsequently they have become more rigorous, leading to the lengthy list of reservations about the 1986 Chirac government's proposals noted earlier. These in effect set out the terms by which ordinances would be assessed in both public discussion and in challenges before the Conseil d'Etat. The Council may also have been reacting to criticisms that governments in a hurry were misusing a facility intended for exceptional circumstances simply to suit their political convenience. Whatever its reasons, the approach it displayed then is likely to have diminished the likelihood of future governments employing Article 38 as a device for short-circuiting the normal legislative process.

In a variety of ways, then, the effect of the Council's rulings has been to broaden Parliament's scope and defend its prerogatives to a degree that would not have been expected in the early days of the Fifth Republic. Not that it has been systematically indulgent towards Parliament. Its attitude to the assemblies' standing orders and to observance of the special procedures for Finance Bills remains strict and literal. The one notable exception was its refusal to uphold a challenge to an Act alleging that a crucial vote had violated Article 27 requiring deputies to vote in person (as had thousands of previous votes, for this 'moralizing' measure fell into systematic disrespect from the dawn of the Fifth Republic). Doubtless to the relief of the Socialist deputies mounting the challenge, it declined to look behind the formal promulgation of the result by the Assembly, though hinting it might have taken a different view had procedural irregularities demonstrably affected the outcome.

However, the same decision invalidated a section of the Act on the ground that the 20 clauses concerned 'by reason of both their breadth and their importance exceed the limits inherent in the right of amendment'. (They originally formed an ordinance that President Mitterrand had refused to sign, which the government opportunistically tacked on to a social affairs Bill which was in its final stages – an incident typical of the infighting of the cohabitation period.) The presidents of both chambers were predictably furious; Chaban-Delmas protested that the Council was 'riding roughshod over the rights of Parliament in the name of constitutional principles which do not figure in the Constitution'. It is unclear whether the Council intended simply to keep Parliament in its place or whether it was effectively warning governments that there were limits to the cavalier

[26] 82–142 DC of 27 July 1982.
[27] C. Eisenmann, *Le Domaine de la loi et du règlement* (Paris, Economica, 2nd edn, 1982), pp. 265-6. Also L. Pezant, 'Loi/Règlement: la construction d'un nouvel équilibre', *Revue française de science politique*, 34:4–5 (Aug.–Oct. 1985).

treatment they might inflict on Parliament. The immediate embarrassment fell on the Chirac government but in different circumstances material of authentic parliamentary origin could be similarly struck down. Beyond the predictable partisan reactions, there was legitimate ground for concern. The idea that the power of amendment is finite is not unusual but it is nowhere to be found in the 1958 constitution. The Council's attempt to deduce it from Articles 44.1 (right of amendment) and 39.1 (initiation of Bills) was laboured and unconvincing, displaying a disquieting readiness to advance on to questionable ground while asserting ill-defined powers of assessment of which it alone would be the judge.

In a variety of ways, then, the Council's behaviour has diverged from its founders' expectations, with consequences they certainly did not foresee and would as surely have resisted. Some of these have proved less straightforward than appears at first glance. This has been most evident with the Council's approach to the statutory domain and, latterly, requests for delegations of legislative authority. Formally the Council has significantly bolstered Parliament's position; in practice, the supportive Assemblies of the Fifth Republic have benefited only marginally and occasionally. Indeed, to the extent that the Council's rulings have resulted in an increase in parliamentary business, they may have exacerbated the perennial problems of dealing adequately with legislation within the limited sessions prescribed by the 1958 constitution. Longer sittings and special sessions have proved no more than partial solutions. The consequences are to be found not only in the unedifying haste and confusion amid which sessions so frequently end, but in the resulting limits on the capacity of reforming governments of whatever hue to carry their policies expeditiously into law.

Thus, although the evidence remains episodic and anecdotal, it seems clear that the Council has made itself a force to be reckoned with at every stage of the policy process, with the executive rather than the legislature its principal 'victim'. Indeed, it could be argued that, in a period of disciplined parliamentary subservience to the executive, it has become a check against 'elective dictatorship'. Major legislation must now be drafted in the knowledge that it is highly likely to be sent for review, leading to earnest discussions about how best the Council's likely requirements may be met (or evaded). There is no way of gauging exactly how much governments have restricted their ambitions in consequence, any more than we can know the extent to which the Council serves as a useful pretext for ministers seeking to water down their policies. What is certain is that every government since at least 1981 has practised 'self-restraint' extensively, whether the Socialists over nationalization, decentralization and the press or the Chirac government of 1986–88 over privatization, the media or electoral reform.[28] These are of course only the high points within a widespread tendency to engage in prudential drafting. The advice governments receive on draft Bills from the Conseil d'Etat is now also heavily conditioned by the Council's jurisprudence, and must be heeded more seriously than was sometimes the case in the past.

The combination of 'self-restraint' and advice from the Conseil d'Etat is by no means a guarantee of a clean bill from the Council; indeed the 'failure rate' has been remarkably high. Typically the Mauroy government took great pains to

[28] Keeler and Stone, 'Judicial-political confrontation in Mitterrand's France' and L. Favoreu, 'Le conseil constitutionnel et l'alternance', *Revue française de science politique*, 34:5 (Aug.–Oct. 1984).

devise acceptable terms for nationalization, only to suffer a humiliating and expensive invalidation. Bills on decentralization in the overseas departments, the universities and concentrations in the newspaper industry suffered similarly, despite intensive efforts to tailor them acceptably. As the Council's jurisprudence becomes better defined (it has at times sent out confusing signals) such incidents may well become rarer, though since the Conseil d'Etat ruling *en contentieux* sometimes disagrees with advice given earlier *en assemblée générale*, they are unlikely to disappear completely. Meanwhile, important though individual instances of disharmony between Council and Conseil have been, they should not obscure the extent to which the Council, through the Conseil d'Etat, has strengthened advisory constitutional review at the drafting stage. This tendency can only be enhanced by the approach displayed in Michel Rocard's exhortation to ministers to 'do everything possible to detect and eliminate risks of unconstitutionality marring Bills and amendments . . . We must be concerned about this even in cases where reference to the constitutional Council is unlikely'.[29] Laudably constitutionalist though Rocard's position might seem, it carried the danger of taking 'self-restraint' to excess, pushing deference to the Council's supposed position to the point where governments might exercise substantially less than their full constitutional powers. Annulments would be rarer but the Council's invisible, immeasurable influence would become even greater. In the event, though, the exhortation seems to have had little impact on the proportion of Bills challenged or the success rate.

The Council is also a force to be reckoned with at the parliamentary stage, despite the reduced importance of its policing of the legislative–executive boundary. There has been a marked juridicization of debates, encouraged by the Council's refusal to entertain certain types of objection unless they have been raised in the course of debate. Motions to declare bills out of order (*exceptions d'irrecevabilité*) on constitutional grounds have become routine. On many occasions threats of reference to the Council have extracted concessions that would never have been granted on straightforward political grounds, sometimes to the opposition, sometimes to wayward supporters.[30] While there is more than a hint of hyperbole in complaints by Michel Péricard that, as *rapporteur*, he had to work 'under fire and threat' from the Council and by Jacques Toubon that the Council is Parliament's 'paralysing muse', François Leótard came reasonably close to the mark in suggesting that Parliament now 'legislates under the shadow of the Council'.[31] This shadow currently falls mainly on governments, which originate almost all legislation; in different circumstances it could fall on a more assertive Parliament.[32]

While reference to the Council has become a routine stage in the legislative process, its influence extends beyond the parliamentary stage to which it seemed initially to be confined. As noted earlier, from time to time it aims injunctions at the central and local government bureaucracies, courts and administrative tribunals. Neither the Cour de Cassation nor the Conseil d'Etat welcomed the

---

[29] His circular also referred to Article 6 of the Declaration of 1789, 'which, as you are aware, has full constitutional status'; *Le Monde* (27 May 1988).

[30] See *Le Monde* (3 Jan., 18 Feb., 15 March 1984, 2–3 Nov. 1985 and 30 July 1987).

[31] Respectively *Le Monde* (10–11 Aug., 5 Sept. and 12 Aug. 1986).

[32] Cf. invalidation on two occasions of amendments introduced by backbenchers requiring Renault to take back dismissed trade unionists. 88–244 DC of 20 July 1988; *Le Monde* (10 July 1988).

newcomer, and relations with them have never been entirely easy – even though the Council has drawn heavily on the Conseil's personnel and jurisprudence. The most serious divergence arose from a 1973 decision, when the Council asserted, more or less in passing, that penalties entailing deprivation of liberty for *contraventions* (the lowest category of offence) could only be introduced by statute. Although directed mainly at the government, this remark overturned a line of jurisprudence the other two bodies had developed over some 15 years. Both made it clear they thought this a cavalier way of proceeding and found ways of bypassing the implications, notwithstanding Article 62.2 which makes the Council's decisions binding on all public authorities.[33] Greatly though legal commentators savour such frictions, what is more remarkable is how few divergences have persisted despite the absence of machinery for resolving them, and how extensively the Cour de Cassation and the Conseil d'Etat have followed the Council. In consequence, the implications of constitutional review as developed by the Council now suffuse the older established legal systems, albeit with occasional contradictions or differences of emphasis. Thus, for example, implementing decrees which are such an important element in the post-legislative phase of French law-making are liable to challenge in the administrative courts much as if they had formed part of the statutory domain.

Yet the Council's emergence as the most authoritative enunciator and interpreter of constitutional norms must not obscure its limitations. It has no *direct* authority over civil, criminal or administrative justice, executive actions or legislation adopted by referendum. (The widening of the scope of referendums, once advocated by François Mitterrand, contained the germ of a stratagem for evading constitutional review.) It does not rule on the conformity of statutes to international agreements. Unlike many of its sister institutions, it reviews legislation only during the brief period before it is promulgated as law. A point missed then can normally never be recovered. Access remains far more restricted than to other constitutional courts. It has no direct means of enforcing its decisions. If, to date, no government has overtly flouted its authority, there have been several instances of wilful evasion, not least in the introduction by decree of further penalties of imprisonment for *contraventions*. One of the Council's most powerfully argued judgements disallowed an Act on police searches of vehicles on the ground that its grant of power was so imprecise and unchecked as to be an infringement of personal freedom – but few would claim that the behaviour of the French police was perceptibly modified in its wake.[34] There is reason to believe that some of the Council's injunctive dicta never reach those at whom they are aimed owing to limited publicity; others are framed so broadly that their intended target and the extent of compliance remain uncertain, though they may prove important in the future and contribute to the Council's 'moral magistracy'.

[33] 73–80 L of 28 Nov. 1973. This was despite the Council's view (62–18 L of 16 Jan. 1982) that the authority of its decisions extends to the *motifs* as well as the *dispositif*. See Favoreu and Philip, *Les grandes décisions*, pp. 308–38; *Recueil Sirey-Dalloz* (1974), *Jurisprudence*, pp. 269–71 and *Chronique*, p. 86, note by L. Hamon; Beardsley, 'The Conseil Constitutionnel and constitutional liberties in France'; Favoreu and Philip, *Les grandes décisions*, pp. 165–71 and Turpin, *Contentieux constitutionnel*, pp. 192–7.

[34] 77–75 DC of 12 Jan. 1977, discussed Favoreu and Philip, *Les grandes décisions*, pp. 354–69; R. Etien, 'L'application des décisions d'annulation du Conseil constitutionnel sur saisine parlementaire', *Revue administrative*, 221 (1984), 472 and *Le Monde* (20–21 Aug. 1978 and 13 Feb. 1980).

Nevertheless, when every reservation has been made, the Council is un-questionably a more substantial body than was expected or intended in 1958. Considering the inhospitable political tradition into which it was grafted, it is scarcely surprising that its enhanced importance has been viewed with mixed feelings by the political class. Today no party advocates abolition of con-stitutional review (though the Communitsts say they would prefer a fully fledged Supreme Court) but wholehearted acceptance is a different matter. That is not helped by a feature that might otherwise be considered an advantage. In the US the status of legislation may remain uncertain for years; in France it is clarified within a month. However, where the Supreme Court has considerable discretion over what cases it accepts, the Council does not. It is often required to rule while passions are high; resort to it becomes one more round in the political battle and its decisions are widely discussed as 'victories' or 'defeats' for the government or its opponents. When, as in 1981, a Council appointed entirely by one side of the political spectrum invalidates major elements in the programme of a newly elected government of the opposing colour, the confrontation between demo-cratic legitimacy and the unelected nine old men of the Palais Royal is inescapable. In the words of Pierre Joxe: '*We* represent the people. *They* represent the political norms of the old majority'. 'You are legally in the wrong because you are politically in the minority', as André Laignel's classic commination put it. In 1986 it was the turn of the right. Although it had systematically sought to overturn the Socialists' legislation of the previous five years, it did not take kindly to being repaid in the same coin. The Council, said one of Chirac's advisers, René de Lacharrière, was 'an aberration, an obscene impairment of democracy'.[35]

However, complaints evoking popular sovereignty, like allegations of partisan balance, have come mainly from the left, while the right (which had appointed a majority of the Council's members up to 1989) has been more inclined to tax it with usurping a role it was never intended to have or of cravenly bowing to government pressure.[36] Some of this sound and fury expressed genuine anger or incomprehension; some was simply calculated to browbeat the Council into a particular course of action (or inaction). Either way, the Council is inescapably a focus of controversy, its decisions liable to the accusation of simply reflecting the partisan origins of its members.

Since it deliberates in secret, issuing a single decision, with no concurring or dissenting opinions, there is no way of investigating conclusively any relationship between decisions and political provenance. However, it is certainly more complex than simplistic interpretations suggest. Several strands in the Council's jurisprudence cut across party lines. An early severity towards Parliament reflected widely held attitudes at the beginning of the Fifth Republic. Its treatment of national sovereignty and its peculiarly French interpretation of the indivisibility of the Republic draw on a wider constitutency than Gaullism. The emphasis on rights since the early 1970s may have reflected the readiness of some

---

[35] See *Le Monde* (19–20 Oct. 1986).
[36] See *Le Monde*, 23 Dec. 1981 (Jospin), 19 Jan. 1982 (Herzog), 20 Jan. 1982 (Leroy, Joxe), 9 Aug. 1986 (Chalandon), 10–11 Aug. 1986 (Péricard, Anciant, Hernu), 12 Aug. 1986 (Léotard); 19 Aug. 1986 (Faure, Poperen), 5 Sept. 1986 (Toubon), 7 Oct. 1986 (Chalandon de Lacharrière), 10 July 1989 (L. Viannet).

MARTIN HARRISON 617

Gaullist nominees to be more assertive after the General's departure, but also matched a wider mood in the wake of the Algerian war, with its massive infringements of human rights. If indeed the Council's jurisprudence displays that greater solicitude for individual over collective freedoms some commentators profess to discern (and this is by no means securely established), this might well reflect the more secure standing of the Declaration of 1789 in the French political tradition over the generous but misty collectivism of the 1946 Preamble, rather than the straightforward ideological bias with which the Council is from time to time taxed.

Again, analysis of the Council's behaviour must take into account its rich jurisprudential heritage from the Conseil d'Etat and the intellectual leadership of particular individuals at certain periods or on certain issues, Georges Vedel over nationalization/privatization being one case in point. Similarly, allowance must be made for the happenstance of interactions between the mix of the classic judicial temperaments of 'activism' and 'restraint' and the issues arising at any particular juncture.

Nevertheless, if Council decisions cannot be read as a mere resultant of members' partisan origins, the scandalized insistence of some of its defenders that they are wholly untinged by politics is no less untenable. It implies a separation between 'law' and 'politics' which denies the realities of constitutional review, and a divorce between judicial attitudes and decisions wholly at variance with the findings of studies of such relationships in other systems. Members are appointed by political office-holders who entertain certain expectations about their behaviour, albeit fairly broad ones which may at times be disappointed. While the partisanship displayed on occasion by the first president, Léon Noel, has been very much the exception, indiscretions about the Council's workings, commentaries by former members such as Luchaire and Goguel, and indeed the argumentation deployed in many key decisions, suggest both a collective ethos, which may shift over time, and the impact of differing personal philosophical positions.[37] On the evidence available it seems difficult to go beyond such a general conclusion, unsatisfyingly vague though it may be. Attempts, for example, to present the Council's record for 1981–86 in terms of antipathy to Socialism have as yet to address its handling of parallel cases in 1986–88, while it is too early to assess the outcome of the change in the Council's 'majority' in 1989. Nevertheless, although the ending of legislative absolutism has brought France closer to *l'Etat de droit* evoked by Carré de Malberg in the last century, as always a 'government of laws' remains, in some measure, a 'government of men'. Much more remains to be done on analysing the consequences.

Meanwhile, the argument over whether France is now under the dreaded 'government of judges' lingers on. Favoreu argues powerfully that it is not; Luchaire, a former member of the Council, is as emphatic that it is.[38] Since the expression is more emotional than technical the debate is inherently inconclusive. Neither it nor any of the alternative terms, such as 'third chamber' or 'countervailing power', encapsulates the Council entirely satisfactorily. It has

[37] Luchaire, *La Protection constitutionnel*; F. Goguel *Le Monde* (19–20 Oct. 1986).

[38] F. Luchaire, 'Le Conseil constitutionnel et le gouvernment des juges' and L. Favoreu, 'Le mythe du gouvernement des juges'; unpublished conference papers, Oxford, 1987: see also Favoreu, 'Le conseil constitutionnel et l'alternance' and his *La Politique saisie par le droit* (Paris, Economica, 1988).

elements of all of these but is also something more. Essentially, whatever purists may say, it is a hybrid – both a court and a political actor of some consequence. A political actor not only because of its constitutional role and the issues it resolves, or because many members have a background in professional politics, but because of the blend of prudence and audacity it has displayed in developing its jurisprudential techniques and the attention it has paid in recent years to presenting fuller and more clearly argued judgements which stress the continuities in its jurisprudence.[39] It is far more aware than once it was of its teaching role and its need to carry legal, political and public opinion with it.

The political class appears to have recognized, however reluctantly and ambivalently, that constitutional review has come to stay, if only because the chances of securing the requisite majorities for change seem remote. Mitterrand's revival in 1989 of the idea of extending access to ordinary citizens received a chilly response from parliamentarians, not least because it would dilute one of their most significant functions. Unless differences between the two Chambers can be overcome, further development of the Council's role must, in the short term, come about informally rather than by outright amendment. Nevertheless, even without the opening up of all existing laws to constitutional review, which Mitterrand's proposals would initiate, the Council's potential remains considerable. Already, in his *La Politique saisie par le droit*, Favoreu sees it regulating the change of parties in office, channelling adversary politics, refereeing cohabitation, legitimating controversial legislation on matters like abortion and nationalization, even promoting 'government from the centre'.[40]

Unlike many French academic lawyers, Favoreu has the signal merit of acknowledging that the Council is a political as well as a legal institution and addressing many of the consequential issues. The evidential underpinning for the roles he identifies is uneven, but experience of constitutional review elsewhere suggests it would not be surprising if at least some emerged as uncalculated by-products of review, legitimation being a case in point. Even at that level the questions of principle are obvious enough; however desirable 'government from the Centre' or the containment of the excesses of adversary politics may be, is a constitutional court an appropriate instrument for achieving such ends? Such questions would gain still greater cogency if the Council were to behave (or to be perceived as behaving) as if the roles Favoreu assigns it were indeed part of its 'mission'.

There is no need here to rehearse the classic debates about the proper scope for judicial discretion, except to note that they gain particular force from the nature of French political traditions and the disparate nature of the material the Council interprets. The *bloc de constitutionnalité*, as defined by the Council, is such as to make it all but impossible to avoid normative judgements about what is 'reasonable' 'necessary' or 'just', which is not to deny that, as critics as diverse as Turpin, Philip, Goguel, Keeler and Stone have argued, the Council is on occasion all too ready to impose its 'appreciations' on matters better left to Parliament.

Where Favoreu's assessment is open to challenge is not only along traditional 'democratic' lines but for being couched largely in short-run terms. The longer-

---

[39] 38 of the 44 members appointed up to October 1990 had legal training, 31 had followed a legal career or were academic lawyers and 24 had parliamentary experience.
[40] Favoreu, *La Politique saisie par le droit*.

run relationship of the Council to the political system cannot lie in its impact on cohabitation or the change of parties in office. Through its constitution the Fifth Republic proclaims certain principles or procedures to be unchanging. Yet its future health may require even these to be adapted or reinterpreted. So far, the Fifth Republic has proved remarkably flexible, but even it needs protection from hardening of the arteries. Given that unfettered popular sovereignty is unacceptable and constitutional amendment onerous, resolution of the tensions between rigidity and flexibility inevitably falls to the Council. There is an obvious irony in so fundamental a political role being exercised by a body whose legitimacy lies in being seen as a judicial institution rather than a political one. Arguably, the preservation of this 'essential myth' is vital to the maintenance of its legitimacy. Favoreu's approach has the single virtue of candour over an attitude of doing good by stealth, but by situating his argument in a very specific political context he runs the risk of compromising the longer-term, and perhaps ultimately more important, function. The Council has come a long way since 1958, achieving a measure of public and political acceptance that could scarcely have been imagined. Nevertheless, if it is to assist the Fifth Republic through its next three decades and beyond, it would be wise to heed other advice from Favoreu on the wisdom of constitutional judges exercising *le self-restraint*. It has, after all, sufficient to do by way of amplifying its existing jurisprudence without succumbing to the lure of still further new worlds to conquer.[41]

---

[41] Favoreu, *La Politique saisie par le droit*, p. 131.

[12]

STANLEY AND INGE HOFFMANN

The Will to Grandeur: de Gaulle as Political Artist

> *"S' élever au-dessus de soi, afin de dominer*
> *les autres, et, par là, les évènements."*
> (*—Vers l'armée de métier*)

THE LEADER, Charles de Gaulle, twice the savior of France, knight-errant for her grandeur, believer in the cultural values embodied in a national tradition, appears all of one piece. It is as if he had chosen to tailor himself to his role in history from the very beginning of his childhood, as if he had carefully selected from his heritage and from his personality the elements that would allow him to play that role to perfection. When the events did not conform to the demands of his self-imposed role, he has waited for the most effective entrance. Once on the scene, he has "arranged" himself so as to meet these demands, and no one, however critical of the play, can deny the merits and mastery of the performance.

It is therefore tempting simply to study from where he derived his characteristic style, how he has shaped his role, and how he has imposed it on his nation—as if he were not really much more complex. Indeed, we do not know whether there is more to him than the public personage. We suspect that there is, behind it, a face both greater and smaller than the public figure: greater, for the public figure draws its life from the man beneath; smaller, because the man is surely restricted by the personage he has chosen to become.

What the man demonstrates is the triumph of the will over personal and national conflict, over inner doubts and external dramas. It is a will to restore, preserve, promote an abstraction, France, which has always been more important to him than any other commitment. That "certain idea of France," of which he speaks, has to be served by a certain kind of leader. And de Gaulle's will has also, indeed primordially, been to be that leader. His career shows a remarkable blend of thought and action, a rare capacity to fulfill one's vocation by giving to oneself and to one's mission exactly the shape of one's dreams and ambitions; in other words, de Gaulle displays an aesthetic talent worked out in a political arena.

It is not the purpose of this paper to pass judgment on de Gaulle as a political leader. Such a judgment would require an evaluation of the intrinsic merit of those dreams and ambitions, a detailed assessment of the means he has used in order to realize them, and a discussion of the lasting effects of his achievements and failures. Our concern is narrower: It is to study de Gaulle as a political artist not by looking at his techniques, at his craft, but by concentrating on what he has called his gift—that is, his "character" and the way in which he has shaped it to fulfill his self-appointed role. We will examine first the development of his personality, then the definition, psychological requirements, and psychological implications of his vocation, and finally, the charismatic link between the political artist and his public—the people to whom he must communicate his gift in order to fulfill his mission.

I. *Genesis*

We will discuss three factors among all those that may have shaped the General's personality and leadership style: his family, his own reactions to his milieu during his youth and adolescence, and the influences of some contemporaries.

The Milieu

A discussion of his family is essential to an understanding of de Gaulle.[1] We are not suggesting that his milieu "determined" him, but it put him on certain tracks that he has never left and also provided him with a point of departure which he both accepted and left behind.

He was born on November 22, 1890, the third of five children, the second of four boys. His father, Henri de Gaulle, descended from a long line of impoverished nobles—belonging both to the *noblesse d'épée* and to the *noblesse de robe*—who lived, at first, in the provinces (Burgundy and Flanders) and, since the seventeenth century, in Paris. The fascination with history which Charles was going to display was already in his family, on Henri's side.

de Gaulle as Political Artist

Henri's father had written a history of Paris, edited one of King St. Louis, and traced the genealogy of the family. One of Henri's brothers, called Charles de Gaulle, was a poet and scholar who, in a book about the Celts in the nineteenth century, anticipated his nephew and namesake, both in celebrating the resilient independence of the Celts (as well as their spread to America), and in writing that "in a camp surprised, at night, by an enemy attack, when each one fights alone, one does not ask his rank of whoever raises the flag and takes the initiative of rallying his men."[2] Henri's mother, a prolific writer of edifying novels, showed sympathy for various revolutionary figures like Proudhon and Jules Vallès, and wrote a book glorifying O'Connell.

Henri de Gaulle was forty-two when Charles was born. He had originally intended to follow a military career, but, according to Charles' biographers, he was stopped by a reversal of his family's fortunes. He was wounded near Paris in the Franco-Prussian War and, later, often took his children to visit the battleground. He became a professor of philosophy, history, and literature and headmaster in a distinguished Jesuit high school in Paris. There is no doubt that his impact on Charles was great; Henri's former students have testified to his mystical love for France, and it is he who supervised his sons' extensive readings in French history and in the classics of French literature.

Charles' mother, Jeanne Maillot, shared her husband's devotion to France and Catholicism; she came from a bourgeois lineage— a line of austere, small businessmen from northern France, in whose families the youngest sons usually pursued military careers. One of her uncles, Charles Maillot, an officer of unusual height, was legendary in the family. Little is known about her.

Charles de Gaulle's milieu was both typical and yet somehow *en marge*, in two essential respects. On the one hand, socially, it is hard to imagine a family more French than one that believes its ancestry goes back to the thirteenth century. Yet de Gaulle was not born in a family typical of nineteenth-century French society: As he pointed out later, his parents' outlook, concerns, and resources were not those of the bourgeoisie, and there must always have been a contrast between the dignified appearances—an apartment in Lille, one in Paris, a summer home in the Dordogne—and the financial realities. De Gaulle's detachment from the class preoccupations of France's social categories thus becomes easier to understand. On the other hand, his family was typical of the values of the French Right: At the end of the nineteenth century, a deep attachment to the monarchy (which the de Gaulle family had served, either as officers or as lawyers), a fervent Catholicism, fierce patriotism, and fear for the decline of France were characteristic of all those families to whom Maurras was pitching his appeal. In one vital respect, however, the de Gaulles did not conform: "*Monarchiste de regret*," Henri de Gaulle was not, it seems, moved in any way by the passionate anti-republican hatred, the anti-Semitism, and xenophobia so characteristic of the Right; there was no sectarianism here, and Henri de Gaulle did not believe that Dreyfus was guilty.

De Gaulle's family thus transmitted to him three essential messages. First, as the preceding example suggests, it was profoundly inner-directed. Not only were the values it believed in, for all their lack of originality, those of a minority of Frenchmen in an impious republic, a fact that did not prevent the de Gaulles from sticking to their beliefs with dignity and firmness. There was also here a willingness to examine issues *independently,* on their own merits, and to judge them from a viewpoint that left its mark on Charles: what might be called intense moderation—intense, because of the depth of Henri's "feeling" and of Mme de Gaulle's "passion,"[3] yet moderate, because the tone of the family, the manners of the father, above all the lessons of French classicism and history all seem to have pointed to the condemnation of excess. Self-respect, later so crucial to de Gaulle, was undoubtedly a family value and achievement.

Secondly, the values inculcated by the parents were above all public values. This was a family where a child would quickly learn to sublimate his private dreams and drives into public ones: the love of France, Christian faith, honor, the lessons of history, respect for culture, the nation as both the highest temporal good and as a cultural partnership of the living and the dead, the virtues of the soldier as both the defender of the nation and the carrier of the Christian faith. Most striking is the way in which, in this dignified but impoverished home of a family whose beliefs ran against the dogmas of the established regime, history—France's past—and the legacy of French culture seem to have served as a consolation for the present as well as a yardstick. Charles' enthusiasm for Rostand's *Aiglon*, seen at the age of ten, fits in easily.[4]

The sentimental story (played by Sarah Bernhardt) of the ailing, oppressed, innocent son of the great Emperor, protected and in-

de Gaulle as Political Artist

spired by a soldier called Flambeau, who symbolizes the average Frenchman and keeps the memories of Napoleon's epic alive in captivity, could not fail to arouse in Charles the patriotic feelings and sense of service cultivated by his family and to strengthen his military vocation, already indicated by his childhood games, where he always insisted on playing the role of France.

Third, and perhaps most importantly, Charles' milieu must have communicated to him a deep sense of distress about the present. Toward the internal situation of France, the emotions must have ranged from discomfort to disgrace, as the nation moved from the unfinished truce of the *ralliement* years, to the turmoil of the Dreyfus case (where all sides, as de Gaulle's father saw it, behaved lamentably), the separation of church and state, the closing of the Jesuit schools (including Henri's), the rise of socialism, labor unions, and strikes. Externally, the dominant feeling was one of persistent national humiliation; the father and mother had been traumatized by the fall of France in the war of 1870 and remained obsessed by the need for *la revanche* and the fear of further French setbacks like Fachoda—another reason why *l'Aiglon,* with its evocation of past exploits to exorcise both the humiliations of the era after Napoleon the First, of which it talks, and those of the era after Napoleon the Third, in which it was written, would appeal to the boy. But the basic fact remains: The de Gaulles' beloved France, the "princess or madonna" of the religious and nationalistic boy, was seen and felt as troubled, threatened, almost tragic rather than healthy, heroic, and expanding.[5] Her present condition could only be deplored, and as for the future, one could and should of course hope, but it was hard to imagine improvement without drama. His martial spirit and his desire to protect thus strengthened each other.

That he picked up all those "messages" we know from the first three paragraphs of the *Mémoires.* For all its opposition to present trends, for all its nostalgia and misgivings, his family life and holidays teamed with activities, fun, and games, of which learning became a part. In short, the family provided a rich and harmonious (*non-conflicted*) cultural legacy.

Childhood and Adolescence

In this setting, the picture of a little boy emerges: a "perfect little devil," who is "neither docile nor naïve"—"when Charles appears, tranquillity disappears"[6]—full of mischief, practical jokes, and energy (books and papers are sent flying around his room). This double concern which never left him: for *statecraft* and for *stagecraft* began in childhood, in his fondness for reliving in his readings and in his games various episodes (usually martial ones) of French history.

This period of joyful ebullience, of passionate abandon in adventure stories and war plays, gradually receded as he approached adolescence. Someone in the family says he must have fallen into an icebox. This fits with his stiff distant bearing in secondary school, where he was reported to have begun to stand apart. Why a child's sense of uniqueness, which it shares with all other growing children, should have matured into a style of life, is a puzzle that we must now try to elucidate.

The key seems to lie in his relation to his family. We see a tension between his respect for it, his acceptance of its beliefs, and his intense desire to make his own mark, to be his own master— *to be himself* and not merely one more relatively undistinguished member of old, respectable, but uncelebrated families. Independence became his claim, not just a family value. The very lessons he received from his father and from his Catholic teachers must have created dissonance. They taught him the honor and pride of loyalty to unpopular values.[7] They, as well as the books he devoured, celebrated service, submission to causes, discipline. But those same books also revealed that history is a tale full of sound and fury, in which whole bodies of doctrines have been blown away, in which, as he was going to write later, "evangelical perfection does not lead to empire."[8] Moreover, the world around him taught him that pure loyalty to traditional dogmas and the perfect practice of Christian values were no way of saving them. His books and teachers, however, provided him with an answer to the dilemma. The young reader of Corneille and history knew that mastery of self and others brings its own rewards[9]; his whole education, at home and in school, was pervaded by the Greek ideal, so powerful in France's classical age and culture (as indeed throughout continental Europe): that of the self-sufficient, self-controlled, and sovereign personality, who controls events, so to speak, from within through force of character. Thus the solution to his tension was sought in a way that was to become typical of his style: by *transcending* the legacy.[10]

He must have experienced, at home, both opulence and de-

de Gaulle as Political Artist

privation—the opulence of affection, example, and high ideals, but also a double deprivation; on the one hand, this obviously remarkable boy seems to have been treated, out of fairness to his brothers and sister, with no special privileges; on the other hand, as one perceptive commentator has put it, it was a "frustrated family,"[11] frustrated socially and politically by France's domestic and external political conditions. There was but one way both to put an end to those frustrations *and* to emancipate oneself from them; to serve the values of the family *and* to save them from obsolescence; to remain loyal to that culture and that history so dear to his parents *and* to remove culture and history from the realm of morose meditations, genealogical explorations, and imaginary recreations; to be a son and brother to his parents and their other children *and* to make a name for oneself: by becoming the man who saves the respected past by shaping a future worthy of it. The solution was to put himself at the service of a great cause that would give him the opportunity to be great by doing great things. The cause could have been that of the church, but the boy seems to have been too fond of battle, too much in love with temporal glory and domination; it thus became that of France, to which he transferred the religious devotion that was in him. He would serve France in such a striking way that the past would be *renewed* rather than just enshrined, and the nation might live according to the family's ideals. This meant accepting—as a precondition for success—the political framework that his parents found so distasteful: to be a nostalgic monarchist and Catholic was not going to help.

It meant, above all, leaping above the family's horizons. De Gaulle says he was tempted by "the play" of French politics, whose permanent confrontation of great characters must have appealed to his imagination and love of drama.[12] But this would have hurt his family's feelings, and the play affronted its and his own values. He could, however, resolve his dilemma harmoniously. In a military career, Charles could try to do what his father had been prevented from doing by fate. He would be at the service of France, rather than of the Republic, and repudiate all divisive ideologies as so many traps. That desire to be France's protector without intermediaries, so characteristic of his career and so clearly marked in the very first page of the *Mémoires* (where he talks first of her, and then only of his "milieu"—his word), had been, after all, authorized, indeed encouraged, by his family and education. Thus, military service was both a family tradition and a personal solution. By serving the cause of the *revanche*, he would begin to solve for all Frenchmen the problems that could otherwise not be solved for his family alone, and he would find glory in it.

He may have found the family horizons stifling, but there was no revolt; rather, there was a kind of externalization: a desire to fight and remove what had made those horizons stifling. Similarly, later, his acts of defiance would never amount to mere rebelliousness, nor would he ever be a revolutionary. But serving France only and directly also asserted his independence from everyone else— as if he had originated from her alone: de Gaulle would appear both as self-made and as the product of two thousand years of history.

There is nothing unique in the case of a young man to whom history and making his mark on it appear the only worthy goals in life. But what is unique is the continuity of concern and purpose. The love affair with France and history, the love of battle and "*rêve de gloire au pied d'un étendard,*"[13] the determination to be at current history's rendezvous so as to be in future history's texts have known no interruption. What is unique is the total identification of his personal destiny with that of his nation, and the strength of will to fulfill the purpose beyond childhood, through a long period of trial and waiting.

In order to understand better how he managed to act out his dreams without losing touch with reality, one has to examine more carefully what seems to have happened in his adolescence, between the ages of fourteen and sixteen. As in every important period of his life, external events coincided with internal developments. The events are well known: France's crisis between church and state (which hit not only France but home) and the Tangiers crisis with Germany. Simultaneously, a *sense* of being different, separate, chosen[14] is strengthened, and a *will to be* unique and self-contained arises in him. These are the years when he grows to be taller than his brothers, to tower over his schoolmates, when he must have felt (and been made to feel) awkward; when he must have also felt the need to distinguish himself from that omnipresent father, who taught him constantly in school as well as at home. Precisely, this is the time when his father, worried by the proliferation of Charles' gifts, by a certain tendency to dispersion, a certain lack of discipline in him, challenges him to study harder in order to be able to enter Saint Cyr, France's West Point. Charles'

de Gaulle as Political Artist

reaction announces his future style: He uses the challenge as an opportunity and makes of the peculiarity not only an asset, but a mark. Tallness becomes the physical symbol of a moral ambition—to be above the others, to be straight and erect. His imagination feeds his will, and his will disciplines his imagination. *Grandeur* becomes his motto, for himself, others, and France: He will join the army because it was then *"une des plus grandes choses du monde."*[15] Aware of how his height and his concerns distinguish him from his schoolmates, he becomes even more aware of his uniqueness and enchanted with it. But if there is narcissism in him, as in every adolescent (and every leader), it is, once more, transcended narcissism, for his reply to the threat of identity diffusion is not totalism, but the mobilization, or, to use two of his favorite words, the *rassemblement* of all his faculties toward the goals of success and service, which will *elevate* him above himself and others.

In this transition from childhood to adolescence, nothing is more interesting than the playlet he wrote at age fourteen and got published the following year: *Une mauvaise rencontre* is the last display of youthful exuberance and the first use of the pen toward the adult goal. It is a frothy skit about an "amiable thief" whose method of robbing is as smooth and painless as Madison Avenue's persuasions, except that there are shiny pistols which underline the persuasion.[16] This theme of coercive persuasion and even the episodes and refrain are taken from an inconsequential *poème à jouer* (poem to perform) by Gustave Nadaud, a popular chansonnier-poet.[17] But Charles transformed its style into sweepy Alexandrines (with a good lacing of Rostand), changed the nameless "amiable thief" of Nadaud into the grand César-Charles Rollet, who declares he was born brigand as others are born kings, officers, . . . or masons (that is, born to their own uniqueness, which they have only to fulfill); a brigand of promise who by great dramatic misfortune lost his superb garb. Unloved and hunted, he "needs" to be comforted by his victim: a ruse indeed, but one which *Charles*, not the original songster, supplied and elaborated. Here are some excerpts of Charles' additions to the original (emphasis added):

. . . *César-Charles Rollet, qu'on connaît en tout lieu*
Voleur de grands chemins par la grâce de Dieu . . .
Certains naquirent rois. . . . Moi je naquis brigand;
On peut le voir d'ailleurs très bien à mon costume.
Sur ma tête, autrefois, s'agitait une plume

. . . (with melancholy)

DÆDALUS

... Pourquoi me rappeler ce superbe panache
Dont un coup de bâton cruel trancha les jours? ...
O jour fatal *et sombre! Eh! Oui, Monsieur,* tout passe! (Epique)

(One wonders what happened "one day" to our young Charles, to transform him from the carefree prankster into the straight, stiff-cordial, but distant schoolboy. . . .) "*Eh, oui—tout passe.*" (How like the style of the grown man, how prophetic of his fatalism half a century later![18])

Oh! Ce fut un combat *terrible,* horrible, laid
Grand, géant, *furieux, effroyable. C'était*
Le chaos monstrueux, sans grâce, *horrible et morne—*
D'un brigand révolté contre un homme à bicorne.
Ma plume *tomba près d'un gendarme à cheval,*
Auquel j'avais ouvert le ventre! ...
... C'est très mal!
Me direz-vous. Ma foi! Je n'en sais rien moi-même.
Personne ne nous voit, personne ne nous aime.

He describes how his featherless hat became sad, and, "*selon la nature,*" gradually lost its *antique* colors.

Il restait sur mon chef droit—*les* grandes *douleurs*
Sont muettes—fier, grand, défiant *la fortune*
Il rêvait, dans le jour serein, dans la nuit brune
Partout, c'était un corps inerte, *laid, rêveur,*
Et pensant à sa plume

And later:

La vie humaine n'est qu'un tissu de misères ...

There are two kinds of messages the play appears to convey. One concerns the young de Gaulle's struggle with his own development, the other foreshadows some of the mature de Gaulle's mastery.

As to the first, the adolescent boy who wrote this play in fun added these characteristic themes of his own to Nadaud's ditty: grandeur, struggle, chaos and loss, loneliness, dreams of glory and fatalism. The idea *great* is repeated again and again. Loss is symbolized by the superb feather which leaves him (that is, his hat) "un corps *inerte,* laid, rêveur"[19]; also, in elaborate jest and as a ruse to arouse pity, he refers to his loss of three sisters and three brothers. This may be a fanciful bit of analysis, but since these

de Gaulle as Political Artist

are de Gaulle's own additions to and transformations of the original, and since they also check (by extrapolation) with the observations reported by his biographers, they warrant being taken seriously, as reflecting the principal preoccupations of young Charles.

Both versions of this boring tale cynically relied on the ultimate persuasive power of force. But Nadaud lacked Charles' subtle blend of flattery and ruse, his lusty and ironic manipulation of gullible pity (de Gaulle's *mépris* for a certain kind of man appeared early), which explained why the use of overt violence was unnecessary. Finally, Charles added the glorification of his hero's pride and egoism; he celebrated his force and his ruse. Compare this with what the mature de Gaulle wrote some twenty years later in his prophetic "credo": *"l'homme d'action ne se conçoit guère sans une forte dose d'égoisme, d'orgueil, de dureté, de ruse."*[20] But the world forgives him because he dares great deeds: "Il séduit *les subordonnés et lors même qu'il* tombe sur la route *garde à leurs yeux* le prestige des sommets *où il voulait les entraîner."* Or: *"Pas d'orateur qui* n'agite *de grandes idées autour de la plus pauvre thèse."*[21] Is it stretching the reader's imagination excessively to ask him to compare these lines with the grand feather which *"s'agitait d'autrefois"* on his hero's head . . . ?

In his childhood play, the seduction is so successful that the victim cries, sincerely, *"enchanté"* at the curtain; later, in his reality play with reluctant opponents (such as General Giraud, or General Salan, or foreign leaders), the victim would often, however, dream of or try for revenge after having been had.

It would seem, then, that at least at the age of fourteen, de Gaulle's fate had been sealed. Obviously, the young man's concern is already for the exercise of power. The play expresses the drive for mastery in a world marked by mediocrity and violence; what is missing from it is what was, so to speak, already *given*—the values and the cause on behalf of which de Gaulle (unlike the brigand) would use the brigand's cynical experience and bouncy dash.

Charles' character now changes and tightens. His sister had described him as "poet and soldier."[22] From now on, his pen will serve first to reflect upon action so as to put action in the lofty perspective that makes it meaningful and, second, as a substitute for action whenever the times are not ripe for it. The sense of fun, so strong in his games and in his playlet, does not disappear, and never will—he will go on performing in plays at Saint Cyr—but a new austerity emerges. Fun will be externalized and transcended, like rebellion: used as a weapon against others and sought in the craft and pleasure of mastery. The sense of drama, so strong in the rambunctious boy, turns into a desire to play a part in a national drama, for which the young man must prepare himself[23]: As he will say later, his gifts must be shaped by skills.[24] The fascination with history continues, but history stops being a playground for childish re-enactments and becomes a judge, a springboard, a reality principle. The need to protect, once turned to the defense of smaller schoolboys mistreated by bullies,[25] is oriented toward France. Already, as throughout his career, the will-to-do or be something feeds on *and* magnifies that something's existence; sensing his difference, he cultivates it. The desire to play a great role leads to double domination—of oneself, as a way of dominating others[26]; the strain increases further the distance from others: Steeped in history, taught to find in its sweep a recourse against the present, he will manifest his ambition by disdaining (once more, *dominer*— that is, both stand above and master) the petty concerns of his contemporaries and all those human entanglements that divert or slow one down. Haughtiness, separateness will be both the condition and the cost of his success.

It is as if, in those years, Charles de Gaulle had experienced a loss that stimulated his creativity and that was reflected or anticipated in his play: the national loss represented by the events recalled above, which made him fear for *his* France, and a more intimate one—the growing awareness of childhood's end, the end of family protection and of mere playacting in a harsh and troubled world, the call of responsibility. Combativeness remains, and indeed grows; but a certain note of bitterness appears—perhaps as a reaction to those events, perhaps also as the by-product of the price the young man felt he had to pay, in his human relations, for his ambition and uniqueness. The years of preparation for action suggest already the double feeling which his whole career inspires: on the one hand, the sense of an extraordinarily effective use of all his resources; on the other, that of a certain repression or compression of ordinary humanity, as if his family and education had provided him with enough human warmth to avoid any real mutilation, yet somehow made him distrustful of his own spontaneity and incapable of dealing with men except on behalf of great abstractions. For such a man, a military career—in which his size and stiffness would be exemplary, where his awkwardness in

de Gaulle as Political Artist

human relations would be concealed by the hierarchy of ranks, and where his need both to serve and to command would be fulfilled—was an excellent choice. And the selection of infantry is equally significant, for it meant both the certainty of being in the thick of battles and the choice of a branch in which he would be in contact not with men recruited from those elites and middle classes who had been his companions in school and for whom he had little penchant, but with those average Frenchmen—mainly peasants—who must have appeared to him as less corrupted, easier to lead, and easier to keep at a distance.

In his later life, after his admission to Saint Cyr, three events are worth noting. One was a national trend. In the years that preceded World War I, a "nationalist revival" brought back prestige to some of the values that de Gaulle's parents and teachers had cultivated—if not Catholicism, at least a militant and passionate concern for the nation's honor and rank spread from the Right to the Republican establishment.[27] Thus de Gaulle learned that if one sticks to beliefs one deems true and great, whatever the costs of temporary unpopularity, one will be proven right when the circumstances at last consecrate the permanent relevance and the specific aptness of those beliefs.

The two other events were personal tragedies which aggravated, on the contrary, his sense of loss, his intense need for self-respect, and his isolation; both also strengthened in him the sense that realities, however sinister, have to be accepted, that they should not crush one's will, but be faced in order to be overcome. First, there were his two years in German captivity—a crushing blow to the dreams of glory of the young officer and also, probably, to his self-respect. It frustrated him of his share in the final victory; it separated him from his comrades and pushed him even more into himself. Since his repeated attempts to escape were defeated by his very tallness, there was only one thing to do: to use this forced separation in order to reflect on the meaning of the great events to which he could not contribute. Out of those reflections, readings, and lectures came his first book[28]—characteristically enough, a study of civil-military relations in Germany in World War I. It was, first, a plea for moderation, for "the limits traced by human experience, common sense, and the law"[29]; second, a study of the crucial role of morale: collective will, confidence, and unity, and of its collapse in Germany largely because of party divisions and the civilian leaders' lack of stamina when faced with the rabid

DÆDALUS

demands of military leaders. The de Gaulle that came out of a German prisoners' camp immediately went to fight in Poland, against the Russian Revolution; he reflected on the strength of the Polish sense of identity across class barriers—seeing both what there was and what he wanted to see. He returned to France in order to marry Yvonne Vendroux, the twenty-year-old daughter of a biscuit manufacturer from northern France, and to teach military history at St. Cyr. As a student at the Ecole de Guerre in 1922-24, he left on his superiors the same kind of impression he had made on his classmates as an adolescent, only stronger—that of a bright but haughty young man. He was contemptuous of strategic "lessons" that enshrined what the French army had learned from the Great War (but that he, who had missed half of it, obviously felt to be foolish, too mechanical, too rigid, too petty); he was extremely sure of himself and disdainful of criticism.[30]

The second tragedy was more intimate. His third child, born in 1928, was a retarded daughter. De Gaulle and his wife decided to keep her with them, and for twenty years, the General was, it seems, the only person capable of making the little girl laugh. His powers of affection were thus lavished on a poor creature with whom no real intimacy was possible.

Influences

During those formative years, it is interesting to see who, among the countless writers the young man was reading, and who, among the several superiors he had, impressed and influenced him most. He picked up what he needed—that is, what resembled him and encouraged him most to "be himself." As a youngster, he had copied a phrase of Hugo's: "concision in style, precision in thought, decisiveness in life" (qualities far more true of him than of Hugo).[31] He read Nietzsche. The vigor with which he resisted him in his own first book shows the appeal which the call for supermen had had on him (and which *Le fil de l'épée* would dramatically display), for one is always marked by what one fights so hard. Yet it also shows the differences between the philosopher's ethics and de Gaulle's; for he denounces in supermen not only "the taste for excessive undertakings," but also the selfishness of an elite that while "pursuing its own glory believes it pursues the general interest."[32] In de Gaulle's own life, personal glory would loom large, but only as the servant of the general interest (as seen, of course, by de Gaulle . . .).

He read Péguy, whose incandescent mixture of nationalism, love for the soil and people of France, and distaste for parliamentarianism (as opposed to the mystique of the Republic), whose celebration of France as the soldier of Christ, repudiation of the formalistic and systematic "systems of thought" derived from Kant, and raising of Hope—active Hope—as the cardinal virtue, corresponded to his own feelings and left their mark even on his style.[38] He read Barrès, but interestingly enough he chose to see in him only the man who "gave back to the [French] elite a consciousness of national eternity,"[34] not the rather xenophobic, intensely conservative and frightened bourgeois writer, turned far more to the past than to a future that spelled possible decadence. He may have appreciated Maurras' (and undoubtedly Bainville's) views on foreign affairs, but there is no sign of any acceptance of the rigid, doctrinaire, and antiquated "system" of integral nationalism with its divisive and "continuous song of hate."[35]

Above all, he read Bergson, whose philosophy of intuition (as against analytic intelligence), *élan vital* (as against established doctrines), emphasis on time as "the vehicle of spontaneous creation," and stress on how personality transcends all "stable, ready-made categories,"[36] obviously seduced a young man eager to transcend and transmute his own categories, to stop his formidable memory from being a museum and to turn it into a fuel for the future. And he could recognize not yet his own destiny, but his own aspirations in Bergson's question:

By what sign do we ordinarily recognize the man of action, who leaves his mark on the events into which fate throws him? Isn't it because he embraces a more or less long succession in an instantaneous vision? The greater the share of the past that he includes in his present, the heavier the mass he pushes into the future so as to weigh on the events in preparation: his action, like an arrow, moves forward with a strength proportional to that with which its representation was bent backwards.[37]

A final influence was even more profound, because it was more direct—it exerted itself in de Gaulle's own chosen career: Pétain's. De Gaulle, as a cadet, served in Colonel Pétain's regiment; he fought under his orders when the war began; he became his aide and protégé in the 1920's. There were obvious differences between the cautious peasant's son and the ardent young officer, but de

Gaulle recognized in his superior what he wanted to develop in himself: "the gift and the art of leadership."[38] He must have recognized himself in that man who "dominates his task through his mind, and, through his character, leaves his mark on his task"; in that "master who . . . has disdained the fate of servants—thus showing the greatness of independence, which receives orders, seizes advice but closes itself to influences—the prestige of secrecy, preserved by deliberate coldness, vigilant irony, and even by the pride in which his loneliness is wrapped."[39] "Too proud for intrigue, too strong for mediocrity, too ambitious for careerism, [Pétain] nourished in his solitude the passion to dominate, hardened by his awareness of his own merit, by the obstacles he had met, the contempt he had for others."[40] He must also have recognized himself in Pétain's impervious disregard for official doctrine, even at a cost to his own career, for Pétain, on the eve of the war, was holding out against the established dogma of impetuous offensive— and de Gaulle was able to observe how costly that dogma proved to be, to conclude (again) that dogmas mislead instead of guiding, and to learn that Pétain's concern for firepower (artillery) and machine guns) was more justified than official emphasis on manpower in a country with a relatively small population.

This is, then, the capital of influences, experiences, and resources that de Gaulle had accumulated by the mid-1920's. Sure of and eager for the great destiny he had announced since he was seventeen,[41] he now turned to his first great task: the intellectual elaboration, clarification, and anticipation of his future mission.

II. *Vocation*

De Gaulle's leadership will be examined from three viewpoints. How has he conceived the character and role of the *leader?* How has he made *himself* the leader he wanted to be? How has he made *France* conform to his own requirements?

Leadership

Whoever examines the General's career as a leader cannot fail to be struck by three aspects. First, the theme of transcendence is essential: de Gaulle is a man who has, so to speak, stretched him-

de Gaulle as Political Artist

self throughout his life so as to be able to meet the needs created by the circumstances and thus to fulfill himself. This has required, on the one hand, the capacity to put himself in a state of readiness and active waiting until the events occur—he was forty-nine when France fell, and he spent twelve and a half years out of power between his two reigns. It also has required, on the other hand, the capacity to grow so as to meet new challenges not with old formulas but with appropriate inner strength.[42]

Secondly, de Gaulle has always been more concerned with being right than with achieving immediate results: There is, throughout his career, a preference for all-or-nothing in every issue he considers important; his uncompromising presentation of the *armée de métier*, his tactics as leader of the R.P.F., his foreign policy all indicate a determination to be right even at the cost of immediate effectiveness or popularity, and to let either events or his own acts prove that any other course than his own is wrong.

Finally, one cannot fail to be struck by the ideological emptiness of Gaullism. It is a stance, not a doctrine; an attitude, not a coherent set of dogmas; a style without much substance—beyond the service of France and French grandeur, itself never defined in its content, only by its context.[43]

All three features reflect de Gaulle's personality and conception of leadership. What he has started with—after studying in his first book what leadership should not be—is not a doctrine, but a portrait. The mission is absent—both because it is *generally* taken for granted and because it *specifically* depends on events. What he presents is a self-portrait in anticipation: the portrait of the leader, in *Le fil de l'épée*—a "Plutarchian hero created in the imagination by the values that will create in History the destiny of this hero, and thereby resembles him."[44] The values that created him were those de Gaulle had picked up from his family, but also from his classical and romantic readings (especially, one senses, in Corneille, with his emphasis on self-mastery, and in Chateaubriand and Vigny, with their glorification of the lonely hero). He had picked up these values, too, from the current of ideas that marked the pre-1914 nationalist revival and that "Agathon's" famous inquiry[45] ascribed then to French youth—a reaction against the Republican dogmas of positivism, optimism (in its liberal or socialist versions), scientism, continuous progress, and prevalence of great forces over individual men. Here, the emphasis is on struggle, competition, and above all on the great men who tame events. Thus de Gaulle, "the

845

man of the day before yesterday and the day after tomorrow,"
indeed goes back to earlier notions than those of the Kantian and
Comtean Republic, so as to shape the future with them.

In de Gaulle's case, the values that created the great man in
his imagination are primarily psychological. Once again, as a true
Corneille hero, and exactly as in Erik Erikson's concept of identity,
he blends what he knows he is and what he would like to be, so
as better to become what he is. The way to tame history and to
leave a mark (for this is the name of the game) is to be and to
have *un caractère*—the *caractère* of the leader. Without such a
character, no set of ideas will help; indeed, they will harm, for
they will interpose a screen between reality and the leader (echoes
of Sorel and also results of de Gaulle's reflections on World War I).
The right *caractère* will, by definition, have the craft and strength
to dominate events. The leader is the man who owes his power
to no one but himself[46]—who imposes himself, who is propelled
by what is in him, not by other people's doctrines. He is literally self-generated and perpetually renewed by challenges, pos-
sessor of and possessed by a gift that is unexplainable and somehow compelling, because men are political animals who need
order and turn to leaders in periods of trouble. When de Gaulle
tries to describe the craft that must shape the gift, again it is not
to techniques of action nor to ideas that he turns, but to psychological traits: secrecy, mystery, distance, silence, and protectiveness—
all summarized as "the contrast between inner strength and self-
mastery,"[47] all enhanced by *"la culture générale,"*[48] his father's
preserve.

No conception could be more alien both to the prevalent style
of French political leadership of his time or to the style of incremental decision-making of modern bureaucratic systems (including armies); yet none could be more fitting to a young man
impatient for action and creation, but reduced—in his mid-thirties
—to expectation and anticipation and endowed primarily with his
own *caractère*, since he accepted neither the attrition of bureaucracy,[49] nor the ideas and habits of the regime, nor the counter-
ideologies that offended his realism or his desire for purposeful
national unity. *Le caractère*, as defined by de Gaulle, would necessarily be the man who stretches his resources to meet the challenges
by "forcing his own nature"; the man whose "contempt for contingencies" and concern for "elevation" would dictate an all-or-
nothing, an *unbending*, attitude; the man whose very condition

de Gaulle as Political Artist

of success would be to combine a stance of energy, responsibility, and domination with doctrinal indifference and flexibility. "His character would be his destiny."[50]

Indeed, the three features of de Gaulle's leadership are all derived from the essence of his conception: Leadership, that mysterious gift, is itself an essence, revealed in acts, in attitudes, and in its very aptitude to outgrow, repudiate, and free itself from specific policies and past courses—an essence that is preserved by constant, conscious effort and renewed by practice.[51] Yet *Le fil de l'épée* does not provide the whole picture: It neither gives the full sweep of de Gaulle's conception of leadership, nor constitutes the single key to his subsequent career.

There is both a backdrop and another side. The backdrop is provided by de Gaulle's cyclical notion of time, in which there are shades of Nietzsche's "eternal return" and of Péguy's "epochs and periods." It expresses itself in the last page of the *Mémoires*[52]: History is made of peaks and depressions; nations, as well as great men and like nature, must ride out the storms and come back up again. At any given moment, the world provides a stage: The great man is the actor, both in the theatrical and in the political sense. The metaphor of the play, of the stage, of the drama, appears in all his works; the actor's duty is not to follow a preconceived script, but to write his own and to play it as well as the circumstances allow.

When one analyzes de Gaulle's idea of the good actor and the right script, the other side of the picture appears. First, the good actor must be able to play on all the registers of history. On the one hand, he must wait for the circumstances to be ripe, and when they are, seize them decisively, for "events, in great moments, tolerate in positions of leadership only men who know how to chart their own course."[53] On the other hand, he must also know "how to put himself on the side of time,"[54] how to discern and work for the long range—to *rise above* the moment. Second, the good actor is not out only for himself: for "the leaders of men—politicians, prophets, soldiers who obtained most from others—identified themselves with high ideas."[55] The notion of the *cause* is crucial to this conception of leadership. The great leader fulfills himself by becoming the militant missionary of a function, at the service of which he puts all the resources of the word and of action. Charles de Gaulle identifies with France, makes of himself a personage—called General de Gaulle in the *Mémoires*—whose vocation is to be the voice of the nation. History calls him in emergencies, and he calls the French on behalf of France. He has to serve the present needs of France, to protect her legacy, and to guarantee her future. He must maintain her personality, so that she can keep playing on the world stage; he must, in his own moves, follow only what he deems the national interest, apart from all categories, ideologies, and special interests. He is a unifier, by being above and lifting others above their daily selves.

Thus, he fulfills a function that "goes far beyond his person"; he serves "as destiny's instrument."[56] His role is to provide "that inspiration from the summits, that hope of success, that ambition of France which sustain the nation's soul . . . something essential, permanent,"[57] whatever specific or institutional role he may be performing at any moment. Malraux speaks of a *dédoublement* of de Gaulle—the man and the personage. But it is really a *détriplement:* There is *Charles;* there is the public-political *de Gaulle,* the temporal leader, who happens to be the head of the Free French, or provisional Premier, or opposition leader, or President; and there is the public-historic person, the embodiment of France's cause, *General de Gaulle,* who dominates the other two, transcending the first and controlling the second.

France provides Charles de Gaulle not only with the transcendence he needs, but also with the limits he craves. To be "France's champion" means depending on no one, yet being oneself completed; but the need to preserve France's personality, the subordination of the self to her service impose prudence, harmony, moderation, and protect both the nation and the missionary from the excesses of those (like Napoleon or Hitler) who use their nation as tools of personal glory or to work out their ideological or psychological obsessions. The vocation is thus all-consuming, yet a restraint. It is all-consuming not only insofar as it must become the leader's *raison d'être,*[58] but also insofar as the missionary and guide, who takes his cue only from history and the national interest, can—as *leader,* as missionary for the cause—take initiatives that are denied to lesser people. (He can rebel against the disgrace of the armistice, but others cannot rebel against him.) It is a restraint, because of the constant need not to do anything that would, by sullying his own public personage, spoil the chances and soil the honor of the nation. The great leader imposes his will and denies fatalism[59]; but he must also know how to balance ends and means, how to distinguish what is irresistible from what is reversible, so as *de Gaulle as Political Artist*

not to be destroyed by *hubris*.[60] The key is provided by the elusive but essential notion of grandeur.

"De Gaulle's" relation to his mission is the relation of a high priest to his God, executing only His will (as he sees it), and leading his flock with a hand that both points to the summits and hides the petty obstacles so as to inflame his people's energies. Hence the mystical quality, noted by many observers,[61] and the lofty assurance of his language. Just as the religious leader must at times protect his people from sin, at times redeem it from sin, de Gaulle's function is to redeem his nation from the secular equivalent of sin, which he himself calls the fall.[62]

It is also the relation of a monarch to his kingship. One can only admire how he has combined his parents' nostalgia, his own acceptance of the Republic as a necessary framework, and his determination to provide that framework with a completely different type of leader, recalled from the monarchic past, detached from heredity, and reshaped for the dramas of the future.

Last but not least, the link between the public figure and his cause is the relation of the artist to his work of art. Charles himself has been very conscious of this. He has pointed to the aesthetic dimension of military leadership[63] and of statecraft,[64] to the analogy between *"le chef et l'artiste."*[65] He has, in his books and speeches which describe or express the public figure, tried to transform ordinary or chaotic experience into aesthetic form, in a style that has two essential features: its deliberateness, reflected in the complexity of highly structured and patterned sentences, and its oratory, as if it were written to be read aloud, for a stage. The calm which surrounds his work is that of the artist who needs deep quiet to transcend the conflicts in himself and the data provided by his experience. The central themes of his published works have remained unaltered since his adolescence; they have been constantly restated, each new statement being superimposed over the last one; each book, each major address has in it *all* of himself (as leader), as well as something about his mission. And each of his major political acts, however tortuous the means or the details, has been whole, indivisible, and unmistakably his own, like any artistic act. There is in him a quality that rises far above force and ruse, beyond the skillful use of all available tactics. But if in de Gaulle's conception the relation of the *leader*—that is, of "de Gaulle"—to the *mission* of "General de Gaulle" is that of an artist to his creation, so, first of all, has been *Charles'* relation to his *public* self. It is to the creation of "de Gaulle" by Charles that we must turn.

The Leader as a Work of Art

How did Charles de Gaulle apply to himself his notion of leadership, make of himself a work of art, and thus "create in History" his own destiny? The answer can be described chronologically and sought psychologically.

It may well be that his captivity in 1916-18, which deprived him of the opportunity to meet his first major challenge in a way that would have satisfied him, both heightened his fervent desire for a future chance and saved him from the risk of rigidity, of mechanically re-enacting later in life the ways in which one has succeeded in meeting one's first test. This accident of fate thus left him *disponible*—in particular, for first building up in his mind and works the image of the leader and also for moving the scene of the mission from military prowess to statecraft. For his choice of a military career, explained above, was not a full nor satisfying answer to his need to serve by saving. The self-portrait that he paints in his two books of 1932 and 1934 goes much beyond military leadership. It already stretches toward statecraft.[66] Only as a national leader could he solve for all Frenchmen the problems— external and domestic—that had plagued his family and his youth. To be sure, if he groped toward supreme power, he did not expect it. His first moves in London, in June 1940, showed that he was still willing to serve under more prestigious French leaders who would reject Vichy's armistice. But he had made himself ready for supreme power and stepped into the void decisively.[67] Eighteen years later, the man who no longer expected a new call again stepped into the void, with supreme ease and tactical skill, because he had, once more, kept himself ready for the unexpected.

One can therefore distinguish in his career two important thresholds: 1940 and 1958. Before June 1940, he is a military man whose concerns, to be sure, far exceed those of his superiors and colleagues; yet they still remain essentially within the realm of strategy. From June 1940 to the early-1950's, he becomes—first as leader of the Resistance, then as head of Liberated France, lastly as head of the Opposition—the political trustee of his beloved France who judges all events from a single yardstick: French substance and

de Gaulle as Political Artist

survival. His fear of loss of and for her is so great that, in his actions on the world stage, he acts primarily as a restorer and preserver of her traditional legacy, conceiving her interests in classical terms, as if the future had indeed to be the prolongation (and rectification) of the past. But finally, with the *Mémoires* and the return to power, a third de Gaulle appears, still concerned above all with France, yet more serene, more willing to let go, more universal (in the sense of being more able to take other peoples' aspirations into account, more eager to adapt and renew than to maintain and restore), and also more detached both from Charles and from his temporal political self, to whom he refers in the third person, *sub specie aeternitatis,* or, rather, from the lofty vantage point of the historic figure.

In each case, the crossing of a threshold has been prepared both by the failure of action within the previous framework, which makes him again *disponible* for action when the framework collapses (for example, the failure of his lobbying for a motorized army in the 1930's, the fiasco of the R.P.F. in the early-1950's) and by the kind of catharsis which his indirect form of action—writing —performed for him. Whereas the man of action, even when he takes so long a view or so high a point of view as does de Gaulle, must take into account the necessities of the moment, the writer can judge those necessities from the viewpoint of future history. The man of action aims at the future, but stands in the present; the writer can put himself already in the future and assess the present from that vantage point. Before 1940 and before 1958, writing both raised his horizon and sharpened his lucidity—about himself, as shown by his call for a "master" in *l'Armée de métier*[68] and by his analysis of "General de Gaulle" in the *Mémoires,* and about the world around him, as shown by his assessment of Germany and France in his two books of 1934 and 1950 and by his re-evaluation of the international scene in the *Mémoires.* There, he also re-judges, and usually absolves, the men he had fought or condemned during the war. He wrote, quoting Faust, that in the beginning was action, not the word.[69] But in his case, although the word is always about action, action was always preceded and defined by the word.

Chronology thus sends us back to psychology—to de Gaulle's double determination not to let failure discourage him from his mission, and to prepare himself through the disciplined reflection of writing for the role that events might allow him to play. It is as

851

DÆDALUS

if *Charles,* the artist, had put all his efforts into shaping *de Gaulle,* the work of art. This has meant, deliberately, an attempt to depersonalize himself, to remove, as Malraux puts it, Charles from the public eye. Yet Charles, the private man, exists. And the public figure, the work of art, is intensely, uniquely personal.

His private self has not been absorbed by his public role: de Gaulle has married a woman whose milieu is very close to that of his mother, he has had three children, has led a normal family life, and is a discreet but devout Catholic. Private affects and public objects have lived side by side. Those who have been able to get through to the man have found him courteous, devoid of arrogance and of awkwardness (indeed the descriptions remind one of those we have of his father).[70]

However, there is a great deal of evidence about the subordination of Charles to de Gaulle: Charles is a rather pale and banal figure, tailored in such a way as to leave all the energies to de Gaulle. His private life is quiet and low key—marked "neither by quarrel nor by laughter."[71] As Malraux has pointed out,[72] other great men have had colorful private personalities. (He mentions Napoleon, but one could add Pétain, who, in addition to episodic liaisons, spent much of life courting a young woman to whom he wrote very intimate letters and whom he finally married.[73]) The private de Gaulle, says Malraux, is merely the one who does not talk of public affairs. His courtesy does not abolish the distance between himself and others; it protects distance—indeed, it is merely, adds Malraux, a feature of his "priesthood." As far as one knows, there is no real intimacy between him and others. His wife is a devoted but reserved figure; his son, physically a carbon copy of himself, has had an unspectacular career as a navy officer; he has had admirers and circles of close acquaintances, but no very close friends, and displays little spontaneity. "He accepts from himself neither impulsiveness nor abandonment."[74] The private self seems always on its guard both against indiscreet questioners who want to get behind the public figure, and against those who, admitted into his restricted privacy, would try to take advantage of it so as to influence the public figure.[75] There is no such thing as happiness, he once "barked out"[76] under this kind of questioning. To such a man, everything that is not public life, service, the personage, and the cause, far from being a haven, a respite, a shelter, means exile and solitude.[77] This does not mean that he is never tempted by it; but when he yields to or chooses that temptation, it is in order to

de Gaulle as Political Artist

pursue his interior monologue, not in order to find ordinary human warmth. The monologue feeds the public figure and prepares him for the next phase of his role; human warmth and entanglements would only distract him from his task.

This task—the exercise of power—is also solitary, if one chooses to perform at such an altitude. Yet in *that* kind of performance lies "the interest of life." The dominant relation between the two selves, between Charles and General de Gaulle, could be characterized by that Lasswellian phrase, the displacement of private affects on public objects. But displacement, here, is deliberate and elaborate— like artistic creation. The first of those public objects is none other than himself, or rather "de Gaulle," the epic figure that has to be shaped so as to fill the part that history and Charles have pre- pared for it. Private feelings have to be transmuted into public service; the requirements of the mission rule out the personage's being influenced either by the whims and demands of the private person or by the pressures and results of others.[78] Hence there is that formidable "internal distance" noted by Malraux and Gide,[79] that refusal to let the internal monologue appear in the open; hence, especially in the months after June 1940 (when the man had to act out the public figure he had created in his mind, when this figure had to meet, to fit, and to make its mission, and when his torment must have been extreme) there is that formidable, gloomy, bitter, and closed look in eyes which "reflected nothing from the world out- side."[80] The sense one gets is of a deeply passionate and sensitive man—indeed, one who, during the war, was so raw and scorched that he did not yet always control his feelings and public face[81]— but one whose real passions are public, whose moods are determined by the state of public affairs, whose serenity, a self-imposed neces- sity for the great leader, is the product of an effort, a conquest, and whose real dialogue is not with specific human beings, but with those abstractions that *to him* are human. Gide's Thesée said: "*Je n'aime pas l'homme, j'aime ce qui le dévore.*" De Gaulle could say: I don't like men, I like what elevates them.[82]

It is as if there were two parallel de Gaulles: the private person with a father and mother of flesh and blood, to whom he was, so to speak, normally attached—yet no part of that trilogy sufficed him. And then there are the higher, public objects of his affections—General de Gaulle as the "national necessity" for troubled times, because he is "alone and erect"[83]; and the General's mythical (or real?) parents: History, the father to whom he is

DÆDALUS

responsible[84] (just as others must report to him), and which will
judge him according to his works; France, his mother—an old
cliché which the long tradition of describing France as a person
had somehow frayed, yet which finds in de Gaulle, the protector
and knight, the new force of authenticity. The feelings that ani-
mate de Gaulle are at that level, in that realm. His failures affect
him not because they are his own, but because they are France's.
The warmth he needs is not the intimacy of equals, but the support
and sympathy of the led. The "melancholy" that is the accepted
price of domination, that willing sacrifice of ordinary human relations,[85] becomes intolerable and leads to "ill-explained retreats"
only when the *leader's* soul becomes engulfed by what Clemenceau
(twice quoted by de Gaulle)[86] called its worst pain: cold—the indifference or hostility of the led. The warmth he needs is public.
Since his goal is not self-expression, but self-fulfillment through
service, and since his mission is to lead men, he cannot perform
his task alone; when they abandon him, then, rather than letting
his private self take over, he remains his public person, but in
waiting.

Between Charles and General de Gaulle, there are undoubtedly
no conflicts. The stoicism with which he faced his third child's
illness resembles his imperial way of facing the realities of power.
Indeed, "de Gaulle" is Charles' accomplishment. If France is "de
Gaulle's" *raison d'être*, "de Gaulle" is Charles'. How could that
double need for glory and for distance be better served than by
stretching oneself into, and merging with, a function of historic
significance, yet one that requires that one keep one's distance
even from oneself, to make sure that the performance will be great?
For a man to be his own creator, what a revenge over solitude
and separateness; also what pride, and, once again, what a way
both of externalizing and of transcending narcissism—for it is in his
historic figure that he takes the pride of the artist who has mastered
his craft; it is not vanity.

The values *Charles* had absorbed from his family have been
grafted on *General de Gaulle's* "parents." He resembles Vigny's
Moses: "*Seigneur, vous m'avez fait puissant et solitaire. Laissez-
moi m'endormir du sommeil de la terre.*" What saves the missionary
from inhumanity is, first, a very Christian sense of man's frailty—
even the great man's (see his astonishing portrait of Hitler:
"but, beaten and crushed, perhaps he became a man again, long
enough to shed a secret tear, at the moment where everything

de Gaulle as Political Artist

ends"[87]). Secondly, rather than serving a harsh God, he serves, on the one hand, History—which requires of its most appreciated servants not only that they court glory, but also that they respect moderation (hence his persistent rejection of dictatorship)—and, on the other hand, France, the beacon of light, the threatened princess, the nation that has to be saved from its vices.

It is by shaping his public figure that de Gaulle has resolved that tension analyzed earlier. The mission is a transmission of the parents' legacy (but as rescued and remade by the leader); the missionary is the receptacle of the cynical lessons that history also teaches, and of the ego's will to power (but to be used for a great cause).

It does not matter if we know little directly about Charles, the artist, who created de Gaulle, the work of art. Even if we knew the last intimate detail of the artist's childhood, schooling, and marriage, what we are able to say about the personal life of the artist is, usually, irrelevant to the evaluation of the work of art. It helps us only to understand the man who made it, rather than the work itself; it may provide the key to the content, but not to the intimate relation of form and content which is the essence of every work of art. Conversely, understanding this relation tells us a great deal about the man.

Indeed, the public figure from whom the Memoir writer who says "I" strived to be detached, and who is supposed to be only the protector of France and incarnation of history, in the real cycle of identifications takes on the features of Charles the artist. The more he bends himself to the public figure and to France, the more the "character" and France resemble the artist—but as in every work of art those features are transformed, re-created, mastered, *dominated*. Charles de Gaulle has continued to marshal all his resources. He has displayed all the qualities associated with artistic creation: the mix of detachment and commitment which allows him to watch his personage from afar, yet to shape its destiny; the blend of passion and decorum, so characteristic of a man whose style often appears as its own reward, yet always serves a cause; the willingness to be dominated by the object—in this case, the character and France, which "haunts" him[88]; the combination of deferral and immediacy. What must be resented as obstinacy by all those who hold dissenting views, and what represents a neurotic flaw in the character of Charles? His old need always to be right reflects the artist's sense of the inner appropriateness of a particular decision, of its perfect fit into the whole vision; his "feel" that his conception "works" or must ultimately work. Very often, his skill as a craftsman (politician) *makes* it work, even as his skill as an artist (statesman) helps him to assess correctly the *"pâte"* (reality) he is trying to reshape. It is an instinctive, instinctual activity, one which involves all the gifts of the artist-leader.

It is easy to see why Malraux should have become fascinated by the General, for the public figure is like the embodiment of Malraux's ideal. He is a character in a novel that Malraux never wrote, but that would combine all of Malraux's strivings; he is also the work of art so much admired by Malraux, that which takes off from past masterpieces, expresses a transcendent faith, and conquers time. De Gaulle is that adventurer with a cause that Malraux had looked for in his early years, and the cause is not the excessively abstract ideology that Communism had represented and that the Soviet Union exploited for its purposes, but the preservation of a cultural entity—the nation, whose importance Malraux had discovered in defeat and whose personality (not superiority) de Gaulle wants to assert. De Gaulle's mission is to leave a scar on history, to shape his destiny, and thus to defy death, chance, oblivion by linking creatively the past and the future. To de Gaulle as to Malraux, men are what they do, what they reveal of themselves not in introspective analysis, but in creative action. If creativity is the "working out of conflict and coalition within the set of identities that compose the person,"[89] then de Gaulle's leadership is highly *creative*, even if it is not so *innovative*.

Some witnesses have seen him as all of one piece. In reality, we find a harnessing of all the pieces. Thus, there is a skillful transformation of his psychological peculiarities into unique tools of leadership. This is true of many of his gifts. His memory has become not only the thoroughly reliable servant of his eloquence, but also a source of prestige and awe. His literary talent and his imagination have blended in the *Mémoires,* written at a time when he seems to have thought that his chances of ever coming back to power were slim; these volumes served not only as a catharsis, as noted before, but also as a reliving in the imagination of the exploits of the recent past and as a legacy of examples for the future. His old gift for drama, acting, and performing on a stage has become ritualized in his press conferences and ceremonial appearances: From his early playacting, he has shifted to role-acting. His energy finds outlets in constant journeys, which feed his curiosity, provide him with the

de Gaulle as Political Artist

"soul's warmth" he needs, allow him to carry his message to all the corners of his widening stage, and preserve his sense of the realities.

We have stated that the army fitted some of the peculiarities of his character—his sense of distance, his shying-away from intimacy, and that incapacity to share decisions that results from his drive for independence. All of those traits have become the trademarks of his political leadership. The "King in exile"[90] has become the Republican monarch. The mold which the army had given to his way of organizing action, its institutionalization of distance, he has elevated and perpetuated in a constitution that makes of the President a kind of commander in chief, aided by a chief of staff, the Premier. His impatience with details that could clutter the mind of the leader has also been institutionalized. His dislike for discussions and debates that dilute the will and confuse the issues,[91] his awkwardness in small groups have led him to replace such negotiations with "consultations" in which he is usually alone with whomever he consults.[92] His preference for infantry, which put him as an officer in direct but dominating contact with average Frenchmen, is relayed by his way of leaning on the people, of short-circuiting the "elites."[93] His preference for a certain protective isolation has driven telephones out of his offices and saved almost all his weekends in France for a return to Colombey. When some feature, left untamed, could have harmed his vocation, he has cursed his own nature. The early reluctance to let himself be interviewed, photographed, or put on display has been disciplined, although not at the expense of the imperatives of mystery and surprise. And even intransigence, his trademark, has gradually been put back into limits—that is, reserved for two kinds of issues, both significant of his leadership: symbolic or protocol issues, involving "nothing but" self-respect, and vital national interests.

Next to the transmutation of personal traits into tools, there is the welding of opposites, or of polarities, in such a way that, far from destroying each other and the man, they complement each other and help him fulfill his mission by becoming ingredients of leadership—externalized and transcended. Some of those polarities can be seen as variations on two permanent themes—picked up from his parents, and later developed in memorable statements: the passionate and the reasonable.[94]

The most obvious are the polarities of rebellion and rallying,[95] or defiance and assertion. The natural *démarche* of de Gaulle is to defy either whatever offends his concept of leadership (such as the instruction he received in military schools, the military policy of the interwar period, or the political styles of the declining Third Republic and of the Fourth Republic), or whatever "insults the future" as he both wants it and deems it possible (such as Vichy's resignation to defeat, or the two-postwar "hegemonies, or the French Communists' servility toward Moscow after 1947). This defiance can be brutal and intransigent. But de Gaulle is neither a nihilist nor (adds Malraux)[96] a Trotsky. The rebel in him wants it known, as he once told a delegation of labor-union leaders, that "General de Gaulle has no predecessors"[97]; but he wants to have successors and to represent historic continuity. The defier, or resister, does so in order to "save and put in order."[98] The purpose of his domestic calls to action was to unify the French; of his external acts of negation, to reshape the world in safer fashion, which to him means, characteristically, into equilibrium. His one substantive domestic notion (beyond the constitutional design he announced in 1946 and realized in 1958-62) has been the association of capital and labor. On the other hand, the unifier and servant of order knows he can succeed only through battle—be it against an overpowering ally, or other French regimes or parties, or business and labor unions attached to their ways.

Another set of polarities, close to the previous one, is the General's romanticism and classicism (his admiration for Chateaubriand, who assured the transition, is no surprise). It is the romantic who says "me and history,"[99] asserts his lack of origins, sees the world as a turmoil in which the man of action, occasionally, discreetly, discontinuously "decides and prescribes . . . and then, after action has been launched, seizes again by spurts the system of his means which facts relentlessly put out of shape."[100] It is, however, the classicist who insists on measure and balance, who sees in the leader a kind of grand entrepreneur, the function of whose investments and innovations is to preserve the continuity and flow of history, who rules like a Cornelian Emperor, and knows that in this century "no man can be the people's substitute."[101] Romanticism and classicism blend in de Gaulle's military programs and use of technological innovations; he has put the radio, during the war, and television, since 1958, at the service of *le caractère;* his old hostility to the "system of armed masses," which inspired first his design for a professional army and, later, his reconversion of the French army to the atomic age, reflects both the romantic love for mobility, decisiveness, lightning action that had made him admire

de Gaulle as Political Artist

Hoche, Foch, and Clemenceau and the classic concern for maximum efficiency in the use of limited resources, which had made him celebrate Louvois and Turenne, Carnot and Pétain.

Two other sets of features that are kept in balance and blended for the mission are, on the one hand, his inflexibility and brutality; on the other, his tactical skill and patience. The former have been displayed abruptly throughout his career—from his relations with Churchill to his speech in Montreal. A psychological tendency that goes back to his childhood and stems both from his loyalty to transmitted values and from his self-assertion has thus been used to shape, delay, or accelerate history. But, on the other hand, there has been—in this transformed prankster and critical *connaisseur* of dubious means to lofty ends—a deliberate use of ambiguity (*"je vous ai compris!"*), a willingness to wait and ponder until the moment is ripe, especially when there was either no other, better way of affecting events or no vital interest involved. Temporization, it seems, was already a trait in the student and young officer whenever his mind was not fully engaged.[102]

Another tension, also resolved, is that which exists between his taste for flamboyance and his sense of finitude. One drives him toward heroic assertions of will, toward grand attempts at making his policies irreversible; the other toward a certain fatalism, a strange readiness, if not to accept defeat, at least to admit partial failure as the price for being human.[103] Once again, he marries the two, and each heightens the other: The more one is aware of the limits of one's possibilities—one's own and those of "the nation as it is in the world as it is"—the more necessary it becomes to do what can be done with *panache*, flair, and style; but those, in turn, are justified only so long as they serve the cause realistically.

One keyword of de Gaulle's political vocabulary illuminates his acts as a leader, his way of mobilizing and welding his resources: "arbitration." It does not mean mediation, finding a common denominator among pre-existing tendencies (within him) or factions (outside); it means deciding—both after taking into account in one's calculations all the givens provided by one's own nature or by the "nature of things," and with the higher interest as a goal. Once again, we find mastery without mutilation; the "arbiter" is none other than *le caractère*, determined to take charge, respectful of the need for equilibrium, and resolving his inner tensions by the tough "internal discipline and heavy yoke"[104] of subordination to the higher goal.

DÆDALUS

But arbitration does not take care of all inner tensions. There is one between him and the cause that is supposed to transcend and elevate both his private and his public selves—between the artist and the mission for which he shaped his work of art. There are, inevitably, opposite pulls. There is, in particular, a contradiction between the *private man*'s desire to assert his personality— his egotism, if you like—his sense of personal adventure, a certain drunkenness with his own destiny, a heady enchantment with having made of himself such a precious capital,[105] and the *historic figure*'s desire to be above all the expression of *France*, his concern for *raison d'Etat*. The former injects occasionally into the leader's acts an element of vindictiveness or into his words a paean of self-praise.[106] The latter may demand some self-abnegation, and in any case prudence in the use of the capital, skepticism about the ego's reach. Yet the reconciliation is usually provided in a way that both protects the mission and satisfies the artist—by exalting the public-political figure. The personality that is spread over the map is the *public* personage, not the private self, and since that personage is nothing but the tool of the state, his successes, resentments, assertions, claims, and setbacks become those of the nation. To leave him "in the desert" (as did the Fourth Republic) is to waste France,[107] to slight him is to slight France, to plan his assassination is a crime against the state, to serve him is to ennoble oneself. If *le caractère* wants full power for himself and denies anyone else's capacity to exert power adequately, it is because there is between "de Gaulle" and his mission a mystical link that allows him to claim historical legitimacy. De Gaulle, quoting Roosevelt who had taxed him with egotism,[108] asks whether F.D.R. thought him egotistic for himself or for France; in fact, he has solved the problem by equating his *public* self with the *higher* interest of France.

Yet this solution poses one more problem: It may reconcile the artist with the *final* work of art—the historic personage which the public-political figure must create. But it does so by boosting the *artist*'s work of art: that public figure. And, like every work of art, this one tends, once it gets under way, to take on a life of its own, with its own demands for wholeness. Since its artist is so closely tied to it by his own needs and in his person, the work tends also to take over the artist. If it does so, he has failed—he is no longer master of himself, of the others, or of his creation. This time he needs to use his resources not to *blend*, but to *separate*. He has

de Gaulle as Political Artist

resorted to three familiar aids, mobilized on behalf of self-distance and perspective: his sense of humor and irony; his habit of describing himself in the third person as an actor on a stage whom he would watch from the audience; and his discipline of detachment by moving away from the all-absorbing present in time (the recourse to history) and space (travels). These three devices have been (as usual) instinctively and deliberately used by Charles to keep himself from fusing entirely with the *éclat* and *grandeur* of his "over-determined" work of art, similar to the over-determination of fantasy and dreams, as of all rich artistic creation. There is a gigantic battle between the artist's attempt to fuse and project his highest aspirations onto *le caractère* who lives for France, and his own narcissistic needs to hold onto that artistic projection by completely identifying with it.

France as de Gaulle

What makes this battle so difficult to win is not only the resemblance of the work of art, "de Gaulle," to the artist, but also the resemblance to the artist of that higher work of art, France, which the public figure has both to serve and to shape as "de Gaulle's" work of art.

Not only have many of Charles' psychological and even physical peculiarities been turned into tools of leadership, they have also been projected by him onto his beloved France. This is especially striking in the case of those traits that are essential to an understanding of the man: his own highest aspirations, blends of the *is* and the *ought* since they reflect both psychological needs and moral values[109] he has assigned to France. A pragmatist in his daily politics, de Gaulle as a political high priest is concerned above all with making France behave according to those values; a Machiavellian in his tactics, he is a moralist in his highest goals. (As an associate has described him, he is "Caesar reshaped by Christianity.") De Gaulle, from adolescence on, has felt the need for a strong internal discipline to guard him against waste and dispersion, to harness his gifts and prevent internal tensions from paralyzing him. The solution, as we know, has been to unify his talents and traits in the service of a great cause, which will provide the harness and heighten the efficiency of his personality. This is exactly what he ascribes to and prescribes for France: France is full of "ferments of dispersion," has often yielded to "chimeras," been threatened by mediocrity and disasters.[110] For France, the harness is to be provided by a unifying and galvanizing "national ambition," a "great undertaking"—by grandeur, by the "choice of a great cause." Once again what he proclaims necessary for her is what he has assigned to himself—"*viser haut et se tenir droit.*"[111] Both he and France need a higher "*querelle*"; without one, he is convinced that she will not "be herself" for she is truly herself neither in mediocrity nor in misfortune. Similarly, he is at his best only when carried by his mission. When he writes of "Old France, burdened by history, bruised by wars and revolutions, relentlessly going back and forth from grandeur to decline, but straightened, century after century, by the genius of renovation,"[112] or describes France as a "great people, made for example, enterprise, combat, always the star of History,"[113] or says that he always felt that Providence "had created her for perfect success or exemplary misfortune,"[114] he is describing himself as much as her.

The identification goes further. Just as he has proclaimed throughout his life that the hero was both his own law and the servant of France, France is seen by him both as *the* nation par excellence and as the servant of what he called, during the war, "*la querelle de l'homme*"—the cause of freedom, of equilibrium, of generosity in a world threatened by mechanization.[115] Just as he has used all his resources in his mission, but put them at its service, he has always wanted to use all the spiritual and political "families" of France, refused to discard any so long as it was willing to contribute to the cause, but tried to convert them all from their separate concerns to the common goal. Just as, for him, grandeur meant an attitude of the will and soul rather than a specific doctrine, grandeur for France means a state of mind and resolve, a rejection of pettiness, an ambition rather than a concrete program: the ambition, more cultural and moral than political, to preserve certain values that are like a blend of Christianity's and of the Revolution's.

The precondition for grandeur, in both cases, is the same: independence. De Gaulle's foreign policy—his central concern—has aimed persistently at giving France "free hands," at restoring her freedom of decision (the more interdependent the nations of the world, the greater the need for a margin of autonomy); in recent years, he has made of this a universal doctrine. It is impossible not to recognize in his philosophy of international relations, in his

de Gaulle as Political Artist

dismissal of ideologies, in his assertion of the primacy of national interests, in his stress on the incommunicable uniqueness of each nation,[116] in his view of states on the world stage as separate national essences with accidental existences shaped by the twists of history and the turns of national consciousness,[117] once again a projection of his own conception of leadership—ultimately, of his personal stance, of his own determination to "belong to all and nobody"[118] (a formula that fits his view of France)—and a blend of the *is* and the *ought* (for his mission and France's as defined by him are justified only if he is right). It was Vichy's crime to have renounced French independence, thus losing its legitimacy.[119] And if he was able to restore France's independence, in 1944 and after 1958, it was because he had never alienated his own.

The emphasis on independence for him and her is tied to another essential notion: that of integrity, meaning both wholeness and faithfulness. Independence is the condition for integrity; integrity is the substance of self-respect; and self-respect, or dignity, a central value, can be found only in grandeur. "Not to disappoint oneself"[120] seems to be the motto he gave both to himself and to France. There is no self-respect in humiliation, or in mediocrity, or in "*bassesse*"[121] (there may be some in failure, if it is honorable). For the leader, there is no loss of self-respect in a resort to deception and cunning so long as the higher cause prevails; there is, for France, no loss of self-respect in revising her alliances and reversing her policies so long as her own higher goals are served. The association of capital and labor that de Gaulle keeps trying to establish, so much like the combination of opposites within himself, makes more sense as a promotion of dignity than as an economic reform. De Gaulle offers France's aid to the French Canadians, who have preserved their independence and integrity and are now claiming a modern role of their own, but the French Algerians, who did not know how to adapt and spoiled the image of France, were less well treated by him.

Grandeur, independence, integrity: just as his leadership tends to give France his own profile, France's leadership aims at making of the world a collection of ideal types of Gaullist nations, each one embodying its unique values and virtues, and kept within the limits of moderation by the balancing of power. There is an underlying assumption here that just as man is truly free and responsible only when he can fully develop and master his personality, there can be no true world order outside that which would be a structured harmony of multiple uniquenesses. And just as the leader sets the example for France, France must set it for the world.

France in international relations indeed behaves as de Gaulle writ large. Just as his conception of leadership consists of discerning what he deems right, providing an example, and asking others to follow rather than forcing them to do so, France's stance on the world stage consists of showing the way imperiously and exhorting others to follow; but just as he has always refused entanglements for himself so as to save his freedom to maneuver, his France refuses commitments with obscure purposes and binding procedures. His difficulty in negotiating, his way of never letting a concession be bargained out of him but, instead, of granting (*octroyer*)[122] concessions to which the other will respond freely become France's vetoes, boycotts, and unilateral moves. His personal intransigence becomes France's intractability; the leader's *âpreté* becomes France's toughness; the man's preference for dealing with other great leaders, lonely masters, and artists becomes France's disdain for taking seriously powers incapable of "charting their course." His need for drama becomes France's stealing the show in world affairs, or attempts to steal it.

The same polarities that he combines in himself he projects onto and harnesses in France. A traditionalist, but also an empiricist thirsty for action, he wants France both to preserve her personality and to innovate—for without innovation, modernization, mechanization, industrialization, there is no way to be great anymore. Yet all these changes must not be allowed to turn France into a bastardized America. (Hence the emphasis on saving her language and culture in which he finds, not surprisingly, her essence.) His own mixture of narcissism and discipline becomes the blend of often strident French self-assertion and recognition of the need for "modesty." And just as the awareness of personal finitude increases the desire for flamboyance, the realistic awareness of the limits of France's present power heightens the need for self-pride: France's foreign policy today combines a colossal *repli* from overseas and abandonment of excessive commitments, with a spectacular determination to exploit every possibility of influence.[123]

III. *Charisma*

The artist does not need a responsive public immediately. He may write or paint for the "happy few" and posterity. The political

de Gaulle as Political Artist

artist needs a public *now*, even if his ambition is to build for the ages; without one, his work of art remains a conception. The political artist succeeds only if public response allows the figure of the leader, privately shaped by the artist for a public role, to become a public figure. Political leadership is a relationship between the leader and his followers; and charisma is not only a gift, it is also a form of authority, a link between a certain type of ruler and the ruled. If charisma is communicated self-confidence,[124] what we must discuss now is why, when, and how de Gaulle has managed to impose his gift to the French, to preserve his authority after coming to power, and at what costs for the nation and for the future of his own work.

Conditions

De Gaulle has always known and said that he could not carry out his mission without public support. From 1940 to 1944, he literally forged it. He resigned in 1946 when he felt it slipping and lacked the institutional means to preserve it *in his style*. He tried in vain to recreate it as leader of the R.P.F. He found it again in 1958. What were the conditions for his success?

He has succeeded in establishing that cycle of identifications—of France to himself, of himself to France, of the people with him, of himself and France to higher causes—whenever the circumstances have been exactly what the script required; whenever he has been able to enact or re-enact on the stage of history the great drama that he had wanted to perform: that of bringing *alone* a decisive and famous service to his nation in distress; whenever history brought his nation to the point where his own need (for drama, leadership, a call, unity, and salvation) became France's, and when France at last had no alternative but to turn to the lonely leader; whenever the missionary who had subordinated his private self to his public function met men whose public drama had become a private crisis.[125] It was the man's great chance that when he projected his formidable will and imagination into the future, events obligingly provided the great dramas that he called for *à la* Chateaubriand (*"levez-vous, orages désirés"*), that World War I foreshadowed in his mind, and that his relative failure in it made even more imperative for his ambition. This was a chance that his political genius has, of course, fully exploited; but it was

865

also part of his genius to have anticipated, announced, and denounced those events clearly.

Here we find the first ingredient of his charisma: the awe-inspiring capacity of *le caractère* to predict the *circonstances*—that is, to be right. Prescience did for him what victory over paralysis had done for F.D.R. in the American people's eyes. (It is no accident if de Gaulle's symbolic domain was public, F.D.R.'s was private.) The somewhat suffocating statement of May 19, 1958: "The Algerians shout: Vive de Gaulle as the French do instinctively when they are deep in anguish or carried by hope,"[126] reflects a reality.

However, what has been required for success has been a perfect adequacy and a perfect prophecy. It is only when the circumstances were those of extreme and irremediable disaster, when the leader could appeal both to the present fears, anxieties, and sufferings of the people and to their hopes, to Péguy's *"espérance"* and Corneille's *"beau désespoir,"* when he could appear as the prophet, the unifier, the remover of the roadblocks to and the guide toward the "summits" of self-respect and greatness that he has succeeded. The counter-example is provided by the long episode of the R.P.F. There, adequacy was missing. The General prophesied titanic turmoil and cataclysmic conflict between East and West: It did not happen. Although his goals were as lofty as ever, he could not appear as a unifier, since his very attempt to "rally" the nation outside and above the parties divided the French—a dilemma that could have been resolved (as in the fight against Vichy) only if they had gradually deserted the parties out of a personal sense of tragedy and need for salvation, the precondition for which would have been the correctness of the prophecy (as shown later, in 1958). Moreover, because "hope had a tragic accent for him," he had to put the spotlight on tragedy in order to justify his call for action; thus, he appealed almost exclusively to people's fears and anxieties, and exploited them stridently, with dismal results. Those who heard him and came were often those who wanted to save not France but their possessions, and of course they deserted him when the fear of loss vanished, but not without having given to the R.P.F. a cramped, regressive, and repressive air, in which Barrès prevailed over Péguy, conservation over innovation.

For de Gaulle to be able to be the voice of hope and effort, the disasters must already have happened. Before, he can denounce

de Gaulle as Political Artist

their coming, but by the very nature of his personage, to try to be more than a *recours* if they come is likely to be counter-productive. If they fail to occur, his prophetic gift will be tarnished, but if he tries as a political leader to contribute to their coming so as to prove himself right and to awaken the missing "great ambition," he will, by *la force des choses*, be forced to exploit the least grand side of men. Moreover, his methods—intransigence, *politique du pire* yet refusal to go all the way to dictatorship (since dictatorship, to his eyes, means excess *unless* it is prompted by a great national ambition or by a national disaster, both precisely absent)[127]—will simultaneously appear like a wrecking operation and keep him and his followers from power. The attempt of the R.P.F. was explainable only in terms, once again, of the man and the mission: At fifty-six, the man had too much energy for internal exile, and he saw his beloved France under mortal threat. The fiasco of the R.P.F. taught him that before catastrophes his strength was in his very solitude,[128] and the writing of the *Mémoires* cleansed the sullied image of the savior: He erased the re-enactment *manqué* in action by a successful re-enactment in writing.

The reason why de Gaulle's effectiveness begins only in the midst of disaster has to do with the second ingredient of his charisma. It is only in the depths of crisis and despair that the fear of losing one's personality breeds millennial hopes of rescue: otherwise, complacency prevails, and the would-be guide has that unsavory choice between frustration and deliberate contribution to the dreaded yet necessary *secousse*. But when the crisis comes, then de Gaulle's peculiar message—that France must regain her greatness by saving her identity—strikes the deepest chord. For the message, as we have noted, is far more pedagogical than ideological (and thus is related to the messages of religious leaders or of a Gandhi): To de Gaulle (as to the Caesar-Charles of his early play), what matters most is *that* one face the turmoil, and *how* one confronts danger, rather than *what* specific measures one should take (for they depend on circumstances). Here is the strength of Gaullism; its roots lie, again, in the adequacy of a personal case to a national one. For de Gaulle, as we know, the goal in life was not to realize a program, but to be a character, to have a firm identity, shaped by internal balance and control for great but pragmatic action, and faithful to certain values; leadership so defined was its own purpose. For France, a very old nation, identity did not have to be defined in substantive, programmatic terms, necessary perhaps for recent nations still unsure of their national consciousness, but positively harmful in the case of a country where an intense feeling of nationhood coincides with fearful divisions on policies. Thus, in times of acute crisis, the thing for a leader to do is to underemphasize the *substance* of action, but to stress the *essence*—which is self-respect and style. There was no need to define a French identity; there was a need to save and proclaim it, to make the French feel proud of being French and relevant to their times: Nobody could *feel* and *understand* this better than de Gaulle.

It is in emergencies that the threat to national identity makes the citizens willing to give up their established way of life, cherished possessions and institutions, in order to overcome the crisis. De Gaulle's personal message—mystical attachment to an idea of France and detachment from any specific social pattern, fixed policy, overseas position, all of which are merely transient manifestations of the mysterious essence that alone must be preserved—could thus only be heard in extreme moments, when he could play his role of innovating protector. His constant and baffling theme—France must be herself—which may seem like gibberish to many foreigners, is the second source of charisma, for it succeeds whenever, in peril, the French feel the need both to assert their personality in the world and to unify and adapt in order to survive. De Gaulle's charisma thus has an element of poetry in it—the sound and the rhythms are more important than the words' actual meanings; they shape or reshape the meanings. In this way, he can preserve the authenticity, the freshness of the nation's *élan vital*, instead of hardening or freezing it in a program.

A third factor in his charisma is his appeal to a certain style of authority, the style of crisis leadership, represented in French literature by Corneille and in French history both by the *Ancien Régime* and by the Napoleonic Empires. The kind of leadership celebrated in *Le fil de l'épée*, for all its distance from parliamentary leadership, was a French archetype. One of us has analyzed this in detail elsewhere.[129] *Le style du Général*—of political action and of eloquence—fits into a mold perfected and conceptualized by Richelieu. His very sense of distance and restraint, his conception of action by individuals each of whom has his own personality to preserve and is linked not to others on the same level as himself, but to a superior (or, in de Gaulle's own case, a higher calling),

de Gaulle as Political Artist

fits both the Frenchman's *horreur du face à face*[130] and his fear of arbitrariness.

One understands, then, the nature of de Gaulle's appeal in a crisis. He tries to address himself to some of the highest qualities in men—a sense of sacrifice and responsibility and duty; he calls on them to find in the crisis an opportunity to *grow*, rather than to succumb to the irrational fears, hatreds, and delusions so often flattered by demagogues. (Indeed, his own lack of "the physique, taste, attitudes and features that could flatter"[131] crowds, his indifference to being loved, and his rejection of a personality cult justify Malraux's comment: His strength lies in authority, not in contagion.[132]) Yet there is no doubt that the crisis itself brings out those fears, hatreds, and delusions, produces a kind of mass regression of helplessness, and makes the helpless eager to let the decisive leader "arbitrate" for them. One finds among his followers different kinds of men whose attachment to him varies in motivation and in intensity. There are some who need idols, or who attach themselves to the hero because of an inner need for a father figure—de Gaulle, this time, is each one of *them* completed; there are many such men in his entourage. Others are attracted more by what is compelling in de Gaulle's mission and message than by a personal need of their own—except for one widespread need, so important in crises or in otherwise mediocre periods, yet neglected by political scientists: the need to admire. Some are fascinated less by the work of art, the mission, than by the artist: They are the romantics of adventure, action, and great-men-defying-history.[133] Others, finally, are occasional followers, attracted by a temporary or partial element of de Gaulle's action, led by their own predilections and by his ambiguity to confuse this element for the essence or to misinterpret its meaning; they are grievously disappointed when they discover their error. The closer they had been to him, the more passionate their rejection.[134]

Preservation

But the qualities necessary for a charismatic (or other) leader's coming to power are not those that he needs in order to stay in power or to protect his work. A number of possibilities arise. One, the charismatic leader, having accomplished his task, responded to, and taken care of the distress that made people turn to him, may lose both his charisma and his power, or at least his power: Having saved, his role is over. Two, he may, in order to stay in office and to avoid the "routinization of charisma," perpetually recreate conditions of distress that will allow him to play the savior (Mao, for example). Three, he may decide that his best way of protecting his accomplishments is to institutionalize, so as to leave to his successors more than a memory of glory; but then there is a problem of preserving, while still in power, his own charisma from the disenchantments of routinization.

De Gaulle's career has managed to embrace all those alternatives. His personality and conception of leadership, on their romantic side, are so much in love with being a lonely savior that the prospects of institutionalization are, at first sight, incompatible with the claim to uniqueness, to direct communication with France and history, with the view of the French as somewhat weak and fickle and ungrateful children or prodigal sons of France: Between them and their big brother, the relations have never been easy. In 1945-46, partly by inclination, partly because of the circumstances (which made of him a national symbol, but put institutionalization into the parties' hands), he had to choose between trying to hang onto power at the expense of his *caractère* and charisma, and saving his charisma by "leaving things before they left me"[135]; which he did, following once again the script of *Le fil de l'épée*.

Since his return to power in 1958, he has succeeded in ruling already ten years. He has applied a fascinating mixture of alternatives two and three. Conditions of distress have been, it is true, provided in abundance by events that were not of his creation—especially during the Algerian war; but he has seized them with characteristic glee so as to re-enact his mission and to renew his charisma: when he put on his general's uniform before the TV cameras while Algiers was rioting in January 1960; when he smashed the army rebellion in April 1961; when he used the 1962 assassination attempt against him as the occasion for a Blitzkrieg on his political enemies. Moreover, the style of his foreign policy since the end of the Algerian drama, while it corresponds to his nature, also serves the function of producing, so to speak, minidramas that rejuvenate his appeal, as if he, too, needed to create crises for whose solutions he will be "erect and necessary" (for example, the press conference of January 1963, the Common Market crisis of 1965, the Canadian venture).[136] The mixture of dread and excitement with which he interpreted the Middle East crisis of

de Gaulle as Political Artist

1967 as a possible gateway to world war is significant and reminds one of the false prophecies of 1947-50.

But precisely because a world drama, today, would be less a challenge than a calamity; because he remains concerned above all with protecting France's heritage and chances to grow; and because he knows (at a time when the problems of economic development dominate people's minds) that the public mood is no more heroic than the international scene is adequate for grand ventures, alternative two is kept in check by his sense of reality and limits. The problem thus becomes how to realize alternative three in a way compatible with the unique personality of the leader and with the preservation of his charisma. Earlier, the challenge was to grow by stretching; now it is to grow by knowing how to fit his enormous and epic frame into a more complacent and limited framework. He has tried to solve this problem by giving France institutions that correspond both to his own personal ideal and practice of leadership and to what he thinks French unity, stability, and efficiency require. The distance that he needs is assured not only by the constitution and by his interpretation of the President's role as one that dominates all other organs and groupings, but also by the ingenious creation of a Gaullist party that provides him with a lever, gives to his supporters highly interested reasons for loyalty, yet maintains the necessary separation between the President of all Frenchmen and a political party with which he has no direct connection, but without which he would be in the same situation as in 1945.

Yet he obviously doubts that institutionalizing his mission will do the trick after him, since leadership remains in essence a personal attribute; and he himself also tries, while alive, to preserve his charisma from the attrition of even well-oiled institutions. His decision to run for office (facing universal suffrage for the first time in his life) at the end of 1965 is highly symbolic, for while it meant that he wanted to give to his "historic" legitimacy the seal of his institutions, it also meant that he doubted that the latter could survive without the benefit of his own charisma. During the brief election campaign that preceded the disastrous first ballot, he resorted again to the apocalyptic language of fall and salvation. Elected, he continues to try to be both the first President of the Fifth Republic and "General de Gaulle." Of the three ingredients of his charisma— prophecy, stress on "being oneself," embodying the style of crisis authority—neither the first nor the third quite fits the present circumstances, not tragic enough to inspire the former nor to justify

871

the latter. But the second one still has its appeal, as shown by the broad approval given by the French to a provocative foreign policy of independence which preserves France's identity even as the French society and polity lose much of their old distinctiveness.

What buttresses, completes, and inspires that appeal are two other factors, of uneven importance. One is memory—his capacity to remind people of the mess they were in, due to the old parties and to outside humiliations, before he came to clean it up. But the very fact of having cleaned it up attenuates the fears of a relapse; and the memories begin to fade away.

The other factor is precisely that which lies behind all his works, that which is most intensely personal, his artistry: de Gaulle's residual charisma lies almost entirely in his own *caractère*, now that the original appeal, the pristine adequacy between his call and the circumstances, has vanished. What people still follow is the great actor on the stage. A charisma that once moved the French to follow him or to cling to him, in circumstances that gave him tasks commensurate with his needs, now persists despite the narrower range of deeds and makes the French watch him as a spectacle—partly because, on the more modest scale where he operates today, they remember how in the past he stretched his potential to whatever scale was required, partly because they sense that even on that smaller scale he performs more impressively than anybody else could, partly because, as Malraux puts it, he is their alibi, and they bask in the sun of his prestige, whose rays illuminate them.[137] And so they watch him accomplishing those grand rites which mark both the institutionalization of his charisma and the periodic occasions of its reassertion, both the symbolic re-enactment of his mission and the reassuring return of normalcy. And they watch him rebelling for France wherever he still can—against the hegemonies, against the power of the dollar, against American violence in Vietnam and English-Canadian "oppression" in Quebec. The times having changed; in an international system that frustrates achievements and multiplies denials, in a nation both dulled and enervated by what Raymond Aron once called the "querulous satisfaction" of an industrial society devoid of deep cleavages but deprived of enthusiasms, a charisma once fed by accomplishments becomes a charisma based on drama. Statecraft becomes stagecraft and thus remains a protest against and remedy for the banality or "melancholy" of a duller period: "Judging the leader capable of adding to the effectiveness of familiar procedures the full weight of a unique authority [*une*

de Gaulle as Political Artist

vertu singulière], confidence and hope keep any obscure trust in him."[138] Indeed, the suspense about how his own drama will end nourishes his charisma.

Costs

Yet the problem of what will happen to his work in the future remains. It cannot be answered fully, but elements of an answer can be found if one looks at some of the costs of de Gaulle's leadership. In the first place, his very identification with France, just as it has subordinated "Charles" to "de Gaulle," and both to "General de Gaulle," has left out of France all that is not in de Gaulle's vision of France: Things have been compressed and repressed that will inevitably reassert themselves, since they have not been suppressed. He has, by his style of leadership, raised in acute form a problem of participation that has been amply discussed elsewhere.[139] His personality and conception of leadership, on the one hand, and his repulsion for French parliamentary politics, on the other, have created a system that may well, once the leader is gone, provoke a swing of the pendulum in the direction that he has so often denounced. His very exclusion of all "intermediaries," because of their discordances and confusion, has only increased their desire for revenge, especially in the old parties' case. His way of unifying the French is to rise above their cleavages and to ignore these cleavages' representatives. But even if some of the alignments they champion have lost much of their relevance thanks to his acts and to circumstances, they are still waiting in the wings. Surrounded by docile men whose docility annoys him, but incapable of bearing near him those who resist him and whom he respects,[140] he may have eased the way for opponents he despises. The great man has dwarfed and distorted his own institutions, which remain both fragile and marginal. The necessary synthesis between the two poles of French political authority—heroic crisis leadership and weak routine authority—continues to elude his nation.

His fascination with long-range national goals—those that can be achieved on the world stage, or whatever is required for playing on it—perhaps also his personal conviction, once more projected onto France, that dignity and greatness are worthier goals than mere material happiness have led him to brush aside or neglect values and concerns of crucial importance to many[141]: hence the re-

current divorce between himself and the French. His own style—
the quest for high drama and distant perspectives—has its reverse
side: a certain indifference, or temporization and lassitude, when
confronted with problems that seem to him less essential than those
lofty goals and on which his advisers differ.[142] As for the French,
their willingness to give priority to France's greatness decreases
whenever the requirements of the latter cease being the same as
their own daily necessities. Once order is restored, independence
insured, the threat of great crisis removed, this divorce leads to
mutual disenchantment, as in the winter of 1945-46, when the
Frenchmen's obsession with the daily difficulties and deprivations
conflicted with de Gaulle's ambitions, or in the years 1965-68: that is,
whenever the French do not live up to the imperative of grandeur,
but satisfy themselves with what he deems mediocrity and, so to
speak, give the lie to his claim that France is not herself without
greatness. *He* may not be himself without it, nor France in *his* eyes,
but France can be in *theirs,* and they do not always crave it. He
needs it always; but he can enact it for France only when both the
circumstances and the French allow him. When they cease being,
to use a famous and autobiographical quotation, an "elite people,
sure of itself and dominating" (master of its fate), the memory of
what they had to do or to give up in order to follow him leads to
"scowling, howling, and growling" (*la hargne, la ronge, et la
grogne*).

No; only have other (to him lesser) goals been discarded
within but—most importantly—higher goals than those that can be
served by the present system of (more or less) cooperating nation-
states have also been ruled out. For the greatness he seeks, for himself and France, is that of the nation-state. A man who sees his
mission as the perpetuation of France and who sees in "being oneself" the highest duty can give to France's higher cause a noble,
humanitarian tone and goals of extensive coordination with others,
but certainly not the "ambition" of disappearing into a higher
grouping: that kind of higher goal would be self-abnegation or
abdication, the opposite of self-assertion; and so every merger of
sovereignties, beyond revocable association, must appear to him
like a fading of the will to live. But whereas, in the domestic realm,
the lack of participation and subordination of "lower" goals may
lead to a reaction that will show the intermediaries and the "lesser"
concerns to be just as destructive as he has always warned (even
more so for having been neglected), outside the mechanism of the

self-fulfilling prophecy may work differently: not through reaction against what he stood for, but through the contagion of nationalism.[143]

Other costs have to do not with things ruled out, but with things created by his leadership. Both his deeds and his style have made enemies—for himself within France, for France in the world. Although he sees international relations as a struggle and puts being right far above being surrounded with friends, the occasional isolation of France in world affairs—when his initiatives or words are not followed by others or when his words and his grand refusal to see things from any perspective but his own antagonize others—is a dangerous price for "grandeur"; for diplomacy does not prosper by, nor morale feed on very distant chances of ultimate success or prospects of final vindication.[144] And the inevitable creation of domestic hostility cannot please the man who wants to unify the French, but who antagonizes many, either because of specific policies they dislike, or because of his haughty style of personal leadership. There can be no greatness without struggle; but the animosities which the struggle provokes impede greatness insofar as, in the temporal world, leadership has to be more than a moral posture: It must bring a payment in cash.

Also, his high image of France and his identification with her have often bred a kind of intoxicating self-delusion in him. A policy followed by other, weaker men can (indeed must) fail. The same policy endorsed by him must succeed—because he can speak for France and because he is "de Gaulle"; he discovered, in dealing with the Algerian F.L.N., that this was not the case. Nor have his pronouncements and visits always been followed by the results he had expected (for instance, in Latin America, or his warning to Israel in May 1967). Thus, hopes have often been dashed, energies wasted, imprudent acts performed, or words expressed because character was not convertible into, or backed by the commitment of, material power, or because he misread events, or because his grand moves were no substitute for those detailed measures of execution with which he does not like to bother.

More serious (because they are more lasting) are the illusions he may have created among the French. His message has bred its own misunderstandings. It is pride that he has wanted to restore in the French; it is vanity that he may have fed. (Their reaction to his Canadian outburst is significant: He wanted to make his people proud of their overseas cousins, both for their past resilience and for their new ambition; French opinion blamed him for having given France a bad name on the world stage.) He has tried to replace a chauvinism of nostalgia, envy, resentment and to displace self-doubt with a national pride in the recovery of independence, harmony, economic progress; yet in its reverberations his own assertiveness has often led to silly manifestations of misplaced gloating or xenophobia. Moreover, in his pedagogic attempt at moving men by making them believe either that they are better than they really are so as to make them better, or that they are doing more than they actually do so as to get them to do more, while knowing the sad truth himself, he has spread myths (such as that of France's almost unanimous role in the Resistance, or share in the victory of 1945, or voluntary decolonization, or atomic prowess). These may in the end detract from the very adjustment to reality that he was also trying to promote and without which the will to greatness would operate in a vacuum.

Ultimately, the reason why the protection of the work remains unsure is quite simple. Some of the deeds are history, irreversibly so: the resistance and liberation of France, and decolonization. Others are fragile—the nuclear force, the stand against supranational integration, the constitution—because they embody a highly personal reading of reality, and above all an attitude rather than a program. Should this attitude be repudiated by the French after him, either by deliberate choice of another course or by incapacity to follow any (through dispersion and discord), then that part of his work would be lost, partly through *their* fault, and—for the reasons just given—partly through his own; but these are so intimately tied to the essence of his personality and leadership that it is hard to see how they could have been avoided. And even if that part of his work disappears, there would always remain the two things which de Gaulle, political master and artist, has most cared about: the trail of glory and the tales of greatness in the history textbooks of the future, and the inspiration and example for action. "Since everything always begins anew, what I have done will sooner or later be a source of new fervor after I have disappeared."[145] For "there is something contagious in greatness."[146]

We have observed that de Gaulle's conception of the leader as missionary of a national cause had religious overtones, and that this missionary figure was itself the creation of a political artist. Indeed, it is the artist, revealed by his work of art, who resembles *de Gaulle as Political Artist*

in many ways the great religious leaders, or the statesmen with a religious dimension, of the past.

A desire to redeem his father and a sense of being chosen; a strong moral conscience and a love for "activity on a large scale"; a long effort of building up in oneself all the resources needed for the task to come; the capacity to make one's childhood crises representative of collective problems, to make of one's personality the answer to a historical crisis, to fill a collective identity vacuum with one's own identity through one's acts or writings; the capacity to wait for the right moment, to engage one's whole personality when it comes, and to prefer settling for nothing rather than compromising one's integrity; a self-fulfilling (and early) sense of omnipotence and omniscience, combined with enormous energy and mental concentration; narcissism absorbed in charisma and lifted into deeds; a sense of being unique and unprecedented—all these traits, assembled by Erik Erikson,[147] apply to de Gaulle. The central values of integrity and fidelity, honor, self-respect developed in adolescence, a kind of telescoping of the adolescent and mature stages of psychosocial identity are also present here, along with the bypassing of intimacy, although there is no apparent bypassing of generativity in the case of a man who has not only had children, but also expressed his concern for the expansion of French youth. At first sight, we do not find one element that characterizes many great leaders: the search for a wider identity than the one that existed before. To him, France remains the highest temporal good; yet the universalist component of French culture, the expansion of de Gaulle's horizons since the mid-1950's, his assertion of the essential equality and dignity of all self-respecting cultural entities, whatever the hierarchy of political power, and, within his country, his effort to transcend traditional class or ideological divisions ought not to be ignored.

If the artist is thus confirmed as a great politico-religious leader, what about the work of art to which he has devoted his life?

For an evaluation of "the work-of-art in history," so much *hubris* is required—even more than that of the artist who created it. In comparison with other art, its ultimate value is dependent on its timeliness, on its permanent "fit" into history, on the lasting appreciation of its audience, as well as on its intrinsic value.

By definition, the intrinsic value of a work of art is to be found not in its timeliness, nor in its social contribution, nor in the applause it gets, but in something hidden entirely within its own complex structure. Whether people like it or not, find it useful, pleasing, or ugly, is irrelevant here—not just because the audience does not matter to its *artistic* evaluation, but because whether it is good or bad is not even the issue. The issue is, rather: Is it or is it not a work of art? If it is, then by definition, "it works, it will last"; it will leave its mark somewhere, sometime.

Just as the artist, at his best, does not care about his immediate impact on his audience, one finds in de Gaulle a certain indifference to it, partly out of faith, partly out of fatalism, partly because he looks to the long-range audience of history, but mainly because he is concerned above all with his artist's work—his public figure and the latter's mission—for its own sake. This concern helps explain the relative ideological poverty of the Gaullist pursuit of grandeur. It also explains de Gaulle's frequent preoccupation[148] with *ending well*. Like Corneille's Augustus, he has the actor's temptation—"*quitter la vie avec éclat.*"[149] What shall the rest of the story be?

The *political* artist, the man of action, needs the support of the public. His mission could end dramatically, if he were to be repudiated by the French after some political crisis. He could then no longer claim—as after January 1946—that he still represented French legitimacy, since the institutions in which the drama would unfold are this time his very own, supported massively by the people. Even rejected as a political leader, however, the historic figure—the ultimate work of art—would continue to exist: "General de Gaulle" could, like any masterpiece, be great (and thus contagious) out of office as well as in power. But for the work of art to persist and endure, the style of the exit would have to be grand, like that of January 1946, and unlike the falls of so many French leaders.

In other words, the real danger lies elsewhere than in the mere withdrawal of assent. It lies in that mysterious and delicate relation of the artist with his creation. Will the artist in him, despite his lucid resolve, become incapable of new creativity? There are two threats, within himself. The artist could become the prisoner of the public figure, from which he would have lost his distance, and which would have turned into a rigidified and uncontrolled caricature of itself, like a huge, heavy fish left on an empty shore. Or else the artist could succumb to the self-indulgence of old age, when all the private fears and flaws, once conquered and transcended, take over, making of the public figure the hostage or the victim of the private man's afflictions. In either case he would be-

de Gaulle as Political Artist

come the captive of his past, which he could no longer renew nor transcend.

Maybe fate will save him from either disgrace. The man who has so eloquently described old age as a shipwreck, who warned himself against Pétain's "majestic lassitude," who watched Adenauer's decline and Churchill's decay must surely be on his guard against personal exhaustion. Against irrelevance, and the tendency to re-enact incongruously his missionary role, he may be protected by his acute sense of reality—and also, one hopes, by his aesthetic concern. For the man who has tried to make of his public figure, of his career, and of his nation an integrated work of art needs an aesthetic end to the script he has written and the character he has shaped. Maybe he will put an end to the work of art—public figure and mission—in time, becoming again, as in his childhood and adolescence, a human being alone with his dreams. Whatever the rest of his story will be, de Gaulle is and has been the incarnation of Bernanos' fragile ideal—the man who has never lost that *"esprit d'enfance"* that consists of all the early aspirations and ardors; he has never betrayed the vision which he formed in those early years and has put a formidable mix of vitality, determination, and sheer exhilarating sense of fun and play into the realization of his dreams.

"On a l'histoire qu'on mérite."[150] This was de Gaulle's first lesson, which he read to his students when he was a young officer. Perhaps it is also his last lesson as an old man.

REFERENCES

1. His biographers do not give much detail, they do not indicate their sources, they copy one another often without acknowledging it, and sometimes contradict each other. The most interesting indications are in: Georges Cattaui, *Charles de Gaulle: l'homme et le destin.* (Paris, 1960); Jean-Raymond Tournoux, *Pétain et de Gaulle* (Paris, 1964)

2. Cattaui, *Charles de Gaulle*, p. 16.

3. De Gaulle, *Mémoires*, Vol. 1, p. 1. (All references to the Memoirs are to the original French volumes; the translations are ours.)

4. Cattaui, *Charles de Gaulle*, p. 20.

5. Compare, André Malraux, *Antimémoires* (Paris, 1967), p. 157: "I think that, ever since his decision of June 18 [1940] hope had a tragic character for him." We think that this tragic vision developed much earlier.

6. Tournoux, *Pétain et de Gaulle,* pp. 24-25; Philippe Barrès, *Charles de Gaulle* (Montreal, 1941), p. 30.

7. Compare, Roger Wild, "De Vaugirard au Quartier Latin," *Revue des Deux Mondes* (March 15, 1962), pp. 275 ff.

8. *Le fil de l'épée* (Paris, 1962), p. 87.

9. The impact of *Cinna* on de Gaulle deserves a long (if hypothetical) discussion. When, in Act II, Augustus appears, his first statement refers to *"cette grandeur sans borne et cet illustre rang"* that he has acquired. His discourse on the melancholy of domination, the *"destin des grandeurs souveraines"* that deprives them of friends they can trust, his call for lucidity, his final mastery—*"je suis maître de moi comme de l'univers"*—all are reflected in *Le fil de l'épée.*

10. There is an extraordinary passage in *Vers l'armée de métier* ([Paris, 1944 ed.], p. 217), where he explains that whoever possesses the germ of leadership qualities cannot develop them by exerting them only in "military categories." *"La puissance de l'esprit implique une diversité qu'on ne trouve point dans la pratique exclusive du métier, pour la même raison qu'on ne s'amuse guère en famille."*

11. Emmanuel d'Astier de la Vigerie, *Les Grands* (Paris, 1961), p. 90.

12. *Mémoires,* Vol. 1, p. 2.

13. Speech at St. Cyr in 1957; quoted in Tournoux, *La tragédie du Général* (Paris, 1967), p. 227.

14. Tournoux (in *Pétain and de Gaulle,* p. 39) suggests that Charles was far ahead in his studies, which would have accentuated his sense of being different and superior. But we have not been able to find a confirmation.

15. *Mémoires,* Vol. 1, p. 2.

16. The text is in Tournoux, *Pétain et de Gaulle,* pp. 29-36.

17. Gustave Nadaud, *Chansons à dire* (Paris, 1887), pp. 303-6.

18. Compare his press conference of Nov. 27, 1967: *à propos* of *"l'après gaullisme,"* he said: *"tout a toujours une fin. Chacun se termine"* (*Le Monde,* Nov. 29, 1967, p. 4).

19. That feather seems to owe a great deal to Rostand's *Cyrano de Bergerac.*

20. *Le fil de l'épée,* p. 87. In his *Mémoires,* de Gaulle talks of several leaders (Churchill, F.D.R., Hitler) as "seducers."

21. *Ibid.,* pp. 86, 87.

22. Cattaui, *Charles de Gaulle,* p. 23.

23. Jean Lacouture, in his *de Gaulle* ([Paris, 1964], p. 15) notes that de Gaulle in his *Mémoires* (Vol. 1, p. 2) describes his ambition to *"rendre à*

de Gaulle as Political Artist

la France quelque service signalé" as "l'interêt *de la vie,*" not as duty. In 1958, when faced, in Dakar, with picketers asking for independence, he exclaimed that when de Gaulle is there, "*on ne s'ennuie pas.*" (Passeron, *de Gaulle parle 1958-62* [Paris, 1962], p. 462.)

24. *Le fil de l'épée,* p. 78.

25. Cattaui, *Charles de Gaulle,* p. 23. Tournoux, *Pétain et de Gaulle,* p. 25.

26. Compare, *Vers l'armée de métier* (Paris, 1944), p. 197. "*Le rôle du chef est toujours de concevoir d'après les circonstances, de décider et de prescrire en forçant sa nature et celle des autres.*"

27. See Eugen Weber, *The Nationalist Revival in France 1905-1914* (Berkeley, 1959).

28. *La discorde chez l'ennemi* (Paris, 1944; first published in 1924).

29. *Ibid.,* p. viii. On p. x, he celebrates the "*jardin à la française*" with its "magnificent harmony," despite the "noble melancholy" that sometimes pervades it because "each element, by itself, could have shone out more," but only "at the expense of the whole."

30. See, on his experiences at the Ecole de Guerre, in addition to Tournoux (*Pétain et de Gaulle,* Part 1, Chs. 5-6, and pp. 380 ff), Jacques Minart, *Charles de Gaulle tel que je l'ai connu* (Paris, 1945).

31. Cattaui, *Charles de Gaulle,* p. 29; Gaston Bonheur, *Charles de Gaulle* (Paris, 1958), p. 32.

32. *Discorde chez l'ennemi,* p. ix.

33. On Péguy's influence, see Edmond Michelet, *Le gaullisme passionnante aventure* (Paris, 1962). The prose poem which ends the third volume of the *Mémoires* closes with the image of the Old Man (de G.) who "never tires of watching, in the shade, for the glimmer of Hope."

34. *La France et son armée* (Paris, 1938), p. 228.

35. Alexander Werth, *de Gaulle* (New York, 1965), p. 60.

36. H. Stuart Hughes, *Consciousness and Society* (New York, 1958), pp. 117-18.

37. Quoted by Lucien Nachin in his preface to de Gaulle's *Trois études* (Paris, 1945), p. xlvi.

38. *Mémoires,* Vol. 1, p. 2.

39. *La France et son armée,* p. 274.

40. *Mémoires,* Vol. 3, p. 60.

41. See Tournoux, *Pétain et de Gaulle,* p. 41.

42. Compare, in *La France et son armée,* p. 191: "*grandir sa force à la mesure de ses desseins, ne pas attendre du hasard, ni des formules, ce qu'on*

> *néglige de préparer, proportionner l'enjeu et les moyens: l'action des peuples, comme celle des individus, est soumise à ces froides règles."*

43. See S. Hoffmann, "de Gaulle's memoirs: the hero as history," *World Politics* (Oct., 1960).

44. Malraux, *Antimémoires*, p. 152. *Le fil de l'épée*, published in 1932, was based on lectures and articles written since 1927.

45. *Les jeunes gens d'aujourd'hui* (Paris, 1913).

46. Compare, *Vers l'armée de métier*, p. 221: *"les puissants se forment eux-mêmes. Faits pour imprimer leur marque, plutôt que d'en subir une, ils bâtissent dans le secret de leur vie intérieure l'édifice de leurs sentiments, de leurs concepts, de leur volonté."* This is a constant theme in this book and in *Le fil de l'épée*.

47. *Fil*, p. 83.

48. *Vers*, pp. 217-18.

49. *Fil*, p. 96-97; *Vers*, pp. 224 ff; Lucien Nachin, **Ch. de G.** (Paris, 1944), pp. 88-89.

50. François Mauriac, *de Gaulle* (Paris, 1964), p. 24.

51. *Fil*, p. 77 ff.

52. See also *Vers*, p. 154, about the "perpetual return" of human affairs.

53. *Mémoires*, Vol. 2, p. 67.

54. Malraux, *Antimémoires*, p. 155.

55. *Fil*, pp. 87-88.

56. *Mémoires*, Vol. 2, p. 312.

57. *Ibid.*, Vol. 3, p. 287.

58. André Passeron, *de Gaulle parle 1962-6* (Paris, 1966), p. 132. (TV interview, Dec. 13, 1965.)

59. Compare de Gaulle's lectures at St. Cyr in 1921, in Tournoux, *La tragédie du Général*, pp. 513 ff.

60. Compare his balanced judgment on Napoleon in *La France et son armée*, pp. 149-50.

61. Compare D'Astier, *Sept fois, sept jours* (Paris, Coll. 10/18, 1961): *"comme un grand prélat glacé dont la France est le royaume qu'il ne veut pas partager et qui n'est peut-être pas de ce monde"* (p. 102). See also: Malraux, *Antimémoires*, p. 135; Pierre Bourdan, *Carnets des jours d'attente* (Paris, 1945).

62. *Mémoires*, Vol. 1, Ch. 2.

de Gaulle as Political Artist

63. Compare *"le caractère esthétique des choses militaires,"* in *Vers*, p. 142.

64. "... *César, qui ne procède que des exigences profondes de son temps, est un homme sur la scène, c'est à dire forcément un artiste"* (emphasis added). Letter to M. de Bourbon-Busset, quoted by Tournoux, *La tragédie*, p. 486. In the *Mémoires*, Vol. 1, p. 47, he called Churchill *"le grand artiste d'une grande Histoire."*

65. *"De même* que le talent marque l'oeuvre d'art *d'un cachet particulier de compréhension et d'expression, ainsi le* Caractère imprime son dynamisme propre aux éléments de l'action. ... *Moralement, il l'anime, il lui donne la vie, comme le talent fait de la matière dans le domaine de l'art."* Fil, pp. 54-5.

66. Compare the quotation in fn 9. The final call for a master, in the same book, is a call for a *"ministre, soldat ou politique."*

67. When General Catroux, a much higher-ranking general, joined de Gaulle in October 1940, there was no doubt any more about de Gaulle's leadership.

68. *"Il faut qu'un maître apparaisse, indépendant en ses jugements, irrécusable dans ses ordres, crédité par l'opinion. Serviteur du seul Etat, dépouillé de préjugés, dédaigneux de clientèles; commis enfermé dans sa tâche, pénétré de longs desseins, au fait des gens et des choses du ressort ... assez fort pour s'imposer, assez habile pour séduire, assez grand pour une grande oeuvre ..."* (p. 227); Robert Aron, in *An explanation of de Gaulle* ([New York, 1966], p. 70), quotes this revealing sentence from de Gaulle's *Mémoires*: "In human endeavors, due to a long and slow effort, a sudden, unique spurt may be achieved in different and disparate spheres:" a good account of de Gaulle's own course.

69. *Fil*, p. 15.

70. See, for instance, Col. Passy, *Souvenirs*, Vol. 1. (Monte-Carlo, 1947), p. 122; André Gide, *Journal 1942-45*, (Paris, 1950), p. 185.

71. D'Astier, *Les Grands*, p. 124.

72. Malraux, *Antimémoires*, p. 150.

73. Compare Henri Amouroux, *Pétain avant Vichy* (Paris, 1967).

74. Malraux, *Antimémoires*, p. 151.

75. Passy, *Souvenirs*, p. 123.

76. D'Astier, *Les Grands*, p. 137.

77. Compare, *Mémoires*, Vol. 3, pp. 288-89. He spent very little time as a "private" person after his resignation in January 1946. He made his first public statement in June, and after the fiasco of the R.P.F., he wrote his *Mémoires*, still unfinished when the Fourth Republic collapsed.

78. In his *Mémoires*, Vol. 3, p. 287, he says that he decided, after his resigna-

tion to stay in metropolitan France so as to show that the flood of insults *"contre moi"* could not touch him. A few lines further, he speaks of "de Gaulle."

79. Malraux, *Antimémoires*, p. 134. Gide, *Journal 1942-49* (Paris, 1950), p. 185.

80. Bourdan, *Carnets des jours d'atteute*, p. 35.

81. Passy, *Souvenirs, passim;* compare also Major-General Edward Spears, *Two Men Who Saved France* (London, 1966), pp. 148 ff.

82. D'Astier, *Sept fois sept jours*, pp. 60-61, writes: *"Il n'aime pas les hommes. Il aime leur histoire, surtout celle de la France, dont il agit un chapitre qu'il semble écrire au fur et à mesure dans sa tête."*

83. *"C'est pourquoi, dans les heures tragiques où la rafale balaie conventions et habitudes, ils (les chefs) se trouvent seuls debout et, par là, nécessaires."* (*Vers*, p. 221.)

84. Pierre Viansson-Ponté, *Les gaullistes* (Paris, 1963), p. 49: insults leave him cold, but he is concerned about how the press treats "his historical figure."

85. *Fil*, p. 89; *Mémoires*, Vol. 2, p. 322.

86. *Fil*, p. 70; *Mémoires*, Vol. 3, p. 243.

87. *Mémoires*, Vol. 3, p. 175.

88. Malraux, *Antimémoires*, p. 135.

89. Jerome Bruner, *On Knowing* (Cambridge, 1962), p. 29; the characteristics listed in the previous paragraph are borrowed from his stimulating essay.

90. Tournoux, *Pétain et de Gaulle*, p. 389 (evaluation by one of de Gaulle's superiors in 1924).

91. *"Le dialogue traditionnel, dans les affaires de l'Etat, lui était étranger."* Malraux, *Antimémoires*, p. 156.

92. D'Astier, *Les Grands*, p. 108.

93. Compare Mauriac, *de Gaulle*, pp. 22-23.

94. Albert Hall Speech, June 18, 1942, in *Mémoires*, Vol. 1, pp. 672 ff; also, *Mémoires*, Vol. 1, p. 1.

95. Compare Jean Lacouture, *de Gaulle*.

96. *Antimémoires*, p. 135.

97. Tournoux, *Secrets d'Etat* (Paris, 1960), p. 351.

98. Portrait of Mussolini, *Mémoires*, Vol. 3, p. 172.

de Gaulle as Political Artist

99. Malraux, *Antimémoires*, p. 156: "nous et le destin du monde."

100. *Vers*, p. 197.

101. *Mémoires*, Vol. 3, p. 232.

102. See Tournoux, *Pétain et de Gaulle*, pp. 383 ff, and d'Astier, *Les Grands*, pp. 119 ff.

103. Compare the portrait of Stalin, *Mémoires*, Vol. 3: He quotes Stalin as saying "after all, only death wins." p. 78.

104. *Mémoires*, Vol. 1, p. 111.

105. Compare *Mémoires*, Vol. 2, p. 294.

106. Compare d'Astier, *Les Grands*, p. 137.

107. Compare his refusal to participate in any public ceremony or go to any public edifice of the Fourth Republic. On his failures, see his press conference of Nov. 1953, in Alexander Werth, *De Gaulle*, pp. 227-28.

108. *Mémoires*, Vol. 2, pp. 240-41.

109. Compare Erik Erikson's concept of *virtue*, in "Human Strength and the Cycle of Generations," *Insight and Responsibility* (New York, 1964).

110. *Mémoires*, Vol. 1, p. 1; see also Vol. 3, p. 21, and Passeron, *De Gaulle parle 1962-66*, pp. 134-37.

111. The epigraph to *Le Fil* is a quote from Hamlet, *"être grand, c'est soutenir une grande querelle"*; see also *Mémoires*, Vol. 1, p. 1.

112. *Mémoires*, Vol. 3, p. 290.

113. *La France et son armée*, p. 277.

114. *Mémoires*, Vol. 1, p. 1.

115. Oxford speech, Nov. 25, 1941: *Mémoires*, Vol. 1, pp. 565 ff.

116. Compare his remarks on Syria and Lebanon, while serving there in 1930: "People here are as foreign to us (and vice versa) as ever." Only two possibilities existed, according to him: coercion or departure (Nachin, *Trois études*, 56-57). He has, later, applied both. At least one possibility was thus ruled out—that which had served as the myth of the French Empire under the name of assimilation and was going to serve as the myth of French Algeria under the name of integration.

117. See the comparison of the French and the Germans in *Vers*, pp. 22-23.

118. See the press conference of May 19, 1958, in Passeron, *de Gaulle parle 1958-62*, p. 5.

119. *Mémoires*, Vol. 2, p. 321.

DÆDALUS

120. Malraux, *Antimémoires,* p. 130.

121. See the portraits of Hitler and of Laval in *Mem.,* Vol. 3, pp. 173-5.

122. Compare Tournoux, *La tragédie,* p. 278.

123. In *La France et son armée,* writing about the 1890's—the years of his childhood—he said: France "cultivates melancholy while enjoying her wealth." His task today seems to be to make her increase her wealth without melancholy, thanks to an active foreign policy.

124. See Lloyd and Suzanne Rudolph, *The Modernity of Tradition* (Chicago, 1968), pp. 199-200.

125. Compare Louis Terrenoire, *de Gaulle et l'Algérie* (Paris, 1964), p. 58, reporting that de Gaulle in March 1958 told him: "People are worried about France, but this feeling of national concern has not yet become a personal anxiety."

126. Passeron, *de Gaulle parle 1958-62,* p. 7.

127. *Mémoires,* Vol. 3, pp. 238, 650 (Bayeux speech of June 16, 1946).

128. Compare Eugene Mannoni, *Moi Général de Gaulle* (Paris, 1964), p. 106: "The R.P.F. merely taught de Gaulle what he had already known: in History's absence, solitude is preferable to promiscuity."

129. S Hoffmann, "Heroic Leadership in Modern France," in Lewis Edinger (ed.), *Political Leadership in Industrialized Societies* (New York, 1967), pp. 108-54.

130. Michel Crozier's expression, in *The Bureaucratic Phenomenon* (Chicago, 1964).

131. *Mémoires,* Vol. 2, p. 311.

132. Malraux, *Antimémoires,* p. 156.

133. Emmanuel d'Astier de la Vigerie is the best example.

134. Soustelle is the best example.

135. *Mémoires,* Vol. 3, p. 271.

136. The photos of his return from Montreal to Orly Airport, in the middle of the night, showed an elated and combative de Gaulle surrounded by sleepy and sullen cabinet ministers.

137. Malraux, *Antimémoires,* p. 140.

138. *Fil,* p. 79.

139. See S. Hoffmann, "Paradoxes of the French Political Community," *In Search of France* (Cambridge, 1963).

140. Compare D'Astier, *Les Grands,* p. 99; Tournoux, *La tragédie,* p. 194.

de Gaulle as Political Artist

141. Compare D'Astier: "I am a French ant, that brings . . . a bit of material for his history. . . . I have been in a theater of history, I want to go back to life, to my life." *Sept fois, sept jours,* pp. 60-61. See also Malraux, *Antimémoires,* p. 131.

142. Compare Paul de la Gorce, *de Gaulle entre deux mondes* (Paris, 1964), Ch. 10, on de Gaulle's hesitations over economy and financial policy in 1944-45.

143. For further details on his European policy, which tries to reconcile a desire for a "European Europe" capable of supplementing France's limited power and voice, with a determination to avoid supranational federalism, see S. Hoffmann, "de Gaulle, Europe and the Atlantic Alliance," *International Organization,* Vol. 18, No. 1 (Winter, 1964), pp. 1-28; "Europe's Identity Crisis," *Dædalus* (Fall, 1964), pp. 1244-97; "Obstinate or Obsolete? The Fate of the Nation-State and the Case of Western Europe," *Dædalus* (Summer, 1968), pp. 862-915; *Gulliver's Troubles, or the Setting of American Foreign Policy* (New York, 1968), Ch. 11.

144. This is the main criticism of his Middle East policy of 1967, which condemned Israel's resort to force from a long-term perspective on war that completely neglected the short-term plight of Israel in the tense circumstances of May 1967.

145. *Mémoires,* Vol. 3, p. 289.

146. *Vers,* p. 154.

147. The authors of this paper express their gratitude to him, from whom they have learned so much.

148. Compare Tournoux, *La tragédie,* pp. 502-3.

149. *Cinna,* Act IV, Scene II.

150. Tournoux, *La tragédie,* p. 514.

[13]

THE POLITICAL PRINCIPLES
OF GENERAL DE GAULLE

Douglas Johnson

THE career of General de Gaulle should be the preoccupation of the historian as well as of the student of international affairs. Too often the historian is tempted to dismiss the General as one of the ghosts of French history, illustrating the tradition whereby authoritarian régimes, such as those of Napoleon, Napoleon III or Pétain, temporarily succeed the more liberal assembly-type régimes. To recall history in this way is to assume that the Fifth Republic is simply a stage in a recurrent process and is to avoid understanding its significance. Too often the historian abandons any attempt to understand the phenomenon of General de Gaulle, by accepting the viewpoint of those who represent the policies and evolution of the Fifth Republic as arising entirely from the character and personality of its creator. Too often articles on, and assessments of, the General concentrate entirely on him, and lack any sense of historical perspective, apart from ironic references to Joan of Arc or to Louis XIV. Together with an exaggerated reliance upon anecdote, the writers employ terms which are purely personal (' pride ', ' egoism ', ' arrogance ', ' pettiness ', ' deceit ', ' showmanship ', if there is hostility to the General, ' courage ', ' patriotism ', ' skill ', ' style ', ' logic ', 'vision' if there is support for him). They do not attempt to understand General de Gaulle as an historical phenomenon; they do not try to discern the principles which he has evolved over a long life, a great part of which has been devoted to the study of history and to the study of ideas.

It is true that there are a number of difficulties which discourage one from doing this. The General himself, some of his supporters and many of his opponents all attempt to dissuade the seeker after such principles. The General has always stressed the need for action, whether political or military, to be based on reality rather than on dogma. In one of his earliest writings he urged his readers to be suspicious of *a priori* theorising, to be sceptical of absolute doctrines, to be disdainful of solutions which are derived from abstractions.[1] In his book *Le Fil de l'Épée*,[2] he claims that once one has made to principles the acknowledgment

---

1 *La Revue Militaire Française.* March 1, 1925.
2 Berger Levrault. 1932. English translation, Faber and Faber. 1960. *The Edge of the Sword*.

which is their due, then men should themselves, and from themselves, decide what they should do in each particular case. In his *Memoirs* [3] he has stated that in economics, in politics and in strategy there exists no absolute truth, but ' only the circumstances '. In countless speeches and communications he has familiarised the world with his insistence upon ' the nature of things ', ' men being what they are ', ' we live in a world where it is realities which dominate '. When dealing with a particular issue, the insistence returns: ' *l'Algérie étant actuellement ce qu'elle est et le monde ce que nous savons* '.[4] When discussing the role of the leader, de Gaulle introduces another quality as a necessity, which is equally inimical to the conception of principles and ideas, namely ' intuition ', which is the indispensable complement to intelligence. And this has been echoed by one of his most illustrious supporters, who has recently written of the General knowing ' by intuition ', ' and from within ', that he has the agreement of the majority of the French people, ' as from within and by intuition, these French people know that they are Gaullists, whilst knowing nothing about General de Gaulle '.[5]

*   *   *

Many Gaullists have maintained that Gaullism is not a doctrine, just as it is not a party. Some have said that there is no such thing as ' *Gaullisme* ', there is only de Gaulle.[6] Other observers, less committed to polemics, prefer to see as the significant feature of de Gaulle's rule, not a movement of ideas or principles, but a movement of personnel, the arrival of a class of capable technicians at positions of authority.[7] De Gaulle's opponents, while considering the cult of reality and ' intuition ' as inappropriate terms for political unscrupulousness and ambition, are no less categorical in their rejection of the General as a man of thought. Jacques Laurent, replying to François Mauriac, reserves his greatest indignation for the suggestion that de Gaulle is a disciple of Charles Maurras. He describes de Gaulle, between 1930 and 1940, as frequenting the most varied political societies (because of the needs of his career) and undergoing a variety of political influences. One of these influences was Maurras (de Gaulle used to attend the Maurrasian *Cercle Fustel de Coulanges*), but according to Laurent he found Maurras too difficult, and rather than representing Maurrasian speculations he simply reflected, and reflects, a number of ideas which were commonplace amongst the smaller and middle bourgeoisie.[8]

[3] *Mémoires de Guerre.* English translation, Weidenfeld & Nicolson. 1960. *War Memoirs.*
[4] Speech of September 16, 1959.
[5] François Mauriac, *De Gaulle* (Paris: Grasset. 1964), p. 118.
[6] J. Gagliardi and P. Rossillon, *Survivre à de Gaulle* (Paris: Plon. 1959).
[7] See, for example, Jacques Bloch-Morhange, *Le Gaullisme* (Paris: Plon. 1963).
[8] Jacques Laurent, *Mauriac sous de Gaulle* (Paris: La Table Ronde. 1965), pp. 171 *et seq.*

It is natural too that the General's methods should have attracted most attention since they have been conspicuously successful, and since they have a particularly dramatic quality. It is noticeable that they also have a certain unity. In the summer of 1940, for example, when the French armies had been defeated on the continent, General de Gaulle insisted on removing the emphasis away from this disadvantageous position, and by insisting that the war was a world-wide war, making the position of France and of the French empire more advantageous *vis-à-vis* the whole world. With the Liberation, preoccupied by the power of the Communists within France, he transformed the question into one of Franco-Soviet friendship; in 1958, faced with the crowds of the Algiers forum, he removed the subject from the uncertain and controversial future of Algeria, and insisted on the renovation of France. Perhaps it is the same tactic which, since the Evian agreements ended the Algerian war, has led the General to emphasise his hostility to the United States. At all events, on each major occasion, General de Gaulle has always elevated the subject at issue away from a position where he is at a disadvantage, and towards an aspect which is more favourable to him. Such a method is also linked to a highly contrived ambiguity in many pronouncements, together with the frankly experimental nature of many of his policies. One saw this most clearly in his Algerian policy, which was more hesitant, less far-seeing and less deceitful than has often been suggested. '*Je crois tout à fait inutile de figer d'avance dans des mots ce que de toute manière l'entreprise va peu à peu dessiner.*'[9] Sometimes it is even suggested that the method is everything, that de Gaulle is presenting a spectacle which is pure illusion, that the realities of power have eluded him, and he compensates for this by being a sort of Walter Mitty amongst world statesmen.

Thus, when one wants to examine '*Gaullisme*' in terms of principles, one not only finds all the usual difficulties which normally beset such an enterprise (the historian of ideas might well find that the differences in terms of ideas between, say, Gaullism, Vichyism and Giraudism is disconcertingly slight), but many particular obstacles are put in the way. Yet it would be strange if Gaullism did not imply a coherent doctrine. Before the war, in 1940, and again from 1958, Gaullism has essentially depended upon words. The written word, the lecture, the discussion group, and the microphone—for a long time these were the only available weapons. Now, better equipped, it is the televised press conference which has been called the absolute weapon of the Fifth Republic.[10] The de Gaulle who emerged from obscurity in 1940 had prepared himself for his task by study and meditation. He had made a theoretical analysis

9 Speech at Constantine, October 3, 1959.
10 Pierre Viansson-Ponté, *Les Gaullistes* (Paris: Seuil. 1963), p. 48.   Reviewed in *International Affairs*, July 1964, p. 518.

of the sort of leader he was to become long before he had any experience
of leadership or power.[11] It is clear, too, that de Gaulle stands in complete contrast to the only two other statesmen who, as leaders of
governments in the Fourth Republic, succeeded in attracting some form
of popular support. In M. Pinay some Frenchmen were pleased to
identify themselves, admiring the respectable head of a family business.
In M. Mendès-France some saw the dynamic, technical leader whom
they thought necessary for a modern state. But de Gaulle is neither of
these. He has always impressed rather than attracted. And one of the
ways in which he has impressed is by placing his utterances within
a large, theoretical framework, by enunciating general principles to
which he remains faithful and which hold the attention of the audience
to which he appeals. Were one to trace the reputation of de Gaulle in
France, after his resignation and the failure of the RPF, one would find
a renewal of respect for him after the publication of the first volume
of his *Memoirs* in 1955. And this was not because they offered any
sensational revelations, but because they dramatically presented a man.
And this man was hardly presented as a person. The *Memoirs* have
remarkably little to say about him, or his family, his thoughts or
emotions. He is presented as embodying a number of aspirations and
assertions.

De Gaulle was unable to appreciate Giraud, as he makes it clear,
because Giraud saw things in an exclusively practical and military way.
He insisted that he gave his concern solely to military matters, he
boasted that he had never listened to anyone who tried to interest him
in a theory or a political programme, he never read a newspaper. As
de Gaulle put it, the moral and political aspects of France's drama
seemed secondary matters to Giraud. In much the same way it seems
likely that the disagreements between Churchill and de Gaulle were
sometimes caused by Churchill's exclusive preoccupation with the
practical matter of winning the war, and his inability, as de Gaulle
claimed, to see ' the moral side ' of the question. Some of the members
of *La France Libre* found de Gaulle's insistence on theoretical questions
rather irritating, but it is this which helped to give him his particular
distinction. He spoke about ' the doctrine of Fighting France '. Others
have spoken about ' a family of Gaullist thought ', and Jacques Soustelle
has distinguished between the ' *gaullistes de foi* ' (who emphasise loyalty
to the General), ' *gaullistes de combinaison* ' (who are careerists) and
' *gaullistes de raison* ' (who believe, or believed, that Gaullism represented a doctrine and an ensemble of beliefs).[12] It is important to examine

---

11 *Le Fil de l'Épée, op. cit.*
12 See the article by Jean de Beer, ' Vivre le Gaullisme ou vivre du Gaullisme ', *Le
   Monde*, April 10, 1964; Jacques Soustelle, *L'Espérance Trahie 1958–61.* (Paris:
   Éditions de l'Alma. 1962), p. 9.

this doctrine and these beliefs. In this way one can place de Gaulle in the tradition of French thought and perhaps assess his significance.

*   *   *

It is impossible to begin any consideration of de Gaulle's thought without '*une certaine idée de la France*'.[13] But this is often misunderstood and is elevated into something mystical, even unreal. It is true that de Gaulle speaks of France as a person, but this is within a long tradition. It is true that he assumes the necessity for the individual to have some sort of patriotism, but this is often found amongst French moralists (such as Saint-Exupéry, with whom de Gaulle can be compared). It is true, too, that de Gaulle makes the assumption that France is important, indispensable, to the rest of the world, but this is also a common assumption; as pacific a statesman as Guizot maintained that France had only to stay still, '*les bras croisés*', to fill her place in the world. But de Gaulle associates this importance of France specifically to the role of France in Europe and to the importance of European civilisation in the world. His conception of France is dramatically explicit ('*Vieille France, accablée d'histoire*'), but it is hardly mystical. He believes that the nation-state is the basis of political action. As recently as June 10 he declared this belief in a provocative manner. '*Les nations, ça existe. Il y a une Italie, une Allemagne. C'est millén-aire, c'est bi-millénaire. Ce ne sont pas des entités qui peuvent dis-paraître comme ça. . . . On peut faire des discours sur l'Europe supra-nationale. Ce n'est pas difficile: il est facile d'être un Jean-foutre.*' As is often the case, the method or the means is an almost pedagogic demonstration of the principle or the end.

It may well be that behind this theory lie many of the assumptions made, for example, by Péguy. But essentially de Gaulle allies a certain contempt for political ideology along with his confidence in national realities. Ideologies such as Communism will pass, or can be accommodated. The nation-state will remain. National leaders, such as Roosevelt or Churchill, may cloak their policies with idealistic phraseology, but essentially they will try to advance the interests and the power of their countries. In a similar way de Gaulle himself will always

---

[13] See, for example, David Thomson, *Democracy in France since 1870*, 4th ed. (London: Oxford University Press for R.I.I.A. 1964), p. 307. Reviewed in *International Affairs*, July 1965, p. 535. As Jean Lacouture has pointed out, ' *la gaullologie se porte bien* ', and his own *De Gaulle* (Paris: Seuil. 1965) is a small but incisive contribution to a large collection of books, too numerous to list. For de Gaulle's thought, special reference can be made to A. C. Robertson, *La Doctrine du Général de Gaulle* (Paris: Fayard. 1959), and to André Passeron, *De Gaulle Parle* (Paris: Plon. 1962). Reviewed in *International Affairs*, April 1963, p. 285. See also Stanley Hoffmann, ' De Gaulle and Democratic Theories ', *World Politics*, October 1960; Charles Morazé, ' La Politique du Général de Gaulle d'après le Troisième Volume de ses Mémoires ', *Revue Française de Science Politique*, 1960 ; R.-C. Macridis, ' De Gaulle: The Vision and the Record ', *Yale Review*, 1960.

endeavour to strengthen the international position of France within the hierarchy of power, whether by attempting to change the frontier, or by a particular defence policy. The whole of de Gaulle's view of the policies of nation-states has obvious resemblances with the policies of the *ancien régime* as described, say, in Albert Sorel's *L'Europe et la Révolution Française*.

From this there are certain conclusions which can be drawn. If the nation-state is the basis of policy, then there are certain political organisations which are not likely to develop, whilst there are new nation-states which can come into being. This would explain de Gaulle's attitude towards colonialism, which many have found puzzling. In the first place de Gaulle does not seem to have been a convinced believer in the realities of colonial rule. After six months in the Levant, during 1929, he wrote to Lucien Nachin his impression that Europe had not penetrated a civilisation which was essentially different, and that a great distance separated the European from the native populations ('*les gens nous sont aussi étrangers—et réciproquement—qu'ils le furent jamais*'). In the same line of thought one can understand his readiness to accept the emergence of new nation-states (*l'Algérie algérienne*), and his reluctance to envisage French settlers as a permanent force in Algeria. One can perhaps understand something, not only of his scorn for international bodies such as the United Nations ('*les nations soi-disant unies*'), but even perhaps for the United States of America, and it might not only have been a *boutade* when he recently recalled the American Civil War and claimed that it was still continuing ('*il leur a fallu une guerre civile, et elle continue*', June 10, 1965). His belief in the nation-state also helps one to understand the episode of his unsuccessful political party, the RPF, since the period of its greatest success coincided with the period of possible war with the Soviet Union (or Russia, as de Gaulle prefers to say). The RPF opposed the French Communists, essentially because they would have introduced alien influence into the country.

Other consequences are of particular interest for France. The French are traditionally divided amongst themselves. In this they contrast strikingly to other countries, such as Great Britain, as de Gaulle pointed out in his Westminster speech. There is conflict between the internal demons which divide the French, and the greatness and permanence of France. Therefore the idea of France not only corresponds to a profound but sometimes obscure reality, it is also a device whereby Frenchmen can be made to forget the elements of discord amongst them. Sometimes it is necessary to do this in some great enterprise, undertaken in the name of France. Sometimes it is necessary for France only to appear to have made the effort. There are passages in the *Memoirs* which reflect such a preoccupation. On the issue of an allied landing in the south of France, or an allied attack on Danubian Europe, de Gaulle favoured the former. ' Was our country to be liberated at a distance and indirectly, without having seen her soldiers and her allies achieve their victory and her rescue on her own soil? . . . By not allowing our forces constituted overseas to fight and conquer in metropolitan France, would we lose our chance to cement French unity, after so many divisions and discontinuities?' And on the question of Indochina he writes, ' . . . I was not distressed by the prospect of taking up arms in Indo-China. . . . I regarded it as essential that the conflict should not come to an end without our participation in that theatre as well '.[14] Those who have found the essence of Gaullism as being a preoccupation with effect and with show should remember that, whether in reality or in appearance, the principle is that the state should remedy the internal conflicts of the country, and that this principle is traditional in France (it was well expressed by Tocqueville, for example).

The question of sovereignty is less familiar outside France, but it has been constantly an issue in France since 1789. Whilst in England it has been customary to assume that sovereignty lies with the Crown in Parliament, and that no law passed by this authority can possibly be questioned, in France the early 19th century saw a quarrel between those who believed that the king was sovereign because of his birth, those who believed that the people was sovereign and that it may or may not delegate its sovereignty, and those who believed that they could escape from the dilemma by designating as sovereign some abstract principle, such as justice. The later 19th century continued the quarrel in different terms, finding in the Third Republic a kind of pluralistic organisation where sovereignty seemed to be distributed variously amongst the President, the Prime Minister, the Assemblies, the administration, a number of corporate bodies and the mass of individual Frenchmen.

In 1940 the question was posed anew when France was defeated and lost her independence. Up to this moment de Gaulle, as he has been frank (or foolish) enough to admit, had felt himself called upon to fulfil some great destiny, but his career had languished, and up to a late moment in the summer of 1940 his main effort was to convince the élites of France to take certain particular actions. But once he realised that these élites had failed him, it was then that he decided that the sovereignty of France had fallen on him. He has reproached Pétain, not so much with capitulating, but precisely with signing the armistice and thus giving up ' *le trésor de la souveraineté française* '. Those who

---

[14] *War Memoirs: Unity 1942–1944* (English edition), p. 261; *Salvation 1944–1946*, pp. 162–163.

regarded Pétain as a legitimate ruler failed to realise that the sovereignty of France had gone to the part of France which was independent. Those who found de Gaulle difficult and touchy during the years after June 1940 failed to realise his need to preserve the reality and the appearance of independence, and thus ' *le trésor de la souveraineté française* '. From this preoccupation came the quarrels with Giraud, who thought that there could be no French government until the end of the war, and the quarrels with Roosevelt and Churchill, who thought that they were dealing with an awkward leader, whose slender means made him dependent upon their support. From this came all the storms and furies whenever someone seemed to dispose of or to disregard France. Therefore, too, all the sneers and references to ' megalomania ', to ' inferiority complexes ', Joan of Arc and so on. But therefore, too, the success of General de Gaulle. According to his own account, General de Gaulle asked Churchill, if he were not the representative of France, then why was Churchill dealing with him? Churchill (it is said) did not reply. ' *Moi, j'étais la France* ', recalled the General, ' I was the independence and the sovereignty of France, and it was for this reason that everyone obeyed me '.[15] The return to Paris of General de Gaulle was in this sense a replica of the return of Louis XVIII in 1814.

The Napoleonic Senate tried to draw up conditions whereby the throne could be offered to the eldest of the Bourbons, but in fact the king recovered his throne by virtue of his right and without objection, so the conspiracies failed. Like Louis XVIII, de Gaulle simply assumed power. When Louis XVIII was told of the abdication of Napoleon, and that he was king, he is reported to have asked, ' Have I ever ceased to be king?' When Georges Bidault, at the Hôtel de Ville, asked de Gaulle to proclaim the Republic, de Gaulle replied that there was no need. The Republic had never ceased to exist, since June 18, 1940 when de Gaulle had made his statement in London. Since then and recently, de Gaulle has spoken of incarnating the sovereignty of France since 1940, discounting the period of his resignation, and embroidering the crown of Lorraine on the tricolour as a permanency. This assertion of sovereignty, derived from the principle of the nation-state as the basis of political reality, is within the framework of discussion which has been important in France for many years.

*   *   *

Everywhere, in de Gaulle's writings and statements, one finds underlined the need for a strong state. It is this which has caused some to compare de Gaulle's thought to that of various European fascist parties of the pre-1939 period. The symptom of the decline of France between the two world wars was the weakness of the French State, unable to take

15 Speech of April 7, 1954.

effective action when danger threatened. De Gaulle's political experience of these years brought him into contact with the ineffectiveness of French institutions. When the Germans were defeated in the Second World War, this did not mean that danger had disappeared. The whole of modern existence represents danger, the whole trend of contemporary developments is to increase that danger. Both supporters and opponents of General de Gaulle associate him with crisis and with disaster. He himself saw his legitimacy as being latent in a period without anxiety, but it would be invoked ' as soon as a new laceration threatened the nation '. Gaullists of all sorts insist that the times in which one lives are exceptional. Edmond Michelet talks of living ' *des années tournantes* ' and Soustelle asks when, since 1940 or since 1914, have times been normal? [16] Opposed to the country returning to what he calls ' *la facilité* ', de Gaulle has always emphasised ' *ce fait écrasant* ', that France is in perpetual danger of sudden death and therefore must have some permanent authority which can take the necessary decisions (January 14, 1963). ' Politics is action, an ensemble of decisions which are made, things which are done, risks which are taken ' (July 23, 1964).

This being so, the government of a country cannot be entrusted to an assembly. An assembly cannot ensure a strong state. It exists for debate and deliberation, it does not exist in order to take decisions. Assemblies, despite their fine speeches, are, according to de Gaulle, governed by fear of action. And although de Gaulle (like other critics of the French parliamentary system) was personally attracted by the Assembly, as he recalls in his *Memoirs*,[17] and as was noticed by observers during his appearances before the Chamber in the 1958 crisis, he has never varied in his opposition to the Assembly as the source of government. He has recognised that his insistence upon a Head of State is in direct opposition to the fundamental principle of the French parliamentary régime, which de Gaulle has characterised as ' let no head show above the trenches of democracy ', indicative of a timorous, anonymous, ineffective system.

In order to make France a strong state, in order to promote change, one man must lead the country, must make decisions and give direction. In a striking and revealing passage in his *Memoirs*, de Gaulle describes his return to the Ministry of War in liberated Paris, and his impression that nothing had changed there since he and M. Reynaud had left on the night of June 10, 1940. Gigantic events had overturned the world, the French Army had been annihilated, France had virtually collapsed,

---

[16] Edmond Michelet, *Le Gaullisme, Passionnante Aventure* (Paris: Fayard. 1962); Jacques Soustelle, *L'Espérance Trahie, op. cit.*
[17] ' I was naturally attracted by the parliamentary body's element of profound yet thwarted life, of ardent yet evasive humanity, of constrained yet violent passions which sometimes subsided as if to belie themselves and sometimes burst into noisy explosions.' *War Memoirs: Salvation, op. cit.*, p. 105.

but at the Ministry of War the look of things was the same. Nothing
had been disturbed. ' Soon I was to learn that this was the case in all
the other buildings in which the Republic housed itself. Nothing was
missing except the state. It was my duty to restore it: I installed my
staff at once and got down to work.'[18] Therefore the task of the Head
of State is to find means of effecting change and reform, and governmental methods have to be examined in the light of this principle rather
than that of ideologies. ' Like everyone else ', as he puts it, he realised
that in our time technology dominated the universe, and the great debate
of the century was whether the working classes would be the victims or
the beneficiaries of this technical progress. Hence the need for profound
and rapid social change. Hence the need for technicians and administrators who would answer the aspirations and fears of the masses and, by
implication, remove the need for the various political banners (Liberal,
Marxist, Hitlerian) which floated over the battlefields. Such a policy as
nationalisation does not exist because it is inherently just or desirable,
but because through nationalisation economic change can be promoted.
Much of the insistence on military and defence projects can be interpreted as ways of promoting economic change. The referendum has
been indicated as a means of effecting reform (April 6, 1962).

*   *   *

Yet the task of the leader is not merely that of providing the
decision-making machinery whereby the state will be strengthened. His
function exists in relation to the principle of the nation-state. As has
recently been remarked, nationalism is nothing else but the desire
to bring together the juridical reality which is the state and the sociological reality which is the national group.[19] De Gaulle sees the leader
as effecting this coincidence. There is the people, the people is sovereign.
The source of power lies with the people, and although he writes of the
occasional value of a temporary period of dictatorship, and of the
temptations of dictatorship, yet his conclusion is simple, ' no man can
substitute himself for a people '. His practice followed his theory. As
he boasted, on May 19, 1958, he could have imposed his dictatorship
with the Liberation; instead he restored the Republic. His resignation in
January 1946 may have been a miscalculation, but he never attempted
to organise a *coup d'état* against the Fourth Republic. During the crisis
of 1958 all the initiatives which he took were based upon the assumption
that he could assume power legally. ' I cannot consent to receive power
from any other source than the people, or at least its representatives.'[20]

   And this contact with the people has to take place directly, and
without intermediaries. The intermediaries pervert and corrupt the

[18] *War Memoirs: Unity, op. cit.*, p. 307.
[19] See Raoul Girardet in *Revue Française de Science Politique*, June 1965, p. 431.
[20] Letter to Vincent Auriol, May 28, 1958.

relations between the leader and the people. Intermediaries tend to mean élites and de Gaulle has always been suspicious of these. He believed, even before the war, that the old élites in France were losing their value, and that whilst men could not dispense with being governed and directed, the respect which had formerly been shown to birth and position was now being accorded to those who showed ability, ' *ceux-là seulement qui ont su s'imposer* '.[21] It has been said that de Gaulle showed a rare perspicacity in realising that ' *la République des notables* ', the product of the French Revolution, was destroyed with the victory of 1918.[22] His experience in 1940 confirmed his impression. The élites failed to support him, and none of the ' *compétences éminentes* ' of France condemned the armistice. With the Liberation came the realisation that the élites had betrayed France, and de Gaulle's realisation, at a meeting at the Palais de Chaillot, that his dealings with the professional politicians would be complicated, and that he must seek his support from the people.

The constitutional change of 1962, whereby the President of the Republic is to be elected by the whole population, and not by an electoral college of 70,000 notables, has also to be seen in the same theoretical framework. Amongst the élites which were to be mistrusted are, above all, the political parties. De Gaulle's contempt for their limitations is well known (he invited Edouard Herriot to help him in the reconstruction of France, but the reply was that he was rebuilding the Radical Party); his mistrust for their sectarianism, for their tendency to represent particular rather than national interests, is allied to the conviction that in modern times there is bound to be a decadence of political parties and of their ideologies. Nothing in de Gaulle is more striking than his alliance of theory and practice, his confidence in the people,[23] his realisation of the value of modern techniques, his insistence that ' *l'affaire est entre chacune de vous, chacun de vous, et moi-même* ' (January 6, 1961). Into this there enters an element of personalisation, of auto-intoxication, comparable perhaps to that of Malraux's heroes who experience ' *un vaste frémissement de fraternité* ' in the night at Canton, but all the deeper because it represents the collusion of theory and reality.

And along with this dialogue between the leader and the people, there is another principle. Harmony is necessary to the state. In his earliest book,[24] on the subject of the German defeat in the First World

---

21 *Le Fil de l'Épée, op. cit.*
22 Jacques Bloch-Morhange, *op. cit.*, p. 48.
23 Which is in contrast to the mistrust of some of the élites, for example, Paul Reynaud: ' *Le peuple français qui a tant de qualités est instable et passionné. En 1889 il aurait élu le Général Boulanger, le général revanche.*' *Et Après?* (Paris: Plon. 1964), p. 106. Reviewed in *International Affairs*, p. 721.
24 *La Discorde chez l'Ennemi.* (Berger Levrault, 1924.)

THE POLITICAL PRINCIPLES OF GENERAL DE GAULLE   661

War, he expresses the view that the harmony of the German State was destroyed when military power invaded civilian power. In the preface he writes: ' *Dans le jardin à la française aucun arbre ne cherche à étouffer les autres de son ombre, les parterres s'accommodent d'être géométriquement dessinés, le bassin n'ambitionne pas de cascade, les statues ne prétendent pas s'imposer seules à l'admiration.*' In his account of the recent past he strives to establish this harmony. Darlan, for example, is condemned because he saw things exclusively from the standpoint of the French Navy. The Communists are treated as dangerous because they seek to control a national movement. The trial of Marshal Pétain is regretted because it became the condemnation of a part of France, whereas it should have been the condemnation of an act, the armistice. The Resistance was not to be allowed to dominate liberated France; France was greater than the Resistance. The Catholic Church should not be allowed to suffer unduly, and the exclusion of Cardinal Suhard from the Liberation mass was regretted by de Gaulle. It is not unreasonable to suppose that de Gaulle was influenced, after 1958, by the same desire not to see the harmony of the country upset, when considering his attitude to the settlers in Algeria, or his policy towards the army.

*   *   *

The General has two fundamental and contradictory beliefs. That France is united, that there is a fundamental unity; that France is diverse and multiple, with many spiritual families. ' *Cela a toujours été ainsi. C'est là notre génie.*' [25] The contradiction is resolved in great moments of crisis and drama. It disappears when de Gaulle, at the Liberation, stands at the Arc de Triomphe and sees the population massed around him. It reappears when the tension slackens. De Gaulle might well have been thinking of his own position when he wrote of Winston Churchill, ' His countenance, etched by the fires and the frosts of great events, had become inappropriate in the era of mediocrity.' [26] It is necessary therefore to maintain the tension and the drama. With Bernanos, Saint-Exupéry and Malraux, de Gaulle believes that man needs something more than material things, that one must take risks, that one must hope. In 1940 he took the side of adventure against what seemed to be the course of history. In 1958 (*pace* Jacques Soustelle) he again chose adventure.

Any attempt to analyse de Gaulle's principles must necessarily be incomplete. He must have written many letters which would reveal more about him than his public countenance allows one to divine. One knows little about his religion. Doubtless since the leader must identify himself with the whole of the nation rather than with a section, de Gaulle

---

[25] November 12, 1947.
[26] *War Memoirs: Salvation, op. cit.*, p. 201.

662 INTERNATIONAL AFFAIRS

has been careful not to emphasise his Catholicism. It is noticeable that he always claimed that the RPF was not a political party, but a Rally, and when it was first formed membership of the RPF did not involve immediate resignation from other political parties. When the RPF got caught up in the political system, then the General abandoned it. He has deliberately chosen to escape from the current French political theorist's insistence on classifying politicians either on the Right or the Left. He unites the traditional values of the Right with the traditional energies and Jacobinism of the Left. Like Cromwell he stands as both the revolutionary and the conservative leader of his epoch. Gaullism as a political phenomenon, as the majority formed in 1962, is more than the thought of the General. Gaullism as a form of political action has developed and changed since 1940, since the days of the RPF, or since 1958. But the preoccupation with unity through diversity remains in Gaullism as it remains essential to French history. And the conviction that history forms a French nature which transcends French division, a conviction represented symbolically by the Fifth Republic's achievement in cleaning the monuments of Paris, emphasises the unity of de Gaulle's thought and brings one back to ' *une certaine idée de la France* '. These principles suggest that de Gaulle is not an isolated phenomenon or an anachronism, but a phenomenon relevant to France.

Douglas Johnson is Professor of Modern History in the University of Birmingham. Author of: Guizot: Aspects of French History 1787–1874, and other studies on French and African history.

[14]

Historiographical Essay

Tony Judt

Une historiographie pas comme les autres: The French Communists and their History

'C'est quoi, la dialectique?'
'C'est l'art et la manière de toujours retomber sur ses pattes, mon vieux.'[1]

As I write this, in the winter of 1982, the secretary of the Confédération Générale du Travail (CGT), Henri Krasucki (a leading member of the Bureau Politique of the French Communist Party, PCF), has just congratulated himself publicly upon boycotting a strike in France to protest against the Polish military coup. In this display of solidarity with the Polish generals, Krasucki was joined by Georges Marchais, secretary-general of the PCF. Marchais denounced the 'adventurism' of the would-be strikers and applauded the communists' role in contributing to the failure of their plans. In the very same week, the Italian Communist Party (PCI) publicly condemned the Polish coup and declared that the militarization of eastern Europe represented the end of an era, the time of hope introduced by the Russian Revolution of October 1917. Santiago Carrillo of the Spanish party made similar, if slightly milder, statements. The French party is the only major western communist organization to have given its unabashed support for whatever actions the authorities in eastern Europe may 'regrettably' have to take.

Review Editor's Note: This essay started life as a review article; a list of the books originally under consideration appears on page 471.

European Studies Review (SAGE, London and Beverly Hills), Vol. 12 (1982), 445-78

The pattern is not new. The French Communist Party has long been remarkable for its rigidity of stance, its reluctance to abandon Stalinist practices and attitudes — but also for the degree of support it can mobilize, these attitudes notwithstanding, in French society. Few of its members remain for very long in the PCF, but a very large number of French men and women (by some estimates as many as 40 per cent of the population today),[2] have been members of the party or are related closely to someone of whom that was the case. Even after its stunning losses in the 1981 elections, the party remains influential — not least through its absolute control of the major union movement. Small wonder, then, that the communist movement in France is a source of undiminished interest and concern for historians and political scientists.

This interest in the French communists began very shortly after their emergence in the December 1920 split from the socialists. What is more, the central problematic — at least for critics of the party — has remained remarkably unaltered. In 1926, Jules Humbert-Droz, the Communist International's representative in Paris, noted that the French branch of the movement was '...un Parti d'un niveau politique au-dessous de tout ce qu'on peut imaginer'. If one but substitutes the word 'moral' for 'politique', this is the substance of the outraged sentiment of much of the French Left at the anti-immigrant actions of the PCF in 1980, when it made a cynical play for the white racist vote in the proletarian suburbs of Paris. What is more, comparison with the Italian, the Spanish or even the British communist parties reveals the French to have an extraordinarily impoverished intellectual inheritance, cause and consequence of its all-but-unswerving adherence to the most banal and static 'Marxist-Leninist' rhetoric.

If these seem somewhat polemical terms in which to couch an introduction to recent literature on the subject of French communism, this should come as no surprise; the historiography of the subject is nothing if not partisan. There have been three generations of writing on the history of the French party. The first, from the late 1930s to the end of the 1950s, comprised mostly memoirs, usually of embittered ex-members, or else official histories in the form, for example, of Maurice Thorez's 'autobiography'.[3] The second generation spanned the 1960s and early 1970s and saw the first serious attempts, in English and French alike, to offer analytical accounts of the party's origins and development.[4] The most recent literature has included a new generation of memoirs,

Judt, *History of the French Communist Party* 447

together with attempts at synthetic histories by people already too young to have experienced many of the events they describe.[5]

Ever since 1964, however, the historiography of the PCF has been dominated by the awesome shadow of Annie Kriegel. Loved, repected or hated, she and her interpretation of the French communist movement have represented, for half a generation, the fulcrum of all debate on the subject. The context of this debate is a threefold claim made in Professor Kriegel's work. The first is that the PCF is a historical accident, the result of a coming together of events and expectations in the years 1914-1920. The party that was born at Tours in December 1920, at the eighteenth congress of the hitherto united French socialist movement, was neither inevitable nor historically 'necessary'. The second Kriegel thesis is that the party which *did* emerge from this conjuncture of circumstances owed more to Lenin and the Bolshevik political model than it did to the indigenous French revolutionary and socialist traditions. Her third proposition is that the way in which this initially alien graft 'took' in France, during the propitious circumstances of the 1930s was by becoming a 'counter society', in but not of French social and political life. Hence both its capacity to endure and its failure to succeed in its stated aim of transforming French society.[6]

Non-communist students of the field can take issue with this account in a number of ways. While agreeing with Kriegel that the birth of the PCF was in no sense 'inscribed' in the years before 1914, they point out that the characteristic weaknesses of the pre-war French Left — bitter socialist-syndicalist divisions, a loosely structured and increasingly parliamentary socialist party, the slow pace of social reform in France — 'over determined' (to use the local jargon) the appearance of a new organization, tighter and more disciplined in structure, claiming political authority over the union movement and committed to a more thoroughgoing rejection of existing social and political arrangements. The war years and the example of the Russian Revolution provided merely the occasion and the example.[7]

A second fundamental area of disagreement concerns the question of inheritance. Although some recent authors such as Robrieux concur with Kriegel in seeing the PCF as the result of the grafting of a degenerated Bolshevik-style apparatus onto a French socialist stem, others (the present writer among them) concede to the communists at least part of their claim upon a peculiarly French tradition. Thus, for example, the Parti Ouvrier Français (POF), which flourished in industrial northern France from 1880 to 1900 under Jules Guesde, surely displayed characteristics of organizational rigidity and Marxist orthodoxy which flowed comfortably into the twentieth-century communist movement, even though the social and geographical bases of the movements were substantially different.[8] There are other areas of continuity: the notably French emphasis upon the state, both as enemy and prize, has firm roots in early socialist analyses of the nature of power in France and very real memories of the effective exercise of that power in 1848, 1851 and again in 1871. It is thus not from Lenin alone that the PCF derives its constant focus on power and authority at the centre, and its relative unconcern with the decentralization of control or with questions of workers' autonomy and shopfloor decision-making. Marx's own thinking has something to do with this orientation, of course, but then Marx himself was a close student of France, especially in his more directly political analyses.

Communists make much of this continuity between early French radical politics and their own concerns and ideals, and have done so since the early 1930s. Before then, of course, the 'Frenchness' of the French communists was a matter for critical condemnation — witness the blistering attack on the PCF in 1928 by 'Ercoli' (Palmiro Togliatti) at the Sixth Congress of the Communist International, where he condemned the 'sort of compromise' that the party represented between the socialist and syndicalist strains in French history.[9] But ever since the Popular Front era the PCF has preferred to invoke that inheritance — and one even older; when Georges Marchais announced in February 1981 that Robespierre was his 'role model' he was but echoing Thorez's invocation of the same hero in 1950. As the official PCF *Manuel d'Histoire* put it in 1964: 'Le parti communiste plonge ses racines au plus profond du sol national et du mouvement ouvrier français. Il est l'héritier d'une tradition démocratique et révolutionnaire riche et ancienne.'[10]

As to Kriegel's characterization of the PCF as a 'counter society', this has aroused perhaps the greatest ire, particularly among partisan communist historians. It is a functionalist and explicitly unsympathetic interpretation of the party's role, emphasizing the inbuilt organizational and stategic stagnation of the movement. For her critics it is thus of all competing interpretations of communism 'la plus subtile et la plus caricaturale'.[11] Noncommunist experts also take issue, though more commonly on

Judt, *History of the French Communist Party*   449

methodological grounds; they have their own analytical categories which they offer in preference to Kriegel's, but do not differ on the central, and often unspoken question: is the PCF (still) a revolutionary movement? If so, what does it exist to achieve and how does it envisage achieving it? For Kriegel, Lavau, Bon, Tiersky and their successors, the answer is in the negative, on a priori grounds. For the Party's own intellectuals, also on a priori grounds, the PCF is what it proclaims to be, means what it says and knows what it means.[12]

In recent years the PCF and its publishing house, *Editions Sociales,* have made considerable efforts to provide a respectable 'house' historiography. At the time of the appearance of Kriegel's two-volume study of the party's origins, the only official alternatives were Thorez's distinctly unreliable memoirs already mentioned, or the 1964 *Manuel,* a gross caricature of a history, ignoring or denying embarrassing episodes or persons and recasting all official decisions such that the course of events from 1870 to 1964 could be seen to have run smoothly, stage-managed by a benevolently evolutionist fate and an omniscient party leadership (from the emergence of Thorez in 1931). There followed a series of lengthy memoirs by ageing leaders, all carefully vetted and confirmatory of the general line, past and present.[13] Only in the mid-1970s, in the high years of the Common Programme and the alliance with the Socialists, did a critical communist literature begin to surface.

One test of this literature, and indeed it is something of a standard hurdle for non-communist histories as well, is how it handles the various turning-points in the chequered history of the PCF. By tradition, the problem did not exist — there *were* no turning-points, only 'developments' and 'advances' in the strategy. This is no longer the case — indeed, a recent collection by nine party historians is conceived in terms of the various moments in question.[14] Broadly speaking, the nodal junctions in the history of the PCF are these: the circumstances of its birth and the social identity of its support at the time; the shake-up of 1930-1, which ended the decade of extreme tactics and political failure and saw the emergence of Thorez; the decision in 1934 to promote a popular front movement; the response to the Molotov-Ribbentrop Pact of 1939 and the ensuing two years of 'anti-imperialist' policy; the question of whether the party desired a revolutionary seizure of power in 1944; the grey years of out-and-out Stalinism 1947-53; the refusal to go along with de-Stalinization after 1956, the move to alliance with the Socialists from 1962 and the break with that alliance in 1977. Of these, the events of the years 1920-47 remain central to contemporary writings on the PCF.

On the issues surrounding the origins of the PCF, there has been some progress towards a consensus. The desire to create as sharp a distinction as possible between the 'old' socialism and its successor communist party is still there, of course; the PCF recently published a two-volume 'Histoire du réformisme en France' whose very title is a polemic, and Danielle Tartakowsky continues to insist that the pre-1920 workers' movement was the prisoner of a reformism which nourished 'democratic illusions'.[15] But Jean-Louis Robert breaks new ground when he gently chides the 1964 *Manuel* for 'overlooking' Zinoviev's telegram to the Tours congress, with its crude and brutal instructions to the delegates to break with Jean Longuet and the historical left-centre of the old party. Although Robert does not spell out the point, this is about as near to an admission from a party writer that the Tours split was manufactured in Moscow as I have seen.

Robert's own work is rather important. Building on the evidence for a wartime boom in large-scale manufacturing (Renault-Billancourt went from 5,000 workers in 1914 to nearly 25,000 in 1918, the Citroen works at Quai Javel from virtually nothing in 1914 to 10,000 plus at the end of the war), Robert offers convincing grounds for overthrowing the conventional view that the split of December 1920 saw workers less enthusiastic than peasants and young people about the communist alternative. Whether this conclusion has significant meaning for the revolutionary character of the new party depends upon the a priori importance you attach to the working class. For Robert and his colleagues it is of course a significant point; and certainly, to the extent that Kriegel rested an interpretative burden on her view that it was enthusiastic but ignorant peasants who helped form the early PCF, one can see that Robert's work matters.[16]

In the years following Tours, the French party followed a path broadly similar to that of the other newly-formed communist movements. For three years it remained in the hands of its founders, men and women whose political education dated from before the war and who were unsuited to the adjustments required by the Moscow-based International. From 1924 it was progressively purged and 'bolshevized' at the hands of an extreme left leadership, itself replaced in the mid-1920s by a more conservative direction. When the latter failed to adapt to the needs of the hardening 'Third Period' line after 1927 it was replaced by a group chosen from the very radical Communist Youth Movement. By 1930 this group in turn was proving insufficiently·flexible and the party was in tatters, with the result that the Comintern stepped in once again and manoeuvred into power the young Maurice Thorez, who would remain in office as head of the party from 1931 until 1964.[17]

The often absurd and self-defeating sectarianism of these years, and the fact that they antedate the emergence of Thorez, and more importantly the final victory of Stalin over his opponents, make them legitimate prey for criticism by even the most orthodox party historian. The theses of the Fifth Congress of the Communist International on organization, requiring that the French movement follow the Russian model of factory cells rather than the traditional French structure based on local geographical sections, certainly broke the PCF from its roots in socialist party organization, but had almost wholly negative results. The working-class base was inadequate to support the whole weight of party communications in this way, and many of the non-factory working members were lost, especially following the attempts in 1925 and 1926 to attach them, willy-nilly, to the nearest factory cell, whatever their occupation. On this much, all can agree. Tartakowsky, however, goes further and sees the years of bolshevization as a sort of spring cleaning, during which the PCF (then still officially referred to as the SFIC — Section Française de l'Internationale Communiste) got rid of the remnants of the old guard and began to renew itself in a revolutionary mould. To the extent to which she insists on this point, she is retreating to a remarkably old-fashioned stance and seems to me to be wrong on two counts.

Firstly, it is a mistake to see the 'left opposition' of Rosmer, Monatte, Souverine and others as a ragbag of romantic syndicalists and crypto-Trotskyists, whose removal enabled 'la lutte contre les déviations qui s'opèrent au nom du marxisme même' [sic] to be pursued in peace. The objections of Souvarine and others to the theory and practice of the new party, as required by Moscow, embodied what little healthy debate on Marxism was to be found at the time, and their loss was never really made good. Secondly, Tartakowsky goes to unnecessary pains to treat the PCF's history in these years as an internal matter, at most a distant reflection of developments in the CPSU. This is foolish and self-defeating; if her aim is indeed to find some rationality in the twists and turns of the 1920s, the source must surely lie in the history of the parent party.

The problem of rationality is at the heart of the next 'moment' in the history of the PCF, the emergence of Thorez (as Robrieux insists throughout his multi-volume history, the role of individuals in general and Thorez in particular is vital to the peculiarity of the French party). The inception of the 'class against class' tactic in the international communist movement from late in 1927 reflected the thesis that post-war capitalism was now entering its 'third period' of sharpening class tensions, during which conflict would become more acute and all persons and parties must take up sides. Socialist and social-democratic parties were lumped with bourgeois and fascist ones as 'fundamentally' similar, with the socialists the greatest threat in their capacity to mislead the workers and their allies. The propitious advent of the 1929 slump lent credibility to this account and sharpened still further the communist attack on the 'social fascists'.

In France, the group led by Barbé and Célor, originally placed in power by the Comintern to implement the sharp leftward turn of the years 1928-30, was edged out, accused of sectarian and dictatorial practices, and replaced by the infinitely more malleable Thorez. So much is common ground and it might readily be thought that this was a somewhat uncontroversial, albeit important, staging post. Not at all. It is clear from the latest batch of party histories that the quasi-Hegelian search for metahistorical rationality in PCF history continues unabated. This is especially the case when it comes to explaining the rise of Thorez, of whom it is not enough to claim that he was sufficient; he must needs have been inevitable. The first task is to diminish the status of the Barbé-Célor group, a task made easier by the rather shady trajectory of some of its members during the Vichy years. Tartakowsky even manages to glean some advantage from the fact that the group had been chosen by Moscow — this explains their 'voluntarism' and distinguishes them from true leaders who spring 'spontaneously' from the masses.[18]

However, the clinching argument runs thus: if the PCF was a mess in the 1920s this is because it was not born of a true crisis in the polity, and thus lacked the thoroughgoing revolutionary character that would have been required of it in such a crisis. This situation could only be resolved when the French state underwent such a total crisis. Danielle Tartakowsky dates this crisis from

1929. The result was a division in the ruling class between the 'true' bourgeoisie and the middle-class state employees on whom the former now turned in order to save themselves. In this situation the PCF was faced with a genuine opportunity, which it accordingly seized by producing a leadership capable of rising to the occasion and mobilizing all the energies of the discontented.

This is a stunning exercise in induction. Thorez emerged in 1931, so 1931 had to be a moment of significance. Since, for Marxists, significant moments are material in character, the moment in question must have been a crisis in the structure of bourgeois state power, and not just in the apparatus of the PCF. Not merely then did Thorez and a genuine communist party *have* to emerge at the start of the 1930s, it *could not* have emerged at any other time! Thorez, the 'intellectuel d'un type nouveau', organically attached to the masses, is the problem of (communist) history resolved (and knows himself to be so...). In the face of this glittering prize, minor difficulties surrounding the exact dating of the economic crisis in France and the Comintern's role in finally identifying a reliable French apparatchik fade quite away.[19]

That Tartakowsky is perhaps unrepresentative of a younger generation of communist historians may be seen in her treatment of the emergence of the Popular Front, whose origins, *élan* and achievements have long been feathers in the cap of the PCF, competing for pride of place with its record in the Resistance. Two areas of doubt lurk here, however. The first concerns the dating of the Popular Front — when did the communists abandon their sectarian opposition to all other parties and begin advocating a common front? The second regards the extent to which the inspiration for a Popular Front came from Moscow. These questions are, as usual, inextricably linked.

On the Moscow origins of the Popular Front we are doomed to remain in some doubt until the Moscow archives of the Comintern are released... The vast literature on the subject leaves little doubt on two points, however. Firstly, that Thorez (and Fried, his *éminence grise*)[20] would certainly have taken no step as momentous as this without full clearance from the executive of the International, so that the question of who first thought of the idea of a popular front is substantially irrelevant. Secondly, nothing happened in France until the USSR had reason to desire it.[21] Some party historians such as Serge Wolikow are content to acknowledge this, keeping their distance from the view of the *Manuel* that there was continuity of strategy from 1931 to 1939 (although even Wolikow covers himself by noting that this view, however erroneous, 'a le mérite d'insister sur la cohérance et la continuité d'action du PCF' — an argument as well invoked in defence of Ptolemaic astronomy).

Here again, however, Tartakowsky takes a last-ditch stand for the old line. The latter depended heavily for its plausibility on the oddities of communist vocabulary. During the class-against-class years of 1928-33, the official slogan was *front unique à la base;* that is, an alliance of members and militants of communist and socialist parties alike, but in outright opposition to the persons and tactics of the socialist leadership, seen as class enemies. In 1934 this changed to *front unique* and thence to *front populaire,* thereby undergoing an important shift of meaning. It now favoured alliance with the socialist (and Radical) leadership. The claim that 'united front' meant the same thing throughout, a claim advanced by PCF leaders like Marcel Cachin from 1935 onwards, is frankly cynical. Yet Tartakowsky adopts it for her own. Pursuing her thesis that the economic crisis rendered formerly protected groups sympathetic to the communist appeal, she writes 'De pédagogique qu'elle était, la question du front unique devient alors politique'.[22]

This is breathtaking — a genuine return to the 'langue de bois' of the old days. If it means anything at all it can only be from within an adoption of the party's strategy of this period and this, to say no more, is an inappropriate perspective from which to write history. Tartakowsky might as well adopt the argument propounded by Cachin in 1935, that the PCF's tactical support of Barbusse's initiative in calling a peace conference in Amsterdam in 1932 (a tactic designed to embarrass the socialists who rejected the invitation) proves that the PCF wanted a popular front in. 1932![23] Unfortunately, Tartakowsky is rather undermined by Thorez himself who, in contributions to *l'Humanité* not referred to in her work, was still writing of 'social fascists' and 'social democratic vomit' as late as April 1934. In the same month he made quite explicit the continuing class-against-class tactic of the communists, when he wrote the following: 'Tous les bavardages sur le mariage entre communistes et socialistes sont foncièrement étrangers à l'esprit du bolchévisme. Nous ne voulons pas nous unir avec la social-démocratie.... Ce que nous voulons, c'est faciliter aux ouvriers socialistes leur orientation vers le communisme, vers Moscou.'[24]

The volte-face of spring 1934, unavoidably linked to the Nazis' destruction of the German communists and Stalin's search for allies in western Europe, is a source of continuing difficulty, in that it *was* a volte-face in a history which some would prefer seamless and linear. But it had the virtue of inaugurating a period which saw the PCF's emergence on to the French political scene as a major force. What is more, the party was on the side of the angels, and benefited accordingly. The same cannot readily be said of the events of August 1939 to June 1941, a period which most PCF historians and militants would simply rather forget. Despite the efforts of the old official history, of the party schools, and even the attempts at the Liberation to destroy the evidence, memory has proven annoyingly resilient, aided by the published memoirs of leading communists of the time who were subsequently purged in the 1950s and have taken their revenge by spilling substantial amounts of dirt. The writings of men like Tillon and Lecoeur have helped document a sad and sordid story whose outlines are already well enough known to an older generation. The massive (600 pages) work by Stéphane Courtois adds little that we did not already know, and in any case leans heavily at crucial points on the aforementioned memoirs.[25]

Immediately following the announcement of the signing of the Molotov-Ribbentrop Pact in August 1939, the French communists began the reversal of their stand against the Nazi threat, placing instead the emphasis of their propaganda upon the growing threat of an 'imperialist' war. They thus provided Daladier's government with the occasion to dissolve the party and its affiliates on 26 September, on the grounds that France was now at war with the ally of the PCF's parent authority, the Soviet Union. Slow to react to the implications of their new position, and in many cases still shocked by the change of line, the communists took some time to establish an underground movement, though they did succeed in expediting Thorez's desertion from the army to spend the war years in Moscow.

During the course of 1940, however, the PCF warmed to its role. It dissociated itself first from the French war effort, then from the ensuing Vichy regime, proclaiming neutrality towards Germany. More seriously, the party took advantage of the German victory to make a formal request of the Nazi authorities (at the end of June 1940) that they allow the party paper, *l'Humanité,* to appear in legal publication. The hope was that the communists would become, de facto, and courtesy of the occupying forces, the only active French political organization and would benefit accordingly. Stéphane

Courtois suggests this was a conscious policy, imitation of the Leninist move of 1917, to exploit the short-term interests of the Germans for the long-term advantage of the domestic revolution. This credits a strategy to the rather frenetic course of communist behaviour at the time. In any event the point is moot, since the Germans rejected the request (a rejection for which the French communists have ever since had cause to be thankful). The PCF, unlike the Danish, Belgian and Norwegian parties, for example, was obliged to remain in semi-clandestinity, thereby enhancing its later claim to have resisted from the start.

Balked in its desire to emerge from clandestinity, the PCF continued none the less to press its new line, that it alone represented the true interests of the nation, interests which France shared with the Soviet Union. The Vichy government was dismissed as an irrelevance, while any criticism of the German occupation (no longer referred to as Nazi) was carefully balanced with attacks on Anglo-, or Anglo-American imperialism. The summa of this epoch came in December 1940 in a letter to party militants, signed jointly by Thorez in absentia and Jacques Duclos, party chief on the spot. The crux of the letter ran thus: '... nous sommes le seul parti exprimant... les sentiments profonds de notre peuple tout entier qui comprend qu'une victoire impérialiste se traduirait par une vassalisation de la France.... Ni domination britannique, ni protectorat allemand, la France aux français.'[26]

In the same month, François Billoux and other prominent communists offered their services to the authorities as witnesses for the prosecution in the notorious Riom trials, where Léon Blum and others were being tried, in an absurd travesty of justice, for their responsibility in precipitating the war and the defeat of France. The communists' desire to obtain official favour here combined with the visceral hatred of the pre-war socialists in general and Blum in particular in a terrible haste to condemn a pre-war government of whose belligerent policies (such as they were) the PCF had been the leading advocate. Here again, the Germans and the Vichy government saved the communists from themselves by declining the offer.[27]

It was not until the very eve of the German attack on Russia that the communists began to waver in their stance, under increasing pressure as they were from the anti-fascist militants in their own movement. In the spring of 1941 Duclos was still condemning as a 'déviation nationaliste' such militants, men and women whose

Judt, *History of the French Communist Party* 457

clandestine actions of the time are now much invoked by the PCF in support of its claim to have resisted throughout the war. It is a bitter irony for Tillon, Lecoeur and others that they should have been purged from the party in the 1950s and their independence of opinion castigated as lack of discipline, while their courageous and often lonely actions in the early years of occupation provide a thin veil of respectability to the otherwise shameful history of the leadership in this period.

In the 630-plus pages of *Le PCF: étapes et problèmes,* six pages are devoted to this period. This is a 300 per cent improvement on the 1964 production, which confined its concern with the Molotov-Ribbentrop Pact to a single paragraph which needs to be quoted in full for maximum enjoyment:

> Ménacée par une guerre qui se serait déclenchée contre elle dans les conditions les plus défavourables, l'Union Soviétique, le 23 août, signe avec l'Allemagne un traité de non-agression. Elle évite ainsi le traquenard qui lui était tendu et brise le front des Etats impérialistes dont elle était ménacée. Le traité conduit à l'isolement ultérieur des Etats fascistes et prépare contre eux la coalition des Etats démocratiques que l'URSS a vainement préconisée pour éviter la catastrophe'.[28]

It is sad to have to report that Germaine Willard's contribution on this subject is little improvement, either on the original or on subsequent publications.[29] She acknowledges that the communists' characterization of the war as 'imperialist' prevented them from grasping correctly the 'whole situation', but claims in the party's defence that it *was* an imperial (and anti-popular) war as well as being against Hitler and that the PCF was correct to take into account its contradictory aspects. There is no mention of the Russian attack on Poland in 1939 — though much is made of the simultaneous German invasion from the west — and the request for permissic⁻ to publish *l'Humanité* is called an 'illusion'. Nor is there anything on the communists' request to be allowed to contribute to the humiliation and punishment of Blum. There is still a long way to go before communist historians come to terms with this period — it may simply be that they never will, and that as militants die and memories fade, the need to explain will quietly disappear.

The disagreements of interpretation surrounding the immediate post-war years are less heated, but of perhaps greater political and theoretical import. At their heart lies a dual question: did the PCF wish to seize power in 1944 and/or 1947? The answer to this question, it is often suggested, would provide the clue to the strategy of the present-day party.

This is a theme on which historians sympathetic to the party are oddly ambivalent, claiming on the one hand that the PCF sought only the liberation and rebirth of French democracy, on the other that there was complete continuity of strategy from the pre-war resolutions at the party congresses of 1936 and 1937. These are incompatible accounts. The emphasis of those congresses was unequivocally on class warfare and a continuing strategy of proletarian revolutionary dictatorship.[30] Non-party historians disagree sharply among themselves. Of the recent writers, Courtois insists that the PCF was aiming in the late autumn of 1944 for a 'stratégie de rupture', with the aim of holding on to arms and preparing the masses for a civil war as the Red Army advanced westward. Except for the well-documented desire of the PCF in the weeks following the Liberation to retain its armed Gardes Civiques, this seems farfetched, and is part of Courtois' rather frantic effort to find consistency and rationality in every communist move.

The most plausible reading of the hectic months that followed de Gaulle's arrival in Paris is this: many members of the PCF, especially in the south-west, undoubtedly had high hopes of a communist-led seizure of power, and kept and hid their weapons to that end. The party leadership may have been divided on this, and would in any case have preferred to keep armed support as a negotiating lever, but Jacques Duclos had the overwhelming urge to re-establish the peacetime party, with its regulated structure, clear lines of authority and coherent political direction, and armed militants led by men whose authority derived not from the party but from their Resistance mystique were inimical to this end.[31]

In any event, the Soviet concern at this stage and until 1946 was with the western alliance. With Thorez in Moscow but due to return any minute, Duclos had even more reason than usual not to act without looking over his shoulder. To the extent that the PCF was genuinely indignant and rebellious when de Gaulle disbanded the Gardes Civiques on 28 October 1944, this opposition melted when he announced, a week later, an amnesty for Thorez's desertion. The party leader duly returned, as part of an arrangement between Stalin and de Gaulle, and proceeded post-haste to direct his party's attention towards domestic and non-revolutionary ends. From then until May 1947 the French communists took a loyal, if sometimes uncomfortable, part in the governments of post-war France, a fact

Judt, *History of the French Communist Party* 459

that de Gaulle himself acknowledged in his memoirs.

The same constellation of interpretations surrounds the events of May 1947, when the socialist premier Ramadier expelled the PCF from his coalition government for ministerial disloyalty. Courtois suggests that the PCF had used the intervening years to build for itself a power base in the state, preparing itself and its syndical affiliate the CGT for the 'march towards a popular democracy in France'. The process was narrowly averted by Ramadier, who received only a slim majority backing in the Socialist Party for his efforts.[32] The communists were forced to resort to *social* pressure, which they applied through a series of strikes in 1947 and 1948, but to no avail, retreating thence to a stance of outright opposition through the Cold War years.

That, it must be acknowledged, is how it seemed to many at the time, including the socialist ministers who had to face the communist pressure.[33] Once again, it is a thesis which has the virtue of tracing a thread of continuity through PCF history — though not the continuity claimed by the party. None the less, it seems radically faulted, and Robrieux (and more generally Kriegel) offers a more appealing case, for 1947 as for the Liberation.

To begin with, it is not clear that the communists had succeeded in placing their own people in strategic locations in government and administration. In contrast with the situation in eastern Europe, they lacked control of the essential ministries. More generally, they seem not to have attempted such an infiltration; if anything, Thorez was so sure that the PCF would be continuing in office that he had actually *reduced* the number of communists serving as cabinet secretaries and advisers and replaced them with full-time *hauts fonctionnaires*.[34]

Secondly, the post-war years were halcyon ones for the party. Whatever one makes of the official membership figures, they show without a doubt that the PCF was a large and thriving organization, bigger and better supported than ever before. From 1946 it was also the strongest party in France, with over 5,000,000 voters. The illusion that they were on the way to a peaceful ascent into power could be excused the PCF leadership in 1947, whatever the passing difficulties they were experiencing in supporting the government's colonial policy or its austerity plans. The shock of the expulsion in May 1947 was a real one. Even after the socialists failed to resign with them, as some hoped, the communists continued to talk and act as though theirs would be a mere temporary passage in the wilderness.

What brought the point home to them, and in many respects confirms the traditional account of these years, was the meeting at Szklarska-Poreba in Poland in September 1947. Ostensibly held to establish the Cominform, successor to the defunct Comintern, this gathering of party leaders served above all to clarify Soviet strategy in the new atmosphere of the Cold War, and to serve notice on foreign fraternal parties, *especially* the PCF, that collaboration with governments was henceforth taboo. Duclos and Fajon from the PCF (Thorez was significantly absent, thus spared the coming humiliation) were abused and condemned for the abysmal myopia of their organization and its snivelling reformism in the years since the Liberation. After descending to the most degrading of self-criticisms, the PCF leadership was let off with what amounted to a warning.[35]

The significance of these events is considerable. They go a long way towards accounting for the care that the PCF took in the next generation never to cross the Moscow leadership, long after the end of the Stalin era, and for the obsession with orthodoxy in theory and practice. They help account for the party's deep suspicion of other fraternal communist parties, nearly all of whom joined in the fun at the Cominform meeting. But they suggest, above all, that there really was nothing very subtle or clever or strategic about the PCF's behaviour in the period after 1944; the party (and Thorez in particular) enjoyed the fruits of power and was loath to abandon them when the world situation altered. Instructed to play a peaceful and secondary role as a result of the Yalta agreements, Thorez had simply been slow to register changing times.

The theoretical thrust of an account on these lines is of course considerable, both for the post-war years and indeed for the whole period under consideration. It reinforces the emphasis on the Soviet Union and its control of the French party, at least until the death of Thorez, it suggests that the PCF lacked any very clear idea of where it was going, and that this confusion can be dated back to the ambivalent stance of the Popular Front years; and it throws into sharper relief the party's setbacks, in that they become not kinks in the linear advance of a self-conscious historical actor, but actions and omissions of political cynicism, moral turpitude or plain incompetence, undertaken for nothing more than the preservation of a political institution, the French Communist Party.

If that is all we are left with, and this is the sense one derives from reading Robrieux, for example, difficult questions of a different kind then emerge. Why should this stagnant institution have survived so long? Why have not its crimes and failures deprived it of any credibility for voters and members alike? What is the value, the meaning of the ideological web it spins about itself and its past? One can see why Courtois strives so to find a method, a reason in all this. In that respect his work is more intellectually satisfying — or would be so, were the facts less recalcitrant. The same is true of the efforts of the party's own historians, and their renewed attempt to ground an account of the PCF in something approaching plausibility. In their case, however, a refusal to go very far in this direction, and a blinkered insistence upon relying on exclusively pro-PCF sources, vitiates the best of intentions.[36]

Paradoxically, any attempt at a synoptic interpretation of the history of the PCF stands a better chance if it *does* acknowledge the insoluble contradictions of the party's behaviour. This can most readily be demonstrated by looking at the two features of the history of the PCF which are peculiar to it and which have proven so very enduring: its obsessively rigid ideological stance and its concern to identify absolutely with the industrial working class.

The French communists' way of talking about Marxism and its aims — the mode of ideological discourse, as it were — has long been conditioned by the crude Stalinism of the PCF's middle years. The spirit of this period (roughly 1948 to the late 1950s) is well captured in the following, a passage from Thorez in 1949:

> Tout le parti, ses militants, ses adhérents, doivent être formés dans l'esprit de la confiance inébranlable envers notre grand et cher camarade Staline. A ceux qui, autrefois, nous criaient 'Staliniens!', en croyant nous faire injure, nous répondions dans la présomption de la jeunesse: oui, nous sommes staliniens. Maintenant, nous disons plus modestement: nous nous efforcerons d'être de bons staliniens.[37]

Four years later, after the death of Stalin, Jacques Duclos, insisting at a meeting at the *Mutualité* that true Marxism was and could only be Stalinist, found no higher praise to offer Thorez than to pronounce him 'le meilleur stalinien français'.

As a way of thinking, Stalinism of course transcended mere pap for the masses. It provided the dialectical rails along which ran even the best-oiled of Marxist brains. Thus Jean-Toussaint Desanti, for long one of the PCF's prestigious intellectuals until he broke ranks, was wheeled in early in this period, and before the onset of Stalinism proper, to justify to young and suspicious members the party's defence of the peasantry. In 1947 working-class and intellectual distrust of the peasant ran deep, both on a priori grounds and because of black market profiteering in the countryside during Vichy. Desanti's solution to the problem of providing an ideological cover for the PCF's search for rural electors was simple: the peasants'...[s'étaient] enrichis individuellement mais appauvris collectivement'. The dialectical charms of this conclusion merit savouring.

Years of this sort of language are not without effect — a poll as late as 1966 found that 68 per cent of communist electors (which would include a very large number of persons not in the party as members) had a 'good opinion' of Stalin and his achievements. As well they might; until 1956, one of the compulsory questions on the application form for new members of the PCF asked the aspiring militant how many of the works of Stalin he or she had read; even if the honest answer was 'none' (and this was not necessarily the case, given the wide diffusion of the French-language versions of Stalin's writings), the implication was not lost on a generation of party activists. Interestingly, just as this question vanished after 1956, so in 1964 (the year of his death) did a similar one concerning the oeuvres of Thorez — and the advent of Georges Marchais required the tactful excision of the hitherto important section of the questionnaire requiring members to specify their wartime activities![38]

Stalinism in style, Stalinism in practice. The close modelling of PCF organizational arrangements upon those of the Stalinized Bolshevik Party is well known, but none the less remarkable, from the establishment of a *commission des cadres* responsible for promoting and demoting members of the Central Committee, the existence of a parallel and unacknowledged power structure answering directly to the party secretaries, the use of the purge (1930, 1951-5, 1961-2, 1981) to curb opposition, to the pyramidal structure of authority and the focus on the person of the general secretary. Some of this can be accounted for in personal terms — the long reign of Jacques Duclos at the heart of the party, guardian of its worst secrets from 1930 until 1971, and perhaps the real 'eye of Moscow' in Paris, undoubtedly provides a continuity that mere structures and habit could not alone ensure. This cannot fully account, however, for the PCF's long-running post-war role as Moscow's poodle, from Marcel Servin's efforts in 1952 to provide evidence for the Prague show trials (concerning the activities of anti-fascist and International Brigade veterans who fought in the French Resistance during the war) to the shameful events of 1968 when, if one credits Robrieux, Jean Kanapa and Etienne Fajon contrived to pass on to the Czech hardliners notes on their private talks with Dubcek in July 1968, thus providing evidence for the 'normalization' process of the following months.[39]

Further documentation of the PCF's inheritance in this respect would be otiose, and would in any case just be another way of narrating the party's history. Nevertheless, rehearsing the highlights of French Stalinism is not *just* an exercise in sadism — it also provides a key to the deeper characteristics of the PCF and the world it has had to make for itself.

To begin with, it is a pity that modern party historians insist on underplaying the Russian links of the party in its early years, since these account for things otherwise hard to explain.[40] The French communists, as we have seen, took a hammering from the Comintern: from 1921 to the early 1930s the French section of the International was the one everyone despised, the fall guy for every failure of official communist strategy (the PCF has internalized this experience, elevating to an art the habit of blaming militants at the base for all failures to implement the party's 'correct' line). Then, from the mid-1930s to the 1950s, the French party became, in the absence of alternatives, the chief foreign representative of the communist movement and thus again the focus of unwonted attention and interference. From 1947 the French learnt to deal with this by awesome efforts to keep in step — broken only by Thorez's refusal to support Kruschev and adopt de-Stalinization for his own (a refusal based on a calculated gamble that neither the man nor the policy would long survive...). Countervailing pressures from within to follow a more independent line, or at least one based on a correct reading of *domestic* politics, ran consistently foul of the leadership's memory of previous such attempts.[41]

The force of this is all the greater when one recalls that the issue on which the old Socialist Party actually split in 1920, the vote which gave birth to the communist movement in France, was precisely over Russian control of the member parties of the International. For communists of *that* generation, accepting direction from above and outside was the only alternative to slipping back into the amorphous polycentrist nationalism which had destroyed the Second International and undermined its stance in 1914. Adopting and adapting Stalinism to the French movement was the natural, if sometimes painful, corollary, to the principle that communism was international or it was nothing, that the methods and lessons of 1917 were necessarily superior to anything the indigenous tradition could offer, and that in any case the defence of the only surviving revolutionary nation must take priority over domestic success, precisely because, in the long run, it was the precondition for any such success.[42]

On the other side there were, and are, purely French and more properly historical elements in the PCF's make-up, and its own historians are right to assert this, though with a different emphasis. This operates in three ways. In the first place the French communists are the heirs of the revolutionary tradition in certain respects — their vocabulary, their geographical implantation, their focus on central authority and their special strength in the Paris region, all these cast them back, beyond the early nineteenth-century Utopians, to the Jacobins of the Revolution and their republican successors. Not that the intervening years are scorned by the communists — the litany of names from St Simon to Cabet is frequently cited in party lectures and the official history began, symbolically, in 1871. But the assorted emphases of the pre-Marxist French socialists on workers' control, autonomy, feminism, co-operatives and the like sit ill with the PCF's own concerns, even today.

In the second place, and even more important, the concerns of the nineteenth-century socialists frequently sat ill with the history of France itself. In this sense the PCF is the more legitimate heir to an altogether more powerful French imperative, the enduring spotlight on the state. This does not make it unique — the much-maligned Guesdists of the late nineteenth century, castigated by Left and Right alike for their rigid, dogmatic Marxism, were remarkably acute in their perception of the locus of power in France and in their organizational and ideological reflection of the fact. The Guesdist *Parti Ouvrier Français* was also, incidentally, more sociologically plausible than the competing and decentralized socialisms of Jaurès and the municipalists, rooted as it was in the emerging proletarian cities and the heavy industrial base of provincial France.

What distinguishes the PCF from the Guesdist POF, and more generally Leninism from Guesde's Engels-derived Marxism, is their respective descriptions of this all-powerful state. For Guesde, the French state, a historical reality and with powerful reactive capacities, had to be captured, not ignored (*pace* the syndicalists), thence to be used against the class which had hitherto controlled it. For Lenin, of course, this was a nervelessly static account of the relations between state and ruling class, relations which could only be shattered by the destruction of both. The PCF grafted its own identity somewhere between, and it has sat there uneasily ever since, sometimes proclaiming that the state can be used neutrally on behalf of the workers (witness Thorez's faith in this prospect in the years 1944-7 and a renewal of such ideas in the era of the common programme since the late 1960s), sometimes retreating to the view that state, high civil servants and ruling monopolists are but one and must be overthrown and replaced accordingly.[43]

The eerie justification for the PCF's ambivalence, and its refusal to displace state and state power from the centre of its concerns, is thus the degree to which it reflects local reality. Nowhere else in Europe are the links between an all-powerful administration, a narrow political class and the interests of an economic elite so complex — and ancient — as in France. It is fully appropriate that one of the earliest attacks on the PCF for its rigidity of dogma and almost military disciplinary structure, made by Monatte and Rosmer in a letter to *Cahiers du Bolchévisme* in December 1924, should have warned that 'bientôt la bureaucratie du Parti fera pige à celle de l'Etat français'.[44] It is not, however, clear whether the targets of such a criticism should not rather be flattered — does not a revolutionary movement *seek* to reflect the historical structures of the society in which it operates, the better to undermine and replace it?

Such a teleological defence, however, reminds us of the third major pillar of the communists' French inheritance. The French party shares the characteristic burden of its predecessors all the way back to Babeuf — the absence of any serious hope of achieving its stated aims. Its strongest suit in the early days was to argue from the failures and compromises of French socialism, from 1830 to 1919, to the consequent necessity of its own emergence. But such reasoning provides hostages to political fortune. If the SFIO did little more than establish a niche for itself in French parliamentary life, and if that is the best evidence of its failure, then what has the PCF to offer in exchange, except a solid grounding in the syndical movement as well as in electoral politics? Each of its 'missed opportunities' — 1936, 1944, 1968 — can be explained away, but only on the presumption of some future occasion which will offer true possibilities and for which the PCF will be uniquely equipped.

Meanwhile, therefore, the PCF has become very much a part of the local landscape and, as with the SPD in Wilhelmine Germany, this is an ambivalent role whose comforts are its embarrassment.[45] Far from generating pressure to reform and thus dispense with the baggage of its early years, this situation reinforces the case for emphasizing the features of those years which justify the party's existence — to wit, precisely the 'revolutionary' and Stalinist traits which seem so redundant if one limits oneself to a functionalist account. This is hardly surprising — faced with not dissimilar stagnation the SFIO of the inter-war years also laid growing emphasis upon its ideological inheritance and the justification this offered for its (passing) ineffectiveness. The difference is that what distinguishes the PCF is its Leninist midwife — beyond that it shares many of the birthmarks of the left wing of the French socialists. Accordingly, it is not at all an aberration that it should be the Stalinist inheritance which remains hardest to shake off, for it is that which gave to the movement its sharpest definition.[46]

One can go further. It is not necessary to adopt wholesale Annie Kriegel's characterization of the party as a counter-society to see the central psychological truth of the idea. To belong to the PCF, or to be drawn close to it through membership of its trade-union and other affiliates, has since the 1930s been a popular way of responding to the anomie of French society — more precisely, it has been a reflection of the enduring exclusion of the popular classes from education, wealth and power. This was never more so than in the 1920s and early 1930s, after the defeats of 1919 and 1920 had reduced the syndical movement to a persecuted minority and returned to the *patronat* some of their absolute power of the previous century. The social explosion of 1936 provided not so much the occasion for any real alteration in the distribution of power in France (by 1938 things were back to where they had been before the strikes of spring 1936), but the opportunity for the communists to emerge as the vehicle for the organization and defence of the working population. The introversion and defensiveness of the modern party reflects this — and reflects too the extent to which it is that counter-social function which most members recognize in their party. Small wonder that the interest in change and reform diminishes the deeper you probe into the PCF's older and more properly proletarian militant base.

Rigidity, then, and the peculiarly but appropriately Stalinist form it has taken in France, has been a condition of the communists' survival as much as it has been a block to their further advance; in similar vein, it has arisen from a combination of genuinely indigenous as well as contingent and exogenous pressures. To this extent, the absence of a French Gramsci, or even a Togliatti, is not just an unfortunate accident of biography or history. The French tradition of Marxist thought is a poor thing, it is true, but communist parties do not just get the philosophers they deserve, they also acquire the ones that they need, and Louis Althusser, in his obscure way, is very appropriately the theorist of the condition of a communist movement in France.[47]

Finally, an interweaving of the Kriegelian thesis with the party's own, ever-renewed emphasis upon its very Frenchness, offers a way of understanding how the PCF can be so seemingly obtuse and obscurantist in its anachronistic emphasis on the contemporary historical centrality of the blue-collar working class. The PCF is the 'parti de la classe ouvrière', a claim that it makes sometimes even to the exclusion of the word 'communiste'.[48] The sociological grounds for the claim are weak — it has never been the party of most of that class, either in membership or in electors.[49] It has assuredly never been the party of most of the *women* of the working class,[50] and this is especially true in its ranks (the PCF makes strenuous efforts to ensure that congress delegates, cadres and parliamentary representatives reflect a favourable self-image, and one thus frequently finds disproportionate numbers of women and former industrial workers in such roles — although even then, in the most favourable circumstances, the number of female delegates at congresses oscillates around 25 to 30 per cent of the total). In some of its strongholds, such as Paris, the proletarian contingent among the party militants is notably drawn from the upper working strata ('labour aristocrats' in the English sense); in 1974 only 16 per cent of the Paris region militants were workers, and 78 per cent of these were *ouvriers qualifiés*.[51]

With the exception of the enduring bias towards men, these features of the party's make-up can all be accounted for by general trends in the French working population. Yet, like Father William, the PCF persists in a stance which is quite inappropriate to its age. Not merely does it insist that it *is* a proletarian party, in some demonstrable sense, but it asserts, as it has done since the 1930s, that the working class is the vehicle for revolutionary change and that the PCF is the motor that propels this vehicle, through its leading and self-conscious sectors. This is a vocabulary and an interpretation now mostly, if quietly, abandoned by other western communist and socialist parties. These have preferred instead to concentrate on capturing the support of the employees of the tertiary sector in particular, without whose votes they are condemned to steady decline. The PCF is not, of course, uninterested in these votes, but it remains adamant in its view of them, as in its schemes for students, intellectuals and peasants, as an adjunct. It is, as Waldeck Rochet put it in 1966, the working class which 'constructs the future'; others take their place alongside, but as allies, nothing more.[52]

The roots of this deeply-felt need to be linked to the proletariat, to measure all things by their proletarian content, to be 'workerist' in thought and deed,[53] lie in a special French paradox (although they have weak equivalents in other countries). Throughout the nineteenth and early twentieth centuries, and largely as a result of the presence of a republican movement that was political in character and revolutionary in origin, the French Left was exposed to the genuine possibility of alliance with the radical middle class, in joint opposition to the regime (as under the Second Empire) or in office during the early Third Republic. In order to carve out an identity of its own under these circumstances, the socialist Left developed, in various forms, a premium upon the rejection of all such alliances, which came to be seen and described as betrayal.

The extremism of this position was a particular result of the following circumstance: the French revolutionary Left had to come to terms with the fact that, in its *own* account, France was a country that had already undergone a bourgeois revolution and in which the task of a Marxist movement *could only be* the preparation and execution of a successor, socialist revolution. This contrasted sharply with the German or Italian experience, where the defence and furtherance of liberal gains and democratic rights (i.e. the achievements of an as yet incomplete 'bourgeois' revolution) were necessary and respectable, the precondition for any further advance. For *French* Marxists of the generation that founded the PCF, however, such emphasis on reform, on 'bourgeois democracy', was a trap and a retreat (a view given popular credibility by the memories, still fresh, of the Commune).

In ironic symbiosis with this outlook went the uncomfortable fact that the industrial proletariat in France was small and lacking in homogeneity; furthermore, the socialist movement had only a very weak purchase upon such industrial workers as there were. None the less, by this time a working-class presence was central to socialist thinking and to the logic of the socialists' growing divorce from the republican tradition. By projecting the achievements of the working-class movement back to 1830, the socialists and their successors could assert that the progress of democracy in France was causally and chronologically linked to the rise of the working class. By extrapolation, social advance in France would depend *exclusively* on the struggles of the workers (upon 'the concrete history of the workers' movement' – Marchais), and not at all on the fortunes of liberal democracy and its spokesmen. For those who saw things this way (and that excludes, for example, Jaurès and many independent socialists), what was offered them was a release from the oppressive mortgage of French republican history. At the same time, their own legitimacy was projected into the future as the heirs to the *true* tradition of revolution (or, more accurately, as the licensed representatives of those heirs).[54]

This helps explain the French communists' dependence upon a hypostasized working class. It also suggests why that class can remain at the centre of communist polemic and attention even as it declines in social and political significance. Here again is an instance of that easy interweaving of a Leninist conception of the avant-garde party and the pressures of the role into which local circumstances have cast the Marxist parties of France. The emotional cost of abandoning both of these strands — and it will now be seen why they cannot be abandoned piecemeal — continues to outweigh the putative advantage to be gained in electoral or political clout. This does not exclude the option of shifting from the Marxist emphasis on exploitation of the worker to the more ecumenical vocabulary of poor and rich when the occasion demands.[55] Nor need it preclude the PCF from promising that it and it alone can defend the interests of a wide range of 'losers' in contemporary monopoly capitalism, from small grocers to low-ranking civil servants and family farmers. But to those who have been mystified at why the PCF persistently reverts to type and reasserts its workerist essence and the unique historical claims of workers and party alike — and it *is* mystifying if one insists upon seeing all ideological pronouncements as interest-related[56] — the historical grounds upon which French Marxism arrived at its identification with the proletariat offer some prospect of enlightenment.

Thus to emphasize the weight of the past upon the present

character of the PCF is not to deny the changes that have taken place. The 'ouverture' of 1976 has at the very least encouraged the mild revisionism we have noted in party histories. Marchais did indeed abandon the concept of a period of 'dictatorship of the proletariat' and mildly critical reference can now be made to aspects of the Soviet and east European experience. However, the tacit disappearance of the 'dictatorship of the proletariat' can be traced to the 1940s, when many parties neglected the phrase, preferring instead to sing the praises of the model of a 'democracy of a new kind' which had replaced it in the Stalinist lexicon.[57]

What is more, the leadership's nods in the direction of reform provoked harsh internal criticism, and the most recent period has seen a reversion to type, with praise for the 'globally positive' record of the eastern bloc, expulsion of many of the leading would-be reformers and unstinting support for Soviet actions in Afghanistan and Poland. Much of this has to do with the strategic success of Mitterand in displacing the PCF into second place on the Left.[58] Losing its grip on the claim it had thought to establish as the natural party of protest and change in France, the PCF can only return to the one role for which there is no serious competition — and this means a retreat to the hardest and most 'workerist' of lines, since that is the way in which the party is most easily recognized and never matched.

One is bound to conclude that, notwithstanding the wealth of literature that offers to account for this strange trajectory — a literature now abating somewhat as interest in France shifts to Mitterand's achievement in re-creating a socialist alternative — the newcomer to the subject remains as ever best-advised to consult Kriegel for an understanding of it all. Professor Kriegel probably underestimates the domestic origins of the party (in part, doubtless, in reaction both to the high Stalinism of the years of her own membership, and the often absurd genealogical efforts of the faithful); she is most likely wrong in points of detail surrounding the party's birth; her thesis of a counter-society is of only limited application to the many young people (aged 17 to 25) who pass through the PCF, remaining less than five years and giving credence to its air of being a 'parti-passoir'.[59]

None the less, few political scientists have come close to her skill in predicting PCF behaviour, and none share her grasp of the central dynamo of the process, the communists' simultaneous sensitivity to ideology and wholly functional practice. Above all, Kriegel has

Judt, *History of the French Communist Party*   471

illustrated better than anyone the oddity contained in this sensitivity: weakest in the field of Marxist doctrine, the PCF is perforce
obliged to lean constantly and heavily in its most vulnerable
quarter. And this is where students of non-French Marxism would
do well to stay alert: if the Kriegelian historico-functionalist account of the PCF is empirically plausible, it points an unerring
finger in the direction of the general history of organized Marxist
parties and their aspirations since 1917. Other parties have only
avoided the French model by ceasing to be Marxist or marginaliz-
ing themselves utterly. It is a charmless reflection, that the study of
the thoroughly unappealing Communist Party of France may not
at all be the circumscribed and unique exercise one imagines, but
instead a mirror to the very history of Marxism itself (and why not
— was France not the paradigm case for the antecedent bourgeois
revolution?). From Marx to Marchais — a vertiginously descending
trajectory, perhaps, but the tracks are surely there.

Notes

This essay originated as a review article, considering the following titles:

Roger Bourderon et al.,   *Le PCF étapes et problèmes 1920-1972*, Paris, Editions
                           Sociales, 1981. 639pp.
Stéphane Courtois,   *Le PCF dans la guerre*, Paris, Editions Ramsay, 1980.
                           585pp.
Jacques Girault et al.,   *Sur l'implantation du PCF dans l'entre-Deux Guerres*,
                           Paris, Editions Sociales, 1977.
Philippe Robrieux,   *Histoire intérieure du parti communiste:* tome I,
                           1920-1945; tome II, 1945-1972, Paris, Fayard, 1980,
                           1981. 735pp.
Danielle Tartakowsky,   *Les premiers communistes français*, Paris, Presses de la
                           Fondation Nationale des Sciences Politiques, 1980.
                           216pp.

1. Jorge Semprun, *Quel Beau Dimanche* (Paris 1980), 99-100.
2. See Cornelius Castoriadis in *le Nouvel Observateur*, no. 895, janvier 1982.
3. Maurice Thorez, *Fils du Peuple* (five editions); also *Maurice Thorez, fils du peuple. La légende et la réalité* (Paris 1953), and Philippe Robrieux, *Maurice Thorez, Vie Secrète et Vie Publique* (Paris 1975). Memoirs from this period include the following: René Andrieu, *Les communistes et la révolution* (Paris 1968); Henri

Barbé et Pierre Célor, 'Le Groupe Barbé-Célor', in *Est & Ouest* Nos. 176, 177 (June-July 1957); Jules Humbert-Droz, *L'Oeil de Moscou à Paris* (Paris 1964); Auguste Lecoeur, *L'Autocritique Attendue* (St Cloud 1955). André Marty, *L'Affaire Marty* (Paris 1955).

Early studies still worth reading are: Alain Brayance (pseud.), *Anatomie du Parti Communiste français* (Paris 1952); Maurice Ceyrat (pseud.), *La trahison permanent. Parti communiste et politique russe* (Paris 1947); 'le Communisme en France', in *Bulletin de l'Association d'Études et d'Informations Politiques Internationales*, No. 126 (March 1955); Mario Einaudi et al., *Communism in Western Europe* (New York 1951); Val Lorwin, *The French Labor Movement* (Cambridge, Mass., 1954); Roy Macridis, 'The Immobility of the French Communist Party' in *Journal of Politics*, November 1958; Charles Micaud, *Communism and the French Left* (New York 1963). Alfred J. Rieber, *Stalin and the French Communist Party 1941-1947* (New York 1962). A faithfully conventional party-line account can be foun. Gérard Walter, *Histoire du Parti Communiste français* (Paris 1948).

4. Among the better-known works from this period are: Daniel Brower, *The Ne⌐. Jacobins. The French Communist Party and the Popular Front* (Ithaca, NY, 1968); J.-P. Brunet, *L'Enfance du Parti Communiste* (Paris 1972); David Caute, *Communism and the French Intellectuals* (London 1964); André Barjonet, *Le Parti Communiste français* (Paris 1969); Frédéric Bon et al., *Le Communisme en France* (Paris 1969); Fernando Claudin, *La Crise du mouvement communiste. Du Komintern au Kominform* (Paris 1972); L. Coutourier, *Les 'grandes affaires' du parti communiste français* (Paris 1972); Jacques Fauvet, *Histoire du PCF* (2 volumes, Paris 1964, 1965); François Fejtö, *The French Communist Party and the Crisis of International Communism* (Cambridge, Mass., 1967); Jedermann (pseud.), *La Bolchévisation du Parti Communiste Français* (Paris 1971); George Lichtheim, *Marxism in Modern France* (New York, 1966); Nicole Racine & Louis Bodin, *Le parti communiste français pendant l'entre-deux-guerres* (Paris 1972); Ronald Tiersky, *Le mouvement communiste en France 1920-1972* (Paris 1973); Robert Wohl, *French Communism in the Making, 1914-1924* (Stanford 1966).

5. See e.g. Giulio Ceretti, *A l'ombre des deux T* (Paris 1973); Pierre Daix, *J'ai cru au Matin* (Paris 1976); Dominique Desanti, *Les Staliniens* (Paris 1974); Henri Fiszbin, *Les bouches s'ouvrent* (Paris 1980); Auguste Lecoeur, *La Stratégie du Mensonge* (Paris 1980); Roger Pannequin, *Adieu, Camarades* (Paris 1977); Philippe Robrieux, *Notre Génération Communiste* (Paris 1977); Jean Rony, *Trente ans de Parti* (Paris 1978); Charles Tillon, *Un 'procès de Moscou' à Paris* (Paris 1971); *On Chantait Rouge* (Paris 1977).

Among the most recent works (and of variable quality) are Jean-Jacques Becker, *Le Parti Communiste veut-il prendre le pouvoir?* (Paris 1981); J.-P. Brunet, *St Denis la Ville Rouge* (Paris 1980); Pierre Daix, *La Crise du PCF* (Paris 1978); Olivier Duhamel & Henri Weber, *Changer le PC?* (Paris 1979); André Harris & Alain de Sedouy, *Voyage à l'Intérieur du Parti Communiste* (Paris 1974); R.W. Johnson, *The Long March of the French Left* (London 1981); Dominique Labbé, *Le Discours Communiste* (Paris 1977); Bernard Legendre, *Le Stalinisme français* (Paris 1980); Lilly Marcou, *Le Cominform* (Paris 1977); Jacqueline Mer, *Le parti de Maurice Thorez ou le bonheur communiste français* (Paris 1977); G. Molina & Y. Vargas, *Dialogue à l'intérieur du parti communiste* (Paris 1978); there are snippets of useful information in Roland Gaucher, *Histoire secrète du Parti Communiste Français* (Paris 1974), and some very good essays in Donald Blackmer & Sidney Tarrow, eds,

Judt, *History of the French Communist Party* 473

Communism in France and Italy (Princeton 1975).

6. Of Annie Kriegel's prolific (and occasionally overlapping) oeuvre, the follow-ing are of greatest interest (important books starred thus*): *Aux Origines du Com-munisme Français 1914-1920** (2 volumes, Paris 1964); *Le Congrès de Tours* (Paris 1964); *La Croissance de la CGT 1918-1921* (Paris 1966); *Le Pain et les Roses* (Paris 1968); *Les Communistes Français** (Paris 1970); *Communismes au miroir français* (Paris 1974); *Un autre communisme?* (Paris 1977); *Le communisme au jour le jour* (Paris 1979); 'The French Communist Party and the Fifth Republic', in Blackmer & Tarrow, op. cit.; 'Les Communistes français et le pouvoir', in Michelle Perrot & Annie Kriegel, *Le Socialisme Français et le Pouvoir* (Paris 1966), 97-215.

7. See e.g. Wohl, *French Communism in the Making,* op. cit.

8. On Guesdism and the Parti Ouvrier Français, see R.P. Baker, *Socialism in the Nord 1870-1924* (unpub. Phd dissertation, Stanford 1966); Edouard Dolléans, *Le Mouvement Ouvrier,* Vol.2 (Paris 1939); Jacques Girault, *Le guesdisme dans l'unité socialiste* (unpubl. diplôme d'études supérieures, Paris 1964); Patricia Hilden, *French Socialism and Women Textile Workers 1880-1914: A Regional Study, Lille, Roubaix, Tourcoing* (unpub. PhD dissertation, Cambridge 1981); Georges Lefranc, *Le mouvement socialiste sous la Troisième République,* Vol. 1, 1875-1920 (Paris 1963, 1977); Aaron Noland, *The Founding of the French Socialist Party 1893-1905* (Cambridge, Mass., 1956); Claude Willard, *Les Guesdistes* (Paris 1965).

9. *'Classe Contre Classe' La Question Française au IXe Exécutif et au VIe Con-grès de l'Internationale Communiste 1928* (Paris 1929), 30.

10. Marchais is quoted thus in *le Nouvel Observateur,* February 1981. For Thorez, see Legendre, *Le Stalinisme français,* 112; the full title of the 1964 publication is *Histoire du Parti Communiste Français (Manuel)* (Paris 1964). See p.7.

11. J.-P. Scot in Bourderon et al., *Le PCF étapes et problèmes,* 235.

12. For the approaches of Kriegel, Bon, Tiersky, see works cited in notes 4,6. For Georges Lavau, see especially 'The PCF, the State and the Revolution', in Blackmer & Tarrow, op. cit., 87-143, and 'Le Parti Communiste dans le système politique francaise', in Bon, *Le Communisme en France,* 7-81.

13. Examples include Jacques Duclos, *Mémoires* (6 volumes, Paris 1968-73); François Billoux, *Quand nous étions ministres* (Paris 1972); Léo Figuères, *Jeunesse Militante* (Paris 1971); Florimond Bonte, *Le Chemin de l'Honneur* (Paris 1950).

14. The contributors to the Bourderon volume are: Roger Bourderon, Jean Burles, Jacques Girault, Roger Martelli, Jean-Louis Robert, Jean-Paul Scot, Danielle Tartakowsky, Germaine Willard, Serge Wolikow. Other recent PCF publications include Jean Burles, *Le Parti Communiste dans la Société Française* (Paris 1979); Jean Elleinstein *Le P.C.* (Paris 1976); Germaine Willard et al., *De la Guerre à la Libération* (Paris 1972). Elleinstein is now persona non grata with the party.

15. *Histoire du réformisme en France depuis 1920* (2 volumes, Paris 1976); see Tartakowsky, *Les premiers communistes français,* 17. The same line is taken in Jean Fréville, *La Nuit finit à Tours* (Paris 1970 — originally published in 1960 as *Né du Feu).*

16. J.-L. Robert in Bourderon op. cit., 14-42; Girault, *Implantation,* 33-4; also Robert, Girault and others in the huge collective work, *Le Congrès de Tours* (Paris 1980).

17. See Brunet, *L'Enfance du Parti Communiste* and Racine & Bodin, *Le Parti Communiste Français pendant l'entre-deux-guerres.*

18. Tartakowsky, op. cit., 118.

19. Tartakowsky, op. cit., 155; also Tartakowsky in Bourderon, op. cit., 66-7. For alternative accounts of this period see Fauvet, *Histoire du PCF*, Vol. 1 and Robrieux, *Histoire Intérieure*, Vol. 1. Strictly speaking, Thorez became secretary of the Bureau Politique in July 1930, but his real control dates from 1931.

20. On the mysterious Fried, his role and the circumstances of his death during the war, see Robrieux, *Maurice Thorez*.

21. There is still no satisfactory English-language history of the Popular Front in France. Alternatives are Georges Lefranc's various general works (*Le Mouvement Socialiste sous la Troisième République*, Vol. 2, 1977; *Juin '36* (Paris 1966); *Histoire du Front Populaire* (Paris 1965)); *Léon Blum, Chef de Gouvernement* (Paris 1967); L. Bodin & J. Touchard, *Front Populaire 1936* (Paris 1961); Guy Bourdé, *La Défaite du Front Populaire* (Paris 1977); N. Greene, *Crisis and Decline, the French Socialist Party in the Popular Front Era*, (New York 1969); Daniel Guérin, *Front Populaire, Révolution Manquée* (Paris 1963, 1970); A. Prost, *La CGT à l'époque du Front Populaire* (Paris 1964); J.-P. Rioux, *Révolutionnaires du Front Populaire* (Paris 1973). There is also a special edition of *Le Mouvement Social* for janvier-mars, 1966.
On the origins of the turnabout in communist tactics, see in addition to the works listed above and in note 4, the following: L. Allen, 'The French Left and Russia: Origins of the Popular Front', in *World Affairs Quarterly*, XXX, 2, 1959; Georges Cogniot, 'Georges Dimitrov et le Parti communiste français', in *Cahiers d'histoire de l'Institut Maurice Thorez*, nos. 25-6, 1978; Jane Degras, 'United Front Tactics in the Comintern 1921-1928' in D. Footman, ed., *International Communism* (London 1960); Albert Vassart & Célie Vassart, 'The Moscow Origins of the French "Popular Front"', in M.M. Drachkovitch & B. Lazitch, eds., *The Comintern: Historical Highlights* (New York 1966).

22. Tartakowsky, op. cit., 160-1.

23. See Marcel Cachin in Cachin, Thorez & Marty, *The People's Front in France. Speeches at the Seventh World Congress of the Communist International* (New York 1935). Also Racine & Bodin, op. cit., 99.

24. *l'Humanité* 13 April 1934. See also *l'Humanité*, 6 April 1934.

25. Of these memoirs the most crucial are Charles Tillon, *On Chantait Rouge;* Tillon, *Les FTP* (Paris 1962); Auguste Lecoeur, *Le Parti Communiste Français et la Résistance, août 1939-juin 1941* (Paris 1968); A. Rossi (pseud. for A. Tasca), *Les communistes français pendant la drôle de guerre* (Paris 1951). See also Guy Rossi-Landi, *La drôle de guerre* (Paris 1971). Among official PCF accounts of the period are three collective efforts: *De la Guerre à la Libération* (Paris 1972); *l'Humanité Clandestine* (Paris 1975) and the dated *Le PCF dans la Résistance* (Paris 1967).

26. This letter is dated 10 December 1940. See Courtois, op. cit., 160. Note, too, the phrase 'La France aux français', traditionally associated in French politics, then and now, with the rhetoric of the far Right.

27. On the visceral communist hatred of Blum, see Annie Kriegel, 'Un phénomène de haine fratricide: Léon Blum vu par les communistes', in *Le Pain et les Roses*, 235-55; also, Kriegel, 'Les Communistes français et leurs juifs', in *Communismes au miroir français*, 177-97.

28. *Manuel*, 368-9.

29. See sources cited in note 25; also Claudie Delattre, 'L'attitude communiste à travers l'Humanité clandestine pendant l'occupation allemande: juin 1940-juin

Judt, *History of the French Communist Party*   475

1941', in *Mouvement Social*, 74, 1971.

30. At the Tenth Congress in June 1945, Thorez studiously avoided *all* such emphases and references.

31. This, if nothing else, emerges unambiguously from his memoirs — especially Vol. 3, part ii, and Vol. 4.

32. The Socialist National Council voted to support Ramadier's expulsion of the communist ministers by 2,529 to 2,125.

33. See in particular the memoirs of Jules Moch, *Une si longue vie* (Paris 1976); Moch was Minister of the Interior at the vital period. Also, R. Quilliot, *La SFI0 et l'Exercise du Pouvoir 1944-1958* (Paris 1972).

34. Yves Roucaute, *Le PCF et les sommets de l'Etat* (Paris 1981), 151.

35. See Eugenio Reale, *Avec Jacques Duclos, au banc des accusés à la réunion constitutive du Kominform* (Paris 1958). Note that it was the Yugoslav delegates, by an acute irony, who did the hatchet work for Moscow at this meeting. Hence, in large part, the vicious attacks by French communists in particular after Tito was expelled from the Soviet bloc — see, as a representative example of contemporary PCF vituperation, Dominique Desanti, *Masques et visages de Tito et des siens* (Paris 1949).

36. Here is Roger Martelli's justification for this absence of real change of line: 'Nul besoin d'exorcisme pour les historiens communistes, de repentir bruyant: ou alors il faudrait que tout le champ politique retentisse des plaintes de tous ceux — et ils sont légion — qui, eux aussi, "utilisèrent" et "torturèrent" la science historique'. Martelli in Bourderon et al., op. cit., 557. Only Martelli himself, and on rare occasions, refers in his sources to books and articles by non-party writers. His colleagues rely exclusively on articles that have appeared in *Cahiers d'histoire de l'Institut Maurice Thorez*, publications of Editions Sociales, the party publishing house, the oeuvres of Thorez and the memoirs of his colleagues.

37. Quoted in Robrieux, *Thorez*, 376.

38. See *Robrieux, Histoire Intérieure*, Vol. 2, 169, for the Desanti quotation. The 1966 data is from *Sondages* 1966, No. 1, 57-73. For Marchais see Robrieux, *Histoire Intérieure*, Vol. 2, 650-78.

39. Robrieux, op. cit., 682.

40. Thus Girault, again, in *Implantation*, p.11 converts a party dogma into a historiographical crusade: 'Nous voulons réagir contre l'historiographie classique qui accorde une importance démésurée au rôle de l'Internationale'.

41. The convenient device of asserting that the party line cannot be in error and that failures are thus the result of incomprehension, incompetence or worse by militants at the grass roots dates from Thorez's emergence in the early 1930s. It is worth noting that it has been adopted by historians for their own purposes — Girault (*Implantation*, p.22) blames the bottom ranks of the party for the disastrous results of the 1932 elections...

42. Compare the vital passage in the Party Statutes of 1926 and 1936 respectively:

'Acceptation obligatoire des décisions des organes supérieures du Parti par les organes inférieures, sévère discipline, exécution rapide et ponctuelle des décisions de l'Exécutif de l'I.C et des organes dirigeants du Parti' (1926).

'Acceptation...du Parti par toutes les organisations qui le composent, selon la discipline librement consentie par tous les communistes et qui fait la force de leur

Parti. Exécution ponctuelle des décisions de l'Exécutif de l'Internationale Communiste' (1936).

43. On the 'soft' view of the state, see Roucaute op. cit., 51, 53, 73. For the 'hard' line one has Thorez speaking to Renault workers in September 1962: '...vous avez devant vous le patron le plus implacable, l'État — instrument de la classe au pouvoir...' quoted in Roucaute, p.24. See also Lavau in Blackmer & Tarrow, op. cit.,

44. Quoted in Racine & Bodin, op. cit., 137. On the general theme of power and the state in France see, from a huge literature, Charles Debbasch, *L'Administration au Pouvoir* (Paris 1969); Jean-Noel Jeanneney, *Francois de Wendel en République: l'argent et le pouvoir, 1914-1940* (Paris 1976). Guy Palmade, *Capitalisme et capitalistes français au dix-neuvième siècle* (Paris 1961); Ezra Suleiman, *Politics, Power and Bureaucracy in France* (Princeton 1974). A good general introduction to the theme is Jack Hayward, *The One and Indivisible French Republic* (London 1973).

45. On the SPD in Wilhelmine Germany, see Dick Geary, 'The German Labour Movement', in *European Studies Review*, VI, iii, 1976; also Geary, *European Labour Protest 1848-1939* (London 1981) and Dieter Groh, *Negative Integration und Revolutionärer Attentismus* (Frankfurt am Main 1973).

46. On the inter-war SFIO, see D.N. Baker, 'Seven Perspectives on the Socialist Movement of the Third Republic', in *Reflexions Historiques*, I, ii, 1974; Tony Judt, *La Reconstruction du Parti Socialiste 1921-1926* (Paris 1976); Gilbert Ziebura, *Léon Blum et le Parti Socialiste* (Paris 1967).

47. There is still remarkably little on French Marxism in English — and little of value in French. Enduringly intelligent is George Lichtheim, *Marxism in Modern France* (New York 1966). See also Lichtheim, *From Marx to Hegel* (London 1971), 142-59, 182-200; Perry Anderson, *Considerations on Western Marxism* (London 1976); Leszek Kolakowski, *Main Currents of Marxism*, Vol. 3 (Oxford 1978), 324-34, 478-523; and of course Edward Thompson's brilliantly polemical 'The Poverty of Theory', in E.P. Thompson, *The Poverty of Theory* (London 1978), 193-399.

48. See Labbé, *Le Discours communiste*, especially 29, table 2. In his 1972 preface to the communist edition of the Programme Commun, Marchais writes; 'Le Parti Communiste...est le parti révolutionnaire de la classe ouvrière....*En conséquence* [my emphasis], sa doctrine, ses méthodes de lutte et d'organisation lui donnent les moyens de jouer ce rôle d'avant'garde de l'union populaire.' Programme Commun de Gouvernement (Paris 1972), 45.

49. In 1962, industrial workers were 51 per cent of the PCF electorate. In 1952 they had been 38 per cent of it, in 1968 they would be 49 per cent.

50. Both as members and voters, women are less attracted to the PCF than men. In 1978, for instance, the voting preference of women was firstly for the Socialists, then for the Gaullists, thirdly the Giscardiens and only lastly for the PCF (see H. Penniman, ed., *The French National Assembly Elections of 1978*, Washington 1980, 69). The percentage of the communist vote coming from women actually *fell* during the Fourth and early Fifth Republics. This is not surprising — the party's attention to women in this period was confined to an outspoken opposition to birth-control, on the grounds that contraception was a form of class oppression, designed by neo-Malthusians to weaken the revolutionary forces in society... See the many pam-

Judt, *History of the French Communist Party* 477

phlets by Jeanette Vermeersch from this period, and the notable article by Marie-Claude Vaillant-Coutourier in *Cahiers du Communisme,* août 1952.

51. See Platone & Subileau, 'Les militants communistes à Paris' in *Revue Francaise de Science Politique,* XXV, v, 1975, 837-70. The average percentage of women in the major federations at the end of the 1940s was between 11 and 14 per cent. In other areas, sample percentages of women members are Alpes-Maritimes 11 per cent. Allier 7 per cent, Côtes du Nord 7 per cent, Corrèze 5 per cent; see Robrieux, *Histoire Intérieure,* Vol.2, 211.

52. It is noteworthy that the PCF's proletarian image works to its advantage in certain respects. In a recent study in Bordeaux, 33 per cent of the members of the local PCF federation claimed that they joined the party because of its identification with the working class. What is perhaps even more revealing, one-third of the party members whom the investigators classed as 'cadres moyens' and three-quarters of those they classified as 'employés' called themselves working-class in that same survey! See Jacques Lagroye et al., *Les Militants Politiques dans trois partis politiques* (Paris 1976), 78, 91.

53. On the 'workerist' imperative that can be traced through the various editions of *Fils du Peuple* and the changes made over time, see Robrieux, *Thorez,* 17.

54. The recasting of the 'tradition of revolution' into a popular, then a proletarian one, can be traced through the historiography of the French Revolution, from Jaurès's *Histoire Socialiste,* through the work of Mathiez, Lefebvre, Labrousse, to the Soboulian synthesis (under constant attack since the late 1960s). On this see William Doyle, *Origins of the French Revolution* (Oxford 1980), 7-41, and G. Ellis, 'The "Marxist Interpretation" of the French Revolution', in *English Historical Review,* XC, 3, 1978, 353-76. It is no accident that Mathiez, Labrousse and Soboul were all closely associated with the PCF.

55. But see Louis Althusser's attack on this sort of opportunism in *Ce Qui Ne Peut Durer dans le Parti Communiste* (Paris 1978).

56. This is a weakness in R.W. Johnson's otherwise absorbing account in *The Long March of the French Left* (London 1981).

57. J.-P. Scot, in Bourderon op. cit., 271, notes that Thorez tended to see as functionally identical the old concept of a proletarian dictatorship and the 'new democracies' of eastern Europe.

58. One aspect of Mitterand's achievement may be the end of a sixty-year inferiority complex towards the PCF on the part of French socialists. A recent study suggests that 47 per cent of socialists in the mid-1970s judged the PCF to be 'tout à fait efficace', but only 27 per cent of them said the same of their own party! See Denis Lacorne, *Les Notables Rouges* (Paris 1980), 108-9.

59. In the mid-1970s the turnover rate was around 14 per cent; in 1977 some 50 per cent of the membership of the PCF in the Paris region had been in the party less than three years.

478   *European Studies Review*

Tony Judt

is Fellow and Tutor of St Anne's College, Oxford, and a University Lecturer in Politics. He
is the author of *Socialism in Provence
1871-1914* (Cambridge 1979), and has also
published various articles on the French Left,
rural politics and social history. He is currently
preparing a collection of essays on aspects of
socialism and the labour movement in France
from the 1840s to the present.

[15]

Does Regional Government Work? The Experience of Italy, France and Spain

MICHAEL KEATING

WHAT IS REGIONAL GOVERNMENT?

Since 1970, regional governments have been established in Italy, France and Spain and have been widely and recurrently advocated in Britain and other western European countries. While the powers, status and circumstances of regional institutions vary considerably among the three countries, the impulses leading to their establishment have a great deal in common. In each case, we are talking of a new set of institutions on a larger scale than traditional local government and occupying an intermediate place between central and local government. Distinct on the one hand from local government in terms of area, functions and the degree of autonomy envisaged for it, regional government is also distinguishable from federalism, at least in the formal sense, in that the regions do not share sovereignty with the national state and their powers are handed down to them from national parliaments. This definition is, admittedly, both formal and a little vague; but one aim of the paper is to establish whether regional government does have its own characteristics. Specifically, it examines how regional government has come into being; how far regional governments have established autonomous political systems around themselves; how far regional governments have succeeded in formulating and pursuing their own policies; and what is the weight of regional governments in intergovernmental relations. In the absence of a theory of regional government in the contemporary western European state, concepts must be drawn in rather eclectic fashion from the study of local government, federalism and intergovernmental relations. It is hoped, however, that further theoretical and empirical work in the years to come, together with the opportunity to observe the dynamics of regional government and regional-central relations over a longer period, will lead to the development of viable theories of regional government as a feature of the contemporary west European state.

Governance: An International Journal of Policy Administration, Vol. 1, No. 2, Apr. 1988 (pp. 184–204), © 1988, Research Committee on the Structure and Organization of Government of the International Political Science Association. ISSN 0952–1895

WHY REGIONAL GOVERNMENT?

A number of factors have brought the question of the need for a regional level of government and administration onto the political agenda in western European countries in the post-war period. An important one has been the need of the central state itself for systems of planning and intervention to pursue its goals of full employment, growth and welfare, particularly in the expansionist years from the mid-1960s to the mid-1970s. Initially, regional development policies in all three countries were organized on a centralized basis, the aim being to satisfy national needs for balanced and non-inflationary growth by bringing into use idle resources in under-developed and declining regions while satisfying regional aspirations for higher living standards. Once regional policy goes beyond a mere system of incentives for industrial location (the British model), however, machinery is required to design and implement it and so, from the 1980s, Italy, France and Spain saw systems of regional administration and planning emerge as arms of the centralized state. Moving from centralized regional *administration* to regional *government* is, of course, a significant step but one which was seen by central administrators in France and Italy and even in Spain (Garcia 1979) as a logical extension of the planning philosophy, tapping regional energies, engaging the collaboration of regional elites in planning and development and freeing the central state from the irksome business of detailed intervention on the periphery. There is undoubtedly a strong technocratic bias to this line of argument, an assumption that central and regional energies will necessarily be united behind common goals of economic expansion and development while skirting around the problem of political conflict but, in the circumstances of full employment prevailing in the 1960s, regional development was seen as a non-zero-sum game in which everyone would win – developing regions through the provision of employment, boom regions through the relief of congestion and pressure on infrastructure and housing, and the national economy through relieving inflationary pressures and bringing into use idle capacity. It thus had a strong appeal, not only to administrators and planners but also to social democrats and political centrists who sought to reconcile the aims of growth with equity and democratic participation.

Regional government has also been sought by decentralists seeking to transform the state and shift power from the center in the interests of democracy and pluralism. With larger areas, populations and resource bases and being more in tune with the facts of modern economic and social geography, regions are seen as having a greater capacity for autonomous action over a wider range of functions than the traditional units of local government. In particular, regional government was seen as being essential if economic and industrial powers were to be decentralized, since local government was at too small a scale to address these issues.

Political oppositions have also favored regional governments as a power basis for themselves. In Spain, the rigid centralization of the Franco regime created in reaction a close association between democratization and regional decentralization. In Italy, the Communists switched from centralism to ardent regionalism when they were expelled from government in 1948 (Villari 1981a) while, in France, the stranglehold of the right on the institutions of the central state was a key factor in converting the Socialists to regional government (Keating and Hainsworth 1986). At the same time, a variety of newly emerging social and political forces have organized on a regional level, seeing it as the scale of unit best adapted to their demands, notably for planning and development, and also as an arena not already colonized by existing power-holders. So France in the 1950s saw the emergence of regional expansion committees while in Italy the demands of industrialists for coherent development policies in the South had produced the policy of *consorzi*, local and regional planning committees (Villari 1981b).

Another source of demands for regional government has been the existence of cultural and ethnic minorities with historic demands for self-determination. The re-emergence of this issue has been a feature of many post-war European states and in our cases has been marked in Britanny, Corsica, Languedoc, Sicily, Sardinia, Catalonia, Galicia and the Basque country, to name only the most prominent examples. This in itself is a complex phenomenon since minority nationalism may be reactionary and *passéiste* or may be aligned with modernizing forces. The doctrine of regional autonomy does not in itself say anything about social or economic issues and regionalists may often try to keep these questions off the political agenda as divisive, or to be postponed until the achievement of autonomy.

Opposed to regional government, we have a variety of forces. There has been a marked fear of regional government among nationally-based administrators and politicians, concerned that regional government would indeed be independent of the center and undermine both national policies and their own power bases. Local politicians, territorial representatives and territorial administrators have often been scarcely less hostile, fearing for their power bases and their monopoly of representation. Local elites have also worried that regional governments, being closer to the ground, might be more interfering than the center. In the case of France, there has also been a preference on the part of local politicians for dealing with the administrative representatives of the state than with fellow politicians who are seen as rivals and as less trustworthy. In Italy, the Christian Democrats turned against regional government as soon as they had consolidated their grip on central power in 1948 while in Spain it goes without saying that the authoritarian Franco regime could not contemplate a dispersal of power.

Ideological opposition to regional government has come from a variety of sources. The "jacobin" philosophy is strong in all three countries. Long detached from its precise historical referents, this now describes an attitude of unyielding centralization based upon the unity of the sovereign people. Diversity and pluralism are seen as undermining national sovereignty and the equality of citizenship; concessions to regional demands based upon cultural or ethnic ideas are particularly dangerous in this regard. The "provinces" are seen as bastions of an archaic social order which must be swept away in the name of progress. So democracy, far from demanding decentralization, requires centralized government (Mény 1974). The Jacobin philosophy is French in invention, a nineteenth century caricature of the spirit of the revolution, but its persistence among republicans of left, right and center, in all three countries reflects an underlying unease about the foundations of national unity.

Social Democrats have often been suspicious of regional autonomy as a threat to equity, the welfare state and national economic and industrial planning. Even when the French Socialist Party, the Spanish PSOE and the Italian Socialists have supported regional government, the commitment has coexisted uneasily with policies in the economic and social spheres which are clearly centralist. Marxists have taken a variety of positions, reflecting their frequently ambiguous attitude to the state itself. On the one hand has been a view that regionalism has been a device to shift power out of the hands of the centralized state before the workers can get their hands on it. This has sometimes been combined with a disdain for the underdeveloped peripheral areas which, under regional home rule, could never shake off feudalism. So, in Italy, the Communist Party long held to the doctrine of the *vento del nord* (Villari 1981a), the wind from the north which would lead the South through capitalism to socialism. The French left long regarded the periphery as a hotbed of reaction to be liberated by Paris and similar attitudes have recurred in the history of the Spanish left. On the other hand, as social and political movements with strong popular bases and progressive ideologies have developed in several peripheral regions, the parties of the left have had to accommodate them. The "new" left in all three countries is less tied to Jacobin notions or the centralist traditions of trade union organization and more receptive to participative and decentralist visions. So there has been a rapproche-ment between the left and regionalism, though acute tensions remain on the issue within the parties of the left.

Opposition to regionalism has also come from conservatives fearful for national unity and the maintenance of traditional power structures – though this has equally led conservatives on occasion to support regions – in Third Republic France, in Italy in the mid 1940s and in parts of Spain at the turn of the century.

So regional government has been surrounded by political argument, has aroused both hopes and fears; and, even within the same political or social groups, indeed within the same individuals, has provoked contradictory reactions. Powerful forces within governments have wanted and needed it but at the same time feared it. It is this which explains the halting experiments over the years, as state elites have sought to obtain the advantages of regional government without conceding power and as the political stakes underlying the issue have become clearer. Franco's Spain provides an extreme example, with the National Plans of 1964, 1968 and 1972 desperately avoiding even using the term "region" though their whole thrust implied the need for a regional level to secure their implementation (Cuadrado 1981), while in both France and Italy the tension between centralized control and the need for a regional dimension of government was acute throughout the 1950s and 1960s.

ESTABLISHMENT OF REGIONAL GOVERNMENT

What we have seen, as a result of these contradictory pressures, is the emergence, in Italy and France, of a "minimalist" version of regional government and, in Spain, a battle between minimalist and more expansive versions.

In Italy, the constitution of 1947 provided for regional government as part of the creation of a new type of liberal democratic regime, a break both from fascism and the centralized and clientilistic political system which had preceded it. Regionalism was tied in closely to the reformist aspirations of the Christian Democrats while the less progressive elements in Christian Democracy saw it as a means of resisting a possible left-wing government in Rome. It was this latter consideration which led the Communists to oppose regional government until the *volte face* of 1948 when the Christian Democrats entrenching them-selves in power at the center on the basis of fervent anti-communism, turned against it, while the Communists came to support it. It was opposition from the left which had removed extensive regional powers

over industry and commerce from the constitution (Good 1976).
Meanwhile, only the "special status" regions in the border and island
areas where there were strong autonomist, separatist and irridentist
movements, had been established. Although still in their anti-
regionalist mood, the Communists had gone along with this, not
without some soul-searching. The case of Sicily was particularly
painful. It was apparent that a self-governing Sicily would be a
stronghold of the clericalist right and the *blocco agrario*; the separatist
movement was supported by the most reactionary opponents of social
and land reform (not to mention the Mafia). On the other hand,
autonomism appeared to be supported by the Sicilian masses, so the
Communists felt obliged to go along with it in order not to lose all
contact with them (Zagarrio 1981; Modica 1972).

Christian Democrat resistance to activating the regional clauses of
the constitution persisted through the 1950s and 1960s, as the party
strengthened its grip on the apparatus of the state at central and local
levels and through the *sottogoverno*, the jungle of state and quasi-
governmental agencies, including those for regional development. It
was the formation of the first center-left governments after 1963 which
brought the issue of planning, and hence regional planning, to the
fore. By the late 1960s, industrialists, as represented in the *Confin-
dustria* were urging regional government as a means of reforming and
cleaning up public administration (Rotelli 1973), as were reformist
elements in the Christian Democrat Party. There was thus a wide
consensus in favour of bringing in regions; but less as a means of
enhancing autonomy than as a way of improving the workings of the
Italian state. The Communists, while supporting regions and seeing
left-controlled regions as an instrument for pursuing the political
struggle against the right, were very cautious about giving them
substantial powers. More widely, regions were seen by some thinkers
as a substitute for the alternation of power which had proved
unattainable in postwar Italy, a means of creating a real political
dialogue. The purpose of regions was thus seen in terms of
modernizing and transforming the Italian state and political system
itself, a monumental task; while the implementation of the transition,
in the absence of alternation in power, remained in the hands of the
existing political elites, notably the Christian Democrat machine.

In France, there was a widespread antipathy to regions in the
postwar years, both on the left, with its traditional Jacobinism and
among Gaullists with their visions of French national unity. All traces
of war-time regional administration were removed; but it was not long
before the Fourth Republic found itself using the regional level for
planning and coordination of local administration. From the late

1950s, *comités d'expansion économique* too, sprung up in various regions, challenging the existing local elites entrenched in the local government system and pressing for planning and development strategies at the regional level (Philipponneau 1982). As regional development became a more insistent theme of state policy, the Gaullists established the *CODER*, regional development committees largely nominated by central government and including the leaders of the *comités d'expansion*, the aim being to incorporate the *forces vives* into institutions which would be subordinate to central policy, the instrument for implementing central policy in the regions rather than a means of promoting regional autonomy (Grémion 1976). Disillusionment rapidly set in. In 1969, de Gaulle, in a frontal attack on the system of territorial representation, proposed the establishment of regional councils and a reform of the Senate. It was the latter which particularly upset the local notables who helped to ensure the defeat of the proposals at the referendum of 1969.

De Gaulle's successor, Pompidou, was more circumspect. Accepting the need for regional government, he entrusted it to the very *notables* who most feared it, setting up regional councils indirectly elected from *départements* and cities and including all the members of Parliament and senators in each region. Regions were thus absorbed in the traditional French system of territorial representation, in which layers of government are inextricably linked through the *cumul des mandats* or multiple holding of elective offices. As nobody was directly elected as a regional councillor but all were there by virtue of some other office, regions could not present a challenge to the existing power holders. Even the boundaries of regions were chosen so as not to encourage autonomist demands, being based on the earlier *Circonscriptions d'Action Régionale* which not only cut across traditional provincial loyalties but also failed to correspond to contemporary social and economic realities.

By the 1970s, the left had been converted to regional government but this coexisted with a strong centralist bias and vested interests in the existing units of local government. So the Communist Party could insist on the need for regions but for strong centralized government at the same time (e.g. Giard and Schiebling 1982), while in the Socialist Party regionalists contested with Jacobins and *notables* (Keating and Hainsworth 1986). Failing to agree on priorities for decentralization, the Socialist program proposed strengthening all three tiers of local government, commune, *département* and region. The result was that, when the Socialists came to power in 1981, their first decentralization law provided for the direct election of the regions, but the implementation of this was postponed to literally the last moments of the

DOES REGIONAL GOVERNMENT WORK?   191

government's life, the general election of 1986. Meanwhile, the *département* had not only survived as an institution of local government but, in comparison with the region, has been greatly strengthened.

In Spain, the establishment of regions owes more to a genuine decentralist impulse, the demands of the "historic" regions of Catalonia, the Basque country and Galicia and the belief among the anti-Franco opposition that regional decentralization was an essential element in the restoration of democracy. Within the historic regions, however, there existed a variety of competing autonomist traditions, emphasizing both different degrees of autonomy and differing social and economic interests. To preserve a semblance of consistency, the constitution laid down that all regions could attain autonomy, of either a weak or a strong form. The historic regions could proceed to the strong form in one stage but other regions would have to go through an elaborate process involving two referendums and absolute majorities of all voters in each province. The whole process was not automatic but depended on initiatives from below. So rapidly did the process of autonomy develop, in fact, that much of it was in place before the final approval of the national constitution (Garcia 1980). The main political parties of the early post-Franco era, the centrist UCD and the socialist PSOE followed rather than led the autonomist trend which appeared at one stage to put in question the very nature of the Spanish state itself. The state might indeed have ended up as a residual entity after regional powers had been carved out; alternatively, some observers saw an inevitable move toward some sort of federalism, in practice if not in law.

By the early 1980s, though, the central parties had begun to get a grip on the process. The UCD initially appeared surprised by the spread of the movement for regional autonomy and, once the statutes for the historic regions were out of the way, sought to slow it down, trying to sabotage the Andalusian attempt to achieve the stronger form of autonomy (Porras 1980). PSOE and the Communists had both long supported the right to autonomy of the historic regions and by the 1970s PSOE's policy was for a federal republic, based on the self-determination of the Catalan, Basque and Galician peoples. Much of this, though, was the product of the clandestine Franco years in which compromises between peripheral nationalists and other opposition forces had been both expedient and (given the distance from power) relatively easy. As the Franco regime collapsed, though, the Jacobin element in PSOE reasserted itself (Blas 1978) and by 1982 Socialist leader Felipe Gonzalez was supporting LOAPA, the measure introduced by the UCD government to limit regional autonomy and harmonize the different forms which it was taking, on the ground that

MICHAEL KEATING

autonomy was not a pact between each region and the state but flowed from the sovereign will of the Spanish people (Gonzalez 1982). This implied decentralization as a reform within the unitary state framework on the French or Italian model rather than a move towards federalism with its implication that the regions possess an element of sovereignty, though the Spanish state is confronted with centrifugal tendencies much stronger than in the other two countries.

THE PERFORMANCE OF REGIONAL GOVERNMENT

To have the basis for an assessment of the performance of regional government, we need to have a well-defined set of criteria. Yet, given the multiple objectives of regionalism, it is arguable that regional government cannot possibly "succeed" in satisfying all of them. There are several dimensions on which we could analyze regional government's performance but here I propose to look at just three themes: the status of regional government; the scope for autonomous action of regional government; and the weight of regional government in negotiation and bargaining with other levels of government.

There is some argument as to whether regional government should be considered a separate category distinct from both federalism and local government. Some observers, such as Bogdanor (1986, p.44) maintain that the distinction between federalism and regional devolution is of little more than formal significance since regional government "serves to create a new locus of political power". Students of federalism, for their part, have also conceded a convergence of the concepts since the vital traditional distinguishing feature of federalism – the independent exercise of constitutionally separated functions – has given way to complex patterns of interdependence, collaboration and conflict (Nice 1987). Frenkel (1986), on the other hand, wishes to retain the distinction between federalism and decentralization for the important reason that, historically, federalism has been a *centralizing* measure, to draw together disparate territories. So the vital part of the federal process is the creation of a central government, not the wrenching away of powers from an existing center. These are not purely definitional issues. They are empirical ones, susceptible to testing. So we can test Bogdanor's view by examining the power relationships around regional government. We have already noted some factors supporting Frenkel's view. In France and Italy, where central governments existed and had established their own networks of territorial support, the process of regionalization was necessarily difficult. The hostility of existing political and bureaucratic elites explains why in many respects regional government has been subordinated to the logic of the existing power systems. This is less true of Spain, where the transition from the Franco regime made necessary the construction of a new state at both central and local levels, in which regions were able to find a place. Even here, though, there was strong resistance to radical decentralization on the part of the military as well a bureaucratic and political elites. Indeed, the attempted coup of 1981 was in part responsible for the slowing down of the regionalization process and the LOAPA proposals.

A point of agreement among all students of decentralization is that interdependence among tiers is an inescapable feature of modern government, so that the question of the status of regions hinges on the effective power of each level within the complex patterns of intergovernmental relations. This, in turn, as Rhodes (1981) has shown, has several dimensions with power resources taking several forms. Here I shall examine the power resources of regional governments in constitutional, functional, political and adminstrative terms.

In constitutional terms, the formal distinction between federalism and devolution, based on the division of powers, is not without importance, the point being not that the lower level in a federal system can exercise its powers independently but that these powers, being entrenched constitutionally, constitute a power resource, forcing the center to negotiate in putting together policies and programs across a wide range of activity. As each level needs powers and resources which are the property of the other, there is a balance of power (though it may be tilted in favor of one level or the other). In none of our cases is this feature present, thus the center can often resolve issues unilaterally, where in a federal system it would be obliged to negotiate. This is most clear in France, where regions are not mentioned in the constitution but are the creatures of statute. It is also true of Italy where, although the regions feature in the constitution, their establishment and the devolution of powers to them depend on acts of the national parliament. Thus parliament, under the doctrine of the supremacy of national law, has continued to legislate on matters of regional jurisdiction (Cammelli 1980). In Spain, much effort has been expended in seeking an adequate term for the new regime, neither unitary nor federalist. Under the Second Republic, in the 1930s, the term *Estado Integral* was coined but the practical content of this formula had not been worked out by the start of the civil war. The 1978 constitution is inconsistent and, in places, confused. The expression *Estado de las Autonomías* has entered general use but again only time will tell what this new formula amounts to in practice. Already, there is evidence that the center is prepared to use its over-ride powers extensively in matters such as educational reform, though it is meeting considerable political resistance in the autonomous communities.

Whether or not they are constitutionally entrenched, the legislative and administrative powers devolved to regional governments are naturally of key importance. The distinction between legislative and administrative devolution is difficult to draw on a comparative basis, given the different boundaries between legislative and administrative activity in different countries – for example, in Italy there is a greater tendency to regulate by legislation than in most countries so that much of the legislative competence of regional councils should be seen as paralleling administrative activity elsewhere. There is not space here to enumerate and compare the functional responsibilities of regional governments in the three countries, but an important issue is whether functions are defined widely or narrowly. Notwithstanding what has been said about interdependence, a wide definition of functions could allow regions a substantial degree of autonomy within the relevant policy fields. A narrow definition, with regions only intervening in restricted areas of policy functions would reinforce interdependence. Where the preponderant influence lies with the center, this inter-dependence leads to regional *dependence*. It also leads to the fragment-ation of regional government as the several departments take their policy lead from the corresponding parts of central government. This tendency has been noted in Italy, encouraged by the way in which functions were handed down. Instead of legislative responsibility for a function being handed over, the administration of existing pro-grams was handed over first, and then a legislative power narrowly defined to correspond to this, thereby inhibiting innovation (Merloni 1982). Bureaucratic interests at the center have continued to ensure that sectoral perspectives prevail, with detailed laws regulating devolved matters (Bassanini 1985; Salerno 1983).

In France, the regions established in 1972 were denied any functional responsibilities of their own and could act only through other agencies, notably local councils and public corporations. Under the recent decentralization program, they have been given their own functions but these are tightly limited so as not to trespass on the power of existing central and local administrations. In Spain, the constitution potentially allows a wide scope for devolution, though in a distinctly confused manner. Each region must have its own statute of autonomy, negotiated between regional representatives and the central govern-ment and approved by the central Cortes. The constitution stipulates a list of items which can be devolved and a list of items which remain under the exclusive jurisdiction of the state. It then goes on to say that any item not exclusively reserved to the state can be devolved to a region in its autonomy statute. In addition, through organic laws, the state can devolve to the regions powers over items which the constitution reserves for the exclusive competence of the center. Not surprisingly all this has given rise to much argument, though the fact remains that the powers are defined more widely than in France or Italy.

The scope for functional devolution of course varies from one field to another and has become severely restricted in the area of cash welfare benefits where national considerations of equity have prevailed, and in that of economic and industrial policy where regional initiatives might impinge on national priorities or those of other regions. Yet we have noted that one of the origins of the call for regional government was the need to translate national development programs into spatial terms. This was to be done through the mechanism of planning – indeed, it has been argued in both the French and Italian cases that the purpose of regional government is not the administration of services directly but is to do with *planning* and *programming* of investments and services to be undertaken largely by other agencies. Just how elected regional government was to be reconciled with national economic planning was an unresolved question but one which, in the conditions of relative consensus and of growth of the 1960s and early 1970s was sidelined. The decline of planning in the 1970s and the end of the Keynesian consensus on economic management put the vision of regions as cooperative partners in national development planning at risk and greatly inhibited their development in both France and Italy. Nor was planning assisted by the delineation of the regions, especially in France. Some, like Nord – Pas de Calais, were relatively homogeneous, under clear party control and able to formulate priorities and place their resources behind them. In other cases, regions do not correspond to economic or social units but are mere federations of *départements*. In the late 1970s, the French Socialists sought to reconcile their new policy of regionalism with their proposals to revive national planning, envisioning a decentralized planning process in which there would be a genuine dialogue between central and regional government. Regions would be encouraged to adopt rational priorities by financial incentives but would have a say in determining these priorities and would in addition be allowed to pursue their independent priorities as long as these were not in conflict with national ones. The process of negotiation, it was recognized, would be a political matter and not a mere question of reconciling technical norms. Thus were the needs of central policy, regional autonomy and central-regional coordination to be reconciled. This was put into effect for the production of the Ninth Plan but the Plan itself was largely by-passed in the major industrial restructurings of the mid-1980s and, in many cases, regional plans were merely the local expression of national sectoral priorities, expressed so as to extract the maximum resources from the center. In the case of Languedoc–Roussillon, for example, officials of the regional council insist that, as there is not a model of the regional economy available, the regional plan is necessarily composed largely of the local end of national sectoral plans (Keating, 1986). What this shows is that regional planning can only be as strong as the technical means and the political, administrative and financial powers which it can mobilize.

Finance of course is an important factor in determining both the scope for independent regional action and the weight of regions in intergovernmental bargaining. National treasuries are always reluctant to concede independent taxation powers, justifying their case by the need for national economic and financial management policies. In France, regions were subject to a taxation ceiling before their direct election and, while they have now been given greater freedom, their tax base remains very restricted (Keating and Hainsworth 1986). In Italy, regions derive 96% of their funds from central grants, of which 70% is tied to specific programs (Buglione and France 1984). In Spain, regions have varying taxation regimes, with the Basque country succeeding, against strong central opposition, in retaining its traditional *concierto economico*, allowing it to raise its own taxes and pass on an agreed sum to Madrid. Elsewhere, taxation powers are more limited.

Bureaucratic resources are another important element in determining the scope and power of regional governments and here again there have been powerful recentralizing forces working against the spirit of devolution. In France, the regions of 1972 were not allowed their own administration, having to act through the prefect, the field administration of central departments, and local councils. While the more inventive regions managed to evade this restriction to some degree by setting up "arm's length" operations for research and policy development, it obviously prevented the development of strong regional government. Since 1981, there has been some transfer of staff but civil servants have striven hard to preserve the unity of their *corps* and the reformed statute for local and regional administrators is highly centralist in effect (Keating and Hainsworth 1986). In Italy, administrative staff were transferred along with their functions but the interlinking of politics and administration especially in Christian Democrat controlled areas through patronage and clientism has emptied this of much of its significance, since patronage and clientism are centralizing forces sustaining existing political elites and their practices. Clientilism apart, Italian bureaucracy is characterized by a highly legalistic approach which concentrates on individual cases at the expense of policy or policy coherence (Dente 1985). Indeed, the Italian intellectual obsession with legalism has greatly hindered the debate about regions and their performance generally. In this as in other respects it is too early to make a judgement about Spain but control over the bureaucracy has been a source of conflict and there do appear to be recentralizing tendencies within the state administration.

The existing pattern of territorial representation and administration can also be an obstacle to regions exercising real power. In all three countries, it has proved impossible to suppress an existing tier of government in order to create the new one. We have noted the resilience of the French *département* despite the fact that many advocates of regional reform had envisioned it giving way to the region. Similarly, in Italy, the provinces have been retained and, in 1982, strengthened, and have remained part of the power base of party politicians. In both cases, all levels deal directly with the central government. In Spain, the town and provincial councils are guaranteed under the constitution, along with the autonomous communities (regions) and, except in Navarre and the Basque country, deal directly with Madrid for most matters including finance. In those cases where the regions comprise a single province, matters are simpler but elsewhere there is potential for conflict. In Catalonia, attempts by regional government to control the provinces have been struck down in the constitutional court. In all three countries, central government has also maintained its territorial administrators dealing with all levels of local government. Certainly, the role of Italian prefects, French prefects (renamed *commissaires de la république*) and Spanish civil governors has been restricted but they remain a central presence in the localities and a source of advice and support to local councils in their efforts to resist regional control.

Many of thee problems can be overcome if regions do indeed become a new locus for political power. This in turn depends on the attitudes and structures of the political parties, the behavior of politicians and electors and the wider interest group formations around regional governments. In both France and Italy, regions have by and large been taken over by existing political elites and subjected to traditional political practices. In France, the indirect election for regions guaranteed that regional councillors would by definition be *cumulards* holding office only by virtue of a power base somewhere else. The lack of direct election not only prevented the emergence of new elites and reduced the democratic legitimacy of regional councils; by presenting regions as federations of *départements*, it also encouraged the practice of *saupoudrage*, the scattering of credits and investments around the region on a proportionate basis rather than according to firm policy priorities. Direct elections as from 1986, together with the limitation of the *cumul* as from 1987 might be expected to reinforce the region as a power base in its own right, though the decision of the Socialist government that the regional elections should be by proportional representation in the *départements* and the political and administrative strengthening of the *départements* since 1981 will work in the opposite direction. With regional and national elections being held on the same day in 1986, there was no significant divergence in regional and national election results and regional lists tended to be led by established *notables*, the exception being Corsica where, as in the Basque country, the lack of a constitutional consensus has prevented the emergence of a stable pattern of regional politics.

In Italy, regions are directly elected, but the national parties, having colonized the whole of the state apparatus, were able to monopolize regional government after 1970. Regional election results follow national trends and the Christian Democrats and, more recently, the Communists, compose their regional lists in Rome, where coalition formation is also decided. In 1985, it was decisions in Rome which led to the Socialists pulling out of local and regional left-wing coalitions to reproduce the *pentapartito* formula of the national government. Factions and client-systems in and around the parties, too, are reproduced at regional level so that the regions, instead of being a focus of political activity and power are reduced to a relay in the existing power system. Resources are distributed on the basis of *pratiche spartitorie* (the Italian version of *saupoudrage*) and client interests rather than in accordance with policy priorities. This has been the fate of many political and administrative reforms and innovations in post-war Italy (including the center-left government formula, economic planning and development policies for the South) – instead of reforming the system they have been corrupted by it. There are exceptions in both France and Italy (examples are cited in chapters in Mény 1982; Putnam et al. 1985). Where regions have been controlled by the left-wing opposition, regional government has sometimes been innovative and used as a political power base and, where there has been strong party control, policies have been focussed and priorities set. In some cases, social and economic interests have also been drawn into the process of regional decision-making, making the regional council a significant focus of attention. This is most likely to occur where regions have some sense of common economic interest and are constructed on a territorial basis suitable for making economic policy choices. Such dialogue is more likely, too, in areas where there are traditions of political participation and partisanship, such as northern Italy and northern France.

In Spain, the existence of separate party systems has strengthened regional government, albeit at the expense of reducing the weight of regional interests at the center, where regional parties, except at times of minority government, can hope to have little leverage. Catalonia provides a clear example of a separate party system, with the dominant CiU tapping both the center-right vote and Catalan nationalism. Indeed, opponents charge that, under its leader Jordi Pujol, the CiU has established its own clientilist network focussed on the Generalitat and the Catalan economic and social institutions fostered by Pujol since the 1950s (Canals *et al.* 1984; Baiges *et al.* 1985). Election campaigns focus on Catalan issues (ESE 1980) and the results diverge markedly from those in national elections. The Socialists were well ahead in Catalonia in the national elections of 1982 and 1986 but dropped sharply behind CiU in the intervening regional elections of 1984. The Basque country, too, has its own party system but, seriously divided on the constitutional status of the region, this serves more as a disintegrative than an integrative force in Basque politics. In the other Spanish regions, the national parties tend to dominate but these must accomodate regionalist pressures from their own ranks and outside, leading to tension in Andalucia.

This brings us to the difficult and imprecise area of political culture. It is apparent that regional government will find it difficult to operate in deeply divided cultures where there is a lack of consensus on basic constitutional norms, as in the Basque country or Corsica, since substantial segments of the population see their interest as lying in the failure of the arrangement. Experience in France, as in Italy (Putnam *et al.* 1985) also suggests that regional government will estabish itself best where there is an established democratic participative culture, social and economic relationships based on exchange rather than tradition, deference and patronage, secular values and social stability – in other words, a 'modernized" political culture. So the most successful French regions have been those of the north where the old clientilist and *notable* system has given way to party politics while in Italy the most successfu regions are those of the North and Center and the least successfu ones those of the South.

There is a certain irony in this since the South and islands in both countries (along with Britanny) are the regions with the strongest sense of regional identity. Much debate has hinged on this question of whether regional government requires a pre-existing sense of "regional identity". This is a complex issue and can be answered at two levels, that of mass opinion and of political elites. At mass level, there are few regions that inspire the kind of "dual identity" with both the region (or "nation") and the state which may be necessary for a "regional political

200   MICHAEL KEATING

system", with its attendant ticket splitting for national and local elections to operate. Catalonia is an example and at times Sardinia and Sicily have appeared to be so. On the other hand, a regional level of politics can develop at elite level around the most "artificial" of units, as has been shown in some French regions and, to a limited extent, Italy, especially in the North; and, by drawing in regional economic and social interests in dialogue and in defense of common regional interests, can create a deeper sense of regional identity (Palard 1983; Chevallier *et al.* 1982). That political institutions should mould identity rather than the other way around should hardly be surprising – this was how the world's "nation states" were constructed. So the development of strong regional government by political and bureaucratic elites could be expected in due course to change popular perceptions. Opponents of regional government have often claimed that few people name it as a policy priority when asked in polls, going instead for substantive issues like unemployment or housing. This, too, is an unreasonable test. Regional government is not a substantive policy but a means for improving the policy process – so the question should be not "would you rather have a regional government or a better house?" but "do you think you would be more likely to get a better house if we had regional government?" The evidence, even from Italy, is that people do think that regional government is more in tune with their needs than national government (Putnam *et al.* 1985). The problem in Italy is that they have little faith in government at all. Regions are not the cause of Italy's political problems and may have made a modest contribution to improving matters.

THE PROSPECTS FOR REGIONAL GOVERNMENT

It is evident that regional government is a different creature both from federalism and from local government. It represents, indeed, an intermediate tier of government between center and locality and this factor, its insertion into an existing pattern of political and bureaucratic relationships, explains many of its difficulties. Despite the radical ambitions of some of its supporters, the capacity of regional government to transform the unitary European state has yet to be demonstrated. On the other hand, it is not to be dismissed out of hand. Political forces in all three countries (and in Britain) have consistently come back to seeking a level of government of a larger scale and greater functional capacity and with more autonomy than local government. It is an issue which will not go away yet which has never been brought to a satisfactory resolution.

Much of the problem hinges on the tension between the centralizing

and decentralizing objectives of regional government, whether it is to
be seen as an extension of unitary government with a greater capacity
for spatial coordination and planning or as a contribution to a more
pluralist and competitive political system. The decline of the substantive
policy consensus on matters for which regional governments have
authority makes this distinction vital. For regions autonomously to
make policy and control its implementation, certain functional pre-
requisites can easily be itemized. These include widely-drawn spheres
of competence, independent sources of revenue, their own bureaucracies and technical capacity. The conditions under which, in a non-
federal system, they will be allowed to acquire and maintain these
attributes, however, are very much in the realm of politics. In the event
of an abrupt regime change, the destabilization of the existing network
of power relationships, both political and bureaucratic, may allow
regional government to establish and consolidate its position. Otherwise, its prospects depend on the vicissitudes of the party system.
Nationally based parties tend to lose whatever interest they may have
had in regionalism once they come within reach of power at the state
level, as the issue will divide their supporters and may create obstacles
for their national administration without providing tangible benefits.
Party realignment, however, may create an opening for forces
sympathetic to regionalism or force national parties to make concessions to regionalist demands. In France, it took the party realignments
of the 1970s to bring direct regional elections onto the agenda and in
Italy the need for the Christian Democrats to broaden their coalition
with the center-left formula was an important factor in the decision to
activate the regional clauses of the constitution. In Spain, the major
parties in the post-Franco era were forced to accommodate regional
pressures to gain their support. In Britain, too, the decline of the old
parties forced accommodation with nationalist interests in Scotland and
Wales in the 1970s and in the 1980s the issue is still with us.

Where regional government has been established, recentralization
may be inhibited by a competitive party system, with regions becoming
power bases for the opposition, especially if regular alternation inhibits
central governments from taking out the territorial bases of the
opposition in the way the British Conservatives were able to do in the
1980s. The effective use of regions by French Socialists and Italian
Communists in the 1970s gained credibility for the idea of regionalism
but recent trends may be less encouraging to regionalists. In France,
the Socialist government, by staging regional elections on the same day
as the legislative, lost nearly all its regional strongholds with its
parliamentary majority. Thrust back into opposition nationally, the
party cannot thus use regions as a counterbalance to central

government. In Italy, shifting alliances have removed the Communists from many regional governments and the only chance for regions to come into their own lies in breaking the Christian Democrat monopoly on the state, with the clientilistic network which this sustains. With a system of alternation of power at central government level, the regions could develop as an important power base for the opposition of the day, as the West German Länder do. Of course, breaking the time honoured tradition of *trasformiso* in favor of alternating governments and pluralistic competition would itself represent a revolution in Italian politics comparable in magnitude to the regime change in France in 1958.

Separate regional party systems may help, if the regional parties are able to exert some leverage in national politics, but this will depend on the accidents of parliamentary arithmetic and cannot be the basis for a stable set of relationships. A similar effect may be achieved where regional elections are at least seen by the electorate as distinct from national contests, so that the parties need to be sensitive to regional issues. This will require the development of regional political leadership, of which there are some signs in all three countries. Failing these, however, regional government is likely to find itself reduced to the status of a planning and administrative arm of the central state, fulfilling some of the goals which the center wants from regionalism but not those of regional autonomy.

Economic trends in the 1980s have led to a strengthening of central economic and financial control while the internationalization of the economy has led many to conclude that the scope for substantial autonomy or influence on economic matters by subnational governments is shrinking to nothing. The influence of economic factors on financial and functional responsibilities, in turn, it is argued, reduces the scope for independent action by subnational governments in all spheres. Yet there have been countervailing factors. As national governments lose their ability to control their economies, particularly the spatial distribution of economic activity, attention is shifting back to the local and regional level. Regional governments may not be able to move multinationals, control foreign exchange movements or influence the price of oil, but neither can states. In the interstices created by global forces, though, there is scope for economic and social intervention geared to the needs of areas and an increasing interest in finding the means to do so. Regions cannot control global forces but the impact of the same international forces can be very different in different regions (Agnew 1987), calling for a differentiated response. It is in coping with these impacts that regional planning has been seen, in the 1980s, as having its greatest contribution.

Elsewhere (Keating 1986), I have drawn a parallel between regionalism and Europeanism, both post-war movements potentially subversive of the nation-state but both largely subordinated to the needs of state policy. Yet both the European Community and regions have survived and, over time, modified political procedures and assumptions. The European and regionalist dreams of the 1960s and 1970s may have been unfulfilled but so are those of the centralists. The centralized state has proved itself remarkably resilient but so has the regional idea. The relation between the two remains unresolved.

Acknowledgements

The research on which this paper is based was supported by a Leverhulme Trust Research Fellowship. I am grateful to Antonio Perreira–Menaut for comments on an earlier draft.

References

Agnew, J. 1987. *Place and Politics. The Geographical Mediation of State and Society*. Boston: Allen and Unwin.

Baiges, F., E. Gonzales, and J. Reixach. 1985. *Banca Catalana. Mas Que un Banco, Mas Que una Crisis*. Barcelona: Plaza y Jane.

Bassanini, F. 1985. La Repubblica delle Autonomie: Rilancio o Declino. *Democrazia e Diritto* 1.

Blas Guerrero, A. de. 1978. El Problema Ñacional–Regional Español en Las Programmas del PSOE y PCE. *Revista de Estudios Politicos* 4.

Bogandor, V. 1986. Federalism and Devolution: Some Juridical and Political Problems. In *Regionalism in European Politics*, ed. R. Morgan. London: Policy Studies Institute.

Buglione, E. and G. France. 1984. Skewed Fiscal Federalism in Italy: Implications for Public Expenditure Control. In *Comparative International Budgeting and Finance*, eds. A. Premchand and J. Burkhead. New Brunswick: Transaction Books.

Cammelli, M. 1980. Cent'anni de Regionalismo e Dieci de Regioni. *Il Mulino* 268.

Canals, R. M., J. M. Valles, and R. Viros. 1984. Las Elecciones al Parlamento de Cataluna del 29 Abril de 1984. *Revista de Estudios Políticos* 40.

Chevallier, J., F. Rangeon, and M. Sellier. 1982. *Le Pouvoir Régional*. Paris: Presses Universitaires de France.

Cuadrado Roura, J. 1981. La Política Regional en Los Planes de Desarrollo, 1964–75. In *La España de las Autoñomias*, ed. R. Acosta España. Madrid: Espasa–Calpe.

Dente, B. 1985. *Governare la Frammentazione. Stato, Regioni e Enti Locali in Italia*. Bologna: Il Mulino.

ESE. (Equipo de Sociologia Electoral – Universidad Autonoma de Barcelona). 1980. Las Elecciones Catalanes del 20 del Marzo de 1980. *Revista de Estudios Políticos* 14.

Fernandez, J.G. 1980. Cronica de la Descentralización: El Panorama Decentralizador al acabar 1980. *Revista de Estudios Políticos* 17.

Frenkel, M. 1986. The Distribution of Legal Powers in Pluricentral Systems. In *Regionalism in European Politics*, ed. R. Morgan. London: Policy Studies Institute.

Garcia Barbancho, A. 1979. *Disparidades Regionales y Ordenacion del Territorio*. Barcelona: Ariel.

Giard, J. and J. Schiebling. 1981. *L'Enjeu Regional*. Paris: Messidor.

Gonzalez, F. 1982. Speech on LOAPA, Congreso do los Diputados, 1 Legislatura. *Diario de Sesiones*, 21 June.

Good, M. H. 1976. Regional Reform in Italy: The Politics of Subnational Reorganization. Ph.D. diss., Boston University.

Gremion, P. 1976. *Le Pouvoir Periphique*. Paris: Seuil.

Keating, M. 1986. Europeanism and Regionalism. In *Regions in the European Community*, eds. M. Keating and B. Jones. Oxford: Clarendon.

——. 1986. Revendication et Lamentation. The Failure of Regional Nationalism in Languedoc. *Journal of Area Studies* 16.

—— and P. Hainsworth. 1986. *Decentralization and Change in Contemporary France*. Aldershot: Gower.

Mény, Y. 1974. *Centralisation et Décentralisation dans le Débat Politique Français, 1945–69*. Paris: R. Pichon et R. Durand–Auzias.

——. 1982. In *Dix Ans de Régionalisation en Europe. Bilan et Perspectives, 1970–1980*, ed. author. Paris: Çujas.

Merloni, F. 1982. Le Processus de Création des Régions en Italie: Problèmes de la Mise en Oeuvre. In *Dix Ans de Régionalisation en Europe. Bilan et Perspectives 1970–1980*, ed. Y. Mény. Paris: Cujas.

Modica, E. 1972. *I Communisti per le Autonomie*. Rome: Edizioni Lega per le Autonomie e i Poteri Locali.

Nice, D. 1987. *Federalism. The Politics of Intergovernmental Relations*. New York: St. Martin's Press.

Palard, J. 1983. *L'Identité Régionale. L'EPR et L'Intégration Régionale en Aquitaine*. Bordeaux: CERVL.

Porras Nadales, A. P. 1980. El Referendum de Iniciativa Autonómica del 28 de Febrero in Andalucia. *Revista de Estudios Políticos* 15.

Putnam, R., R. Leonardi and R. Nanetti. 1985. *La Pianta e le Radici*. Bologna: Il Mulino.

Philipponneau, M. 1982. *Décentralisation et Régionalisation*. Paris: Calaman–Levy.

Rhodes, R. 1981. *Control and Power in Central-Local Relations*. Farnborough: Gower.

Rotelli, E. 1973. *Dal Regionalismo alla Regione*. Bologna: Il Mulino.

Salerno, G. 1983. Governo, Parlamento, Regioni ed Enti Locali. In *Annuario 1983 delle Autonomie Locali*. Rome: Edizioni delle Autonomie.

Villari, R. 1981a. Autonomismo e Mezzogiorno. In *Autonomismo Meridionale: Ideologia, Politica e Istituzioni*, ed. G. Mori. Bologna: Il Mulino.

Zafario, V. 1981. La Tradizione Meridionalista e il Dibattito Sulle Autonomie nel Secondo Dopoguerra. In *Autonomismo Meridionale: Ideologia, Politica e Istituzioni.*, ed. G. Mori. Bologna: Il Mulino.

[16]

The Impact of Party Reform on Party Systems

The Case of the RPR in France

Kay Lawson

A political party is never an end in itself. It is composed of men and women who are seeking control of other institutions or access to those in control, who are in turn sporadically supported by men and women who also seek, to a different degree and often for different purposes, access to power.

Like any other instrument of power, to be effective for those who use them parties must continually be adapted to changing conditions. The nature of the territory to be conquered or held in subjection changes from time to time: institutional change provokes party change. Opposing forces may develop superior tactics that must be met by at least equivalent advances: party change provokes party change. And the purposes or other characteristics of those who support the party may undergo a transformation: electorate change provokes party change.

Each of these kinds of change is usually multifaceted, is seldom found singly, and is seldom entirely absent. Parties live in the vortex of change and to survive must be able to adapt and adapt appropriately. Not all do.

Parties may fail to adapt because they are weak and lack the necessary resources: leadership capable of recognizing the need for change, channels available for communicating the message of change, followers ready to accept—perhaps even to help create—change. But they may also fail to adapt because they are strong and have alternate, nonparty resources, such as leadership secure in governmental positions of power. Party leaders in power may be tempted to respond to change by using the institutions they control to suppress, or at least to channel and "guide," the transformations they observe. If the institutions of power are inadequate to the task, the party (or parties) in power may attempt to change the institutions. This attempt may work. However, if not carried far enough to include the suppression of dissent, induced institutional change is likely to be only transiently successful; other parties adapt to the changed institutions, and the known fact of manipulation may it-

0010-4159/81/0715-0002/$05.00/1

401

self cause a decline in electoral support for the party in power, compelling it to return to the battlefield. If it has been in power for a long time, it will be all the more poorly adapted to the struggle.

When a party finds itself seriously outdistanced by change, for whatever reasons (the abrupt end to a long period of shelter in power is only one of many conditions likely to be productive of that result), it must find a way to catch up. Incremental adaptation will be too slow. It will be time for self-generated party reform.

(Externally imposed party reform is reform decreed or legislated by government and is usually applied to all parties within a system; this article is concerned exclusively with self-generated reform, and the term ''party reform'' will be used in that sense only.)

Such reform will itself stimulate further changes. Other parties will be compelled to make adaptive changes in response. In a coalition system, the reformed party will interact differently with its alliance partners and may even change partners. The electorate will respond differently to all these changes, shifting loyalties and/or varying the intensity of support offered. Party reform has an impact, inevitably, on party systems. When a key party in a political system announces it is undertaking extensive reform, it is worthwhile to undertake an examination of that impact.

In order to do so, it is important to find out first what the reforms really are. There are good reasons why this is almost always a difficult task.

Party reform is different from incremental party adaptation not because it is wider-ranging (it may or may not be) and not because it is prompted by moral considerations (it may or may not be). It is different because it *claims* to be wider-ranging and *claims* to be morally motivated; it demands respectful attention. The mere assertion of reform, if credited, may strengthen the party's capacity to compete.

This means, then, that the reforms must be announced in moral terms. Different parties (and their supporters) have different notions of how parties might serve moral ends, but one theme is common to all: all political parties, even in totalitarian states, claim to serve as popular intermediaries, as linkage agencies between the citizenry and the state. Although many doubt its feasibility, nearly everyone accepts the idea that party linkage is desirable. In order to sustain a claim to respectful attention, parties undertaking reform are almost compelled to describe that reform as in some way improving the party's capacity to serve as an agency of linkage. However, caveat spectator: when a claim must be made, it must be doubted. A good close look is always in order.

These, then, are the considerations that shape the following inquiry into the impact of party reform on party systems. The key example will be the Rally for the Republic (RPR) party in the French party system. Our purpose will be to explain the circumstances forcing the Union of Democrats for the Fifth Re-

Kay Lawson

public (UDR) to change intself into the Rally for the Republic; to describe the nature of the change, with particular emphasis on the extent to which internal linkage processes have or have not been improved; and to assess, in preliminary terms, the probably impact of these changes on the French party system. A final section will explore, in broader terms, the relationship of party change to system change, indicating how the reform discussed here fits within the postwar pattern of political change in France, and stressing the importance of studying party systems not as fixed entities but as structures that, like all other social structures, change in response to change.

This study is based on recent (1977-78) field work in France, including over 100 interviews with approximately equal numbers of RPR militants, local officials, federal officials, and national leaders; and attendance at numerous party meetings at the base, including several called after the elections for the purpose of electing party officers. The field work was conducted in Paris (for contacts with national leadership) and the Department of Les Yvelines (for contacts at the local and federal levels).

Why the UDR Changed to the RPR

The UDR, first known as the Union for the New Republic (UNR), was formed in 1958 out of a coalition of small groups, some new and some old, which had in common the wish to support the return of General Charles de Gaulle to power in the midst of the political and institutional crisis provoked by Algerian rebel activity and the French army's efforts to take control of response to that activity out of the hands of the civilian government, if need be by taking over the government itself. From the beginning, the new party was characterized by its unstinting and undemanding loyalty to de Gaulle and by its remarkable and enduring success at the polls.[1]

However, although the UDR was France's strongest party in the Assembly, Fifth Republic France has not been a regime of parties, nor has power been located in the Assembly.[2] De Gaulle created a semipresidential system in 1958, reinforced it institutionally in 1962 by engineering a constitutional amendment for direct election of the president, and protected it politically by never according the strongest party, even though it was also the party most loyal to him, the strength in governmental ministries seemingly warranted by its success with the voters.[3] His popular but noncharismatic successor, Georges Pompidou, was obliged to base his power somewhat more directly on the party, but only somewhat.[4] When he died in 1974, at least three UDR leaders announced their readiness to step into his place, but none of them succeeded either in rallying the party or in assuming the presidency. The lukewarm support given Jacques Chaban-Delmas, the candidate who finally carried the

403

party's colors into battle, gave the presidency to Valéry Giscard d'Estaing of the Independent Republicans and the prime ministership to the member of the UDR who apparently did the most to deflect his party's votes to Giscard, Jacques Chirac.

It seems clear now that the fate of the UDR hung in the balance from 1974 to 1976, and that the scales were held by Jacques Chirac. Never one to act blindfolded, this pragmatic technocrat kept his vision sharply focused on his own political future and saw clearly that the UDR required serious reform in order to survive and that he himself would require a strong party to back his own quest for power. He was no doubt helped to the first understanding by the ease with which UDR voters had been shifted to Giscard even on the first ballot in 1974 and by declining membership rates; to the second by Giscard's tendency to rely more on his minister of the interior, old friend and ally Michel Poniatowski, than on his prime minister, Jacques Chirac.[5]

Chirac did not wait long to act. Less than six months after the presidential election, he moved in on the party he had betrayed. The power of the prime ministership may have been limited in government, but in party affairs it gave him sufficient leverage to make the post of secretary general his almost for the asking, and in December of 1974, he asked. Efforts by the UDR "barons" (the half-derogatory, half-admiring title given the party's old guard, formerly close associates of Charles de Gaulle) to find alternate leadership more acceptable (and more tractable) than Chirac proved unsuccessful, and the new secretary general was installed. During the next two years, Chirac progressively strengthened his control over the UDR and weakened his bonds to the president. When he left the prime ministership in mid-1976 only a few strategy meetings with his closest allies were necessary to rough out the scenario for the next act in the drama. Very soon, the call went out for Assises Nationales Extraordinaires, i.e., a special meeting of the UDR, to be held in Paris, December 5, 1976. At this meeting the party was renamed the Rally for the Republic, and a new set of statutes was adopted.[6]

How the RPR is Different from the UDR

The RPR is a direct continuation of the UDR. The new statutes begin, "there is formed among the adherents to the present statutes an association named Rally for the Republic" (Title I, Article 1) and end, "The present association is substituted for the rights and obligations of the association named 'Union of Democrats for the Fifth Republic'" (Title XV, Article 46).[7] What then are the changes? In general terms, they may be summarized as (1) giving the appearance of "deconcentrating" power to the base, (2) developing new sources of

Kay Lawson

power by strengthening intermediate agencies of communication and control, and (3) keeping all power, including that newly developed, concentrated at the top. We will discuss each in turn.

Giving the appearance of deconcentrating power to the base The most important statutory changes affecting the base are (1) local party leaders are now elected (Title I, Article 4), (2) membership applications may be made directly to socioprofessional associations within the party (Title II, Article 7), (3) French citizens residing abroad may join the party via a new "overseas federation" (Title II, Article 7), and (4) application for membership may be made directly to any party office—local, federal, or national (elimination of the clause stating, "Every application for membership presented to a party office other than the Federal Committee, is considered null"—Title II, Article 10, Statutes of Nice, 1975).[8] In addition, the party has recently set up a program of study groups, is expanding the work of its "leadership schools," and is undertaking to improve the methods of welcoming new members into the organization.

Interviewing and observing at the base leaves no room for doubt that these changes are having an impact. The party claims to have more than doubled its membership since the creation of the RPR (from 285,256 to over 620,000), and this claim is echoed and even magnified in its constituencies: "I had 35 members in my canton [a subdivision of the legislative district] in 1976; now we are 68."[9] And: "We were 200 in this district in 1976; now there are 600, and of those 150 are *militants*."[10] The party leadership urged that 50 percent of all local party posts be accorded to the new adherents and has invited both old and new members to join study groups and to attend courses in leadership at "centres de formation et de perfectionnement."[11]

Jacques Chirac, now president of the party, says, "Since our leader is gone, we must rediscover our Gaullist inspiration at the base and for that we need the members' participation."[12] However, only brief reflection is required to realize that all of the above changes may be motivated more by the desire to form a mass movement of committed, informed, and trained militants, ready to follow the party where it leads, than by a felt need to improve the party's means of basing its politics on "intransigent respect for the sovereignty of the people" (Title I, Article 2). And indeed, in interviews with other party leaders this alternate motive was frankly expressed: "A political party is a machine for gaining power." And : "We need members more like the Communists—you cannot talk to a Communist for ten minutes without hearing *the* Communist position on whatever you are talking about. That's *good*; that's what *we* should have." A question regarding a militant's obligations elicits a ready enumeration: recruit other members, paste up posters, distribute tracts, attend all meetings, be ready to do whatever is asked of him.

405

The next, asking what a militant's rights are, is far more likely to provoke doubt, a pause, and often the blunt reply, "I don't think he has any rights; it is much more a matter of obligations." [13] Or the answer might be, "The right to be informed, to know what is going on inside the party, not to have to find it out in the papers."

Attendance at Gaullist meetings of district executive bureaus, district committees, district general assemblies, the federal committee, the federal bureau, and selected meetings of youth, workers, and teachers also helps to discover the real meaning for the membership of these changes. [14] The same format prevails at all: the chair leads the proceedings with a firm hand, giving a report on local developments. Reports are given by those in charge of various activities, e.g., for youth, for women, and so on. Then the speaker, if there is one, is introduced. This might be the local deputy, a leader from the next level up of the party, or a party "personality." Finally, the audience is asked if there are questions, and usually two or three questions of information are asked and courteously replied to. Very occasionally, information on a new subject is volunteered from the floor, but this does not lead to the presentation of motions or any other action from the floor. The mood in all might best be described as affable and disciplined. Interviews with militants reinforced this view of meetings. They commonly felt that they were free to speak out if they wanted to, but were most concerned to be given full information by those in a position to know what was going on. Interviewees spoke frequently of the need for discipline, of every organization's need for someone who can make decisions, of an appreciation for order.

It is also at local meetings that one can discover how meaningful is the reform permitting the membership to elect its local chief, the party secretary for the district. Both observation and report suggest that the incumbent secretary is almost always reelected unopposed (the case in the three elections observed) and that when he is opposed the choice indicated by the departmental secretary easily carries the day. A district secretary who becomes persona non grata can be removed by the secretary general (Title III, Article 11). Members also elect the party committee for the district. In theory anyone may nominate himself, and some nonofficial nominations are occasionally offered. The most common situation appears to be that a printed "ballot," listing just as many candidates as there are positions on the committee, is passed out and then collected; names may be crossed out and others written in, but this rarely happens.

On the other hand, it should not be taken for granted that these still relatively new reforms will not produce some democratization of the party. Interviewees quite frequently made such complaints as, "It is very hard to move anything *up* in the party, to reach the higher levels," and expressed the wish that there would be "more real consultation with the base" in the setting of party policy and the choice of candidates for national office (the latter at pre-

Kay Lawson

sent rests exclusively in the hands of a small committee at national headquarters). A few believed meetings should be held more frequently, with more opportunity for substantive discussion. Not everyone was content with the procedures for internal elections: one woman, just reelected herself to the district committee, said, "To tell the truth, I only knew one or two other names on the list. I am going to write to M. _____ [the Department Secretary] and tell him that next year we must have some system requiring the candidates to present themselves. We should know whom we are voting for."

Developing new sources of power by strengthening intermediate agencies for communication and control The most important changes made by Chirac and his advisers are those at the intermediate level of the party, the Department Federation. Here, too, statutory changes have been supplemented by further modifications in practice. The net effect has been to strengthen the usefulness of the federations as agencies of communication and control by headquarters, to weaken their capacity to operate independently of the national party, and to build the power base of the national party.

The thrust of statutory change has been mostly in the last direction. In the previous statutes, respect for hierarchical channels was strictly enforced, to the benefit of the federations: applications for membership went only to the federal committee (Title II, Article 10, 1975), only the federations were permitted direct correspondence with the national direction of the movement (Title I, Article 6, 1975), the federations could call for regional conferences (with the consent of the Central Committee [Title I, Article 6, 1975]), and "electoral problems and internal affairs of the movement" were the "domain of the federations" (Title I, Article 6, 1975). None of these clauses can be found in the party's present statutes. Furthermore, although each federal secretary is still named by the secretary general and ratified by the departmental committee, he can now be replaced by the secretary general, with no right of appeal (Title II, Article 11).

What national headquarters wants, and good federal secretaries are working to help provide, is an RPR influence in every domain of French life. Merely having more and better-informed members is not enough—the national leadership wants these members working purposively within domains appropriate to their lifestyles and interests. In the days of the UDR, the party had a set of functional representatives at the national level who worked, often on a volunteer basis, to strengthen the party's impact among women, workers, students and other youth, the handicapped, sport associations, educational institutions, local government bodies, and so on. However, inadequately staffed and financed, and with nearly nonexistent local implantation in most cases, this effort was of little impact until the party was reformed in 1976. Now, what was little more than a part-time pious hope in the UDR is in the process of becoming grass-roots reality in the RPR. Functional representatives now are more

407

likely to have a full set of federal counterparts; federal representatives are in turn gradually being provided with district representatives. Supporting structures can be very elaborate and well publicized or discreet and simple—or somewhere in between. One or two illustrative examples will make clearer what is involved in this level of party reform, as well as the key role played by the federations.

Action Ouvrière et Professionelle (AOP). The AOP is the Gaullists' answer to left-wing domination of the trade union movement in France. It is not a union and does not operate within factories or other enterprises. It consists instead of various cells (the RPR prefers the word "sections"), each composed of RPR supporters who work in a particular enterprise, join the party via that enterprise's AOP section, and try to spread the party's ideas among their fellow workers. Intended to be a concrete manifestation of the hitherto obscure notions of "participation" first promulgated by de Gaulle (a philosophy of worker involvement in management that calls for sharing profits, holding stocks, and having a voice in decisions and that Gaullists envision as the "third way" between Marxism and capitalism), the AOP has begun to come to life in the RPR. Over 600 sections have been created. The goal is to have over 2,000 in operation, at which point its national representative, Georges Repeczki, optimistically claims it will be "irreversible." At present, resistance remains strong on four fronts: workers are afraid that the AOP is too ready to cooperate with management; management fears loss of control over decision-making processes; regular local party leadership resents the loss of revenue represented in AOP dues; and traditional party members are not quite sure what they think of the influx of workers qua workers. The cooperation of the federal secretaries is crucial in finding departmental and district AOP representatives who will have the patience to repeat the AOP message wherever an appropriate forum can be found and the skill to set up new sections whenever possible. The federal secretary must also encourge regular party acceptance of the AOP, by example and by exhortation. It is not an easy part of his job; as one committed AOP representative put it with a wry smile, "L'AOP gêne." ("The AOP disturbs.")[15]

The representatives in education.   The party's efforts to build influence among teachers represent an entirely different approach but are also dependent on the cooperation and support of the federations. No issue agitates RPR members more than what they see to be the tactics of Marxist indoctrination by left-wing teachers in the public schools. But Gaullist teachers seem unanimously persuaded they are victimized by left-wing administrators and colleagues once their politics become known. Respecting this perhaps well-founded fear, the party is simply urging them to join existing "autonomous"

Kay Lawson

(i.e., not Communist-dominated) parent-teacher associations, as individuals, not as party militants, and to attempt to shift decisions in the appropriate direction. In addition, federal level representatives work with local representatives to bring teachers together in study groups to help formulate proposals for government action in this area of education. At these sessions, the RPR label is not stressed; where possible, the work is organized around the idea of presenting results to the local RPR deputy for his consideration. Teachers who are not party members but who seem sympathetic are also invited to these loosely organized ad hoc meetings. It is delicate work and can only succeed where the federal secretary knows how to set up a local team in touch with local sensibilities.

As these two examples illustrate, every domain presents its particular problems. Efforts to organize the RPR women require finding the private settings in which women with no experience in public affairs will feel comfortable in developing new skills, yet at the same time keeping the women fully involved in the life of the party. The youth, too, must be kept involved in the regular party while they are provided opportunities for militantism and socializing appropriate to their inclinations. Here the threat is not a drift into privatism, but the contrary: the RPR has a clear and unhappy memory of the days when the UDR youth broke away to endorse François Mitterrand, the Socialist candidate for the presidency! Overseas members are allowed, for local political reasons, to form organizations with a different name "which are really RPR." In short, the stress is on finding the tactics and the leadership that will extend the RPR communication network into all spheres of French life. In this thoroughly pragmatic approach, little thought is given to protecting or building democratic processes. Functional representatives are appointed, by the secretary general at the national level, by the federal secretary at the department and district levels, and anyone who does not work out can be summarily replaced—it happens all the time.

Keeping power concentrated at the top Throughout most of the lifetime of the UDR it was widely understood that, whatever the statutes might say, central control of the party (itself not particularly meaningful in the days of subservience to de Gaulle and Pompidou) was a matter of informal negotiations among "the barons," most of whom owed what power they had in the party to the closeness of their association with de Gaulle and the high government offices that that proximity had secured for them.

As long as the party kept its close ties to popular presidents, it could afford to follow the comfortable old lines of a loose cadre organization, summoning the troops at the time of elections. However, even before de Gaulle left office, signs of the party's attrition in power were setting in, most noticeably in lower returns for the 1967 legislative elections. Recognition of these problems

409

prompted minor reforms at the National Congress of 1967 (Statutes of Lille), most important among them being an effort to expand membership and improve local implantation. The impetus for change was undercut in 1968, when student riots and worker demonstrations propelled many frightened French back into de Gaulle's aging embrace, boosting the party's legislative bloc to unprecedented numbers. Nevertheless, the 1967 modifications were crucial in the crisis years of 1974-76: they meant the existence, however rudimentary, of a structure through which the message of change could be communicated and ratified once the party came under the dominion of a leader capable of recognizing the need for change.

The 1976 statutes provide a new set of structures at the top, eliminating some, adding others, and changing all the rest. The National Congress is changed from its predecessor in two respects: the new statutes say that there will be substantive preparation at the base for these national meetings and that those with the right to vote are charged with electing the president of the party. To assist in the first, the agenda for the meetings is to be distributed two months in advance to the federations, which in turn are to send it out to the districts. At the end of one month, federations are to send back local relevant propositions to the secretary general. Fifteen days before the meetings the Central Committee, on the proposal of the secretary general, is to establish a synthesis, which is to be submitted to the Congress for the vote.[16]

The new statutes give special status to the role of the Extraordinary Congress (Title V), and indeed that mechanism has already proved a formidable tool for centralized control. In the March 1978 election, the RPR won over 150 seats in the 491 member legislature, maintaining its status as France's leading party. As expected, the party presented a candidate for the presidency of the National Assembly, Edgar Fauré. However, the parliamentary party was divided and gave enough votes to another member, Jacques Chaban-Delmas, to tip the balance to him. Chaban-Delmas has frequently contended, not coincidentally, against Chirac for power within the party (and could not have won without the cleverly marshalled support of President Giscard d'Estaing's supporters in the Assembly). Chirac was quick to retaliate. An Extraordinary Congress was convened within the month to change the statutes so as to exclude any member "named to the Constitutional Council, to ministerial functions or elected to the presidency of parliamentary assemblies" from all party offices. The decision was not a popular one in the party, but was dutifully voted into effect, making very clear the leadership's control.[17]

The old National Council and Central Committee have in effect been combined in a new expanded Central Committee, which now includes all RPR deputies and senators, all federal secretaries, members elected from the districts, 100 members elected on a national list, and all members of the Political Council not elected by the Central Committee, for a total of approximately

410

Kay Lawson

300. The functions of the Central Committee remain much the same as before, except that no mention is made of regulating the conditions of the association of other groups to the party, and the committee now has the additional function of being able to pronounce, upon the recommendation of the secretary general, the dissolution of a Federation or a District Union (Title VII). In statutory theory, each meeting of the Central Committee is to last for two days, with the first day being devoted to the work of six permanent committees; in practice, the committee meets for a few hours at a time, hears speeches, and votes, usually unanimously, for the proposals presented to them by the party leadership.[18] As one member put it, "I don't go anymore; I prefer to sleep at home."

The closest equivalent now to the former Executive Bureau is the Political Council, consisting of the president of the party, the secretary general, fifteen members elected by the Central Committee, members appointed by the president, and the RPR "personalities" who "formerly directed the government of France." This group meets at the request of the president, and prepares recommendations for the Central Committee (Title VIII). In practice, however, the daily work of the national party is carried out by the Executive Committee, an entirely new body, all of whose members are named by the president. How many members it has and what its functions are "are fixed by the president upon the recommendation of the secretary general" (Title X), and no mention is made of the frequency of its meetings. The Executive Committee in fact normally meets at least once a week and is composed of those who have been asked to take responsibility for particular functions, for example, four assistant secretary generals (for information, associations, participation, and elections) and sixteen national functional representatives (for such domains as youth, the family, aged persons, women, and so on); the closest counselors of President Chirac, who may or may not have official titles; and of course the secretary general and the president. Problems are thrashed out, pragmatically and matter-of-factly, "among friends."

According to the statutes, the two top men of the party are the president and the secretary general. According to all informed observers, the top decision maker in the party is the president, who takes advice from whom he wishes. The first secretary general of the reformed party, Jérome Monod, was a skilled technocrat brought in to give the party the organization and discipline it needed to win as many legislative seats as possible. When his job was finished, Monod left, as he had always said he would, to be replaced by Alain Devaquet, a personable young man whom very few had ever heard of before and who cannot possibly have had any independent power base in the party. A university professor by métier, Devaquet said he was "always ready to return to [the] laboratory," and was indeed replaced in 1979 by a third loyalist, Bernard Pons.[19]

411

In short, power in the RPR is still concentrated at the top, but in different hands. De Gaulle's "barons" are out; Chirac's "copains" are in, at least so long as they prove useful. Power is greater, thanks to the continuing development of federal and local structures, but so is its concentration, more and more in the hands of a single man. One of the party's most distinguished former leaders put the matter very simply: "The RPR is a political machine for one man." One of the party's most widely distributed election posters was equally succinct: "Support Jacques Chirac; Vote RPR." And many of the men and women interviewed for this study volunteered, in remarkably uniform language, "No party counts in France unless it has a leader considered capable of becoming president. We now have that leader in Jacques Chirac."

Thus, the RPR is on the way to becoming a presidential party. The ever growing militant base is being trained and closely involved in the leader's crusade. The intermediate leadership is hard-working and disciplined. The superstructure provides for instant popular ratification of the leader's decisions and a diligent corps of functional experts to carry them out.

It is tempting to employ the anthropomorphic metaphor to summarize the nature of the reforms: the party survived the death of its fathers and achieved responsible adulthood. It recognized that it could not count any longer on benign if distant paternalism but must itself wage the battle for control. However, a party is never a single organism, with immutable interdependency among its parts. It is true for now that the party must have its candidate-leader and that the candidate must be backed by the party; it is less clear that upon success the head would still need the body.

The Impact of Party Reform on Party Systems: The Case of France

Party systems are frequently discussed as if they were (1) permanently fixed systems within larger permanently fixed systems and (2) composed of units (parties) that (a) differ from each other significantly only in ideological orientation and (b) are active only within governmental structures and processes. Emphasis is placed on the number of parties in a system and the extent to which one party or one coalition strategy appears dominant in the government of that system. Such an approach is often very useful for understanding how a given government system is functioning at a given time; it is less useful for understanding system change, the role of parties in effecting that change, and the impact of change on parties.[20]

Nevertheless, change takes place, and one kind of change leads to another. To understand what is going on in a system, to be able to make informed guesses about what may happen next, each kind of change and each example of the kind must be studied. It is an unending job; we may gradually become

Kay Lawson

familiar with particular configurations of change, but new ingredients are always being stirred into the brew, producing unanticipated effects. The table of political elements is far from complete.

The change in the RPR is helping to change the French party system. But the impact it is having cannot be understood without seeing where this latest change fits in the overall pattern of change in postwar France. The change in the international system that flowed from World War II led to changes in the relationship between France and her colonies that in turn provoked internal system change. The move from the Fourth to the Fifth Republic set off other reactions. The institutional change, from a parliamentary to a quasi-presidential regime, stimulated party change, especially among the parties out of power, as manifested first in a quest for federated action (excluding the Communists) and then in the transformation to the loosely organized Section Française de l'Internationale Ouvrière into the more disciplined and more coherent Parti Socialiste.

At the same time, the change of leadership brought changes in government policy, with an emphasis on strengthening the French economy and the role of France in the world. During this period France became more prosperous, and so did most French citizens, but at the same time the gap between rich and poor grew greater. Then the leadership changed again: first de Gaulle and then Pompidou died, removing the two leaders who had been most capable of persuading the French that the Fifth Republic was—or would bring into existence—the best of all possible worlds. Social discontent and leftist party reform were ripening and merging; the Socialists and Communists produced an electoral pact and a common program, and more and more voters chose leftist candidates in local elections and expressed a readiness to do so in national elections (and did shift in that direction in the 1967 and 1973 legislative elections). The international energy crisis sharpened the growing sense of malaise. Left-wing party change coupled with the change in electoral preferences provoked further party change. Right-wing formations struggled to reform themselves into more powerful organizations, the RPR as described in this article, the Giscardists by transforming their Independent Republicans into a newly prominent "Republican party."

This, in very broad outline, is the pattern of political change in France from war's end to mid-1977. At each stage of this process, the operative party system was the transient product of these forces for change, including party reform. Three quite different party systems came into existence. The first, the postwar party system, was a series of constantly shifting coalitions, forged in the crucible of war, but inadequately resistant to the heat of postwar skirmishes for power and thoroughly vulnerable to the spreading flames of dissent over Algeria. The conditions that brought de Gaulle to power shifted power within the party system over to right-wing parties, but more importantly also

413

shifted power away from the parties altogether; the new party's most important characteristic was its powerlessness. When leftist leaders began to seek
new modes of party alliance to enable them to take over the presidency,
France began moving toward yet another party system, this time a party system composed of more centralized, more tightly organized parties, maximizing their strength internally and in cooperation with their closest allies, and
focusing on the presidency. The support Mitterrand won from the Communists and Giscard d'Estaing elicited from UDR supporters demonstrated in
1974 how serious the change was. France's parties were preparing to be powerful again, this time within the quasi-presidential system of the Fifth Republic.

Then came the beginnings of the campaign for the 1978 legislative elections. Suddenly all was changed. The Socialist-Communist pact broke up
almost completely, in September 1977. In January of 1978, the Republican
party joined forces with other small centrist parties to form the Union for
French Democracy (UDF). Although this latter move at first seemed consistent with the move toward stronger, more cohesive parties, when the UDF
began to register candidates in constituencies that earlier electoral agreement
on the Right had declared to be the inviolable turf of the RPR, it became clear
that division was growing on this side of the political spectrum as well. The
result was that France's four major parties went into the elections deeply divided, warring more bitterly against erstwhile allies than putative opponents,
made only minimal pretense of intra-alliance amity during the period of pragmatic "désistements" between the first and second "tours" of the elections
and ended by splitting the electorate neatly among themselves; the Communists won 18.62 percent of the popular vote; the Socialists, 28.31 percent
the UDF, 23.18 percent; and the RPR, 26.11 percent (the remaining 3.78 percent going to smaller groups).[21]

Since the 1978 election the political battle has if anything grown more bitter
and has extended into the internal councils of the various parties. Communists
continue to accuse Socialists of moving to the right; the national meeting of
the Parti Communiste Français in 1980 was characterized as a "congrès"
dénonciation du Parti Socialiste."[22] The Socialists claim they are ready to
reestablish the pact with the Communists at any time, but have instead been
restoring links with international socialism (while campaigning for the European Parliament elections in 1979) and have openly discussed the possibility
of an all-Socialist government for France.[23] Both leftist parties have been
plagued by internal problems as well. Communist intellectuals waged an open
debate regarding the wisdom of the party's 1977-78 tactics and were only
slowly brought back into disciplined conformity with the party line. Socialist
leader François Mitterrand was unable to prevent fellow Socialist Michel
Rocard either from announcing his candidacy for the presidency or from with-

Kay Lawson

drawing it precipitously upon his own announcement (observers speculated that Mitterrand had hoped for a decisive victory over his younger competitor in the quest for the party's endorsement; instead, Rocard's speedy and respectful withdrawal left him well defended against charges of either *lèse majesté* or divisiveness—and thus able to resume his battle for the party's leadership at a more convenient moment).[24]

The parties of the government are almost equally at loggerheads with one another and show similar signs of internal discord. For the RPR the two problems are closely intertwined. Following the advice of close counselors Pierre Juillet and Marie-France Garaud, Chirac carried his denunciations of the politics of the government to new extremes following the 1978 elections. His party's poor showing in the subsequent 1979 European Parliament elections was blamed in part on widespread discontent with Chirac's style, which puzzled and dismayed those RPR supporters who believed a party "of the majority" should not be constantly taking arms against its partners in that coalition. Twenty-four RPR deputies were sufficiently concerned to hold a meeting to discuss how to counteract their party leader's intransigence. Taking the warning, Chirac parted company with Juillet and Garaud, single-handedly reconstituted the Political Council more to the deputies' liking (thus reasserting his personal control of the party apparatus at the same time that he acknowledged his need to exercise that control in a manner at least marginally acceptable to other powers within the party), and temporarily softened his attacks on Giscard.[25] Such conciliatory tactics had their cost and were only minimally effective in rallying the "legitimistes" back around their putative leader. A sign of the first was Marie-France Garaud's announcement of her own candidacy for the presidency; a sign of the latter was the same announcement by former prime minister Michel Debré (a far more serious challenge to Chirac's hegemony, since many old-guard Gaullists have never ceased to regard Debré as the proper spiritual and ideological heir to de Gaulle).[26] Nor did the forces behind Giscard show any signs of being placated by Chirac's momentarily milder tone. On the contrary, Prime Minister Barre lashed out with particular virulence against the RPR's refusal to vote the government's budget in the fall of 1979, despite that party's promise not to vote for any motion of censure, or against any motion of confidence, brought against or by the government.[27] Internally, the small parties composing Giscard's UDF have shown no signs of revolt against the president, but neither have they formed a strong organisation to campaign on his behalf. His supporters' losses in late 1980 legislative by-elections and repeated reports of "childish quarrels" within the centrist movements indicate that even those seemingly most secure in power are not immune from the centrifugal forces pushing them apart—from each other as well as from more distant allies.[28]

What are the forces that have acted so relentlessly to halt France's move

toward a party system based on rational bargaining by cohesive parties focused on the presidency? Why is it that even when France's parties manage
temporarily to coalesce, singly and in alliance, and to make a few of the
pragmatic cooperative moves most unambiguously dictated by political reality, one can so confidently expect their redivision into warring movements
and factions? Four causes of this phenomenon may be suggested. The impact
of RPR reforms on the French party system is a key aspect of the fourth.

The first cause for the failure of French parties to maintain a degree of
coherence and alliance is the fact that France did not adopt a fully presidential
system in 1958. Under the terms of the present constitution, the president
must govern through a prime minister, and the prime minister must have the
confidence of parliament. Any legislature with a firm majority against the
president can successfully wrest power back from the president by consistently voting against the bills presented by the government. A motion of censure can be filed, or the government's effort to make the passage of a bill a
motion of confidence can be repudiated. If the nation were behind it, an opposing majority could be sustained in the elections that would then have to be
called, and the president would be forced either to appoint a prime minister
from the opposition or to resign.[29] All this means that it is still worthwhile to
wage the battle for parliament and to gain as many seats as possible, if only in
order to have the power to maintain or break the power of presidents.

However, once in Parliament, individual deputies must exercise power (including the making or breaking of presidents) in conjunction with others—a
majority has to be achieved to control Parliament just as it must control the
presidency more directly. Thus, the "only a quasi-presidential system" argument cannot stand alone.

The second probable cause for the recurring divisiveness of the parties is
the fact that the French are still deeply divided over unresolved issues: the role
of France in the world, the distribution of wealth, the role of government in
the economy, and the extent to which individual liberties should be protected.[30] Allowing their opinions on these issues to be aggregated sufficiently
to allow the emergence of four major parties, capable of forming only the
most tenuous alliances on each side of the political spectrum, may be as far as
the French electorate can go for the present, no matter what the institutionalized incentives for further cooperative effort may be.

The French electoral system has a feature that has received remarkably little
scholarly attention but that has sufficient impact to count as our third
explanatory factor: the runoff. Because there are so many parties, the only
way to get a clear majority in many constituencies for local and legislative
elections and in the nation for the presidency is to hold two elections, one a
week after the first, between the leaders in the first polling. But this system
works both ways: it is partly because there is a runoff that France continues to

Kay Lawson

Figure 1 System, Party, and Party System Change in France, 1962-81

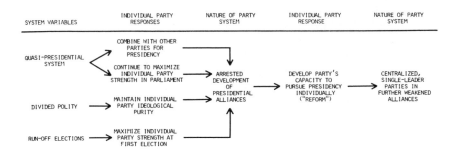

have "so many parties" and that preelectoral alliances are likely to be loose and contingent upon first ballot results. The first vote becomes (and is now often called) a primary election within the alliance, and one week is a very short time to heal the wounds inflicted in a long primary battle. Those who warred throughout the electoral period find it difficult to forgive and forget when the votes are counted.

The fourth factor explaining the arrested development of presidency-oriented alliances between cohesive parties is that that has been the topic of this article: party reform in the direction of presidential politics. This is not the contradiction it may at first appear to be. The three factors already discussed have the combined effect of making presidency-oriented alliances tenuous and fragile in France, and of ensuring that there will be recurrent periods when the individual parties will operate independently and hostilely vis-à-vis even their closest ideological allies. At the same time, the fact that so much (even if not all) power is now concentrated in the French presidency means that each individual party has naturally begun to reshape itself in response to the imperatives of that power. Unable to combine more effectively, each endeavors to transform itself, by itself, into a majority party. Since "no party counts unless it has a leader considered capable of becoming president," a party bent on achieving majority status constantly seeks such leadership and conspires in its own transformation into an electoral machine for that leader. When his chances of success dim, others endeavor to take his place, but the effort to build and/or maintain a powerful party apparatus, characterized by centralized power and a mass membership, does not falter.

In sum, at the present writing, institutional and electoral factors (the remaining powers of the legislature, runoff elections, and divided opinion) keep the parties divided, and a further institutional factor (the powers of the presidency) compels those divided parties to try to build strong centralized organizations largely subservient to the will of a single leader, who, in the effort to attract attention and support, exercises his leadership in a fashion to reinforce the divisiveness among (and often within) the parties. The relationship among these variables is diagrammed in Figure 1.

The French electorate may grow sufficiently weary of this new round of elitist power-seeking to compel change—or otherwise respond in a fashion the parties cannot afford to ignore. Internal factionalism may prevent the emergence of unchallenged leaders. Current leaders may be forced out of office by illness, scandal, or death. We cannot be certain what will stimulate the next, set of changes in French politics, nor when it will take place. But understanding the nature and interrelationships of past changes suggests what to watch for, how to interpret what we see, and above all, the importance of expecting the party system of France, like all other party systems, to respond to change and to be itself a force for further change.

EPILOGUE (May 1981)

In the recent presidential election, all the candidates pursued the new strategy of independence. Attacks on former allies were frequent and sharp. Chirac overcame the challenges of Debré and Garaud by winning a respectable 18 percent on the first ballot (to their respective 1.7 percent and 1.3 percent). His lukewarm endorsement of Giscard prior to the second ballot probably increased the margin of Mitterrand's victory and in any case helped to dissociate the RPR leader from the former president's fall from grace. Chirac is now well placed to appear as the only possible *recours* for France when and if her citizens weary of their new experiment with socialism. Thus, for Chirac as for Mitterrand, the strategy of turning a decaying party into a well-organized mechanism and of moving that party free from significant commitment to interparty alliances has proved the currently correct response to the ever changing dynamics of the French political system.

NOTES

1. Jean Charlot, *L'U.N.R.* (Paris: Armand Colin, 1967), p. 37; and Philip Williams, *French Politicians and Elections 1951-1969* (London: Cambridge, 1970), pp. 110-112.

2. Henry Ehrmann, *Politics in France* (Boston: Little, Brown, 1976 3rd ed.), pp. 298-316.

3. Throughout de Gaulle's tenure in the presidency, the party held either a minority or a very slim majority of seats in the cabinet. See John S. Ambler, "The Democratic Union for the Republic: To Survive de Gaulle," *Rice University Studies, Papers in Political Science*, 54:33 (1968).

4. For a detailed study of Pompidou's shifting relationship with the party, see Frank L. Wilson, "Gaullism without de Gaulle," *Western Political Quarterly*, 26 (Spring 1973), pp. 485-506.

5. Pierre Crisol and Jean-Yves Lhomeau, *La Machine R.P.R.* (Paris: Fayolle, 1977), pp. 17-93.

6. Ibid.

7. See the National Statutes adopted by the Extraordinary Congress of December 5, 1976. All further references to these statutes will be indicated in the text by title and article number.

Kay Lawson

8. See the National Statutes adopted by the National Council and completed by the National Congress of June 14-15, 1975. All further references to these statutes will be indicated in the text by title, article number, and the year 1975.

9. All quotes not otherwise identified are from interviews conducted in France between April 1 and July 15, 1978. Information regarding party characteristics and procedures not otherwise documented was obtained from these interviews or from attendance at party meetings.

10. Most of this growth took place prior to the 1978 legislative elections and can be ascribed (as it frankly was in many interviews) to the quest of many of the French for some way to combat what appeared to be the serious threat of left-wing victory in those elections. See, for example, the extensive poll data reported in the newsweekly *Le Point*, September 12, 1977, pp. 46-56, and December 12, 1977, pp. 87-97.

11. To sustain these and other *formation* efforts, the party has prepared over thirty brochures, which provide the party's positions on issues such as Europe and government policy for the handicapped, copies of several of Chirac's speeches (also available in a full-length volume), and advice on such matters as "How to Act in Your Commune." These small brochures, from ten to thirty pages long, have been printed under the general headings *Rassemblement Actualité* and *Le R.P.R. Propose*. They are available from party headquarters, 123 rue de Lille, Paris. Other key party publications are *Propositions pour la France* (Paris: Stock, 1977) and *Discours pour la France à l'heure du choix* (Paris: Stock, 1978). The latter consists of the printed speeches of Jacques Chirac.

12. Interview, July 1978.

13. It should be noted that this kind of answer came even more frequently from militants (19 percent so commenting) than from leaders (of whom 14 percent gave such an answer). A full report of interview data will be presented in a forthcoming study, *Political Parties and Change: Rally for the Republic*.

14. The author attended meetings in Paris, in a rapidly developing middle-class suburban area, in a well-established, traditional and wealthy area, and in a district approximately half-industrial, half-rural.

15. The AOP puts out its own monthly bulletin, *Inter A.O.P.*, and maintains its own headquarters at 11 rue Solferino, Paris.

16. However, given past habits of ignoring the more cumbersomely democratic provisions of statutes and present techniques of controlling party meetings, it would be foolish to take these provisions as predictive of what practice will actually be in the future.

17. At the same meeting, the statutes were also changed to make it the secretary general (rather than the federal secretary) who removes an unsatisfactory district secretary and to bring in all deputies and senators as members of the Central Committee (*Le Monde*, 11 April 1978).

18. See, for example, the report of the meeting of the Central Committee given in *Le Monde*, 30 June 1978.

19. Devaquet was interviewed by the author in July, 1978.

20. Giovanni Sartori, *Parties and Party Systems* (London: Cambridge, 1976).

21. French electoral constituency boundaries have been drawn to favor the Right: the popular vote was translated into Assembly seats as follows: Communists, 86; Socialists, 115; UDF, 123; RPR, 154; other, 13.

22. *Le Monde Hebdomadaire*, week ending November 12, 1980.

23. Ibid., May 24, 1979 and February 27, 1980.

24. Ibid., November 12, 1980.

25. Ibid., May 2, 9, June 13, July 4, and September 26, 1979.

26. Ibid., July 2 and October 29, 1980. Interviews with militants in 1978 gave ample evidence of the esteem in which Debré is held, and Debré himself openly acknowledged in an interview with the author (July, 1978) both his dissatisfaction with current RPR proceedings and his awareness of his continuing popularity among older Gaullists.

27. Ibid., November 21, 1979.

28. Ibid., December 10, 1980. Also to be noted in this regard is Giscard's steadily declining popularity in opinion polls through 1980 (*New York Times*, February 1, 1981, p. E5).

29. See Titles II through V and Title XIV, of the French constitution.

30. Suzanne Berger, *The French Political System* (New York, 1974) and David Thomson, *Democracy in France since 1870*, (London: Oxford, 1969 5th ed.).

419

[17]

Economics and the French Voter:
A Microanalysis

MICHAEL S. LEWIS-BECK

IN THE United States, the impact of economic conditions on voting behavior is a subject of extensive research. Initially, this work focused on establishing aggregate relationships between national economic indicators and party vote totals in congressional elections over time (Arcelus and Meltzer, 1975; Bloom and Price, 1975; Goodman and Kramer, 1975; Kramer, 1971; Lepper, 1974; McCracken, 1973; Stigler, 1973; Tufte, 1975). These macrolevel findings were rather confusing. While most showed an economic effect, a few did not. Further, among those which did, there was little agreement on the nature of the effect. That is, was it unemployment, income, or inflation which influenced the voter? And, what form did this influence take? Such perplexing questions could not be resolved at the aggregate level, where results were compatible with several patterns of individual voter choice. Therefore, analysis of the impact of economics on the vote had to descend to individual level survey data (Fiorina, 1978; Kiewiet, 1981; Kinder and Kiewiet, 1979; Kuklinski and West, 1981; Klorman, 1978; Sigelman and Tsai, 1981; Weatherford, 1978; Wides, 1976, 1979). As Fiorina (1978:430) stated, "The existence of some relationship between the two [in the survey data]

Abstract In the United States, uncertainties surrounding the aggregate time series evidence on economic conditions and voting behavior led researchers to explore the relationship through individual level survey data. For France, aggregate time series studies have begun to appear but, as yet, no microlevel analysis has been done. My investigation attempts to resolve doubts arising from the macrolevel work, by looking at individual economic perception and vote intention in surveys of the French electorate. I find that economic conditions, both personal and collective, exert a significant influence on party choice in French legislative elections. Moreover, this economic influence appears more pervasive in France than in the United States.

Michael S. Lewis-Beck is Professor of Political Science at The University of Iowa. The author wishes to thank anonymous reviewers for their comments, and Jo Ellen Childers for computer assistance.

would appear to be a necessary condition for the existence of a 'true' relationship between the time series of aggregate data. . . .''

With regard to Western Europe, research on economic conditions and electoral behavior is in its youth (see Whiteley, 1980, for an introduction). For France, some aggregate level time series work has been carried out. There are now four papers which look at national economic measures and executive popularity. Lafay (1978), Lewis-Beck (1980), and Hibbs and Vasilatos (1981) all agree that the popularity of the president and/or the prime minister suffers from economic downturns, although they disagree on which indicators are important. In contrast, Norpoth and Yantek (1981) find that French presidential popularity is unrelated to the state of the economy. Unfortunately, these popularity studies shed no direct light on the issue of whether the economy shapes the vote. Here, only two papers exist, one by Rosa and Amson (1976), another by Lewis-Beck and Bellucci (1982). Both discover a relationship between macroeconomic indicators and the legislative vote share for Leftist parties. However, they are not consistent as to which are the key economic variables, and they share the handicap of a small sample size. As with the United States research, to establish firmly the presence of a link between economics and the voter, one must drop to an individual level of analysis, which is my purpose. I ask the basic question, "Do individual economic perceptions influence the voting decision in France?" The answer is clearly affirmative, as I demonstrate below.

Preliminary Considerations

As noted above, there are two studies, both at the aggregate level, which relate economic conditions to voting in legislative elections in France. Both employ the dependent variable, percentage of the first-ballot National Assembly vote going to Leftist parties, relating it to various national economic indicators. The Rosa and Amson (1976) study covers legislative elections through 1973, while the Lewis-Beck and Bellucci (1982) study is more current, reaching to the 1981 election. The final regression model in the latter article indicates that increases in the unemployment rate and decreases in real per capita income significantly enhance the vote share of the Left. The equation fits the data rather well ($R^2 = .63$), and it was actually able to forecast the Leftist victory in 1981. However, the foundations of the model are shaky, due to a severe multicollinearity problem, and a sample size of only seven (the seven legislative elections from 1956–1978). Further, as the authors themselves admit, "Because the data are aggregate, we must perforce speculate about individual motive." Clearly, until individuals are examined, the actual link between economic circumstance and voting in France cannot be known, and the possibility remains that the reported aggregate relationship is in fact spurious.

If one thinks about it, there are many reasons why French citizens might not take their personal economic situation into account when deciding how to vote. First, they may simply fail to perceive their deteriorating economic circumstance (e.g., the price of groceries inches up so slowly that its impact on real purchasing power goes unnoticed). And, if they do perceive it, they might blame themselves, their boss, the community, rather than hold elected officials responsible (e.g., Giscard tries very hard over a long time period to lower the inflation rate; hence, it is not rational to blame him for failing). Or, even if the politicians are blamed for the economy, they could still be supported for other reasons (e.g., a man who is unemployed votes Gaullist because he is strongly committed to a "France First" foreign policy). More subtly, only certain elected officials may be held culpable (e.g., the voter reasons that the president can direct the economy, but a mere deputy cannot). Finally, one may steadfastly refuse to vote for the Left on policy grounds, despite their opposition role. That is, voters may be dissatisfied with their economic situation, but feel that the Left would make things worse (e.g., someone suffering from inflation under Giscard might argue that the Socialists, with their generous program of spending, would stimulate still more price rises).

These possibilities can be tested through analysis of the French survey data in the *Euro-Barometers,* directed by Jacques-René Rabier and Ronald Inglehart. Although the interview schedules were not designed with these research questions in mind, there are still enough items available to provide a solid beginning. Let us explore an example (from *Euro-Barometer 9*).[1] In the election year of 1978, a national sample of the French public was asked, "I want to talk about the last 3 years. . . . During this time have you ever been unemployed [yes or no]?" They were also asked, "If there were a general election tomorrow, which party would you support?" The responses to this item can be ordered from Left to Right as follows: Communist, Unified Socialist, Socialist, Left Radical, Centrist, Union for French Democracy, Gaullist. The association of these two variables ($r = .19$) suggests unemployment affects party support. Of those who responded yes, they had been unemployed during the last three years, 78 percent said they would support a party on the Left (i.e., Com-

---

[1] See Jacques-René Rabier and Ronald Inglehart, *Euro-Barometer 9, April, 1978,* Inter-University Consortium for Political and Social Research (ICPSR) Edition, 1980, P. O. Box 1248, Ann Arbor, Michigan 48106.

munist, Unified Socialist, Socialist, Left Radical). Appreciation for
this apparent impact of unemployment increases upon comparing it to
the "normal" vote for Leftist parties, which equaled 45 percent in
Fifth Republic first-ballot legislative elections to this time.[2]

That the unemployed should vote Left is not really surprising.
First, it reflected dissatisfaction with President Giscard d'Estaing's
ruling Center-Right Majorité. Under his administration, the unemployment rate had reached a level without precedent in the Fifth
Republic (in 1978, the unemployment rate was 5.3 percent). Therefore, it would not be difficult for the unemployed to blame the Giscardian government for their personal misfortune, and cast a ballot for
the Left opposition. Furthermore, a vote for a Leftist party might be
dictated on strict policy grounds. That is, voters may believe that the
Left, perhaps because of its working class base, is more likely to
initiate programs that will reduce unemployment. Contemporary survey research certainly bolsters this notion. Just before the 1978 election, an *Institut Français d'Opinion Public* (IFOP) poll asked a national sample of French voters why someone would vote for the Left.
The leading reason cited was the unemployment problem. In fact,
fully 67 percent of the survey felt the unemployment problem was a
"fundamental" reason for supporting the Left. (Interestingly, the economic issues of inflation and income ranked as the second and third
most important reasons; see *Sondages,* 40, nos. 2 & 3, 1978:132–34).

An immediate concern is whether the above finding is atypical. Or,
put another way, are individual economic conditions, variously measured, consistently related to voter choice? Lamentably, none of the
economic items appearing in the *Euro-Barometers* are routinely administered. For instance, in contrast to the Michigan Center for
Political Studies (CPS) surveys, the electorate is not regularly asked
something like, "During the last few years, has your financial situation been getting better, getting worse, or has it stayed the same?"
Hence, my strategy of analysis was to begin by locating all items
which appeared to tap individual economic perceptions. Across these
11 national surveys, stretching from 1970 to 1978, I uncovered 55 such
items.[3] With very few exceptions, these 55 questions were administered no more than once. When the bivariate correlations of these

[2] The first-round vote share for Leftist parties in the legislative elections of the Fifth
Republic through 1978 is reported in Lewis-Beck and Bellucci (1982).
[3] These 11 national surveys of France come from the 1970, 1971, and 1973 *European
Communities Studies,* and the *Euro-Barometers* numbered 3, 4, 5, 7, 8, 9, 10, 11, all
directed by Jacques-René Rabier and Ronald Inglehart, and available from the ICPSR,
P. O. Box 1248, Ann Arbor, Michigan 48106. Neither the original collectors of the data
nor the ICPSR bear any responsibility for the analyses or interpretations presented.

items with the above Left-Right party preference variable are examined, the results are highly suggestive. All the relationships are in the expected direction, with adverse economic conditions appearing to push voters to the Left. Further, the average $r=.20$. It is noteworthy that the strength of this relationship is markedly greater than that reported for the United States case, where unemployment and income dissatisfaction variables were only weakly correlated to voting in 11 congressional elections (Kinder and Kiewiet, 1979:503–4).

A Model of Economic Voting

These moderate, consistent bivariate correlations encourage me to believe that personal economic perceptions are significantly related to party preference in France. Nevertheless, until relevant control variables are successfully introduced in a multivariate explanation of the vote, the possibility of spuriousness remains serious. The American literature on the subject dictates two essential controls: party identification and other economic variables.

With respect to the former a stumbling block is that, in the tradition of French electoral surveys, the *Euro-Barometers* never directly measure the respondent's party identification. (This does not mean that the typical French voter fails to identify with a party. I consider the topic at length elsewhere; Lewis-Beck, 1983). However, there are other "standing commitments," in V. O. Key's phrase, which over time reliably point the French voter in specific directions (Campbell, 1974:74–75). The most important of these is ideology, a variable that the *Euro-Barometer* surveys have sometimes asked about. The question takes the following form: "In political matters people talk of 'the Left' and 'the Right.' How would you place your views on this scale? [the respondent is shown a 10-point scale ordered from 'Left' to 'Right']." The American voter, at least until recently, has not responded well to such ideological self-placement scales. But, because of the historic salience of the Left-Right cleavage, the French voter does not show a similar reticence. For example, in the above-mentioned 1978 survey, only 10 percent of the sample would not locate themselves on this 10-point scale. Like party identification in the United States, ideological commitment serves potently to structure voter choice in France. When this ideology measure is correlated with the 1978 vote variable, $r=.79$. Remarkably, this is exactly the magnitude of correlation between actual French party identification and vote reported from a 1967 survey by Barnes and Pierce (1971:645). Clearly, then, in the French context, the ideology variable appears an acceptable substitute for an absent party identification variable, acting as its functional equivalent.

Returning to the issue of spuriousness, the possibility exists that a "third variable," ideology, is acting as a common prior influence on individual economics and party choice. For instance, Left-leaning respondents might tend to express more dissatisfaction with their income prospects and, at the same time, favor Leftist parties. This situation would generate a bivariate correlation of income satisfaction and vote, even if there were no causal connection between the two. To test for such spuriousness, one can hold constant the ideology variable in a multiple regression equation, and observe whether the coefficient for the economic variable is significant.

Besides ideology, it is necessary to include more than one economic variable in the equation. At the microlevel of analysis, at least two basic types of economic variables may enter into a voter's decision: personal and collective (on this distinction, see especially Kinder and Kiewiet, 1979). "Personal" variables measure the citizen's own individual economic circumstance, e.g., the respondent says he or she is unemployed, dissatisfied about income, upset over an expanding grocery bill. "Collective" variables tap the citizen's evaluation of the economic well-being of the larger community, e.g., a respondent judges that, for the nation as a whole, unemployment is up, the general economic situation is deteriorating, inflation is accelerating. Writing on the United States, Kinder (1981) denotes these as "pocketbook" versus "sociotropic" concerns, respectively. For France, I have speculated, from my aggregate time series analysis, that citizens draw both on their "personal experience" of economic conditions and on their "policy evaluation" of them in deciding whether to support the president; however, to determine if this is so, one needs to study individuals (Lewis-Beck, 1980:311, 321–22).

Obviously, both kinds of economic variables should be considered before arriving at a final model. Nevertheless, as Kinder (1981:3) notes, most models that have been offered focus on either a "personal" or a "collective" explanation. An evident problem with these approaches is that any positive findings might be spurious, a product of the excluded economic variable. For instance, suppose that because respondents are unemployed (a personal variable), they project a bleak unemployment picture for the nation (a collective variable) and, at the same time, express support for the Left. Then, when this personal economic variable is brought into the equation, it will tend to show a significant effect, whereas the collective economic variable will not. Still, on the basis of their United States work, Kinder and Kiewiet (1979) conclude that the opposite is in fact the case. More specifically, they find that it is collective economic judgment, rather than personal economic experience, that matters in shaping the congressional vote. With regard to the French case, then, it is not clear exactly what kind of an economic effect will be found, if any. Therefore, to test whether one, none, or both of the personal and collective economic variables are influential, they must each be included in any microlevel model of legislative voting in France.

The foregoing considerations indicate that, in order to control major sources of spuriousness and to estimate reliably the nature of the economic effects, the following basic model is necessary:

$$V = b_0 + b_1 P + b_2 C + b_3 I + e \qquad (1)$$

where V = legislative vote; P = personal economic situation; C = collective economic judgment; I = Left-Right ideology; b_0, b_1, b_2, b_3 = the parameters to be estimated; e = error.

My approach, then, was to estimate this model using all the available *Euro-Barometer* surveys which measure these relevant variables. Unfortunately, the 10-point ideological self-placement scale was usually not administered, and there were not always personal and collective economic items in the same survey. Nevertheless, I still was able to locate surveys from the actual legislative election years of the period, 1973 and 1978, which met these criteria. On the basis of the preliminary considerations, I hypothesize that ideology is positively associated with the vote, and that worsening personal and collective economic evaluations heighten the Leftist vote. That is, $b_1, b_2, b_3 > 0$. In Table 1, the ordinary least squares (OLS) estimates of Equation 1, from these 1973 and 1978 surveys, are reported.

Evaluation of the Findings on Economic Voting

The central question is whether individual economic perceptions influence the French voter. They certainly do, according to the Table 1 results. All the coefficients of the economic variables are in the expected direction, indicating that citizens who discern personal or collective economic difficulties are more likely to vote for a party on the Left. Further, these slope estimates are statistically significant (at .05, $t > 1.65$), even after controlling for the powerful influence of the ideology variable.

This economic effect is induced by both personal and collective cares. With the former, feelings about one's own economic conditions mold party preference. More precisely, those who were dissatisfied over their income or who had been unemployed expressed stronger

Table 1. An Economic Model of Voting in French Legislative Elections, 1973 and 1978 (OLS Estimates)

	1973 [a]	
$\hat{V}_3 = .72 + .20^*P_3 + .23^*C_3 + .52^*I_3$		(2)
$\quad\quad\quad (.04) \quad\quad (.07) \quad\quad (.01)$		
$\quad\quad R^2 = .55 \quad\quad\quad N = 1311$		

	1978 [b]	
$\hat{V}_8 = -.57 + .39^*P_8 + .24^*C_8 + .67^*I_8$		(3)
$\quad\quad\quad\quad (.12) \quad\quad (.07) \quad\quad (.02)$		
$\quad\quad R^2 = .63 \quad\quad\quad N = 840$		

Correlations of the Independent Variables

1973	P_3	C_3	I_3		1978	P_8	C_8	I_8
P_3					P_8			
C_3	.14				C_8	.16		
I_3	.21	.03			I_8	.15	.30	

SOURCE: The data are from the *1973 European Communities Study* and *Euro-Barometer 9, April, 1978*, directed by Jacques-René Rabier and Ronald Inglehart, and available from ICPSR, P.O. Box 1248, Ann Arbor, Michigan 48106.

NOTE: The R^2 = the coefficient of multiple determination, the N = the sample size, the values in parentheses = the standard errors.

* Significant at .05.

[a] V_3 = vote intention (1 = Communist, 2 = Unified Socialist, 3 = Socialist, 4 = Left Radical, 5 = Reform Movement, 6 = Gaullist); P_3 = income satisfaction (1 = not at all satisfied, 2 = not very satisfied, 3 = fairly satisfied, 4 = very satisfied); C_3 = the country should fight inflation (0 = the country should give priority to fighting inflation, 1 = give priority to something noneconomic); I_3 = Left-Right Ideology (from 1 to 10 on a Left-Right self-placement scale).

[b] V_8 = vote intention (1 = Communist, 2 = Unified Socialist, 3 = Socialist, 4 = Left Radical, 5 = Centrist, 6 = Union for French Democracy, 7 = Gaullist); P_8 = unemployment (1 = unemployed during last 3 years, 2 = not unemployed during last 3 years); C_8 = job opportunities in the area (1 = very bad, 2 = rather bad, 3 = quite good, 4 = very good); I_8 = Left-Right ideology (from 1 to 10 on a Left-Right self-placement scale).

support for Leftist parties. But discontent over personal circumstance does not exhaust the economic response of the French voter. Beyond that, evaluations about the economics of the larger community guide the vote. Specifically, voters who believe that the nation should pursue the inflation fight more vigorously, or who perceive area employment opportunities as limited, tend to favor the Left.

This microlevel investigation was inspired by uncertainties over the results from aggregate time series research on French national economic fluctuations and mass electoral behavior. Do individual French voters actually respond to economic changes, as the bulk of these studies suggest? And, if so, what is the nature of that response? My analysis indicates that these aggregate patterns do indeed reflect individual behaviors. Further, although the same survey items were not administered repeatedly, a few tentative generalizations emerge about the specific variables involved. Most important, the French voter appears to respond to variations in income, unemployment, and inflation, the three independent variables most commonly examined in the research on economics and elections. Moreover, that electoral response may be elicited either by personal experience of the economic condition (e.g., "I'm unemployed") or collective judgment about it (e.g., "the nation's unemployment rate is up").

The existence of a personal and collective economic reaction on the part of the French electorate represents a central difference from the United States microlevel findings. In the American case, economics appears to influence the congressional vote, but most of the evidence indicates this impact derives from collective, rather than personal, economic events. Kinder and Kiewiet (1979:499) summarize this view well, concluding that "voters draw not on their recent personal economic experiences, but on information about aggregate economic conditions. . . ." An interesting question is why these French and American differences in economic response appear. This issue cannot be resolved here, but I would like to suggest a "cultural" explanation for the findings.

According to this cultural argument, Americans have such a strong sense of individualism that they blame themselves, not government, for their personal economic difficulties (see Feldman, 1982; Kinder and Kiewiet, 1979:522–23; Kinder and Mebane, 1982). For instance, if they are out of a job, they see it as their own fault, perhaps feeling they did not work hard enough, or were not really qualified. To better their economic lot, then, they believe they must change themselves, rather than change their congressional representative. From an individualist perspective, such self-blame for one's financial problems is to some extent rational, because government in the United States is relatively fragmented and nondirective, at least with regard to people's economic life.

For France, by way of contrast, individualistic values are not so strong. The vaunted individualism of the past has been eroded by many years of continuing centralization of political and economic authority in the national government. Thus, it is reasonable for the French to express their personal economic grievances at the ballot box, for government decisions may well be responsible for their financial plight. This cultural explanation for the presence of a personal economic vote in France, as opposed to the United States, is buttressed by data from Britain. Butler and Stokes (1974:404) found that in Britain, a nation with a weak individualistic tradition and a strong central government, support for the Conservative government varied with the voter's own financial situation.

A final matter needs to be dealt with. The model of Table 1 was developed to assess the effects of economic conditions, rather than to provide a complete explanatory model of French voting behavior. As the equations stand, they perpetuate the parochial character of much of this research, neglecting other variables that ought to be included. A more fully specified model would broaden our understanding of the French voter and, at the same time, apply a still more rigorous test of spuriousness to the coefficients of the economic variables. We cannot elaborate here a detailed rationale for a particular explanatory model of French voting behavior. However, there are several variables, representing well-known cleavages in French politics, which certainly must be incorporated in any model that aims to be complete (see, for example, Cerny, 1972:445). The most important of these is Left-Right ideology, which I have already included. In addition, social class, religion, and region clearly demand consideration. This suggests the following expanded model of French voting choice:

$$V = b_0 + b_1 P + b_2 C + b_3 I + b_4 S + b_5 R + b_6 G + e \tag{4}$$

where V, P, C, and I are defined as with Eq. (1), and S = social class, R = religion, G = region.

Below are the OLS estimates of this model for our most recent election year, 1978. (The results for the 1973 election parallel these and, therefore, are not reported):

$$\hat{V}_8 = -1.21 + .31^*P_8 + .20^*C_8 + .65^*I_8 + .33^*S_8 + .18^*R_8$$
$$\quad\quad (.13) \quad\quad (.08) \quad\quad (.03) \quad\quad (.06) \quad\quad (.05)$$
$$\quad -.24G_{18} - .03G_{28} - .24G_{38} - .36^*G_{48} + .21G_{58} - .40^*G_{68}$$
$$\quad\quad (.17) \quad\quad (.18) \quad\quad (.22) \quad\quad (.18) \quad\quad (.24) \quad\quad (.17)$$
$$\quad\quad\quad R^2 = .66 \quad\quad\quad N = 608 \tag{5}$$

where V_8, P_8, C_8, I_8 are measured as in Eq. (3); S_8 = the occupation of the head of the household (worker = 1, peasant = 2, middle class = 3); R_8 = church attendance (1 = no religion, 2 = never attend, 3 = a few times a year, 4 = once a week, 5 = several times a week); G_{18} to G_{68} = dummy variables for region (1 if in the region, 0 otherwise), e.g., G_{18} = 1 if the respondent lives in the northwest, 0 if not (there are seven regions, with Paris serving as the base category); R^2 = the coefficient of multiple determination; N = the sample size; the figures in parenthesis = the standard errors; the asterisk (*) = significant at the .05 level.

This model explains the legislative voting behavior of the French electorate rather well, as the $R^2 = .66$ indicates. Further, as expected, the additional variables significantly influence party preference. And, what is more interesting, the variables of personal economic situation and collective economic judgment manifest a statistically significant impact, even after imposition of these extensive controls. Such a finding strengthens the notion that the French public, in deciding which party to vote for, takes economic conditions into account.

Summary and Conclusions

This microlevel analysis demonstrates that economic conditions help determine the vote in French legislative elections. Individual perceptions of personal economic hardship, such as inadequate income or joblessness, and national economic difficulties, such as rising inflation or unemployment, move the French voter to the Left opposition. Especially when joined with aggregate studies, the influence of economic circumstance on the vote seems more pervasive, more important in France than in the United States. A contemporary example is the 1981 victory of Mitterrand and the Left, which can be accounted for by economic voting. My research has shown that the more economic malcontents there are, the more Leftist votes are expected. Relevant data point to the presence of an unusually large number of economic malcontents prior to the 1981 elections. Under the Giscard administration, national unemployment and inflation had reached annual rates of 7 and 14 percent, respectively, figures unequaled during the Fifth Republic. Moreover, these sorry aggregate indicators were reflected in the public perception of the state of the economy. Since 1972, the European Community has conducted consumer surveys in member states three times a year. A central item asks about the "general economic situation in the country now compared to 12 months ago." In the last survey before the Mitterrand election, this subjective index of national economic well-being stood at 77, its lowest level ever (Directorate-General, 1981:3). These readings, taken together, suggest an exceptional number of voters who were dissatisfied with their own economic situation, or with the course of the economy as a whole. This group of economic malcontents was large enough that, when they went to the polls, they tipped the scale to the Left.

Clearly, an economic vote for the Left opposition is often a simple vote against the incumbent, who is blamed for adverse economic conditions. But it can be more complicated. French economic voters, by casting ballots in favor of a Leftist party, could be engaging in policy voting. That is, they may be expressing a preference for particular economic policies of the Left, regardless of whether it is in power. For example, in the United States, Kiewiet (1982:chap. 4) found that the unemployed American voter almost always favors the Democrats, even if the party controls the White House. Returning to France, the 1978 IFOP survey cited earlier revealed that, for two-thirds of the electorate, the "fundamental" reason for voting with the Left would be its unemployment policy. This suggests that economic voting in France is distinguished by a policy component, as well as the more obvious incumbency component. Unhappily, separation of the effects of these two components is difficult, because for all the elections under the Fifth Republic the Left has been in opposition. Hence, unlike the situation in the United States, there has not been an opportunity to observe whether economic hardship translates into a vote for a Left-leaning party when that party itself holds office. However, the Mitterrand triumph of 1981 has provided a way out of this research dilemma.

With the arrival of the next legislative election, the French voter will finally have the chance to decide whether or not to vote for a Left that is in power. On the one hand, if economic voting were based exclusively on an evaluation of the incumbent, then the signs of the economic conditions coefficients would merely reverse themselves, showing that the Right opposition now benefited from economic trouble. On the other hand, if French economic voting is some combination of policy and incumbency orientations, as seems likely, then the future signs of these coefficients are less predictable. The incumbency status of the Mitterrand coalition will undoubtedly cost the Left votes among those who have suffered economically. Nevertheless, this vote loss might be at least partially offset if the Leftist government pursues promising economic policies. But, as of this writing (late 1982), the Socialist economic policies have not been notably successful on either the unemployment or inflation fronts. Thus, the possibility exists that any policy component in French economic voting which favors the Left is being eroded by their weak economic performance in office. In the long run, if Left and Center-Right parties begin to alternate in power with some regularity, then we might expect policy-oriented voting to fade further, as these different ruling coalitions struggle with the rather intractable economic realities confronting the closing years of the twentieth century.

References

Arcelus, Francisco, and Allan Meltzer
  1975 "The effects of aggregate economic variables on congressional elections."
       American Political Science Review 69:1232–39.
Barnes, Samuel H., and Roy Pierce
  1971 "Public opinion and political preferences in France and Italy." Midwest Journal of Political Science 15:643–60.
Bloom, Howard S., and H. Douglas Price
  1975 "Voter response to short-run economic conditions: the asymmetric effect of prosperity and recession." American Political Science Review 69:1240–54.
Butler, David, and Donald Stokes
  1974 Political Change in Britain. New York: St. Martin's Press.
Campbell, Bruce A.
  1974 "The future of the Gaullist majority: an analysis of French electoral politics." American Journal of Political Science 18:67–94.
Cerny, P. G.
  1972 "Cleavage, aggregation, and change in French politics." British Journal of Political Science 2:443–55.
Directorate-General for Economic and Financial Affairs, Commission of the European Communities
  1981 "Economic prospects-consumer survey results." European Economy, No. 2-July 1981, Supplement C. Luxembourg: Office for Official Publications of the European Communities.
Feldman, Stanley
  1982 "Economic self-interest and political behavior." American Journal of Political Science 26:446–66.
Fiorina, Morris P.
  1978 "Economic retrospective voting in American national elections: a micro-analysis." American Journal of Political Science 22:426–43.
Goodman, Saul, and Gerald H. Kramer
  1975 "Comment on Arcelus and Meltzer, 'the effect of aggregate economic conditions on congressional elections.'" American Political Science Review 69:1255–65.
Hibbs, Douglas A., Jr., and Nicholas Vasilatos
  1981 "Economics and politics in France: economic performance and political support for Presidents Pompidou and Giscard d'Estraing." European Journal of Political Research 9:133–45.
Kiewiet, D. Roderick
  1981 "Policy-oriented voting in response to economic issues." American Political Science Review 75:448–59.
  1982 Macroeconomics and Micropolitics. Chicago: University of Chicago Press.
Kinder, Donald R.
  1981 "Presidents, prosperity, and public opinion." Public Opinion Quarterly 45:1–21.
Kinder, Donald R., and D. Roderick Kiewiet
  1979 "Economic discontent and political behavior: the role of personal grievance and collective economic judgments in congressional voting." American Journal of Political Science 23:495–527.
Kinder, Donald R., and Walter R. Mebane, Jr.
  1982 "Politics and economics in everyday life." In Kristen Monroe (ed.), The Political Process and Economic Change. New York: Agathon Press.
Klorman, Ricardo
  1978 "Trend in personal finances and the vote." Public Opinion Quarterly 42:31–48.
Kramer, Gerald H.
  1971 "Short-term fluctuations in U.S. voting behavior, 1896–1964." American Political Science Review 65:131–45.

Kuklinski, James H., and Darrell M. West
  1981 "Economic expectations and voting behavior in United States Senate and House Elections." American Political Science Review 75:436–47.
Lafay, Jean-Dominique
  1977 "Les conséquences électorales de la conjoncture économique: essais de prevision chiffrée pour Mars 1978." Vie et Sciences Economiques 75:1–7.
Lepper, Susan
  1974 "Voting behavior and aggregate policy targets." Public Choice 18:67–82.
Lewis-Beck, Michael S.
  1980 "Economic conditions and executive popularity: the French experience." American Journal of Political Science 24:306–23.
  1983 "France: the stalled electorate." In Paul Allen Beck, Russell J. Dalton, and Scott C. Flanagan (eds.), Electoral Change in Industrial Democracies. Princeton, New Jersey: Princeton University Press.
Lewis-Beck, Michael S., and Paolo Bellucci
  1982 "Economic influences on legislative elections in multiparty systems: France and Italy." Political Behavior 4:93–107.
McCracken, Paul W.
  1973 "The practice of political economy." American Economic Review 63:168–71.
Norpoth, Helmut, and Thom Yantek
  1981 "Economic conditions and government support: deflating a popular myth; or, can political economy survive Box-Jenkins and live to find true significance?" Prepared for delivery at the 1981 Annual Meeting of the American Political Science Association.
Rosa, Jean-Jacques, and Daniel Amson
  1976 "Conditions économiques et élections: Une analyse politico-econometrique (1920–1973)." Revue Française de Science Politique 26:1101–24.
Sigelman, Lee, and Yung-mei Tsai
  1981 "Personal finances and voting behavior: a reanalysis." American Politics Quarterly 9:371–400.
Stigler, George J.
  1973 "General economic conditions and national elections." American Economic Review 63:160–67.
Tufte, Edward R.
  1975 "Determinants of the outcomes of midterm congressional elections." American Political Science Review 69:812–26.
Weatherford, M. Stephen
  1978 "Economic conditions and electoral outcomes: class differences in response to recession." American Journal of Political Science 22:917–38.
Whiteley, Paul, ed.
  1980 Models of Political Economy. London and Beverly Hills: Sage.
Wides, Jeffery W.
  1976 "Self-perceived economic change and political orientations: a preliminary exploration." American Politics Quarterly 4:395–411.
  1979 "Perceived economic competency and the Ford/Carter election." Public Opinion Quarterly 43:535–43.

[18]

Decentralisation in Socialist France: The Politics of Pragmatism

Yves Mény

Most observers of French political life were surprised in June 1981 that the first bills presented to Parliament by the new Socialist Government were about decentralisation. There were several reasons for this: for thirty years it had been the subject of continuous, almost ritual declarations and grandiose plans but always combined with extreme caution when it came to translating them into action;[1] there was a general assumption that decentralisation was something to be championed in opposition and to be quietly forgotten once in power; the question was not even mentioned during the presidential and legislative election campaigns of April-June 1981.

The suddenness and extent of the reforms (14 laws proposed of which ten have already been passed) can be explained by a combination of factors: the ideological evolution of the Left, which from being Jacobin became progressively more decentralist and regionalist in the 1960s and 1970s under the influence of moderate elements of the political clubs; the increasing strength at the local level of the Socialist Party, which caused so much trouble in the 1970s between elected local socialist officials and the Giscard d'Estaing Government;[2] and lastly, the desire on the part of Gaston Defferre (Minister of the Interior and of Decentralisation) to associate his name with a local government reform purporting to be the most important since the French Revolution and the Local Government Act of 1884. This last factor is not simply anecdotal: the timing of the reforms and their nature owe a great deal to the personality of the minister who, as an old hand at politics, was well aware that the successful introduction of the reforms would depend on the speed of their adoption by Parliament: too many worthy reforms had been promised by Mitterrand and some would inevitably be squeezed out of the political agenda. On the other hand, the new minister illustrates almost to the point of caricature the prototype of a French politician: Gaston Defferre has been a Deputy since 1945, but is also Mayor of Marseilles, a member of the *Conseil général*, Chairman of the Regional Council, Chairman of numerous para-State bodies, without counting all the other organisations which he controls through faithful subordinates. In short, he is a prime example of *ces notables rouges*,[3] whose national strength is underpinned by a powerful local base. In such circumstances it is hardly surprising that the reform which is currently going through Parliament has little to do with the somewhat radical *autogestionnaire* programme of the Socialist Party. Not only does one search in vain for the slightest trace of *autogestion* in the texts of the adopted laws; there is not even a semantic allusion to it.

Certain observers were surprised. Mark Kesselman, for example, after pointing out that 'the socialist project looks to a new political formula to restructure the State, civil society and their mutual relations in an era of capital crisis', deplored the disappearance of *autogestion* in the reforms.[4] The astonishment would have been somewhat less had more attention been given to the promoters of the reforms and to the composition of the group of principal beneficiaries of the party in power – namely the mayors of Socialist towns. The reforms are not for idealistic activists. They satisfy the needs and aspirations of urban elites and *notables* and in particular the 'bosses' of the big cities, *départements* and regions.

By June 1983 ten laws had been adopted: the first concerns the 'rights and freedoms of the communes, *départements* and regions'. The others deal with the organisation of the regions in Corsica and French Overseas Territories, modify the local electoral system, reorganise the cities of Paris, Lyons and Marseilles and implement the first transfers of powers and finance. Among the plans being discussed, other than a new law for transferring powers, there is the important reform of the civil service which aims at harmonising the status of local and State officials.

There is no need to give all the details of these reforms,[5] but the principal elements are as follows:

– The executives of the *départements* and regions are in future to be chosen by elected bodies, the regional council of each of the 22 regions being itself elected by direct suffrage as from 1984 or 1985.
– Prefects are to be known as *commissaires de la République* and are the representatives of the State in the *départements* and regions; but they cease to be the executives of these territorial units.
– The *a priori* supervision of the prefect and the representative of the Ministry of Finance in the decisions of communes, *départements* and regions is to be replaced by *a posteriori* legal control exercised by administrative tribunals or the new regional courts of accounts.
– New powers are or will be transferred to the three levels of local government (commune, *département*, region) in the areas of town-planning, housing, professional training and social matters; although each level has the main responsibility for certain areas, the transfer of the requisite powers has *not* led to a clear division of respective roles.
– Corsica and the French Overseas Territories (Guyana, Martinique,

Guadeloupe, Réunion) are granted specific statutes which will result in a number of new institutions rather than the acquisition of important new powers.
– The cities of Paris, Lyons and Marseilles have been divided into separate units with mayors whose task is to run local services.
– Lastly, in the place of a fiscal reform which has been shelved, the Government has done two things: it has transformed a number of specific subsidies into a block grant and will guarantee the transfer of the necessary resources to enable decentralisation to be effective.[6]

At the present time the legislative load is considerable and implementation continues apace. The legal texts and a preliminary view of their implementation does allow, however, an appreciation of the outlines of the reforms and enables a number of hypotheses to be formulated on the potential implications for the politico-administrative system as a whole and centre-periphery relations in France in particular.

It is meant as no insult to politicians to suggest that there are certain purely political reasons for introducing a particular reform. These reasons, though not overwhelming, were far from absent from the present policy of decentralisation. The first reason was that this was a propitious moment for such a reform. For the first time under the Fifth Republic, there existed a concordance of views between the national political majority and the majority of local elected representatives in the large cities. The Government was, therefore, able to benefit from the support of two-thirds of the mayors of towns with more than 30,000 inhabitants, whereas the governments of De Gaulle, then of Pompidou and Giscard d'Estaing had had to face the hostility either of the national opposition parties and the majority of local elected representatives or the passive resistance of the *notables* whom no one wanted to upset. The fact that the Left was in power at both national and local levels along with the temporary collapse of morale of the Centre and the Right provided the right circumstances for change. But Gaston Defferre, the Minister of the Interior (and almost alone in the new Government in having had ministerial experience under the Fourth Republic), understood that the honeymoon period would be short-lived and that he had therefore to act quickly.

The timing of the reforms is not the only element in which political reasons played a crucial role. From numerous points of view the adopted laws are less inspired by a desire for decentralisation than by politically-partisan considerations. Examples are not lacking: regional reform in the French Overseas Territories was designed to give the Left a majority which the electoral system did not provide at a departmental level. When the Constitutional Council annulled the law voted by Parliament the Government could achieve its ends only by creating in the same territory both a departmental assembly and a regional assembly. In the same way, the electoral system in the towns with more than 3,500 inhabitants pays only lip-service to the promise of the Socialist Party to introduce proportional representation: the clever combination of both proportional and majoritarian systems guaranteed to the party, which obtained either an absolute or even relative majority

of the votes cast, over-representation in the town council.[7] The paradox is
that such a system, considered in Italy as beyond the pale since it allowed the
victory of the Fascists, is considered as liberal in France, because for the first
time since 1965 it permitted opposition representation in the councils of
towns with more than 30,000 inhabitants. Under the previous electoral
system in these towns a party which won a majority took all the seats.

The reform which has created the most stir, however, was the decision to
divide Paris into 20 areas with their own mayors and councils elected within
each *arrondissement* and responsible for the affairs of that *arrondissement*.
Whilst the city, the mayor and the city council of Paris were to continue, it
was obvious that the 'balkanisation' of the capital would have been a
considerable blow to the Mayor, Jacques Chirac, the Gaullist leader, who
had made of his post a show-case for his managerial abilities, an instrument
for the mobilisation of resources and a platform for the eventual acquisition
of the Presidency. The violent reaction of the Mayor of Paris and the
opposition obliged the Government to beat a hasty retreat: in addition it did
not go unnoticed that, although the initial plan was confined to Paris, there
were further plans for extending the process to Lyons and to Marseilles (of
which Gaston Defferre, the Minister for the Interior, is Mayor). What could
have turned out to be a disaster for the Government finally saved the Mayor
of Marseilles his post. Whilst Paris and Lyons were divided respectively into
20 and nine *arrondissements* corresponding to the traditional administrative
and electoral divisions, the 16 administrative divisions of Marseilles were
transformed into only six electoral constituencies, the limits of which were
cleverly drawn to protect a marginal seat. Defferre did not achieve his aims
in Paris and Lyons since the opposition won all the newly divided constituencies in the 1982 elections. On the other hand, he rescued the situation in
Marseilles: even though the opposition was elected to two *mairies d'arrondissement* out of five, Gaston Defferre remained Mayor of Marseilles despite the fact that the Left obtained 5,000 votes fewer than the
Right in the city as a whole!

Apart from these inevitable partisan and political aspects, the reforms
themselves showed great prudence, despite symbolic and spectacular ges-
tures, such as the 'suppression' of the prefect. Even though the Socialists are
often accused of being inexperienced and dogmatic, it seems that at least in
the area of decentralisation, they have demonstrated pragmatism and have
clearly shown that they can learn from experience. The experience in
question comes first of all from the Fifth Republic which for more than 20
years has played with radical reforms in regrouping communes. Failure had
been so obvious (after twenty years there were still more than 36,000 of the
original 38,000 communes in France) that all the politicians had rallied to the
politics of the status quo. The cry is: 'Hands off the communes!' This total
consensus of opinion confirmed that, at least in the matter of fusion and
regrouping communes, local reform could not be introduced over the heads
of the local elected representatives. The latter constitutes a large pressure
group (approximately 500,000) of whom virtually all are from the rural
areas. Their influence in the appointment of senators, the local links of
national politicians (80 per cent of whom hold local elected office) all

contribute to fossilising the present situation. Just as the communal map could not be redrawn, so the Government has been unwilling – or unable – to decide which is the more important, the *département* or the region, or radically to reform and extend the basis of inter-commune cooperation – especially in urban areas (districts and urban communities). The changes were, therefore, only marginal and achieved more by encouragement than by constraint and more by addition than by suppression.

The experience of previous governments is not the only one to have inspired Socialist reformers. A large number of the changes introduced were based on the experience gained in local affairs by the Socialists in the large towns and the *départements*. The reforms being introduced reflect as much the past exasperation of locally elected representatives with the men and methods of the central executive as they do any traditional conception of the exercise of local power in France.[8] The suppression of prefectoral super-vision over the decisions of the departmental, regional and municipal coun-cils, the introduction of juridical control of finances at the expense of the representative of the Ministry of Finance, the *Trésorier-payeur-général* (TPG), the removal of the prefect as the executive of the *Conseil général* and regional council are substantial and symbolic reforms which bear witness to the irritation of elected Socialists with the central administration under Giscard d'Estaing. On the other hand, the absence of reform on citizen participation or the French habit of accumulating elected offices (*cumul des mandats*)[9] is ample demonstration that there exists a considerable area of agreement amongst politicians as to the 'untouchable' elements of the political system, despite all the election speeches and ministerial promises to the contrary.

In other respects, reform is indeed merely a legal recognition of former practices of the elected representatives – particularly the Socialists – in the most dynamic urban areas or *départements* and regions. Put another way, the Minister of the Interior, Gaston Defferre and the Prime Minister, Pierre Mauroy, have enshrined in legal form the practices used in Marseilles and in Lille (where they are the mayors) which work well but have been hindered by the rules and regulations which the central government and its local representatives can use from time to time to make things difficult. This view is supported by a number of empirical observations: the mayors of the large towns, the chairmen of influential *conseils généraux*, some chairmen of regional councils, had already made for themselves powerful local bases from which to apply strong pressure[10] on the prefectoral administration, the local administrators and financial and accounting services. One recent study from Lille and Valenciennes in collaboration with Jack Hayward[11] has confirmed just how powerful are the innovating *notables*, just how ingenious and inventive are their extra-legal practices, and just how powerless the administration is to control this policy of continuous harassment from local elected representatives. In short, the State administration, despite its theoretical and traditional *imperium* is exploited by the most powerful local *notables*. As may be seen, such a perception is at odds with the contention that most of the power and the source of the so-called '*mal français*' is to be found in the central administration. In the struggle between the 'boss' (the mayor) and the 'manager' (the prefect) it is the former who, during the past two decades, has got the better of the latter who has now been downgraded from the prestigious title of prefect to the more prosaic *Commissaire de la République*. In the same way, the suppression of prefectoral supervision over the regional, departmental and local authorities is less revolutionary than supporters and opponents would like to admit. Prefectoral supervision was no longer the meddlesome nuisance often described, but had increasingly become a source of legal guidance particularly useful to the small communes. According to a recent colloquium[13] the Prefect of the Somme pointed out that in his *département* only seven councillors out of 9,000 had been sacked between 1975 and 1980. The number of decisions which have been taken in any one year by local councils has varied from three to 22 for 783 communes (out of a total of over 36,000) and in 1975, for example, only two were annulled. At the national level the figures given in a debate in Parliament are of the same order. So was the 1981 reform merely a gesture so far as the smallest communes were concerned? By and large, it was. The possibility of a prefect telling a commune that he intends taking one of its decisions to an administrative tribunal merely formalises *a posteriori* something which occurred *a priori* informally and often at the request of the mayor himself.

On the other hand, compared with what has happened in other European countries over the past two decades, the 1981–83 French reform was not mainly justified by questions of public management – even if the problems of the division of labour, of laws and of personnel management played an important role. In the eyes of the Left, the local system, quite independently of its defects, suffered from two main problems: a lack of democracy in its institutions and the arbitrary character of State intervention. '*Changer la vie, changer l'Etat*' meant that at the local level priority should be given to changes which were considered indispensable to justify the activity of local elites. Put another way, even before modifying or extending the powers to be devolved to the various decentralised levels, the Left considered it essential to invest them with a new legitimacy. In this respect the beliefs of the Left are well known and have been reasserted in two centuries of political combat: the election is the source of all powers and the rule of law protection against arbitrary power. The Left taken together (Socialist Party, Communist Party, Radical Party) have, since the last World War, unceasingly demanded 'democratisation' at the local level and denigrated central control. The Constitution of the Fourth Republic which was considerably influenced by the Left was the first in French history to express this political aspiration, but it was never put into practice. It was, therefore, no surprise that the reforms of 2 March 1981 give formal recognition to the democratic beliefs repeatedly voiced by the Left.

So from now on the legitimacy of power is to be assured at all local levels by recourse to elections: local assemblies, departmental and regional assemblies are now all elected by direct universal suffrage and appoint their own executive bodies. This innovation should not hide the fact that the other mechanisms for the control of executive authority were not considered: referendums, public hearings, neighbourhood councils and other means of practising a participatory and responsive democracy are totally absent. One might be glad about this, since some of these latter methods are less than perfect: they are too often manipulated by unrepresentative pressure groups or are administratively disruptive. But it must be said that the channels for expressing opinions and applying pressure in society are singularly limited. 'One of the unwritten principles of French public law is that people are incapable of self-government', states Michel Bouissou,[14] and Céline Wiener has added, 'Citizens are merely able to choose good representatives, they have no direct role, merely that of electing delegates who will in their name manage or control the managers'.[15]

The inadequacy of the reforms in this respect is forcefully pointed out by the urban associations, the ecologists and the extreme Left – in short, by all those whom the politico-administrative system tries more or less to marginalise. As early as the summer of 1981, for example, *Lutte Ouvrière* expressed its disappointment by saying that decentralisation as proposed would effect only a modest transfer of powers from the centre to the prefects and from the prefects to the electors. But 'for the population as a whole, the changes will by and large be invisible'.[16]

Furthermore, the control of local authorities will henceforth be governed by a legal system, as is the case in most other Western systems – that is to say, answerable to a *judge*. The organisation of centre-periphery relations tends therefore to follow the example of the majority of Western countries. Their experience leads us to expect at least two sorts of difficulty in putting such a new system into operation: on the one hand, a great lack of flexibility in the exercise of jurisdictional control (as seen in Britain) compared with the margin for manoeuvre and negotiation which always characterised prefectoral supervision; on the other hand, there is a considerable risk of a politically-motivated supervision from one tier of local government to another, cutting right across planning procedures and the subsidising of investment projects. These possible developments represent real fears for numerous mayors, especially those of small communes. Something similar has already occurred in Italy where municipal and provincial elected representatives complain *mezza voce* that elected regional representatives have replaced the prefect in exercising supervision.

This process of legitimisation is not, however, going so far as to modify the fundamental character of the politico-administrative system. One of the most significant features of the French local government system is the personalisation, indeed, the authoritarianism which characterises the exercise of power. The length of time that people hold an elected office, the fact that many elected posts are handed on from father to son, the multiplicity of electoral offices held by a single individual (*cumul des mandats*), the methods of decision making are just some of the manifestations of a phenomenon which has little – or no – equivalent in the other countries of Western Europe.[17] This model has until now had two variants: the prefectoral and the mayoral. The first has now been abolished, but the model otherwise remains fully intact. The prefects have been replaced by elected executives, but the concept of a strong power remains – as shown by the rejection of the proposals of the Communist Party which sought a more collegial system of decision making. It is not the task here to assess the advantages (definite) or the inconveniences (no less definite) of such a method, but from the point of view of society the change in the elites has not resulted in any substantial modification in the way things are run.

Quite the contrary: the new opportunities which can be exploited by local and national elites may well result in reinforcing the *cumul des mandats* (against which so far nothing has been done, despite declared intentions to the contrary) and to exacerbate the problems of 'government by delegation'. Since some individuals are holding multiple offices and cannot exercise all of them effectively, they often have recourse to *eminence grises*. The latter are the real managers of day-to-day affairs (and often more), since the mayor, the chairmen of the *Conseil général* and the regional council are simply unable to accomplish all the tasks, any one of which would take up most of their time.

Well-staffed private offices (*cabinets*) which have already been in existence in the big towns for some years are now being recruited at departmental and regional level. Already about 60 prefects and sub-prefects run things in *départements* or regions on behalf of the new elected representatives after having been seconded from the prefectoral corps. Thus one sees now a strange game of 'musical chairs', with one part of the old prefectoral corps removed but reappearing in other slots. And the local system is run by public servants even more than before. Already numerous observers have pointed out the part played by public servants in the elective functions at local and national level in the last few years. But the phenomenon is even more striking if one looks at what has happened in the most important functions. Overall, hardly 10 per cent of the mayors are also public servants – but the proportion is greater in larger towns and more urbanised areas. For example, A. Mabileau and P. Sadran have shown that in the region of Aquitaine, more than half the mayors of towns with more than 10,000 inhabitants are also public servants, and also note that 'the higher you go in the hierarchy of local political responsibilities, the larger the proportion of public servants' (26 per cent of all town councillors, 32 per cent of assistant mayors and 52 per cent of mayors).[18] Similarly, whereas less than 20 per cent of departmental councillors are public servants amongst the members of the departmental executives this proportion rises to more than a quarter.

We are thus witnessing a situation where local government posts are being increasingly taken over by public servants by two means: *sociologically* in the candidates elected and *functionally* by the growing practice of public servants carrying out the administrative and policy tasks of elected individuals. Incidentally it is interesting to note that the reform of the local public service provides, amongst other things, some form of solution to the problem of legitimation by applying to local public servants the rules governing recruitment and careers similar to those of State civil servants. The period when the elected representatives could recruit just whom they wanted '*selon leur bon plaisir*' seems to have disappeared – at least in principle.

One of the obsessions of political debate in France has been the fear that a loosening of the centralised hold would lead to problems in French society and thereby threaten the State. The parliamentary debates in 1981 and 1982 echoed this phobia and were sustained by certain self-interested pressure groups (amongst top officials in particular). Until these recent reforms the only response to calls for greater local and regional autonomy had been chilly. Such an attitude, far from lessening the arguments and dissatisfaction only exacerbated them. Most importantly, in view of its sociological and ideological evolution, the Socialist Party had even suggested these reforms whilst in opposition. Once in power, the Left had no intention of abandoning its promises, all the more so since their implementation no longer involved the apocalyptic consequences which had been threatened *ad nauseam* for two centuries.

The attitude of the Right-wing parties, in power until 1981, had been neither consistent in substance nor intelligent in form. In the Western democracies, social integration is strong since it is based on consensus rather than constraint. This may be seen at the level of social groups, and it also applies at the territorial level, provided that the central government displays some flexibility. The United Kingdom deserves its title, since it tolerates a great diversity of institutions and cultures, particularly in its four principal parts. In matters of local government, education and cultural policy, the absence of uniformity is the rule.[19] Can one imagine Corsica or Belle-Île striking its own coinage or France being represented in the World Cup by four separate teams each with their own anthems and emblems? What a national scandal that would be! Can we imagine the people from the Saar or the Walloons living in France enjoying the right to vote in French national elections? And yet Jersey and the Isle of Man have their own coinage, and the Irish from Eire may take part in British elections if they reside in Great Britain.

The reforms introduced since 1981 have been carried out with the conviction that decentralisation or regionalisation reinforces rather than diminishes national unity. 'Decentralisation and deconcentration', declared M. Defferre in June 1981, 'in giving to the regions the potential to be themselves, to be faithful to their traditions, to their language, to their culture and in creating a harmonious equilibrium between the central power and local authorities, will abolish the causes of conflict'.[20] Certainly this declaration of faith is over-optimistic. As Jacques Chevalier has written, 'The reinforcement of the region promotes the unity of the politico-administrative system only up to a certain point. ... There is, therefore, a threshold above which the effect may be reversed',[21] and 'the process of evolution or transformation is unlikely to stop simply because a policy of decentralisation or regionalisation has been carried out: institutionalisation itself causes problems for the creation of new organs or new relationships constitute a disruption of the system'.[22]

The reforms already agreed illustrate this integrative capacity of a policy of decentralisation and regionalisation. The stakes have now shifted from the area of confrontation with the State and its apparatus to the competition for the exercise of local power. Even if regionalisation in Corsica is far from having resolved all its problems – and indeed has created some new ones – at least it has allowed the inclusion within the overall political system of problems that violent minority groups attempted to solve outside it because of a lack of suitable channels and means of discussion. As Peter Eisinger has rightly pointed out, 'The manner in which individuals and groups behave within a political system is not simply a function of the resources which they control, but depends also on its weak points, the accessibility, the barriers and the resources of the political system itself.'[23] If this strategy of integration is *mainly institutional* it will be by that very fact limited in impact. The events in Corsica have given us a topical example, recently cited by a magistrate during the 15th *Congrès de la Magistrature*: 'The real cause of the present situation', he declared, 'is that, despite the reforms achieved, the socio-political structure has not evolved with them . . . the establishment of the rule of law and a respect for universal suffrage would, in Corsica, be revolutionary'.[24]

Integration may be promoted by means less spectacular than those of structural reform, but they may be more effective. Thus, if the State gives a grant to the regions for cultural purposes this allows certain demands to be satisfied – especially in matters of language. The progress can be seen in the respect both for individual and regional personal identities. But the advantages are no less negligible for the State which by effecting reform calms a situation where the absurd was as evident as the ridiculous, whilst maintaining partial control of the regional cultural policy. It is, of course, a 'block grant', but negotiating and signing a contract imply that a consensus between the signatories has been reached. The State, which provides the money, defines in some way the limits which it will allow to be transgressed whilst preventing the protests of a partner – the region – which by signing the contract has accepted the means by which it was negotiated and its contents.

Apart from its democratic virtue decentralisation has, according to its supporters, another important advantage, that of simplifying administrative procedures by placing decision making at the appropriate level. Such a view would need careful scrutiny because of the numerous factors involved: the transformation of the tasks of local government, the fiscal system, the inter-dependence of territorial units of government and the external constraints they face. It is worth pointing out that the experience of federal states reveals that the relations between the centre and the constituent States far from being simple are becoming increasingly complex. It would be more correct to argue about the administrative unwieldiness (*lourdeur*) which is inherent in the excessive centralisation of decision making. Central ministries which are theoretically omnipotent by virtue of their regulatory and supervisory powers are often unable to ensure proper implementation of their policies. Decentralisation would, therefore, be a means of making the bureaucracy more efficient and simplifying the decision-making process. However, for that to occur the implemenation of a policy of decentralisation should be sensitive to the desired ends. But the present reforms do not appear to be aimed at simplification and efficiency. As we might expect from a long tradition the introduction of new structures has not been accompanied by the abolition of old ones. Although it is difficult at this stage to measure the extent of the phenomenon, it already seems that the local authorities (communes, *départements* and regions) are in the process of creating and reinforcing their services even though those of the State still exist and are to be at least in part transferred to them. A few examples will serve to illustrate this rapid growth which no doubt will be limited only be economic factors: 70 members of the prefectoral corps have been recruited to strengthen the services of the departmental and regional executives; in the region Ile-de-France the running costs rose by 42 per cent between 1981 and 1982; the Auvergne region has announced the creation of a cultural affairs agency.

Corsica, which has barely 200,000 inhabitants has become a caricature of multiple assemblies and bureaucratisation: two departmental councils, a regional council, an economic and social council, a cultural, educational and environmental council, a regional council for the media, without counting the coordination committee for its industrial development of Corsica and the State-Regional employment committee, both of which are limited to the Prime Minister's office. Furthermore, other bodies have been or will be created – one for transport, one for agricultural and rural development and one for hydroelectric power in the Corsican region – and other agencies may be created by Corsica itself under the law of 2 March 1982. The complexity of the political situation in Corsica does not by itself account for this overlapping of powers and institutions. Corsica is but one example of a general phenomenon. The creation of mayors for each of the *arrondissements* in Paris, Lyons and Marseilles will considerably encumber the administrative machine, especially for Lyons where the conurbation, comprising scores of communes, is organised into an 'urban community'. Any important investment will, therefore, have to involve the State, the region, possibly the *département*, the urban community, specific communes and in the case of Lyons, the new councils of the *arrondissements*. The complexity of such a combination results not only from the number of institutions involved but springs also from the multiple roles played by urban individuals. Where previously the prefect used to be the representative of the State, the regional and departmental executive there is now the *commissaire de la République*, who represents the State, a chairman of the regional council and a chairman of the departmental council. Criticism of the present reforms does not imply that the past situation was ideal – that was far from being the case – but the refusal to define the appropriate level of decision making might well increase administrative confusion, stimulate local political rivalries or increase conflicts between local administrations and State field services.

Up to now the risk of such conflicts was limited by the constraints imposed upon State and local officials, even though the most dynamic towns and regions displayed during the 1970s a great deal of imagination and activity in weakening State control. Henceforth the choice is between maintaining a relationship which ensures the predominance of the expert from the State services and the creation of local competitive centres of expertise. But there is a problem: official prefectoral supervision has been abolished and a promise has been made to reduce technical supervision, yet the State field services remain untouched. It is difficult to imagine that the officials of these services whose power has been somewhat reduced both as experts and as decision-makers will for long tolerate this lesser role. The re-emergence of technical control in one form or another is highly probable. The law of 2

March does, of course, forbid the imposition of 'technical norms' except by way of a law or a regulatory decree. But in this matter it is difficult to know whether it is easier to admire the Machiavellianism or the naïvety of the authors of that measure. Such confidence in the importance of form is scarcely justified, because there will be considerable pressure to impose universal technical norms on the jungle of local functions and territorial institutions.

The confrontation between the centre and the localities was avoided either by real or purely formal concessions. But the logic of such concessions is either chaos or the reimposition of uniformity. It is impossible to retain 36,000 communes and completely decentralise powers to that level. In that respect the decision to decentralise urban planning to the commune is either absurd or misleading. Either the communes will be completely responsible (unless they form some kind of intercommunal cooperative agencies or come to some form of intercommunal planning agreements) in which case disastrous consequences are to be feared because of the total inadequacy of the average commune to deal with the problems of urban planning,[25] if the State or the regions have to impose planning norms which are numerous, precise and highly detailed, then decentralisation will become a fiction, a source of frustration and disillusion.

Finally, one may wonder about the consequences which are likely in the event of harmonising the statutory conditions of State and local officials. The purpose of the reform is both to increase mobility between the two types of officials and to give to each the same rights with respect to recruitment, promotion and unionisation. It is still difficult to forecast the consequences of a bill which is still being debated in Parliament but it may well be that the measure will combine the negative aspects of both 'nationalisation' and 'localism' which is already noticeable in certain parts of the State service, for example, in education. 'Nationalisation', that is to say the imposition of universal rules, is already highly developed in the State administration. But, in return for these guarantees, State officials have always sought to ensure at least a minimum of geographical mobility both in appointments and promotions. Local officials on the other hand who were recruited and promoted under conditions which were frequently undesirable and precarious were guaranteed almost total geographical stability, since they depended on a local authority and the opportunities of moving from one authority to another were virtually non-existent. State officials will exert strong pressure to obtain the same stability: henceforth if they are threatened with a transfer they will try to move to a local authority which will give them the same advantages without the inconveniences of mobility. The high degree of bureaucratisation of the local services might then well spread to the State administration.

Moreover, the local authorities may become highly attractive for the top officials working for the State, particularly amongst the younger generation who find it increasingly difficult to obtain responsible posts in the State administration. Since local authorities lack high quality personnel they may become highly attractive for all those who view a post as general secretary of a big town or *département* as a better prospect than a humble job in the

Ministry of Education. Once again, it is the possibility of moving from one level to another which may accelerate a process, evident since 1981, resulting in scores of prefects and sub-prefects joining local services.

If the two trends discussed above were to become pronounced, the local services would become *quantitatively* more important because of the transfer of State personnel linked largely to the transfer of powers and *qualitatively* more dependent upon the State administration. The increasing uniformity of local policies would not result, as it has in Great Britain, in the mobility of local officials who move from one local authority to another to improve their personal position but rather would result in a one-way movement from the State administration to local authorities. The rigidity of the resulting system might then be maximised.

CONCLUSION

The Defferre reforms are being introduced in curious circumstances: despite several protests of a purely formal nature, the Right has given them its blessing and has even complained about their being implemented too slowly; the Left and the unions give their support to a policy in which elements of decentralisation (for example, the abolition of prefectoral supervision and the transfer of powers and financial resources) are combined with elements of unquestionable centralisation, for instance, in the conditions relating to local officials; the elected representatives in the small communes feel completely unaffected by a reform which does not conern them and which they are incapable of implementing (to understand the ministerial circular which explains in 20 pages of small print the changes in supervision, one would need to have a law degree!); finally, the population is totally uninterested in the process, even though the local elections of March 1983 could have been the opportunity for a serious debate on the issue. The only significant reaction took place in Paris when the first governmental bill threatened the capital with being broken up.

The reforms therefore have served neither to change the management of local authorities nor to enhance the participation of the population. Nor do they constitute a simplification of procedures or decision making. Quite the opposite is the case: they do not fundamentally change the basic mechanisms and structures of the French politico-administrative system since they leave untouched the *cumul des mandats* and existing organisational structures.

If the reforms have provoked so little reaction it is because in very large measure they merely confirm processes which had been under way for the previous 10 to 15 years. They give legal blessing to a *de facto* situation – the accession to power of the major local elected representatives – and at the same time legitimises the increased intervention of local authorities in economic and social affairs. It is this congruence between the previous practice and the new legislation which explains the moderate reactions of certain pressure groups. The prefectoral corps, for example, made no protest against a reform which nonetheless profoundly affects its conditions and its role. But certain members of the corps drew the immediate consequences by taking up posts with the new departmental and regional executives:

despite the redistribution of roles, the osmosis between administration and politics at the level of executive authority remains a basic characteristic of the French system.

The reforms do not constitute a revolution but rather a shift in the balance of power and influence from representatives of the State to those of the local authorities. Both have somewhat different cards to play and the rules of the game have been modified, but it is premature to predict the final outcome. One thing is, however, certain: just as during the 1970s, the differences and variations between *départements* and between regions are likely to be accentuated. The previous legislation was more suited to rural rather than urban France, to a hierarchical system rather than to one of inter-dependence. The present reforms bring the law into line with the require-ments of urban and regional elites. But a new problem has arisen because the reforms are without real consequence for most communes and probably for some *départements* and regions. Doubtless it is the price to be paid in a country which, in spite of its policy of decentralisation, has some difficulty in conceiving a reform other than in terms of uniformity and universal implementation.[26]

NOTES

1. Yves Mény, *Centralisation et décentralisation dans le débat politique français, 1945–1974* (Paris: LGDJ, 1974).
2. Vincent Wright, *Continuity and Change in France* (London: Allen and Unwin, 1984).
3. Denis Lacorne, *Les notables rouges* (Paris: Presses de la Fondation Nationale des Sciences Politiques, 1980).
4. Mark Kesselman, 'The Tranquil Revolution at Clochemerle: Decentralisation in France and the Crisis of Advanced Capitalism', Unpublished paper, *Conférence de Bellagio*, March 1982.
5. For further details, see D. E. Ashford, 'Reconstructing the French 'Etat': Progress of the *loi Defferre*' *West European Politics*, July 1983, pp. 263-70.
6. For details of these measures, see *Administration 1982* (Paris: Editions Economica, 1982).
7. Law of 19 novembre 1982, *Journal Officiel*, 20 November 1982, p. 3487.
8. Jeanne Becquart-Leclercq, *Paradoxes du pouvoir local* (Paris: Presses de la Fondation Nationale des Sciences Politiques, 1976).
9. M. Reydellet, 'Le cumul des mandats', *Revue de Droit Public*, no. 3, 1979, p. 693 *et seq.*; and Jeanne Becquart-Leclercq, 'Cumul des mandats et culture politique', Unpublished paper, Bordeaux, December 1982.
10. Jacques Lagroye, *Société et politique: Jacques Chaban-Delmas à Bordeaux* (Paris: Pédone, 1973); Yves Mény, 'Permanence and Change; The Relations between Central Govern-ment and Local Authorities in France', *Government and Planning*, Vol. 1, 1983, p. 17-28.
11. Jack Hayward and Yves Mény, 'Economic Incentives in Lille and Valenciennes', working paper, Princeton, 1981.
12. Howard Machin, *The Prefect in French Public Administration* (London: Croom Helm, 1977).
13. Fédéralisme et décentralisation', *Revue française d'administration publique*, January-March 1982, no. 21.
14. Michel Bouissou, 'La pratique référendaire en France', *Revue Internationale de Droit Comparé*, 1976, no. 2, p. 276.
15. Céline Wiener, 'Service public ou autogestion: d'un mythe à l'autre?', *Mélanges Charlier* (Paris: Ed. de l'Université, 1981), p. 330.
16. *Lutte Ouvrière*, 8 August 1981.
17. Yves Mény, 'Le maire, ici et ailleurs', *Pouvoirs*, no. 24, 1983, p. 19.

POLICIES OF DECENTRALISATION 79

18. A. Mabileau and Pierre Sadran, 'Administration et politique au niveau local', in J. L. Quermonne, *Administration et politique en France sous la Ve République* (Paris: Presses de la FNSP, 1981).
19. R. A. W. Rhodes and Ed Page, 'The Other Government of Britain', in Ian Budge, (ed.), *Political Processes in British Society* (London: Longmans, 1983).
20. *Le Monde*, 10 June 1981.
21. Jacques Chevallier, *Le pouvoir régional* (Paris: PUF, 1982), p. 183.
22. Yves Mény, 'Les crises de l'Etat', *Pouvoirs*, no. 19, p. 18.
23. Peter Eisinger, 'The Conditions of Protest Behavior in American Cities', *American Political Science Review*, March 1973, p. 11.
24. *Le Monde*, 20 November 1983.
25. Yves Mény, 'Urban planning in France: Dirigisme and pragmatism, 1945–80', in David McKay, (ed.), *Planning and Politics in Western Europe* (London: Macmillan, 1982).
26. The uniformity of rules does not preclude, however, considerable variations in practice. See, on this 'pragmatic' interpretation of the French system, Douglas Ashford, *British Dogmatism and French Pragmatism – Central-Local Policy-Making in the Welfare State* (London: Allen and Unwin, 1982).

[19]

The Executive Divided Against Itself:
Cohabitation in France, 1986–1988

ROY PIERCE

From March 1986 to May 1988 France was headed by a leftist President and a rightist Prime Minister. The background to this unusual situation is presented, and the experience itself — referred to as 'cohabitation' — is discussed in detail.

The complex game that the two executive leaders played during the period was regulated by the constitutional rules, conditioned by the electoral calendar and the narrowness of the prime minister's coalition majority, and moderated by public approval and the existence of a bipartisan foreign and defense policy.

The 1986–1988 experience did not overtax the constitutional system, but 'cohabitation' under different conditions could be destabilizing. 'Cohabitation' is like the possibility of the US president being selected by the House of Representatives: not highly probable but possible, not necessarily dangerous but possibly so, and something that arouses little enthusiasm.

For slightly more than two years, from March 1986 to May 1988, France was headed by a leftist president (François Mitterrand) who had been popularly elected in 1981 and by a rightist prime minister (Jacques Chirac) who was supported by a razor-thin legislative majority that had been returned in March 1986. This unusual governing formula, called 'cohabitation', had been anticipated for decades, more often than not with some unease, because it carried the potential for sharp clashes within the very apex of the executive branch, for deadlock, and even for constitutional crisis.

This article discusses, first, the complex constitutional and political background to 'cohabitation'; secondly, the 'cohabitation' experience itself; and finally, the extent to which 'cohabitation' may still carry risks in the future, despite the lack of any seriously destabilizing consequences from the 1986–1988 experience.

'Cohabitation' was not, as has been suggested, a French version of

Governance: An International Journal of Policy and Administration. Vol. 4, No. 3, July 1991 (pp. 270–294), © 1991. Research Committee on the Structure and Organization of Government of the International Political Science Association. ISSN 0952-1895

THE EXECUTIVE DIVIDED AGAINST ITSELF   271

divided government, as it is practiced in the United States under the
separation of powers. The rival executive leaders in France did not
avoid paralysis or crisis through compromise, but rather because of the
pacifying effects of special conditions: the nature of the electoral calendar, mass attitudes toward the °cohabitation° experience, the narrowness of the prime minister's parliamentary majority, and the existence
of a bipartisan foreign and defense policy. Those conditions may not
prevail during future cohabitation experiences.

THE BACKGROUND

The Constitution of the Fifth French Republic is a hybrid system that
grafts a popularly-elected president with a fixed term of office and
extensive constitutional powers onto an otherwise more or less conventional parliamentary system in which the prime minister and the cabinet
are responsible to the popularly-elected legislative chamber, the National Assembly. The French constitutional structure is not unique; the
ill-fated German Weimar Republic was also a hybrid regime, and so are
several small contemporary democracies, including newly democratic
Portugal. But systems in which executive power is divided or shared
are unusual, no doubt because of considerations of the kind expressed
in the 70th *Federalist* with regard to the necessity for unity in the executive.

The structure was designed by Charles de Gaulle and his followers
in 1958 in order to give energy and stability to the executive branch that
earlier, under the parliamentary systems of the Third and Fourth Republics, had generally been weak and unstable. Accordingly, both the
president and the government (the prime minister and the cabinet)
were strengthened relative to Parliament.

To this end, the president was given the power to dissolve the National Assembly once within any 12-month period, to permit the government to hold referenda on certain questions, and to exercise emergency powers. The government was given strict control over the agenda
of Parliament, whose legislative powers are enumerated and not general; the government can require Parliament to vote on complete texts
of bills, thereby avoiding serial amendments; and the government can
be censured only by the vote of a majority of the total membership of
the National Assembly (what the French call an "absolute" majority),
as opposed to a majority of the deputies voting. In addition, an attempt
was made to "separate" the government from Parliament, even as it
remained responsible to it, by requiring newly appointed cabinet ministers with seats in Parliament to resign them and preventing ministers

resigning from the cabinet from returning to their parliamentary seats before the next election.

This structure rested, in part, on the assumption that France would always have a highly fractionalized party system that would make it difficult to produce stable parliamentary majorities and, by extension, stable governments. De Gaulle appears to have believed that the new arrangements would permit French governments to operate in the face of shifting parliamentary majorities the way the United States presidency does, by drawing on support from variously constituted majorities, depending on the issue involved, as opposed to the customary parliamentary model, in which governments normally rely on a single-party majority (as in Great Britain) or on a particular coalition majority (as in most continental European countries) for the entire life of the government.

In fact, the French system worked in the intended fashion only during the first four years of the Fifth Republic, between 1958 and 1962 when, with de Gaulle as president and Michel Debré as prime minister, the government was alternately supported by the Socialists and opposed by the conservatives on Algerian policy, and supported by the conservatives and opposed by the Socialists on economic policy. In what in retrospect turns out to have been an abnormal period, de Gaulle wielded his presidential powers freely, by-passing Parliament by using the referendum, counter-attacking rebellious army officers by using emergency powers, and ultimately dissolving the National Assembly.

After 1962, the French party system began to change in a fundamental way, and by 1967 it had become completely transformed. The earlier electoral and parliamentary fractionalization gave way to two opposing coalitions, each consisting mainly of two rival but allied parties: the Communists and Socialists on the left, and the Gaullists and Giscardians on the right. This left-right configuration, somewhat erroneously described as "quadripolar," characterized the scene until the mid-1980s.

From 1962 to 1981, the rightist coalition was electorally victorious; the rightist parliamentary parties displayed unusual parliamentary discipline; and France experienced a period of comparatively stable right-wing governments.[1] The leftists gained power for the first time when François Mitterrand was elected president in 1981, and parliamentary elections the following month returned a parliamentary majority for the Socialists alone, who naturally provided the requisite parliamentary support for ensuing leftist governments.

From 1962 to 1986, therefore, the pattern of governance in France was one of comparatively stable coalition majorities, and even — for about ten of those years — of single-party majorities, rather than the pattern of shifting parliamentary majorities that the Constitution of the

THE EXECUTIVE DIVIDED AGAINST ITSELF 273

Fifth Republic was designed to permit, but which were evident only from 1958 to 1962.

While the development of two opposing electoral blocs facilitated the creation and maintenance of governing majorities, it also focused attention on the potentiality of the presidency being held by one partisan bloc and the National Assembly being controlled by the opposing bloc. If a parliamentary majority opposed the president, the prime minister supported by that majority would also be opposed to the president, and unity in the executive branch — taken as a whole — would vanish. The ironic outcome could be that the presidency, designed at least in part to help bolster the government in its relations with the legislature, would contribute toward undermining a government that the legislative majority was prepared to support.

In addition to the powers already mentioned above, the French constitution confers numerous powers on the president that can be used to frustrate the prime minister.[2] And quite without regard to the special problem of the two main branches of government being controlled by opposing blocs, the French constitution is less than wholly clear concerning executive powers. Article 15 states that "the President of the Republic is the chief of the armed forces," while Article 20 says that "the Government determines and directs the policy of the nation" and that "it has the administration and the armed forces at its disposal," and Article 21 says that "the Prime Minister directs the activity of the Government" and that "he is responsible for the national defense."

These specific possibilities of conflict within the executive branch and the broader constitutional ambiguities concerning executive power produced occasional commentary but posed few operational problems during the period from 1962 to 1986, when French governments were supported by more or less coherent coalition majorities.[3] The president and the prime minister belonged to the same political tendency if not the same party. There were differences of opinion, sometimes of considerable importance, but the prime minister normally deferred to the president in public. When relations between the two top executive officials became strained to the breaking point, the prime minister resigned.[4] But these were disputes within the same political family. The stakes would be higher if the division within the executive branch were not simply between leaders from the same political bloc but rather between leaders of the two opposing blocs.

With regard to the possibility of divided political control of the presidency and the legislature, and therefore divided control of the presidency and the premiership, it is useful to recall that presidential and legislative elections are not simultaneous in France, as they are every four years in the United States, punctuated regularly by mid-term

274   ROY PIERCE

congressional elections. The French electoral calendar for the presidency and the National Assembly is not permanently fixed. The presidential term is seven years, without restrictions on reeligibility; there is no vice-president; and a new presidential election must be held promptly if the presidency is vacated. The National Assembly may sit no longer than five years, but it may be dissolved by the president at any time (but not more than once within any 12-month period).[5] The intervals between presidential elections, between legislative elections, and between presidential and legislative elections may and do vary.

Divided political control of the presidency and the legislature can come about in one of two ways: a president from one bloc can be elected while there is a majority in the Assembly from the opposing bloc, and a majority from one bloc can be returned to the Assembly while the incumbent president is from the other bloc. In the first situation, there is a way open for the president to try to break the deadlock promptly: he can dissolve the National Assembly. It is not inevitable that the new legislative elections will produce a new majority to support the president, but thus far that has been the case in France. François Mitterrand dissolved the assemblies containing right-wing majorities after each of his two presidential election victories, in 1981 and 1988. In 1981 his Socialist party triumphed spectacularly; in 1988 it did less well, but the legislature has supported a Socialist-led government since that date.

It is the second situation, the election of a legislature with a new majority opposed to the party of the incumbent president, that carried the greater risk of major constitutional and political conflicts. Each time the possibility presented itself, various scenarios were passed in review.[6] During the legislative election campaign of 1973, President Pompidou hinted that if the leftist coalition won a parliamentary majority he would use his constitutional powers to prevent a left-wing government from being formed, although he did not say how he could accomplish that. During the 1978 legislative election campaign, however, when pre-electoral polls were predicting a left-wing victory, President Giscard d'Estaing warned rightist voters that he could do nothing as president to prevent a left-wing majority from enacting its program, but he did not say what he *would* do.

Those were occasions when the presidency was held by the right, and threats to right-wing control were coming from the left. These did not actually come to fruition until 1981, when François Mitterrand was elected president and his Socialist party won a landslide victory at the ensuing legislative elections of the same year. After 1981, relative political positions were reversed. Now it was the left that was in the ascendancy, and the next drive toward divided political control had to come from the right.

THE EXECUTIVE DIVIDED AGAINST ITSELF   275

The popularity of President Mitterrand and of his Socialist party dropped sharply and rapidly after their electoral triumphs of 1981, and by 1984, all the signs were pointing toward a right-wing victory at the legislative elections that would be held no later than 1986. The right was so confident of forthcoming success that something of a debate occurred among rival rightist leaders concerning the stance they should take in such a situation. The most surprising contribution to this debate came from former Prime Minister Raymond Barre (the most favored right-wing politician in the presidential horse-race being conducted at the time by the pollsters). Barre argued that the logic of the constitution required that the president, prime minister and parliamentary majority come from the same political family and that the president should resign so that the voters would have the opportunity to elect a president in conformity with the political views of the newly-elected right-wing parliamentary majority. Barre did not indicate what should be done if the president chose not to resign, other than by inference from his statement that he would not personally cast his vote in parliament in favor of any government that agreed to serve under a left-wing president. If a new rightist parliamentary majority systematically boycotted all prime ministers proposed by the president, government would be paralyzed. That tactic drove President Alexandre Millerand from office in 1924, but circumstances had been very different then from what they were in the 1980s. Such tactics directed against a popularly-elected president acting constitutionally could easily backfire.

The most measured contribution to the discussion came early in the period in the form of a newspaper article by Edouard Balladur (*Le Monde*, 16 Sept. 1983) in which he argued that a left-wing president could continue to serve in office even with a right-wing parliamentary majority, that he would continue to retain his constitutional powers, and that cohabitation between the president and the prime minister would be possible. It was necessary only that the protagonists avoid excessive confrontation, that the new majority not try to paralyze the president, and that the president not refuse to acknowledge that there was a new parliamentary majority.[7]

While rightists debated how to behave after what they confidently believed would be their forthcoming legislative election victory, President Mitterrand took steps to try to prevent it from happening or, at least, to minimize its magnitude. He persuaded his party to change the electoral system for the National Assembly from the single-member district, two-ballot, majoritarian system that had been used for every legislative election since the Fifth Republic was founded, to a list system of proportional representation. The French two-ballot system is highly leveraged with respect to the conversion of votes into seats; the leading coalition (on the left-right basis characteristic of the period from 1962 until the early 1980s) in terms of votes gains a huge premium in seats (Converse and Pierce 1986, 436–40). The French Socialists profited greatly from that effect in 1981; the prospect for 1986, however, was that it would be the rightist coalition that would benefit. Proportional representation, on the other hand, distributes seats to each party roughly proportionately to the votes they receive. Thus proportional representation would closely tie any rightist gains in parliamentary seats to the size of the rightist vote. Moreover, Mitterrand and his supporters had reason to believe that overall gains in the vote for their traditional right-wing opponents, the RPR (Rassemblement pour la République) — the latter-day version of the Gaullists — and the UDF (Union pour la Démocratie Française) — a federation including the old Giscardians and centrist supporters of Raymond Barre — would in any case be limited. Since the previous legislative election, in 1981, a new extreme right-wing party, the National Front, had emerged, and there were grounds for believing that it would cut into the electoral support of the respectable right, thereby capturing seats that would otherwise go to Mitterrand's traditional opponents.

Mitterrand's effort to frustrate the ambitions of the right-wing coalition almost succeeded. The legislative elections of 1986 produced an Assembly in which the RPR and the UDF, with the help of a handful of sympathetic independent deputies, constituted a razor-thin majority. Mitterrand appointed Jacques Chirac, the leader of the RPR and the Mayor of Paris, as Prime Minister. The stage was set for 24 months of cohabitation.

THE EXPERIENCE

The experience of cohabitation between a Socialist president and a right-wing prime minister and parliamentary majority was *conditioned* above all by the electoral calendar and, to a lesser extent, by the narrowness of the government's majority, *regulated* by the constitutional rules, and *moderated* by general popular approval and by the existence in France of a bipartisan foreign and defense policy.

The Electoral Calendar

The importance of the electoral calendar was primordial, not only in shaping the strategies of the main protagonists during the period of 'cohabitation' but also in their decisions to undertake the experience itself. A presidential election had to be held no later than May, 1988, some 26 months after the 1986 legislative elections. It was as certain as such things can be, that François Mitterrand, Jacques Chirac, and Raymond Barre would be candidates at the presidential election. Every aspect of their political behavior was affected by this electoral perspective.

The timing of the presidential election was as important as its inevitability. Two years gave Chirac the minimum amount of time in which to try to enlarge his visibility, produce tangible economic and social changes, and increase his popularity. A shorter period of time might have looked less inviting to him. A longer period might also have been discouraging because of the more prolonged and greater effort required to maintain a parliamentary majority, which would have all the less incentive to remain united as the next presidential election receded in time.

Of course, there was no guarantee that the presidential election would not be held at an earlier date. President Mitterrand could alter the date of the presidential election simply by resigning, just as he could call new legislative elections by dissolving the National Assembly.[8] But if Chirac needed time to establish a record and to try to increase his popularity, so did Mitterrand. The president's popularity was not very high early in 1986, and his Socialist party, while doing rather better at the 1986 legislative elections than had been generally expected, nevertheless had won only slightly more than 30 percent of the votes. Mitterrand, like Chirac, needed time to raise his standing with the public. The constitution gave the president an advantage over the prime minister by allowing him to control the electoral timetable, but he had no immediate reason for altering it. Indeed, to the extent that he benefited from the divisions within the majority, it would be to his advantage to give them maximum exposure rather than to curtail the life of Chirac's government.

The electoral perspective, combined with the novelty of the situation, made the president and the prime minister even more than normally sensitive to public opinion. They exploited their constitutional powers to the fullest but avoided exceeding them in order not to antagonize a public that viewed the 'cohabitation' experience tolerantly and even, at least throughout 1986, with increasing favor (Duhamel and Jaffré 1987; Sofres 1988). "Whoever draws first is dead," said Edouard Balladur (Balladur 1989, 78–79). But within those limits, there was implacable hostility within the French executive branch, between two protagonists who were squaring off for the main bout to come at the presidential election.

Strategies and Constitutional Resources

The Prime Minister

President Mitterrand did almost everything he could to make life difficult for his prime minister, but Chirac had as much or more difficulty
in maintaining his parliamentary majority as he did in fending off the
president's efforts to frustrate him. Chirac's objective was simple: to
enact a legislative program consistent with goals agreed upon in principle by the two parties constituting his majority, the RPR and the UDF.
This was difficult to do in practice, however, because the UDF contained
deputies whose preferred presidential candidate was not Jacques Chirac
but Raymond Barre. Barre's supporters had not done as well in his
home town of Lyons at the 1986 legislative elections as Chirac's forces
did in Paris, and Barre was forced to renege on his earlier pledge not
to support any cohabitation government. But Barre felt that he had to
distinguish himself from Chirac's positions, even though there were
few real programmatic differences between the two men, and Chirac
had to contend regularly with a group of deputies within his majority
that was bent on advertising more or less marginal differences of opinion.

   One result of this sticky situation was that the prime minister bran-
dished more often than is customary the constitutional provision (Art.
49) that permits him, after discussion in the Council of Ministers (a
formal meeting of the cabinet, at which the president presides), to
terminate parliamentary debate on a measure and, in effect, to dare the
deputies to introduce a motion of censure. If such a motion is introduced
and passes, by an "absolute majority" of the total membership of the
Assembly, the government is defeated and must resign. If such a motion
fails to pass in those terms, or if no such motion is introduced within
the prescribed period, the legislative measure in question is deemed to
have been adopted. Chirac did not actually invoke this procedure in
the Assembly much more often than other prime ministers (including
Socialist ones) had done in the past, but he sometimes did so very early
in the parliamentary discussion of an issue, thereby seriously curtailing
debate, and he secured authorization from the Council of Ministers to
do so some 30 times in 1986, in effect putting Barre's supporters (and
other potential troublemakers) on notice with regard to his intentions
(Duverger 1987, 100–101).

   Chirac made much more frequent use of the package vote (governed
by Art. 44). This provision permits the government to avoid serial votes
on a succession of amendments by requiring that a measure be voted
straight up or down, with only those amendments attached to it that

the government accepts. Chirac employed that procedure 14 times in 1986 and 22 times in 1987, more frequently than any previous prime minister.

But maintaining the voting discipline of a narrow and sometimes grudging majority is not exclusively a matter of applying restrictive constitutional provisions.[9] The government was also unusually attentive and responsive to their parliamentary supporters. Ministers and their staffs brought them into the policymaking process, took them seriously, and satisfied them when they could (Duverger 1987, 31).

If Jacques Chirac had to work particularly hard to maintain parliamentary support, he was the most powerful prime minister of the Fifth Republic as long as he could do so. From de Gaulle to Mitterrand, it had been the president and not the prime minister who set out the broad objectives of government policy, and French presidents had also intervened more or less directly in its day-to-day administration. Chirac, who had resigned as prime minister in 1976, alleging that President Giscard d'Estaing did not allow him the freedom he needed to carry out his functions properly, no longer had to accept instructions from the president and no longer ran the risk of having his ministers go over his head to the president.[10] The president could and did do much to disturb Chirac's tranquility, but one of the quips making the rounds was "Why does Chirac want to be president? He already is."

The President

President Mitterrand insisted on the primacy of the president in foreign affairs, exploited his capacity to command the attention of the public, frequently registered his disapproval of the government's conduct, relied on certain veto powers specifically conferred on the president by the constitution, presented himself as the champion of parliament in the face of an overbearing government, sought to delay enactment of several of the government's measures, but never sought to create a situation from which a united parliamentary majority could not extricate itself.[11]

One important domain in which the president can exercise a veto concerns senior appointments. The president alone appoints the prime minister; he also appoints the other ministers on the proposal of the prime minister; and while his appointments must be countersigned by responsible ministers, he also makes the appointments that are decided on in the Council of Ministers (Art. 13). By withholding his signature, the president can, therefore, block major appointments.

Cabinet appointments went smoothly enough. Mitterrand turned down Chirac's initial choices for the ministries of foreign affairs and defense, but the two men quickly agreed on alternates.[12] Lower level appointments were constant bones of contention. During his first five weeks in office, Chirac removed some 170 officials who had been installed by previous Socialist governments (Pfister 1986, 146). Mitterrand was most concerned about sharing in the appointment process for the highest, most sensitive posts, as well as those central to foreign affairs and defense, while allowing the government a free hand for lesser posts, provided he was given adequate notice of the government's intended personnel changes and that appropriate equivalent jobs were found for the officials being removed (Colombani and Lhomeau 1986, 184–185). Reaching common accord was difficult but, more often than not, the prime minister prevailed.

A second area in which the president holds a constitutionally based veto power concerns ordinances prepared by the Council of Ministers pursuant to special grants of power given to the government by parliament under the terms of Article 38. This provision permits the legislature to delegate its legislative powers to the government for a given period of time, during which the government may in effect legislate by ordinance on matters covered by the delegation of power, including the amendment or repeal of standing legislation. The government must give the legislature an opportunity, prior to the expiration of the specified time limit, to reject some or all of the ordinances issued under the grant of authority. The provisions of Article 38 have been employed by virtually every government of the Fifth Republic, including those headed by the Socialists, when they have wanted to move quickly, when they have wanted to enact unpopular measures that the legislature might not want to support, or when they believed that they would have a difficult time persuading a parliamentary majority to accept the detailed formulation of general propositions on which they were nevertheless agreed in principle. Article 13 of the constitution says that the president signs the ordinances decided on in the Council of Ministers, and Article 19 makes it clear that the president's signature must be countersigned by one or more responsible ministers.

No French president had ever before refused to sign the ordinances prepared by a government, but on three occasions, when the Chirac government obtained parliamentary authorization to legislate by ordinance under Article 38, President Mitterrand refused to sign the ordinances prepared by the cabinet. The first veto, solemnly announced by the president from his office on the 14th of July, 1986, against a backdrop consisting of the French flag, concerned the government's plan to privatize 65 financial and industrial enterprises that had been nationalized by the Socialist administration that took power in 1981. Claiming that his decision was a matter of conscience, he justified his refusal to

THE EXECUTIVE DIVIDED AGAINST ITSELF   281

approve the relevant ordinances on the ground that they offered no protection against the nation's property falling into the hands of foreigners. Thus, nationalizations that had been undertaken to alter the balance of economic power within France were defended on grounds of national independence. If the Parliament wanted to assume responsibility for privatization, let it do so, said the president. He would have no part of it.

Chirac's supporters fulminated against the president's decision, and the prime minister went on television to counter the president's arguments, but he indicated that he had no wish to provoke a political crisis. Instead, he went to work, rallied his supporters in the legislature, and produced a proper privatization law within two weeks of the president's refusal to sign the ordinances.[13]

There was a virtual replay of the same scenario in the fall of 1986 concerning two sets of ordinances that the government had prepared, on the basis of parliamentary authorization conferred pursuant to Article 38, in order to restore the old two-ballot electoral system and redistrict the country. Once again the president refused to sign the ordinances, arguing that the details of the electoral system should be determined by the Parliament. The prime minister rallied his troops and, with very little discussion in Parliament, secured adoption of the ordinances in legislative form three weeks later.

The third and last time the president withheld his signature from a set of ordinances produced more severe difficulties and delays for the government. Toward the end of the 1986 legislative session, the government obtained authorization to issue a set of ordinances relating to hours of work which, against a background of labor unrest, the president refused to sign. This time the government was in a difficult position because it could not secure parliamentary approval of a new bill without either holding a special session of Parliament or waiting until the regular spring session, which begins in April.[14] The government tried to solve its problem by persuading Parliament to adopt the substance of the ordinances as an amendment to an omnibus bill that was already in the legislative process. The Socialist deputies and senators appealed to the Constitutional Council, which held in January 1987, that the procedure had expanded the concept of an amendment beyond constitutional acceptability. It was not until June 1987, some six months after the president's pocket veto, that Parliament adopted the legislation that the government had wanted to enact by ordinance.

In that fashion, the president succeeded in delaying, but not preventing, the enactment of the government's legislative program. In addition, throughout the entire 'cohabitation' period, the president freely criticized virtually every governmental initiative in domestic affairs (in-

282   ROY PIERCE

cluding matters concerning the overseas territory of New Caledonia)
and supported demonstrating university students who forced the government to withdraw a bill to reorganize the university system.[15]

He also succeeded in seizing control of the parliamentary agenda
away from the prime minister. Political tempers naturally rose feverishly
as the 1988 presidential election approached, and various political scandals bubbled to the surface late in 1987. One of these was a mini-version
of the US Iran-Contra episode known as the Luchaire affair. This involved the delivery to Iran, under the previous Socialist administration,
of munitions that had been authorized for delivery to other countries.
This might have turned out to be just another embarrassment for the
hapless Charles Hernu, the Socialist minister of defense at the time,
who eventually resigned because he had not been informed that French
agents technically under his jurisdiction had sunk the Rainbow Warrior
in New Zealand, except that there had been some misuse of funds, and
an internal administrative document, divulged by the press, "did not
exclude" that some of these funds had ended up in the coffers of the
Socialist party. At more or less the same time, the prime minister's
majority, minus a few troubled deputies and senators, but joined by
the Communists, voted to lift the parliamentary immunity of a Socialist
deputy and former minister of cooperation (essentially the minister for
foreign aid) and to indict him before the High Court of Justice for misuse
of public funds, including their expenditure for political purposes. This
was the first time since 1930 that Parliament had voted to bring a former
minister to justice.

Mitterrand counterattacked by claiming that it was high time to put
an end to the numerous insinuations that were being raised, that legislation regulating the financing of elections and even parties was ur-
gently needed, and that the government should promptly introduce
measures to that effect. The prime minister's supporters wondered
aloud why, if the matter was so urgent, the president had not asked
the Socialist governments between 1981 and 1986 to tackle the problem,
but Chirac felt compelled to take action. He tried to produce a measure
that would obtain broad inter-party support, across the frontier between
left and right, but was unable to do so. At a special session of Parliament
held early in 1988, shortly before the presidential election, two laws
governing the financing of parties and elections were adopted over the
opposition of the Socialists and Communists.[16]

Foreign Policy

At the beginning of April 1987, after meeting with United States President Reagan about the question of intermediate range nuclear missiles

based in Europe, Prime Minister Chirac said that President Mitterrand had sent President Reagan a letter setting forth the French position, and that he, Chirac, had given Reagan the same message. "France has a single position," he said, "a single policy, and speaks with a single voice" (*Le Monde*, 2 April 1987). Several months later, he repeated the statement: "Our partners understood perfectly that a Socialist President and a government that is not Socialist speak with the same voice" (*Le Monde*, 8 July 1987). To a great extent that affirmation was correct, although it was not so in all particulars.

Foreign policy is the domain that puts divided executive power to the most difficult tests. Divided authority in domestic affairs can be troublesome, but ambiguity and uncertainty in foreign affairs can be dangerous. It is unlikely that 'cohabitation' would have endured for over two years, or even been undertaken in the first place, if France had not had what amounts to a bipartisan foreign and defense policy with regard to the United States, the Soviet Union and, by and large, the European Community.

On those big issues, the two protagonists were agreed. Early in the 'cohabitation era', in April 1986, they both made it clear that it would be an intolerable violation of French policy to permit US aircraft to fly over France on their mission to bomb Libya. They did not differ with regard to the Euromissile issue. President Mitterrand pronounced the government's military program for 1987–1991 to be "serious, reasonable and coherent," and it was among the handful of legislative measures that the Socialist deputies and senators supported in Parliament (*L'Année Politique 1987*, 1988, 96). But there were other issues on which the president and the prime minister did not agree: the response to President Reagan's strategic defense initiative, the pace of normalization of relations with Iran, sanctions against South Africa, European integration, and Central America, to cite the most obvious ones.[17]

Even where there were no or only marginal differences between them, there was competition for attention. "What is essential, in the 'cohabitation' framework, is to assert one's preeminence" (Pfister 1986, 234–235). For the first time, the prime minister, as well as the president, attended summit meetings of the Big Seven and the European Community, where there were occasional skirmishes over protocol or precedence. Particularly on the prime minister's side, foreign policy considerations sometimes seemed governed more by considerations of short-term political advantage than by long-term objectives (July 1987, 199). The interstices of divided authority were exploited by the French military to increase its autonomy (Colombani and Lhomeau 1986, 199).

Nevertheless, there were no direct, public confrontations between the two executive leaders in the area of foreign affairs, and the two men showed greater restraint in that domain than in domestic matters. The prime minister had operational capabilities that the president lacked, but the most numerous channels of communication between the government and the president's office related to defense and foreign policy. It appears that the government fulfilled the letter of its constitutional obligation (under Article 52) to inform the president of its international negotiations, and when these were delicate — as in the case of the liberation of hostages and dealing with New Zealand over the Rainbow Warrior affair — the president maintained diplomatic silence (Colombani and Lhomeau 1986, 191). The same formally correct relationship between the government and the president was even maintained when, between the two ballots of the presidential election of 1988, the government negotiated the release of the three last surviving hostages being held by the Islamic Jihad in Beirut. In a separate operation on the same day, French military forces attacked a nationalist group in New Caledonia that, two weeks earlier, had taken a number of French gendarmes hostage in a raid that resulted in the deaths of four other gendarmes. Two French soldiers and 19 members of the nationalist movement were killed during the military attack. The president was in deep and open conflict with the prime minister over policy in New Caledonia, but he had approved the military operation, he said, in the expectation that there would be few casualties.

Party Distance

The French experience with 'cohabitation' is sometimes described as a species of divided government similar to that which regularly occurs in the United States, when the presidency is held by one party and one or both houses of Congress are held by the other party (Duverger 1987, 165–168). This is wide of the mark. In France a leftist president faced a right-wing Parliament, but the executive branch itself was divided on a partisan basis as well. To approximate the French situation in the United States would require something like, say, Jim Wright serving as Ronald Reagan's secretary of state and director of the Office of Management and Budget at the same time as he was speaker of the house.

As real and important as the structural differences between France and the United States are, however, they are not at the heart of the difference between 'cohabitation' in France and divided government in the United States. The main difference is not so much structural as behavioral. United States parties are more disposed to compromise than French parties are, with the result that there is genuine power-sharing between the president and Congress while there was virtually no co-operation in France between the president and the prime minister or between the president and the legislative majority.

In the domain of foreign affairs, where 'cohabitation' produced the fewest confrontations, the only visible sign of negotiation between the president and the prime minister appeared during the initial appointments of the ministers of foreign affairs and defense. Such other demonstrations of agreement as the two leading executive officials displayed in those fields were the expression of similar policy positions that they had adopted earlier and separately rather than the convergent results of bargaining between them.

The government and the presidency during the 'cohabitation' period did not together constitute a decision-making *system,* in the sense in which the US presidency and the Congress, with its two competing parties actively participating, constitute a system (Peterson 1990). In the United States, it is not always easy to distinguish the institutional component from the partisan component of legislative-executive bargaining, but the partisan element is invariably present and inter-party agreements are frequently arrived at. There is power-sharing, between branches and between parties. In France, there was, of course, bargaining and compromise between the government and the deputies and senators that it counted on to provide it with a parliamentary majority, and this included negotiations between the two parties that constituted the majority, the RPR and the UDF. But the president and his Socialist followers were outside that circuit and, by all accounts, preferred to remain outside it.

Communication between the government and the president was carefully structured and limited. The prime minister's and the president's chiefs-of-staff were in regular communication with each other; the ministers of foreign affairs, defense, and cooperation reported directly to the president, and members of the president's staff could contact officials at the foreign ministry or the prime minister's office with regard to those subjects; liaison had to be maintained concerning European affairs, which touch on a host of domestic issues. Formalities were respected concerning the agenda and the minutes of meetings of the Council of Ministers, over which the president presides. All the proprieties were upheld, but except for the designated exceptions (and Edouard Balladur), no minister or ministerial aide was permitted to communicate with the president's office without the authorization of the prime minister's chief-of-staff (Pfister 1986, 54).

While the president insisted on being fully informed in the diplomatic and military domains in which he holds constitutional powers, he had no interest in having his staff involved in any way in the elaboration or the administration of government policy, for which he did not want to share responsibility (Pfister 1986, 53–54; Colombani and Lhomeau 1986, 157). There was coexistence, but no power-sharing.

On the parliamentary level, there was almost unrelenting antagonism between the government and its supporters, on the one hand, and the president's Socialist party, on the other. The Socialists voted with the majority on only four measures enacted during the 'cohabitation' period: the four-year military program referred to above; ratification of the Single European Act, which had been negotiated by the previous Socialist administration; and two bills that were adopted unanimously, one concerning the responsibility of divorced parents for their children and the other designed to protect public monuments. They abstained on a few others. They flatly opposed the great majority of the bills passed during 'cohabitation'.

This record of partisan conflict is not unique to the 'cohabitation' era. It is characteristic of French party politics generally and, indeed, of the politics of most democratic systems outside the United States. It is the loose, undisciplined congressional parties in the United States that are atypical, not the more hierarchical and disciplined parliamentary parties elsewhere.

The fact remains, however, that the French experience with the pattern of governance that they called 'cohabitation' was only remotely comparable to that of divided government under the separation-of-powers system in the United States. The characteristic patterns of French elite political behavior are not, at present, well adapted to the power-sharing that divided government requires. French political leaders project greater distance between themselves and their parties than US leaders do.[18] At the same time, they make the barriers surrounding the parties impermeable by the imposition of parliamentary party discipline, while US parties tolerate cross-voting on virtually all legislative roll-calls. French elite behavior can be accommodated by parliamentary government, and by the hybrid constitutional system of the Fifth Republic when the president and the parliamentary majority are in political accord. But when French partisan divisions, at least those that parallel the left-right fault line, are projected upward into the dual executive, severe strains are placed on the constitutional system.

THE LEGACY

Prior to the 'cohabitation' experience, the French constitutional system had been placed under great stress on two occasions. The first was in 1962, when President de Gaulle decided to amend the constitution by referendum to provide for the direct popular election of the president, and outraged deputies produced the only successful censure motion against a government of the Fifth Republic. The second occurred in 1968, when rioting students, striking workers, and middle-class demonstrators almost brought the regime to its knees. On both occasions the system held, in that the challenging forces were defeated at the polls and acquiesced in the outcomes. In the language of institutional equilibrium theory, on those two occasions the French constitutional system proved to be highly robust (Shepsle 1989, 141–143).

'Cohabitation' never reached as dangerous a point as those two earlier events. It produced severe strains between the president and the prime minister, but it did not produce a fundamental political or constitutional crisis. There were no prolonged deadlocks between the two executive leaders; neither contested the other's right to remain in office; neither tried to alter the constitutional rules. There was never a need for the electorate to decide whose interpretation of the constitution was the proper one. But the presence of the electorate hovered over the two main protagonists. The possibility that the voters might be called upon to render such a verdict helped to prevent the president and prime minister from letting matters go that far.

'Cohabitation' worked as well as it did because of four main factors:

1) the 25-month time frame leading to the next presidential election;
2) the comparatively favorable opinion of 'cohabitation' held by the electorate;
3) the fragility of the parliamentary majority; and
4) the existence of a bipartisan foreign and defense policy covering the most sensitive foreign issues.

The comparatively short time span between the 1986 legislative election and the latest date at which a presidential election could be held made the efforts that 'cohabitation' required tolerable, especially for the prime minister. Both the prime minister and the president needed time: the former to build a record, the latter to recover from declining popularity; but the prime minister (and possibly also the president) would not have regarded a long period of 'cohabitation' with equanimity.

'Cohabitation' was a novelty of which, on the whole, the electorate approved, especially during 1986 (Duhamel and Jaffré 1987; SOFRES 1988). Except early in 1987, more French men and women thought that cohabitation was working well than thought it was working badly, usually by a wide margin. Overwhelming majorities in 1986 and 1987 thought that the experience should be allowed to continue until May 1988, the latest date at which a presidential election could be held. Although the polling data were not wholly free from ambiguity,[19] it was clear that it might be electorally damaging to either of the executive leaders if he provoked a stalemate bordering on crisis. In this sense, it was helpful for the cause of constitutional stability that both the principal actors were presidential candidates.[20] The potential risks of breakdown were high for both men.

The fragility of the parliamentary majority ruled out aggressive challenges to presidential power by the prime minister. Jacques Chirac had enough trouble as it was securing agreement within his majority on the specifics of matters on which the RPR and UDF were agreed in principle, without widening the range of potential disagreement by taking on new issues designed specifically to embarrass or weaken the president. There is evidence as well that the RPR/UDF electorate was sensitive to the limits that the narrow parliamentary majority imposed. On the day of the March legislative election, but before the results were known, 73% of the RPR-UDF voters thought that the president should resign "if the RPR and UDF gain sharply (nettement)." The next day, when the results were in, only 46% of the RPR-UDF voters expressed the same defiant opinion, "taking the results into account" (Duhamel and Jaffré 1987, 59). The smallness of the majority would not only make it very difficult for Chirac to hold it together for untried ventures, but it also helped to undermine popular support for doing so.

Lastly, the bipartisan foreign and defense policy, concerning in particular relations with the United States and the Soviet Union, withdrew a large domain, in which there was considerable activity at the time, from contention between the president and the prime minister. The importance of this fact can hardly be overemphasized, for two reasons. The first and most obvious reason is that on essential matters the two executive leaders did indeed speak with one voice, thereby avoiding ambiguity in Washington and Moscow. The less obvious reason is that what passed for the maintenance of presidential leadership in foreign and military affairs was actually due to the absence of a conflict between the president and the prime minister that, as long as the prime minister had the support of a parliamentary majority, the president would necessarily lose.

None of the four conditions that prevented 'cohabitation' from deteriorating into political crisis — the 26-month electoral horizon, the favorable popular attitude toward the experiment, the narrow parliamentary majority, and the bipartisan aspects of French foreign and military policy — is necessarily likely to prevail again if and when another cohabitation episode appears.

A glance at the past electoral calendar (see Figure 1) suffices to show that if the leftist alliance had won parliamentary majorities in 1973 (when the possibility was not excluded) or 1978 (when that outcome seemed highly probable), the maximum length of the 'cohabitation' period would have been 14 months or 38 months, and not the more or

THE EXECUTIVE DIVIDED AGAINST ITSELF   289

FIGURE 1. **Maximum Duration of Real and Hypothetical 'Cohabitation' Periods, 1973–1988 (Based on Actual Election Dates)**

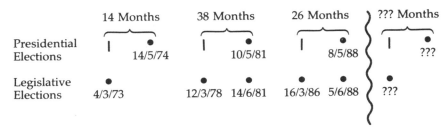

FIGURE 2. **Maximum Duration of Hypothetical 'Cohabitation' Periods, 1973–1983 (Assuming that Georges Pompidou had completed his presidential term)**

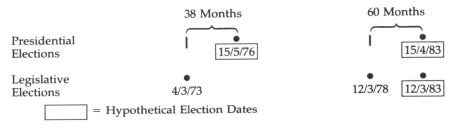

less happy mean of the 26 months that elapsed between the legislative elections of 1986 and the presidential election of 1988.

'Cohabitation' periods of still different lengths of time might have occurred if past circumstances had been different in other ways. If we assume that President Pompidou had not died in office, but had survived long enough to complete his presidential term, the possible 'cohabitation' periods would have been of different maximum durations (see Figure 2). On the assumption of Pompidou's survival, if the left had won a majority at the 1973 legislative elections, the 'cohabitation' period could have been 38 months. If a rightist had won the hypothetical 1976 presidential election, and the leftists had won a majority at the 1978 legislative elections, the immediate prospect would have been that of a 'cohabitation' period of 60 months, the entire life of the legislature.

None of this means that if there were the prospect of a new 'cohabitation' experience of 38 or 60 months, it would necessarily last that long. The president controls the electoral calendar to a considerable extent, and there is no constitutional reason why the National Assembly could not dissolve itself if it wished to do so. Moreover, the behavior of a 'cohabiting' president might well vary considerably, depending on the point in the president's term that the 'cohabitation' experience began.

Former prime minister Pierre Mauroy said that he thought ʻcohabitationʼ had worked fairly well during 1986 because the president was experienced and near the end of his term, while a newer, less experienced president might have reacted differently (*Le Monde*, 12 Feb. 1987).

Similarly, a new ʻcohabitationʼ experience might begin at a time when public opinion was less approving, possibly because one political coalition had succeeded in acquiring parliamentary dominance. In those circumstances, a new prime minister — far from being restrained by considerations of public censure — might well feel the need to act aggressively toward a president of a different persuasion in order to satisfy the swell of mass opinion. The prime minister might appoint a heavyweight to the ministry of foreign affairs that the president would find hard to veto.[21] A determined majority might alter the 1964 legislation which confers ultimate control over the use of France's nuclear forces on the president, and shift it instead to the prime minister. A strong parliamentary majority could erode the president's authority in foreign affairs, leaving him only with the shell of power in the form of courteous but empty communications about decisions taken elsewhere.[22]

Such a situation would be the more likely to occur if there were substantial differences in policy outlook between the president and the prime minister. It is not engraved in stone that France will always have as much of a bipartisan foreign and military policy as it did between 1986 and 1988. That has certainly not always been the case during the Fifth Republic, and it may well not be the case in later years. In the late 1960s and early 1970s, French foreign policy and military policy were fiercely debated. The left-wing parties opposed the nuclear striking force until well into the 1970s; if the left had won a parliamentary majority in 1973, military policy would have been a bone of contention between the president and the prime minister. If the left had won the legislative elections of 1978, European policy would have been a major issue within the dyadic executive. And so on.

The future is no more likely to resemble 1986–1988 in this regard than those years resembled the past. With the collapse of the Soviet Union, the restoration of separate independent states in Eastern Europe, and the strong possibility that the United States will reduce its commitments to and in Western Europe, a foreign policy based on "national independence" may well lose much of its recent appeal. Instead, there is likely to be heated debate within France concerning how it should adjust to the new configuration of forces in the world.

These remarks are not meant to be a prophecy of doom if the ʻcohabitationʼ formula is repeated in France. They are meant only to suggest that the experience of 1986–1988 took place under favorable circumstances, perhaps the most favorable that can be imagined, and that problems avoided then might not be avoided at a later time (just as our brief survey suggests they might not have been avoided if 'cohabitation' had occurred in the past). But the variables are numerous, and naturally lend themselves to a large number of combinations. The incentives of the protagonists depend on the policy distance between them. Their strategies are the joint result of the time frame and, within it, the allocation of patience, the perceived risks of breakdown, the tolerance for those risks, and the estimates of the differential impact of the "transaction costs" of making basic institutional changes (Shepsle 1989, 144). The outcome of the contest (game) depends upon the resources which the actors can accumulate, among which electoral approval is paramount.

Disequilibrium may be the characteristic condition of politics (Riker 1980, 443), and in the democratic world, French politics may be among the least stable, but it must quickly be added that the Constitution of the Fifth Republic is a capacious structure, capable of sheltering various more specific forms of governance: shifting coalitions from 1958 to 1962, more or less stable coalitions from 1962 to 1981, something approaching party government from 1981 to 1986, and 'cohabitation' from 1986 to 1988. It remains true, however, that 'cohabitation' is a governing formula that carries risks of institutional paralysis or breakdown. Those were avoided between 1986 and 1988, because of circumstances that may not prevail during some future 'cohabitation' experience.

The possibility of 'cohabitation' in France is something like the possibility that no US presidential candidate will receive a majority of the electoral votes, thereby transferring the presidential electoral decision to the House of Representatives, voting by states. The probability of it occurring is not particularly high, but it is real. How it would work out would depend on circumstances, albeit — in the French case at least — these can be specified with some precision. The event might unfold without unduly raising tensions; it might place such severe strains on the system that the system itself would be changed. Neither possibility is necessarily a time bomb with explosive force, but both possibilities are potentially destabilizing, and few national political leaders anticipate them with enthusiasm.

Notes

1. I do not mean to suggest that the period was one of uninterrupted tranquility. The discipline of the rightist coalition began to fray badly after the election of 1967, and France exploded in an unprecedented display of anti-Gaullist sentiment in May 1968. But elections in that year produced a

Gaullist landslide that gave the Gaullists alone a majority in the National Assembly until 1973.

2. These will be cited specifically later in the context of the 'cohabitation' experience of 1986–1988.

3. And even fewer problems from 1958 to 1962, when the legislature had more confidence in the president than in the prime minister.

4. Jacques Chaban-Delmas in 1972, when Georges Pompidou was president, and Jacques Chirac in 1976, when Valéry Giscard d'Estaing was president.

5. And not while the president is exercising emergency powers.

6. The scenarios included some highly imaginative fiction. For summaries, see Poulard (1990, 250–251).

7. Balladur had been President Pompidou's chief-of-staff; he was a friend and adviser of Jacques Chirac; and when Chirac eventually became prime minister of a 'cohabitation' government after the legislative elections of 1986, Balladur became not only minister of finance, but also the key man on the prime minister's side in negotiating the ground rules for cohabitation with the president's chief-of-staff, Jean-Louis Bianco (Colombiani and Lhomeau, 149–55).

8. Prime Minister Chirac had the electoral law changed back to the old two-ballot, majoritarian system early in the cohabitation period, because he did not want to risk new legislative elections being held under proportional representation.

9. To say nothing of the fact that Articles 44 and 49 permit deputies to go on record with amendments without actually requiring them to vote for them.

10. Although the president outmaneuvered the prime minister at the end of 1987, when he effectively seized control of the parliamentary agenda by pressuring the government to bring in a bill relating to the public financing of parties and elections. See below.

11. Although on numerous occasions the Socialist members of Parliament sought to have laws enacted by the majority declared unconstitutional by the Constitutional Council.

12. Some cynics doubt whether Chirac was serious about his first suggestions in any case.

13. On this occasion, and two later ones as well, the French Senate, which is not popularly elected, which participates in the legislative process but which cannot veto legislation that is adopted by a majority of the National Assembly, and which contained a large majority supporting the government, found an ingenious way of speeding up its deliberations so that the government would lose no time in having the privatization bill passed. It simply defeated the bill on a preliminary motion, thereby killing it in the Senate and sending it immediately to the National Assembly, where the Senators knew it would be adopted despite their insincere rejection of it.

14. Constitutional Article 30 states that special sessions of Parliament are opened and closed by presidential decree, and President de Gaulle established the precedent in 1960 that the president can refuse to hold a special session (but not a regular session) even if a parliamentary majority requests one. President Mitterrand never denied any of Prime Minister Chirac's requests for special sessions, but he did refuse to allow Chirac to include the privatization of the Renault automobile company on the agenda of a special session held just prior to the 1988 presidential election campaign.

15. The proposed legislation would have permitted the universities to limit

THE EXECUTIVE DIVIDED AGAINST ITSELF   293

    enrollments in certain programs, to raise fees, and to inscribe the name of the university on the diplomas awarded to the graduating students.

16. The former minister was never brought to trial, as his case fell within the terms of legislation adopted in January 1990, that amnestied persons for infractions relating to the financing of political parties (*Le Monde* 6 April 1990).

17. The two men were constantly at loggerheads publicly over policy toward New Caledonia. The French regard this as an internal matter, but it is an overseas question that can be deadly (see below).

18. In 1984, the US electorate perceived a mean difference of 1.51 between the locations of Ronald Reagan and Walter Mondale on the seven-point liberal/conservative scale (American National Election Study, 1984, ICPSR No. 8298). In 1988, the French electorate perceived a mean difference of 2.44 between the locations of François Mitterrand and Jacques Chirac on a seven-point left/right scale (a national sample survey conducted by SOFRES for the author under Grant No. SES-8801639 from the National Science Foundation). The placements of the leaders' parties was virtually identical to that of the leaders.

19. As usual, the polling data varied with the question wording. More people thought that "cohabitation" was good for France than thought so when it was spelled out that cohabitation was between "a leftist President of the Republic, François Mitterrand, and a rightist Prime Minister, Jacques Chirac" (Duverger 1987, 52).

20. Edouard Balladur, however, thinks that that exacerbated conflicts, instead of moderating them, and argues that cohabitation would work better if the president and prime minister were not direct rivals (*Le Monde* 13 June 1990, 8).

21. Some observers thought that Chirac should have appointed former President Valéry Giscard d'Estaing to the post in 1986. Chirac was unlikely to name such a potential rival to the important post, but it would have been interesting if he had: Giscard, unlike Mitterrand and Chirac, thought that France should have approved US overflights en route to Libya.

22. Although the president could appeal to the Constitutional Council, which might find solutions that would be less costly to the president.

References

American National Election Study. 1984. ICPSR No. 8298.

L'Année politique, économique et sociale en France 1987. 1988. Paris: Editions du Moniteur.

Balladur, Edouard. 1989. *Passion et longueur de temps*. Paris: Fayard.

Colombani, Jean-Marie and Jean-Yves Lhomeau. 1986. *Le Mariage blanc; Mitterrand-Chirac*. Paris: Bernard Grasset.

Converse, Philip E. and Roy Pierce. 1986. *Political Representation in France*. Cambridge MA: Harvard University Press.

Duhamel, Olivier and Jérôme Jaffré. 1987. La découverte de la 'cohabitation'. In SOFRES, *L'Etat de l'opinion; Clés pour 1987*. Paris: Editions du Seuil.

Duverger, Maurice. 1987. *La Cohabitation des français*. Paris: Presses Universitaires de France.

Hamilton, Alexander, John Jay and James Madison. 1941. *The Federalist*. New York: Modern Library.

294   ROY PIERCE

July, Serge. 1987. *La Drôle d'année; Radio-croquis.* Paris: Bernard Grasset.

Peterson, Mark. 1990. *Legislating Together.* Cambridge MA: Harvard University Press.

Pfister, Thierry. 1986. *Dans les Coulisses du pouvoir; La Comédie de la cohabitation.* Paris: Albin Michel.

Poulard, Jean V. 1990. The French Double Executive and the Experience of Cohabitation. *Political Science Quarterly* 105:243–267.

Riker, William H. 1980. Implications from the Disequilibrium of Majority Rule for the Study of Institutions. *American Political Science Review* 74:432–446.

Shepsle, Kenneth A. 1989. Studying Institutions; Some Lessons from the Rational Choice Approach. *Journal of Theoretical Politics* 1:131–147.

SOFRES. 1988. *L'Etat de l'opinion; Clés pour 1988.* Paris: Editions du Seuil.

[20]

THE REAFFIRMATION OF A MULTIPARTY SYSTEM IN FRANCE

JOSEPH A. SCHLESINGER
MILDRED SCHLESINGER
Michigan State University

The Fifth Republic's most impressive accomplishment is its solution to the problems of political parties that plagued its predecessors. Unlike its predecessors, the Fifth Republic has a party system capable of performing the basic task asked of parties in a democracy—the production of alternative stable governing majorities. Nevertheless, the Republic's party system remains the same as that of its predecessors in one critical aspect; it remains a multiparty system. It is, however, a multiparty system renovated to achieve what the Third and Fourth Republics could not.

To understand the renovation and its consequences we turned to the office-seeking theory of parties. The office-seeking theory assumes that in democracies elective office goals dominate political parties. Within parties, then, elected officeholders and candidates for office are the most important individuals. It follows that parties' organization and behavior will reflect the aspects of a political system that guide politicians' expectations about elective offices and the means for achieving them (J. Schlesinger 1965, 1984). If the Fifth Republic's parties perform better than their predecessors, we must seek the explanation in how politicians' expectations have been altered.

Two aspects of a political system, we feel, are crucial to the organization of political parties. One is the structure of political opportunities. This structure consists of all the elective offices in a political system. It therefore lays out the goals and directs the ambitions of politicians. The other aspect is the structure of electoral competition. This structure lays out how offices can be won. Together, these two factors provide the impetus for the development of party organization (J. Schlesinger 1960, 1965, 1966). Those who would renovate parties and the party system must therefore renovate one or both of these structures. The Fifth Republic altered both structures.

The Renovation of the Structure of Political Opportunities in the Fifth Republic

By redesigning the structure of political opportunities in France, the Fifth Republic's founding fathers clarified the office-seeking base of French parties. During the Fifth Republic the relationship between the maintenance of parties and their chances at gaining important offices has become blatant. The most striking innovation in the structure of opportunities was the establishment of a popularly elected presidency. In response, every significant party of the Fifth Republic has emerged as a national organization, renovated or newly minted for the purpose of serving presidential ambitions (Charlot 1967, 1970; Colard 1983; Colliard 1972, 1979; Duhamel 1980; Ponceyri 1985; Portelli 1980; Schonfeld 1980; Wilson 1982).

Moreover, the newly established office of the presidency imposed more concerted and disciplined action on French parties than in the two previous republics. The president gained formidable powers over the legislature, impelling party organizations to provide the executive with consistently reliable majorities for the first time in French republican history. In response there emerged for the first time a unified opposition with realistic aspirations for providing a reliable governing alternative.

All the same, despite the novelty and importance of the presidency, we must not overlook the continued importance of popularly elected national legislative office in the renovated structure of political opportunities or its consequences for party organization.[1] Despite the considerable

power granted to the president over the popularly elected national assembly, the assembly came to play an increasingly important role in the implementation of the president's program. As a result, partisan organization within the assembly has had a critical role to play. Efforts on the part of the president to impose his stamp on legislative elections and their parliamentary outcome have been successful only when the president has identified with the dominant legislative group. Indeed, Converse and Pierce (1986, 552) have called disciplined voting in the assembly the clearest manifestation of partisan organizational behavior.

The Renovation of the Structure of Electoral Competition in the Fifth Republic

Important as the renovation of the structure of political opportunities has been for party organization in France, we wish to emphasize the effect of renovating the structure of *electoral competition*. The structure of competition has a major bearing on the nature of party organization in democracies. The structure of opportunities defines what choices the voter makes. Electoral rules define how the choices are made and how they translate into electoral victory (Grofman and Lijphart 1986; Rae 1967). The most important choice voters make in democracies in electing the officials who govern them; but office seekers must heed the way voters make those choices. Electoral rules then become guidelines for organization.

In two of the three oldest democracies, the United States and Great Britain (the third being France), electoral rules allow the voter only one choice for each office. In these two democracies single candidates win by capturing a plurality of votes in one round of elections. No provision is made for the ranking of preferences. Under these circumstances, many voters

A Multiparty System in France

will respond sincerely by voting for their first preference among the candidates presented. Others, however, will vote strategically by choosing the candidate they prefer most or dislike least among the candidates they believe have a chance to win.[2] As a result, those organizing to capture office must be sensitive to a whole range of voter preferences. In nominating candidates and taking stands on issues, they cannot rely on the voter's firm allegiance to a first choice. The British and U.S. electoral systems then, encourage the formation of a few broad partisan organizations seeking to balance within themselves the range of choices that the systems deny the voter.[3]

The two-ballot system reintroduced in the Fifth Republic for most important elective offices frames the choices before the electorate differently, with different consequences for political organization.[4] Under this system candidates are chosen in single-member districts in two rounds of elections. Candidates can win on the first ballot by receiving an absolute majority of the valid votes cast. On the second ballot candidates win by receiving a plurality of the votes. French electoral rules therefore allow the voters more options than U.S. and British rules.[5] Knowing that a second ballot will occur if no candidate wins on the first ballot, voters may well choose to vote sincerely on the first ballot, leaving their strategic choice for the second ballot. Or they may underline their sincere choice by abstaining on the second ballot or casting a blank vote. Conversely they may choose to cast what the French call a "useful" vote on the first ballot, passing up their sincere choice to ensure that their second preference is guaranteed a place for the second contest. They may even choose to underline their strategic vote by voting only on the second ballot, after the field has been narrowed.[6]

Given the greater options offered the voters in ordering their preferences, it follows that those organizing to capture office will also have more options. The most obvious option is to form more, rather than fewer, organizations to rely on coalitions between, rather than within, organizations. The two-ballot system also encourages other organizational options. One is to create an organization whose candidates and policies will be the voters' first choice. Another is to construct an organization aimed at appealing to voters as a second, or compromise, choice. Still a third is to try to construct an organization aimed at appealing to some voters as a first, and to others as a second, choice—although this is undoubtedly the more difficult organization to construct. Qualities that make a party an attractive first choice for some can make it an unattractive second choice for others.

In effect, the French two-ballot electoral system encourages the organization of parties that specialize. It is true that across the range of constituencies parties can play the game differently depending on their strength. Certainly, variations in constituencies make it unlikely that any party will be exclusively a first- or second-ballot organization. Yet in a parliamentary system there are limits to the degree to which parties can vary their appeal from constituency to constituency, hence the likelihood of some form of verifiable specialization.

A Typology of Parties in a Dual-Ballot Electoral System

We can test our proposition about specialization by examining how legislative groups (which we have singled out as the core of partisan organization) win in the single-member-district, two-ballot arrangement for elections to the national assembly. Since legislators can win on the first or second ballot, we have devised two measures of winning.[7] The most

American <u>Political</u> Science <u>Review</u> Vol. 84

Figure 1. A Typology of Parties in a Two-Ballot,
Single-Member District System of Electing Representatives

WAYS OF WINNING

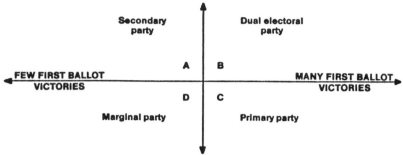

direct measure of a group's success on the first ballot is the percentage of its members who win by taking an absolute majority of the votes.[8] The significant measure of a group's success on the second ballot, where candidates need only a plurality to win, is the shift in the average electoral margin of the group's members from the first to the second ballot. This measure can be positive or negative, since it measures the increase or decrease in a group's voting strength between the two ballots relative to that of its competitors.[9] We stress the relative position because winners on the second ballot always increase their vote, given the withdrawal of candidates due to agreements between parties or to the legal requirement for access to the second ballot.[10]

Together, the two measures reveal four distinct ways of winning, each of which fosters a prototypical party (see Figure 1). Winning mostly on the first ballot or mostly on the second ballot fosters two basic types of organization, the *primary*

and the *secondary party*, respectively. Their variants are the *dual electoral party* (which does well on both ballots) and the *marginal party* (which has difficulty winning on either ballot).

The primary party (whose candidates win mostly on the first ballot) is designed to appeal to voters as their first choice. Since first choices are likely to be firmer than second, or compromise, choices, this means creating an organization whose candidates and policies have a strong appeal and whose resources are ample, allowing the organization to maximize its vote on the first ballot. A strong appeal should not be confused with a sharply defined ideological message, which in fact tends to restrict, rather than attract, the broad support needed for many first-ballot victories. Rather, the primary party's appeal is to the basic instincts of a broad spectrum of the electorate, for instance, to the instinct to conserve or maintain stability. A popular individual can personalize this appeal. Thus, the pri-

A Multiparty System in France

mary party emerges as an organization dominated by a single individual who overshadows all others, making them dependent for election on his drawing power. In turn, mutual dependence forges links among officeholders. The primary party, then, is likely to be a centralized, orderly organization.

The secondary party, whose candidates take most of their victories on the second ballot, is constructed to appeal to voters as their second choice. Note that this does not mean aiming only at second-ballot votes. Recall that voters have the option of voting strategically on the first ballot for a second-choice candidate who, they feel, is more likely to win. Nevertheless, the organization is designed to maximize its support on the second ballot. This means constructing an organization whose candidates and policies are capable of attracting voters with other partisan preferences on both ballots. Flexibility and adaptability, then, characterize this organization. But this is not achieved by putting forth a broad, vague appeal. Rather, it requires targeting different groups of voters with specific appeals without antagonizing other groups whose votes the party also seeks to win. Nor do flexibility and adaptability mean loose organization. On the contrary, the mutual need to attract support beyond the partisan base forges strong links among all those holding and seeking office.

The dual electoral party, whose candidates do well on both ballots, is a variant of the primary party. Many of its candidates win on the first ballot. Those who win on the second ballot win handily (unlike the primary party's candidates). This organization is designed to appeal to some voters as their first choice, and to others as their second choice. Since it attempts both types of appeals, it differs markedly from both the primary and secondary parties. Dual behavior allows for the greatest degree of independence among officeholders. Unlike the primary

party, it cannot be overshadowed by a single, dominant personality. Unlike the secondary party, the widespread need for mutual assistance is absent. It is then likely to be a looser, more heterogeneous organization than the other two parties, an umbrella organization encompassing notables or officeholders who operate with considerable freedom in the single-member districts that the electoral system prescribes.

The marginal party, whose candidates have difficulties with both ballots, is a variant of the secondary party. Its candidates have difficulty winning on the first ballot, (like the secondary party's). And though most of its candidates win on the second ballot, they win unimpressively. The marginal party is an organization that many voters are reluctant to accept as either a first or second choice. The most likely reason is a sharply defined message targeted at a limited group of voters. In this it differs from the other prototypical parties. It does not rely on a broad instinctive appeal or a popular personality (as the primary party does). It is unwilling or unable to target multiple groups of voters (as the secondary party does). Unlike the dual electoral party, it is incapable of dual behavior. Thus, we infer a rigid organization, whose officeholders and office seekers are bound and confined together by limited options.

The two-ballot system, which fosters four distinctive ways of winning, also fosters two distinctive strategies of alliance, which derive from the needs of the two basic prototypical parties. These strategies in turn reinforce the primary and secondary parties. As the party designed to be the voters' first choice and win on the first ballot, the primary party favors the strategy of the unique candidacy. This means it uses its resources to try to get likely allies to agree on a single or unique candidate in each constituency before the first ballot. This strategy has the best prospect for amassing the abso-

American Political Science Review Vol. 84

lute majority of votes needed to win on the first ballot. Faced with a second ballot, however, unique candidates will have no sizable pool of new support to draw on. In contrast, as the party designed to appeal to voters as their second choice and win on the second ballot, the secondary party favors the strategy of the trial run. This means that the party seeks to get likely allies to agree to withdrawal for the second ballot on behalf of candidates who have demonstrated in the first round of elections the best chance for ultimate victory.[11] By encouraging competitive candidacies, this strategy naturally reduces the chances that the secondary party's candidates will amass an absolute majority on the first ballot. Conversely, it guarantees them a new source of support for the second ballot.

At the same time, the tensions inherent in alliances reinforce the positions of the variant prototypes, the dual electoral and marginal parties. Since the two alliance strategies are incompatible, tension is likely to be greatest between the primary party and its likely ally, the dual electoral party, which also aspires to win on the first ballot. Because the dual electoral party also seeks to appeal to voters as a first choice, it too finds an advantage in coming to terms with the primary party on a single candidate in many constituencies. Yet the dual electoral party may be less content with the strategy of the unique candidacy. For one thing, it requires hard bargaining between parties: the balancing of resources, of incumbency, of control of local offices in order to distribute candidacies. In such negotiations the advantage may well rest with the organization best constructed to win on the first ballot. For another, the dual electoral party also encompasses those who propose to win by expanding their support on the second ballot and who will therefore press for the strategy of the trial run. This pressure reinforces the dual electoral party's position as a distinctive type of organization.

Tension is more muted between the secondary party and its likely ally, the marginal party, which also takes most of its victories on the second ballot. This is because the trial run is the easier strategy to implement. Unlike the unique candidacy, the trial run can be implemented without much prior agreement or commitment between parties. While prior agreements and promises of mutual assistance can facilitate the alliance, they are not essential. Ultimately, the implementation of the alliance rests with the voters. The resolution of the difficult problem of whose candidate is to benefit from the alliance is turned over to the electorate. Nevertheless, the very nature of the alliance derives from the existence of two distinct types of organizations, one of which is adaptable, the other rigid. Hence, it eliminates neither tension between allies nor the pressure for the marginal party to maintain itself as a distinct organization.

The four prototypical parties should be stable over time regardless of the electoral outcomes in individual elections. The obvious reason is that officeholders whose techniques and strategies have been successful will dominate their organizations. Differences in electoral fortunes, on the other hand, will affect the two variant prototypes. While electoral prosperity will bolster their distinctive styles of winning and the organization traits that derive from these styles, electoral adversity will make the two variant parties look more like their prototypical allies. The reason is that in times of adversity, the variant parties will win in their strongholds where they have been most successful in negotiating the alliance strategies that derive from the two basic parties. Thus, in difficult times the dual electoral party's relatively fewer victories will come in districts where it is able to command a unique candidacy based on its ability to attract an absolute majority of the votes on the first ballot. Similarly, the marginal party's relatively few victories

A Multiparty System in France

will come in districts where it can be expected to expand its support on the second ballot. This of course will also be true of the two basic prototypes. But there is an important difference. In good times and bad the two basic prototypes will rely mostly on their characteristic styles of winning. The variant parties will rely on the basic types' styles only in difficult times. Any improvement in variants' electoral fortunes will depend on candidates who win by departing from the styles of the two basic parties in the ways described. The variant parties will therefore retain the distinctive organizational traits we assigned them.

While the two-ballot system fosters four stable types of parties, it also allows parties to come and go. In the legislature this means the appearance of new groups that resemble one or the other of the prototypes, in part because they will draw some of their members from these sources. But it also means the disappearance of groups because their members choose to migrate to the prototype their previous group resembled. The two-ballot system may also encourage new political organizations to try their luck in electoral contests. At the same time, the greater inducement the system offers to the existent prototypical parties to continue to form alliances among themselves will give novice organizations little chance of electoral success.

The Dual Ballot Typology and the Parties of the Fifth Republic

Our typology reveals the basis for the principal accomplishment of the Fifth Republic: the provision of reliable governing alternatives by means of four stable partisan organizations. In the 1960s, the period of Gaullist dominance, political observers called attention to the majoritarian government produced by the

new Republic's party system. By the 1970s, as differences emerged in both governing and opposition coalitions—between Gaullists and the Independent Republicans–Union for French Democracy and between Socialists and the Communists—observers acknowledged the quadripartite character of governing alternatives (Dupoirier and Platone 1974; Duverger 1964; 1978, 154–75; Goguel 1967; Kesselman 1988; Le Gall 1977; Parodi 1977, 1978, 1979; Pierce 1980). Our typology reveals that both majoritarianism (in which one ally dominates the governing coalition) and quadripartism (in which coalitional allies are more equal) derive from the two-ballot arrangement introduced with the Republic's renovated structure of political opportunities.

Before applying our two measures of winning to the Republic's parties, we wished to test whether the relationship that produced our typology was built in to the two-ballot system of elections arithmetically. We looked first, therefore, at the overall results for the deputies elected to the seven assemblies between 1962 and 1988 on two ballots. We found that analysis of the overall electoral data, using our two measures of winning, produced results at variance with our theoretical assumptions. With the exception of 1968 there was a strong positive correlation between our two measures: the more first-ballot victories, the greater the positive shift in electoral margins on the second ballot (see Figure 2).

Only when we analyzed the results for each election by party did we find the negative relationships we expected. Figure 3 shows the breakdown of electoral results by partisan legislative groups for each of the seven assemblies.[12] In seven assemblies with strikingly different outcomes for the groups, the relationship between the two measures was always strongly negative. The positive relationship that emerged when electoral results were analyzed without regard for party, then, only

American Political Science Review Vol. 84

Figure 2. France: The Two-Ballot System of Elections to the National Assembly—
All Groups Combined, by Assembly

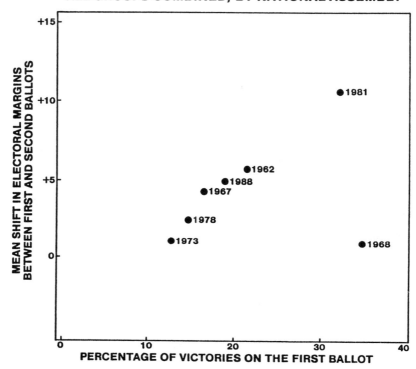

ALL GROUPS COMBINED, BY NATIONAL ASSEMBLY

Sources: Electoral data and group membership, 1962–1981 from Ministère de l'intérieur, *Les élections législatives de 1962, 1967, 1968, 1973, 1978, 1981* (Paris: Imprimerie Nationale); electoral data and group membership, 1988 from Le Monde, *Les élections législatives, 5 juin, 12 juin 1988* (Paris: Le Monde, Dossiers et Documents), and *Le Monde* 25 June 1988, p. 8.

Note: The total number of deputies was 488 in 1981 and 575 in 1988. The change in electoral rules in 1986 to proportional representation resulted in an increase in the number of deputies, which was retained with the return to the former electoral system. Correlations—$r = .98$ (excluding 1968); $r = .39$ (including 1968).

A Multiparty System in France

Figure 3. France: Political Groups and the Two-Ballot System of Elections to the National Assembly, 1962–1968

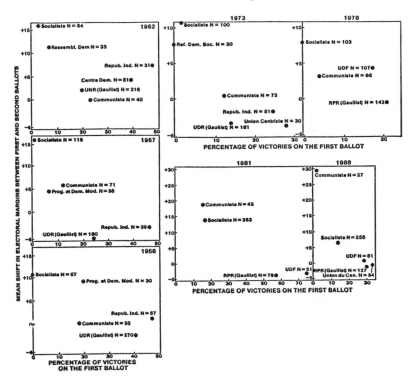

Sources: Electoral data and group membership, 1962–1981 from Ministère de l'intérieur, *Les élections législatives de 1962, 1967, 1968, 1973, 1978, 1981* (Paris: Imprimerie Nationale); electoral data and group membership, 1988 from Le Monde, *Les élections législatives, 5 juin, 12 juin 1988* (Paris: Le Monde, Dossiers et Documents), and *Le Monde* 25 June 1988, p. 8.

Note: Correlations—1962, $r = -.53$; 1967, $r = -.75$; 1968, $r = -.74$; 1973, $r = -.86$; 1978, $r = -.70$; 1981, $r = -.95$; 1988, $r = -.91$.

American Political Science Review Vol. 84

Table 1. Average Electoral Margins on the First Ballot of
Deputies Having To Go to a Second Ballot, by Groups

Groups	1962	1967	1968	1973	1978	1981	1988
Communist	6.63 (31)	4.47 (63)	5.09 (27)	8.38 (65)	9.13 (82)	4.68 (36)	11.50 (26)
Socialist	.80 (62)	.67 (115)	−1.20 (57)	1.58 (99)	4.45 (103)	3.11 (217)	7.58 (222)
Gaullist	13.21 (173)	15.46 (138)	14.86 (161)	13.37 (140)	12.20 (112)	11.49 (33)	10.21 (89)
Independent Republicans	10.36 (16)	11.93 (20)	13.20 (30)	13.06 (39)	—	—	—
Union for French Democracy (UDF)	—	—	—	—	8.58 (87)	8.96 (13)	8.51 (58)
Centre Démocratique	7.47 (31)	—	—	—	—	—	—
Rassemblement Démocratique	4.05 (32)	—	—	—	—	—	—
Progrès et Démocratie Moderne	—	7.79 (36)	7.32 (24)	—	—	—	—
Union Centriste	—	—	—	10.68 (22)	—	—	—
Réformateurs Démocrates Sociaux	—	—	—	2.85 (30)	—	—	—
Union du Centre	—	—	—	—	—	—	5.50 (23)

Sources: Electoral data and group membership, 1962–1981 from Ministère de l'intérieur, Les élections législatives de 1962, 1967, 1968, 1973, 1978, 1981 (Paris: Imprimerie Nationale); electoral data and group membership, 1988 from Le Monde, Les élections législatives, 5 juin, 12 juin 1988 (Paris: Le Monde, Dossiers et Documents), and Le Monde 25 June 1988, p. 8.
Note: Number of deputies are in parentheses.

serves to confirm that the partisan differences we found were real and not a product of the arithmetic of the two-ballot system. Applying our two measures of winning to each of the groups elected in the seven assemblies, we did indeed find four groups that consistently resembled our four prototypical parties.

The Gaullists

Emerging clearly as the primary party was the Gaullist group in the national assembly. Only in 1973 did the group's proportion of first-ballot victories fall below 20% (see Figure 3). In every election after 1962 its proportion of first-ballot victories exceeded those of all other groups except its allies. Moreover, in every election except 1988, even Gaullist candidates who had to win on the second ballot amassed the highest average electoral margins on the first ballot (see Table 1). On the second ballot, however, these candidates won by compiling average margins of support that registered declines in every election except 1962. No other group's margins declined so consistently from one ballot to the other. This was a party whose support peaked on the first ballot, a party of first choice.

In the 1960s, as the fate of the new

A Multiparty System in France

Republic and its institutions remained unsure, the Gaullist, or primary, party dominated the regime. It did so by identifying the fortunes of the Republic with its own fortunes and identifying its own fortunes with Charles de Gaulle. This posture brought it strong support throughout the French electorate, as voting studies have demonstrated (Goguel 1963, 1971; Labrousse 1971; Lancelot and Lancelot 1971; Lancelot and Weill 1971).[13] As the elections of 1968 proved, numerous French voters had no firmer preference than the stability of the regime identified with Charles de Gaulle. (Converse and Pierce 1986, 417–43). Student and worker unrest brought the Gaullists the largest electoral victory that any party was to achieve through the eighties; 40% of these victories came on the first ballot.

In the 1970s and 1980s, however, once the Republic's institutions emerged as safe even in the event the opposition came to power, the status of the primary party became less secure. Gaullist representation in the national assembly declined, along with its margins of support between ballots (see Figure 3). No other group showed such large declines. Indeed, in 1981 the party suffered its worst electoral defeat, while emerging as a purer primary party than ever. In the 1981 elections almost 60% of the Gaullist group were elected on the first ballot—its record high; but between ballots the average margin of support for its winning candidates declined by 3.8%, the largest decline since 1967. As we had expected, in a period of political adversity the party had reverted even more to type. Even as the party's fortunes declined, it clung to its original organizational trait—domination by a strong personality seeking to personify a strong broad appeal. Now, however, the dominant personality was the controversial deputy mayor of Paris, Jacques Chirac, seeking to personify appeals incapable of achieving the consensus produced by the defense of the republic.

These appeals ranged from the free market economy to Europe 92 and included an ambiguous flirtation with the anti-immigrant rhetoric of Le Pen's National Front.

The Socialists

Using our two measures of winning, we found the Socialist party to be the other basic type of organization, the secondary party. Even more than the Gaullists, the Socialists resembled the basic type of party: Figure 3 reveals strikingly the extent to which the Socialists were a secondary party. In the five elections from 1962 to 1978 only four of their candidates won on the first ballot. In two of these elections, 1968 and 1978, no Socialist candidate won on the first ballot. Even as the Socialist party was achieving its greatest electoral victory in 1981, it was electing only 17.5% of its deputies on the first ballot. In stark contrast, the Gaullists had elected 40% during their greatest victory in 1968. Moreover, except for the election of 1988, Socialist candidates who won on the second ballot compiled the lowest electoral margins on the first (see Table 1).

On the other hand the Socialists' second-ballot performance consistently outshone that of their competitors, except for the elections of 1981 and 1988. In these elections, as we shall see, the Communist party, faced with electoral adversity, moved toward the style of the secondary party. In these elections, however, the Socialists still continued to outperform the opposition by far on the second ballot, as they had in all previous elections. Even in 1962, as the Socialists were electing their second smallest number of deputies, their second-ballot margin of support improved by 16% compared with the Gaullists' 2.3%. In the electoral debacle of 1968 the Socialist party improved its second-ballot margin of support by 10.5%, while the Gaullists' margin declined by 2.1%. Of course, at this electoral low point, the Socialists were falling back on their basic technique of winning: in 1968 all their deputies won election on the second ballot.

The Socialists' performance certainly reflects Mitterrand's recognized transformation of their party into an acceptable governing party. Our analysis shows that Mitterrand was able to accomplish this by utilizing the party's appeal, visible since 1962, as the voters' preferred second choice. Under Mitterrand, the Socialists became increasingly successful at attracting Communist voters by assuring them of a continuing concern for their specific needs, while reassuring centrist voters that such concern would not threaten their interests.[14] Other electoral and voting studies have traced the Socialists' growing ability in the 1970s and 1980s to attract center as well as Communist votes for their candidates on the second ballot (Charlot 1973, 1981; Denis 1978; Frears and Parodi 1979; Goguel 1983b, 177–98; Jaffré 1981; Le Gall 1981; Martin 1981; Ysmal 1986). Our analysis underscores the party's growing success in targeting multiple groups of voters, in becoming the compromise choice of larger numbers of voters with different first ballot prefererences.

The Independent Republicans and Union for French Democracy

Apart from the two basic prototypes, our measures also revealed an organization resembling the dual electoral party: the Independent Republicans, together with its expanded version, the Union for French Democracy (UDF). In four out of the seven elections these groups had the highest percentage of deputies winning on the first ballot (see Figure 3). In the election of 1973, the Independent Republicans' percentage of first-ballot victories was exceeded only by the Union Centriste, which disappeared in 1978, its personnel mostly migrating to the UDF, as

the theory led us to expect (see Table 2). In 1988 the highest percentage of first-ballot victories was achieved by the new Union du Centre, much of whose personnel came from the UDF, as we were also led to expect (see Table 3). Moreover, in every election except 1988 Independent Republican or UDF candidates who won on the second ballot were second only to the Gaullists in the size of the average electoral margins they compiled on the first ballot (see Table 1). On the second ballot the group consistently showed greater improvement in its average margin of support than the Gaullists; in three out of the seven elections it showed greater improvement than the Communists as well. Faced with electoral adversity in the election of 1981, the UDF did move clearly in the direction of the primary model: 75% of its deputies won election on the first ballot, the highest percentage won by any group in the seven elections; on the second ballot the decline in its average margin of support was its highest, equalling that registered in the 1967 elections by the Independent Republicans.

All the same the Independent Republicans–UDF were our prototypical dual electoral party. The small Independent Republican party was able not only to resist absorption by the Gaullists but also to expand its organization by joining with even smaller officeholders' fiefs to form the UDF as a confederation. Our analysis reveals a firm basis for the Independent Republicans' resistance to Gaullist pressures to transform a majority coalition into a majority party—a different and potentially more effective mode of winning. Here was a partisan organization that appeared to be capable of appealing to some voters as a first, to others as a second, choice. The potential was clearly present in the 1960s when in all three elections the smaller Independent Republican group always ran better than the Gaullists on both measures. With the organization of the UDF in 1978 the Gaullists found

A Multiparty System in France

Table 2. Ephemeral Groups: Migration of Their Personnel in the Succeeding Legislature

Groups	Socialist	Prog. et Dém. Mod.	Independent Republicans	UDF	Union Centriste	Ref. Dém. Soc.	Gaullist	No Group	Total
				Number in Next Legislature					
1962									
Rassemblement Démocratique (35)	22 + 1ᵃ	3	1ᵃ		—	—		1	28
Centre Démocratique (51)	—	18 + 1ᵃ	1		—	—	5 + 1ᵃ	1	27
1968									
Progrès et Démocratie Moderne (30)	—	—	1		12	9 + 2ᵃ		1	25
1973									
Independent Republicans (51)	—	—		24		—	1	1	26
Union Centriste (30)	—	—		9 + 3ᵃ		—	1ᵃ	1	14
Réformateurs Démocrates Sociaux (30)	1ᵃ	—		13 + 2ᵃ		—	—	1	17

Sources: Electoral data and group membership, 1962–1981 from Ministère de l'intérieur, *Les élections législatives de 1962, 1967, 1968, 1973, 1978, 1981* (Paris: Imprimerie Nationale); electoral data and group membership, 1988 from Le Monde, *Les élections législatives, 5 juin, 12 juin 1988* (Paris: Le Monde, Dossiers et Documents), and *Le Monde* 25 June 1988, p. 8.

Note: Number of deputies in the group are in parentheses.

ᵃ*Apparentés* (allied with the group).

their ally substantially increased in numbers; the improvement in UDF strength relative to the Gaullists was maintained in the 1980s (see Table 4). Examining the relationship between Gaullists and Independent Republicans, some electoral studies highlighted the similarity in their electoral and geographic support, implying a weak base for the smaller group's continued viability.[15] After the 1978 election other studies examined the UDF's ability, like the Socialists', to attract votes on the second ballot beyond their expected base of support (Charlot 1980; Frears and Parodi 1979, 83–97; Jaffré 1980; Laurens 1988; Parodi 1978, 26, 29). Our analysis confirms this advantage over the Gaullists while demonstrat-

ing that it was observable early on in the Republic.

The Communists

Finally, our two measures of winning revealed the Communist legislative group as the one most closely resembling the marginal party. After 1962 the Communist group always lagged far behind the Gaullists and the Independent Republicans–UDF in first-ballot victories (see Figure 3). Even the Communist candidates who won on the first ballot usually piled up smaller average margins than Gaullists and Independent Republicans (see Table 5). Until 1981 the Socialists always outshone the Communists on the second

American Political Science Review Vol. 84

Table 3. Source Groups of Ephemeral and Most Recent Groups' Personnel

Groups and Source Groups	National Assemblies						
	1962	1967	1968	1973	1978	1981	1986
Progrès et Démocratie Moderne, 1967 (38)							
Centre Démocratique	17 + 1ᵃ	—	—	—	—	—	—
Rassemblement Démocratique	3 + 2ᵃ	—	—	—	—	—	—
No group	2	—	—	—	—	—	—
Réformateurs Démocrates Sociaux, 1973 (30)							
Socialiste	—	2	2	—	—	—	—
Rassemblement Démocratique	4	—	—	—	—	—	—
Centre Démocratique	4	—	—	—	—	—	—
Progrès et Démocratie Moderne	—	8	—	—	—	—	—
Républicains Indépendants	—	1	—	—	—	—	—
Union Centriste, 1973 (30)							
Socialiste	—	1	—	—	—	—	—
Rassemblement Démocratique	2 + 1ᵃ	—	—	—	—	—	—
Centre Démocratique	5 + 2ᵃ	—	—	—	—	—	—
Progrès et Démocratie Moderne	—	11 + 1ᵃ	12 + 1ᵃ	—	—	—	—
Gaulliste	1	2	4	—	—	—	—
No group	—	1	—	3	—	—	—
Union du Centre, 1988 (34)							
Progrès et Démocratie Moderne	—	1	1	—	—	—	—
Union for French Democracy	—	—	—	—	9	11	22
Union Centriste	—	—	—	3	—	—	—
Réformateurs Démocrates Sociaux	—	—	—	3	—	—	—
No group	—	—	1	—	1	1	—

Sources: Electoral data and group membership, 1962–1981 from Ministère de l'intérieur, *Les élections législatives de 1962, 1967, 1968, 1973, 1978, 1981* (Paris: Imprimerie Nationale); electoral data and group membership, 1988 from Le Monde, *Les élections législatives, 5 juin, 12 juin 1988* (Paris: Le Monde, Dossiers et Documents), and *Le Monde* 25 June 1988, p. 8.

Note: Number of deputies in the group are in parentheses.

ᵃ*Apparentés* (allied with the group).

ballot. Moreover in three of the five elections before 1981 the Independent Republicans–UDF also outperformed the Communists on the second ballot. Here was an organization that clearly had difficulty appealing to voters as a first or second choice. Our findings merely confirm the rigidity of the Communist party, its inability to adapt to the alterations made in the structures of political opportunities and of electoral competition and to broaden its electoral appeal.

Only in the elections of 1981 and 1988, because it was doing more poorly than in any legislative elections since 1932, did the Communist group emulate the style of the secondary party and improve its performance on the second ballot. Certainly, the Communist performance in the election of 1988 corroborates our hypothesis that in times of adversity the variants would emulate the basic prototypes because of the need to fall back on their strongholds. In this election the Communists won almost entirely with candidates who demonstrated an impressive

A Multiparty System in France

Table 4. Relationship in Size between Principal Allies in the National Assemblies of the Fifth Republic

National Assembly	Socialist-to-Communist Ratio	Gaullist Ratio to		
		Independent Republicans	UDF	All Center Groups
1962	1.6	7.0	—	2.6
1967	1.6	4.6	—	2.3
1968	1.7	4.7	—	3.1
1973	1.4	2.0	—	1.5
1978	1.2	—	1.3	1.3
1981	6.1	—	1.6	1.6
1988	9.6	—	1.6	1.1

Sources: Electoral data and group membership, 1962–1981 from Ministère de l'intérieur, *Les élections législatives de 1962, 1967, 1968, 1973, 1978, 1981* (Paris: Imprimerie Nationale); electoral data and group membership, 1988 from Le Monde, *Les élections législatives, 5 juin, 12 juin 1988* (Paris: Le Monde, Dossiers et Documents), and *Le Monde* 25 June 1988, p. 8.

Table 5. Average Electoral Margins for Deputies Who Won on the First Ballot, by Groups

Groups	Elections						
	1962	1967	1968	1973	1978	1981	1988
Communist	33.4 (5)	28.9 (8)	23.2 (6)	33.7 (8)	33.8 (4)	27.8 (7)	25.9 (1)
Socialist	34.9 (2)	22.5 (1)	— (0)	22.7 (1)	— (0)	22.8 (46)	25.2 (36)
Gaullist	36.2 (43)	32.0 (42)	36.2 (109)	36.9 (21)	31.8 (30)	25.8 (46)	29.2 (38)
Independent Republicans	45.8 (15)	35.7 (19)	43.0 (27)	37.9 (12)	—	—	—
Union for French Democracy	—	—	—	—	34.8 (20)	25.9 (38)	26.5 (23)
Centre Démocratique	36.3 (20)	—	—	—	—	—	—
Rassemblement Démocratique	30.6 (3)	—	—	—	—	—	—
Progrès et Démocratie Moderne	—	26.7 (2)	32.6 (6)	—	—	—	—
Union Centriste	—	—	—	27.2 (8)	—	—	—
Réformateurs Démocrates Sociaux	—	—	—	— (0)	—	—	—
Union du Centre	—	—	—	—	—	—	31.7 (11)

Sources: Electoral data and group membership, 1962–1981 from Ministère de l'intérieur, *Les élections législatives de 1962, 1967, 1968, 1973, 1978, 1981* (Paris: Imprimerie Nationale); electoral data and group membership, 1988 from Le Monde, *Les élections législatives, 5 juin, 12 juin 1988* (Paris: Le Monde, Dossiers et Documents), and *Le Monde* 25 June 1988, p. 8.

Note: Number of deputies are in parentheses.

ability to improve their support on the second ballot. In 1988 the Communists registered the greatest improvement in the margin of support between ballots of any group in the seven elections. They did so by fielding a record number of candidates who ran on the second ballot without opposition: of the twenty candidates who ran without opposition in the 1988 election, nine were Socialists, while eleven were Communists. Coincidentally, the Communist candidates demonstrating unusual prowess on the second ballot were predominantly elected officeholders. Over half the Communist deputies elected in 1988 had served two or more terms in the assembly. Of the six new deputies, five were local officeholders elected in districts previously held by the Communists. Unfortunately for the Communists, officeholders capable of expanding their support on the second ballot were in short supply. In the 1988 election the Communists for the first time failed to win enough seats to form their own group in the national assembly. Only through the indulgence of the Socialists, who supported a rule change lowering the thirty-member minimum requirement for a group, were the twenty-seven Communist deputies elected to the 1988 assembly able to form their own group.

In analyzing the balance of power within the Communist-Socialist alliance of the Fifth Republic, electoral studies have traced the shift in dominance from Communists to Socialists to the 1970s. At that time Socialist candidates began to outpoll Communist candidates on the first ballot in elections. Voting and electoral studies accredited the shift in power to the Socialists' ability to attract a broader spectrum of support than the Communists. They found that voters were consistently more likely to support a candidate of the Left if the candidate were a Socialist (Baudoin 1981; Bon and Jaffré 1978; Charlot 1973; Frears and Parodi 1979, 89–97; Goguel 1983b, 59–92; Grun-

berg 1986; Grunberg and Schweisguth 1981, 152–55; Jaffré 1980; Jaffré and Ranger 1974; Lavau and Mossuz-Lavau 1980; Le Gall 1978; Parodi 1978; Platone and Ranger 1986; Ranger 1986).

Our analysis reveals that the Socialists' favored position was evident from the elections of the 1960s. In every election from 1962 on, the Socialists always elected noticeably more deputies than the Communists. From the elections of 1962 on, the Socialists' dominance of the second ballot was never in doubt. In the four elections between 1962 and 1973 the Socialists improved their electoral margins on the second ballot, as compared with the Communists, by at least 10 percentage points. Even in the election of 1978, when difficulties between the two parties undoubtedly cut into the improvement in the Socialists' second-ballot margins, they did better than the Communists by four percentage points. The Communists' larger second-ballot margins after 1978 came only as the ratio of Socialist to Communist strength in the national assembly increased dramatically. In the elections before 1981 the ratio of Socialist deputies to Communist deputies remained relatively stable (see Table 4). In 1981 the ratio rose to 6.1, in 1988 to 9.6. Our analysis, then, clearly relates the Communists' difficulties in the Fifth Republic to their emergence as the organization most closely approaching the marginal party. Only in times of adversity did the winning style of the secondary party become conspicuous.

Alliances between the Legislative Groups

We hypothesized that specialized parties devise strategies of alliance that reinforce their special positions. As our discussions of the Fifth Republic's legislative groups imply, this was the case. As the Republic's primary party, the Gaullists from their initial dominant position had sought conquest of, rather than coopera-

A Multiparty System in France

tion with, their allies. Faced with determined resistance, they had used their considerable superiority of resources to impose upon the Independent Republicans the strategy of the unique candidacy. As the dual electoral party, the Independent Republicans were ambivalent toward but accepting of this strategy, given their junior status (Charlot 1971; 1973, 139-40; Goguel 1983a, 500-503).

In 1978, however, strengthened as a dual electoral party, the Independent Republicans, reincarnated as the UDF, came closest to practicing the strategy of the trial run. Even as tensions between the two allies reached their highest point, the UDF, bolstered by its newly confederated forces, as well as its control of the presidency, contested a record number of districts with the Gaullists, allowing the electorate to decide between them in contests that went to a second ballot (Charlot 1980, 81-87; Colliard 1979; Frears and Parodi 1979, 23-27, 32, 38-42). The result was an election that most strongly confirmed the UDF's status as the dual electoral party while bringing it closest to the Gaullist group in size. Faced with the prospect of defeat in the subsequent two-ballot elections, the UDF did revert to practicing the strategy of unique candidacy with the Gaullists (Charlot 1988, 62-69; Le Monde 1988, 36-37; Ysmal 1986, 177-78, 194-95). In these elections, the UDF also emulated more closely the primary party's style.

As we hypothesized too, the Socialists as the secondary party consistently engaged in trial runs with the Communists, the marginal party. For all seven elections the Socialists were able to implement this strategy with a more or less willing Communist party. It is true that during the 1970s, as it became increasingly clear the alliance was working to the Socialists' advantage, the Communists became increasingly uncooperative. For the election of 1978 they held aloof from any formal agreement until the eve of the

second ballot for the first time since 1962. In this election Socialist progress was in any event affected by the explosion of candidates from minor parties, who in some instances deprived the Socialists of their favored status within the alliance on the first ballot (Boy and Dupoirier 1986; Frears and Parodi 1979, 18-23, 42-44, 73-75, 85-97; Parodi 1978).[16] In the two subsequent elections provoked by the Socialist president, however, the Communists had no choice but to accept without objection the strategy of the trial run. In these elections the strategy worked to the overwhelming advantage of the Socialists. But it also helped salvage the Communist legislative organization, which in adverse times had fallen back on the style of the secondary party.

As we hypothesized, the encouragement the two-ballot system gave to new electoral organizations did not disrupt the stability of the party system. Thus, the explosion of minor party candidacies in 1978, at most affected the distribution of power among the four major, stable groups rather than bringing new parties into the assembly. Given the increase in first-ballot contests between Gaullists and the UDF, the explosion of candidates affected the distribution of wins between these allies, as well as between the Socialists and Communists. Only the proportional representation system used for the 1986 election to the national assembly brought Le Pen's National Front into parliament. While the return to the single-member-district, two-ballot system in 1988 destroyed Le Pen's organization in the assembly, it allowed the Communist organization to survive. The legislative election of 1988 then left the multiparty system composed of our four prototypical parties intact.

Legislative Groups and the Presidency

We should note that the organizational and coalitional arrangements originating in the legislature have had their impact on partisan organization for the presidency. Also conducted in two rounds, the presidential elections have produced, for the most part, candidates from the four major legislative groups. The Communists, regretting their decision to sit out the presidential elections in 1965 and 1974, fielded candidates in 1981 and 1988. Neither the Gaullists nor their allies have been willing to pass up a try for the presidency. Certainly, the insistence of both on running candidates contributed to the close election of the Independent Republican Giscard in 1974, his defeat in 1981, and the defeat of the Gaullist Jacques Chirac in 1988. Rather than inspiring unity, defeat has exacerbated the differences between allies, thereby strengthening the multiparty system whose origins derive from the legislature.

The Dual-Ballot Typology and the Parties of the Third Republic: A Retrospective

Since the *Third* Republic also used the single-member-district, two-ballot system for elections to parliament, we speculated that in the Third Republic, as in the Fifth, parties specialized in ways of winning elections. Since the four types of parties we discovered in the Fifth Republic could all trace their political ancestry in some fashion to the Third, we wondered if their specializations had originated there. To test our hypotheses we applied our two measures of winning to the groups formed by deputies elected in 1936 to the final legislature of the Republic. We were thus able to glimpse the parties of the Third Republic in their final stage of organization. The first thing that strikes us in Figure 4 is the large number of groups compared with the legislatures of the Fifth Republic.[17] A more careful examination shows the groups clustering according to our two basic forms of organi-

zation: the primary and secondary prototypes.

Emerging as secondary parties were the Radicals, Socialists, and Communists.[18] The placement for the Radicals is the expected one. Throughout the Third Republic the party reigned as the pivotal political organization. From its founding in 1901 the Radical party had laid claim to the reformist position, translating its message—neither reaction nor revolution—into an effective electoral strategy for garnering second-ballot support (M. Schlesinger 1974). In 1936, however, the Socialists demonstrated that they had not only adopted the Radical style of winning, but were capable of using it more effectively. In 1936 the Socialists for the first time surpassed the Radicals in the number of deputies elected; for the first time they became the single largest group in the chamber (M. Schlesinger 1978). In the 1962 legislature both Radicals and Socialists reemerged as secondary parties. But the Radicals' small group, the Rassemblement Démocratique, was gone in the next legislature, its personnel having merged for the most part with the Socialists. The remaining Radicals merged with groups, bordering on dual as well as secondary parties, which ultimately joined the UDF (see Table 2). The Socialists' durability as a secondary party outlasted not only the Radicals but also the Communists. In 1936 the Communists' placement as a secondary party brought them their greatest electoral success in the Third Republic: they elected a record number of deputies, reversing the humiliating defeat of 1932 when their representation in the chamber had sunk to its all-time low. Unlike the Socialists, the Communists were unable to reemerge as a secondary party in the Fifth Republic, as we have seen.

In 1936, as in the Fifth Republic, the secondary parties employed the alliance strategy we predicated from our theoretical assumptions. Running on their own on

A Multiparty System in France

Figure 4. Political Groups and the Two-Ballot System of Elections
to the Chamber of Deputies, 1936

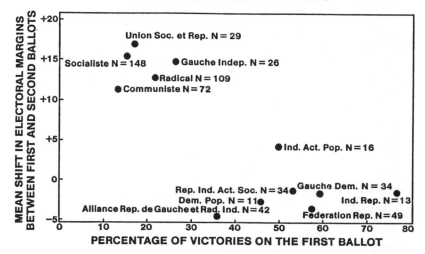

1936 CHAMBER OF DEPUTIES

Sources: Electoral data and group membership, 1936: Georges Lachapelle, *Élections législatives, 26 avril et 3 mai 1936, résultats officiel.* Paris: *Le temps; Journal officiel,* Chambre débats, 2d sess., 19 June 1936, pp. 1522–24.

the first ballot, they agreed on the second ballot, for the most part, on a single coalitional candidate. There is no question that the electoral success of the Communists and Socialists in 1936 resulted from the formation of the Popular Front alliance that made possible the implementation of this strategy. The Popular Front, formed two years before the elections as an antifascist coalition among Communists, Socialists, and Radicals, allowed Socialists and Communists time to mute their sharper ideological images and to reach out to a broader spectrum of voters than had been their wont (M. Schlesinger 1978). Thus, in the elections they were able to pick up support on the second ballot not only from each other but also from their more moderate partner, the Radical party.

Almost all the remaining groups cluster as primary parties. While the lines to the parties of the Fifth Republic are less clear, most can qualify as ancestors of the Gaullists or the UDF, having participated in governing coalitions that excluded Socialists, Communists, and sometimes Radicals. Looking most like a precursor of the Gaullist organization was the Fédération Républicaine. Founded in 1903 to combat the recently formed Radical party, the Fédération emerged over the course of the Third Republic as the most sharply defined conservative organization, bearing a strong Catholic and nationalist message. Moreover, during the interwar years it became identified with a single strong personality, the deputy Louis Marin. It is not surprising, then, to find this organization, like the subsequent Gaullist organization, a first-choice party. Equally long lived though less sharply defined were the two groups the Gauche Démocratique et Radicale Indépendante and the Alliance des Républicains de Gauche et des Radicals Indépendants. In this respect they were the forerunners of the Independent Republicans and the UDF. Their status as primary parties in 1936 undoubtedly reflects their fallback position in a polarized election where they were not favored.[19]

Indeed, in the elections of 1936 primary parties also followed the alliance strategy we posited for them. This finding is even more impressive, given the number of primary parties that participated. All the same, Georges Dupeux, in his excellent monograph on the 1936 elections, found that the opponents of the Popular Front had agreed on unity or quasi-unity candidates in more than half of the contested districts. Commenting on this strategy, he observed, "This tactic prevented the voters from expressing their preference for such and such political nuance; it allowed them only to show their hostility for candidates of the Popular Front" (Dupeux 1959, 125). These findings on the alliances of 1936 and the parties that formed them lend additional support to our assumptions about the dual ballot's effect on party organization in France.

Conclusions

Our findings about the parties of the Fifth Republic lend strong support to the central assumption of the office-seeking theory of parties in democracies: party organization reflects, above all, the response to the structures of political opportunities and of electoral competition. By introducing the popular election of a president endowed with considerable

powers over the legislature, the Fifth Republic forced the restructuring of parties as national organizations capable of concerted, disciplined action in government. At the same time, the alterations in the structure of political opportunities did not diminish the key role played in party organization by the legislative group. Moreover, the structure of electoral competition that the Fifth Republic adopted, dual-ballot elections in single-member districts, ensured that the legislative group would be the core party unit in a multiparty system.

The multiparty system was, however, distinctive, consisting of parties tailored to the two-ballot mode of winning. Students of electoral systems have for some time recognized the effects of voting arrangements on the number of effective parties in a democracy. Our study reveals the impact of these arrangements on the parties themselves.

As we have shown, the parties of the Fifth Republic specialized in their approach to the dual-ballot election. Thus, the Gaullists emerged as a primary party, maximizing their strength on the first ballot largely because of their ability to create an organization with a strong appeal (defense of the regime) identified with a popular personality (Charles de Gaulle). They were also able to use their organizational strengths to implement a distinctive strategy of alliance—the unique candidacy—which reinforced their position as a primary party. On the other hand, the allies with whom they practiced this strategy, the Independent Republicans–UDF, had their own organizational response to the two-ballot election, that of the dual electoral party. This created tensions within the alliance, while reinforcing the position of the Independent Republicans–UDF as a distinct political organization. At the same time, the Socialists emerged as a secondary party, maximizing their support on the second ballot, largely by creating an organization

A Multiparty System in France

that appealed to multiple groups of voters as the acceptable second choice. They, too, implemented a distinctive strategy of alliance that worked to their advantage, the strategy of the trial run. Yet tensions also existed within this alliance because the Socialists' allies, the Communists, had their own organizational response to the two-ballot election, that of the marginal party. These tensions reinforced the Communists' independent position. We have also shown that in the *Third* Republic the same electoral rules produced similar organizations, to which the parties of the Fifth Republic could trace their ancestry. These findings are important because they allow us to see significant similarities and differences in French parties that would otherwise be obscured.

Our findings also have broader implications. The French dual-ballot election exposes a problem inherent in all democratic elections, the problem of voters' preferences. In societies of any size or complexity we should not expect any single candidate or party to be the first choice of large numbers of voters. This basic insight tends to be overlooked, however, because most electoral systems give voters only a single option, the option to vote once for a single candidate in a plurality election or the option to vote for a list of candidates in an election determined by proportional rules. In these situations the problem of voters' preferences must be resolved within the party and among its candidates. The French dual-ballot election, however, while not offering voters the opportunity to rank all their preferences, does invite parties to approach voters so as to allow them to express either their first or compromise choices. Thus, analyzing the French structure of electoral competition for its impact on party organization can shed light on the tensions that exist within and between political parties in all democracies.

Notes

We thank Didier Maus, Jean-Luc Parodi, Roy Pierce, Marie-France Toinet, and Colette Ysmal for helpful discussions on our approach to the parties of the Fifth Republic.

1. On the relationship between president and parliament see "Le parlement français sous trois présidents 1958–1980," 1981, and "La constitution de la Cinquième République," 1984. See also Andrews 1978, Baumgartner 1987, Maus 1987, and Toinet 1988.

2. The problems of preference ordering and the "sincerity" of the vote are focal issues in positive political theory. Early discussions are Arrow 1951 and Black 1958. See also Riker and Ordeshook 1973, chap. 4.

3. For the effect of the single-member plurality election on the number of parties see E. E. Schattschneider's (1942, chap. 4) classic explanation and Duverger's (1951, 236–309) comparative analysis.

4. The Third Republic used the two-ballot system for elections to the chamber of deputies. For elections to the national assembly, the Fourth Republic used a list system, which distributed seats in some proportional fashion. Except for the legislative election of 1986, which used a form of proportional representation, the Fifth Republic has used the two-ballot system for legislative, presidential, and cantonal elections. For municipal elections a combination of the two-ballot system and a list, proportional representation system is used. A list, proportional representation system is used for elections to the European parliament and was also used in 1986 for the first popularly elected regional councils.

5. In the United States, primary nominating elections give voters additional options, thus greatly affecting U.S. party organization. In most primaries, however, voters, again, have only one option, since winners need only a plurality of the votes. Only run-off primaries offer voters a range of options similar to the range offered by the French two-ballot system.

6. Converse and Pierce (1986, chaps. 10–13) examine the behavior of the French electorate in the two ballots of the 1967 election.

7. In all of our calculations we have used the total votes cast (*votants*) in each constituency, rather than the more commonly used total of valid votes cast (*suffrages exprimés*). Since voters casting blank (*nul*) ballots can be expressing a preference for none of the candidates and since our theory rests on the importance of voters' preference ordering for parties, we decided to include their votes in the totals.

8. Since, as we shall see, the dual-ballot system encourages multiple parties, legislators who win on the first ballot by an absolute majority usually win by very comfortable margins. For the seven two-ballot elections held between 1962 and 1988, the

first-ballot winners' average electoral margin—that is, the difference between the winner's vote and that of the nearest rival—was 32.3%. In two-party terms that is equivalent to winning by over 65% of the vote.

9. The electoral margin is the difference in percentage of the total vote received by the winning candidate and the candidate receiving the next highest number of votes. On the first ballot, if the eventual winner did not come in first, the margin is negative, because it is calculated as the difference between the winning candidate's vote and that of the candidate who led on the first ballot. The figures we have used are the differences between the electoral margins on the second and first ballots, averaged for each group as a whole.

10. Contrary to the rule in the Third Republic, new candidates cannot enter for the second ballot and candidates can run on the second ballot only if they receive a certain percentage of the votes on the first ballot. The requirement was, for the election of 1962, 5% of the *suffrages exprimés*; for the elections of 1967, 1968, and 1973, 10% of the registered voters (*electeurs inscrits*); for the elections of 1978, 1981, and 1988, 12.5% of the *electeurs inscrits*. The law does provide that if only one candidate meets the requirement, the next highest vote getter can contest the second-ballot election; if no candidate qualifies, the two highest vote getters on the first ballot contest the election.

11. This type of alliance is often referred to as a "primary" to suggest a similarity to the U.S. nominating primary. A significant difference is that electorates in U.S. primaries are restrained or restricted.

12. In analyzing the groups, we include deputies from both metropolitan France and the overseas possessions. We did not include those allied to a group (*apparentés*), because we considered their organizational commitment weak. Nor did we include the small number of deputies listed in each legislature as "belonging to no group."

13. The Gaullists played up their identity with the new Republic with the labels they used for their candidates in the elections of the 1960s: in 1962, Union pour la Nouvelle République; in 1967, Comité d'Action pour la Ve République; in 1968, Union pour la Défense de la République.

14. Mildred Schlesinger, "Why Mitterrand Is Qualified To Make Power Sharing Work," *Christian Science Monitor*, 13 April 1986.

15. Studies of the elections held in the 1960s did not even distinguish between the support of the Independent Republicans and the Gaullists (Goguel 1963, 1971; 1983a, 500–503; Lancelot and Lancelot 1971; Lancelot and Weil 1971). Colliard (1972, 207–34) raises the difficulties of distinguishing between the Gaullists' and the Independent Republicans' electoral support in the sixties. Converse and Pierce (1986, 30, 32, 38, 114–15, 189, 218, 262–63, 266, 435–36) stress the similarities between the two

in the sixties. Analyzing the results of the 1973 election, Charlot (1973, 81–144) found the Independent Republicans and the Gaullists sharing the same electoral fate. See also Hayward and Wright 1973.

16. In the 1978 election the Socialists also faced competition on the first ballot for the first time from the small Mouvement des Radicaux de Gauche (MRG). In the past the Socialists and the MRG had easily come to terms on candidates before the first ballot, thanks to the special relationship between the Socialists and this remnant of the Radicals that had carried over from the Fourth Republic.

17. In the Third Republic only 13 deputies were needed to form a group. Institutional rules also favored small groups and their pivotal bargaining power for positions in the executive (M. Schlesinger 1989).

18. The two other groups that emerged as secondary parties were organizations whose personnel always associated with the Radicals or Socialists. The Gauche Indépendante was an ephemeral organization that appeared only in 1936 and disappeared from the chamber of deputies by 1938. The Union Socialiste et Républicaine had a more continuous history, tracing its origins to the founding of the Socialist party in 1905, whose revolutionary rhetoric its members rejected. In 1936 the group received new recruits from those breaking with the Socialist party over its refusal to support Radical cabinets in the previous legislature.

19. The remaining primary parties, all newer, more ephemeral organizations, nevertheless had sharper images than these two groups. They ranged from the tiny Groupe Démocrate Populaire (a Catholic party) and the Groupe des Républicains Indépendants et Agraire Indépendant (an agrarian party) to the Groupe Indépendant d'Action Populaire (formed to defend the interests of Alsace-Lorraine)—all of which appear appropriately as primary parties. The tiny Groupe des Indépendants Républicains (to be distinguished from the Independent Republicans of the Fifth Republic) consisted of deputies brought together by the rule that required all deputies to form some type of group. Their first ballot strength supports their position as political powers in their own right (Anderson 1974; Irvine 1979).

References

Anderson, Malcolm. 1974. *Conservative Politics in France*. London: George Allen & Unwin.

Andrews, William G. 1978. "The Constitutional Prescription of Parliamentary Procedures in Gaullist France." *Legislative Studies Quarterly* 3:465–506.

Arrow, Kenneth. 1951. *Social Choice and Individual Values*. New York: Wiley.

A Multiparty System in France

Baudoin, Jean. 1981. "L'échec communiste de juin 1981" [The Communist defeat of June 1981]. *Pouvoirs* 20:45–54.

Baumgartner, Frank. 1987. "Parliament's Capacity To Expand Political Controversy in France." *Legislative Studies Quarterly* 12:33–54.

Black, Duncan. 1958. *The Theory of Committees and Elections.* Cambridge: Cambridge University Press.

Bon, Fréderic, and Jérôme Jaffré. 1978. "Les règles d'élection au scrutin majoritaire" [Electoral rules for majority voting]. *Revue française de science politique* 28:5–20.

Boy, Daniel, and Elisabeth Dupoirier. 1986. "Le poids des petits candidats" [The influence of minor candidates]. In *1981: Les élections de l'alternance* [1981: The elections of alternation]. Paris: Presses de ia Fondation des Sciences Politiques.

Charlot, Jean. 1967. *L'U.N.R.* Paris: Armand Colin.

Charlot, Jean. 1970. *Le phénomène gaulliste* [The Gaullist phenomenon]. Paris: Fayard.

Charlot, Jean. 1971. "Les préparatifs de la majorité" [The preparations of the majority]. In *Les élections de mars 1967* [The elections of March 1967]. Paris: Armand Colin.

Charlot, Jean. 1980. "The Majority." In *The French National Assembly Elections of 1978,* ed. Howard Penniman. Washington: American Enterprise Institute.

Charlot, Jean. 1981. "Le double enchaînement de la défaite et de la victoire" [The dual relationship between defeat and victory]. *Revue politique et parlementaire* 83:15–28.

Charlot, Jean. 1988. "The End of the 'Majority'." In *France at the Polls, 1981 and 1986,* ed. Howard Penniman. Durham, NC: Duke University Press.

Charlot, Jean, ed. 1973. *Quand la Gauche peut gagner* [When the Left can win]. Paris: Alain Moreau.

Colard, Daniel. 1983. "Réflexions sur le renouveau des clubs politiques après l'alternance du 10 mai 1981" [Reflections on the renewal of political clubs after the change in power of 10 May 1981]. *Pouvoirs* 14:157–70.

Colliard, Jean-Claude. 1972. *Les Républicains Indépendants* [The Independent Republicans]. Paris: Presses Universitaires de France.

Colliard, Jean-Claude. 1979. "Le parti giscardien" [The Giscardian party]. *Pouvoirs* 9:115–29.

Converse, Philip E., and Roy Pierce. 1986. *Political Representation in France.* Cambridge: Harvard University Press.

Denis, Nicolas. 1978. "Les élections législatives de mars 1978 en métropole" [The legislative elections of March 1978 in metropolitan France]. *Revue française de science politique* 28:977–1005.

Duhamel, Olivier. 1980. *La Gauche et la Ve République* [The Left and the Fifth Republic]. Paris: Presses Universitaires de France.

Dupeux, Georges. 1959. *Le Front populaire et les élections de 1936* [The Popular Front and the elections of 1936]. Paris: Armand Colin.

Dupoirier, Élisabeth and François Platone. 1974. "Une nouvelle étape dans le déclin du social-centrisme" [A new stage in the decline of social centrism]. *Revue française de science politique* 24:1173–1204.

Duverger, Maurice. 1951. *Les partis politiques* [Political parties]. Paris: Armand Colin.

Duverger, Maurice. 1964. "L'éternal marais: Essai sur le centrisme français" [The eternal swamp: Essay on French centrism]. *Revue française de science politique* 14:33–51.

Duverger, Maurice. 1978. *Échec au roi* [The king in check]. Paris: Albin Michel.

Frears, J. R., and Jean-Luc Parodi. 1979. *War Will Not Take Place.* London: C. Hurst.

Goguel, François. 1963. "Le référendum du 28 octobre et les élections du 18–25 novembre 1962" [The referendum of 28 October and the elections of 18–25 November 1962]. *Revue française de science politique* 13:289–314.

Goguel, François. 1967. "Bipolarisation ou rénovation du centrisme" [Bipolarization or the renovation of centrism]. *Revue française de science politique* 17:918–28.

Goguel, François. 1971. "Analyse global des résultats" [Overall analysis of the results]. In *Les élections législatives de mars 1967* [The legislative elections of March 1967]. Paris: Armand Colin.

Goguel, François. 1983a. "Les élections législatives des 23 et 30 juin 1968" [Legislative elections of 23 and 30 June 1968]. In *Chroniques électorales* [Electoral chronicles], vol. 2, Paris: Presses de la Fondation Nationale des Sciences Politiques.

Goguel, François. 1983b. "Les élections législatives des 14–21 juin 1981" [The legislative elections of 14–21 June 1981]. In *Chroniques électorales* [Electoral chronicles], vol. 3, Paris: Presses de la Fondation Nationale des Sciences Politiques.

Grofman, Bernard, and Arend Lijphart, eds. 1986. *Electoral Laws and Their Political Consequences.* New York: Agathon.

Grunberg, Gérard. 1986. "Causes et fragilités de la victoire socialiste de 1981" [Causes of, and weaknesses in, the Socialist victory of 1981]. In *1981: Les élections de l'alternance* [1981: The elections of alternation]. Paris: Presses de la Fondation Nationale des Sciences Politiques.

Grunberg, Gérard, and Etienne Schweisguth. 1981. "Profession et vote: La poussée de la Gauche" [Profession and vote: The upsurge of the Left]. In *France de gauche vote à droite* [Leftist France votes Right]. Paris: Presses de la Fondation Nationale des Sciences Politiques.

Hayward, Jack, and Vincent Wright. 1973. "Presidential Supremacy and the French General Elections of March 1973." *Parliamentary Affairs* 26:

274–395.

Irvine, William D. 1979. *French Conservatism in Crisis: The Republican Federation of France in the 1930s.* Baton Rouge: Louisiana State University Press.

Jaffré, Jérôme. 1980. "The French Electorate in March 1978." In *The French National Assembly Elections of 1978,* ed. Howard Penniman. Washington: American Enterprise Institute.

Jaffré, Jérôme. 1981. "De Valéry Giscard d'Estaing à François Mitterrand: France de gauche, vote à gauche" [From Valéry Giscard d'Estaing to François Mitterrand: Leftist France votes Left]. *Pouvoirs* 20:5–28.

Jaffré, Jérôme, and Jean Ranger. 1974. "Les structures électorales de la gauche" [The Left's electoral structures]. *Revue française de science politique* 24:1149–72.

Kesselman, Mark. 1988. "The Notables' Revenge." *French Politics and Society* 6:8–15.

Labrousse, Jean. 1971. "L'opinion publique" [Public opinion]. In *Les élections législatives de mars 1967* [The legislative elections of March 1967]. Paris: Armand Colin.

Lancelot, Alain, and Pierre Weill. 1971. "Les transferts de voix du premier au second tour des élections de mars 1967" [The transfer of votes from the first to the second round of the elections of March 1967]. In *Les élections législatives de mars 1967* [The legislative elections of March 1967]. Paris: Armand Colin.

Lancelot, Marie-Thérèse, and Alain Lancelot. 1971. "Géographie des élections de 5 et 12 mars 1967" [Geography of the elections of 5 and 12 March 1967]. In *Les élections législatives de mars 1967* [The legislative elections of March 1967]. Paris: Armand Colin.

Laurens, André. 1988. "De l'ouverture ratée à l'obligation d'ouverture" [From the failed opening to the obligations of opening]. In *Les élections législatives, 5 juin, 12 juin 1988* [The legislative elections of 5 June, 12 June 1988]. Paris: Le Monde, Dossiers et Documents.

"La constitution de la Cinquième République." Special issue of *Revue française de science politique* 34, nos. 4–5 (1984).

Lavau, Georges, and Janine Mossuz-Lavau. 1980. "The Union of the Left's Defeat." In *The French National Assembly Elections of 1978,* ed. Howard Penniman. Washington: American Enterprise Institute.

Le Gall, Gérard. 1977. "Élections législatives: L'alchimie du second tour" [Legislative elections: The alchemy of the second round]. *Revue politique et parlementaire* 79:21–29.

Le Gall, Gérard. 1978. "A gauche toujours le rééquilibrage" [On the Left always readjustment]. *Revue politique et parlementaire* 80:33–43.

Le Gall, Gérard. 1981. "Du recul de la Droite vers l'hégémonie du P. S." [From the setback of the Right toward the hegemony of the P.S.]. *Revue politique et parlementaire* 83:29–41.

Le Monde. 1988. *Les élections législatives, 5 juin, 12 juin 1988* [The legislative elections, 5 June, 12 June 1988]. Paris: Le Monde, Dossiers et Documents.

"Le parlement français sous trois présidents 1958–1980." Special issue of *Revue française de science politique* 31, no. 1 (1981).

Martin, Pierre. 1981. "Le basculement électoral de 1981" [The electoral upheaval of 1981]. *Revue française de science politique* 31:999–1014.

Maus, Didier. 1987. "Le parlement français de l'alternance à cohabitation, 1981–1987" [The French parliament from alternation to cohabitation]. Maison Française d'Oxford (Paris). Typescript.

Parodi, Jean-Luc. 1977. "Après les élections municipales: La fin de la transition?" [After the municipal elections: The end of the transition?]. Revue politique et parlementaire 79:6–18.

Parodi, Jean-Luc. 1978. "L'échec des gauches" [The failure of the Left]. Revue politique et parlementaire 80:9–32.

Parodi, Jean-Luc. 1979. "La France quadripolaire à l'épreuve de la proportionelle" [Quadripolar France tested by proportional representation]. *Revue politique et parlementaire* 81:9–32.

Pierce, Roy. 1980. "French Legislative Elections." In *The French National Assembly Elections of 1978,* ed. Howard Penniman. Washington: American Enterprise Institute.

Platone, François, and Jean Ranger. 1986. "L'échec électoral du parti communiste" [The failure of the Communist party]. In *1981: Les élections de l'alternance* [1981: The elections of alternation]. Paris: Presses de la Fondation Nationale des Sciences Politiques.

Ponceyri, Robert. 1985. *Gaullisme électoral et Ve République* [Electoral gaullism and the Fifth Republic]. 2 vols. Toulouse: Presses de l'Institut d'Études Politiques de Toulouse.

Portelli, Hugues. 1980. "Le présidentialisation des partis français" [The presidentialization of French parties]. *Pouvoirs* 14:97–106.

Rae, Douglas. 1967. *The Political Consequences of Electoral Laws.* New Haven: Yale University Press.

Ranger, Jean. 1986. "Le déclin du parti communiste français" [The decline of the French Communist party]. *Revue française de science politique* 36: 46–63.

Riker, William, and Peter Ordeshook. 1973. *An Introduction to Positive Political Theory.* Englewood Cliffs, NJ: Prentice-Hall.

Schattschneider, Elmer E. 1942. *Party Government.* New York: Rinehart.

Schlesinger, Joseph A. 1960. "The Structure of Competition in the American States." *Behavioral Science* 5:197–210.

A Multiparty System in France

Schlesinger, Joseph A. 1965. "Party Organization." In *Handbook of Organizations*, ed. James G. March. Chicago: Rand McNally.

Schlesinger, Joseph A. 1966. *Ambition and Politics.* Chicago: Rand McNally.

Schlesinger, Joseph A. 1984. "On the Theory of Party Organization." *Journal of Politics* 46: 369–400.

Schlesinger, Mildred. 1974. "The Development of the Radical Party in the Third Republic." *The Journal of Modern History* 46:476–501.

Schlesinger, Mildred. 1978. "The Cartel des Gauches: Precursor of the Front Populaire." *European Studies Review* 8:211–34.

Schlesinger, Mildred. 1989. "Legislative Governing Coalitions in Parliamentary Democracies: The Case of the French Third Republic." *Comparative Political Studies* 22:33–65.

Schonfeld, William R. 1980. "La stabilité des dirigeants des partis politiques: Le personnel des directions nationales du parti socialiste et du mouvement gaulliste" [The stability of leaders of political parties: The personnel of the national leaderships of the Socialist party and the Gaullist movement]. *Revue française de science politique* 30:477–505.

Toinet, Marie-France. 1988. "The Elections of 1981: Political Background and Legal Setting." In *France at the Polls, 1981 and 1986*, ed. Howard Penniman. Durham, NC: Duke University Press.

Wilson, Frank. 1982. *French Political Parties under the Fifth Republic.* New York: Praeger.

Ysmal, Colette. 1986. "D'une Droite en sursis à une Droite défaite, 1974–1981" [From a Right in reprieve to a Right defeated]. In *1981: Les élections de l'alternance* [1981: The elections of alternation], Paris: Presses de la Fondation Nationale des Sciences Politiques.

Joseph A. Schlesinger is Professor and Mildred Schlesinger is Adjunct Professor of Political Science, Michigan State University, East Lansing, MI 48824.

[21]

B.J.Pol.S 17, 257–279
Printed in Great Britain

State Structures and Clientelism: The French State Versus the 'Notaires'

EZRA N. SULEIMAN*

The power of a state to act independently of civil groups is widely seen to depend on the state's structure. This view of the policy-making process has given rise to an assertion that is now accepted as an almost self-evident truth: that states that have centralized administrative structures are better able than are decentralized states to formulate and implement policies independently of societal pressures. Put simply, decentralized states are said to be more permeable than centralized ones.

In this article, we treat this widely credited assertion as a hypothesis and subject it to an empirical examination. The theoretical concern of our study is the capacity of what is generally considered to be the quintessential example of a 'centralized', or 'strong' or even 'omnipotent' state to act independently of societal groups. This concern is tested by reference to an empirical study of the relationship between this centralized state, the French, and a specific group, a liberal profession, the *notaires*.

THE STATE AS AN ACTOR

We are all aware of the revival of interest in the state and of the outpourings of works that lay claim to having rediscovered the state.

From the late 1950's until the mid-1970's the term state virtually disappeared from the professional academic lexicon. Political scientists wrote about government, political development, interest groups, voting, legislative behaviour, leadership, and bureaucratic politics, almost everything but 'the state.' However, in the last decade 'the state' has reappeared in the literature.[1]

* Department of Politics, Princeton University. Earlier versions of this article were presented to the XIII World Congress of the International Political Science Association, Paris, July 1985, and at the conference on 'Continuity and Change in Mitterrand's France', Harvard University, Cambridge, December 1985. I am indebted to Anthony King for his careful reading and helpful comments on that version. This article was written under the auspices of the Center of International Studies, Princeton University.

[1] Stephen D. Krasner, 'Approaches to the State: Alternative Conceptions and Historical Dynamics', *Comparative Politics*, XVI (1984), 223–46, p. 223.

258   SULEIMAN

The state as such has not merely reappeared in the literature. It has, according to Theda Skocpol, come to represent a new paradigm in the study of politics.

There is no gainsaying that an important paradigmatic shift is underway in our understanding of the relevance of 'the state' as actor and structure in social life. One does not have to be very old ... to remember when the dominant theories spoke of anything and everything but the 'state.'[2]

To announce the imminence of a revolution is not the same thing as announcing the revolution itself, for even if the state today represents the paradigm that political development or voting behaviour represented two decades ago, it still needs to be shown how our understanding of the political process has thereby been advanced. Gabriel Almond has spoken of the 'professional amnesia'[3] that is characteristic of those who have 'discovered' or 'rediscovered', as the case may be, 'the state' and suggests that the refusal to cumulate knowledge by the 'statists' in the end helps to undermine the propositions they put forward:

The impairment of professional memory has become common in political science and helps to explain its fragmented and faddish character. The behavioral movement buried the memory of the institutionalists, only to have a 'statist' counterrevolution take place in the last year or two. The 'dependency' movement in comparative politics vilified and buried the modernization and pluralist theories, and now has come to terms with its own exaggerations and distortions.[4]

Almond's critique suggests that the current vogue of 'the state' has little to do with the promise of a bright future for political science; it is due simply to a degree of forgetfulness about what political science has been about in the past. This is the position taken by David Easton, though he emphasizes more strongly than does Almond the dangers that the study of politics runs if it follows the 'statist' path. Easton argues that the reintroduction of the concept of the state after it had been abandoned almost three decades ago merely returns us to the 'vapid debates of the nineteenth and early twentieth centuries' and 'to a conceptual morass from which we thought we had but recently escaped'.[5]

Whatever the respective merits and claims of the old and the new schools and whatever the outcome of the debate, it remains true that only the refinement of the state as a concept and only after the concept has been subjected to empirical investigation can we really have clear indications of its potential contributions and utility. One of the earliest champions of the 'statist' approach,[6] Stephen

[2] Theda Skocpol, 'Bringing the State Back In: False Leads and Promising Starts in Current Theories and Research', paper presented at a conference on 'States and Social Structures', Mount Kisco, New York, 1982, p. 1.

[3] Gabriel A. Almond, 'Corporatism, Pluralism. and Professional Memory', *World Politics*, XXXV, (1983), 245–60, p. 252.

[4] Almond, 'Corporatism, Pluralism, and Professional Memory'.

[5] David Easton, 'The Political System Besieged by the State', *Political Theory*, IX (1981), 302–25, pp. 321–2.

[6] See Stephen D. Krasner, *Defending the National Interest* (Princeton, NJ: Princeton University Press, 1978).

Krasner, has rightly observed that to maintain 'that terms have changed, that certain scholars have self-consciously adopted a new vocabulary (or readopted an old one), does not necessarily imply that there has been a change in substance.'[7] How are we to know if there has been a change in substance? The confidence in a new paradigm can only come about by the exercise of empirical exploration within the context of theoretical models. In the absence of such an undertaking, it is inevitable that discussions about the state will be forced to fall back on what we already knew from more general (or, as some would call them, 'old-fashioned') analyses.

Perhaps nowhere is this more evident than in the attempt to assess the power of a state by reference to the administrative organization of the state. A state may be more, or less, than the sum of its administrative parts, for when new administrative organizations are created this does not always lead to a concentration or an effective and authoritative use of power.[8] Indeed it is precisely for this reason that a purely institutional approach to the study of the political process was found wanting.

Yet most analyses of state power, whether pluralist or statist in orientation, have been based on rather formalistic or institutional approaches to the study of politics. The understanding that France possesses a 'strong' state because 'the French state is centralized ... united and controls an atomistic society', whereas the American state is weak because it is 'decentralized ... divided and is controlled by a pluralist society', is based on straightforward expositions of institutional structures.[9] It need not represent an accurate description of the French and American states.

In order to assess the capacity of a state to act 'upon its preferences', and to act autonomously 'even when its preferences diverge from the demands of the most powerful groups in civil society',[10] we need to go beyond a simple analysis of administrative capabilities. A state needs to be viewed as constituting a multitude of organizations interacting with one another and interacting separately with civil groups. This interaction helps to some extent to shape and to define the state's preferences, which in turn shape and define the state's relationships to civil groups. Figure 1 depicts these multiple relationships, which serve to define state interests.

A state's preferences in democratic polities are not formulated in a vacuum.

[7] Krasner, 'Approaches to the State', pp. 223–4. It happens that Krasner believes that there has definitely come about a change in substance. This is not a view that is widely shared, as the views of Gabriel Almond and David Easton indicate. A recent survey of changing trends in comparative politics makes no mention of the 'state' paradigm. See Ronald Inglehart, 'Changing Paradigms in Comparative Political Behavior', paper presented at the 1982 annual meeting of the American Political Science Association, Denver, Colorado, 1982.

[8] See Stephen Skowronek, *Building a New American State: The Expansion of National Administrative Capacities* (New York: Cambridge University Press, 1975).

[9] Peter J. Katzenstein, 'International Relations and Domestic Structures: Foreign Economic Policies of Advanced Industrial Societies', *International Organization*, xxx (1976), 1–45, p. 17.

[10] Eric Nordlinger, *On the Autonomy of the Democratic State* (Cambridge, Mass.: Harvard University Press, 1981), p. 1.

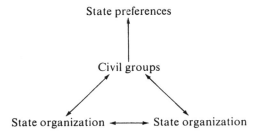

Fig. 1. The interaction of state organizations and civil groups

Figure 1 indicates that, regardless of the type of administrative organization that the state has at its disposal, it does not follow that the multitude of state organizations that go to form the totality of the state's administrative capacity will act to insure that the state's preferences (as they are defined, say, by government policy) will actually be put into effect. The state's organizations will themselves shape the state's preferences, whether as a result of considerations of bureaucratic politics, whether because they represent powerful client groups, or whether because of ideological considerations. In all cases, the interactions between civil groups and state organizations, and the impact of both in shaping what becomes the state's preferences, serve to determine what the state will or will not be able to do. This is precisely why the state is able to implement its preferences more easily in some policy areas than in others. States, like societies, are neither uniformly 'strong' nor uniformly 'weak'.

CENTRALIZATION AND STATE POWER

Centralized structures have long been assumed to possess power and to be able to use that power for the good of the community, whereas decentralized structures are seen to be an ideal terrain for take-over by private groups and as allowing for the undue influence of such groups over the policy-making process.[11] Hence, it is argued, public values 'will fare best at the hands of large diverse constituencies – the presidency (and perhaps the Senate) rather than the House; the national government rather than the states and the local governments.'[12]

But does a unitary state with a centralized state apparatus in fact resist the encroachments and power of private groups more effectively than a decentralized one? This would surely be the case only if the centralized state was not constituted by a multitude of administrative agencies pursuing separate goals and only if the private groups in the state were poorly organized. Centralization cer-

[11] See Grant McConnell, *Private Power and American Democracy* (New York: Alfred A. Knopf, 1966).
[12] J. David Greenstone, 'The Public, the Private, and American Democracy: Reflections on Grant McConnell's Political Science', in J. David Greenstone, ed., *Public Values and Private Power in American Politics* (Chicago: The University of Chicago Press, 1984), p. x.

tainly concentrates jurisdictions. It does not necessarily concentrate effective power. Private groups organize themselves in response to an administrative structure in which jurisdictions are centralized. They are thus able to concentrate their activities effectively on a given structure.

We examine in this article not only the room for manœuvre available to a centralized state but also whether a centralized state is in fact capable of resisting the hegemony of private groups. We find, in effect, that centralized structures that allow for the concentration of jurisdictions in an arm of the state often do not prevent, but on the contrary facilitate, the take-over of the state by such groups. McConnell assumed that a centralized authority necessarily represented a large constituency and that dispersion of power necessarily strengthens the hands of private groups. Our analysis does not bear this out. We find that centralization offers a remarkable advantage to private groups: they need not disperse their efforts in accordance with jurisdictional dispersion, as is the case in decentralized structures. All of their efforts at influencing the policy process can be directed at one central organizational structure. Once a close, symbiotic relationship is established with a state structure that is given the power to regulate an economic or social sector, the relevant private group can often succeed in using public power for private gain. It does not need to disperse its efforts. Clientelism may thus actually be more dangerous in a centralized system than in a decentralized one.[13]

A state's organizational structure does not, then, define the degree of power, or strength, or autonomy that the state possesses. A centralized state encourages the development of relatively centralized private organization (or counter-power), which more often than not comes to regard the centralized agency as its spokesman and defender. The investment of regulatory power in – or the granting of a *tutelle* to – an administrative agency implies the granting of power and authority over a private group. But regulation and *tutelle* often come to mean, both to the agency and to the group in question, the defence of the group. When that occurs, the public overseer is transformed into the spokesman of a private group, possibly without the state's even noticing the subversion of its proper role.

The extension of the state's role is not directly tied to an extension of its power or capacities. Indeed it often leads to an extension of the state's protective role: agencies are created to *protect* sectors and groups. And this protective role leads to a clientelistic relationship between the state and private groups, a relationship that ends up circumscribing the state's power to define and implement policies that do not protect the interests, goals and privileges of the groups. The providential state thus becomes a protector and defender of groups rather than an independent entity with the power to affect important changes of a redistributive nature. Neither the extension of the public sector nor the centralization of the state apparatus necessarily implies an increase in the state's independence and

---

[13] This theme is treated more fully in my *Private Power and Centralization in France* (Princeton, NJ: Princeton University Press, forthcoming).

262   SULEIMAN

autonomy. Administrative centralization is often welcomed by private groups precisely because it facilitates their task of creating a close, reciprocal relationship with the state.

The centralized state, moreover, almost never (save perhaps in a totalitarian system) confronts society in a unified manner. The pluralism of society is likely to be mirrored in an administrative pluralism that is more than an illustration of the bureaucratic-politics phenomenon. Administrative pluralism refers to interests going beyond the preservation of budgetary allocations. It refers to shared interests between an administrative agency and a private group; and, as interests change, so an administrative agency may establish a new complicity with a new group. When this occurs, it becomes difficult for the policy of the state as defined by the political authorities to be implemented in a consistent way.

In order to arrive at a more precise understanding of the mechanism of the policy process and the role that the state plays in this process, we have chosen to concentrate on the relationship between one state and one group. It does not matter much whether this group is typical of others that interact with the state apparatus. It matters only that the interactions and relationships we are about to describe give us a perspective on the policy-making process that we had not previously associated with a centralized state. Legion are expositions of the centralized, omnipotent nature of the French state. Much rarer are examples of the French state's being hemmed in and constrained by the relationships it has established with society.

We have indicated thus far that the theoretical underpinnings of the study will lead us to assess the ability of the state to determine and to implement its preferences and also to examine the extent to which a centralized administrative apparatus can resist the dominance of private groups. We hope in dealing with these critical issues to come to an increased understanding of the process of political change.

THE CASE

The case we have chosen to examine, given the theoretical concerns outlined above, is that of a group that maintains a close, if sometimes conflictual, relationship with the state and that manifests characteristics both of an archaic and of a highly modern society. The group in question is the legal profession of *notaires*. Its functions have remained essentially intact over a long period of time, but the profession now carries them out in a distinctively twentieth-century setting. In concentrating on the case of the notarial profession, we intend to explore the critical issue of the relationship of the state to civil groups. What is the nature of the relationship between the state and the notarial profession? Is it merely one that involves the state's playing a protective role? Does the state consider the profession as a public service, and hence does it see its own role as being the profession's defender? Or do the state's interests diverge from the *notaires*'? If there is conflict, what is usually the outcome?

First, a word about the group in question. The law grants the *notaire* a monopoly over the drawing up of contracts that the party or parties to them wish to have legalized. Rather than the state taking it upon itself to legalize contracts, it delegates this authority to officials whom it names but who purchase their practice in the open market. The *notaire* is an official who exercises his public monopoly in a private context.

Once the aspiring *notaire* has fulfilled a number of specified conditions, his candidacy for purchasing an office is presented to the Minister of Justice. He can purchase an established practice or may be granted by the state a newly created one. Each individual practice belongs to a specified territorial entity and cannot be moved to another part of the country. Hence, the presence of notarial offices is widespread across the country; but competition among *notaires* within a specified territorial unit is limited because the state fixes the fees that can be charged. The *notaire* thus enjoys a functional, as well as a territorial, monopoly.

What does the functional monopoly consist of? To understand what a *notaire* actually does, one merely has to know that a call for his services cannot be avoided where the sale or purchase of a property is involved (whether it be an apartment, a house, a factory, a parcel of land), where a marriage contract is desired by a couple, where a mortgage is obtained from a bank, where an inheritance has to be allocated among friendly or vying members of a family, where a business is bought or sold, where a merger between individual fortunes or companies is desired. In all such cases, an agreement is considered legal only when a notarial contract has been drawn up. The *notaire* is responsible for the verification of the contents of the document as well as for its legalization. Just as only a doctor can perform an operation, so only a *notaire* can legalize a contract. He is also responsible for the conservation of documents, which is why notarial archives represent such a rich fund of materials for historical research.

In some societies, the functions that the *notaire* performs in France are carried out, on a voluntary basis, by a lawyer. Such is the case in the United States. In other societies, a legal profession has been able to maintain a monopoly over specific legal functions such as the purchase of property, as in the case of solicitors in Britain.[14] In still other societies where the notarial profession exists (Belgium, Latin America, Italy, Spain) the principal responsibilities are much the same as in France, but the mode of operation may differ; essentially, the public function in certain societies receives greater emphasis, in that *notaires* are (as in Spain and Italy, for example) admitted to the profession through a state-sponsored examination and not through the purchase of a practice. Even in Alsace and Lorraine, where the impact of German law is still felt, *notaires* do not buy and sell the (public) office; they are more akin to civil servants than to members of the free professions. The French *notaires*, except those in Alsace and Lorraine, enjoy the purest form of a state-granted monopoly (both territorial and functional), the greatest degree of state protection and, the setting of fees apart, the widest latitude for operating as a commercial enterprise.

Though the case of the *notaires* may be unusual, and may lack the grand aura or significance of business or labour, the preservation of such an unusual status

---

[14] The UK Administration of Justice Act of 1985 removes the conveyancing monopoly of solicitors.

indicates that a complex relationship with the state is at work. Whether the state grants a tax concession to business or a wage increase to labour does not by itself reveal a great deal about the interaction of these groups with it. The attempt and subsequent failure by a long series of governments to break with patterns of *notaire*–state relations gives us considerable insight into the workings and mechanism of a centralized state. Apparently unusual cases may reveal more than more obvious ones about the politics and policy processes in so-called 'strong' states.

The history of the notarial profession shows varying degrees of closeness to, and alienation from, different regimes. It is true, as one author noted at the end of the last century, that *notaires* tend to believe that 'in high governmental or parliamentary spheres, one is poorly disposed towards entertaining the grievances of the *notaires*, and consequently, the reforms would certainly be made against them.'[15] But, if this really had been the case, it is doubtful whether the profession would still be in existence in the last part of the twentieth century.

That the profession has generally had a closer relationship with conservative regimes is beyond dispute. If the kings generally showed a kindly disposition toward *la corporation des notaires*[16] it was because the corporation, 'whether or not it was sincerely devoted to the monarchy, knew how to give back in respectful affection what it received in noble protection.'[17] The Revolution was less accommodating to the profession, which had to wait for Napoleon to father the law of *25 ventose an XI* (1803) that constitutes even today the profession's legal basis. This law has been referred to as 'one of those works of art that is untouchable; it nobly assumed its place of honour among those immortal laws which, one dependent on the other, were the most lasting glory of an era which itself was so full of glory.'[18]

The fortunes of the profession changed a number of times in the course of the nineteenth century. If the Restoration was particularly kind to it, the regime that came to power in 1848 was markedly less so, for this was the 'era in which socialism dealt it a fast and deadly step backwards which has left the foundations and the notarial profession trembling ever since.'[19] Nevertheless, although the Third Republic made numerous attempts to undo Napoleon's work in this area, it did not succeed. The image of the socialists – 'the enemies of private property' – seeking to take away from the profession what was their legal right could not, however, be effaced. Hence, the socialists' return to power in 1981, with an unprecedented majority, must have conjured up for many in the profession images of 1848. 'In the darkest times of our history, the *notaires* have found themselves invariably placed in the ranks of the friends of order and stability.'[20]

[15] R. Hurson, *Etude sur une organisation du notariat en France* (Paris: A. Chevalier-Marescqe (1984), p. 11.

[16] A. Jeannest Saint-Hilaire, *Du Notariat et des offices* (Paris: Durand, 1858), p. 209.

[17] Saint Hilaire, *Du Notariat et des offices*, p. 209.

[18] Saint-Hilaire, *Du Notariat et des offices*, p. 240.

[19] Saint-Hilaire, *Du Notariat et des offices*, p. 245.

[20] Saint-Hilaire, *Du Notariat et des offices*, p. 210.

It may be that the *notaires* have preferences as to the kinds of regimes they like to see governing the country. The history of the profession suggests that some regimes are less hostile to it than others. But the profession's preference for one regime over another has meaning only in the context of sharp political turns. In general, the profession has to establish relationships with the state, whoever controls it; and it soon discovers that the state is not always defined by the name of the party that won the last election.

MULTIPLE STATE RELATIONS

The *notaires* sometimes perceive that a tension exists between the profession and the state. When 'the friends of unions' and 'the enemies of private property' came to power in 1981, the *notaires* took the view that the state had been 'captured', had fallen into the hands of those who would be hostile to their cause. Of course, the *notaires* were not the only ones to think, in the wake of the Left's victory, that freedom had come to an end in France. The *notaires* rightly recognized, however, that it was now ideologically respectable to denounce the privileged castes in society.

If the Left was not well disposed towards the privileged groups, the notarial profession none the less successfully warded off attempts by the Socialists to do away with those privileges. This was so even though the Socialists did not propose a revolutionary reform that threatened to do away with the profession; they merely sought to open it up and grant it limited market freedom. The government's project called for (1) freer entry into the profession, that is, the end of *numerus clausus*; (2) the end of the *ancien régime* practice whereby a *notaire* presents his own successor to the public authorities; and (3) a less rigid fee structure that would allow for greater competition within the profession. The profession viewed all three provisions as dangerous to its own well-being in large part because they implied an end to the protective role of the state. Paradoxically, the profession objected to the Left's liberal, market-oriented project.

The notarial profession is a well-organized interest group. It has a wealthy national organization that represents the profession, and it is decentralized in that decisions affecting the profession are made at the departmental level. The profession also has a distinct advantage in that, having the ambiguous status of being both a public and a private group, it has an official link to the public authorities through the Ministry of Justice. It is this ministry that exercises administrative (regulatory) authority – the *tutelle* – over all the legal professions. Just how this notion of state authority has been interpreted, and how it would be more accurate to interpret it, will be become clear.

The Ministry of Justice was not only the *tutelle* ministry for the *notaires* prior to 1981: it was then the profession's most important ally and staunchest defender. Until 1981 there was no talk of serious reform, no threats from the government to the profession, and the Ministry of Justice could be counted on

266   SULEIMAN

to come to the profession's defence. Indeed, it is clear that, for the notarial profession, *tutelle* was synonymous with *defence* since after May 1981, when the
Ministry of Justice shared a willingness to entertain reforms of certain of the
notarial profession's outdated practices, the *notaires*'s President actually wrote
to the Minister of Justice reminding him that 'vous assurez notre tutelle, donc
notre defense'.[21]

After June 1981, however, it was no longer possible for the notarial profession
to consider the Ministry of Justice its chief ally. This led the profession to choose
other allies to thwart reforms proposed by the Ministry of Justice or the government. It worked with those allies in the state bureaucracy to undermine the projected reforms – and with considerable success. One should not forget that we
are referring to a state in which, at that time, one party controlled the executive
and legislative branches and which still has great patronage powers and controls
over a major segment of the economy. None of this matters when a policy is not
a top political priority (and few policies can be) and when bureaucratic agencies
pursue specific goals and ally themselves with groups that help them attain those
goals.

How was the profession able to thwart the government's reforms? If it has succeeded in preserving its status, this has been owing in part to its organizational
strength, in part to the weakness of the state and in part to the complicity
between the state and the *notaires*. Organizational strength is important, but it is
not sufficient by itself to undermine a state's will. The question arises: did the
state undermine itself?

The first thing that emerges from an examination of the relationship between
the state and the profession is that there is in fact no clear-cut relationship
between them, certainly none that can be characterized unequivocally as either
hostile or complicitous. Generally there is both hostility and complicity. The
task of any professional organization is to decide where it can find allies and
then to decide how it can use those allies to undermine those who are attempting
to upset the 'natural order'. In the 1980s, it was not always clear whether the
notarial profession understood that it was engaged in a political game. It may be
that the interests of the lenders of the profession were served by the picture they
gave of the members of the profession being under siege. It adopted throughout
an alarmist tactic, projecting the government and the state as being determined
to break the back of the 'closed' and 'privileged' professions.

From meeting to meeting, from reports to reform projects, the officials of the professions
in question tried to define a reasonable evolution of their duties. But they realized with
bitterness and uneasiness that while extolling *concertation* [negotiation] the government
had taken the irrevocable decision to completely change everything.[22]

This melodramatic language is only a reflection of what the profession was trying to get across to its members. On the eve of the 1984 Congress of Notaires, the

---

[21] Letter of Henri Chardon, President of the Conseil Supérieur du Notariat, to Robert Badinter,
Minister of Justice, *VIP*, 83/8 (December 1983).

[22] François Terre, 'Haro sur les officiers ministériels', *Le Figaro*, 14–15 January 1984.

very congress at which the Minister of Justice announced the abandonment of his reform projects, the President of the Conseil Superieur du Notariat in an interview with *Figaro-Magazine* stated that 'these reform projects shake the profession's foundations'.[23]

But one has to separate the public relations aspect of pressure from the more political and mundane pressures that are also applied. The first is used as a means of mobilizing the profession and of gaining support for the profession's main organization – the Conseil Supérieur du Notariat. In maintaining the membership in a state of agitation, the Conseil Supérieur strengthens its hand in negotiations with the state. The second involves separating allies and enemies and utilizing alliances with different segments of the state. This, however, is not made explicit, since the state needs to be presented as a cohesive entity if it is to be successfully portrayed as being menacing.

The notarial profession always has multiple relationships with the state. The configuration of such relationships may change over time, depending on political circumstances, but at any given time the profession has allies, enemies and others who may be swayed into becoming either allies or enemies. The profession generally has one important advantage over the state it confronts: it is unified and its goal of survival is shared by all of its members, whereas the state is an amalgam of diverse institutions each of them pursuing separate goals. Only those who saw a Marxist plot underlying all of the state's actions after 1981 claimed that the state was a solid entity pursuing certain goals single-mindedly. The more sophisticated leaders of the profession expressed this view in their public pronouncements while privately seeking alliances with segments of the state apparatus. As one such leader put it: 'Yes, this is a socialist state, but it doesn't do only socialist things.' Another put the same point slightly differently: 'There is a socialist majority in power. Does this change the fact that parts of the state need us and we need them? We just have to find each other.'

Once the profession understood that the new era of socialism did not bring with it an end to administrative pluralism, it quickly set about finding allies and identifying enemies. The search did not take long, for its potential allies were at the same time searching for them and also saw in the new political circumstances an opportunity to turn the *notaires* into clients. The *notaires* succeeded in thwarting reform because, operating politically, they were able to drive a wedge into the government's projects, which depended on policy co-ordination among diverse state institutions. Clientelism is as much part and parcel of the French state's interaction with society as it is of a decentralized state. Centralization even offers advantages to the client group over a structure in which power is widely dispersed.

The key actors in this political battle were all ostensibly part of the state machine: the Ministry of Justice, which had a legal tie to (and authority over) the notarial profession; the Ministry of Finance, for whom the profession was an

---

[23] *Figaro-Magazine*, 26 May 1984, p. 130. In his address before the Congress of Notaires two days later, Robert Badinter expressed his bitterness at Chardon's remarks.

important arm of its tax-collecting function and whose interest in a more market-oriented fee scale was a means of curbing the structural causes of inflation; the Caisse des Dépôts et Consignations, the state development bank that received the vast deposits of cash deriving from the private (individual and company) transactions that the *notaires* had the responsibility to legalize; and the notarial profession itself, which was a delegatee of public authority.

THE FICTION OF 'TUTELLE'

The relationship between the notarial profession and the state is multifaceted. Its legal function makes it a ward of the Ministry of Justice, which has the role of *tutelle* over the profession. The Service des Professions in the Direction des Affaires Civiles of the Ministry of Justice oversees the notarial as well as the other legal professions. Since the Ministry of Justice exercises the *tutelle* function, it might be thought to have a clientelistic relationship with the *notaires*. It does, though after 1981 the Ministry demonstrated considerable ambivalence with respect to its *tutelle* function, sometimes considering its duty to be to transcend the mere defence of a group under its jurisdiction, at other times considering its duty to be to come to the defence of the very group it sought to reform.

It should be noted that this ambivalence came about in the wake of the Left's victory in 1981. As we saw earlier, prior to 1981 harmony reigned in the *notaire*–Ministry of Justice relationship. The profession had no need to seek other allies – though it did have them – because it had a comfortable clientelistic relationship with the Ministry. No Minister of Justice prior to 1981 would have attempted even a mild reform without the profession's full accord. The Ministry was there to serve and defend the profession. The profession knew this to be the case, and the Ministry accepted this role.

The nature of a *tutelle* defines to a large extent the policy options available to a Ministry with respect to its wards. A distinction needs to be made between a regulatory *tutelle* and a policy *tutelle*. In the regulatory case, the group in question is dependent on the Ministry for the conditions that regulate its functioning. It is the Ministry that insures that the public service in question is well provided for. No legal text that might alter the conditions under which the group in question functions can pass without the *tutelle* Ministry's accord. In the policy case, the *tutelle* does not involve direct regulation of, or involvement in, a specific group. Groups may have an anchor in a public agency (labour in the Labour Ministry, industry in the Industry Ministry), whose interest in a given sector extends to questions of policy; but there is no direct regulation involved, since most policy questions are distributed over, or involve, a wide segment of the state apparatus. Hence, the policy *tutelle* of a public agency is necessarily diluted by its limited capacity for intervention and by the lack of concentration of jurisdictions and policy-making authority.

It should not be thought that the regulatory *tutelle* controls all policy options concerning its wards and is able therefore to deliver on all the requests that are made by the group in question. All financial matters – and in the case of the *notaires* this involves the central question of the fixed fee scale – must be approved by the Ministry of Finance. Moreover, because the *notaires* are also tax collectors, since the state imposes a tax on all transactions, the treasury's involvement in this profession is of considerable importance. The Ministry of Finance has an interest in seeing that the notarial profession operates efficiently so that it can perform the critical task of tax collection on the state's behalf.

However, the regulatory *tutelle* does mean that the Ministry exercising the *tutelle* becomes the chief representative of the group in the state apparatus. What is not directly under its control, it tries to influence on the group's behalf. Prior to 1981, the Ministry of Justice did a fine job of representing the notarial profession and of procuring fee increases and other advantages.

Why does an agency charged with a regulatory *tutelle* take it upon itself to defend and represent an interest group? The answer is fairly clear: the public agency is charged with a mission, and to accomplish what the law obliges it to do it must gain the loyalty of the group that carries out this mission. It therefore begins to perform services for the group, which in turn leads the group to request further services. Gradually a symbiotic relationship of the kind described by Philip Selznick in *TVA and the Grassroots* develops.[24] The original mission of the public agency gets blurred; or, rather, it becomes entangled with the specific aims of the group it is supposed to regulate. When this occurs, the group itself comes to believe that the central mission of the public agency is not to look after the general interest but to defend the specific interests of the group. This is what leads to a situation in which the President of the Conseil Supérieur de Notariat is able to remind the Minister of Justice: 'Vous assurez notre tutelle, donc notre defense.'

The symbiotic relationship between a public agency and a group does not follow iron-clad principles. It is susceptible to change, especially when ideological and political winds drastically shift. This is precisely what occurred in the case of the Ministry of Justice–*Notaires* relationship. Looking back at the full cycle of events, we see the relationship going through several stages: an assertive Ministry produces a document warning the profession that things will be done differently and that serious reforms must be envisaged; this is followed by an aggressive counterattack by the profession and a mobilization of all its forces within the state apparatus; the Ministry then ends up abandoning the reforms it had originally put forward and defending the profession against other segments of the state apparatus that had taken at their face value the Ministry's original proposals; finally, an agreement is reached whereby the profession is asked to undertake a study based on a simulation model and to submit the results, together with a set of proposals (a *contrat de programme*), to the Ministry.

On coming to power the Left sought to bring about reforms in different sectors, including the administration of justice. The Minister of Justice, Robert Badinter, a lawyer with a liberal background, sought among other things to abolish the death penalty. It was not surprising that his Ministry should also

---

[24] Philip Selznick, *TVA and the Grassroots* (New York: Harper Torch Books, 1966).

270   SULEIMAN

have wanted to reform the *offices ministériels*. The Minister informed them of his intentions and asked them to provide the ministry with a wide array of information about their professions. The *notaires* were the first to respond with the necessary documentation. There began a series of meetings and exchanges between the profession and the Ministry. The profession continued to provide the Ministry with documentation, arguing that their *tarif* was not excessive or inflationary, that access to the profession had been opened up, that they were performing a public service but also ran commercial enterprises that required capital investment, that the profession's economic situation had substantially deteriorated in recent years. The constant discussions and meetings between the profession and Ministry were not regarded as *concertation*. The president of the Conseil Supérieur du Notariat, Henri Chardon, expressed the view that genuine *concertation* means that the public authorities adopt the positions recommended by the profession; otherwise the profession is being merely confronted with a *diktat*. 'Of course,' the president said to the officials of the Ministry of Justice, 'we advanced arguments. And, of course, no account was taken of them. It was clear that it was a political decision. But then we should be honestly told. If it was a political decision, we would have yielded to it. Why speak of *concertation*?'[25]

More specifically, did the profession regard as *concertation* the adoption of its own proposals, or the abandonment by the Ministry of Justice of all of its? More than a year before Badinter announced, at the Congress of Notaires in 1984, that future proposals by the Ministry would not be made before the profession had had a chance to provide the Ministry with the results of its own detailed survey, the same suggestion had been made to the Ministry by Chardon. At a meeting on 2 February 1983, Chardon stated that it would be irresponsible to accept a reform of the *tarif* without having first undertaken a 'scientific' study, and he volunteered to study the problem with 'experts' and by means of 'simulations'.[26] Apparently, the Minister in 1984 simply made his own what the profession had earlier proposed. This was what *conceration* amounted to.

It becomes evident that *tutelle* is a juridical notion and by no means conveys the reality of the relationship between a public agency and a group. This is the case even where a regulatory *tutelle* is concerned, because the control that the public agency exercises over the group is often rudimentary and because its protective role comes to assume greater importance. The Ministry of Justice's control over the profession does not extend beyond the confirmation of a *notaire* to the office he has purchased. For the rest, the profession is left to police itself. The profession is of the view that this is an ideal distribution of roles and responsibilities. As Maître Cordier, Chardon's successor as president of the Conseil Supérieur, put it:

Finally, the constant concern of the Conseil Supérieur du Notariat is improvement of control, not only in the financial domain, but also in its other aspects (deontology,

[25] Entretien du 5 janvier 1983 à la Chancellerie (CSN), p. 5.
[26] Intervention du Président Chardon, Entretien du 2 fevrier 1983 à la Chancellerie (CSN), pp. 5–6.

notarial technique): and on this last point, it is essential that the control be put into effect, under the supervision of the state prosecutors, by the profession itself, which appears technically the best placed to judge the quality of the service rendered.[27]

THE REALITY OF PROTECTION

Thus, the *tutelle* function of the Ministry of Justice is insignificant when compared to the protective function it fulfils. In the end, the Ministry in the 1980s neither sought greater controls over the profession nor made serious attempts to push through the reforms it had originally claimed were essential. Quite the contrary, it began to undermine its own proposals, and it became more attentive to the profession's claims once it observed that its ward was under attack from the outside.

Prior to 1981, when the Ministry fully accepted that its protective role *was* its *tutelle* function, it did not countenance reforms proposed by other public authorities. The reasons it gave for its opposition were reasonable, just as the reasons it gave after 1981 for wanting the reforms that it had earlier objected to were reasonable. When the Ministry of Finance made a number of proposals concerning the fee structure of the notarial profession in late 1970s, the Ministry rejected them out of hand. The proposals were not very different from what was proposed after 1981:

- to do away with the fee on transactions having to do with corporations;
- to put a ceiling on fees for transactions concerning individuals;
- to make optional the recourse to a *notaire* in certain cases;
- to authorize the *notaire* to grant reductions in accordance with the fee scale, which would no longer be fixed, but would have a maximum level;
- to free up those fees corresponding to transactions for which the recourse to the *notaire* is not obligatory.[28]

The Ministry of Justice did eventually ease its position, recognizing that corporations were severely penalized by the present fee structure; but it was loathe to tamper with the profession's monopoly and with the *tarif*. It was also totally opposed 'to the proposition to give the scale the character of a maximum fee scale rather than one with a compulsory fee.'[29] The reasons given by the Ministry were those that the profession itself had always given:

- equality in public service;
- the risk of threatening the financial equilibrium of the profession;
- the existence of the possibility of adjustment, under the control of the profession, in case of clear irregularities.[30]

Despite the line taken by the Ministry of Justice, the Ministry of Finance believed that Justice had in fact moved from its earlier position. It was therefore

---

[27] Michel Cordier, 'Le Controle de la profession,' Entretien du 20 Janvier 1983 à la Chancellerie (CSN), p. 3.

[28] 'Réforme de la tarification des notaires', Ministry of Finance, 1979, p. 1.

[29] 'Réforme de la tarification des notaires', p. 3.

[30] 'Reforme de la tarification des notaires', p. 3.

272   SULEIMAN

hopeful that further discussions would lead to further compromises. Clearly, it would take some doing to get the Ministry of Justice to compromise the *notaires*' monopoly and get it to a point where it would accept competition over fees within the profession. The matter was left in abeyance until the elections of mid-1981. The Ministry of Justice then reversed its earlier positions and now pushed for the very reforms that under the previous government it had refused to consider.

Why did the reform of the notarial profession not turn out to be a simple issue? The answer lies in the fact that, once the Ministry of Justice realized that a serious reform was a probability, given the intentions of the government, the resurrection of the Ministry of Finance's pre-1981 projects and its own projects and intentions, it became aware that it was about to abandon, to a large extent, its traditional role of protecting the profession. Rather than assert its *tutelle* functions, it decided to reassert its protective functions. In interministerial meetings, the Ministry of Justice became the defender of the profession against the projects of others.

The Ministry of Finance was basically concerned with one reform: the *tarif*. It had no interest in the reforms concerning the *numerus clausus* and the *droit de présentation*. The *tarif* was central to its preoccupation with eliminating the structural causes of inflation. Any reform that helped bring about competitive pricing would receive its support. When the Ministry broached the *tarif* question with the Ministry of Justice, even after 1981, it received only a lukewarm response. One official from the Finance Ministry explained that 'when we ask the Ministry of Justice to look into the question of the *tarif*, they usually suggest that we examine the profession as a whole – its functions, role, utility, etc. All this so that we discuss things other than the *tarif*.' Now, to many people in the administration and in the government, the only reform that meant anything was the reform of the *tarif*. According to the same Ministry of Finance official, 'After we suggested a serious reform [i.e., the *tarif*], the Ministry of Justice suddenly tells us that, after all, the *notaires* are useful! The truth of the matter is that the Ministry of Justice doesn't really want to do anything. They make up a lot of noise, but they don't want reforms.'

The Ministry of Justice was not much interested in reforming the *tarif*. According to a Ministry official: 'Mr Badinter can't get excited by this sort of problem,' adding, 'all the more so since this has become a burning issue. This is why he prefers to throw it in the lap of the Ministry of Finance.' But the issue was not returned to the Ministry of Finance to do with it as it pleased. On the contrary, the Finance Ministry could not obtain the support of the Ministry of Justice for a reform of the *tarif*. The Justice Ministry argued that the *notaires* were in dire straits because of the downturn in the economy and that care should be taken not to impose such a serious reform at a time when they were so vulnerable. The *notaires* were vulnerable and now once again useful for the Ministry of Justice. Despite all the proposals put forward by the Ministry of Justice and the Ministry of Finance, an official in the latter observed in April 1984 that, because of the Ministry of Justice's position, 'we are exactly at the same point that we were at five years ago.' This was essentially confirmed a month later when the Minister of Justice oficially confirmed that his Ministry was no longer concerned with initiating reforms on its own – that is, reforms that did not have the profession's prior accord.

While the shifting positions of the Justice Ministry were somewhat baffling to officials elsewhere in the state apparatus, they were not always seen in the same light by others. The *notaires* did not always see their *tutelle* ministry as having a balanced position. They saw it – and sometimes chose to see it – as uniformly hostile. 'They got scared when they saw who was around Badinter,' said one Ministry of Finance official.

A look at the record of some of the interministerial meetings shows quite clearly that the Ministry of Justice generally came to the profession's defence. While to the profession it may have indicated that it was spearheading a reform movement, to others in the state apparatus it was providing a model example of a bureaucratic agency defending its client. While officials like Pierre Lyon-Caen may have appeared to the profession as being bent on its destruction, neither he nor any other official in the Justice Ministry gave this impression when meeting with officials from other departments.

In fact, one official from the Caisse des Dépôts et Consignations, the public agency that acts as the profession's banker, saw things very differently. He believed that the *notaires*' fright was not wholly unjustified but that the Ministry of Justice should not be considered as the cause for this. 'The Ministry isn't really very hostile to the *notaires* despite the impression the *notaires* have.' He explained that the Ministry did not have much weight in the policy-making process – certainly not when acting alone – and that it was not a true believer in a profound reform because 'in comparison with other professions – the *huissiers, syndics, commissaires priseurs* – it doesn't see the *notaires* as being so bad'.

The so-called *tutelle* relationship creates over time a particular form of co-operation. One official put it this way:

There is a complicity between the Ministry of Justice and the *notaires*. The *notaires* give the Ministry a lot of information which it needs to be able to do its job. Also, the *notaires* are part of the *services* of the Ministry of Justice. The Ministry needs them, and it needs them to be present everywhere; otherwise people will start howling and it's the Ministry that will bear the brunt of the public's outcry.

The Ministry was, in effect, tied down by its *tutelle* mission for it could not attack a group that carried out functions for which it bore responsibility. All this means that any structural reform that undermines, or appears to undermine, the *notaires* not only cannot come from the Ministry of Justice but will in fact be opposed by this ministry. One official from the Caisse des Dépôts explained that the Ministry of Justice's hostility to the *notaires* was more apparent than real. 'If you look,' he said, 'at the three points that are being discussed now as possible reforms, two – the *droit de présentation* and the *notaire's* freedom to establish a practice in a locality of his choosing – were initiated by the Ministry; the third – the *tarif* – came from the Ministry of Finance, *et ça c'est plus sérieux* because it's the reform that really counts.'

274   SULEIMAN

'TUTELLE' AND CLIENTELISM

We have seen the extent to which *tutelle* is a juridical notion that is belied by the
reality of its functioning. This reality is more akin to practices that we tend to
associate with different political systems. Indeed neither French jurisprudence
nor observers of the French political system have ever seen a connection
between the concepts of *tutelle* and clientelism, which are *a priori* contradictory.
Yet centralization clearly facilitates the clientelistic relationship, allowing the
client to concentrate his efforts and energies within a circumscribed set of institutions that set the agenda and determine the outcomes of public policies.

Usually the group that seeks to influence public policy in its favour does not
have to reach further than its *tutelle* agency. But, as sometimes happens, political
shifts may threaten to upset the relationship between agency and client and
another public agency, and the *tutelle* agency will then seek to reassert its *tutelle*
and its ties to the group. Ultimately, and herein lies a key paradox, the *tutelle*
agency cannot afford a divorce from its client. And so it attempts to return to its
client's good graces.

This is a curious way to view a policy process that has so often been described
as centralized, powerful and cohesive. Nevertheless, in the rare instances where a
tutelle has been examined, it has been found to bear no relationship to its juridical sense.[31] For example, to carry out his function effectively, the prefect was
compelled to establish a complicity with mayors, which meant that he could
never be merely the representative of the central authorities in the departments.
He could therefore not dictate orders to the mayors, on whom it turned out he
was heavily dependent.

Similarly, the Ministry of Justice can exercise only a minimum authority over
the notarial profession; and, as we have seen, it cannot control the profession,
which has largely been successful in remaining self-regulatory. The profession
screens its own candidates, sets its own organizational procedures, polices itself,
determines its own budgetary allocations and enjoys an independence from its
tutelle agency that is perhaps greater than many a private group. The profession
even determines for the Caisse des Dépôts whether a *notaire* should receive a
loan from the Caisse, since even the Caisse does not wish to intrude on the profession's prerogatives.

The *tutelle* agency maintains this relationship, devoid of genuine powers over
its ward, because it needs the ward to carry out a mission on its behalf and also
because it does not want to lose either its formal role *vis-à-vis* the group or an
important area of jurisdiction. For its part, the group does not want the relationship broken because it is a relationship that brings only advantages. As a private
group without a 'mother agency' the *notaires* might find themselves in the wilderness. Instead they now enjoy all the advantages of a private group – notably
independence and self-regulation – and also all the advantages of being able to
call on the state to come to their aid. The president of the profession can tell the
state with utter conviction that it has to intervene on the profession's behalf.

[31] Jean-Pierre Worms, 'Le Préfet et ses notables', *Sociologie du travail*, VIII (1966), 249–75.

For the *notaires* who are responsible for a public service, and whose continuity has the value of a principle, things are simple. If the firm cannot maintain the normal and regular operation of the service, it is up to the State to intervene and give it the means to carry out its mission.[32]

The profession can even tell the state that its job is not to limit its monopoly but 'on the contrary to extend it'[33] – something that a private group would have a very difficult time doing and getting accepted. Hence, a client group, particularly if it can claim to be linked to public service, can derive from a *tutelle* relationship advantages that caricature a centralized state's alleged power. It can exploit its relationship with the state by creating yet another client–state relationship. It can thus place itself in the enviable situation of being a client courted by one, or indeed several, state agencies. When this occurs, it may result in a marriage of convenience, which is likely to produce a clientelistic relationship that is difficult to envisage in a centralized state. But such relationships exist and they relegate the general interest to secondary importance. The Ministry of Justice in the end was more concerned to calm and satisfy the profession than it was to push ahead with reforms that were undoubtedly in the general interest. It did not exercise the power of its *tutelle* because it had seen to it over the years that its *tutelle* could exist only if it were devoid of power. This is why the profession could understand *concertation* with the government to mean only that the public authorities accepted by and large what was good for the profession.

If the Ministry of Justice's *tutelle* is fictional in the sense that it is devoid of authoritative power, the chances for implementing a genuine reform quickly vanish. All the more is this the case when the profession discovers a powerful ally in the state apparatus willing to give full support to the profession and at the same time to the status quo.

CONCLUSION: POLICY-MAKING UNDER CENTRALIZATION

A state-centred approach to the study of the policy process is useful precisely because it can illuminate the extent to which the state has, and does not have, the means to impose its will, once that will is clearly defined. The most accurate conclusion that one is likely to reach is that state power, or autonomy, varies across sectors and that there is no predetermined constellation of factors that renders a state either a prisoner of civil society or wholly independent of it. In effect, an examination of state power in different societies would reveal the existence of sectors where state power is evident in the state's ability to impose its will; sectors where the state is unable to impose its will or where it concedes its authority; and, finally, sectors where the state's power is shifting and indeterminate. Care must therefore be taken not to substitute a formalist approach for the

[32] Henri Chardon, 'Allocution au Congrès des Notaires de France', Versailles, 28 May 1984, p. 23.
[33] Chardon, 'Allocution au Congrès des Notaires de France', p. 15.

necessary empirical investigations, the lack of which has led to conclusions
about the degree of power of different states that are based on institutional
analyses and deviate considerably from the reality of power. One cannot help
but agree with the statement that 'If the state were a less complex entity, the task
of statist-oriented scholars would be easier.'[34] What are implications of this with
regard to the permeability of a centralized state?

A centralized state, as we have seen, evidently failed to carry through a proposed reform that ran counter to the interest of an ostensibly private group.
What are the implications of this as far as policy-making in a centralized state is
concerned? In the first place, it has to be remembered that a state is dependent
on structures that have a past. Any attempt by the political authorities that control the state apparatus to do away with long-established patterns of interaction
between private groups and the state is akin to a major transformation in the
way the state conducts its relations with the society.

When the Socialists came to power in 1981 it was understood that after the
initial sweep of reforms there would be a 'pause'. Having mobilized public
opinion and the bureaucracy to support the major reforms – nationalization of
industry and banks, and decentralization – there would follow the process of
reassuring the middle classes that the basic social and economic institutions
could continue to function without threat from the government. Hence, the
government would cause limited ruptures in the normal way that the state conducted its relationship with the society.

Secondly, a state may be administratively centralized without being administratively coherent. A government does not dispose of a readily available and
malleable administrative machine. To dispose of an integrated policy-making
machine is a *task*, a task of any government in a centralized as well as a decentralized system. Mastering the bureaucratic apparatus is no less of a task in a
centralized administrative system than in a decentralized one. To overcome the
resistance of individual bureaucracies, to mobilize different agencies in the service of a single objective and, finally, to insure the implementation of a political
reform are the typical ingredients of a policy process. Once this is understood as
a *process*, it becomes clear that it is not a given and cannot be assumed to exist
simply because the charts of the administrative structure indicate that the
administration is centralized.

The policy process that we have examined through our case study suggests
that, when the structure is centralized, the processes of co-ordination, mobilization and implementation may be much harder to achieve, given that a central
agency may have such a large stake in the status quo ante. In such an instance, it
may be much harder to break the clientelistic relationship between the private
group and the administrative agency. In the case of President Reagan's attempts
to achieve policy co-ordination in the federal bureaucracy, this was done essentially by appointing to high positions officials committed to Reagan's pro-

---

[34] Howard Lentner, 'The Concept of the State: A Response to Stephen Krasner', *Comparative
Politics*, xvi (1984), 367–77, p. 373.

grammes and also by leaving top positions vacant for long periods.[35] Since in any case bureaucratic clients had been distributing their efforts among legislative committees and different levels of the governmental (federal and state) bureaucracies, it was not as difficult as might have been expected to break ties between the bureaucracy and regulatory agencies. This is not the case in France where a client may be wholly dependent on one or two central agencies. Hence, the impulse for collusion is much greater. The potential for control of the administrative agencies and for their mobilization in the service of a common policy is apparently greater under a centralized system. In reality, it may be more elusive.

Thirdly, a party's ideology may encourage the kind of clientelism that it needs to break in order to introduce its new policies. This is especially the case with social democratic parties who need to show their commitment to democratic norms and so encourage *concertation*. The Ministry of Justice entered into lengthy and innumerable meetings with the *notaires* and so expected to gain greater legitimacy as a result of attempting to arrive at an agreement over the new policies to follow. Such governments try to avoid giving the impression that they are proceeding in undemocratic ways. In acting as the guardian of democratic institutions, in advocating a more decentralized and democratic political system and in encouraging greater participation, such governments may actually lend legitimation to the *corporatistes* groups that they see as impediments to social progress. This is an important consequence of the rhetoric, and the process, of decentralization.

Emphasis needs to be placed on the state's role in encouraging the development of a societal group, which leads to a clientelistic relationship, which in the end leads to severe constraints on the power of the state to effect changes in the group's position in the society. State capacities are therefore greater when the state seeks to strengthen societal groups than when it seeks to reform them after it has endowed them with strong organizational capacities and granted them privileges.

The clientelistic relationship that exists between private groups and bureaucratic agencies, and the effect this may have on subverting an agency's mandate[36] or in subverting democratic norms,[37] have long been recognized. And yet a centralized state was seen as a mechanism for co-ordinating policies and for preventing private groups from unduly influencing public policies in their favour. That the centralized state may be more inefficient than a decentralized state, or that it may not allow for the same degree of citizen participation, may or may not be the case. But its central characteristics have generally been thought to be its capacity for setting policies, co-ordination in the policy process

[35] See Richard P. Nathan, 'The Reagan Presidency in Domestic Affairs', in Fred I. Greenstein, ed., *The Reagan Presidency: An Early Assessment* (Baltimore, Md.: The Johns Hopkins University Press, 1983), pp. 48–81.

[36] Selznick, *TVA and the Grassroots*.

[37] Grant McConnell, *Private Power and American Democracy* (New York: Alfred A. Knopf, 1966).

and efficient implementation of policies. But that is an administrative view of the world, one that leaves out the *political* process.

A number of recent studies have moved, some more explicitly than others, away from this administrative and static view of the policy process in a central-ized state. Such studies have recognized that clientelism is part and parcel of the policy process and, as a consequence, hardly depends on the precise structure of the state.[38] Indeed, once the policy process is recognized to be a derivative of the political system, it becomes understandable why an array of obstacles to policy co-ordination are possible in a centralized state. Studies on local politics,[39] on transportation policy,[40] on the petroleum industry,[41] on agriculture[42] and on the media,[43] as well as on other sectors, have recognized the extent to which the state's clients shape public policies. To be sure, the groups in question shape policies to different degrees, so that the state's autonomy depends on a number of variables: contextual conditions, its set of priorities, its capacity for mobilizing political support and, perhaps most important, the nature of the policy issue in question, whether it is an issue involving redistribution or whether it is a more all-encompassing issue affecting several groups, all indirectly.

Can we, then, speak of state 'interests' or 'preferences', as opposed to simply *policies* that governments adopt? A state-centred approach requires that states and state preferences be divorced from ties to an ephemeral leadership and be considered in Rousseauistic terms, that is to say, as the embodiment of an over-arching will that is not merely a representation of the sum total of interests in the society. How, then, to distinguish between a government policy and a state policy?[44] It is possible to speak of a state independently of its government, because it has a stability of rules, laws, structures and procedures. But the inter-

[38] See Jean G. Padioleau, *L'Etat au concret* (Paris: Presses Universitaires de France, 1982) and *Quand la France s'enferre* (Paris: Presses Universitaires de France, 1981); Douglas Ashford, *Policy and Politics in France: Living with Uncertainty* (Philadelphia: Temple University Press, 1982).

[39] See Worms, 'Le Préfet et ses notables'; Jacques Rondin, *Le Sacré des notables* (Paris: Fayard, 1985).

[40] See Elliot J. Feldman, *Concorde and Dissent: Explaining High Technology Project Failures in Britain and France* (New York: Cambridge University Press, 1985).

[41] Harvey B. Feigenbaum, *The Politics of Public Enterprise: Oil and the French State* (Princeton, NJ: Princeton University Press, 1985).

[42] See John T. S. Keeler, 'Agricultural Reform in Mitterrand's France', in John Ambler, ed., *The French Socialist Experiment* (Philadelphia: Institute for the Study of Human Issues, 1985), pp. 60–92.

[43] Jean-Noel Jeanneney, *Echec à Panurge: L'audiovisuel public au service de la différence* (Paris: Editions du Seuil, 1986). See also, Valerie Rubsamen, 'The Media and the State in France', unpub-lished doctoral dissertation, Princeton University, 1987.

[44] That even as committed a statist as Theda Skocpol can slip into using the terms 'government' and 'state' in an interchangeable way shows how difficult is both the analytical and practical distinc-tion between them. 'Government itself was not taken very seriously as an independent actor, and in comparative research, variations in governmental organizations were deemed less significant than the general "functions" shared by the political systems of all societies.' See Theda Skocpol, 'Bringing the State Back In: Strategies of Analysis in Current Research,' in Peter Evans, Dietrich Ruesche-meyer, and Theda Skocpol, eds, *Bringing the State Back In* (New York: Cambridge University Press, 1985), p. 4.

action of the state with civil society is what in the end structures the state's 'interests' or 'preferences'. This is why a concentration on the state does not obviate the need to explore the class or group basis of state actions.

In the case of the French state, once we begin to move beyond the formal aspects of state structures and begin to examine the political and policy process, it becomes evident that definitions of state interests are most often derivate of a dialectical process with private groups. There can be no such thing as a study of the state – its autonomy, its capacities, its interests – without a deeper understanding of the relationship between the governmental and administrative structures on the one hand and between these structures and civil groups on the other. Only the cumulativeness of such empirical studies will allow us to speak with any degree of assurance about 'the state'. Whether or not states can be said to be propelled by a 'logic',[45] that logic can only be uncovered by an analysis of the various forms of interaction between the state and civil groups.

If we examine the process in the formation of states and the gradual development of societal powers, what is striking is the increasing affirmation of the latter. Although this development may be regarded as the natural consequence of the democratic process, it is above all a process encouraged by the state. The democratic process requires the state to have interlocutors and intermediaries. This is why the state encouraged the formation of organized private groups. It needed them both to fulfil important governmental functions and to act as its 'legitimate' interlocutors.[46] The logical consequence of this process was the development of corporatist modes of interaction. But whether the process by which the state strengthened private groups led to corporatism or not, it did create a situation whereby the strengthening of societal groups eventually compromised the state's own power.

The failure of the post-1981 French government to reform the *offices ministériels* is a consequence of the state's past policies to strengthen these groups. It was in large part through the state's efforts that the notarial profession acquired its modern organizational strength, modernized its modes of operation and gained its adaptive capacities. Once the profession had succeeded in effecting its own transformation, the *rapport de force* between it and the state changed. Before this change got under way, the state was in a position to crush the profession, and contemplated doing so. Instead, it chose to work towards its renewal. So well did the state succeed that it is no longer in a position to dictate to the *notaires*. Hence, the relationship between the notarial profession and state typifies the cyclical historical process through which a state's strength ultimately leads to symbiosis with and then to dependence upon private groups.

[45] See Pierre Birnbaum, *La Logique de l'Etat* (Paris: Fayard, 1982).

[46] The state bureaucracy has always preferred to interact with more powerful private groups, considering them more representative, and hence, more legitimate. See Ezra N. Suleiman, *Politics, Power and Bureaucracy in France* (Princeton, NJ: Princeton University Press, 1974), pp. 337–45.

[22]

SOCIAL PROTEST AND POLICY REFORM
May 1968 and the *Loi d'Orientation* in France

SIDNEY TARROW
Cornell University

The politics of reform has most often been viewed as incremental process—which indeed it is, under most circumstances. The model for this mode of analysis is found in Aaron Wildavsky's (1974) work on the budgetary process. The best predictor of the size of a public budget in year *n*, Wildavsky observes, is the size of its predecessor in year $n - 1$. Given the number of constraints and inhibitions that prevent policy innovation under most circumstances, writes John Keeler (1993 [this issue]) "those rare governments that have surmounted such obstacles . . . have thus commonly

AUTHOR'S NOTE: *This article is dedicated to the memory of Annick Percheron, who both experienced the events described here and immeasurably facilitated the author's research. This is a much revised version of an earlier report on social protest and reform in Western democracies, funded by a National Endowment for the Humanities Interpretive Research Grant. I am grateful to Denis Barbet, Beldon Fields, David Goldey, Peter Hall, John Keeler, René Mouriaux, René Rémond, and Ezra Suleiman for their help and advice on the earlier report, as well as to the people cited herein who agreed to be interviewed. I would also like to thank Mark D. Bayer, Anita Lee, and Sarah Soule for their invaluable assistance in preparing the tables and graphs. Of course, only I am responsible for the accuracy of any claims made.*

COMPARATIVE POLITICAL STUDIES, Vol. 25 No. 4, January 1993 579-607
© 1993 Sage Publications, Inc.

been discussed simply as interesting exceptions to the patterns of what might be termed ordinary policy-making" (p. 434).

But from time to time, major waves of policy innovation emerge above the gentle plain of ordinary politics. For understanding these breakthroughs, incremental models of policy-making are not nearly as helpful as models based on changes in political opportunity structure. Major electoral realignments; political crises, the ends of wars or military threats, leadership succession; and the emergence of new social coalitions. Such nonincremental changes frequently trigger periods of reform. What Valerie Bunce (1981) writes of succession can be extended to a number of different types of political change: "Major changes," she writes, "if they occurred at all, tended to be introduced in conjunction with the rise of new chief executives" (p. 225). But what of the effect on policy innovation of the threats to routine politics coming from challengers to the polity? Although Bunce's (1981) *Do New Leaders Make a Difference?* examines the impact of leadership succession, Rose (1980) has analyzed the impact of party differences on policy, and Keeler (1993) analyzes the importance of political crisis and electoral landslides, we still know little about the impact of social protest on policy change. As Marx and Wood (1975) write:

> Given the variety of places that one can look, the extreme difficulty in most cases in determining causal relations, and the long time periods that may be involved, most statements about the consequences of social movements are primarily descriptive or taxonomic. The systematic study of social movement consequences is much less developed than that of the prior conditions that give rise to movements. (p. 403)

Most scholars of movements have assumed with Turner and Killian (1972) that one of the necessary aspects of a social movement is "a program for the reform of society" (p. 256). But how often do movements bring about anything as global as "the reform of society"? Even in less grandiose terms, we have very little idea of the impact of movements on reform for few scholars have looked systematically at the effects of movements on reform.[1]

One of the reasons for this gap is that reform has often been conceived of as a top-down extension of citizenship (Marshall, 1964), either through incorporation (Rokkan et al., 1970) or by elite policy diffusion (Heclo, 1974). A second reason is that social movements often coincide with political changes of a more conventional type, making it difficult to sort out their degree of responsibility for a particular policy change (Burstein & Freudenberg, 1978). A third is that scholars most often focus on movement *emergence*, giving less attention to the slower, less dramatic processes of policy elaboration, negotiation, and implementation. Rare is the movement that is sufficiently focussed and powerful to stimulate a direct and visible policy response—except where that response is repression.[2]

MAY 1968: A WINDOW FOR REFORM

But we do have a near-laboratory case for studying the political impact of a major wave of protest on policy innovation—May 1968 in France. As two of that period's most acute historians observe:

> despite the retreat of the movement and its rejection in the ballot box, the events were the carriers of potentialities that, by one means or another, durably mortgaged the French political scene in a way that had to be immediately faced. (Capdeveille & Mouriaux, 1988; p. 219 [my translation])

This is a puzzle; for how could the May crisis "durably mortgage the French political scene" when it produced few coherent policy proposals, left a disorganized and almost-collapsed movement in its wake, and led to an enlarged conservative majority and a dispirited and divided opposition? The answer we give to this question depends on how we think social movements influence reform—either directly, through the power of the people, or indirectly, through changes in the political opportunity structure that they trigger. If we proceed from a pure "protest leads to reform" model, we will have difficulty explaining why *any* reform effort should have followed the May movement, for that movement was soundly defeated. But if we understand policy innovation to be mediated by changes in the political opportunity structure—for elites as well as for the mass public—it is less surprising that a wave of protest was followed by a major reform.

In the months following the June 1968 national elections, in which the Gaullist party achieved a major electoral triumph, the government—not without internal dissent—boiled down the jumble of demands for educational change that had erupted during May into a major law for educational reform—the *loi d'orientation* of Minister Edgar Faure. The movement of May arose suddenly and unexpectedly and collapsed just as quickly, but the policy response was rapid and directly addressed the universities, where the events had begun.

The law that resulted was intended to restructure the university system around three broad goals: autonomy, pluridisciplinarity, and participation (Chalendar, 1970, parts 2, 3; Fomerand, 1974, chap. 5). It replaced the old faculties with departments (UER), it broke up the massive University of Paris into 12 different "campuses," and it provided the machinery for all the French universities to elect governing councils and create their own internal statutes.[3] It would be difficult to imagine so major a change being introduced into the sclerotic structure of French education without the impulse of a major political earthquake.

What is the implication of this story for the theory of policy innovation? In what follows, I will show that, as Keeler suggests in his contribution to this volume, an exceptional electoral mandate and a threatening political crisis open a window for policy innovation. But the brevity of the French crisis and the disorganization of the movement of May left the initiative for reform to elites, leaving it to become ensnared in the mechanisms of parliamentary politics. As the political struggle receded from the streets to the halls of Parliament and the cabinets of ministers, the game of ordinary politics decided its future. As I shall argue in the conclusions, this has implications for reform that go beyond the case at hand.

POLITICAL OPPORTUNITIES AND REFORM CYCLES

Before reviewing these events and my interpretation of them, it will be important to make clear what I mean by the term "the structure of political opportunity" and how it can be used to link the *enragés* of May—few of whom were at all interested in reform—to the reformers of October. The social movement literature on political opportunities has usually employed the concept to understand when movements emerge and the strategies they choose when they do so.[4] It has less often been extended to understanding the political opportunities opened up by a wave of protest for a movement's allies and opponents and for political elites.

Scholars of movement emergence and strategy have mainly emphasized four elements of political opportunity structure: electoral realignments (Piven & Cloward, 1977), the opening of institutional access (Eisinger, 1973), the presence of influential allies (Gamson, 1991; Jenkins & Perrow, 1977), and divisions within the political elite (Tarrow, 1989a, chap. 2) and how these provide incentives for movement formation and collective action.[5] A fifth element—the availability and extension of new frames of meaning— has received far less attention but can also be critical in triggering of a new movement (Snow & Benford, 1988, 1992).

But new movements themselves sometimes produce changes in political opportunity: for participants in the original movement who can see what succeeds and what fails; for allies and opponents who adopt their models of collective action and use their collective action frames for new purposes; and for members of the political elite who use the movement to gain political advantage. Major waves of movement create opportunities for others by demonstrating new or innovative forms of collective action, placing new frames of interpretation on the agenda, and making clear either the threat of an opponent or the promise of a new constituency.

For example, the protest cycle initiated by the American civil rights movement demonstrated how nonviolent resistance tactics, employed in the spotlight of national television, could gain majority support for a minority movement. Second, it provided a dramatic and fungible "rights frame" that other minority groups were quick to take up—what Snow and Benford (1988) call a "master frame." Third, it demonstrated the existence of a large African-American constituency for reform, a signal that the Kennedy and Johnson administrations were quick to exploit (Piven & Cloward, 1977, chap. 4).

But the American movements of the 1960s also show how a protest cycle's endogenous development helps to produce its demise. As the nonviolent movement in the South gave way to more aggressive collective action in the North and to a more violent rhetoric from younger militants, a split was induced between moderate older organizations and their newer competitors and—in part because of the rhetoric of exclusiveness of the latter—between the movement as a whole and its White "conscience constituents." Militant tactics and violent rhetoric, although in a distinct minority in the movement, helped to turn public opinion against it and to justify a shift from the facilitative policies of the reformist Johnson administration to the punitive ones of the Nixon years (Button, 1978).

This parabolic model of a protest-reform cycle can also be applied to France after May. Spurred by fear of renewed agitations in the streets and encouraged by a constituency for reform, the French reformers of July 1968 quickly drew up a scheme for the reform of higher education. But as in the United States—although far more rapidly—the cycle had an internal dynamic from protest to reform to consolidation and retreat. As the threat of contestation evaporated, the reformists were forced to scale down their ambitions to meet the objections of their conservative opponents (Fomerand, 1974, chap. 8). And by the spring of 1969, with the defeat of de Gaulle's referendum and his sudden retirement, the reform lost much of its sting, resulting in a greater gain for the conservative professorate than for the dissatisfied students. This is a story that French specialists know well; what can we learn from it about the politics of policy breakthrough?

THE OPPORTUNITY FOR REFORM

Three major factors facilitated the reformers' task in the summer and fall of 1968: first, an informed debate about higher education that predated May by several years; second, the very suddenness and brevity of the May-June crisis; and, third, the strength of the Gaullist electoral mandate. Taken together, these factors provided Education Minister Faure with fertile polit-ical ground and gave the reform an unusually smooth beginning.

THE REFORMIST BACKGROUND

In thinking back to the conflagration of May 1968, it is easy to forget that the 1960s were a decade of discussions, debates, and attempts at educational reform—in France as elsewhere.[6] From the reform projects of the Resistance, which culminated in the never-implemented Langevin-Wallon report of 1947, to the two important *colloques* of Caen in 1956 and 1966, through the passage of the Fouchet reform of 1965, "the 'modernisation' of the universities became a major issue in certain sectors of education, in certain industrial circles and among certain groups in the world of politics and the higher administration" (Bourricaud, 1982, p. 37).

Groups of reformers, including some of the most distinguished names in French academia, called at one time or another for most of the reforms that would later appear—admittedly in different form—in the loi d'orientation. Summarizing these proposals from Bourricaud's (1982) extensive treatment, they included, notably: increased support for research, the opening of the university to society, the modernization of teaching, the replacement of the faculties with something approaching the American department, the removal of barriers between universities, a degree of autonomy in the financing of research units outside the state's annual budgets, the elimination of certain chairs, and even—in one version—the limited participation of students in university governance (pp. 38-44).

Nor were the reformers either isolated or disorganized. They had an interest group—the Association for the Development of Scientific Research —and maintained close ties with important officials in the Ministry, even succeeding "in enlisting the support of a number of politicians" (Bourricaud, 1982, p. 37). Although the shift from the Fourth to the Fifth Republic denied them the help of some of their closest allies—for example, Mendès-France— they retained a position of trust with the Ministry and especially with two successive directors-general for higher education, Gaston Berger and Pierre Agrain (Bourricaud, 1982, pp. 40-41, 44-45). This coalition for reform was partly responsible for placing—and for keeping—educational reform on the policy agenda during the 1960s.

But the reforms did not attack all the defects of the system with equal vigor. Grignon and Passeron's (1970) summary of the major reforms that were implemented between 1954 and 1967 in four of the five main faculties shows that the significant reforms were mainly concerned with the organization of degrees. They left out the problem of the structure of the faculties or universities, methods of teaching, and the relation between teaching and research. Although the faculties of law and medicine implemented significant reforms under government prodding, where the arts and sciences were concerned, the "new system . . . [did] not necessarily imply a break with the old teaching organization and still less with the system of traditional attitudes" (Grignon & Passeron, 1970, p. 32).

What was important about this for the period of *l'après-mai* was that, by 1968, a cadre of educational reformers could be identified by Faure for his cabinet and as an elite support base. These had ties throughout the educational establishment and could draw on ideas that had been circulating since the colloques of Caen. May brought new and unruly actors on to the stage, but it exploded onto the political scene in the context of an ongoing debate about the future of higher education.[7] Faure had only to pick up the existing threads of proposals and use the fear of a renewed May to produce a political response. He could do this, first, because of the extraordinary nature of the crisis.

A SHORT AND ABRUPT CRISIS

The May crisis was quite short, which strengthened the reformers' hand, against both those whose instinctive response was for greater law and order and against their sworn enemies. Even adopting the kind of broad definition used by Schnapp and Vidal-Naquet (1988), the French May was over very quickly compared, for example, to its German and Italian counterparts. In fact, the sudden beginning, the lightning diffusion, and the rapid collapse of the May-June events were its most visible characteristics.

The actual beginning of the cycle is in some dispute. Some see the agitation against the Fouchet educational reform in 1964-66 as the most important gestation stage (Passeron, 1986, pp. 376-377), a view that is reinforced by Converse and Pierce's (1989) findings about the widespread dissatisfaction with the educational system before May.[8] Others find the beginning in the anti-Vietnam War protests of 1966, while still others see it in the early signs of working class insurgency in 1967 (Capdeveille & Mouriaux, 1988). What is certainly true is that the rise in collective action associated with the actual *themes* of May began in the fall of 1967 and continued sporadically through the winter and early spring of 1968.[9]

The same suddenness marked the end of the events. But while most would regard the sudden drop in collective action after the elections of June as the sign of the collapse of the movement of May, some see the end of the cycle coming much later—in the conflicts over reform that succeeded the passage

586   COMPARATIVE POLITICAL STUDIES / January 1993

of the loi d'orientation and ended with the last major university strike in 1976 (Passeron, 1986, p. 394).

It is certainly true that the movement was effectively neutralized when the Sorbonne and other faculties were cleared out at the end of May and that the movement as a whole suffered a major collapse with the Gaullist electoral victory of June. By the *rentrée*, solidarity had so broken down among student groups and between the students and their supporters among the faculty that they posed no real threat to the authorities. It was this lassitude, against the general fear of the renewal of contestation, that gave the reformers the pause they needed to shift the center of gravity from the streets to the political arena.

But the demobilization of the students over the summer of 1968 was only a part of the picture—and perhaps not the most important part. The major reason why the French crisis can be said to have ended by June 1968 was the return to work of the working class with the signature of the Accords of Grenelle.[10] To the extent that factory militancy continued, it was linked to the issue of union rights in the workplace in December 1968 and to the favoring of collective bargaining by the Chaban-Delmas government in September 1969 (see Bridgford, 1989, pp. 103, 111 for these changes).

The May events largely exhausted the capacity for collective action of the other major sectors of French society too. Although groups as different as cadres (Groux, 1988), white-collar workers, public employees, farmers, Catholics (Hervieu-Leger, 1988), parents' associations (Vernus, 1988), and even football players (Wahl, 1988) were swept into the movement of May, their attitudes to the crisis were sharply divided. By June the Parisian middle class—which had been outraged by police brutality in the Latin Quarter in May—voted in overwhelming proportions for the Right.

THE CRISIS AND THE MANDATE

The movement of May was surely one of the shortest springs in the history of French protest cycles. But as it ended, no one could predict what the students would do at the rentrée and how their actions would affect the workers and others who had joined them in May. We know that uncertainty is one of the major resources of protest movements (Eisinger, 1973; Tarrow, 1989a). This uncertainty, and the desire of the shaken Gaullist party to provide palliatives for the masses of students who had turned out in May, provided a major opportunity for reform.

With the virtues of hindsight, we can see that there was little prospect for a renewed May at the rentrée of the fall of 1968. But in July, when Faure was appointed, no one really knew whether the movement of May was dead. The rapid paralysis of the university system and of virtually every part of French society in May had shocked the political elite out of its *suffisance* and convinced reformists that something had to be done to prevent a recrudescence of revolt. The fact that the summer vacation brought a deadly quiet to the educational establishment might have meant that the movement was over or it could have meant that its leaders were regrouping for the next round of contestation.[11] Faure's appointment was a response to this fear and he was quick to take advantage of it, as the major studies of his tenure as minister show (Chalendar, 1970: Fomerand, 1974, 1975).

The most direct source of the opportunity for reform lay in the enormous triumph of the Gaullists in the elections of June. Their success was even more remarkable when we consider that, as late as May 24th, General de Gaulle had attempted to deal with the crisis through a referendum on participation— one that he might well have lost. How great their success was can be judged from Table 1, which compares the swing in votes to the Gaullists and their allies in June to previous electoral swings in the Fifth Republic.

It was not only the Gaullist victory that explains the strength of Faure's mandate but the humiliation de Gualle suffered in May, when he found his political space constricted by the enormity of the conservative victory and the refusal of his supporters to organize the referendum he wanted (Charlot, 1989). By putting a reformer like Faure in charge of the Education Ministry and giving him a sweeping mandate for reform, General de Gaulle hoped to strengthen his own position vis-à-vis the Gaullist party.

This can best be understood in the coalitional terms used by Peter Gourevitch (1978) to understand de Gaulle's later resignation after the referendum of 1969. The Gaullist coalition had never been limited to loyalists and conservatives; it had from the beginning appealed to "modernizers" who wanted to make France into an advanced industrial nation. As in the stillborn referendum that spelled his defeat the following spring, de Gaulle may have seen educational reform of 1968 as a way to regain the support of the modernists, short-circuit the power of the conservatives, and reestablish his personal links with the electorate.

For such a coalitional juggling act, Edgar Faure fit the bill very well.[12] A former radical who had never been central to the Gaullist coalition, he was suspect to many in the Gaullist party because of his identification with many of the Fourth Republic's excesses. But he was far more palatable to the General, whose previous efforts at educational reform had been undermined by Pompidou and Peyrefitte.[13] More than anything, Faure's leadership was characterized by a deft political touch and a degree of light-footedness that some saw as opportunism. He was once quoted as saying that "France is not ungovernable. It can be ruled by skill and dissimulation" (quoted in Wright, 1987, p. 527).

Table 1
Electoral Change in France, 1958-1968

Year of legislative election	First ballot		Total swing from Left to government[a]
	Left parties	Government	
1958			
Percentage	41.9	17.6	—[b]
Seats	90	212	—
1962			
Percentage	42.1	36.4	18.6
Seats	107	269	8.8
1967			
Percentage	41.5	37.7	1.9
Seats	194	242	−71.3
1968			
Percentage	36.5	43.6	11.9
Seats	83	354	103.5

Source. Ehrmann (1983, p. 220).
a. Index for votes: Percentage of change in governmental vote from last election minus percentage of change in Left vote from last election. Index for seats: Percentage of change in governmental seats from last election minus percentage of change in Left seats from last election.
b. Excludes changes from Fourth to Fifth Republic.

POLITICIZATION AND FACTIONALIZATION

Given the conflicts surrounding higher education in May, it might be supposed that a reform like the one Faure proposed in October 1968 would stimulate tremendous controversy from the activists of May. But movements arise quickly and seldom focus on the details of reform. In addition, *this* movement had rapidly left educational issues behind to focus on national politics and had internal divisions that were so severe as to reduce its capacity to return to the issue of university reform. Both of these features of the movement of May gave Faure a relatively free hand to enunciate a major reform project.

A FOCUS ON NATIONAL POLITICS

If the May movement began in the universities, once it had evolved from the terrain of student demands to that of political power, there was no turning back. As Passeron (1986) observes:

If the raging conflict in the universities acquired a privileged position for the tensions that triggered the escalation of the revolt, the student movement soon ceased to have—if it had ever had them—goals that were strictly speaking related to the university. (p. 382 [my translation]).

Encouraged by the overreaction of the Minister of Education in clearing out the courtyard of the Sorbonne in May and by the police brutality that met the ensuing demonstrations, the students quickly focused their energies on the political arena. Their main slogans were at first largely tactical: the reopening of the faculties, amnesty for the arrested students, an end to police presence. But once these goals were achieved—and they were effectively achieved soon after Pompidou's return in mid-May—the movement could not rest on its laurels if it was to survive. As Passeron (1986) writes: "The united front against the traditional university exploded as soon as the disdained institution was no longer available to bring together its attackers and paper over their opposing criticisms" (p. 382 [my translation]).

Scanning the documents that have been assembled by Schnapp and Vidal-Naquet (1988, parts 2, 3), one cannot help but be struck by the rapidity with which a great number of student groups focussed their attention on politics. The major exceptions were the *instances de fait* that had sprung up in faculties around the country, which devoted themselves over the summer to questions internal to the university. But these were divided and dispersed and were easily coopted into the reform projects of the Minister and his cabinet. The result was that the greatest student mass movement in the country's history lacked an educational counter-program at precisely the time when a strengthened Gaullist majority put forward a major program of university reform.

Whether the movement's rapid concentration on national politics was the result of the inherent centralization of the French system (Schnapp & Vidal-Naquet, 1988, p. 50), of the instinctive Jacobinism of the Left, or simply of the pace and direction of events, it is difficult to say. What was unusual about the French May was the rapid diffusion to movement organizations around the country of slogans that invested the national political system and the rapid disappearance of a radical discourse about the need for educational change. This was in part responsible for the gravity of the May crisis, but when it was over, it left open a window of reform for the elite.

FACTIONALIZATION

Nor was there any such thing as a unified movement for university reform in French society. Had Edgar Faure and his collaborators wished to reflect movement opinion in the law they proposed to Parliament in October, they could not have found a coherent representative of these views among the student organizations, the teacher's unions, or the universities in general. This was as true of students and teachers as it was of the relations between various student groups and of various levels of the educational establishment.

Students and Teachers

The most obvious cleavage was between students and teachers. The mythology of May '68 has left the impression that the students enjoyed considerable faculty support. This is in part the result of a few, highly publicized translations of books by university professors and in part due to a confusion between the "heroic," national phase of the movement—when the stakes were the installation of a new kind of regime—and the more prosaic concerns of students and teachers. In terms of the latter issue, there was a deep cleavage between the radical student groups that emerged from May and the bulk of university professors—even those on the historic Left.

This cleavage had already emerged in the debates of the large, unorganized assemblies that developed in many faculties in May. A number of younger faculty and even some professors joined these student groups to design ambitious schemes for university reform (Salmon, 1982, pp. 67-68). In June, even full professors were encouraged to participate by the Ministry. But these instances de fait, rather than soldering a reform coalition around the goals of May, demonstrated the great gap in perspective between the students and most of the teaching staff and produced humiliation and resentment among the latter. As Salmon (1982) writes: "Even to those who had favoured reform, many of the ideas developed in the assemblies and seconded occasionally by colleagues seemed both childish and certain to cause a complete collapse of all forms of higher education" (p. 68).

The shock administered to conservative professors by these reform schemes[14] was reinforced by the reform strategy of Minister Faure, who appeared ready to embrace the students' demands for *co-gestion*. The differences went well beyond the assemblies of May and June, as professors, maîtres, maîtres-assistants, assistants, and technical and administrative personnel carved out different positions on the prospect of changes in the university.[15]

Students and Students

If there were sharp cleavages between teachers and students, the ideological differences among the student groups were even sharper. Before May, some of these groups had been reformist; others had reformist tendencies within them; whereas others rejected the university as a relevant arena from the beginning.[16] Although these differences were obscured by the unifying target of the state in May, by June they began to emerge more clearly, both in the debates in the unofficial assemblies being held in various faculties and in the tactical attitudes of various groups toward participating in the elections. Differences in strategy that preceded May, together with those that resulted from clashing interpretations of the events, combined to produce divergent attitudes toward the reform.

The Union Nationale des Etudiants de France (UNEF) provides a well-documented example. The organization was deeply split when the movement of May exploded, between a "universitist" tendency that "gave primacy to the allocation of studies," and a "structuralist" one that "insisted on the need to present 'counter-plans' to the government's projects" (Monchablon, 1988, p. 17). Competition for the support of newly radicalized students led UNEF to adopt a more radical stance as the movement of May ended. Its leaders were "conscious that 'in many places the struggles [of May] had taken place outside' of l'UNEF" (p. 11). To gain their support, it needed to maintain a radical *élan* that went beyond reforming the university. Faced at its national assizes in July by the presence of many delegates outside its control, the UNEF leadership proposed a new charter that would make it "a mass political movement" and liquidate the vestiges of unionism (p. 11).

Teachers and Teachers

The bulk of the French professoriat had never been enthusiastic about a movement that some of its members saw as juvenile, whereas others feared it for what they saw as its subversive dangers. Influential conservative groups like the Société des Agrégés and professional associations like the Syndicat Autonome of university professors weighed in heavily against *any* student participation in university policy-making. Distinguished academics like Georges Vedel and Charles Debbasch argued forcefully against the dangers of encroachment on professors' freedom of choice.[17]

Divisions among the teachers' organizations that had participated in the May movement were almost as broad as those within the student movement. The best example was the Fédération de l'Education Nationale (FEN), which was constitutionally only a federation of teachers' unions, but that had considerably increased its importance during May. Even at the height of the movement, FEN's internal constituencies were divided. Although the Syndicat National de l'Education Superieur (SNESup), under gauchiste control, joined the students in their movement in the university, the secondary school union, SNES, which was controlled by the Communists, opposed *contestation* and tried to brake the movement in the *lycées*.[18] Although some of the FEN's leaders were present at Charléty, others took a more moderate line, hoping to increase the organization's influence with the government after the crisis ended.[19]

These divisions may well have been partly responsible for the Federation's incapacity to put forward a viable alternative to the Faure reform when, in October 1968, it held its "Etats Généraux de l'Université Nouvelle" (FEN, 1969). The constituent unions divided at the conference on mainly sectoral lines.[20] Remarkably, this national conference failed to discuss the forthcoming university reform altogether (FEN, 1969). It was only through a focus on "common demands for the allocation of greater financial credits" that the cleavages among FEN's main constituent unions were covered up (FEN, 1969, pp. 207-208).

It should be obvious from this brief survey that, in the highly politicized crucible of tendencies and organizations that emerged from the movement of May, there was no unified movement for university reform. Had Faure and his collaborators wished to reflect the movement's views in the law they proposed to Parliament in October, they could not have found a coherent representative of these views among the student organizations, in the teacher's unions, or in the universities in general.[21] The absence of such a coherent movement made it easy for Faure to manoeuver, but, as we shall see, the collapse of the movement and its internal divisions after the rentrée removed the threat that was the major incentive for reform.

REFORM AND THE POLITICAL PROCESS

Faure's strategy was to build a coalition for reform out of some elements of the former movement, some educational modernizers, and Gaullist loyalists. He wasted no time in making contact with modernists who wanted to build a university in tune with the modern world, and with radicals who wanted to see the Napoleonic system dismantled. Distrusted by the conservatives, he nevertheless made contact with representatives of the Catholic educational hierarchy and met surreptitiously with student leaders in the evening.

Faure's first formal move was to set up a number of study commissions and to make contact with many of the instances de fait that had organized spontaneously in the effervescence of the spring, and began a series of meetings with interested groups—some of them sub rosa.[22] He drew the FEN into his plans and met privately with Confédération Général du Travail leader Georges Seguy, convincing him—and through him his Parti Communiste

Français comrades—not to oppose the reform.[23] In the months following his appointment, Faure diverted attention from the much-feared renewal of mobilization in the streets by creating a *"bouillonnement au sommet"* around himself and his cabinet.[24]

Faure sounded very like a progressive in the fall of 1968, but his true strategy was to take advantage of the political opportunity structure of a disorganized, but still potentially dangerous movement and a strengthened gaullist majority. He built a political and ideological coalition based on the desire of the conservatives to preserve social peace, of the modernists to create universities that would be adequate for a modern society, of liberals who wanted university autonomy from the state, and of progressives who hoped for real student participation in university decision making. In legislative terms, the coalition-building exercise was a success; by November 7th, only 4 months after he took office, the reform passed both houses of Parliament with overwhelming majorities (Fomerand, 1974, chap. 4).

But Faure's coalition was temporary, depending as it did on fear of a renewed May among the government's supporters, the disorganization of the opposition, and General de Gaulle's personal support. It also failed to take account of the institutional power of the professorate to turn reforms to its own advantage—a capacity that the reform actually increased. As fall gave way to winter and winter to the following spring, with the reform's implementation and de Gaulle's sudden resignation, the cracks in the reformist coalition became fissures.

THE WEAKNESSES OF THE REFORM

Seldom had so many sweeping changes been proposed in such haste or had to be implemented in so short a time.[25] In fact, at the end of the legislative process, even the idea for a provisional year to put the system into gear was scrapped. By December 31, 1968—within 2 months of the law's passage— some 600 provisional UERs had been created. By April, elections for new councils had been held for students and faculty all over the country. The new universities almost immediately elected their presidents and submitted draft statutes to a commission of the Conseil d'Etat. By the 1970 *rentrée* even the thorny problem of dividing the University of Paris into 13 new universities had been largely completed.[26]

The UER Problem: Creating Resources for Your Opponents

But a number of unfortunate results followed from this haste.[27] The greatest problem had to do with the creation of the new departments—or

UERs—and their integration into the newly created universities. For rather than following the educationally rational course of first creating the new universities and then allowing them to define their own internal structures, Faure's cabinet created a "provisional" list of UERs very rapidly—by December 1968—and only then moved to the broader step of aggregating them into universities.

The problem that this created was that the provisional UERs—some of them no more than new names for old faculties and institutes—quickly gained an institutional base from which they could defend their interests and constrain the shape of the new universities. Although the fear in governing circles was that radical students would take over the provisional UERs, the real danger in this procedure was that the professorate could use them to consolidate its position and prevent real educational innovation from being carried out. Although, here and there, creative new interdisciplinary units were created as a result of the procedure, one disappointed reformer writes that "a certain number of associations were created only to gain greater autonomy and control over more resources, while many were created from the desire of teachers from the same political or philosophical tendency to stay together" (Chalendar, 1970, p. 177).

The problem was reinforced by the reluctance of the Prime Minister's cabinet to see the law implemented in the frenzied atmosphere of l'après-mai. Not everyone in the administration shared Faure's enthusiasm for reform.[28] Under French constitutional procedure, only the Prime Minister or the President had the right to pass the decrees that would be necessary to create the universities.[29] If the Prime Minister—or members of his staff—were unconvinced of the necessity of the law, serious delays could result.

Although Faure and his staff proceeded almost immediately to the designation of the new universities—naming 17 of them by March 1969 and 37 more by June (Chalendar, 1970, p. 192)—the Prime Minister's office was not happy over the plans to apply the law to the *grandes écoles* (p. 189). "Under different pretexts," his staff found reasons for delay and "the signature of the Matignon was held back until Faure's departure as Minister" (p. 193).[30] There was an even longer delay in the case of Paris, but this related more to the need to find a solution to feuds and political differences within the old Sorbonne than to high politics. But while the government delayed, academic mandarins who had no enthusiasm for reform had time to regroup.

The Revenge of the Mandarins

Faure and his cabinet expected the newly created UERs to be provisional for two reasons: "The Minister could himself complete or modify [the plan], and the councils of the new universities, once elected, could equally question them in creating their statutes" (Chalendar, 1970, p. 175). But they calculated without taking account of two factors: First, it would require a continued commitment to reform in the political system for the spirit of the reform to survive; and second, they took insufficient account of the power of the academic establishment to delay or reshape the reform.[31]

The power and factional divisions of the academic community were particularly important in the big cities, where more than one university was created. In smaller towns like Caen, Clermont, Dijon, Nice, and Poitiers, where only one university was created, true "pluridisciplinary" institutions resulted (Salmon, 1982, p. 78). But in the bigger cities, like Aix-Marseilles, Lyon, Lille, Bordeaux, Strasbourg, and Toulouse, the law set numerical limits on the number of students and more than one university had to be created.

In principle, there was no reason why this could not have been done on an educationally rational basis. But most often, professors would collect on personal, political, or disciplinary bases.[32] Some who favored reform found their way to experimental universities like Vincennes or to Paris VII; others created solutions of convenience like Paris I; and those who dreaded change could remain in the old faculties of law and medicine in Paris, which were virtually unchanged, or join conservative "new" universities like Lyon I. The reformers' urgency in beginning the reform with the UERs, while the government delayed in creating authoritative university institutions, left it hostage to the revenge of the mandarins.

Business as Usual

No doubt, had an actively reformist Education Ministry remained in place, led by a minister with the political will to defend his reform, provisional arrangements that were based on hasty decisions or on poor educational policy could have been revised. But the season for reforms, like the season of protest, was very short. After less than 1 year in power, and as the result of de Gaulle's ill-considered referendum and resignation, Faure was removed from power by the new Pompidou government and his reformist cabinet dispersed. An educational conservative whose brother-in-law was president of the Société des Agregés, Pompidou replaced Faure with Olivier Guichard, a Gaullist loyalist who administered the law without personal conviction or political imagination. And Guichard's tenure coincided with a series of administrative and management shakeups of the Ministry that left little time or energy for reform. He was followed by Joseph Fontanet and, after Pompidou's death, by Jean-Pierre Soisson, Valery Giscard d'Estaing's first Education Minister.

This merry-go-round of ministers and their cabinets did little good for the newly formed universities. Each new government attacked the problem of educational reform anew, unintentionally contributing to the turmoil in the universities by reinventing the wheel many times over (Passeron, 1986, p. 390). In the absence of a reformist hand at the helm, the orientation law was "diverted according to local power relations, here to the profit of the continuity of the powers in place; there as a camouflage for demagogic practices" (Passeron, 1986, p. 386). These constant changes gave the Ministry the chance to reaffirm its tutelage over many aspects of educational life and left room for an educational conservative like Alice Saunier-Seité to attack the spirit of the law when she became Minister for the Universities in 1978 (pp. 394-395).

THE NARROWING WINDOW OF REFORM

But if the reform failed in its boldest aspirations, it was not primarily because of the power of the educational establishment or because Faure had lost his position. The reform passed so swiftly because Faure and his collaborators had built a coalition on the fear that—barring a reform—there was danger of mobilization in the streets. Their coalitional base was wide but temporary. Some favored reform for its own sake, but many others supported it only because of their fear that the rentrée would bring renewed student strife and a return of insurgency to French society. When that fear abated, so did the impulse for reform.

Even before de Gaulle's resignation and Faure's replacement at the Ministry, Faure lost the marginal power he had enjoyed over the summer and during the fall. This was not only because of the normal wearing away of reformist initiatives by the give-and-take of the political process or of administrative resistance, but more fundamentally because the industrial and educational rentrée provided evidence that—except for small groups of isolated agitators—the movement of the previous spring was dead.

It was the challenge from outside the polity that had given the reformers their political opportunity and it was the decline of that threat that reduced their leverage vis-à-vis a cautious government, a conservative Parliament, and an aroused academic establishment. This can be seen in the sharp decline in collective action in general—and of confrontational protest in particular—at the rentrée. As the reported time line of student demonstrations, public marches, and violence from July 1968 through June 1969 in Figure 1 shows, it was mainly *after* the reform was passed, and during the period of the election of student councils, that contestation was renewed.

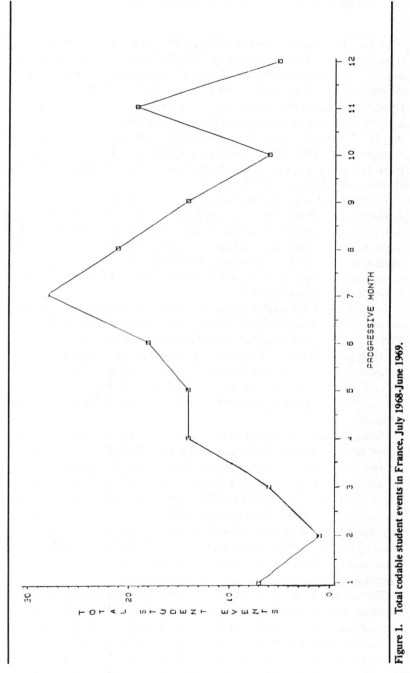

Figure 1. Total codable student events in France, July 1968–June 1969.

In fact, the reform helped to bring student protest back to where it had started. In contrast to West Germany and Italy, where the same period saw a move out of the universities into the streets on the part of student radicals, the election campaign for the student councils envisioned by the reform law brought the student movement back to the campus, where both violent and nonviolent collective action accompanied the election campaign. Although the press featured the most violent encounters when radical groups attempted to stop students from voting, in fact, most of the collective action surrounding these elections was peaceful and the 60% quorum of participation was not always reached (Fomerand, 1974, p. 240).[33]

It was in Parliament that the first signs of the declining threat of mobilization appeared. Each step of the legislative process led to a whittling down of the liberality of the initial reform plan. Many of the amendments were inspired by the academic establishment, either working through the Prime Minister's office or through individual members of Parliament. As a result, in the final text and in the implementation of the law, each of the bill's original principles was compromised.[34]

Second, in the electoral colleges, the weight of the maîtres-assistants and assistants was reduced from Faure's generous proposal of August (Chalendar, 1970, p. 117), and that of the students made dependent on their level of electoral participation—a limitation that was never suggested for the other categories of voters (pp. 149ff.). As for the cherished goal of opening up the university to the outside, little was said about it in the final text of the law, but external groups held a statutory proportion of seats on the university councils.

Third, the regional councils foreseen by Faure to coordinate educational policy were never created, for after de Gaulle's ill-fated referendum on the regions, there was little enthusiasm in the government that succeeded him for decentralization. Instead, the group of university presidents who had begun meeting informally as an Association was turned into an official Council by ministerial decree and eventually came to exercise real power.[35] The replacement of Faure's cabinet of reformers by Guichard's, which was made up largely of current or future members of the Conseil d'Etat and had come mainly from the conservative law faculties, set the seal on reform for a generation.[36]

The defects of the loi d'orientation will be familiar from a number of countries that attempted systematic educational reform; whereas other defects appear to be results of the traditional French system and cannot be blamed on the law or on its implementation; and others have to do with characteristics of later periods of French politics. But in assessing the outcome of this case of extraordinary policy-making, it should not be forgotten how far the French system had come from its Napoleonic roots.[37] If the universities that emerged from the Faure reform were less autonomous, less pluridisciplinary, and less participatory than the reformers had hoped, they were an advance on the situation they replaced, where there had been no structure even resembling the university system common to other advanced countries. Faure may have failed in his more ambitious undertakings; but given the parallelogram of forces resisting reform, his achievement was no mean feat (Passeron, 1986, p. 389).

CONCLUSIONS

The major implications of the loi d'orientation for the comparative theory of extraordinary policy-making are three.

First, like critical elections and major crises, protest waves like that of May, 1968 do not simply take advantage of an existing political opportunity structure but become an important component of that structure and, through it, provide a window for reform.

Second, although they may help unleash a reform process, protest waves are not sufficient to produce significant reforms—they also require the presence and entrepreneurship of well-placed reformists who can turn the impetus for change into concrete proposals and pilot them through the political process.

Third, waves of mobilization can produce a temporary coalition for reform, but they are often too brief, too divided, and too multivoiced to supply reformers with sustained support when the fear of disorder evaporates.

These conclusions can be highlighted and illustrated by comparison of the French educational reform of 1968 with other recent mobilization waves. First, with respect to the co-occurrence of protest and reform, although there is no evidence that reform *must* result from protest, sustained collective action frequently impels elites to move in the direction of reform. In the United States, argue Piven and Cloward (1971), "relief arrangements are initiated or expanded during the occasional outbreaks of civil disorder produced by mass unemployment" (p. xiii). Similarly, Shorter and Tilly (1974) concluded from their analysis of the history of French strikes that "the great wave-year mobilizations . . . were invariably rewarded with some kind of legislative success, the ultimate touchstone of the value of political action" (pp. 145-146).

Periods like the Popular Front in France, the New Deal and Great Society in the United States, and the 1968-72 period in Italy all saw a co-occurrence between protest and reform. As the Tillys concluded from their study of a century of conflict in Europe:

> No major political rights came into being without readiness of some portions of those [protesting] groups to overcome the resistance of the government and other groups, consequently without considerable involvement of those groups in collective violence. (Tilly, Tilly, & Tilly, 1975, p. 184)

This occurs not through a direct translation of protest into reform, but because protest movements become part of the political opportunity structure and provide reform-minded elites with openings they otherwise would lack.

Second, it was not the movement of May itself that produced the educational reform in France, but a realignment in the governing coalition triggered by that movement and exploited by skillful political entrepreneurs. In analytical terms, much of the variance in the outcomes was explained not by the independent but by intervening variables.

The same was true in the reform period of the 1960s in the United States. "Protest," to paraphrase the work of Browning, Marshall, and Tabb (1984), was "not enough" to produce reformist outcomes for minority groups without the intervening influence of elections, political realignments, and leaders able to take advantage of a widening political opportunity structure. This suggests that the study of social movements will remain fatally incomplete unless scholars become more sensitive to the relations between protest and politics.

Third, the implementation of the French Orientation Act shows that, although protest is necessary for a reform process to begin, it is not sufficient to sustain it. A reform that takes shape during a period of crisis quickly loses its steam when the threat of crisis has passed. It took the May crisis to give French reformists the political opportunity to put in motion reform plans that predated May; they seized it by constructing a broad coalition for reform stretching from some elements of the student movement to educational modernizers and Gaullist loyalists. But the window of opportunity opened by May was not wide enough, nor did it stay open sufficiently long to allow the reform to be implemented in its original spirit.

In the same way, the distributive policies of the Johnson administration in response to the riots gave way to the "law and order" expenditures of the Nixon administration (Button, 1978). In Italy, the repressive policies of the authorities followed rapidly on their initial confusion and permissiveness faced by the protest wave of the late, 1960s (della Porta, 1992). Like the French May and its reformist aftermath, these examples suggest that although protest can put reform on the agenda, it is insufficient to guarantee its success.

Whether this is equally true of other sources of extraordinary policy-making will only be known as the result of systematic comparative analyses.

One final note: The outcomes of a cycle of protest and reform cannot be measured only by its immediate results. Like the troughs of major movements in other countries—for example, in the United States (Rupp & Taylor, 1987) and Italy (Lange, Tarrow, & Irvin, 1990), the doldrums following a period of mass mobilization like that of May 1968 can disguise a slow and capillary process of cultural transformation that leaves a heritage of values and practices for the next cycle of protest.

NOTES

1. For some exceptions, see Astin, Astin, Bayer, and Bisconti (1975), Burstein and Freudenberg (1978), Button (1978), Gamson (1991), Gurr (1980), Piven and Cloward (1977), and Tarrow (1989a, 1989b).

2. But see the study of the U.S. ghetto riots by Button (1978), who demonstrates a fairly clear cross-sectional relationship between the intensity of violence and increases in federal spending in cities.

3. Jacques F. Fomerand's (1974) thesis, "Policy-Formulation and Change in Gaullist France: The 1968 Orientation Act of Higher Education" is the best existing analysis of the policy process surrounding the Orientation Act and its policy outcomes. Fomerand also includes a basic chronology of the policy process (pp. 6-7) and the full text of the law (pp. 342-355). Also see Fomerand (1975) for a summary of his most important findings.

4. For the development of the concept of political opportunity structure in relation to social movements, see the survey in Tarrow (1988). The most important signposts are Eisinger (1973), McAdam (1982), Kitschelt (1986), Katzenstein and Mueller (1987), Tarrow (1989a, 1989b), Kriesi (1991), and Rucht (1990).

5. The most systematic study based on a political process model is that of Doug McAdam (1982), who argued in the case of the American civil rights movement that a model based on the political process provides a far better explanation of when the movement emerged than other available models.

6. See Bourricaud (1982); Fomerand (1975, chap. 2); Grignon and Passeron (1970); Passeron (1986). As Grignon and Passeron (1970) write:

The immobilism of the university and the inflexibility of its organization and curricula have been constantly denounced over the past 15 years, until finally denunciation became unanimous and the effects of the rise in enrollments succeeded in rousing even the most conservative academics. (pp. 27-28)

7. In fact, an examination of the reform proposals of Education Minister Alain Peyrefitte was scheduled for an Assembly debate on May 14th (Aubert, Bergounioux, Martin, & Mouriaux, 1985, p. 204).

8. Converse and Pierce (1989) conclude from their analysis of the relationship between public opinion in 1967 and demonstration participation in May, 1968 that

Attitudes towards educational opportunities and the role of government in promoting education, *expressed more than a year before the events*, had more independent impact on the May demonstrations than either the classic leftist issues of unionism and income distribution or even lack of trust in the governing authorities generally. (pp. 232-236, emphasis added; see also Table 2)

9. The first event that Schnapp and Vidal-Naquet (1988, pp. 106ff.) relate to the May crisis took place on November 25, 1967. No other major conflicts appear in their careful itinerary of university protest until the celebrated events of March 22 at Nanterre.

10. Statistics provided by the French Ministry of Labor show that the number of days lost to strikes in the years following the May outbreak was actually lower in 1969 and 1970 than it had been in 1966 and 1967 (Capdeveille & Mouriaux, 1988, p. 107). Although there were signs of continued worker militancy after May—for example in a greater willingness to occupy plants during strikes (p. 108)—the accords of Grenelle of June 1968 effectively closed the crisis as far as industrial relations were concerned.

11. In a personal interview, Michel Alliot recalls that, when visitors would complain to General de Gaulle of the damage that the Faure reform might do to higher education, he would remind them of the collapse of the system in May (interview, April 2, 1990).

12. Faure had ambitions for the post well before May 1968. Alliot recalls discussing it with him as early as 1964. Although Faure was not named to the post until July, it was in June that the two had their first conversation about Faure's plans for the ministry (interview, Alliot, April 2, 1990).

13. I am grateful to David Goldey for reminding me of this, as well as for identifying the Faure quote that follows.

14. The most serious were produced by the "Conférence InterFacultés," meeting in Toulouse in July (Chalendar, 1970, p. 13).

15. As Schnapp and Vidal-Naquet (1988) conclude:

Pour nombre d'assistants ou de maîtres-assistants, la revendication de la suppression des hiérarchies à l'intérieur des universités passait par leur propre élevation au rang de professeurs. Des professeurs de province estimaient que l'occasion était unique de se faire nommer à Paris, d'autres qui avaient moins de 40 ans déclaraient avec candeur que la direction de l'Université devait être confiee aux professeurs de moins de 40 ans. (p. 47)

16. Before May, for example, the Union des Etudiants Communistes were "divided among 'orthodoxes', 'italiens,' and several varieties of extremists" (Schnapp & Vidal-Naquet, 1988, p. 16). The various maoist groups, both before and after May, never had much interest in the university—except as a site for the recruitment of militants for the factories (p. 151). The one surviving maoist document on the university, which is reproduced by Schnapp and Vidal-Naquet (pp. 359-360), called for the subordination of the movement to the cause of "serving the people." Even the movement of the 22nd of March rejected what its leaders called "a corporatist spirit" (p. 149), and viewed the movement for transforming the university with a critical eye, affirming that "ni pratiquement ni theoriquement on ne peut créer un îlot socialiste à l'intérieur d'une société capitaliste" (p. 152).

17. Divisions could by no means be reduced to a Left-Right axis. Although many conservative Catholic supporters of the *école libre* were in favor of educational reform (the same was true for the majority of Jewish professors), the lay Left was divided. For to the extent that the reform was thought to attack the unity of French education (and Edgar Faure tried to project exactly this impression), it could be understood as undermining the foundations of the secular

education that was thought to be a foundation of the republican tradition. Some of the attempts to modify the bill in a conservative direction as it passed through the political process would come from liberal academics who had voted stalwartly for the Left in the elections of June (interview with Gérard Conac, March 21, 1990).

18. Astre interview, April 5, 1990.

19. Although SNESup, under Alain Geismar, opposed compromise with the authorities even before May (Aubert et al., 1985, p. 204), the Syndicat National des Instituteurs (SNI) was quick to vote for a return to work after the general strike of May 20th, whereas SNES decided to continue the strike a while longer. FEN experienced contestation from insurgent teachers even before the end of the crisis: first on June 7, when some 200 radical *instituteurs*, opposing the organization's support for the end of the general strike, occupied the courtyard of the federation in Rue de Solferino (Barbet, 1988, p. 12). Although its leaders' basic instinct was to defend its members' professional interests, May saw the FEN develop a strategy of political mediation (Barbet, 1988, p. 15) that made it difficult for the federation to act when its constituent national unions were divided.

20. Although the SNI pushed for a platform on the school-leaving age and problems of curriculum and professional mobility for teachers, the SNES "insisted on the development of socioeducative activities, on the need for dialogue between parents and teachers, and on the reorganization of students' employment of their time" (Aubert et al., 1985, p. 207) and the SNESup opposed the reform altogether as a *"reformette"* (p. 205).

21. In an early stage of his Ministry, Faure and his collaborators wanted to include participants in the former movement in the early stages of participation. In fact, Faure's first plan for the election of the councils of the future university—bodies that would also draft their statutes—was to create informal bodies—which in many cases would in fact end up to be the instances de fait which had emerged in May and June—to act as the bodies which would elaborate the new statutes for the universities (Chalendar, 1970, p. 174). But this was too much for the government, which feared the influence of the instances de fait of May on the future universities (p. 117), and the idea of provisional committees had to be abandoned. As we shall see below, this defeat turned out to be crucial in the creation of the new university structures during the 1968-69 academic year.

22. Interview, Gérald Antoine, March 21, 1990; interview, Chalendar, March 17, 1990. Between his appointment in early July and the end of the summer, Faure and his collaborators reportedly saw over 4,000 individuals interested in one way or another in educational reform. Reported by Michel Alliot, in an interview, April 2, 1990.

23. Interview, Gérald Antoine, March 21, 1990.

24. Interview, Astre, April 5, 1990.

25. The haste was not accidental. Alliot was of the opinion that "in France, the only decisions that are taken are taken quickly" (interview, April 2, 1990).

26. Because several of these new units would continue to share the same facilities, the task was far more delicate than the creation of provincial universities (interview, Gérard Conac, March 23, 1990).

27. The first was that the law left a number of substantive gaps to be filled in later. Some of these would be dealt with in supplementary legislation in 1971 and 1975, whereas others—for example, the provision for regional councils—remained a dead letter. A large number of details were also left to be dealt with by administrative negotiation. The most crucial issue that the law left open was the nagging problem of selection—a problem that no one, either in the delicate atmosphere of l'après-mai or since, has been willing to broach (Gaussen, 1990, p. 10). Another result was that an enormous number of amendments were proposed to deal with the ambiguities

of the project. From Faure's original draft of 9 pages, a document of 39 pages finally emerged, "codifying a large number of situations and mechanisms, balancing general and generous principles with precise and numerous restrictions" (Passeron, 1986, p. 385).

28. Michel Alliot reports that on the morning after the law's passage, he was congratulated by a member of the Prime Minister's cabinet for its passage without a single dissenting vote. The same official promptly confided to him that now it was time to decide how to avoid its implementation (Alliot interview, April 2, 1990).

29. Under French constitutional procedure, although the Minister could effect the *arrêtés* necessary to create new units within the universities, only the Prime Minister or the President could effect the *décrets* necessary to create new *établissements publiques*, which is what the Universities would become.

30. I am following Michel Alliot's reconstruction of these events (interview, April 2, 1990).

31. Faure was aware of the danger. As Chalendar (1970) notes, he warned at the time that "simply transforming the existing units into UER's will carry the risk of quickly denuding the reform of its content" (p. 175).

32. As Salmon (1982) judiciously writes, "there were many anomalous collections of disconnected UERs" (p. 79). The biggest problem was in Paris. Here the overgrown university had to be divided into 13 units, and the process was so complicated that discussions and conflicts lasted up until the rentrée of 1970. Many of the "universities" that emerged were pluridisciplinary in name only, with odd collections of UERs existing cheek-by-jowl in uneasy cohabitation and frequently offering no more of an interdisciplinary training to their students than had the old faculties (Chalendar, 1970, p. 177). In some cases, different universities had to share the same premises—for example in the Sorbonne—which could lead to territorial disputes over wings of the building, rectorial apartments, even corridors. The UER of history ended up with 6,000 students; that of English literature more than 10,000 (Salmon, 1982, p. 177). Although changes were later made, the quality of university education in the capital never recovered.

33. Fomerand reports that 77% voted in the university Institutes of Technology and 68% in the former Medical faculties, but only 53% in Law, 43% in Sciences, and 43% in Liberal Arts. Fomerand—and Faure—regards these as successful figures, but it is difficult to know what to compare them to. What was certainly true was that the extreme Left groups were soundly defeated (Fomerand, 1974, pp. 241-243).

34. Consider the principle of the autonomy of the universities. Although the reformers achieved the liquidation of a priori administrative tutelage of the university's budgets, the autonomy of the new institutions would continue to be restricted by a Ministry of Education that had the power to define "programs of study leading to national diplomas" (Passeron, 1986, p. 387) and continued to exercise a posteriori control over their budgets.

35. Interview, Gérard Conac, March 23, 1990.

36. The one *universitaire* was Gerald Conac, himself a member of the Paris Faculty of Law and Economic Science.

37. Fomerand (1974), whose careful study is the most dispassionate one around, shares this view. He writes: "Often described as a mere political 'mesure de circonstances,' the Orientation Act, in several respects, was also an epoch making event" (Fomerand, 1974, p. 232).

REFERENCES

Astin, A. W., Astin, H., Bayer, A., & Bisconti, A. (1975). *The power of protest*. San Francisco: Jossey-Bass.

Aubert, V., Bergounioux, A., Martin, J.-P., & Mouriaux, R. (1985). *La Forteresse enseignante. la Fedération de L'Education Nationale*. Paris: Fayard.

Barbet, D. (1988, November). *La FEN en Mai-Juin 1968*. Paper presented to the Colloque sur Acteurs et terrains du mouvement social de 1968, Paris, CRSMSS.

Bourricaud, F. (1982). France: The prelude to the *loi d'orientation* of 1968. In H. Daalder & E. Shils (Eds.), *Universities, politicians and bureaucrats* (pp. 31-61). Cambridge: Cambridge University Press.

Bridgford, J. (1989). The events of May: Consequences for industrial relations in France. In D. L. Hanley & A. P. Kerr (Eds.), *May '68: Coming of age* (pp. 100-116). London: Macmillan.

Browning, R. P., Marshall, D. R., & Tabb, D. H. (1984). *Protest is not enough: The struggle of Blacks and Hispanics for equality in urban politics*. Berkeley: University of California Press.

Bunce, V. (1981). *Do new leaders make a difference? Executive succession and public policy under capitalism and socialism*. Princeton, NJ: Princeton University Press.

Burstein, P., & Freudenberg, W. (1978). Changing public policy: The impact of public opinion, antiwar demonstrations and war costs on Senate voting on Vietnam War motions. *American Journal of Sociology*, 84, 99-122.

Button, J. W. (1978). *Black violence: Political impact of the 1960s riots*. Princeton, NJ: Princeton University Press.

Capdevielle, J., & Mouriaux, R. (1988). *Mai 68: l'entre-deux de la modernité. Histoire de trente ans*. Paris: Presses de la Fondation Nationale des Sciences Politiques.

Chalendar, J. de (1979). *Une loi pour l'université*. Paris: de Brouwer.

Charlot, J. (1989). The aftermath of May 1968 for Gaullism, the Right and the Center. In D. L. Hanley & A. P. Kerr (Eds.), *May '68: Coming of age* (pp. 62-81). London: Macmillan.

Converse, P. E., & Pierce, R. (1989). Attitudinal roots of popular protest: The French upheaval of May 1968. *International Journal of Public Opinion*, 1, 221-241

della Porta, D. (1992, August). *Social movements and the state: First thoughts from a research on the policing of protest*. Paper presented to the Conference on European/American Perspectives on the Dynamics of Social Movements, Catholic University of America, Washington, DC.

Ehrmann, H. (1983). *Politics in France* (4th ed.). Boston: Little, Brown.

Eisinger, P. K. (1973). The conditions of protest behavior in American cities. *American Political Science Review*, 67, 11-28.

Fédéderation de l'Education Nationale. (1969). Les Etats généraux de l'université nouvelle. *Enseignement public*, 5 bis.

Fomerand, J. (1974). *Policy-formulation and change in Gaullist France: The 1968 Orientation Act of Higher Education*. Unpublished doctoral dissertation, City University of New York.

Fomerand, J. (1975). Policy formulation and change in Gaullist France. The 1968 Orientation Act of Higher Education. *Comparative Politics*, 7, 59-89.

Gamson, W. (1991). *The strategy of social protest* (2nd ed.). Belmont, CA: Wadsworth.

Gaussen, F. (1990, January 19). Universités 68-90: Même causes, mêmes effets? *Le Monde*, pp. 1, 10.

Gourevitch, P. A. (1978). Reforming the Napoleonic state. In L. Graziano, P. J. Katzenstein, & S. Tarrow (Eds.), *Territorial politics in industrial nations* (pp. 28-63). New York: Praeger.

Grignon, C., & Passeron, J.-C. (1970). *Innovation in higher education: French experience before 1968*. Paris: OECD Case Studies in Higher Education.

Groux, G. (1988, November). *Les cadres et le mouvement de mai; un moment, une rupture*. Paper presented to the Colloque sur Acteurs et terrains du mouvement social de 1968, Paris, CRSMSS.

Gurr, T. R. (Ed.). (1980). *Handbook of political conflict: Theory and research*. New York: Free Press.

Heclo, H. (1974). *Modern social policies in Britain and Sweden: From relief to income maintenance*. New Haven, CT: Yale University Press.

Hervieu-Leger, D. (1988, November). *May 1968 et les Catholiques: Les cas de la Mission Etudiante*. Paper presented to the Colloque sur Acteurs et terrains du mouvement social de 1968, Paris, CRSMSS.

Jenkins, C., & Perrow, C. (1977). Insurgency of the powerless: Farm worker movements (1946-1972). *American Sociological Review, 42*, 249-268.

Katzenstein, M., & Mueller, C. M. (Eds.). (1987). *The women's movements of the United States and Western Europe: Consciousness, political opportunity and public policy*. Philadelphia, PA: Temple University Press.

Keeler, J.T.S. (1993). Opening the window for reform: Mandates, crises, and extraordinary policy-making. *Comparative Political Studies, 25*, 433-486.

Kitschelt, H. (1986). Political opportunity structures and political protest: Anti-nuclear movements in four democracies. *British Journal of Political Science, 16*, 57-85.

Kriesi, H. (1991). *The political opportunity structure of new social movements: Its impact on their development*. WZB Occasional Paper No. 91 - 103.

Lange, P., Tarrow, S., & Irvin, C. (1990). Party recruitment: Mobilization, social movements and the Italian Communist Party since the 1960s. *British Journal of Political Science, 22*, 15-42.

Marshall, T. H. (1964). *Class, citizenship and social development*. Garden City, NY: Doubleday.

Marx, G., & Wood, J. L. (1975). Strands of theory and research in collective behavior. In A. Inkeles (Ed.), *Annual review of sociology* (Vol. 1, pp. 363-428). Palo Alto, CA: Annual Reviews.

McAdam, D. (1982). *The political process and the development of Black insurgency*. Chicago: University of Chicago Press.

Monchablon, A. (1988, November). *L'UNEF en Mai 1968*. Paper presented to the Colloque sur Acteurs et terrains du mouvement social de 1968, Paris, CRSMSS.

Passeron, J.-C. (1986). 1950-1980: L'université mise à la question: changement de décor ou changement de cap? In J. Verger (Ed.), *Histoire des universités en France* (pp. 367-420). Toulouse: Privat.

Piven, F. F., & Cloward, R. (1971). *Regulating the poor: The functions of public welfare*. New York: Pantheon.

Piven, F. F., & Cloward, R. (1977). *Poor people's movements: How they succeed and why they fail*. New York: Vintage.

Rokkan, S. et al. (1970). *Citizens, elections, parties*. New York: David McKay.

Rose, R. (1980). *Do parties make a difference?* Chatham, NJ: Chatham House.

Rucht, D. (1990). Campaigns, skirmishes and battles: Anti-nuclear movements in the USA, France and West Germany. *Industrial Crisis Quarterly, 4*, 193-222.

Rupp, L., & Taylor, V. (1987). *Survival in the doldrums: The American women's rights movement, 1945 to the 1960s*. New York: Oxford University Press.

Salmon, P. (1982). France, the *loi d'orientation* and its aftermath. In H. Daalder & E. Shils (Eds.), *Universities, politicians and bureaucrats* (pp. 63-101). Cambridge: Cambridge University Press.

Schnapp, A., & Vidal-Naquet, P. (1988). *Journal de la commune étudiante: Textes et documents, novembre 1967—juin 1968* (2nd ed.). Paris: Seuil.

Shorter, E., & Tilly, C. (1974). *Strikes in France*. Cambridge, MA: Harvard University Press.

Snow, D., & Benford, R. (1988). Ideology, frame resonance, and participant mobilization. In B. Klandermans, H. Kriesi, & S. Tarrow (Eds.), *From structure to action: Comparing social movements across cultures* (pp. 197-218). Greenwich, CT: JAI.

Tarrow, S. (1988). Social movement and national politics. *Annual Review of Sociology, 14,* 421-440.

Tarrow, S. (1989a). *Democracy and disorder: Protest and politics in Italy, 1965-1975.* Oxford: Oxford University Press.

Tarrow, S. (1989b). *Struggle, politics and reform: Collective action, social movements, and cycles of protest.* Western Societies Papers No. 21, Cornell University.

Tilly, C., Tilly, L., & Tilly, R. (1975). *The rebellious century, 1830-1930.* Cambridge, MA: Harvard University Press.

Turner, R., & Killian, L. (1972). *Collective behavior* (2nd ed.). Englewood Cliffs, NJ: Prentice-Hall.

Vernus, M. (1988, November). *La F.C.P.E. en Mai 1968.* Paper presented to the Colloque sur Acteurs et terrains due mouvement social de 1968, Paris, CRSMSS.

Wahl, A. (1988, November). *Le mai des footballeurs.* Paper presented to the Colloque sur Acteurs et terrains du mouvement social de 1968, Paris, CRSMSS.

Wildavsky, A. (1974). *The politics of the budgetary process.* Boston: Little, Brown.

Wright, G. (1987). *France in modern times: From the enlightenment to the present.* New York: Norton.

Sidney Tarrow is Maxwell M. Upson professor of government at Cornell University, where he teaches comparative politics and social movements. He has recently published Democracy and Disorder, *a study of protest and politics in Italy, 1965-1975, and is at work on an interpretive study of social movements called* Power in Movement.

[23]

Ronald Tiersky

FRANCE IN THE NEW EUROPE

Fr om de Gaulle through Mitterrand, France saw its historic task to be one of repairing the damage of Yalta—the division of Europe into Cold War blocs. Moving "beyond Yalta," it was said, would free Eastern Europe from communism and leave Europe as a whole free from domination by the superpower rivalry. That historic geopolitical change has now occurred— unexpectedly, astoundingly, within only a few years. And the healing of Europe's division has now been guaranteed by the astonishing disappearance of the U.S.S.R. as a state and an empire. French long-term policy has thus been served. Yet hard dilemmas confront the French in the new Europe.

To some, France emerged a big loser among the winning Western powers. Prior to the Cold War's passing a divided Europe and a divided Germany profited France geopolitically. France's main postwar foreign policy stage was Western Europe, and its main dilemma was how to maintain a political edge over West Germany's ever-growing economic influence.

Thus France supposedly had a geopolitical interest in avoiding both German unification and the end of superpower spheres of influence. In a divided Europe, built on a divided Germany, French overall influence was maximized. By extrapolation, the end of divided Europe meant for France above all else German ascension.

The consequence for the French is a rapid evaporation of France's ability inside the European Community to be the political/diplomatic engineer of the German economic locomotive in pivotal Franco-German relations. Or worse, with the probable expansion of the EC into a larger European Union— centered geographically more in the east and north—the Franco-German relationship will be put under stress, if not completely thrown into question.

Ronald Tiersky is Professor of Political Science at Amherst College. He recently completed a fellowship at the Centre d'Etudes des Relations Internationales in Paris.

132 FOREIGN AFFAIRS

II

In 1989 President François Mitterrand was initially reluctant about encouraging German unification, not as a principle, which he saw as inevitable and right, but as a practical matter—about the pace at which it was coming, the risks West German leaders created by moving so quickly and the nature of the resulting entity. To the French reluctance was added the deeper British reservations of Prime Minister Margaret Thatcher, not to mention the initial Soviet opposition of President Mikhail Gorbachev and Foreign Minister Eduard Shevardnadze. For all three, France, Britain and the Soviet Union, German unification was not on the agenda.

In contrast the Bush administration showed early and broad confidence in the political instincts of West German Chancellor Helmut Kohl, and the American public also demonstrated solid support for unification. This divergence created strains within the EC's central leadership and within the Franco-German "couple" in particular.

President Mitterrand shocked the Germans, for example, during his talks in Kiev with Gorbachev in early December 1990, from which rumors filtered out that the French leader was hoping to cooperate with the Soviets in slowing the pace of unification. Then Mitterrand, against West German wishes, went ahead with a state visit to a clearly collapsing East Germany on December 20–21, 1990. The Bonn government could only think that Mitterrand, received by the East Germans as the first Western head of state to visit, must be trying to prop up the East German regime. The visit was termed "anachronistic" by West German leaders, who viewed it as an unfriendly act.

Naturally German leaders did not appreciate Mitterrand complicating their own strategies.[1] Yet France, as any Gaullist leader would have said, has a right to its own policy. Nevertheless Kohl and Foreign Minister Hans-Dietrich Genscher were in the more delicate position. Mitterrand's behavior was, at worst, risking some measure of the trust that had been built up in the German-French EC relationship.

It goes without saying that President Mitterrand, along with Prime Minister Thatcher and other EC leaders, was seriously

[1]For all these events, a good source is the memoir-diary of Kohl's former foreign policy adviser, Horst Teltschik, *329 Tagen*, Berlin: Siedler, 1991.

concerned about the political power consequences of German unification in the European equation. In addition Mitterrand wanted to keep the process of unification under control, recognizing the explosive character of the situation. While insisting repeatedly that France was "not afraid" of unification and that the Germans had the right, according to the 1975 Helsinki Final Act, to decide their own future, the French president emphasized that it would enhance future relations if Germany's leaders carried forward the unification process in a spirit of close consultation and even some deference to the allies, bilaterally and in the "two-plus-four" talks involving the two Germanys, Britain, France, the United States and the Soviet Union.

Kohl and Genscher, for their part, achieved a strict separation between the "external" and "internal" aspects of unification, and a strict limitation (accepted by Washington, Paris and London) of what had to be decided by the Four Powers. The latter included skirting a Soviet suggestion that certain Four Power rights carry over for a transition period after unification.

Once President Mitterrand accepted the German timetable, presaging the most rapid possible unification of the two Germanys, a last point became crucial: to imbed German unification firmly in the Atlantic alliance and in the European integration process. Consequently French policy firmly supported unified Germany's full membership in NATO. Mitterrand several times deflected suggestions by Gorbachev and Shevardnadze that unified Germany should have a "French status" in NATO—that is, holding full political membership yet remaining outside the integrated military command. Finally, to assuage a French concern that unification might lead German policy eastward and away from plans for EC monetary and political union, Kohl agreed with Mitterrand that German unification and further EC "deepening" must go together. The Germans, in turn, understood well that legitimacy for German unification required deeper EC integration, that German unification and the unification of Europe were two sides of the same coin.

As proof that Kohl and Mitterrand, after a period of friction, were again on the same wavelength, they introduced in April 1990 a joint French-German initiative to revive momentum toward EC political union. There were two purposes: to complement the economic side of the integration process, that is, the 1992 single-market project and the plan for European Monetary Union; and to give practical assurances that German unification was not derailing European integration. It was this proposal, stimulated at the time by tensions over German unification, which turned into the Political Union Treaty initialed at Maastricht last December.

III

This kind of linkage had already been part and parcel of German policy. Kohl and Genscher consistently emphasized that German unification had to be "embedded" in European unification and that NATO, including a unified German membership and continued American military presence in Europe, was a "vital" requirement not only for American but also for German policy. Kohl, for example, emphasized repeatedly in the course of 1990 that neutrality, as Gorbachev and Shevardnadze were then suggesting, was not a price he would pay for German unification. Genscher remarked to Germany's EC partners that if they were worried about growing German power, their best strategy was not to isolate Germany into some *sonderweg* that the Germans did not want anyway, but rather to tie up Germany in a deepened, thickened and more federalized European Community, which the Germans would happily accept because it had been their proposal all along. Unification would not change Germany's EC and Western policies. And both Kohl and Genscher often repeated the powerful slogan that German leaders wanted a "European Germany," not a "German Europe."

Kohl's overall view, as summarized by his former foreign policy adviser, Horst Teltschik, was that all "thoughts of neutrality, demilitarization and alliance or bloc-disaffiliation he described as 'old thinking.' Kohl founded his position in the experience of German history, that peace, stability and security in Europe had always been guaranteed when Germany— the country in the middle of Europe—had lived with all its neighbors in firm ties, with contractual equality and mutually beneficial exchanges."[2]

As early as January 1988, in view of the cracks in Eastern Europe, Kohl had proposed a joint Franco-German Ostpolitik to the French. Mitterrand held back, since the Germans would

----

[2] *Ibid.*, pp. 244–5.

doubtless be the leading force and because a vigorous Franco-German Ostpolitik would cost the French excessively. As an alternative Mitterrand preferred to keep France's freedom of maneuver, even for a second-level and mainly diplomatic presence, in Eastern Europe.

One result of this French attempt to play a significant diplomatic role—without the economic and political means to be convincing—was the disastrous Prague conference on the proposed European confederation. There Czechoslovak President Václav Havel and Mitterrand apparently quarrelled bitterly. Havel was furious at Mitterrand's determined resistance to moving quickly to admit the former communist central European countries into Western institutions, especially NATO and the EC. Mitterrand instead offered the vague waiting room of his "confederation" idea, including a long association status (later Mitterrand spoke of "tens and tens of years") before east European economies would meet EC standards. This was an approach reminiscent of Mitterrand's go-slow recommendation on German unification, and may explain why many commentators, rightly according to the evidence, thought French policy was lagging during this period when others were forcing the pace.

Elsewhere in central and eastern Europe and in the former Soviet Union a similar policy could be found. There was French support for all of the prodemocracy revolutions of course, but there was also French concern about changes that would be destabilizing or simply too rapid.

In general Mitterrand's foreign policy, though it has moved case by case, has supported the maintenance of existing states over secession movements. In the most important instance, that of policy vis-à-vis the crumbling Soviet Union, this meant support right up to the end for Gorbachev and the retention of some kind of "center" against the breakup of the U.S.S.R. led by Boris Yeltsin. During the attempted putsch of August, Mitterrand had even pushed his preference for continuity to the point of a huge diplomatic blunder—an uncharacteristic error of precipitous reaction, of appearing to assume right away that the long-dreaded coup against Gorbachev was successful. On television Mitterrand called the perpetrators "the new leaders" of the Soviet Union and read from a letter he had received from one of them, Gennadi Yaneyev, to the effect that reform would continue, as if to reassure French opinion that the worst had not happened and that France had

136 FOREIGN AFFAIRS

a special diplomatic status (since the coup leaders were explaining themselves to the French leader). This was surely misjudgment masquerading as serenity.[3]

In the Yugoslav civil war Mitterrand's policy was to prefer integrity of the Yugoslav federation and negotiation among the republics. This contrasted sharply with the German push for immediate recognition of self-declared Slovenian and Croatian independence. Some observers argued, plausibly but unconvincingly, that the operative factor was in some fuzzy historical sense the traditional French bias toward "centralism." Another argument was that French policy was dictated by an old Quai d'Orsay preference for Serbia and anti-German coalition maneuvering, dating from World Wars I and II.

French policy was not this kind of woolly anachronism, but rather a calculation that in the long run the principle of national self-determination must be given limits before it becomes self-destructive. It did not make sense, in terms of peace and development, to encourage the emergence of a whole host of economically unviable, politically and militarily threatened states. It is a strategy of geopolitical prudence to limit civil wars and prop up stability inside the east European powder keg. The French approach might be mistaken, but rather than nostalgic it is at least forward-looking to the new dangers of the post-Cold War era.

Immediately after Maastricht in December 1991, however, two events suddenly signaled a new German assertiveness, the one a monetary decision, the other a German *alleingang* on the Yugoslav imbroglio.

First, the Bundesbank abruptly raised German interest rates to their highest level in 30 years. The German central bank, by law independent from government influence, acted for domestic economic reasons (German inflation, at 4–5 percent, was double the French rate at the time, reflecting both higher than expected costs of unification and union wage demands), but of course all partners in the European Monetary System (EMS) were immediately and sharply affected. The "deutsche

---

[3]Later, when Gorbachev's book, *The Coup*, appeared, there was a similar flap. In at least one edition Gorbachev wrote of his disappointment, which he said he still remembered painfully, that Mitterrand did not telephone him as soon as possible after his liberation, as opposed to George Bush's quick reaction. In other language editions this reference did not appear. In a fence-mending meeting with Mitterrand at the latter's country home following the Middle East peace talks' opening in Madrid, Gorbachev unconvincingly denied that he had ever written such a comment.

mark zone"—including governments inside and outside the system's "snake" of currency ranges—followed the German interest-rate lead immediately. The Bank of France also raised interest rates, reluctantly, following the German initiative for the second time in a few months; whereas French policy for a year had been to break free of the need to emulate Bundesbank policy—to create, through low inflation, a "strong franc" no longer a deutsche-mark zone currency.

The French and other governments were critical of the Bundesbank's nationalist unilateralism, while defenders of the German measure argued that outsiders failed to appreciate how dangerous German inflation had become. In any case those EC governments that planned to relax monetary and fiscal policy to pull their respective economies out of recession were put under unwelcome pressure by the unilateral German decision and then whipsawed between the German move upward and the Federal Reserve's lowering of the U.S. discount rate to 3.5 percent, the lowest level in decades.

Second, Chancellor Kohl, concerned about looking weak at home, decided his government could now—after Maastricht—afford to take a strong, even if unpopular, lead to do something to stop the bloody fighting in Yugoslavia. Foreign Minister Genscher, in a divisive EC Council of Foreign Ministers debate, forced diplomatic recognition of Croatia and Slovenia on several recalcitrant EC allies, among them France, and in the process rebuffed American and U.N. preferences for a prior ceasefire and, if necessary, deployment of a peacekeeping force. The strong-arm tactics of German diplomacy, threatening its EC partners with a go-it-alone decision, amounted to an unprecedented postwar German policy sortie.[4] Then Germany shortcircuited the Council of Ministers' compromise resolution (which had a January 15 deadline for recognition if the EC's conditions had been met) in order to announce recognition by Christmas, as Chancellor Kohl had earlier promised the Croats and Slovenes. Germany thus stood by its initial position that the EC had not been very effective and that recognition would pressure the Serbs, perhaps stopping the killing earlier. The German diplomatic fig leaf was to

[4]French Foreign Minister Roland Dumas summed up Germany's partners' attitude by saying, "The attitude of unilateral recognition could be damaging for the Community. . . . It would be prejudicial for Europe as a whole." Many commentators noted the irony of Germany's adopting at Maastricht the goal of a common foreign policy, then taking such a unilateral attitude in the first post-Maastricht crisis.

138 FOREIGN AFFAIRS

separate recognition from its actual implementation, which was put off to the agreed January 15 date. No one was fooled, but reactions were mixed, with many observers, including some Americans who had been critical of Germany in the past, commending Germany's decisiveness and new leadership role. *Der Spiegel*, the leading German newsweekly, pointed out: "It was the first time since 1949 that Bonn has taken a unilateral action in foreign policy."[5]

Did this mean that a "Fourth Reich" was in the making? Not likely, if one is talking literally about some sort of authoritarian-minded German zone in Europe, run from Berlin with an accumulation of suspicious, damaging ambitions. But if one means a Germany with time working in its favor and that is growing stronger, then, as a high German official sympathetic to foreign worries told me, "the Fourth Reich is coming unless others, first of all France and the United States, do something about it." The right strategy for this new version of containment, indeed suggested by the Germans themselves, must be to thrice bind German strength: into the European Community, the Atlantic alliance and the all-European Conference on Security and Cooperation in Europe (CSCE) frameworks. An "ordinary" Germany will be strong, and should be. But Germany need not be hegemonic. The German and French leaders have been remarkably united and effective at the origin of most important initiatives in EC forward movement.[6] Old worries about Germany have not entirely dissipated, but no one can believe that forty years of Federal Republic history have not created a modern Western political culture, including as in France and elsewhere, a too-often apolitical or apathetic youth, or that all the sturdy safeguards in the new German system are about to spring loose.

Nevertheless there are legitimate concerns about the rise of German political power. France in particular must play a significant role in balancing Germany and what will be an unavoidable tendency toward the establishment of a German sphere of influence in the complex framework of the new European arena. For example, Genscher has mounted a campaign for EC ties and association agreements with the new republics in the Commonwealth of Independent States. This is all the more important for France in that "Europe," meaning

[5]*Der Spiegel*, Jan. 6, 1992, p. 22.
[6]Axel Krause. *Inside the New Europe*, New York: HarperCollins, 1991.

both the EC and Europe writ large, is France's stage, where France can act "in the front rank" and, through the Franco-German couple and other multiplier coalitions, maintain a world role through the coming European Union.

IV

Or is Mitterrand's policy narrowly nationalist, a kind of Florentine calculation of his own—that is, France's—power interest? Mitterrand, for all his habits and moments of pettiness, is undoubtedly a statesman. He summarized his broad view, extemporaneously, in his 1990 Bastille Day interview on French television:

I would like to tell you what my plan, my *grand projet*, is. It is to turn the whole of Europe into one space, . . . a single and vast market and, at the same time, constant and structural links established among all the European countries. This is why I have talked about a confederation. . . . I would like the Community of the 12 to strive for its own economic, monetary and political entity. . . . I would like to see a strong nucleus capable of making political decisions collectively. This is the Community. Within the Community and Europe, I would like to see France—we are working at it, and it is not easy—become a model of economic development and social cohesion. That is my plan.

This is genuine Mitterrand, a long-term view—vague yet plausible—of the concentric circles of French policy for Europe: the Community within the confederation and, though not mentioned specifically, the Franco-German axis at the center.

The problem is that this conception remains the French frame of reference even though conditions have meantime changed radically in Europe—even though it is clear to everyone, including the French, that new EC members are likely to emerge fairly quickly. The Germans, by contrast, without wanting to damage close relations with their French partners, are already reasoning in terms of a larger community.

Was Maastricht a success for French policy? Like every government, the French won their specific rounds, including even a few against the Germans. France led the fight against extensive powers for the European parliament and against awarding the unified Germans 18 new parliamentary seats. The Germans made concessions to everyone and, though it may not have "won" any single big point at Maastricht, Germany emerged strengthened overall in that German uni-

140   FOREIGN AFFAIRS

fication was legitimized and Germany's new strength was
cloaked in integration.

The two central Maastricht advances for the French were
the agreement on monetary union and the beginnings of a
European security and defense policy. Both involved remarkable French and German concessions on national sovereignty.
By accepting a single European currency, by 1999 at the latest,
Germany sacrificed the deutsche mark on the altar of Europeanism. In agreeing with the Germans prior to Maastricht to
an integrated military command for a French-German military
entity pledged to the Western European Union (WEU),
France's Gaullist obsession with maintaining a strictly national
defense was also sacrificed. At Maastricht the reference to an
eventual European military force seemed to concern conventional defense only. But in January President Mitterrand
volunteered, in an obviously premeditated declaration, that
France's nuclear force itself would inevitably become part of
the debate about a European defense. The trade amounted to
German abandonment of monetary sovereignty for French
abandonment of military sovereignty. This Franco-German
understanding was the keystone of the entire Maastricht
accord, a vision of full political union to complete a vision of
full economic and monetary union.

France's primary gain was EC commitment to monetary
union. Paris achieved two historically stunning goals: adoption
of a single European currency and creation of a European
central bank. The European Currency Unit is to replace
national currencies sometime between 1997 and 1999, while
the EuroFed will take form within a transition structure, a
so-called European Monetary Institute, during the second
phase of monetary union beginning in 1994.

Paradoxically, the French want monetary union as their
chance to regain some control over their own monetary policy.
In the European Monetary System, in place since 1979, French
interest rates have been obliged by financial markets to follow
Bundesbank decisions on German rates. With a single currency, however, the French will have a voice in "pooled
sovereignty" EuroFed decisions on interest rates, reached by
an international board of directors. The French wanted this so
much that in the final Maastricht negotiation President Mitterrand himself proposed a mechanism to make the launching
of a single currency automatic in 1999 if it is not decided in
1997. Apart from an unlikely British opt-out, the number of

FRANCE 141

countries to join will depend on their meeting a certain number of so-called convergence criteria (low inflation rates, interest rates, budget-deficit and public-debt levels). At the present moment, with Germany suffering the burdens of unification, France would meet the criteria but Germany would not!

The French also scored points in the adoption of a modest beginning of social policy legislation, including Community-wide labor laws. A controversial British veto on putting this in the EMU treaty, however, forced the other 11 governments to make a special outside agreement on social policy. The French argument, ideologically inspired by social democracy but also by recognition that labor must benefit from integration, was that economic and political union should not go forward without providing a "social," or worker-oriented dimension to "Europe." At Maastricht the decision was made to adopt a joint foreign and security policy, beyond the informal European political cooperation forum that has existed for years. But, mainly at British insistence, the move from unanimity to qualified majority voting—which would be the key to a pooling of sovereignty in foreign and security policy—was limited to implementation. Another proviso was added on specifying that the council must decide by unanimous vote which foreign policy actions should be decided by majority vote.

On defense the Maastricht summit followed up agreements of the important November 1991 NATO summit. There the Bush administration finally agreed, after some rigorous debate, that it would not object to elevating the nine-nation WEU to a formal connection with the European Community, meaning that such a move would not be taken as anti-NATO. The British, who had earlier echoed American concerns about the WEU's becoming a European caucus within NATO, now signed on to the principle of an eventual European defense.

Yet the commitment to have a common defense policy, with EC decisions executed by the WEU, does not yet provide for a European military force. France and Germany, on the other hand, have been cooperating for several years (with ups and downs) to produce a Franco-German military force, and as early as 1988 Chancellor Kohl himself endorsed the idea of an eventual "European army." An initial 5,000-man binational brigade has struggled for several years to work out its numerous problems, even though the mixing of nationalities there occurs at the lowest levels, that is, at those easiest to work out.

142   FOREIGN AFFAIRS

Overall, multinational fighting forces seem likely to be political crowd-pleasers more than effective fighting units, whereas an integrated WEU command and standardization policies (in coordination with NATO) would be of clear military efficiency.

Just prior to Maastricht in another Franco-German joint initiative, Mitterrand and Kohl announced that the brigade would be expanded to a corps-sized element, open as the Maastricht treaty specifies to any WEU member. If the corps is ultimately attached, as planned, to the WEU as its military force, French troops would be permanently placed for the first time under an integrated, nonnational command. Thus the post-Gaullist French are willing to do for a European force what they refuse to do for NATO. Or, to put it another way, the French have signaled their willingness to pool military sovereignty with a European force, as part of a larger pooling of aspects of sovereignty in the European Union.

In any case there is little necessary contradiction between NATO and the EC-WEU, or at least little need to choose for at least several years, and no European government, the French very much included, wants to see the U.S. military presence removed. Defense Minister Pierre Joxe has even announced that the French, without rejoining NATO's integrated command, are going to increase their participation in NATO's military affairs by attending the meetings of the Military Committee and the Defense Planning Committee. This French step forward—a quid pro quo for the American acceptance of a WEU attached to the EC—indicates that everyone's goal is to create compatible NATO/WEU structures.

Yet the new European security problems are anything but solved. NATO, even if it remains the overall background European guarantee, is not the answer to the real post-Cold War security problems in Europe. It is at best a limited solution because of "out of area" constraints but even more because American administrations will not want to get involved in land wars, especially civil wars, on the European continent. The point of a WEU military contingent would be to implement any European Union defense policy decisions, in particular to have a force that could act in Europe outside the NATO area (remembering that NATO is a defensive alliance that reacts only to attack on a member state). But what exactly would have been the mission, one that could have been accepted politically, of an EC military force in the Yugoslav civil war?

In any event a much higher and sustained degree of

FRANCE   143

European political union will be necessary before a military force to defend it, or to intervene elsewhere, would be possible or justified. For the meantime it is worth pointing out that European states are certainly not without military recourse in the unlikely event of border defense or a need for intervention.

Beyond this, the question of a European defense leads sooner or later to a discussion of pooling nuclear deterrence, hitherto a Gaullist taboo. On January 10, 1992, at a national forum on the results of Maastricht, President Mitterrand surprised French opinion by hinting that the doctrine and strategy of *force de frappe* could be ripe for revision: "The beginnings of a common defense raise problems that have not yet been resolved and which will have to be resolved. I am thinking in particular of nuclear weapons." He said of the British and French forces that "they have a clear doctrine for their national defense. Is it possible to imagine a European doctrine? That question will very quickly become one of the major issues in the construction of a European defense." In principle the answer is that France's nuclear umbrella could indeed be raised over the entire Community, in a kind of European extended deterrence, one that would keep control in French hands. A great reexamination of the French defense consensus will thus apparently take place. Its content may surprise some who thought the only answer about France is that *plus ça change, plus c'est la même chose.*

V

Mitterrand believes that his greatest legacy will be the making of "Europe." As he has said, "France is our home, Europe is our destiny." In the shadow of de Gaulle's legacy, this is statesmanship. Yet in France EC integration is not yet a trigger of great political mobilization. This may change in the next year, as the Maastricht treaties come up for parliamentary ratification, but moreso over the next decade.

Who will lead the new Europe? The answer thus far is Germany. Over the longer term that may change. It may be that neither Germany nor France will do so; both will have leading roles, in different ways and in a shifting pattern of coalitions and problems.

Is the Franco-German alliance likely to survive? No doubt. It is not surprising that there have been tensions and misunderstandings between the two, but rather what is sur-

144 FOREIGN AFFAIRS

prising is that overall French-German cooperation has held up so well. The fact remains that each country is the other's most important partner. Even if the United States remains Germany's key security ally, and even if the geopolitical center of the European Community moves eastward, building the French-German relationship is, as one high German official put it, the most important task for each country's diplomacy in the period ahead. Broadly speaking, the two countries together embody most of the contrasting characteristics of the other EC countries: North/South, industrial/agricultural, Protestant/Catholic and so forth. So where France and Germany can agree, others can usually accept. France, or *le fait français*, to use a Gaullist term, has been in a way the point of reference in the Community for Spain, Italy, Portugal, Greece and, to some extent, even Belgium. And in an enlarged Community, countries such as Sweden and Norway, and especially Poland, would see France as a natural ally in dealings with Germany and *le fait allemand* for historical reasons not yet out of mind.

French leadership, given German unification and the new German assertiveness, obviously is not likely to be stronger in the next few years than it has been in the Mitterrand period generally. Rather, the question is whether it can continue as strong as before.

So much depends on the president. Mitterrand, at 75 and in the third year of his second seven-year term, is in effect a lame duck. Moreover his modus operandi has always been to prefer the waiting game, to play for the longer term, to let others agitate themselves and defeat rivals, leaving himself to pick up the pieces and to close out adversaries. And he has been more successful than many observers are willing to admit. Now, however, Mitterrand no longer has so much time, but he has a knack for turning situations around. Indeed he has announced that he will this year propose several constitutional reforms, one of them concerning the length of the presidential term. If the term is shortened, to five or six years, he may (though he would not be constitutionally obliged) choose the noble exit and resign—bringing on an earlier transition. Moreover his Socialist Party is lagging in the polls, and the 1993 parliamentary elections seem at this point likely to produce either a conservative majority or some heterogeneous realignment, perhaps involving a large ecologist group, which would make strong government unlikely. Mitterrand surely would not relish ending his tenure with another French

FRANCE 145

political "cohabitation," which either gives over most of the president's powers to the prime minister or at least reduces the president's freedom to maneuver.

VI

Is France for all that a "loser" in the end of the Cold War? France is not so much a loser as one who pays a price in Europe's evolution "beyond Yalta."[7] There are also gains and opportunities for France arising from European integration.

The French dilemma in power terms is not zero-sum but that of finding the best, or least bad, alternative. For geopolitical reasons—relative industrial might, relative population weight and dynamism—the strength of *la France seule* was always in danger, even in a divided Europe. The French search for influence, rank and grandeur was increasingly perceived as an obvious mismatch between the goal and French means. De Gaulle was French grandeur and rank. With time it becomes less and less imperative to measure French presidents against the General.[8]

On the other hand, France in the new Europe may well continue to be "only" the second-ranking power. But France in the new Europe will be relatively stronger and more prosperous than it would have been over the long term in the old Europe.

VII

European integration has often been underestimated. Today it is easy to be overenthusiastic, to jump to conclusions in the wake of Maastricht.

What has been built in the EC, plus the new plans, constitutes a partial transformation of sovereignty, of the European nation-state in the modern age. What is required in understanding international relations is a readiness to rethink the geopolitical unity of national power. Sovereignty can be broken into parts, parts of sovereignty can be pooled.

The future of the nation-state needs to be debated again.

---

[7]In the same sense, Lech Walesa feared that Poland "would pay the price" for the disappearance of the Berlin Wall, because West German policy and economic aid would naturally concentrate on the former East Germany. Horst Teltschik, Kohl's adviser, writes in his recent memoir that the German reply to the Polish leader sounded thin, "because at bottom I knew that he was right." Teltschik, *op. cit.*

[8]See Ronald Tiersky, "Mitterrand, France, and Europe," *French Politics and Society*, vol. 9, no. 1, Winter 1991, pp. 9–25.

146   FOREIGN AFFAIRS

Nationalism did not defeat European integration but merely stalled it. European integration is not destroying states but comforting them. European nations will not disappear even if European integration goes deeper. The nation-state as an entity can be broken apart, and both parts of the term can evolve independently. Nations, or peoples, will persist even as they change through modernization and immigration. States will adapt to survive—some of their functions reassumed at the international level, some at regional and local levels.

Europe seems once again a leading edge of political development. Even if an integrated European Union were to become merely a new, larger geopolitical player, its internal structure would reveal one possible evolution of the international system.

[24]

B.J.Pol.S. **18**, 145–170
Printed in Great Britain

Nested Games: The Cohesion of French Electoral Coalitions

GEORGE TSEBELIS

Coalition building involves both co-operation and competition, but the dynamics between these two has not yet been systematically analysed. The existing game-theoretic literature focuses exclusively on the co-operative aspect of participants in a government coalition.[1] The question posed by this literature is which coalition will form, and not which coalitions (once formed) are likely to dissolve. Moreover, the zero-sum game assumption made either explicitly or implicitly by these authors implies that the coalitions formed will be of minimum size. More recently, Grofman has presented a model of proto-coalition formation, based on ideological proximity, where coalitions might not be minimal. His model, however, also assumes that 'proto-coalitions, once formed, remain nondissolvable'.[2]

Recognizing that co-operative and competitive strategies coexist inside an alliance implies that the unity of an alliance is itself a variable to be explained. To analyse this problem, I shall use a game-theoretic framework and I shall develop the concept of Nested Games. Political parties will be considered as pursuing strategies in two different but connected arenas. Their choices affect the

Department of Political Science, University of California, Los Angeles. I would like to thank Robert Bates, David Brady, Pam Camerra-Rowe, John Ferejohn, Bernie Grofman, Steve Krasner, Peter Lange, Jack Levy, Tom Rochon and Paul Sniderman for many useful comments in previous drafts and oral presentations. Anonymous referees and especially Ivor Crewe greatly improved the manuscript. None of them is responsible for any remaining errors.

[1] See W. Riker, *The Theory of Political Coalitions* (New Haven, Conn.: Yale University Press, 1962); R. Axelrod, *Conflict of Interest: A Theory of Divergent Goals with Applications to Politics* (Chicago: Markham, 1970); L. Dodd, *Coalitions in Parliamentary Government* (Princeton, N.J.: Princeton University Press, 1976); G. Luebbert, 'Coalition Theory and Government Formation in Multiparty Democracies', *Comparative Politics*, 15 (1983), 235–49.

[2] See B. Grofman, 'A Dynamic Model of Protocoalition Formation in Ideological N-Space', *Behavioral Science*, 27 (1982), 77–90, p. 86.

balance of forces *within* each coalition, and the balance of forces *between* coalitions. The game between partners is, therefore, nested inside the game between coalitions.

Technically, the partners of each coalition will be considered to be playing a game with variable payoffs. The payoffs vary according to the outcome of a (competitive) game between coalitions.

Substantively, Nested Games are a way of transplanting context into game theory. In fact, instead of assuming that people play games in a vacuum, it shows that these games are embedded in some higher-order network. In my approach this higher-order game determines the payoffs of the players. Parties therefore find themselves in a situation where their payoffs vary according to the specific balance of forces between coalitions, and have to choose strategies that will have implications for the balance of forces both within each coalition and between coalitions.

Several social and political situations represent a structure which can be captured adequately by the Nested Games framework. Class conflict can be modelled in terms of Nested Games, because each social class confronts the other, while facing its own collective action problem, and political influence will ultimately depend on which class solves the collective action problem more effectively. Or the balance of forces might be so favourable to the one side that it does not need to overcome its collective action problem.[3] Factions within political parties face similar Nested Games. Their decision to split from, or remain inside, the party will have implications in the national political game. Primary elections in the United States present another case where the same framework can be useful. Competition between candidates for party nominations may leave incurable wounds, and thereby handicap a party's chances of winning. So initiatives undertaken in the primaries have to be regarded (both by the actors and by observers) as having an impact on the general election.

The framework is general enough to permit empirical tests in different situations. For reasons that will become obvious, the French elections of 1978 have been chosen as the test case. The article is organized into the following sections. Firstly, the choice of France as a case study will be explained and the possible outcomes of French elections will be presented diagrammatically so as to facilitate intuitive speculations about choices of party strategies (Section i). Secondly, the theoretical framework of Nested Games will be presented, in order to examine the validity of these intuitions (Section ii). Thirdly, empirical proposi-

[3] C. Offe and H. Wiesenthal, 'Two Logics of Collective Action: Theoretical Notes on Social Class and Organizational Form', *Political Power and Social Theory*, 1 (1980), 67–115, argue that this was the case for class conflict at the end of last century: capitalists did not need to organize at the national level. J. Elster, *Making Sense of Marx* (Cambridge: Cambridge University Press, 1985), p. 346, and A. Przeworski, 'The Challenge of Methodological Individualism to Marxist Analysis' in P. Birnbaum and J. Leca, eds, *Sur l' Individualisme* (Paris: Presses de la FNSP, 1985), provide evidence that the Marxian conception of class struggle can be captured by this formal approach, since the force unifying each class is competition against another class. In other words, classes become classes *against* someone before they become classes *for* themselves.

tions derived from the theory of Nested Games will be tested with French electoral data (Section III). Fourthly, an anomaly in the data will lead to the distinction between visible and invisible politics, and to laws that rule this distinction (Section IV). Finally, Section V will summarize and discuss the argument.

I: WHY FRANCE?

The French Fifth Republic is an excellent case for studying the stability of coalitions. Under the Fifth Republic, and at least up to 1984, the four major political families (the Gaullists, currently named the RPR; the Giscardians, currently called the UDF; the Socialists, called the PS since 1971; and the Communists, the PCF) formed two competing coalitions, the Right and the Left. The competition between the Right and the Left led to the progressive elimination (under the Fifth Republic) of centre parties.[4] Duverger describes this system as *quadrille bipolaire* and explains that its mechanics are due to the particular electoral system which is used in the French Fifth Republic (with the exception of the 1986 elections), namely the two-round plurality system in the National Assembly elections.[5] In each constituency (*arrondissement*), each of the four major political families presents candidates for the first round of voting. If no candidate receives an absolute majority, then a second round is held one week later. The party that came second *within* each coalition usually endorses and supports the strongest candidate of the coalition (*desistement*). This intra-coalition discipline is the result of agreements between the parties but is not enforced by the electoral law. Due to the difficulty of sticking to this decision, cases of 'triangular competition' (one candidate from one coalition and two candidates from the other competing against each other) have been reported in France.

At the national level, the stability of French coalitions has been challenged several times.

(1) The Right moved from a period of Gaullist dominance (1958–74) through a slow re-equilibration of forces under Giscard d' Estaing to ambivalent support for Giscard by the Gaullist party in 1981.
(2) The Left presented a single candidate in the first round of the presidential elections of 1965, split in the presidential elections of 1969, signed the Common Programme of government in 1972, remained united until just before the legislative elections of 1978 when the Common Programme was shattered, reunited for the elections of 1981 and in the first period of government (under Pierre Mauroy as prime minister), only to split again in the summer of 1984 (after the withdrawal of the Communist ministers from the government).

[4] See J. Chapsal and A. Lancelot, *La Vie Politique en France Depuis 1940* (Paris: Presses Universitaires de France, 1969).
[5] See M. Duverger, *Institutions Politiques et Droit Constitutionel*, 10th edn (Paris: Presses Universitaires de France, 1968).

148   TSEBELIS

This history of conflict and co-operation is not unique. In all European democracies parties join or leave coalition governments; the cases of the French
Fourth Republic and Italy are the most obvious examples. What is unique to
France is that both the co-operative and the competitive forces are magnified in
front of the public because the electoral system favours both competition (in the
first round) and co-operation (in the second round).

Duverger has demonstrated the implications of electoral laws for party systems.[6] Under proportional representation the parties stress their differences to
the electorate. After the election, government coalitions are formed and the previous pre-electoral competitiveness is replaced by co-operation within the
government (at least as long as the coalition lasts). In plurality electoral systems,
the two major parties try to build their electoral coalitions and reduce intra-
party differences in front of the public as the elections approach.

In France, however, each party must do two things. It must affirm its own
political line (otherwise it will lose its supporters in the first round); but in the
second round it has to promote the coalition. This situation is very similar to the
American, in which primaries are followed by Congressional or Presidential
elections. The important difference is that in the United States a National Convention or the simple passage of time *may* heal the wounds of the primaries;[7] in
France, the two rounds are only seven days apart, so the parties do not have
time to change their strategies. It is the simultaneity of elections and the visibility
of strategies (coalitions are made *before* the election, and *in front* of the electorate) that makes the study of French politics so suitable for the theory of coalitions.

If the two partners of a coalition go too far in criticizing each other in the first
round, they will not have the time to change their strategies in the second round,
even if they wish to. The votes of the loser within each coalition will not be transferred to the winner, and, therefore, in the decisive second round the coalition
might lose because it has been too competitive in the first round. On the other
hand, if a party is not critical enough towards its partner in the first round, it
might lose the crucial votes which would make it the frontrunner in that round
and thereby give it the right to represent the coalition in the decisive second
round (and maybe win the seat).

Having set out the situation which we seek to model, let us now lay out the
model itself. We shall begin by considering a single constituency represented in a
particular space. This representation will improve our understanding of the dynamics of cohesion and competition at the local level.

Ignore for the moment the internal divisions of the Right, and the existence of
smaller parties of both the Right and the Left, and consider the following (sim-

---

[6] See M. Duverger, *Political Parties* (London: Methuen, 1954) and M. Duverger, *La Monarchie
Republicaine* (Paris: Laffont, 1974).

[7] Several times, however, the passage of time has not been enough to heal the wounds and candidates have not endorsed their fellow-party runners, nor have activists of a defeated candidate in the
primaries joined the other party (see D. B. Johnson and J. R. Gibson, 'The Divisive Primary Re-
visited: Party Activists in Iowa', *American Political Science Review*, 68 (1974), 67–77.

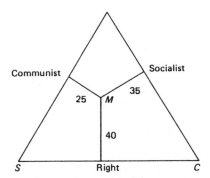

Fig. 1. Barycentric system of coordinates

plified) electoral competition: the Right (as a whole) confronts the two partners of the Left, the Socialists and the Communists. We can use the equilateral triangle of Figure 1 to represent this triangular competition.[8]

It can be shown that the sum of the distances for any point inside the triangle to the sides of the triangle is equal to the altitude of the triangle. This geometric property can be used to map different electoral outcomes in a three-party contest on points inside the equilateral triangle. Each side of the triangle will be named after a party (or coalition), and the distances of any point M from each side of the triangle will represent the percentage of the vote of the corresponding party (or coalition). By definition (if we ignore other parties) these percentages sum to 100 per cent, so if the altitude of the triangle is 100, there is a perfect correspondence between the percentage of the vote of a party and the distance from the corresponding side of the triangle. Figure 1 represents the electoral outcome in a constituency where the Right coalition received 40 per cent of the vote, the Socialists 35 per cent and the Communists the remaining 25 per cent. Once the mechanics of this particular spatial representation are understood, it can provide interesting intuitions. One additional reason for the reader to become familiar with this particular representation of outcomes is that, as will be argued later, the distribution of constituencies on this outcome space accounts for the variations in the cohesion of coalitions.

Figure 2 presents the same outcome space, but with some additional significant lines. C', S', and R' are the midpoints of the sides representing the Communists, the Socialists, and the Right respectively. $C'S'$ represents all the possible ties between coalitions. Indeed, at any point of $C'S'$ the Right receives 50 per cent of the vote; the two parties of the Left, therefore, receive the remaining 50 per

---

[8] Figure 1 focuses on the internal divisions of the Left. If one wanted to examine the Right, then the dual triangular competition (between the Left, the Gaullists and the Giscardians) would be relevant. Generally, the appropriate space to represent electoral outcomes would be an n-dimensional Euclidian space (where n is the number of parties) and the corresponding n-1 dimensional simplex. The triangle of Figure 1 is in fact a two-dimensional simplex, or a barycentric system of coordinates.

150   TSEBELIS

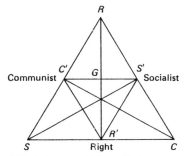

C'S': tie between Right and Left
RR': tie between Socialists and Communists
GC'R': Socialists need Communist support to win
GS'R': Communists need Socialist support to win

Fig. 2. *Ties within and between coalitions*

cent. The segment GC' represents all the cases where the following two conditions hold: (1) the Socialists dominate the Left, and (2) the two coalitions tie.
The segment GS' represents the opposite case of a Communist-dominated Left.
The vertical line RR' represents the ties within the Left. Along this line, the Communists and the Socialists get the same percentage of votes. However, in the
upper part of the segment (GR), the Left coalition is defeated, while in the lower
part (GR') the Left wins the seat.

The area $C'GR'S$ represents all electoral outcomes where the Left wins and the
Socialists are the stronger partner of the coalition. The area $S'GR'C$ represents
the case of a Communist-dominated and victorious Left. Within these areas, one
has to distinguish between two cases: Case A, where one of the two coalition
partners receives an absolute majority (triangles $SC'R'$ and $CS'R'$) and Case B,
where in order to win in the second round, one of the two partners needs the
support of the other (triangle $C'R'G$ for the case of the Socialists and $S'R'G$ for
the case of Communists). Clearly, in such a situation we may reasonably expect
the weaker partner to possess considerable blackmail potential.

With respect to electoral outcomes, one can distinguish two sensitive zones:
the vertical zone around the segment RR', and the horizontal zone around $C'S'$
(see Figure 3). Electoral outcomes inside the vertical zone are uncertain about
which of the two partners will represent the Left in the second round. One might
expect that in this area the competitive aspect of party politics would win over
the co-operative one. Note also that the nature of the competition is very different if the Left is expected to win a seat (lower part) or to lose one (upper part). In
the former case, a seat is at stake, while in the latter case, only an honorary title
is at stake.

Electoral outcomes anticipated to be inside the horizontal zone of Figure 3
are uncertain as to which coalition will win. The co-operative aspect of intra-
coalition politics is therefore likely to dominate.

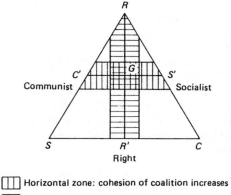

	Horizontal zone: cohesion of coalition increases
	Vertical zone: competition between partners increases

Fig. 3. Areas where co-operation or competition between partners increases

In summary, co-operation is likely when a seat is at stake (horizontal zone), while competition is likely when the two partners are almost equivalent in size (vertical zone). However, these geometrically-generated political intuitions are incomplete in several ways. Firstly, the two zones are not mutually exclusive; our intuitions will therefore be in conflict at the intersection of the two zones (the area around G) where each partner of the Left has approximately 25 per cent of the vote. Secondly, the two zones are not collectively exhaustive of the outcome space; thus, for points outside the zones we have no predictions at all. Thirdly, the two zones are not defined in any theoretical or precise way; it is therefore difficult to say whether a point belongs to each one of them or not. Can we then deal with these circumstances within the same framework? It is to this question that we now turn.

II. THEORY OF NESTED GAMES

Let us now have a closer look at the game between the two partners of a coalition. Assume that each party has two alternative strategies: to co-operate with its partner (C) or to defect (D). By 'co-operation' I mean the promotion of the coalition's interests, and by defection the promotion of partisan interests and open criticism of the partner. Clearly, in the real world coalition and partisan interests need not necessarily be in conflict, nor are parties restricted to two alternative strategies. For example, one can promote partisan interests without explicitly criticizing the coalition partner, or by attacking the partner directly or indirectly. These assumptions will be relaxed shortly, and replaced with probabilistic statements. For the time being, however, let us examine the outcomes of this two-player game and try to imagine the payoffs for the two players.

A party (player) benefits most when it follows a partisan line, while its partner promotes the interests of the coalition; in terms of strategies, when it uses D, while its partner uses C. This most preferred outcome for player i is called T_i (for temptation). The worst possible outcome is the converse situation: when a party carries the weight of the coalition, while the partner promotes its own interests. This is the intersection of strategy C with D of the opponent. This least preferred outcome is called S_i (for sucker).

The other two possible outcomes are mutual co-operation with payoffs R_i (for reward), and mutual defection with payoffs P_i (for penalty) for player i. We know that both these payoffs lie in the $[S_i, T_i]$ interval, but we do not know which of the two outcomes is preferred by each player. Disregarding ties, two orderings are possible:

$$T_i > P_i > R_i > S_i, \qquad (1)$$
$$\text{and } T_i > R_i > P_i > S_i. \qquad (2)$$

If (1) describes the preferences of parties, then the game between parties is known as Deadlock, and parties would never form coalitions, because when a party defects, it gets either the best, or the second-best outcome. If co-operation is to occur, the order described in (1) cannot hold.

If (2) holds, then the game between the parties is a Prisoners' Dilemma game. Each player is better off using a partisan strategy (no matter what the other party does), but if they both pursue this strategy, they find themselves worse off than if they had promoted the coalition.

Two more orderings of payoffs are possible and theoretically interesting:

$$T_i > R_i > S_i > P_i, \qquad (3)$$
$$\text{and } R_i > T_i > P_i > S_i. \qquad (4)$$

If (3) holds, the game between the two coalition partners is known as Chicken where the worst possible outcome for each partner is mutual defection. If (4) holds, the game is known as an Assurance Game where the best possible outcome is produced by mutual co-operation.

Table 1 represents the game between partners at the *national* level, which is most likely to be a Prisoners' Dilemma game.[9] But this is not the only game in town. In fact, it is subsumed in a competitive game between coalitions. The parliamentary seats accrue to the stronger member of the winning coalition. The incentives for co-operation or defection are therefore, modified by the electoral game at the *constituency* level. What are the mechanics of these nested games? To answer this question we shall proceed as follows: (i) a new payoff matrix will be constructed, in order to take into account the utility of events at the constituency level (like winning a seat or helping your partner win a seat); (ii) the impact of the new payoff matrix on the likelihood of co-operation will be assessed.

---

[9] Arguments can be made that (3) or (4) hold and that, therefore, the game is Chicken or Assurance. These modifications of the payoff matrix, however, while important by themselves, will not influence the subsequent results of this article (see G. Tsebelis, 'An Algorithm for Generating Cooperation in a Prisoners' Dilemma Game', Duke University Program in International Political Economy, Working Paper no. 7, 1986).

TABLE 1 *Payoffs of the Game Between Two Coalition Partners*

	C(ooperate)	D(efect)
C(o-operate)	R_1,R_2	S_1,T_2
D(efect)	T_1,S_2	P_1,P_2

$T_i > P_i > R_i > S_i$: Deadlock
$T_i > R_i > P_i > S_i$: Prisoners' Dilemma
$R_i > T_i > P_i > S_i$: Assurance
$T_i > R_i > S_i > P_i$: Chicken

(i) The New Payoff Matrix

This matrix will be constructed by adding to the payoffs of the original matrix of the game at the national level (Table 1) the *expected* payoffs from the game at the constituency level. In order to calculate these expected payoffs, we have to define the utilities and the probabilities of different events at the constituency level.

Two probability distributions have to be defined over the space of electoral outcomes (the triangle in Figure 3). The probabilities p_v (v for victory) and p_{prox} (*prox* for proximity) are defined, respectively, as the probabilities that the antici-pated outcome will be a tie between coalitions or a tie between partners. More precisely, p_v is an increasing function of the closeness of the outcome to a tie between coalitions (p_v is equal to 1 on the $C'S'$ segment of Figure 3 and 0 on the segment SC and the point R). In algebraic terms,

$$\partial p_v / \partial \text{victory} > 0. \tag{5}$$

Similarly p_{prox} is an increasing function of the closeness of the outcome to a tie between partners of the Left (p_{prox} is equal to 1 on the RR' segment of Figure 3 and 0 on the points C and S). In algebraic terms,

$$\partial p_{prox} / \partial \text{proximity} > 0. \tag{6}$$

Call V_i the utility of a seat to the coalition for party i. This utility will differ according to whether the seat goes to party i, or to its partner. Call these two dif-ferent possible values of V_i, W_i (for Win) and A_i (for Ally winning) respectively. The values of W_i and A_i are an empirical matter. It seems reasonable, however, to assume that in all cases $W_i > A_i$, since it is better for a self-interested player, such as a party, to win a seat than to leave it for its partner. Moreover, the value of A_i may be negative; a party might prefer its partner to lose the seat. Local rivalries, or long-term considerations, might account for such payoffs.

The expected value of a seat can now be calculated as the product of its utility (V_i) and the probability of winning it (p_v). In the case of a disputed seat, the vic-tory can be assured only if both parties co-operate. In the case of competition the stronger partner is likely to forgo the necessary transfer votes in the second

154   TSEBELIS

round and thus lose. This reasoning suggests that the utility of mutual co-operation at the local level is higher than at the national. More precisely, the expected utility of a seat has to be added to the utility of mutual co-operation. In algebraic terms,

$$R_i = R_i' + p_v V_i. \tag{7}$$

where R_i is the new utility (at the local level), R_i' is the utility at the national level, p_v is defined by inequality 5 and V_i is either W_i or A_i.

The previous thoughts concern the dispute between coalitions for a parliamentary seat. What happens with the intra-coalitional dispute over who is to represent the coalition in the second round? Call U_i party i's utility from representing the coalition in the second round. If defeat is anticipated, this representation will have purely symbolic meaning. Call REP_i the value of U_i in this case. Representation of the coalition may, however, be of paramount importance when a seat is at stake. Call SE_i the value of U_i in the case of anticipated victory.

The value of SE_i is always positive, and greater than REP_i because parties prefer to win seats. However, it is not clear, theoretically, whether the value of REP_i is positive or negative. Arguments can be made both ways. A party might prefer to represent the Left, despite the probability of defeat, because it thinks that this would improve its position *vis-à-vis* its partner, and the probability of winning the seat in the future, with a more favourable balance of forces between coalitions. However, the party might also think that representing the Left when it loses is a liability for the future.

The expected value of representation of a coalition can now be calculated as the product of its utility (U_i) and its probability (p_{prox}). This expected utility will modify the payoffs at the national level: it will increase the temptation to defect and decrease the sucker's payoff. Indeed, partners will have an additional incentive to be aggressive against each other if they can ensure themselves representation of the coalition, and (maybe) a seat down the road. Conversely being treated as a sucker will be more painful. In algebraic terms

$$T_i = T_i' + p_{prox} U_i, \tag{8}$$
$$\text{and } S_i = S_i' - p_{prox} U_i, \tag{9}$$

where T_i and S_i are the new utilities (at the local level), T_i' and S_i' are the utilities at the national level, p_{prox} is defined by inequality 6 and U_i is either REP_i or SE_i.

Table 2 represents the new payoff matrix (for the Nested Game). For reasons of simplification, only the payoffs of the row player are presented, and the subscript i, therefore, has been dropped.[10] The nature of the Nested Game represented by the new matrix is variable. For appropriate values of the different

[10] It is, however, useful to remember that all parameters are indexed by party and the value of an additional seat for Communists may be very different from that for Socialists. Consequently, all the comparative statements that follow concern the behaviour of the *same* party (under different expected outcomes) and not comparisons of different parties.

TABLE 2 *General Payoff Matrix for One Coalition Partner (Row Player)*

	C(o-operate)	D(efect)
C(o-operate)	$R = R' + Vp_v$	$S = s' - Up_{prox}$
D(efect)	$T = T' + Up_{prox}$	P

Note: Payoffs are functions of the probability of a tie between coalitions (p_v) or a tie between partners (p_{prox}).

parameters it can become an Assurance game (in the area close to the segment $C'S'$ of Figure 3 and for sufficiently high values of V) or it can remain a Prisoners' Dilemma, or it can become a game of Chicken (in the area close to the segment RR' of Figure 3 and for negative values of U).

(ii) The Cohesion of the Coalitions

It has been proved that in a Prisoners' Dilemma, a Chicken, or an Assurance game, the likelihood of Co-operation increases as the payoffs of Co-operation (R or S) increase, and decreases as the payoffs of Defection (T or P) increase.[11] Let us now examine the impact of variations of payoffs or distances from the lines RR' (tie between partners) and $C'S'$ (tie between coalitions). We can distinguish the following cases:

1. V *is negative.* If V is negative, the value of winning an additional seat (W) or the value of one's partner winning an additional seat (A) is negative. Earlier we excluded the first but not the second possibility. If A is negative, the closer an ally is to winning a seat, the higher the probability of winning (inequality 5), and the more the reward from mutual co-operation (R in Table 2) decreases. However, the more R decreases, the more Defect becomes an attractive strategy, because its dominance becomes more pronounced. So, if A is negative, that is, if for one party the value of its partner winning a seat is negative, then the closer the coalition is to disputing the seat the more likely the party is to undermine its partner.

2. V *is positive.* Similar reasoning for V when positive indicates that the cohesion of the coalition increases when victory is near. In particular, since for each party $W > A$, the dominant partner of a coalition will be more sensitive to

[11] R. Axelrod, *The Evolution of Cooperation* (New York: Basic Books, 1984) pp. 202–3, and J. Maynard Smith, *Evolution and the Theory of Games* (Cambridge: Cambridge University Press, 1982), pp. 207–8, prove such propositions concerning the Prisoners' Dilemma game. Tsebelis, 'An Algorithm for Generating Cooperation in a Prisoners' Dilemma Game', proves the proposition for all three games. The proof presupposes the possibility of correlated or contingent strategies, which is the case here since the two partners can adjust their strategies to each other over time.

the proximity to victory. We can summarize these results in the following proposition:

Proposition 1. The cohesion of a coalition increases the closer the anticipated outcome is to a tie between coalitions when V is positive. It decreases when V is negative.

3. *U is positive.* When U is positive the value of winning a seat (*SE*), or simply representing the Left (*REP*) is positive. We have provided arguments why this is always the case for *SE* and true, most of the time, for *REP*. It is always true that the closer the anticipated result is to a tie between partners, the higher the probability of a tie (inequality 6), so, as Table 2 indicates, if U is positive the value of T (the temptation to Defect) increases, and the value of S decreases (fear of being cheated increases). This means that the dominance of Defection becomes more pronounced and, therefore, the choice of strategy D is more likely.

4. *U is negative.* Similar reasoning for U when negative indicates that the cohesion of the coalition increases when the two partners are approximately equal. We have argued that the condition for this event to occur is if a party does not want to represent the Left when it is about to lose (*REP* < 0). We can summarize these results in the following proposition:

Proposition 2. The cohesion of a coalition decreases the closer the anticipated outcome is to a tie between partners when U is positive. It increases when U is negative.

Taken together, Propositions 1 and 2 indicate (1) that most of the time (except when the value of the victory of a seat by the ally is negative), the cohesion of a coalition increases when the anticipated outcome is close to a tie *between coalitions*; and (2) that most of the time (except when the value of representing the coalition when it is about to lose is negative), the cohesion of a coalition decreases when the anticipated outcome is close to a tie between *partners within the coalition*.

The most simple algebraic representation of these two propositions is the following equation:[12]

$$cohesion = c + (aV)victory - (bU)proximity \qquad (10)$$

where *cohesion* stands for the cohesion of the coalition, c is a constant, *victory* stands for the closeness of the anticipated outcome to a tie between coalitions, and *proximity* stands for the closeness of the anticipated outcome to a tie

[12] Equation 5 can be formally derived as a Taylor series first-order approximation of the likelihood of mutual co-operation (that is cohesion), if one uses the chain rule, since the signs of the required first derivatives are given in the text. This remark indicates that one could increase the precision of approximation, and use non-linear estimation routines for the empirical part. However, since this approach is a first approximation, I shall not follow this direction here.

between partners. The Appendix gives the exact algebraic definition of these variables. The coefficients *a* and *b* are positive as Propositions 1 and 2 indicate.

A comparison of these conclusions with the intuitions proposed at the end of the previous section indicates the following:

1. The epistemological status of propositions 1 and 2 and of Equation 10 is different from the conclusions of the previous section. Similar propositions were *conjectured* in the end of Section I. They are *derived* here from the Nested Games approach. The emphasis on this difference is not a statement of epistemological preference. Deriving propositions instead of positing them has the advantages of generality, better approximation, and specification of the conditions under which the propositions hold. Each one of these advantages will be treated as a separate point.
2. Equation 10 does not concern French politics alone. It can cover cases of coalition cohesion such as those mentioned in the introduction, provided we can measure the independent variables. This point is developed further in the last section.
3. Equation 10 covers the entire outcome space. We can therefore generate and test predictions about the intersection of the vertical and horizontal zones, as well as the areas not covered by the zones. In fact, the crude dichotomies generated by the two zones are now replaced by continua of outcomes. Moreover, calculus techniques permit us to replace the linear formula of Equation 10 with more precise approximations.
4. Although our conjectures were largely correct, they were misleading on two points. It is not always the case that cohesion increases when the two coalitions are of equal strength. The condition for such behaviour is that the weak party of the coalition wants the partner to win the seat. This is neither a trivial assumption nor, as we shall see, factually correct. Moreover, it is not always correct that cohesion decreases when the two partners are of equal strength. The condition for such behaviour is that both parties want to represent the coalition even when it is about to lose. This, again, is not a trivial assumption, but it turns out to be empirically correct.

III. TESTING FOR COHESION

In order to test Equation 10, the results of the March 1978 elections for the French National Assembly will be used. The reasons for choice of year will become clear from a schematic reminder of the history of the French Fifth Republic.

From 1958 to 1974 the Gaullists dominated the Right and the Right was in charge of government. From 1974 to 1981, under the Presidency of Giscard d'Estaing, a new balance of forces was created inside the Right and the Gaullist dominance was challenged. In fact, the UDF was created one month before the elections of 1978, in order to challenge the Gaullist dominance more effectively at the electoral level.

This same period was characterized by a change in the balance of forces within the Left, when the new Socialist Party created in Epinay (1971) became the most popular party of France. In fact, 1978 was the first national election in which the Socialist party became the most popular party in France and the dominant force inside the Left. Finally, although the Left came close to winning in 1978, it was only from 1981 to 1986 that it held power.

From this brief overview it becomes clear that 1978 presents two very important characteristics for our study:

1. *The two coalitions were competitive.* In 1978 the two coalitions were of almost equal strength; the vote for the Left in the first round was 49.5 per cent, compared with 46.3 per cent in 1973, and 55.8 per cent in 1981.[13] Since the two coalitions were of approximately equal size, one would expect, given the theory just developed, maximum cohesion within the coalitions.
2. *The two coalitions are not cohesive.* An important shift in the internal balance of power took place within both the Left and Right. It was in 1978 that the two political families of the Right competed widely in the first round for the first time and also the first time that the Socialist party demonstrated its dominance within the Left.

For these two reasons, both centripetal and centrifugal forces were more pronounced during the 1978 election. Thus this particular election is especially appropriate as a test case for a theory of coalition cohesion: the election results of the 474 constituencies of metropolitan France in 1978 were therefore used as the data base.[14]

Before proceeding to empirical tests, the variables of the theory have to be operationalized in terms of the data. Two remarks are in order here. Firstly, how do we operationalize the variable 'anticipated outcomes'? The results of the first round will be used as a proxy for this variable. This choice assumes that the parties have a fairly accurate perception of the electoral outcome, a legitimate assumption given the feedback from the electoral campaign that parties receive both from their activists and the polls (which in France can be conducted but not published during the last week of the campaign). Once the anticipated result is equated with the actual result in the first round, the operationalization of the positioning variables *victory* and *proximity* is straightforward.

Secondly, how do we operationalize the variable *cohesion*? I have already argued that if a party does not co-operate with its partner, but instead aggressively denounces its partner's policy positions, then even if this position is modified the day after the first round, its supporters will find it difficult to transfer their votes to the party considered to be their enemy only a few days previously. Competition, therefore, results in the inefficient transfer of votes between the two partners in the second round. I will use *the difference between the vote for a*

---

[13] See V. Wright, *The Government and Politics of France* (New York: Holmes and Meier, 1983), p. 190.

[14] Overseas Departments (DOM) and Territories (TOM) are omitted.

coalition in the second round and the sum of the votes for the coalition partners in the first round as the best indicator of the *cohesion* of the coalition.[15]

In this discussion, the interaction between party leadership, local party officials and voters is ignored. In fact, the empirical outcomes may be attributed to strategies elaborated at the national or the local level, strategies which were followed precisely by the voters. Alternatively, they can be considered the result of independent decisions made by the voters themselves in the specific political environment. This does not preclude strategic voting (that is, voting contrary to one's nominal preferences) since, as we shall see, parties (or voters) sometimes do not transfer *all* the votes to their partner (defective transfer of votes). More realistically, one could argue that different parties have different levels of control over their voters and that this control increases *ceteris paribus* from Right to Left and from moderate to extreme parties. However, this part of the interaction between voters and parties is deliberately ignored. In what follows it will not matter whether vote transfers originate from party headquarters, from local candidates or from the voters themselves. The reasons for this choice are the obvious simplifying consequences for modelling.

One more point needs to be clarified. One might think that the maximum cohesion of a coalition occurs when the votes in the second round are the same as the sum of the partners' votes in the first round. In this case, the partner delivers to the coalition as many votes as it had in the first round. What happens, however, if the coalition gets more votes in the second round than it got in the first? This happens quite frequently in fact given that turnout increases between the two rounds by approximately two percentage points.[16] But if turnout rises in the second round, this may be due to general factors (like the perceived closeness or political significance of the result) rather than specifically local conditions. Thus, cohesion should account for the variance of vote transfers once this general increase in turnout in the second round is taken into account. Therefore, the consistency where the coalition gains the highest percentage point increase in votes is the most cohesive. Note that this conceptualization of the problem leads to more conservative tests because transfer of all the first round votes to the representative of a coalition is no longer considered all a party can do for its partner.

This conceptualization of cohesion leads to the exclusion of several constituencies from the data analysis. Firstly, it excludes all constituencies where the winner was decided in the first round. Secondly, it excludes constituencies with a triangular competition (two candidates of the same coalition running in the

[15] This operationalization presents a problem because it ignores vote transfers that do not appear on the aggregate level. For example, if the Socialist represents the Left in the second round, one cannot discriminate between the following cases: (1) all Communists transfer their votes and (2) some Communists abstain, while some abstainers in the first round vote Socialist (or vote for the Right, while some votes from the Right are transferred to the Socialist). Unfortunately, there is no way to correct for such ecological fallacies with aggregate data. However, because of the polarized electoral climate, I do not think that the 'invisibility' of the aggregate transfers is very significant.

[16] See N. Denis, 'Les Elections Legislatives de Mars 1978 en Metropole', *Revue Française de Sciences Politiques*, 28 (1978), 977–1005.

second round). In this case, it would be inappropriate to sum the votes of candidates who run against each other. Thirdly, it excludes constituencies where only one candidate is represented in the second round. In this case, one of the two coalitions could not present a candidate in the second round (owing to the threshold imposed by the electoral law) or would not (because it understood that there was no chance of winning); there is, therefore, no way to measure its cohesion. Of the 474 constituencies, seventy (15 per cent) fall into one of these three categories. The first is by far the most frequent: it includes forty-four constituencies where there was a unique candidate of the Right who won in the first round. Such cases are, in fact, cases of maximum cohesion of the Right; cases where one of the two partners puts the interest of the coalition over its own. Such cases should therefore be included in the accounts of the Right and will be assigned the maximum cohesion (which turns out to be 0.091). On the other hand, they cannot be included in the accounts of the Left because no indication of the cohesion of the Left is given. Thus, our empirical investigation will concern 448 constituencies for the Right, and only 404 constituencies for the Left.

For the convenience of readers, the equation to be tested (Equation 10 is repeated here.

$$cohesion = c + (aV)victory - (bU)proximity \qquad (10)$$

Readers are also reminded that this equation was derived under the simplifying assumption that the vote was divided into three parts: the two partners of one coalition and the opposite (unified) coalition. This simplification was necessary in order to introduce a two dimensional outcome space (the equilateral triangle), instead of an $(n - 1)$ dimensional simplex. It is time now to relax this simplifying assumption and take the other parties into consideration. Equation 10 indicates that the smaller the difference in size between the two partners of a coalition the weaker the cohesion of the coalition (if U positive). In other words, the stronger the second partner of a coalition, the less cohesive the coalition. Similar reasoning in a more complicated multidimensional space suggests that other important allies reduce the cohesion of the coalition, in the same manner as one ally does. This reasoning indicates that an additional term expressing the strength of other allies has to be introduced into Equation 10 for reasons of theoretical consistency.

$$cohesion = c + (aV)victory - (bU)proximity \div (d)others. \qquad (11)$$

Examination of Equation 11 indicates that it is the same as Equation 10, with one additional term. This term is introduced to control for the importance of other allies in the coalition.

One improvement on these results can be considered: the value of an additional seat is not the same regardless of the identity of the opponent. For example, in France, where the Communist party was excluded from the political game for a long period of time, and the Right-wing parties were deliberately using anti-Communist propaganda to undermine the Socialists, one would expect that the transfer of votes inside the Right would be much easier and more

TABLE 3   *Cohesion of French Coalitions as a Function of Their Probability of Winning, the Distance Between Partners, the Existence of Other Allies, and the Identity of the Adversary*

Coalition	Repr	N	R^2	Cons	Victory	Prox	Adv.	Others
Left	PC	141	0.56	−0.36	0.43	−0.06	0.002	−0.36
				(−10)	(10)	(−2.2)	(0.5)	(−5.8)
Left	PS	263	0.09	−0.07	0.06	0.037	−0.00	−0.25
				(−1.9)	(2.2)	(1.55)	(−0.4)	(−4.5)
Right	UDF	205	0.44	0.05	0.09	−0.10	−0.02	−0.35
				(1.1)	(1.9)	(−6.7)	(−4.7)	(−8.1)
Right	RPR	243	0.53	0.07	0.05	−0.08	−0.02	−0.44
				(2.0)	(1.4)	(−6.8)	(−6.3)	(−11.6)

Note: Adv. is considered to be RPR for the Left, and PS for the Right.

effective against a Communist than a Socialist opponent. Similar results could be expected for the cohesion of the Left when its Right-wing opponent was the RPR under Jacques Chirac, which was considered very conservative. In fact Jaffre reports survey evidence which corroborates the second conjecture but not the first.[17]

Table 3 indicates the outcome of the estimation of Equation 11[18] using OLS procedures.[19] The first row of the table represents the results of the estimation of Equation 11 in the 141 cases where the PC was representing the Left (and the PS had to transfer its votes in the second round). The R^2 of the estimation and the values of coefficients (top) and t-statistics (in parenthesis) are presented.

Out of twelve estimated coefficients (for *victory*, *proximity* and *others* for each of the four political families), one has a wrong sign, two are not significant at the 0.05 level ($t < 2$) and the remaining nine are significant at practically any confidence level. The fit of the model is quite satisfactory in three out of the four cases (R^2 from 0.44 to 0.56). The only exception is the case of the vote transfers of the Communist party, which produces both a very poor fit and the only coefficient with a wrong sign. Contrary to Jaffre, the results indicate that the opponent does not make any difference for the cohesion of the Left, but it does for the Right.

There is one remaining problem: the non-satisfactory fit of the model for the Communist voters. Why do Communist voters behave in a different way from the supporters of other parties? To the student of French political life this finding should not come as a surprise. The Communist party began a vigorous campaign against the Socialists in the summer of 1977 when the negotiations for the

[17] See J. Jaffre, 'The French Electorate in March 1978' in H. R. Penniman, ed., *The French National Assembly Elections of 1978* (Washington, D.C.: American Enterprise Institute, 1980).

[18] With the additional dummy variable for the identity of the adversary.

[19] It might be argued that OLS is not appropriate in this case, since the residuals may be correlated. However, the use of OLS will not bias the estimates, but will decrease their efficiency, making hypothesis-testing more conservative. Thus, if OLS coefficients turn out to be statistically significant, this holds *a fortiori* for the GLS coefficients.

162   TSEBELIS

Common Program of the Left came to an impasse. During the entire electoral campaign, the Communist party refused to commit itself to the 'discipline of the Left', because it considered the discussions of vote transfers premature and a distraction from the major issue, which was the negotiations for the Common Program.[20] So the electoral strategy of the PCF remained the big unknown of the election until literally the last moment. It was *after* the first round (and only one week before the second), on 13 March, that the three parties of the Left met and signed a vague political agreement which included vote transfers. This agreement operated only for one week, and it was denounced by all partners after the second round.

In the absence of a clear strategy for PCF voters, it is not surprising that the vote transfers look like random noise and the fit of the model is poor. This is, however, part of the explanation, and not the most interesting one.

IV. VISIBLE AND INVISIBLE POLITICS

Another way to explain the electoral tactics of the Communist party is to divide the electoral outcomes into two subsets: when the total of Left votes in the first round is over 50 per cent and when it is under 50 per cent. In the first case, the public's attention is concentrated on the weak partner of the winning coalition while, in the second, it is not. The reason is that the weak partner can determine the electoral outcome if the coalition seems to be winning in the first round. A bad transfer of votes is enough to undermine the strong partner and assure the defeat of the coalition. On the other hand, if the total votes of a coalition places it behind the rival coalition in the first round, the excuse can be made that the coalition would lose anyhow, and the attention of the public is focused on the vote transfers of the weak partner of the opponent.

If the previous reasoning is correct, one would expect supporters of the weak partner of a coalition to run to the rescue of their partner (as Section II indicates) only when the combined votes of the coalition place it ahead in the first round, and their game is visible. In this case they attract the attention of the public, and, therefore, expect that they will be sanctioned for failing to support their partner. So 'fair play' will be expected only when the coalition totals more than 50 per cent of the vote in the first round. Let us examine this conjecture with respect to the Communists. Table 4 indicates that the conjecture is correct. The R^2 of the model jumps from 0.09 to 0.58, and the coefficients are highly significant with the correct sign.

Were the Communists excellent tacticians after all? Did they behave as they should whenever they were visible? The answer seems to be positive if one considers two pieces of evidence. The first is the survey reported by Jaffre,[21] where the Communists appear to vote massively for the Socialist in the second round

---

[20] See G. Lavau and J. Mossuz-Lavau, 'The Union of the Left's Defeat: Suicide or Congenital Weakness?' in Penniman, ed., *The French National Assembly Elections of* 1978, p. 138.

[21] See Jaffre, 'The French Electorate in March 1978', p. 74.

TABLE 4   Cohesion of French Coalitions When Each Coalition Comes First in the First Round

Coalition	Repr	N	R^2	Cons	Victory	Prox	Adv.	Others
Left	PC	98	0.74	−0.34	0.47	−0.13	0.003	−0.25
				(−12)	(14)	(−6.2)	(1.2)	(−5.4)
Left	PS	109	0.58	−0.26	0.31	−0.04	0.00	−0.24
				(−8.2)	(11)	(−1.8)	(0.17)	(−4.5)
Right	UDF	118	0.61	−0.04	0.19	−0.13	−0.00	−0.29
				(−0.7)	(3.4)	(−7.7)	(−0.82)	(−6.2)
Right	RPR	123	0.70	−0.13	0.28	−0.12	−0.00	−0.35
				(−2.7)	(5.6)	(−8.2)	(−1.0)	(−6.9)

(while the Socialists do not reciprocate); the other is the analysis of vote transfers done in a special edition of *Le Monde*. The newspaper reports two different patterns of vote transfer inside the Left and provides tables which show that Communist votes were transferred to the Socialist candidate but not vice versa. Spatial voting explanations can account for such a difference: the Communist voters have no choice but to vote for the Socialist candidate in the second round whereas the Socialists can choose the Right instead of the Communists. However, it is interesting to note that, as Table 4 indicates, supporters of the other parties adopted exactly the same strategy as the Communists. In fact, the fit of the model and the significance of the coefficients increases substantially when in each case the only constituencies to be considered are the ones where each coalition was ahead in the first round.

What happens when a coalition appears to lose in the first round? Table 5 addresses this question. The fit of the model drops sharply and the significance of the coefficients decreases. However, the competitive aspect of coalition partners remains: the closer they are to each other, the more votes there are missing in the second round. On the other hand, the closer the coalitions are to

TABLE 5   Cohesion of French Coalitions When Each Coalition Comes Second in the First Round

Coalition	Repr	N	R^2	Cons	Victory	Prox	Adv.	Others
Left	PC	43	0.22	0.22	−0.16	−0.06	−0.00	−0.46
				(1.7)	(−1.5)	(−0.74)	(−0.41)	(−2.3)
Left	PS	154	0.08	0.05	−0.04	0.01	0.00	−0.16
				(1.4)	(−1.4)	(0.58)	(0.42)	(−2.8)
Right	UDF	87	0.24	0.11	0.01	−0.08	−0.03	−0.29
				(1.2)	(0.19)	(−2.3)	(−3.8)	(−2.5)
Right	RPR	120	0.46	0.23	−0.13	−0.07	−0.01	−0.24
				(5.9)	(−3.8)	(−4.5)	(−5.2)	(−5.2)

victory, the more partners undermine each other. In view of the theory of Nested Games developed in Section II of this paper, the interpretation of this result is straightforward: each party attributes negative utility to its partner winning an additional seat. So, whenever there is an official excuse, or whenever the attention of the public is not concentrated on its behaviour, each party undermines its own partner.

Thus, the difference in behaviour that arises from winning as distinct from losing in the first round can be attributed to the difference in the visibility between the two cases. The pattern of helping the partner when needed if politics are visible, while undermining the partner when invisible, is reflected in the behaviour of the UDF towards the Gaullists, and to both partners of the Left, but it is not observable in the behaviour of the Gaullists. These results indicate that the confusion of the political line in the leadership of the Communist party did not produce outcomes different from other parties. The strategies and behaviour are fundamentally the same. It is just the degree of precision which varies.

Close examination of Table 5 indicates readily available measures to compare this similar behaviour of parties. The coefficients of *victory* indicate the increase (or decrease) in cohesion caused by approaching the 50–50 split between coalitions in the first round. The coefficients of *proximity* indicate the increase (or decrease) in cohesion caused by an equal split of the vote between partners in the first round. We can see from Table 5 that in visible politics, cohesion is more sensitive to variations of victory than to variations of proximity. Moreover, the ratio of the coefficients (victory/proximity) is a rate of substitution, that is a measure of how many points of increasing *proximity* will produce the same impact on cohesion as a one point decrease of *victory*. This ratio is 3.6 ($=47/13$) for the Socialist party, 7.8 ($=31/4$) for the Communist party, 1.5 ($=19/13$) for the RPR, and 2.3 ($=28/12$) for the UDF. So, although the behaviour of all parties is regulated by the same rules, in general the Right is more competitive than the Left (smaller coefficients), and the Communist party is by far more co-operative than the Socialists. Another indicator of the cohesion of coalitions is the estimated intercepts of cohesion, presented in Table 4. The reader can verify that the Right here is more cohesive (-0.04 and -0.13 respectively) than the Left (-0.26 and -0.34), and the Communists (-0.26) more co-operative than the Socialists (-0.34).

A similar analysis could be made with the coefficients in Table 5. It should be kept in mind, however, that the coefficients are not statistically significant, and the results are less reliable. Besides, in this case there is no trade-off effect because the coefficients are all negative, and therefore the comparison is not interesting.

Because of this difference between visible and invisible politics in each constituency, the dominant party of the coalition which is ahead in the first round, can expect the support of its partner, but the dominant party of the losing coalition will find that some of the votes of its partner are missing. As a result, the winner of the first round can almost be assured of success in the second round. Indeed, out of the 404 constituencies there were only thirty-five where the Left came first in the first round but lost (8.5 per cent) and eighteen cases where the same happened to the Right (4.2 per cent).

One final observation can be made from a comparison of Tables 4 and 5: the competitive behaviour inside the Right is reduced in front of a Communist opponent, regardless of whether politics is visible or invisible.

To summarize, there are two major differences between visible and invisible politics. Firstly, visible politics has much clearer rules than invisible politics. Secondly, while the competitive aspect of coalitions is always present, and while the closer the two partners are in the first round, the more votes will be missing in the second, the co-operative aspect is doubtful: parties attribute positive value to a seat for their partner only in visible politics. In invisible politics, there is only competition.

V. CONCLUSIONS AND DISCUSSION

Several of the results of this article should be considered in a broader framework. The discussion will distinguish three different subjects: (1) conclusions about France; (2) thoughts about the theory of Nested Games; (3) speculations about the distinction between visible and invisible politics.

France

In a recent article, Rochon and Pierce examine the cohesion of French coalitions and conclude that: 'The general rule for both sympathy and cooperative behaviour between the two parties will be that the coalition is most harmonious when it is least needed, that is when the success of one of the two parties in capturing a legislative seat is not at stake'.[22] The data that Rochon and Pierce use are completely different from the data presented in this article and their analysis captures dynamic rather than cross-sectional characteristics. To the extent that they generalize their results, however, it seems that they are correct only part of the time. Contrary to their assertion, it is precisely when a coalition is about to win (visible politics), that votes are transfered when they are needed, that is, when a close outcome is expected. On the other hand, their conclusion holds for invisible politics. In that case the more the support of a partner is needed, the less it is offered.[23]

The conventional wisdom that the Communists transferred their votes while the Socialists did not can be explained to a certain extent, but can also be challenged. As we saw in Section IV, there is no fundamental difference between the behaviour of Communists and that of other parties. The same equation can account for the behaviour of all parties. What changes is the size, not the sign, of coefficients. Both Jaffre and Le Monde find the Communist behaviour different

[22] See T. R. Rochon and R. Pierce, 'Coalitions as Rivalries: French Socialists and Communists, 1967–1978', Comparative Politics, 17 (1985), 437–51, p. 493.

[23] For an extended comparison between their results and the results reported in this article see G. Tsebelis, 'When Do Allies Become Rivals?' Comparative Politics (forthcoming).

166   TSEBELIS

because they are interested in the description, and not in the explanation, of vote transfers. The appropriate explanatory variables are therefore absent from their analysis. How can the previous analysis explain their findings?

Spatial explanations have been offered to account for the difference in the pattern of vote transfers inside the Left. Indeed, we saw that, overall, the Communists are more faithful partners than the Socialists. However, this policy explanation is not sufficient. An additional reason for defective vote transfers, according to the theory of Nested Games, is intra-coalition competition. This competition is the result of closeness in the scores of the two parties in the first round. If, therefore, the Socialists appear to be more competitive than the Communists, it must be that when the Left is led by a Communist at the constituency level, the Socialist is usually only slightly behind, whereas when the Socialist is ahead, the Communist is a long way behind.

Table 6 confirms this explanation. On the one hand, the first column of this table indicates that in constituencies where the Socialists lead the Left, the Communists remain some 10 percentage points behind, no matter how close the coalition is to victory at the constituency level. On the other hand, the second column demonstrates that in constituencies where the Communists lead, the closer the coalition is to a victory, the smaller the difference between the two parties in the first round.

The Left was close to victory in 1978 because of the rapid growth of the Socialist party. This rapid growth, however, had its negative effects for the cohesion of the Left. Political commentators at the time stressed the fact that it created reactions from part of the Communist leadership. This analysis shows that the rapid growth of the Socialists created an additional problem for the unity of the Left: the Socialists started making claims over constituencies which were traditionally represented by a Communist candidate. This dispute created tensions and resulted in defective vote transfers *from the Socialist party*.

Figure 4 gives a graphic representation of the differential distribution of the relative strength of the two parties of the Left. The constituencies of metropolitan France are plotted on the two dimensional simplex (triangle) of Section I.

TABLE 6   *Proximity of the Two Partners of the Left When They Approach Victory*

	Socialist lead	Communist lead
General	0.908	0.916
–	(302)	(146)
victory > 0.95	0.909	0.938
–	(158)	(85)
victory > 0.97	0.907	0.943
–	(113)	(53)
victory > 0.99	0.910	0.959
–	(38)	(11)

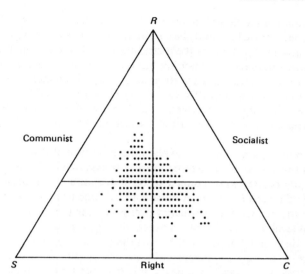

Fig. 4. Representation of first round electoral results (PS, PCF, Right) in barycentric coordinates

Figure 5 presents the differential distribution of constituencies with respect to the Right. Again, the different constituencies are plotted on a triangle, which this time represents UDF, RPR and the Left. The scale of Figure 5 is the same in order to facilitate visual comparisons with Figure 4. Note, by comparing the two triangles, the difference in the spatial distribution of the two coalitions. The

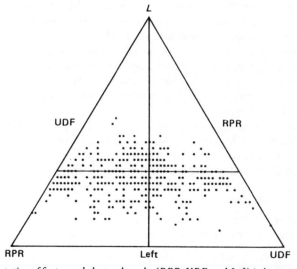

Fig. 5. Representation of first round electoral results (RPR, UDF, and Left) in barycentric coordinates

168   TSEBELIS

Right is expanding along and below the horizontal axis (visible politics), while the Left is concentrated around the origin and expands along the vertical axis. But, as we have said, whenever the distribution of election results is along and below the horizontal axis the coalition has the maximum cohesion, while whenever the distribution is along the vertical axis, competition increases.

The victory of the Right in 1978 can therefore be attributed to two factors: (1) an overall better quality of transfers; (2) a more favourable (asymmetric) distribution of strength between the partners which further improved the quality of transfers.

This last remark can be used to explain the evolution of strategies of different parties over time. Since only one election was considered in this paper, the political line of the parties was assumed to be stable, and was represented by the original payoff matrix (Table 1). A more sophisticated framework would be concerned with the impact of constituency politics on the political line of parties at the national level. It is reasonable to expect that if the election results are anticipated to be distributed along (and below) the horizontal axis, the national line will be more co-operative, whereas if the election results are expected to be distributed across the vertical axis, deviations towards more competitive politics are likely. Thus, plotting the distributions of election results over time on the triangle is a way of providing an explanation for the strategy of the parties at the national level.

Nested Games.

The introduction to this article mentions cases where actors are involved in several games, and the choice of strategies in one game has implications for the other games. Nested Games help us to examine situations in which the payoff matrix itself is a contextually dependent variable. The field of application of such an approach is limited only by the information about the distribution of the relative strength of actors or the different payoffs.

In the formal approach, the payoffs were considered to be dependent on only one distance: from either the horizontal or the vertical axis. Moreover, a first-order approximation was used to derive the formulas to be tested empirically. Both moves were simplifications; more realistic, sophisticated (and complicated) conclusions can be derived.

Finally, all the previous discussion assumed that the internal game was a Prisoners' Dilemma, Chicken or Assurance game, while the external game was competitive. There is no reason to restrict Nested Games to these situations. Any game could be used to develop the theory further.

Visible and Invisible Politics

This terminology is borrowed from Sartori[24] who argues that Duverger's law(s) do not operate at the party-system level, but only at the party level. The reason

[24] See G. Sartori, *Parties and Party Systems: A Framework for Analysis* (Cambridge: Cambridge University Press, 1976).

that Duverger's laws do not operate at the party-system level is that party strategies are part of visible politics, and therefore electoral considerations cannot be the exclusive basis for party choices. Inside a party, however, factions operate without any constraint (invisible politics) and, therefore, electoral considerations determine faction politics. There are several cases where we suspect that visible and invisible politics follow different rules. We know, for example, that secret diplomacy has different rules and different results from open diplomacy, but we do not know what the differences are because the former is secret. On the theoretical level, all the principal-agent literature in economics builds on this distinction and on the opportunities that a loose monitoring procedure provides for an agent.[25]

The principal-agent literature suggests that whenever a monitoring mechanism is installed, the behaviour of people is modified according to its effectiveness. No matter how self-evident this proposition seems to be, we have very few empirical examples. The reason is precisely the secrecy of invisible politics. This paper speculates that in visible politics people comply with the 'official' rules of the game, no matter what these rules are, while in invisible politics different rules apply. It also conjectures that the threshold point between visible and invisible politics is 50 per cent of the first round votes. We saw that in the case of French coalitions, visible politics means more intelligible behaviour in terms of the Nested Games model, while invisible politics generally means more confusing outcomes. Moreover, we saw that in invisible politics the game between partners is always competitive. Because of these differences between visible and invisible politics, the winning coalition in the first round is very likely to win in the second round, since it will enjoy the advantage of better vote transfers than its opponent. In fact, in only 12 per cent of the constituencies did the winner of the first round not win the seat.

To sum up, the differential distribution of strength at the local level accounts in large part for the variance of vote transfers inside coalitions. Parties (all parties) are more co-operative with their partner when a seat is at stake, and more competitive when they have approximately equal strength. However, if the first round suggests that a defeat is probable, each party undermines its own partner.

Finally, although France was chosen as the case study for the theory of Nested Games, there is nothing in the theory that restricts its applications to this particular country or this particular election. More analysis of these and other election results is necessary in order to examine and further refine the propositions of this article.

APPENDIX: DEFINITION OF VARIABLES

npr   Number of votes for the Gaullists
udf   Number of votes for the Giscardians

[25] See M. Jensen and W. Meckling, 'Theory of the Firm: Managerial Behaviour, Agency Costs, and Ownership Structure', *Journal of Financial Economics*, 3 (1976), 305–60 and B. Klein, R. Crawford and A. Alchian, 'Vertical Integration, Appropriable Rents, and the Competitive Contracting Process', *Journal of Law and Economics*, 21 (1978), 297–326.

170   TSEBELIS

ps	Number of votes for the Socialists
pc	Number of votes for the Communists
reg	Number of registered voters
fround	Number of voters in the first round
sround	Number of voters in the second round
tleft	Number of votes for Socialists, Communists and allies in the first round
tright	Number of votes for Gaullists, Giscardians and allies in the first round
left	Number of votes for the candidate of the Left in the second round
right	Number of votes for the candidate of the Right in the second round
victory	$1-abs(fround/2-tleft)/reg$
proxl	$1-abs(ps-pc)/reg$
proxr	$1-abs(udf-rpr)/reg$
otherl	$(tleft-ps-pc)/reg$
otherr	$(tright-udf-rpr)/reg$
advl	Dummy variable with value 0 if the adversary is Socialist
advr	Dummy variable with value 0 if the adversary is Gaullist
cohl	$(left-tleft)/reg$
cohr	$(right-tright)/reg$

[25]

French Interest Group Politics: Pluralist or Neocorporatist?

FRANK L. WILSON
Purdue University

In recent years, many observers of western European politics have discerned an ineluctable and irreversible trend toward the emergence of a neocorporatist pattern of interest group and government interaction (Harrison, 1980; Lehmbruch & Schmitter, 1982; Schmitter & Lehmbruch, 1979). Neocorporatism is seen as a polar opposite to the pluralist pattern of interest group politics. Each pattern has its own distinctive organizational forms and types of interest group activities. Despite a growing body of neocorporatist literature on theoretical questions and some empirical case studies of the causes and consequences of corporatism, the extent of neocorporatism at the level of national politics is more often assumed than established by empirical research.

This article proposes to examine the extent of neocorporatist or pluralist interest group practices in France. France offers a good testing ground for an empirical study of interest group and government interaction. First, there are divergent views on the nature of French interest group politics. Some observers have claimed to find strong evidence of corporatism in France (Crouch, 1978, pp. 215-216; Ehrmann, 1961; Harrison, 1980, pp. 67-97; Keeler, 1981; Kilinsky, 1974, p. 174; Schmitter & Lehmbruch, 1979; and Wilensky,

1976, p. 50). Others see France as having only a very low level of corporatism and as characterized by traditional pluralist interest group patterns (Lehmbruch & Schmitter, 1982, pp. 245, 294). These varying views are based primarily on impressions, since there has been no comprehensive study of French interest groups since those of Meynaud 20 years ago (1958, 1962). Empirical research on the nature of interest group activities in France may help to clarify whether or not the neocorporatist trend has affected France. Second, the Socialist victories in 1981 give us an opportunity to determine if the trend toward neocorporatism has been encouraged by the presence in power of a socialist party. Many neocorporatist theories assert that the movement toward neocorporatism is made possible by the presence of a social democratic government that eases the fears in the labor movement about too much collaboration with government.

To determine the extent of neocorporatism in France, two sets of interviews were conducted by the author with interest group leaders. In the fall of 1979, 99 interest group representatives were interviewed for their accounts of how they tried to influence government policy. These group leaders included both elected officials and professional administrators from most of the principal interest groups identified by Meynaud at the beginning of the Fifth Republic, with the exception of those groups that have since ceased to function. I added representatives from groups whose existence resulted from schisms since the Meynaud list was compiled and from the emergence of new issues (Table 1). To reflect better the real impact of these groups, the sample included several representatives from the reputedly more active groups and

The author expresses his sincere appreciation to the American Philosophical Society, whose fellowship made possible interviews in France in 1982.

895

only one or two from the smaller organizations.[1] The interviews included both closed and open-ended questions, with an average length just under two hours. In the spring of 1982 follow-up interviews were conducted with several of the initial subjects and others. These interviews probed, through open-ended questions, the changes interest group leaders saw in their activities since the 1981 socialist victory. Group leaders' reports of their activities in these two sets of interviews are supplemented by the available case studies of specific groups, policy decisions, and bureaucrats, as well as by my own observations of actual practices.

Patterns of Interest Group-Government Interaction

To test the extent of corporatist interest group politics in France, we must first determine the kinds of interest group activities that might be expected under corporatism and those that would prevail under pluralist forms of interest group-government relations. According to most versions of the neocorporatist pattern of interest group politics, one of its most prominent features is a set of statutory institutions to accommodate direct contacts between government officials and repre-

[1] It is difficult to prove the representativeness of this sample, since the universe of interest groups is not known and since it is not possible to establish a priori the weight that should be accorded to individual groups. However, it is my belief that the sample is broadly representative of the major interest groups now actively trying to influence governmental decisions at the national level.

sentatives of authorized interest groups. These contacts may take the form of corporatist chambers, or they may be commissions with interest representatives and government officials sitting regularly to consider policy matters. These bodies assure the obligatory involvement of the interest groups in the decision-making process through direct bargaining over policy between government and a cartel of organized interests. In addition, interest groups are often charged with implementing the policy decisions, permitting the groups further influence over policy and encouraging the acquiescence of group members to the policies adopted through elite accommodation. The collaboration of government and interest group leaders is so close and constant that it is difficult to distinguish government action from that of the groups. In Lehmbruch's (Schmitter & Lehmbruch, 1979, p. 150) words, corporatism involves "the intimate mutual penetration of state bureaucracies and large interest organizations."

Under corporatism, the presence of institutionalized access to the decision-making process for all recognized groups diminishes the importance of personal ties between interest group representatives and government officials. Parliamentary lobbying is also of lesser importance because the consensus agreed upon by the government and group elites is regularly sustained by parliament. Interest group leaders avoid appealing to the public at large to mobilize public opinion or electoral forces. They recognize that compromise among the elites is usually easier when public attention is not focused on the issue at hand. Similarly, where corporatism prevails, interest groups do not organize demonstrations or strikes. However, when the elites lose control of their organizations, there may be periodic revolts

Table 1. Membership Affiliation of Interview Subjects

	1979 N	1982 N
Farmers' associations	15	6
Trade unions	24	6
Business groups	24	9
Others		
Educational groups	6	1
Liberal professional groups	5	3
Environmental and consumer groups	5	3
Finance and insurance associations	5	1
Family associations	4	1
Artisan groups	4	1
Others	7	2
	99	33

Table 2. Forms of Interest Group Activity Associated with Alternative Patterns

Activity	Pluralist	Neocorporatist
Institutionalized or statutory contacts between interest groups and government	rare: groups operate outside formal governmental institutions	well-developed, frequent, and very effective major form of interest group activity
Involvement in administrative or implementing stages of policy-making	occasionally but usually only in consultative capacity	frequent and very important; groups sometimes become implementing bodies
Personal contacts between interest group representatives and government officials	frequent, especially with elected officials; very effective; major form of interest group activity	frequent, especially with civil servants; very effective
Importance of "old boy" networks between interest group representatives and government officials	very great importance; key factor in affecting policy	some importance
Parliamentary lobbying and/or contacts with parties	very important and frequent	unimportant and rare
Public opinion campaigns to shape attitudes on policies or to affect electoral politics	very important and frequent	unimportant and rare
Protest demonstrations, strikes, and other forms of direct action	occasional but normally for extreme cases only	rare by recognized groups
Policy sabotage or noncompliance	occasional but usually reserved for extreme cases	rare

of the rank-and-file members in the form of wild-cat strikes or spontaneous protest demonstrations.

Under pluralism, statutory contacts between interest groups and government officials are less frequent or nonexistent. The groups act from outside the institutional framework of government to influence policy through political pressure rather than become directly involved in the decision-making process itself. The more common forms of group action under pluralism are personal contacts between interest representatives and government officials. Because there are no institutionalized channels for group access to policy-making, "whom you know" becomes important in opening up opportunities to influence policy decisions. Informal contacts provided by personal friendships and old-boy networks are very important in a group's effectiveness. Since parliament exerts an influence over policy content either directly through its legislative acts or indirectly through its members' contacts with government officials, interest groups usually devote considerable attention to lobbying parliament. The groups use partisan channels in order to influence government policy. They seek to mobilize public support through propaganda or public relations drives "either to win support or at least to neutralize opponents" (Ehrmann, 1957, p. 4). They also

attempt to persuade elected officials by trying to impress them with their electoral strength. Groups resort to public demonstrations, strikes, and policy boycotts only under extreme conditions, when they fear that vital interests are endangered. Table 2 provides a summary of the kinds of activities expected under the two patterns. As we look at French interest group activities, we need not expect to find only one pattern. It is probable that the activities will vary with the interest group, the issue, and the personality of the government. Neocorporatist writers suggest that such a mix is normal during the transition from pluralist to corporatist interaction, but the nature of the combination may help to determine where France fits on the continuum between these two ideal types.

An Overview of Interest Group Activity in France

Before closely analyzing patterns of group action in France, it is useful to review quickly the general picture of interest group activity as painted by group leaders. Group representatives were asked in 1979 to describe how frequently their groups engaged in ten forms of interaction with government in order to influence policy (see

Table 3).² There is clearly no single pattern of interest group action that is predominant. Indeed, many of the interest group leaders stressed the need for flexibility in their approaches according to the issue at hand and the political context. They indicated that a combination of several approaches was usually necessary for success in shaping policy. One leader of an environmental interest group expressed a common theme: "We must saturate the whole political atmosphere. We must make our issues talked about everywhere."

The form of interest group action most listed as undertaken "often" by their groups was a method linked with corporatist forms of interest representation: participation in the activities of government committees. Action in the Economic and Social Council, a formal government institution designed to bring the opinions of interest groups into the policy process, was also rated as a frequent approach by a number of groups.³ Other activities cited as most frequently undertaken included traditional pluralist activities such as formal and informal meetings with government officials, public relations campaigns, and legislative lobbying. However, two other pluralist forms of action, contacting parties and legal proceedings, were least mentioned as frequent activities. Interest group leaders generally claimed that their

groups avoided or only rarely engaged in direct action or policy sabotage.

There are some notable variations in reported activities among different types of interest groups. Table 4 presents the frequencies of "often" and "never" responses for the three major occupational groups. The small numbers in each category suggest caution in interpreting these data. In general it appears that trade union leaders, facing a hostile conservative government in 1979, were less likely to claim frequent contacts with government officials. Labor leaders were especially wary of admitting to frequent informal contacts with the government out of fear that behind the scenes involvement would leave them open to accusations that they were collaborating with the government. This continued to be true in 1982, even with a more favorable left-wing government. As one trade union leader said: "We really do not seek confrontation now with the government—and we did not really seek it before either. We continue to exert pressure on government in order to counter the pressure exerted by other groups, especially by the employers." Business and farm groups were not very interested in shaping public opinion or in protest action in 1979, but after the change in government, both these types of groups, especially small businesses and farm interests, expressed a much greater willingness to turn to direct action.

Later in the 1979 interviews, respondents were asked which of the forms of action were the most effective (see Table 5). Although the question referred specifically to the list of ten forms discussed earlier, group leaders often ignored it to emphasize other actions. For example, many specified that contacts with senior civil servants, as opposed to political figures, were most effective. This response was particularly common among business representatives, who felt that they had very good links with key ministerial staff

²The data in this and subsequent tables are drawn from the 1979 interviews. The open-ended questions in 1982 do not lend themselves to quantification.

³The figure of 26.1%, which rates this method as often used is artificially low, since some 20.4% of those interviewed reported that their groups were not members of the Economic and Social Council and therefore were not ever able to use this forum. One-third of those representatives whose groups belonged to the Council indicated that they used it often as a means of influencing policy.

Table 3. Reported Frequency of Interest Group Actions

	Often %	Sometimes %	Rarely %	Never %
Participation in government committees	55.2	31.3	8.3	5.2
Action in the Economic and Social Council	26.1	26.1	17.4	30.4
Formal meetings with government officials	53.6	32.0	12.4	2.1
Informal private contacts with government officials	46.9	29.2	15.6	8.3
Public relations campaigns	33.0	43.6	21.3	2.1
Legal action	7.8	20.0	36.7	35.6
Parliamentary lobbying	32.3	59.4	7.3	1.0
Influencing parties and their leaders	9.9	37.4	40.7	12.1
Demonstrations, strikes, or other direct action	12.8	20.2	24.5	42.6
Attempts to block or sabotage policy decisions	9.9	22.0	37.4	30.8

Text of question: "Here is a list of types of actions that some groups use to influence policy. Would you indicate if your group uses them often, from time to time, rarely or never"? (*N* = 96)

French Interest Group Politics

Table 4. Reported Frequency of Interest Group Action by Type of Group

	Occurs Often			Never Occurs		
	Business %	Farm %	Labor %	Business %	Farm %	Labor %
Participating in government committees	63.6	72.3	41.7	6.1	0	4.2
Action in the Economic and Social Council	25.0	21.4	35.0	37.5	21.4	5.0
Formal meetings with government officials	69.7	78.6	41.7	3.0	0	0
Informal private contacts with government officials	72.7	92.9	8.7	0	0	13.0
Public relations campaigns	29.0	14.3	56.5	3.2	0	0
Legal action	6.5	0	9.1	41.9	50.0	9.1
Parliamentary lobbying	32.4	23.1	21.7	0	7.7	0
Influencing parties and their leaders	9.7	16.7	4.5	12.9	25.0	0
Demonstrations, strikes, or other direct action	3.1	7.7	21.7	71.9	38.5	13.0
Attempts to block or sabotage policy decisions	6.5	7.1	20.0	51.6	21.4	5.0

(Business, N = 33; Farm, N = 14; Union, N = 24)

members. On the other hand, farm leaders thought that they fared better in contacting the minister directly. Many respondents volunteered that the most effective means was to have a favorable "rapport de force," in that the group was able to demonstrate that it had broad support from the public or determined support from a small but dedicated following, so that the government could not afford to ignore its interests. This was the approach that some 41% of the labor leaders spontaneously mentioned as best for their unions. Many leaders also volunteered that the key to success was to have well-prepared presentations. As one leader of a white-collar union said, "A clear, reasoned argument does have an impact." Several leaders also stressed the need for the groups to be regarded as "serious" by their

governmental counterparts. Leaders from groups basically supportive of the government felt that groups which made demogogic appeals or which systematically opposed the government were not seen as "serious" by the government and thus lost their impact. It is interesting to note that only one representative out of the entire sample rated participation in government committees as the most effective means of influencing government, even though this activity was most frequently given the rating of a course of action often followed by groups.

French interest group leaders claimed to have recourse to a wide range of different approaches to influencing policy. They varied these approaches with the issues and the political setting. Groups out of favor with the government major-

Table 5. Most Effective Means of Action

	All	Business	Farm	Union
Participation in government committees	1.1	0	0	4.5
Contacts with ministers	21.3	12.1	38.5	22.7
Contacts with civil servants	17.0	30.3	15.4	0
Public relations campaigns	9.6	9.1	0	9.1
Parliamentary lobbying	4.3	6.1	0	4.5
Demonstrations, strikes, or other direct action	3.2	0	0	4.5
Grass-roots pressure	5.4	9.1	0	0
Well-thought-out proposals and presentations	8.5	12.1	23.1	0
"Rapport de force"	18.1	9.1	7.7	40.9
Others	11.7	12.1	15.4	13.6
N	(94)	(33)	(13)	(22)

Text of question: "From the list of actions which groups use to influence policy, would you cite those which you believe are the most effective?" This table reports the means of action listed first by the respondents.

ity felt obliged to press for their position by seeking to demonstrate strong public sympathy for their claims. In general, representatives from both groups favorable to the government majority and groups opposed to it seemed to perceive themselves as having problems in getting the government's attention even if they had access to it. A frequently repeated complaint in both 1979 and 1982 from leaders of all types of groups was, "We are usually listened to but not heard."

Forms of Analysis of Specific Interest Group Action

Interest Groups on Government Committees

There is a long tradition in France, dating back to at least Colbert, for the government to form consultative committees that bring together public officials and representatives of private interests. Since World War II, the number of these bodies has literally exploded. By the mid-1960s, one estimate (Mignot & d'Orsay, 1968, p. 92) pegged the total at 15,000: 5,000 at the national level plus at least 10,000 in the departments.[4] In the 1979 sample, 89.6% reported that their groups sat on one or more such committees. Those who did not were usually small dissident groups regarded as "unrepresentative" by the government and often as undesirable by other interest groups. Nearly all of the group representatives commented on "the unbelievable quantity" of committees, councils, and working groups on which they were represented. Even small groups showed me lists of 30 to 50 committees where they sat alongside public officials. Several group leaders complained that they did not have enough personnel to fill all the positions assigned to them on the various committees. A representative of an employers' association noted:

> Sometimes I feel that there are several ways to ignore the ideas of others: never consult them or consult them so often that they don't have time to really think out the problem. The latter seems to be the case at times. There are too many meetings of too many committees. Such a multiplication of consultation makes it difficult for us to follow the issues closely.

After 1981, the Socialist government further increased the number of committees as a means of

---

[4]This estimate is in line with an earlier one of some 4,000 in Paris (Williams, 1966). The numbers of individuals involved are also impressive. In 1965 more than 4,000 people participated in the planning commissions' work on the Fifth Plan, most of whom were associated with interest groups (Harlow, 1966, p. 7).

promoting greater democratic participation. The growth was especially noticeable at the departmental and regional levels as part of decentralization. At the national level membership in existing committees was expanded to include formerly excluded groups; some inactive committees were revived, and a few new ones were created. But both friends and opponents of the new government were cautious in evaluating the importance of these statutory consultative bodies. As one leader stated: "They often seem formalities to amuse the gallery."

In fact, many committees are moribund and have only a paper existence. As an illustration, President Valéry Giscard d'Estaing created a Haut Comité de l'Environnement in 1975 to evaluate the environmental problems of economic growth. Four years later, one of its principal figures, a supporter of the president, resigned complaining that the committee had not even met in the previous year and a half. Even committees that do meet seem to have little effect on policy decisions. But, as Hayward (1979, pp. 36-37) notes, "To abolish the inactive or uninfluential bodies would give offense to the groups represented on them, so they are seldom scrapped even when they no longer meet."

Nearly all respondents claimed that the government dominated the committees. Very few committees had anything more than a purely consultative or advisory task; the government could, and often did, ignore the advice. In some cases, the government is legally obligated to submit proposals to the appropriate committee. But even in these cases, the committees are rarely the forums for the major decisions. Most proposals necessitate consulting several ministries, especially the Ministries of Finance and Interior. By the time they reach the committees, the proposals are relatively fixed, leaving little room for input from the interest group representatives. Even if interest group opposition blocks the proposal, the result would be to return it to the interministerial stage. The new proposal might then be drastically different, but the changes would not come from the groups but from the new round of interministerial bargaining. Thus, most respondents felt that the committee consultation phase of policy-making came too late to be really effective. One respondent told of attending a committee meeting one day to discuss proposed measure and then saw it printed the next day in the *Journal Officiel*, suggesting that the decision was made and the measure sent to the printer before the committee even met.

Interest group representatives stressed the limits of the committees. The leader of a major physicians' association noted that "Often, committees or councils are formed not to come to a decision but to gain time, to cool off issues, or to deflect public opinion." A leader of a craftsmen's association quoted de Jouvenal to explain the situation: "If you want to bury an issue in France, create a committee." Despite this pessimistic outlook, most interest group leaders continued to emphasize the importance of committee work. The feeling was often expressed that "it is better to be there than not to be there." Several leaders mentioned past experiences when their groups followed an "empty chair" policy by refusing to sit on powerless committees. They explained that they had returned to the committee because of the information and discussion that came through the committee meetings.

Farm representatives were the most positive in 1979 about the role of joint government-interest group committees: 69% of them rated committees as rather effective or very effective and not one farm spokesman said that committees had no or very little policy impact. This positive assessment of committee work resulted from the very special relationship that developed between the dominant farm associations and the Gaullist-Giscardian government (Keeler, 1981).[5] This relationship was formalized into an Annual Agricultural Conference to discuss farm problems, possible policy responses, and government financial assistance to agriculture (see Caillois, 1977). The Annual Conference culminates in a formal meeting between the farm leaders and the Prime Minister and other members of the Council of Ministers. Between Annual Conferences, ministerial officials and farm representatives met for a monthly conference on farm issues. In addition to these formal conferences, farmers' associations were present on numerous other committees. Without exception, the farmers' representatives interviewed in 1979 emphasized the importance and effectiveness of their work in these various bodies.

By 1982 the situation had changed. For two decades, government and the principal farm groups had collaborated closely in agricultural policy-making and in administering some government farm policies. Now the Socialists wanted to end this. The Annual and Monthly Conferences continued, but farm representatives felt that they lacked meaning given the new government's coolness for the established farmers' groups. The Mitterrand government ended the monopoly of the four principal agricultural associations—which in fact are closely intertwined—and invited small dissident farm groups from the far left and right

to participate in the conferences. Whereas in the past these conferences were important in setting government farm policy, they are now new fields of battle. The sharp conflict between the farmers' associations and the ministry of agriculture turned the conferences into meetings where two monologues are presented without real dialogue or negotiation.

The Economic and Social Council

The Economic and Social Council (ESC) brings representatives from major interest groups together to discuss all bills dealing with economic and social matters before they are debated in parliament. Three-fourths of its members are appointed by the interest groups; the others are "qualified individuals" named by the government. The Council issues advisory opinions on this legislation which parliament can consider or ignore. It has the reputation of having at best a negligible effect on the policy process. My respondents echoed this evaluation: 59% saw the ESC as having very little or no effect on policy. Even though they felt that the ESC advisory opinions were often of outstanding quality, most group spokesmen, including those who served personally on the Council, admitted that neither the government nor the parliament paid much heed to its work. An employers' association representative despaired: "Parliament almost always votes exactly the opposite of the ESC opinion." A trade union leader sitting on the ESC said: "Two days ago, we adopted a report on the economic situation that was really outstanding. But unfortunately, this enormous effort and well-executed report will probably not be taken into account by the government because it is not in the line of Barre's current policy." The groups that seemed to assign more importance to their activities in the ESC were those that lacked more effective direct contacts with the government.[6]

There are other benefits from the ESC to compensate in part for its lack of impact on the policy process. Participation in the ESC facilitates gathering information through the direct contacts that it provides with other groups and through the access to the bureaucracy that membership in a government institution affords. Several noted the importance of interaction in the Economic and Social Council with rival groups. An employers'

[5]Earlier in the Fifth Republic, more traditional leaders of the FNSEA clashed frequently and futilely with Gaullist leaders bent on reforming agriculture. See Tavernier (1966, 1972).

[6]One farmers' group representative admitted that his organization did not send its best people to the ESC because it had better access elsewhere. Ehrmann (1957, p. 255) had noted similar conduct on the part of business leaders.

association representative said: "It is the best place to meet with opposing groups. It helps build the habit of talking with each other." ESC membership also opens the door to the press and eases the way for contacts with local governments. Finally, there are important financial benefits as well since ESC members receive a generous salary, secretarial and staff assistance, and office space. One environmental leader said that he received 9,000 francs a month tax free with which he was able to finance the operations of his group. Trade union ESC members turn their salaries from the Council back to their unions, and this provides the unions with an important hidden subsidy.[7]

Formal and Informal Contacts between Interest Groups and the State

I noted earlier that group leaders believed formal or informal contacts between their groups and government officials were the most common form of interest group political action, and that they regarded these means as the most effective in influencing policy. When interest group leaders were asked to be more specific about the frequency of such contacts, more than half reported that the contacts occurred very often or almost every day (Table 6). Business leaders were more likely to claim very frequent contacts in 1979. One business leader expressed clearly his group's preference for the discrete, one-to-one contacts with government in contrast to the more institutionalized contacts between the "social partners" of government, business, and labor representatives: "We are very jealous of our role and our privileged position. We try to avoid tripartite meetings and prefer our privileged private meetings." This preference is well founded, as there is evidence to suggest that these unofficial contacts are more influential on

policy decisions than are the more official multilateral meetings (Suleiman, 1974, p. 343). As long as the conservatives held power, the trade unions were not optimistic about their ability to use such direct contacts. However, in 1982 labor leaders reported improved access and effectiveness, and it was the business and farm groups which complained about access to the government. They found once friendly public officials replaced by leaders who regarded them as class enemies and who examined issues from a political or ideological rather than a technical viewpoint.

In these direct contacts, the personal ties of the interest group leaders were often very important in getting access and in being listened to. While the conservatives ruled, business leaders had an advantage since their common social background facilitated informal contacts with ministers and senior civil servants. As one employers' group leader said in 1979, "We speak the same language as our interlocutors in government." This was no longer true in 1982. One business leader complained: "When I meet with these people it is like meeting with Martians. The underlying truths are not at all the same; we talk using two different sets of reference." Several observers (Crozier & Friedberg, 1978; Suleiman, 1978) have noted the importance of old-boy networks from the elite grandes ecoles linking interest groups, especially those from the business sector, with political leaders and high-ranking officials. Senior civil servants are sometimes recruited by interest groups or more frequently by private enterprises, which then use their knowledge of the ministries to aid their new employers in influencing government policy.[8] Those in my 1979 sample (N = 14) who

---

[7] In the mid-1960s, this subsidy from ESC salaries accounted for one-seventh of the CFDT's total revenues and one-eighth of the CGT's income (Hayward, 1973, p. 62).

[8] There is also a sometimes-ignored transfer of the administrative mentality into private business and interest groups as a result of the recruitment of such individuals. A consequence of such recruitment in France is that the ex-civil servants bring an "anti-profit mystique" resulting in a tendency to run private enterprise "for the sake of the country rather than for the long run good of the stockholder" (Granick, 1972, pp. 43, 370-371).

Table 6. Reported Frequency of Contact Between Groups and State

	All %	Business %	Farms %	Trade Unions %
Never	2.1	0	7.1	0
Rarely	9.4	6.3	7.1	12.5
Sometimes	32.3	21.9	21.4	45.8
Very often	31.3	25.0	35.7	37.5
Almost daily	20.7	43.7	28.7	4.2
Varies	4.2	3.1	0	0
N	(96)	(32)	(14)	(24)

were graduates of these prestige schools empha-sized their personal contacts. However, there was no firm evidence they had greater influence except for their self-proclaimed importance.

In Suleiman's study (1974, p. 325) of the ad-ministrative elite, two-thirds of the senior civil ser-vants indicated that the initiative for contacts with interest groups always came from the groups. In contrast, most interest group leaders (57.6%) claimed that the initiative was shared equally; on-ly 10.9% felt that the first step was always taken by the group.' Generally, the unions and outsider groups (environmentalists, consumer advocates, family groups, and veterans' groups) saw it as more common for the groups to take the initiative than did the government. Under the Socialists there are signs that the government is more willing to take the initiative. All groups reported a much more open-door policy in the ministries and ad-ministrative offices as part of the Socialists' move toward greater democracy. Many, however, re-mained openly skeptical about the likely conse-quences on policy of the increased contacts.

Regarding prior consultation with government concerning legislation affecting their members, most group spokesmen saw this as happening at least on occasion. Only 17.7% asserted that the government never consulted them on legislation directly touching their members. Judgments on the significance of prior consultation varied with the groups' political orientation: those favorable to the government at the time saw it as often ef-fective and those opposed regarded it as usually formalistic and ineffective. However, even leaders from groups openly hostile to the government claimed that the government consulted them and that they were often able to shape the legislative proposals to meet their objections.[10] When legis-lation is aimed directly at one specific sector of society, the representatives of that sector are usually consulted and their viewpoints carefully considered by government in drawing up its final proposal. Thus, for example, the government consulted heavily with representatives of the in-surance industry when it was drafting the in-surance code. The resulting laws can be con-sidered as "negotiated laws" where nearly all dis-cussion and controversy take place between government and its social partners before the legislation is proposed to parliament. But when the legislation is broader, consultation even with groups whose interests are affected is spottier.

Suleiman (1974, p. 323) suggested that the bureaucracy is the most important branch of government activity for interest groups. The in-terest group leaders interviewed for this study only partly confirm this. In response to a question asking whether it was most effective to contact politicians or civil servants, there was just a slight preference in 1979 for the bureaucrats: 34.8% claimed contacts with the administration were more effective; 26.1% preferred political con-tacts. The others insisted that they needed both types of approaches (26.1%) or that the choice depended on the issue at hand (13.0%). Most respondents stressed the limits of strictly admin-istrative channels of access, especially when the issue was a broad one as opposed to narrow, tech-nical details. A common theme was: "The admin-istration only applies the decisions of the political leaders; it is simply the transmission belt of the ministry."

Representatives from all types of groups stressed the variable nature of their direct contacts with government depending on the personality of the officials involved. Some ministers and senior civil servants were identified as genuinely inter-ested in dialogue with nongovernmental groups; others were seen as hostile to such contacts. The quality and usefulness of the direct contacts thus varied with the particular individuals involved. Suleiman (1974, pp. 337-340; 1975) pointed out that senior civil servants distinguish between "good" and "bad" interest groups, according more attention to the former. This observation was confirmed in my interviews. Representatives from groups that are regarded favorable by the administrative elite tended to be the most optimis-tic about receiving satisfactory responses from their contacts with government and those from groups deemed to be "pressure groups," "lob-bies," or "class enemies" were the most critical of government responses. Definitions of "good" groups tend to shift with the party in power. After the 1981 change, business and farm leaders indi-cated that their contacts with once-friendly civil servants had deteriorated. Bureaucrats seemed to them to have less latitude than in the past. They also felt that civil servants tried to demonstrate their loyalty to their new political masters by according cool receptions to business and farm in-terests. Some interest groups appeared to exclude themselves from an influential role because of their own negative evaluations of close contacts with government and their preference for con-frontation rather than cooperation.

The great variability of these relationships according to the personalities involved on both parts suggests the absence of an institutionalized

'The others thought that although both sometimes took the initiative, the groups (27.2%) or the govern-ment (3.3%) usually made the first move.

[10]For a documentation of effective labor input under a conservative government see Reynaud (1978, p. 116).

pattern of regular interaction between interest groups and government in France. Very often the success of a group in attracting government attention to its concerns depended upon the personal skills and contacts of its leader. To define the changing, subtle, and informal networks of personal relations that prevail in French interest group politics is "somewhat analogous to trying to draw a topographical map of a desert of slowly but ever-shifting sands" (McArthur & Scott, 1969, p. 308).

Public Relations Campaigns

For most groups, public relations means the publication of a house magazine or newspaper destined for the groups' membership and the periodic issuance of press releases to the Paris newspapers. The public relations staffs are small and often amateurs rather than trained specialists. The question of whether or not their group used an advertising agency elicited sharp denials: "We are not a commercial product!" or "That's not the French way." Only eight of the respondents said that their groups used professional public relations firms, and these groups used them for technical tasks, such as preparing a film. Until recently, most groups were shy about any kind of publicity beyond their own clienteles.[11] Groups unable to succeed in getting their points of view across in the confidential negotiations with government or the administration would sometimes try to go public in order to politicize the issue. Sometimes such action forced concessions (Thoenig & Despicht, 1975, pp. 400-401), but more often the results were meager (Roussillon, 1970, pp. 133-134). A major public relations campaign by apartment owners, including billboards and full-page advertisements, failed to deter passage of an important bill expanding renters' rights in 1982.

Legal Action

In the United States and elsewhere, interest groups frequently go to the courts for legal redress when other means of influence fail (Orren, 1976). Such an option is available to French interest groups through the administrative courts topped by the prestigious Council of State. Groups have the right to stand as plaintiffs in these courts, but they are limited to challenging the correctness of the procedures rather than the constitutionality of the laws. The group representatives interviewed

regarded judicial action as the last resort. Most could not give a single example of their group being involved in such a case. In general, the French legal system seems to offer fewer recourses for interest groups than is true elsewhere.[12] The legal process was too slow, too expensive, and too easily thwarted to be an effective means. An ecological group leader told of a successful court action to overturn a building permit. Then, the next day, the prefect issued a new permit avoiding the technical error that had invalidated the previous permit. A labor leader summarized a widely held view that politics counted more than legal principle: "We have no illusions about the effectiveness of legal action. We believe that the strength of the social forces is more influential and that it even influences the judges as they render their decisions."

Parliamentary Lobbying

Interest group leaders gave a surprisingly strong assessment of the policy-making role of parliament. Only 4.1% of these leaders felt that parliament had no influence; 45.4% felt it had some influence; and 49.5% felt that it had an important place in the policy-making process. Several of my respondents admitted that parliament was less powerful than it had been during the Fourth Republic, but argued that it was now more powerful than it had been in the 1960s and early 1970s. In 1979 they attributed increased parliamentary power to the conflicts within the Gaullist-Giscardian coalition that allowed them to play one party against the other. In 1982, the judgments were more mixed according to political outlooks, but most group leaders acknowledged a greater legislative impact for deputies. Many supported their optimistic views by providing examples of important legislative changes in government bills. Nearly all groups made some attempt to affect policy through pressuring deputies. After 1981, the Socialist parliamentary leadership introduced new controls on lobbyists, ostensibly to improve security. Group representatives now have to wear identification badges and are no longer permitted access to parts of the Palais Bourbon where they used to mingle with legislators. The new restrictions are more petty annoyances than real obstacles to lobbying.

Often the results of interest group lobbying are indirect but nevertheless satisfying. In 1979, a renters' association leader reported that his

---

[11]The CNPF, the largest employers' group, did not even have a press service or public relations office until 1970 (Brizay, 1975, pp. 165-169).

[12]A comparative study of opposition to nuclear energy showed that legal action produced few results in France. See Nelkin and Pollak (1981, p. 155).

organization had mounted a major campaign in the National Assembly against the public housing budget. He won the support of many government and opposition deputies. Party discipline nevertheless assured the victory of the government's proposal. But the next year, the government consulted the group in the drafting stage and incorporated some of its ideas in order to forestall the parliamentary battle of the previous year. "The minister's fear of a bad night in parliament led him to make concessions to us."

The forums of influencing parliament varied. No group admitted to giving financial support to reelection campaigns of friendly deputies. Since there is no public accounting of campaign contributors, it is not possible to verify this. But the low cost of French election campaigns and general revulsion against financial contributions from special interests make such interest group action unnecessary and unlikely. Most of the activities mentioned in the interviews involved simply conveying information to deputies and senators. In most cases it meant no more than mailing a letter or information packet to the members of parliament.[13] Almost 80% of those interviewed claimed to submit draft amendments to friendly deputies, and some pointed to specific amendments adopted by parliament that were "written right here in this office."

Most leaders reported that their groups did not devote many resources to parliamentary lobbying. Only 8.5% said that their organization had a full-time lobbyist; another 20.2% said they had a part-time lobbyist; 71.3% had no one specifically assigned to work with the legislature.[14] For groups without lobbyists, the attempt to reach deputies and senators was made by the same officials who worked with ministers and administrators. Several groups stressed that they relied heavily on their local units for lobbying deputies. The farm groups appear to be the most active in parliamentary lobbying. Despite their access to the ministries, they were ready to work on the floor of parliament for what they could not get through consultation with the ministry. There are numerous *amicales parlementaires* linking sympathetic members of parliament with interest groups. One out of four of the people I interviewed indicated that their group had an *amicale*. The memberships of these are often large and cross party lines. For example, the *amicale* associated with small business interests

had 160 deputies and over 100 senators in 1979.

The shift of political power from parliament to the executive has reduced interest group attention to parliament. By no means, however, do interest groups ignore the legislative branch. Indeed, there appears to be a renewal of interest in parliament among groups now. A number of important government proposals in the late 1970s were paralyzed in parliament by interest group pressure on the deputies or senators. Ministers have on occasion mobilized interest groups to lobby parliament on behalf of legislation backed by both the groups and government. Some observers (Rimareix & Tavernier, 1963) note that a "triangular game" has developed in which groups act on the administration and on parliament to get their will. The French "triangular game" lacks the interdependencies of the American "iron triangle," but does permit interest groups to modify the details of government proposals and sometimes block them in either the ministries or parliament.

Interest Groups and Political Parties

The development of well-disciplined parties substantially altered the political terrain for interest groups compared to the weak and fragmented parties of the past. With deputies voting en bloc according to their parties' decisions, interest groups might be expected to redirect their pressure from the individual deputy to the party, but there is no evidence that this shift took place. Instead, interest groups redirected their activities toward influencing government and the bureaucracy. My respondents seemed uncertain in responding on how frequently they contacted political parties. Many were unable to distinguish attempts to influence parties from their lobbying of deputies. Over half (52.8%) said that their groups rarely or never contacted the parties as such. Many of the contacts that were reported were perfunctory and not likely to produce results.

Ehrmann (1957) claimed that under the Fourth Republic organized interests had power "equivalent if not superior to that of political parties." In 1951, the Chambers of Agriculture succeeded in electing some fifty deputies and had their own parliamentary group on the floor of the National Assembly. Under the Fifth Republic, changes in the electoral system made such a direct election strategy on the part of interest groups unlikely to succeed. Ecologists tried the direct electoral approach, but they have never had more than 4% of the vote in a national election (1.08% in 1981) and have not elected a single deputy. The strengthening and consolidation of the parties reduced their vulnerability to interest group colonization and pressure. Their broader social

---

[13]This kind of activity is apparently not frequent. One analysis of mail to a deputy found a total of only 15 letters from interest groups in a three-year period (Lancelot, 1962, p. 426).

[14]Since I interviewed several people from some large groups, these data include duplications.

bases and better internal discipline made it impossible for special interests to capture the parties, as the defenders of church schools captured the Christian Democrats or as the civil servants colonized the Socialist party under the Fourth Republic.

The overlapping of party and interest group leadership is common in western European countries, with prominent trade unionists filling leadership positions in left-wing parties and employers' group leaders often among the elected officials from conservative parties. But this has never been common in France. The strong syndicalist tradition separates the trade unions from parties. Conservative parties avoid too-close ties with business interests because of a strong antibusiness sentiment in the electorate, and the business groups reciprocate with the antiparty sentiments of traditional French conservatism. Giscard attracted several farm leaders to active partisan politics, and a number of union officials accepted administrative posts under Mitterrand. This, however, was not common. Those group leaders who did enter partisan politics resigned their interest group positions, thus maintaining the traditional separation of parties and groups.

Demonstrations, Strikes, Direct Action

In a country where rioting is a "national sport" (Peyrefitte, 1981, p. 263), it is not surprising that interest group leaders regard demonstrations, marches, strikes, and other forms of direct action as effective means of pressuring government. When asked about such forms of pressure, 60% of my respondents asserted, sometimes with expressions of regret, that direct action was productive in influencing policy decisions; only 22.2% denied that demonstrations were effective. Leaders from all types of groups agreed with this positive evaluation of direct action. A leader of a parent-teacher association stated: "The most effective means is the most violent one. I regret this . . . but governments are more susceptible to crises than they are to more peaceful overtures and arguments." Some of those who thought demonstrations ineffective did so because these tactics were impractical for their group. Such was the case with a veterans' group leader who said his members were too old to turn out for street demonstrations. Beyond attracting the government's attention by a massive strike or demonstration, interest groups see such direct actions as having other benefits. Interest groups do not have access to the government-controlled radio and television to publicize their concerns. Only the spectacular or violent demonstration brought some coverage of a group's complaints on the air (Frears, 1981, pp. 195-196). Demonstrations or

strikes were also the means to forge unity among otherwise undivided groups within a single interest sector. This was especially true in the fragmented labor movement, where a "day of action" was designed less to influence government than to bring the unions together (Barjonet, 1968).

When asked if direct action worked, most claimed that it did. However, in the open-ended question asking for two or three of the most effective approaches, only 3.2% placed demonstrations first, and only 15.7% mentioned it as a second or third choice. This apparent contradiction is explained by the difficulties of mounting a national demonstration. There is not only the lost salaries of those who engage in the action, but also the tremendous expenses in personnel, time, and money for the groups organizing it. In addition, most groups are unable to gauge accurately ahead of time whether or not a demonstration will succeed in mobilizing their sympathizers. Trade unions, for example, often announce publicly a "hot spring" or "hot autumn," but nothing happens as workers remain indifferent to the unions' organizing drives. And then a crisis will occur when the union leaders do not expect one. Strikes and political demonstrations are processes with their own momentum and not easily controlled for use as an organizational weapon to support particular political causes (Mothé, 1970; Schain, 1980). Even if an organization directs a successful demonstration, the achievement may cause problems because future demonstrations will be measured with its earlier success. One educators' group leader told of a successful march by 100,000 supporters that set a very difficult record to match: "What is dangerous is to announce a major demonstration and then fail to produce. . . . Our opponents would see such a check as a decline in our strength. We must put 100,000 people into the streets to match the previous demonstration."

Finally, the frequency of direct action in France means the government is experienced in handling demonstrations, strikes, and other forms of unconventional political participation. The government has a "feather quilt strategy" to handle such events, whereby it can absorb blows and limit violence without responding to the issues raised by the demonstration (Berger, 1972, pp. 237-238). It simply waits for the demonstrators to tire or to dissolve in internal conflicts. The government may offer headline-attracting concessions during the heat of a protest, only to retract or deform them after the demonstrators have demobilized. In most cases these approaches are successful. As a result, most groups avoid national demonstrations except under extremely provocative circumstances. Their local units often organize direct actions, and their members may engage in spontaneous grass-roots actions. But the costs and risks of national actions are seen as too great unless vital interests are at stake.

Veto Group Politics

In complex, democratic societies, the growing intervention of government into the economy and social life fosters interdependency between government and groups representing economic and social forces. As governments adopt more policies that affect social and economic life, they are increasingly dependent upon the voluntary compliance and cooperation of groups at a number of decision points and clearances during implementation of the policies. There is evidence in many western democratic countries that interest groups are using the powers granted by this interdependency to veto duly adopted policies that they regard as unacceptable (King, 1975; Richardson & Jordan, 1979). Such an approach is obviously a last-ditch effort for groups with no other recourse. There are observers of French politics (Crozier, 1964, 1974; Hoffmann, 1974; Pitts, 1965; Shonfeld, 1976; Wylie, 1965), however, who assert that this negative approach is more typical of French political behavior than positive efforts to shape policies before they are adopted.

There was little evidence from my interviews to support such a disposition among French interest group leaders. Those groups with some privileged access to the government worried that an attempt to block a policy would result in closing doors that had proven useful. One representative of an industrial association told of a success in blocking a policy formulated by an administrative section other than his group's usual point of access. The consequence was an internal administrative conflict between the two departments, and the director of the preferred section resented the resulting tensions. It destroyed the carefully developed relationship between the group and its most important bureaucratic contact. The group leader concluded: "It is dangerous to block policy, but sometimes it is necessary."

Veto group politics in France is risky because it usually fails. Several group leaders responded to the question of whether their group engaged in attempts to block policy by shrugging their shoulders and saying such an approach did not work in France. The strength of the government and its ability to ignore public outcries and even parliamentary pressures make it difficult for interest groups to block government decisions. In some issue areas where the appropriate ministries are weak or paralyzed by their own bureaucratic rigidity, organized interests have attained the status of veto groups. Examples include educa-

tion[15] and some sections of the ministry of industry (Crozier & Friedberg, 1978). The combined resistance of business and unions have blocked government policies to reform private industry management and proposals to establish an incomes policy. But in most issue areas, organized interests are unable to block government policy even when they see the government action as detrimental to their issues (see also Hayward, 1975). There may be a few face-saving consultations and perhaps a token "concession" here and there, but ultimately the groups' bluff is called and government wins.

Conclusions

Organized interests engage in a wide variety of activities, and many groups follow a "politics of presence" in any setting where they think they may have some chance of influencing policy. This survey of group action in France suggests that the predominant pattern is pluralist. The most frequent activities, and the ones regarded as most effective in shaping policies, were formal and informal contacts between separate interest groups and political or administrative officials. Other basically pluralist practices, especially legislative lobbying and public relations campaigns, are important forms of group action.

Interest group leaders reported that their groups did engage in some activities which are common in the corporatist pattern. But most leaders rated the multipartite committees, clearly corporatist in form, as ineffective. The Economic and Social Council, a corporatist chamber, was almost unanimously discounted as at best of marginal use to interest groups. There was no evidence of organized interests forming a cartel of varied groups concerned with a specific policy area to present government with a common front. Only in agriculture were there signs of extensive corporatist interaction, and this disappeared in 1981 with the change in government. The presence of corporatist-type structures does not mean the prevalence of corporatist patterns of interest group politics when governments fail to give any power to these bodies. In France, neither conservative nor leftist governments have shown any inclination to grant real power to the various committees they have proliferated.

The French version of interest group pluralism has its peculiarities. The first is the sharp distinction that the government and administration draw between their friends and foes among groups

[15]A forceful minister supported by the president can sometimes overcome the department's divisions and the entrenched interest groups (see Fomerand, 1975).

seeking to influence policy. Groups opposing the government see themselves as second-class participants denied privileged access to the policy process. They sense that their view of society is so different from that of the government that they have little hope of changing the government's course of action except in its technical details. The excluded groups shift with the parties in power. Under the Gaullists and Giscardians, the trade unions perceived themselves as constrained to minor adjustments as they operated within the conservative government's exploitative capitalist framework. Under the Socialists, business interests and farmers felt themselves to be regarded disdainfully as "class enemies." The exclusionary pluralist politics is not complete. Although groups opposed to the government see important limits on their ability to influence policy, they claimed success, sometimes important successes, in adjusting legislation to accommodate their needs. This was especially true with the trade union representatives in 1979, nearly all of whom regarded their overall records as successful in influencing government. In 1982, employers, farmers, and especially small business interests were less sanguine about their abilities to protect their clienteles from damaging socialist legislation. This may be only a temporary result of the difficulties for both government and groups to adjust to the new balance of political power. The interests were frustrated in finding ways to deal with a less friendly government, and the Socialists were still exercising their new power to make up for what they perceived to be past injustices.[16]

A second unusual feature is the frequent recourse to protest policies. Some (for example, Crozier, 1964, 1974, and Hoffmann, 1974) see this as so important as to constitute a distinctive pattern of interest group politics. The interviews provided ample evidence of the willingness of French groups to engage in protest actions. Groups as ordinarily pacific as doctors, dentists, and businessmen reported on their use of demonstrations to press their views on government. In 1982 small businessmen and trucking interests even alluded to the Chilean experience to warn of the possibly dangerous path France was embarking on under the Socialists. As widespread as protest is in French interest group politics, it is a supplement to traditional pluralist patterns, not a replacement for them.[17] Thus, in the spring of 1982, angry

French farmers chased the minister across a field, forcing her rescue by helicopter, and the very same day the president of the leading farmers' association sat with President Mitterrant in the Elysee to exchange views on farm policies.

Since France seems to be an exception to the purported trend toward corporatism, it is useful to consider some explanations of the French resistance to corporatism. One important reason is the French concept of the State as aloof from the squabbles of selfish interest and as charged with the duty to pursue a Rousseauian general will. Shonfield (1966) argues that the specialized training in defense of the State and the corporate self-consciousness of the higher civil service are important sources of resistance to corporatism in France. Government thus protects its autonomy, but the groups are equally jealous in defending theirs. Most groups face competition within their own sectors from rival groups. They cannot afford to appear to be too closely aligned with the government for fear that members will see them as captive of the government and switch allegiance to a rival. Syndicalist traditions among the unions and antiparty philosophies of conservative groups reinforce this desire for complete autonomy from the government.

In other European countries, trade union resistance to close involvement with the state was overcome by the presence of a social-democratic government. This does not appear to be happening in France under the Socialist government. Because of loyalty to their syndicalist traditions and the sharp rivalries among them, French unions are unwilling to engage in corporatist practices. Nor does the Socialist government, like preceding conservative governments, seem disposed to grant any of its authority to trade unions or any other interest groups.

Another important explanation of the absence of a corporatist trend in France is the lack of a political consensus at the elite level. There may well be an incipient or even a well-developed consensus at the mass level. But the elites are still fighting old battles and are far from an agreement on the basic ends and means of government that must underlie any corporatist relationship. Ideological and personality clashes prevent the emergence of a single organization to represent the interests of workers or businessmen. Rival unions and alternative employers' associations conflict with each other within their social categories as well as between categories. These divisions weaken the groups in facing government. Finally, given the conflictual nature of French politics, the few areas that have been "hived off" to corporatist bodies have not functioned well. A prime example is the administration of social security funds. Ashford (1981) argues that a triangular

[16]One Socialist trade unionist admitted in an 1982 interview: "One of the characteristics of French politics is the tendency to take revenge once you get in power."

[17]For a case study of the protest model, see Fomerand (1975). Fomerand concludes that the protest model is inadequate as an explanation of French interest group behavior in this case.

conflict over "the values of society itself, the authority of the state, and the organizational complexity of the social security system itself" is fought out on the various social security boards as unions contend with each other and with employers' associations. The experience is not one that many would like to extend to other policy areas.

The French experience suggests that corporatist patterns of interest group-government interaction may simply be a form of pluralism to which government and interest groups may have recourse for specific issue areas or certain periods. In France the government clearly controls the use of corporatist forms. It has formed statutory bodies to promote "concertation" among groups and government representatives, but it has refused to give these bodies decision-making or other powers. In the various experiments with corporatism during the Fifth Republic, the corporatist practices developed in a structural framework that was strictly pluralist. There was no sign of either the government or the groups losing their autonomy; there were no representational monopolies within social categories nor was there any inter-group accommodation to present a joint front to government.

The most extensive network of corporatist relations was in agricultural policy. The government initiated corporatist relations with the major farm groups in the late 1960s and early 1970s (after bitter and successful battles with these same groups earlier in the 1960s over the most important postwar agricultural reforms). It ended the corporatist ties in 1981 when the new Socialist government rejected the farm groups' influence over agricultural policy. The ease with which the government was able to end this relationship suggests the lack of institutionalized ties even where cooperation was best developed.

The principal exponents of neocorporatist theory define it as the polar opposite of pluralism. However, case studies of corporatism point to its presence in certain issue areas and its use by only some groups. Other areas and groups, usually not carefully examined by neocorporatist writers, seem to be pluralist. For these theorists this mix suggests that evolution toward neocorporatism is still incomplete. Another possibility, and one which I believe is supported by the French case, is that corporatist practices can be found in a pluralist setting and indeed are simply some of several ways that groups approach government. None of the interest group leaders, except for a single farm representative in 1979, felt that the few corporatist forms that did exist marked a novel approach to interest group action; these forms were among the varied means that groups used to cover all points of access in trying to make their influ-

ence felt in the policy process. Further studies of the overall pattern of interest group politics in other countries, not just of groups or issues prone to corporatist patterns, would be useful to test this hypothesis, based on the French experience, that corporatist forms of interest group-government interaction are no more than forms of action within the pluralist pattern.

A final general conclusion from this study is the aloofness of French government from interest group pressure. So powerful is the executive that it is perhaps accurate to discuss the current situation as one of limited pluralism. In contrast to the permeability of the Fourth Republic to interest group pressure through parliament, the ministers, the administration, and the parties, the remote and sometimes authoritarian power of the executive in the Fifth Republic places important limits on interest group influence. The executive exercises controls over most of the avenues of access for interest groups. It closes off some of these points of access to certain groups deemed too hostile, too demogogic, not representative, or not "serious" enough. Other groups exclude themselves by ideological disagreements with the government and by the desire to avoid appearances of collaborating with class enemies (see Wilson, 1982). The interviews support Hayward's (1976) conclusion that organized interests in France are less likely to impede or even affect government action in France than in other western democracies; they are sometimes more pressured groups than pressure groups.

References

Ashford, D. E. The British and French social security systems: welfare state by intent and by default. Paper presented at the annual meeting of the American Political Science Association, 1981.

Barjonet, A. La CGT. Paris: Seuil, 1968.

Berger, S. Peasants against politics: rural organizations in Brittany, 1911-1967. Cambridge, Mass.: Harvard University Press, 1972.

Brizay, B. Le patronat. Paris: Seuil, 1975.

Caillois, J.-P. Sept années de conférence annuelle. Information Agricole. October, 1977, pp. 23-31.

Crouch, C. The changing role of the state in industrial relations in Western Europe. In C. Crouch & A. Pizzorno (Eds.). The resurgence of class conflict in Western Europe since 1968, v. 2. New York: Holmes & Meier, 1978.

Crozier, M. The bureaucratic phenomenon. Chicago: University of Chicago Press, 1964.

Crozier, M. The stalled society. New York: Viking, 1974.

Crozier, M., & Friedberg, E. L'acteur et le système. Paris: Seuil, 1978.

Ehrmann, H. W. Organized business in France. Princeton, N.J.: Princeton University Press, 1957.

Ehrmann, H. W. French bureaucracy and organized interests. *Administrative Science Quarterly*, 1961, *5*, 534-555.

Fomerand, J. Political formulation and change in Gaullist France: the 1968 Orientation Act of Higher Education. *Comparative Politics*, 1975, *8*, 59-89.

Frears, J. R. *France in the Giscard presidency*. London: George Allen & Unwin, 1981.

Granick, D. *Managerial comparisons of four developed countries: France, Britain, United States, and Russia*. Cambridge, Mass.: The M.I.T. Press, 1972.

Harlow, J. S. *French economic planning: a challenge to reason*. Iowa City: University of Iowa Press, 1966.

Harrison, R. J. *Pluralism and corporatism: the political evolution of modern democracy*. London: George Allen & Unwin, 1980.

Hayward, J. Institutional inertia and political impetus in France and Britain. *European Journal of Political Research*, 1976, *4*, 341-359.

Hayward, J. *The one and indivisible French republic*. New York: Norton, 1973.

Hayward, J. The politics of planning in France and Britain: the transatlantic view. *Comparative Politics*, 1975, *7*, 285-298.

Hayward, J. Interest groups and the demand for state action. In J. Hayward & R. N. Berki (Eds.). *State and society in continental Europe*. New York: St. Martin's Press, 1979.

Hoffmann, S. *Decline or renewal: France since the 1930s*. New York: Viking, 1974.

Keeler, J. T. S. Corporatism and official union hegemony: the case of French agricultural syndicalism. In S. Berger (Ed.). *Organized interests in Western Europe*. Cambridge: Cambridge University Press, 1981.

King, A. Overload: problems of governing in the 1970s. *Political Studies*, 1975, *23*, 284-296.

Klinsky, M. *Continuity and change in European society*. New York: St. Martin's Press, 1974.

Lancelot, M.-T. Le courrier d'un parlementaire. *Revue Française de Science Politique*, 1962, *12*, 426.

Lehmbruch, G., & Schmitter, P. C. *Patterns in corporatist policy-making*. Beverly Hills, Calif.: Sage, 1982.

McArthur, J. H., & Scott, B. R. *Industrial planning in France*. Cambridge, Mass.: Harvard Graduate School of Business Administration, 1969.

Meynaud, J. *Les groupes de pression en France*. Paris: Armand Colin, 1958.

Meynaud, J. *Nouvelles études sur les groupes de pression en France*. Paris: Armand Colin, 1962.

Mignot, G., & d'Orsay, P. *La machine administrative*. Paris: Seuil, 1968.

Mothé, D. Comment prendre la température des masses? *Esprit*, February, 1970, pp. 352-354.

Nelkin, D., & Pollak, M. *The atom besieged: extralegal dissent in France and Germany*. Cambridge, Mass.: The M.I.T. Press, 1981.

Orren, K. Standing to sue: interest group conflict in the federal courts. *American Political Science Review*,

1976, *70*, 723-741.

Peyrefitte, A. *The trouble with France*. New York: Knopf, 1981.

Pitts, J. R. Continuity and change in bourgeois France. In S. Hoffmann et al. (Eds.). *In search of France*. New York: Harper, 1965.

Reynaud, J.-D. *Les syndicats, les patrons, l'état: tendances de la négociation collective en France*. Paris: Presses Universitaires de France, 1978.

Richardson, J. J., & Jordan, A. G. *Governing under pressure: the policy process in a post-parliamentary democracy*. London: Martin Robertson, 1979.

Rimareix, G., & Tavernier, Y. 1963. L'élaboration et le vote de la loi complémentaire à la loi d'orientation agricole. *Revue Française de Science Politique*, 1963, *13*, 389.

Roussillon, H. *L'association générale des producteurs de blé*. Paris: Armand Colin, 1970.

Schain, M. A. The dynamics of labor policy in France: industrial relations and the French trade union movement. *The Tocqueville Review*, 1980, *2*, 86-88.

Schmitter, P. C., & Lehmbruch, G. (Eds.). *Trends toward corporatist intermediation*. Beverly Hills, Calif.: Sage, 1979.

Schonfeld, W. *Obedience and revolt: French behavior toward authority*. Beverly Hills, Calif.: Sage: 1976.

Shonfield, A. *Modern capitalism*. New York: Oxford University Press, 1966.

Suleiman, E. N. *Politics, power, and bureaucracy: the administrative elite in France*. Princeton, N.J.: Princeton University Press, 1974.

Suleiman, E. N. Industrial policy formulation in France. In S. J. Warnecke & E. N. Suleiman (Eds.). *Industrial policies in Western Europe*. New York: Praeger, 1975.

Suleiman, E. N. *Elites in French society: the politics of survival*. Princeton, N.J.: Princeton University Press, 1978.

Tavernier, Y. Le syndicalisme paysan et la Cinquième République, 1962-65. *Revue Française de Science Politique*, 1966, 16.

Tavernier, Y. *L'univers politique des paysans dans la France contemporaine*. Paris: Armand Colin, 1972.

Thoenig, J.-C., & Despicht, N. Transport policy. In J. Hayward & M. Watson (Eds.). *Planning, politics, and public policy: the British, French and Italian experience*. Cambridge: Cambridge University Press, 1975.

Wilensky, H. L. *The "new corporatism": centralization and the welfare state*. Beverly Hills, Calif.: Sage, 1976.

Williams, P. M. *Crisis and compromise: politics in the Fourth Republic*. Garden City, N.Y.: Doubleday Anchor, 1966.

Wilson, F. L. Alternative models of interest intermediation: the case of France. *British Journal of Political Science*, 1982, *12*, 173-200.

Wylie, L. Social change at the grass roots. In S. Hoffmann et al. *In search of France*. New York: Harper, 1965.

Name Index